THE VICTORIA HISTORY
OF THE
COUNTIES OF ENGLAND

A HISTORY OF
MIDDLESEX

VOLUME VI

THE VICTORIA HISTORY OF THE COUNTIES OF ENGLAND

EDITED BY C. R. ELRINGTON

THE UNIVERSITY OF LONDON
INSTITUTE OF
HISTORICAL RESEARCH

Oxford University Press, Walton Street, Oxford OX2 6DP

OXFORD LONDON GLASGOW
NEW YORK TORONTO MELBOURNE WELLINGTON
KUALA LUMPUR SINGAPORE HONG KONG TOKYO
DELHI BOMBAY CALCUTTA MADRAS KARACHI
NAIROBI DAR ES SALAAM CAPE TOWN

ISBN 0 19 722750 3

Printed in Great Britain
at the University Press, Oxford
by Eric Buckley
Printer to the University

INSCRIBED TO THE

MEMORY OF HER LATE MAJESTY

QUEEN VICTORIA

WHO GRACIOUSLY GAVE THE TITLE TO

AND ACCEPTED THE DEDICATION

OF THIS HISTORY

Highgate: the Chapel and Gatehouse in 1750

A HISTORY OF
MIDDLESEX

EDITED BY T. F. T. BAKER

VOLUME VI

PUBLISHED FOR
THE INSTITUTE OF HISTORICAL RESEARCH
BY
OXFORD UNIVERSITY PRESS
1980

LIST OF ILLUSTRATIONS

For permission to reproduce material in their possession thanks are rendered to: the Greater London Council Photographic Library; Highgate Literary and Scientific Institution; the National Monuments Record; North London News Ltd. Photographs dated 1979 were taken by A. P. Baggs. The coats of arms were drawn by C. W. Scott-Giles and H. Ellis Tomlinson.

LIST OF ILLUSTRATIONS

LIST OF MAPS

All the maps except that of Highgate were drawn by K. J. Wass of the Department of Geography, University College, London, from drafts prepared by Diane K. Bolton, T. F. T. Baker, and M. A. Hicks. The map of Highgate is taken from Ordnance Survey Map 6″ (1873 edn.).

EDITORIAL NOTE

THE revival of the *Victoria History of Middlesex* in 1955 is described in the Editorial Note to Volume III, and later modifications of the arrangements are mentioned in that to Volume I. The University of London again records its appreciation of the generous grants made by the Local Authorities. The membership of the Middlesex *Victoria County History* Council in 1979 is set out below. Mr. R. M. Robbins, C.B.E., chairman of the Council since 1963, resigned in 1976 and was succeeded by Mr. I. W. Davies. Dr. M. A. Hicks resigned from the editorial staff in 1978, when he was succeeded as an Assistant County Editor by Miss P. E. C. Croot.

The present volume is the sixth to be published in the Middlesex set and broadly follows the usual scheme of 'topographical' volumes of the *Victoria History*. The structure and aims of the *Victoria History* series as a whole are outlined in the *General Introduction* to the *History*.

Many people have helped in the compilation of the volume by providing information or by reading and commenting on parts of the text. Those who have read the drafts of individual parish articles are named in the footnotes. The co-operation of the town clerks and other officers of the various Local Authorities is gratefully acknowledged. Special thanks are due to the Clerk to the Governors of Highgate School, for allowing access to the governors' records, to Mr. H. V. Borley, for help with the information on railways, and to the staff of the Greater London Record Office (Middlesex Records).

MIDDLESEX
VICTORIA COUNTY HISTORY
COUNCIL

As at 1 June 1979

Chairman

I. W. DAVIES, ESQ.†

Representatives of the following Local Authorities

The Greater London Council

London Boroughs

Barnet	Enfield	Hillingdon
Brent	Haringey	Hounslow
Ealing	Harrow	Richmond-upon-Thames

District

Hertsmere

(The District Council of Spelthorne, formerly represented on the Council, has declined to make any contribution since 1975)

Representatives of

The London and Middlesex Archaeological Society

The Institute of Historical Research

Co-opted Members

MISS F. M. GREEN†

R. M. ROBBINS, ESQ., C.B.E.†

Hon. Secretary: MISS J. COBURN†

Hon. Treasurer: G. M. NOBLE, ESQ.†

General Editor: C. R. ELRINGTON, ESQ.†

Executive Committee

MISS A. CAMERON	DR. F. H. W. SHEPPARD
J. F. HEYWOOD, ESQ.	K. A. BAILEY, ESQ.
A. H. HALL, ESQ.	D. CLARK, ESQ.

together with the persons marked with a dagger

LIST OF CLASSES OF DOCUMENTS IN THE PUBLIC RECORD OFFICE

USED IN THIS VOLUME WITH THEIR CLASS NUMBERS

Chancery

	Proceedings
C 1	Early
C 2	Series I
C 3	Series II
C 5	Six Clerks Series, Bridges
C 6	Collins
C 7	Hamilton
C 8	Mitford
C 9	Reynardson
C 10	Whittington
C 43	Pleadings, Rolls Chapel Series
C 54	Close Rolls
C 66	Patent Rolls
C 88	Records upon Outlawries
C 108	Masters' Exhibits, Farrar
	Inquisitions post mortem
C 133	Series I, Edw. I
C 135	Edw. III
C 136	Ric. II
C 137	Hen. IV
C 142	Series II
C 143	Inquisitions ad quod damnum
C 146	Ancient Deeds, Series C
C 147	Ancient Deeds, Series CC
C 219	Writs and Returns of Members to Parliament
C 263	Tower and Rolls Chapel Series, Legal Miscellanea

Court of Common Pleas

C.P. 25(1)	Feet of Fines, Series I
C.P. 25(2)	Feet of Fines, Series II
C.P. 40	Plea Rolls

Exchequer, Treasury of Receipt

E 36	Books

Exchequer, King's Remembrancer

E 126	Decrees and Orders, Series IV
E 153	Escheators' Files
E 179	Subsidy Rolls, etc.
E 210	Ancient Deeds, Series D
E 214	Modern Deeds

Exchequer, Augmentation Office

E 301	Certificates of Colleges and Chantries
E 305	Deeds of Purchase and Exchange
E 315	Miscellaneous Books
E 318	Particulars for Grants of Crown Lands
E 326	Ancient Deeds, Series B

Exchequer, Lord Treasurer's Remembrancer's and Pipe Offices

E 352	Chancellor's Rolls
E 368	Memoranda Rolls
E 372	Pipe Rolls

Ministry of Education

Ed. 7	Public Elementary Schools, Preliminary Statements

Registry of Friendly Societies

F.S. 2	Indexes to Rules and Amendments, Series II

Home Office

H.O. 67	Acreage Returns
H.O. 107	Population Returns
H.O. 129	Ecclesiastical Returns
	Entry Books, Various
H.O. 136	Miscellaneous
H.O. 137	Reformatories

Justices Itinerant, Assize and Gaol Delivery Justices, etc.

J.I. 1	Eyre Rolls, Assize Rolls, etc.

Court of King's Bench, Crown Side

K.B. 9	Ancient Indictments

Exchequer, Office of the Auditors of the Land Revenue

L.R. 2	Miscellaneous Books

Ministry of Agriculture, Fisheries, and Food

M.A.F. 9	Deeds and Awards of Enfranchisement
M.A.F. 68	Agricultural Returns: Parish Summaries

Prerogative Court of Canterbury

Prob. 11	Registered Copies of Wills proved in P.C.C.

Office of the Registrar General

R.G. 9	Census Returns, 1861
R.G. 10	Census Returns, 1871

Court of Requests

Req. 2	Proceedings

Special Collections

S.C. 2	Court Rolls
S.C. 5	Hundred Rolls
S.C. 6	Ministers' and Receivers' Accounts

State Paper Office

S.P. 1	State Papers, Hen. VIII, General Series
	State Papers, Domestic
S.P. 12	Eliz. I
S.P. 44	Entry Books

Court of Star Chamber

Sta. Cha. 8	Proceedings, Jas. I

Court of Wards and Liveries

Wards 5	Feodaries' Surveys
Wards 7	Inquisitions Post Mortem
Wards 9	Miscellaneous Books

SELECT LIST OF CLASSES OF DOCUMENTS IN THE GREATER LONDON RECORD OFFICE (MIDDLESEX RECORDS)

USED IN THIS VOLUME WITH THEIR CLASS NUMBERS

Deposited Records	
Acc. 262	Stowe Collection
Acc. 351	Allen-Cooper Estate and Family Papers
Acc. 410	Banks Collection
Acc. 1038	Records of Colney Hatch Asylum
Acc. 1289	Records of Manor of Topsfield Hall, Hornsey
Cal. Mdx. Rec.	Calendar of Sessions Records, 1607–12
Cal. Mdx. Sess. Bks.	Calendar of Sessions Books, 1638–1752
D.R.O. 12	Diocesan Records, Friern Barnet Parish Records
D.R.O. 20	Diocesan Records, Hornsey Parish Records
F	Facsimile
EA	Enclosure Awards
MJ/SR	Sessions Rolls
MR/LV	Licensed Victuallers' Lists
MR/TH	Hearth Tax Assessments
PR	Prints
TA	Tithe Awards

NOTE ON ABBREVIATIONS

Among the abbreviations and short titles used the following may require elucidation, in addition to those noted in the V.C.H. *Handbook* (1970):

B.L.	British Library (used in references to documents transferred from the British Museum)
B.L.H.L.	Barnet Local History Library
Brewer, *Beauties of Eng. and Wales*, x(5)	J. N. Brewer, vol. x (1816) of *The Beauties of England and Wales* (1810–16), ed. E. W. Brayley and J. Britton. The part of the work cited is alternatively known either as the fifth part, or as the second part of vol. iv, of *London and Middlesex*, which is itself vol. x of *The Beauties.*
Calamy Revised	A. G. Matthews, *Calamy Revised* (1934)
Educ. Enquiry Abs.	*Education Enquiry Abstract*, H.C. 62 (1835), xli
Educ. of Poor Digest	*Digest of Returns to the Select Committee on Education of the Poor*, H.C. 224 (1819), ix(1)
Ft. of F. Lond. & Mdx.	*Calendar to the Feet of Fines for London and Middlesex*, ed. W. J. Hardy and W. Page (2 vols. 1892–3)
Foot, *Agric. of Mdx.*	P. Foot, *General View of the Agriculture of the County of Middlesex* (1794)
Freshfield, *Communion Plate*	E. Freshfield, *The Communion Plate of the Parish Churches in the county of Middlesex* (1897)
Guildhall MSS.	City of London, Guildhall Library. The collection includes bishops' registers (MS. 9531), diocesan administrative records (MSS. 9532–60), and records of bishops' estates (MSS. 10234–51)
Hennessy, *Novum Rep.*	G. Hennessy, *Novum Repertorium Ecclesiasticum Parochiale Londinense* (1898)
Hist. Lond. Transport	T. C. Barker and M. Robbins, *A History of London Transport* (2 vols. 1975 edn.)
Hist. Mon. Com. *Mdx.*	Royal Commission on Historical Monuments, *An Inventory of the Historical Monuments in Middlesex* (H.M.S.O. 1937)
Kelly's Dir. Mdx.	The Post Office *Directories*. The directories for Middlesex between 1845 and 1863 were published as part of the *Home Counties Directory*
Lond. Dioc. Bk.	*Yearbook* of the diocese of London (1940 to date)
Lysons, *Environs*	D. Lysons, *The Environs of London* (1792–6), vols. ii and iii (1795), Supplement (1811)
M.L.R.	Middlesex Land Registry. The enrolments and indexes are at the Greater London Record Office (Middlesex Records); the volumes are at the Greater London Record Office
M.R.O.	Middlesex Record Office. On the incorporation of Middlesex within Greater London on 1 April 1965 the office became known as the Greater London Record Office (Middlesex Records)
Mdx. Cnty. Rec.	*Middlesex County Records* [1550–1688], ed. J. C. Jeaffreson (4 vols. 1886–92)
Mdx. Cnty. Rec. Sess. Bks. 1689–1709	*Middlesex County Records, Calendar of the Sessions Books 1689 to 1709*, ed. W. J. Hardy (1905)
Mdx. Sess. Rec.	*Calendar to the Sessions Records* [1612–18], ed. W. le Hardy (4 vols. 1935–41)
Middleton, *View*	J. Middleton, *View of the Agriculture of Middlesex* (1798)
Mudie-Smith, *Rel. Life*	R. Mudie-Smith, *The Religious Life of London* (1904)
Newcourt, *Rep.*	R. Newcourt, *Repertorium Ecclesiasticum Parochiale Londinense* (2 vols. 1708–10)

NOTE ON ABBREVIATIONS

Norden, *Spec. Brit.*	J. Norden, *Speculum Britanniae* (Middlesex) (facsimile edn. 1971)
P.N. Mdx. (E.P.N.S.)	*The Place-Names of Middlesex* (English Place-Name Society, vol. xviii, 1942)
Pevsner, *Mdx.*	N. Pevsner, *The Buildings of England, Middlesex* (1951)
Potter Colln.	British Museum, Department of Prints and Drawings, Potter Collection of North London Topography
Rep. on Bridges in Mdx.	*Report of the Committee of Magistrates Appointed to make Enquiry respecting the Public Bridges in the County of Middlesex* (1826) in M.R.O.
Rec. Com. Eccl. Revenues	*Report of the Commissioners Appointed to Inquire into the Ecclesiastical Revenues of England and Wales* [67], H.C. (1835), xxii
Rep. Cttee. on Returns by Overseers, 1776	*Report of the Select Committee on Returns by Overseers of the Poor 1776*, H.C., 1st ser. ix
Robbins, *Mdx.*	M. Robbins, *Middlesex* (1953)
Thorne, *Environs*	J. Thorne, *Handbook to the Environs of London* [alphabetically arranged in two parts] (1876)
T.L.M.A.S.	*Transactions of the London and Middlesex Archaeological Society* (1856 to date). Consecutive numbers are used for the whole series, although vols. vii–xvii (1905–54) appeared as N.S. i–xi
W.A.M.	Westminster Abbey Muniments
Walker Revised	A. G. Matthews, *Walker Revised* (1948)

OSSULSTONE HUNDRED

OSWALD's stone, from which the hundred took its name,[1] may well have been the Roman geometric stone standing at the point where Watling Street (Edgware Road) joined the road (Oxford Street) running westward out of Essex. It was in position up to 1822 but was then earthed over.[2] After Marble Arch had been erected upon approximately the same site in 1851, the stone leant for a while against that edifice but it has not been seen since 1869.[3] Between 1285 and 1312 there are references to a field called Ossulstone and by 1341 Ossulstone seems to have been a settlement.[4] In 1484–5 it possessed 'pits',[5] where the county court met in 1554.[6] On a map of 1614 Ossulstone was spot-marked as lying at the western end of South Street, Mayfair, where that street joins Park Lane.[7] While this may then have been the centre of the settlement and even the hundred meeting-place, it need not be concluded that the hundred originally met there,[8] for the stone itself is the more likely location.

After the Middlesex county court had been reorganized by the Small Debts, Middlesex, Act of 1750[9] the court for Ossulstone hundred suitors was held further eastward. In 1793[10] and 1808[11] it was in Fulwood's Rents (now Fulwood's Place), Holborn, and by 1827 in Kingsgate Street, Holborn,[12] where it remained[13] until, after the passage of the County Courts Act, 1846, it ceased to exist in that form.[14]

In 1086 the components of the hundred that were named and can be identified were Chelsea, Ebury, Fulham, Haggerston, Hampstead, Harlesden, Holborn, Hoxton, Islington, Kensington, Lisson, Stepney, Stoke Newington, Tollington, Tottenham Court, Twyford, Tyburn, and Willesden. In addition there must be added St. Pancras, Westminster, and an area outside Bishopsgate, all of which are identifiable but unnamed, and 'Nanesmaneslande', Rugmoor, and 'Stanestaple' which are named but unidentifiable.[15] A survey of documents listing the components of the hundred from the early 13th century to 1801[16] shows that 14 of the 24 places recorded in 1086 continued to be named more or less regularly, but that Haggerston, Harlesden, Tollington, Tottenham Court, and the 3 unidentified places were not so named after 1086, Ebury and Lisson not after the early 14th century, and Hoxton only in the 16th century and early seventeenth. Three places newly occurred as members of the hundred in the

[1] *P.N. Mdx.* (E.P.N.S.), 81.
[2] *V.C.H. Lond.* i. 32.
[3] *T.L.M.A.S.* iv. 63.
[4] Grosvenor Estate Off., C. T. Gatty's scrap bk., f. 67 (notes by Ethel Stokes taken from W.A.M.).
[5] C. T. Gatty, *Mary Davies and Ebury Manor* (1921), i. 58.
[6] C 219/23/84.
[7] Gatty, op. cit. ii, map after p. 238.
[8] Sir Cyril Flower seems to imply this: *Public Works in Med. Law*, ii (Selden Soc. xl), 40.
[9] 23 Geo. II, c. 33.
[10] *Univ. Brit. Dir.* i. 408.
[11] *Holden's Triennial Dir.* (1808), 115.
[12] *Pigot's Commercial Dir.* App. 38. The street disappeared in the metropolitan improvements of *c.* 1905.
[13] *P.O. Lond. Dir.* (1847), 1464.
[14] 9 & 10 Vic. c. 95.
[15] *V.C.H. Mdx.* i. 119–22, 124–6, 128–9.
[16] The following sources have been examined: J.I. 1/536 rott. 7, 9 (1235); S.C. 5/Mdx./1 rott. 1–2 (1278–9); J.I. 1/543 rott. 47, 55, 60, 60d., 61, 62d., 66, 66d., 68; *Plac. de Quo Warr.* 475–9 (1294); *Feud. Aids*, iii. 373–4 (1316); E 179/141/5 (1336); *Feud. Aids*, iii. 383 (1428); E 179/141/114 (1522–4); *L. & P. Hen. VIII*, iv(1), p. 422 (1524); E 179/141/118 (1525); E 179/141/122 (1534–6); E 179/141/131 (1540–1); E 179/141/138 (1542–4); E 179/141/140/, E 179/141/154 and E 179/141/155 (1545); *Mdx. Sess. Rec.* ii. 103 (1614); *Cal. S.P. Dom.* 1635, 283 (1635); Hist. MSS. Com. 4, *5th Rep. I, H. L.* 120 (1641); *Census*, 1801.

early 13th century, Bromley, Finsbury, and Knightsbridge; 23 in the late 13th century, Acton, Brentford, Chancery Lane, Chiswick, Clerkenwell, Ealing, Finchley, Hackney, Highbury, Hornsey, Kentish Town, Leicester soke, Paddington, Portpool, St. Clement Danes, St. Giles-in-the-Fields, St. Mary-le-Strand, Shadwell, Shoreditch, East Smithfield, Sutton, Westbourne, and St. Margaret, Westminster; and 6 in the 14th century, Friern Barnet, Bloomsbury, West Smithfield, Stratford, St. Martin-in-the-Fields, and Worcester soke. Fifteen of those places dropped out of the lists before 1801. There were 13 permanent additions to the lists of the 16th century, Bethnal Green, Charterhouse, Haliwell, Holborn, Limehouse, Marylebone, Norton Folgate, Poplar,

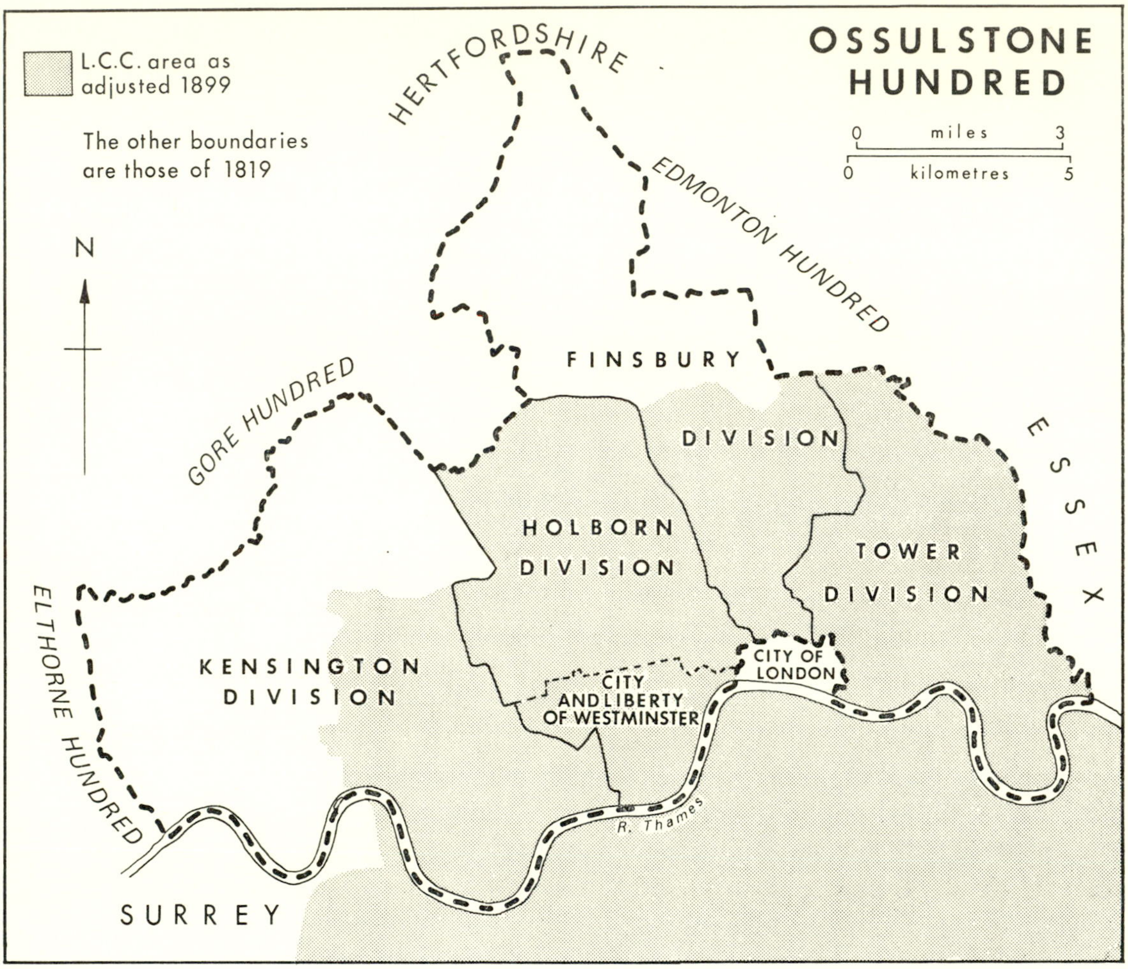

Ratcliff, St. Katherine, Savoy, Tower, and Whitechapel, and 4 temporary ones. Of these the Savoy replaces St. Mary-le-Strand, which lost its church *c.* 1548, did not regain it until 1723, and meanwhile was partially divested of parochial status.[17] In the 17th century 13 new names were listed, of which only Duchy of Lancaster, Hammersmith, Mile End, Saffron Hill, and Spitalfields were listed in 1801, when 6 other names were added, Old Artillery Ground, Glasshouse Yard, St. Luke (Old Street), St. George in the East, Wapping, and Holy Trinity (Minories). The foregoing analysis omits the inns of court and Chancery, some of the parishes in the city and liberties of Westminster, and most of the parishes in the city of London without the walls. The components of Ossulstone hundred as they were *c.* 1841 are listed elsewhere.[18] The conclusion is that the extent of the hundred remained unaltered from

[17] R. Somerville, *Savoy* (1960), 48 sqq.

[18] *V.C.H. Mdx.* ii. 113–14. For the components of the city of London without the walls and the city and liberty of Westminster see ibid. 118–19.

1086 onwards, the changes in the names of the component places reflecting variable onomastic usage and the contraction and spread of population. In 1881 the hundred covered 50,593 a. (20,474·2 ha.).

The hundred was never alienated by the Crown.[19] In 1086 it was assessed at 219¾ hides.[20] Otherwise its value is never stated, but it cannot ultimately have been high. By 1294 it was admitted that the bishop of London and the abbot of Westminster ought each to hold view of frankpledge in 7 manors, the chapter of St. Paul's in 6, the earl of Oxford in 2, and the prior of St. John of Jerusalem, the abbot of Abingdon, the master of the Temple, the prioress of Stratford, the prior of Holy Trinity, Aldgate, and Thomas de Moese each in one. Moreover the prior of St. John, as lord of Clerkenwell and Highbury, and the abbot of Westminster, as lord of the soke of Mohun, were expressly quit of suit of hundred. The same prior, as lord of Highbury, and Edmund, earl of Cornwall, as lord of the soke of Leicester, claimed a like acquittance, the former with some show of probability.[21]

The hundred was represented at the eyre of 1294 by 4 electors of jurors and 8 other jurors. Westminster was represented separately.[22] From *c.* 1384 the hundred often presented nuisances in the King's Bench[23] and between 1397 and 1496 there are references to tourns held at Ossulstone.[24]

For the purpose of mustering the people to arms or of organizing the county funds the hundred was from 1559[25] to 1729[26] almost invariably associated with Edmonton and Gore. In 1593, however, the eastern part of Ossulstone was associated with Edmonton hundred,[27] and in 1627 the whole of Ossulstone with the whole of Edmonton.[28]

A hundred bailiff is mentioned in 1314–15.[29] By 1572 the Crown had usurped the patronage of the office of bailiff errant in the hundred, an appropriation of shrieval rights paralleled elsewhere.[30] In that year life appointments were made to Richard Lorchyn[31] and Robert Lawton.[32] Lawton surrendered his patent almost at once and was reappointed by the corporation of London, to whom the appointment was said to belong in virtue of their right to farm Middlesex.[33] On Lawton's death in 1585 the corporation again appointed, choosing Rowland Scudamore, who was a nominee of Secretary Walsingham, and William Sebright, the then Common Clerk.[34] In 1613 the Crown pressed that the office should revert to one John Owen,[35] who a little later inaccurately claimed that he had been possessed of it since 1585.[36] Owen seems to have been bought off and between 1615 and 1617 he, Scudamore, and Sebright surrendered their rights.[37] In 1621, however, after a suit between the Crown and the city had been started, Owen petitioned the Crown for the bailiwick.[38] The action was still in progress in 1638.[39] The incident may be of importance as indicating the profit potential of the bailiwick. On Lorchyn's death *c.* 1608 the Crown ordered that the office be granted to Thomas Ayrey.[40] There is nothing, however, to prove that either he or Lorchyn ever took the emoluments.

Hundred bailiffs, whose relationship with the foregoing bailiff errant is uncertain,

[19] In 1294 it is expressly stated to belong to the Crown: J.I. 1/543 rot. 62.
[20] *V.C.H. Mdx.* i. 83.
[21] *Plac. de Quo Warr.* (Rec. Com.), 475–9; J.I. 1/543 rott. 61, 62d.
[22] J.I. 1/543 rott. 47.
[23] *Public Works in Med. Law*, ii. 41 sqq.
[24] Grosvenor Estate Off., Gatty's scrap bk., f. 81.
[25] *Cal. S.P. Dom.* 1547–80, 122.
[26] M.R.O., Cal. Mdx. Sess. Bks. 1727–9, 126.
[27] Hist. MSS. Com. 3, *4th Rep., Westm. Abbey*, p. 188.
[28] *Cal. S.P. Dom.* 1627–8, 323.
[29] *Cal. Pat.* 1350–4, 247, quoting Pipe R. of 1314–15.
[30] R. B. Pugh, *Imprisonment in Med. Eng.* (1968), 149.
[31] *Cal. Pat.* 1569–72, no. 3286.
[32] Ibid. no. 2987.
[33] City of Lond. R.O., Rep. 17, ff. 395v.–396v.; cf. ibid. Rep. 28, f. 4.
[34] Ibid. Rep. 159, f. 159.
[35] *Acts of P.C.* 1613–14, 334–5; cf. City of Lond. R.O., Rep. 31(1), f. 155v.
[36] *Acts of P.C.* 1615–16, 57.
[37] City of Lond. R.O., Rep. 32, f. 132v.; 33, f. 49v.
[38] Ibid. Rep. 35, ff. 241v., 242.
[39] Ibid. Rep. 52, f. 177.
[40] *Cal. S.P. Dom.* 1603–10, 402, 428.

were appointed by quarter sessions. The number rose from five (1608)[41] to ten (1617)[42] and averaged eight. In 1655 there were under-bailiffs.[43] A chief constable of the hundred is mentioned in 1574.[44] Between 1608[45] and 1618[46] four chief constables, always 'gentlemen', were appointed in quarter sessions and no doubt the practice long continued. It was decided in 1614 that their terms of office, unless extended by re-election, should be limited to three years[47] and this principle was still observed in 1743,[48] although in 1740 an incumbent served more than five years before he was relieved.[49] From 1631 the title 'high constable' was preferred[50] and was still in use in 1745.[51] By 1692 the high constables were individually associated with the four divisions.[52]

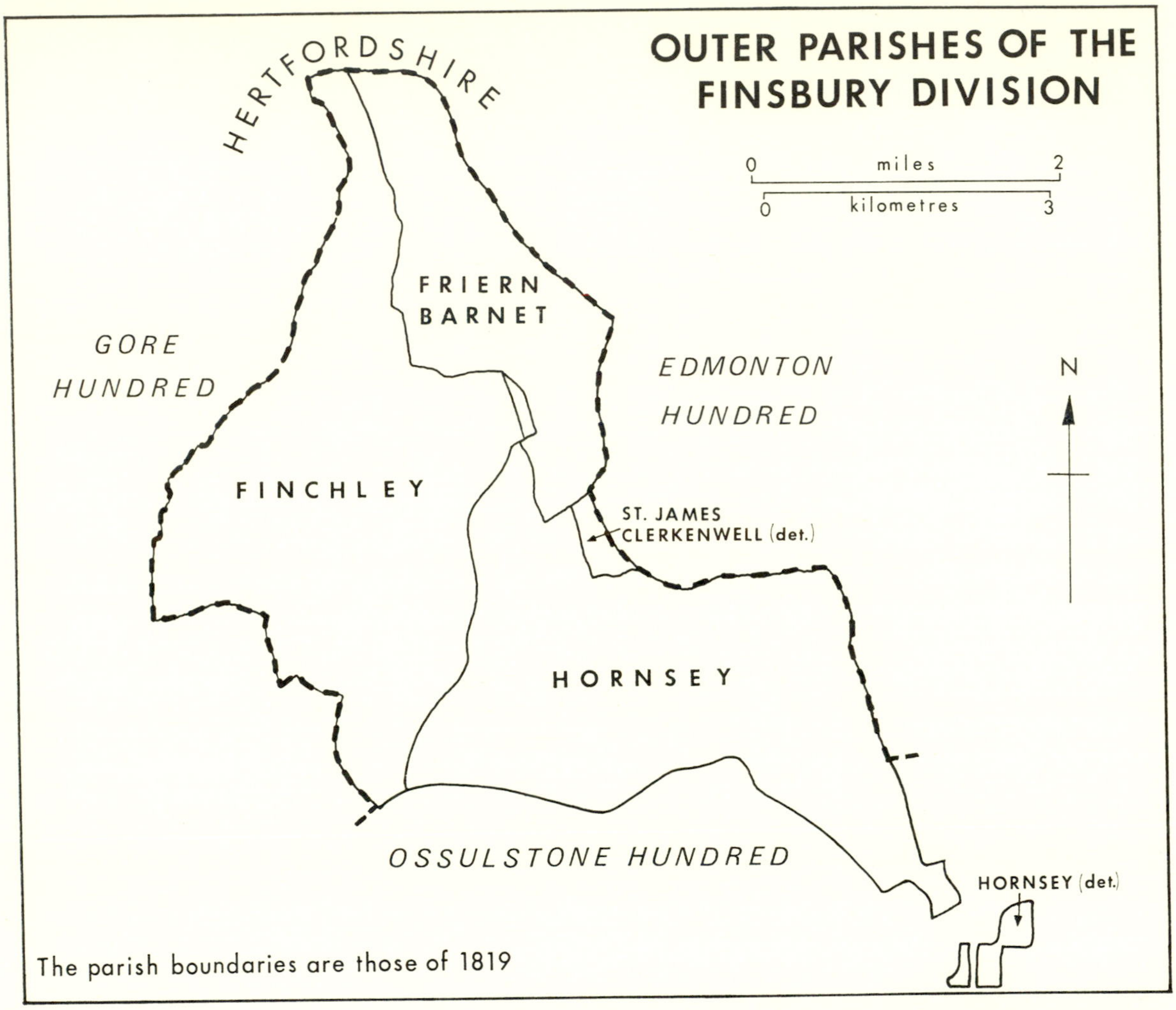

Under-constables were similarly appointed between 1608 and 1612. They averaged 95 a session.[53]

By the late 16th century the relatively dense population of the hundred, described in 1635 as very large and populous,[54] had begun to make some sub-division necessary. In 1593 an 'east' part was allied with Edmonton hundred in the conduct of an inquiry.[55] By 1613 there was a 'northern' part to which one of the high constables was attached.[56] By 1627 there were eastern and western divisions.[57] By 1634 there were four divisions.

41 M.R.O., Cal. Mdx. Rec. 1608–9, 99.
42 *Mdx. Sess. Rec.* iv. 277.
43 M.R.O., Cal. Mdx. Sess. Bks. 1652–7, 118.
44 *Mdx. Cnty. Rec.* i. 89.
45 M.R.O., Cal. Mdx. Rec. 1608–9, 221.
46 *Mdx. Sess. Rec.* iv. 329.
47 Ibid. ii. 117.
48 M.R.O., Cal. Mdx. Sess. Bks. 1742–3, 74.
49 Ibid. 1739–41, 66.
50 *Mdx. Cnty. Rec.* ii. 40.
51 M.R.O., Cal. Mdx. Sess. Bks. 1745–7, 31.
52 See below.
53 M.R.O., Cal. Mdx. Rec. i–x.
54 *Cal. S.P. Dom. Addenda*, 1625–49, 508.
55 Hist. MSS. Com. 3, *4th Rep.*, *Westm. Abbey*, p. 188.
56 *Mdx. Sess. Rec.* iii. 342.
57 *Cal. S.P. Dom.* 1627–8, 333.

They were *inter alia* petty sessional divisions, areas which appear to have originated in Middlesex.[58] The Tower and Finsbury divisions are named in 1634,[59] Holborn division in 1635.[60] Kensington division has not been noticed *eo nomine* until 1689 but was obviously much older.[61] To some degree the four divisions were treated as separate hundreds. Until 1675, when the practice was forbidden, alehouses were licensed at divisional sessions,[62] and in the census report of 1801 Finsbury division succeeds Elthorne hundred in the alphabetical sequence.[63] The Registrar General was still grouping the Ossulstone parishes by divisions in 1841 and divisional population totals were published in the census up to 1861.[64] By them the histories of the parishes and districts in the hundred will be grouped in this and succeeding volumes. The map on p. 2 shows their boundaries.

The city and liberties of Westminster, as defined in a patent of 1604,[65] were from the 16th century to the 19th in many ways distinct from the parishes of the hundred, as indeed were the liberty of the Tower and the inns of court and Chancery. Westminster, for example, had its own high constable from 1585[66] and its own commission of the peace from 1618.[67] It is clear, however, that in the 17th and earlier 18th centuries it was for fiscal purposes regarded as part of the hundred. In 1635 the whole county was rated to ship money, Westminster paying far more than the rest,[68] and in 1670[69] and 1727 Westminster was forced to contribute to fines under the Statute of Winchester (1285) for failing to arrest robbers.[70] In 1723 it was rated for certain but not for all county purposes with the rest of the hundred in which it was expressly said to lie.[71] In 1703 the high constable of Westminster along with the high constables of two of the Ossulstone divisions was ordered by the Middlesex magistrates to observe an order concerned with the quartering of soldiers.[72] By the early 18th century, however, Westminster was sometimes treated as a distinct 'division' for rating purposes[73] and is so called in the 1851 and 1861 censuses.

In this *History* the city and its liberties are not included in the Middlesex volumes but are reserved for treatment under the *History* of London. The excluded areas consist of the parishes of St. Anne, Soho, St. Clement Danes, St. George, Hanover Square, St. James, Piccadilly, St. John, Smith Square, St. Margaret, St. Martin-in-the-Fields, St. Mary-le-Strand, St. Paul, Covent Garden, part of the parish of St. Leonard, Foster Lane, London, and the extra-parochial places of St. James's Palace, the Privy Gardens, Whitehall, the close of Westminster abbey, and the verges of the palaces of St. James and Whitehall. The inns of court and Chancery are likewise excluded.

The hundred is remembered partly because it gave its name to the barony of Ossulston conferred upon John Bennet in 1682. John was the brother of Henry Bennet, earl of Arlington (d. 1686), a member of the Cabal,[74] who built Ossulston House, formerly nos. 1 and 2 St. James's Square and afterwards demolished.[75] The barony was absorbed into the earldom of Tankerville in 1714.[76] Ossulston Street, St. Pancras, laid out by 1799,[77] has existed under that name since 1807.[78] It has been subsequently extended.

[58] S. and Beatrice Webb, *Parish and County* (1924), 401; E. G. Dowdell, *Hundred Yrs. of Quarter Sessions* (1932), 10.
[59] *Cal. S.P. Dom.* 1634–5, 105.
[60] Ibid. 1635, 283.
[61] M.R.O., Cal. Mdx. Sess. Bks. 1686–9, 87.
[62] Ibid. 1673–4, 66.
[63] *Census*, 1801.
[64] *Census*, 1841–61. In 1851 and 1861 Westm. is treated as an Ossulstone division.
[65] *Archaeologia*, xxvi. 236.
[66] Westminster Act, 27 Eliz. I, c. 31.
[67] *Guide to Mdx. Sess. Rec.* ed. K. Goodacre and E. Doris Mercer (1965), 14.
[68] *Cal. S.P. Dom. Addenda*, 1625–49, 507–8.
[69] M.R.O., Cal. Mdx. Sess. Bks., 1664–73, 95–6.
[70] Ibid. 1727–9, 38.
[71] Ibid. 1722–7, 117.
[72] *Mdx. Cnty. Rec. Sess. Bks. 1689–1709*, 257.
[73] e.g. 1703: ibid.; 1726: M.R.O., Cal. Mdx. Sess. Bks. 1722–7, 293–4.
[74] *Complete Peerage*, s.v. Ossulston.
[75] *Survey of Lond.* xxx. 77 sqq.
[76] *Complete Peerage*, s.v. Ossulston.
[77] *Bowles's Plan of Lond. and its Outskirts* (1798–9).
[78] Didier and Tebbett, *New Plan of . . . Lond.* (1807).

FRIERN BARNET

FRIERN BARNET,[1] home of Colney Hatch asylum, is a small parish 7 miles north of London and, with Finchley, protrudes into Hertfordshire.[2] Its maximum length along the main north-north-west axis is 3 miles and nowhere is it more than 1½ mile wide. The extent of the civil parish was 1,304 a. in 1871. In 1891 a small detached portion of Hornsey at Colney Hatch was included in Friern Barnet. The area increased to 1,340 a. between 1931 and 1937, through adjustments to boundaries on the incorporations of Finchley and Southgate, and to 1,342 a. in 1951.[3] The parish acquired a local board in 1884, became a U.D. in 1895, and from 1965 was included in the London Borough of Barnet.[4]

There are no natural boundaries, the location of estates having probably determined the border with Hertfordshire to the north and north-east. Edmonton and Tottenham lie to the south-east, Clerkenwell detached (later part of Hornsey), and Hornsey to the south, Hornsey and Finchley to the south-west, and Finchley to the west. Boundaries with Clerkenwell detached were marked by 1339 and with Finchley and Hertfordshire by 1515.[5] Where woods extended into Tottenham, Edmonton, and Finchley,[6] the boundary may have been fixed later. The bounds were beaten annually by 1781[7] and marked by posts from 1855.[8]

Most of the ground lies on London Clay. A narrow deposit of brickearth lines Bounds Green brook. Boulder clay from Finchley stretches into the north part of the parish as far as All Saints' Avenue and along the whole western boundary the clay is flanked by glacial gravel, which extends eastward to Russell Lane in the north and through Colney Hatch to New Southgate in the south. The Friary, Manor House Farm, and St. James's church stand on an outcrop of gravel beside Friern Barnet Lane.[9] The highest point is Whetstone High Road in the north, on a ridge of over 300 ft. which recedes gradually southward along the Great North Road in Finchley. The whole of Friern Barnet south and east of that line falls away sharply as far as Bounds Green brook. The 250-ft. contour curves from Oakleigh Park station to the parish church. The only areas below 125 ft. are farther east, including part of Bethune recreation ground, and to the south on either side of Bounds Green brook, south of which the land rises steeply to 250 ft. towards Muswell Hill.[10]

The streams are all tributaries of Pymme's brook. Blackett's brook, mentioned *c.* 1513,[11] runs southward from a re-entrant in the North Middlesex golf course, eastward across Friern Barnet Lane, and under the railway towards Hertfordshire. Streams also flowed eastward under Friern Barnet Lane from Friary park by the so-called Queen Elizabeth's well in 1826 and through a culvert near the alms-houses. Farther south Bounds Green brook flows along the line of the North Circular Road to Southgate.[12] Bridges called Ruffins bridge and Stone bridge were decayed in 1519[13] and Queen's bridge at 'Mr. Graham's Bottom' was to be repaired in 1765,[14] but in 1783 and 1846 Blackett's and Bounds Green brooks crossed the road in watersplashes.[15] Both brooks had been bridged by 1865 and the two northernmost streams were later mainly culverted.[16]

About 1197 the church, lands, and woods lay in 'Barnet',[17] which was not distinguished from the neighbouring Barnets in Hertfordshire. The name denoted a 'place cleared by burning', which may have been only recently assarted and presumably was relatively unimportant in 1237, when Barnet in Middlesex was termed Little Barnet. Not until 1274 was it called Frerenbarnet,[18] recording the lordship of the brotherhood or knights of the Hospital of St. John and later crystallized into Friern Barnet. The name was applied not only to the parish but to the manor, which from the 15th century, however, was usually called Whetstone.[19]

There were early settlements at Whetstone in the north-west part of the parish, at Friern Barnet in the centre, and at Colney Hatch to the south-east. The name Whetstone occurred from 1398[20] and so cannot have derived from a stone used to sharpen swords before the battle of Barnet.[21] Colney Hatch was first mentioned in 1409,[22] the 'hatch' perhaps being a gate of Hollick wood.[23]

Friern Barnet parish remained largely rural until after the First World War. The building of Colney Hatch asylum in 1851 helped to cut off the area to the south, and the location of railways caused the edges of the parish to be built up first. In 1883 the most populous and prosperous district was that of All Saints', Whetstone. Sixty-one per cent of the total population, however, lived in the Freehold, Avenue, and Holly Park districts,[24] which had grown up around Colney Hatch. The working-class

[1] The article was written in 1975. Any references to later yrs. are dated. The help of Mrs. J. M. Corden in commenting on the article is gratefully acknowledged.
[2] Except where otherwise stated, the following four paras. are based on O.S. Maps 6″, Mdx. VI. SE., VII. SW., XI. NE., XII. NW. (1863 and later edns.).
[3] *Census*, 1871–1951; *V.C.H. Mdx.* v. 179.
[4] See p. 27.
[5] See p. 25.
[6] Natives of Friern Barnet had rights of common in Finchley until 1814: M.R.O., EA/FIN.
[7] M.R.O., D.R.O. 12/I/C1/1.
[8] Ibid. C1/4.
[9] Geol. Surv. Map 1″, drift, sheet 256 (1951 edn.).
[10] O.S. Map 1/25,000, TQ 29 (1969 edn.).
[11] St. Paul's MSS., box B 17, m. 11.
[12] M.R.O., MA/A/J3/19; *Finchley Press*, 17 July 1925; *Rep. on Bridges in Mdx.*
[13] St. Paul's MSS., box B 17, mm. 11, 14d.
[14] M.R.O., D.R.O. 12/I/C1/1.
[15] Guildhall Libr., map case 247; M.R.O., TA/FRI; *Rep. on Bridges in Mdx.*
[16] O.S. Map 1/25,000, TQ 29 (1969 edn.).
[17] *Rot. Chart.* (Rec. Com.), 16; *Feet of Fines, 1196–7* (P.R.S. xx), no. 37.
[18] *P.N. Mdx.* (E.P.N.S.), 99–100.
[19] St. Paul's MSS., box B 17.
[20] See p. 38.
[21] *P.N. Mdx.* (E.P.N.S.), 100–1.
[22] *Sel. Cases in K.B.* (Selden Soc. lxxxviii), pp. 186–7.
[23] Hollick wood is more likely than Enfield Chase, suggested in *P.N. Mdx.* (E.P.N.S.), 100.
[24] *Barnet Press*, 13 Oct. 1883.

Freehold, so called in the late 19th century when the original ownership of the land had been forgotten, lay south of Bounds Green brook and east of Colney Hatch Lane. The Avenue was a similar area north-east of Colney Hatch, in the angle between Oakleigh Road South and Friern Barnet Road and separated by the railway from Holly Park, to the west.[25] Relative densities of population were altered by building in the central and northern parts of the parish after 1920.[26] More than ten per cent of the land was still open in 1975, most of it in the southern part. From the mid 19th century newcomers have worked mainly outside the parish, which by 1933 was largely residential.[27]

John Walker (d. 1807), actor and lexicographer, was born at Friern Barnet in 1732.[28] The philanthropist Dr. Samuel Wilson Warneford (d. 1855) was married at Colney Hatch in 1796. Charles Macfarlane (d. 1858), miscellaneous author, lived in a cottage at Friern Barnet in 1846.[29] Among those buried in the parish were Sir William Oldes, gentleman usher of the Black Rod, in 1718;[30] Admiral Sir Thomas Pasley, Bt. (d. 1808), whose hatchment hangs in St. James's church;[31] the song-writer Helen Selina Sheridan (d. 1867), later Lady Dufferin and countess of Gifford; and Herbert Kynaston (d. 1878), hymnologist and high master of St. Paul's school. Other notable inhabitants are mentioned below.

COMMUNICATIONS. Friern Barnet's road system was established by the late 15th century. The main north–south route of that date became known as Whetstone High Road in the north, as Friern Barnet Lane between Whetstone and Colney Hatch, and as Colney Hatch Lane from there to Muswell Hill. According to Norden, it had been the principal highway from London to Barnet and the north of England but by the early 14th century the main road ran through Hornsey park to Finchley and thence to rejoin Friern Barnet Lane at Whetstone, along the route of the modern Great North Road.[32] Thus only Whetstone High Road, in the extreme north-west part of the parish, was left as a major line of communication.

Friern Barnet Lane, also known as Friern Lane, which was realigned *c.* 1790,[33] was Wolkstreet *c.* 1518.[34] Colney Hatch Lane, so called from 1846,[35] was Halliwick Street (Halwykstrete) in 1398[36] and Muswell Hill Lane or Aspen Lane in 1801.[37] No route led westward, except via Whetstone. To the east a road led from Colney Hatch to Betstile, where it met roads to Enfield, Tottenham and Wood Green, East Barnet, and the modern Oakleigh Road. It was known in turn as Betstile Lane between 1549 and 1785,[38] Southgate Lane in 1801,[39] High Road in 1879,[40] and Friern Barnet Road from 1889.[41]

Oakleigh Road runs north-west from New Southgate parallel with Friern Barnet Lane to Whetstone High Road. The northern part or perhaps the whole was Avernstreet in 1499,[42] Hungerdown Lane from at least 1823 until 1881,[43] Blackhorse Lane in 1851,[44] Station Road from 1863 to 1871, and Oakleigh Road by 1873.[45] The stretch north of the Brunswick railway bridge became Oakleigh Road North, the rest Oakleigh Road South. Leading north-east from the centre of Oakleigh Road to East Barnet was Mare Lane, so called in 1522 and 1825[46] but also known as Beldams Lane before 1820, when it was described as Blackhorse Lane,[47] and as East Barnet Lane by 1863.[48] In 1975 it was Russell Lane. By 1754 the modern Coppetts Road ran from Crouch End along the south-west parish boundary north towards Colney Hatch,[49] which by 1846 was linked by a track south of Bounds Green brook to Colney Hatch Lane.[50] At the northern end Coppetts Road met a route running westward from Colney Hatch shortly before it forked into two tracks crossing Finchley common, later Woodhouse Road and Summers Lane.[51] In the late 15th and early 16th centuries many copyhold lanes apparently led to individual holdings.[52]

South of Whetstone, in addition to Woodhouse Road and Summers Lane, roads on the lines of the later Torrington Park and Friary roads were planned in the 1820s[53] and had been laid out by 1863[54] as Friern Park North and South.[55] Friern Barnet Lane and Oakleigh Road were linked only after 1903 by Myddelton Park.[56] Oakleigh Park North and South, following earlier footpaths, were laid out by 1888.[57] The principal roads of the Freehold in the south part of the parish existed by 1863, but access to Colney Hatch station was made difficult by the asylum to the north and the railway to the east, which apparently impeded growth in 1895.[58] A route across the railway line was not provided until the construction of the North Circular Road

25 See pp. 11, 13.
26 See p. 14.
27 D. H. Smith, *Industries of Gtr. Lond.* (1933), 73.
28 Except where otherwise stated, the para. is based on *D.N.B.*
29 M.R.O., TA/FRI.
30 Lysons, *Environs*, ii. 24.
31 J. Phillips, *Sht. Hist. of Par. of Friern Barnet* (1967), 15.
32 See p. 39.
33 Guildhall MS. 14223/3, p. 287.
34 St. Paul's MSS., box B 17, m. 14d.
35 *Finchley Press*, 19 Nov. 1948.
36 *Pub. Works in Med. Law*, ii (Selden Soc. xl), p. 38.
37 M.L.R. 1801/2/150.
38 St. Paul's MSS., box B 16, m. 7; box B 17, m. 21; B.L.H.L., Acc. 9888 (highway surveyors' acct. bk. 1785).
39 M.L.R. 1801/2/150.
40 M.R.O., D.R.O. 12/I/G7/1.
41 *Kelly's Dir. Barnet* (1889).
42 St. Paul's MSS., box B 17, m. 5.
43 Barnet Mus., Pandora box, P.B. 15/189; Barnet Mus. 1287.
44 H.O. 107/1701/1A ff. 319–31. In 1827 Blackhorse and Hungerdown lanes were distinct: M.R.O., D.R.O. 12/I/C1/2.
45 R.G. 10/1334 ff. 93–101, 109; M.R.O., D.R.O. 12/I/C1/4; O.S. Map 6", Mdx. VII. SW. (1863–4 edn.).
46 St. Paul's MSS., box B 15, m. 15; M.L.R. 1857/3/294.
47 Guildhall MS. 14223/5, p. 194.
48 O.S. Map 6", Mdx. VII. SW. (1863–4 edn.).
49 J. Rocque, *Map of Mdx.* (1754).
50 M.R.O., TA/FRI.
51 Rocque, *Map of Mdx.* (1754); see below, p. 41.
52 St. Paul's MSS., box B 17.
53 M.R.O., MA/A/J3/19t, u.
54 O.S. Map 6", Mdx. VI. SE. (1863–6 edn.).
55 B.L.H.L., Acc. 9888 (deeds). The colln. mainly comprises Friern Barnet loc. bd. and U.D. min. bks. and deeds.
56 M.R.O., D.R.O. 12/I/A12/6.
57 Barnet Mus. 99.
58 *Barnet Press*, 2 Mar. 1895.

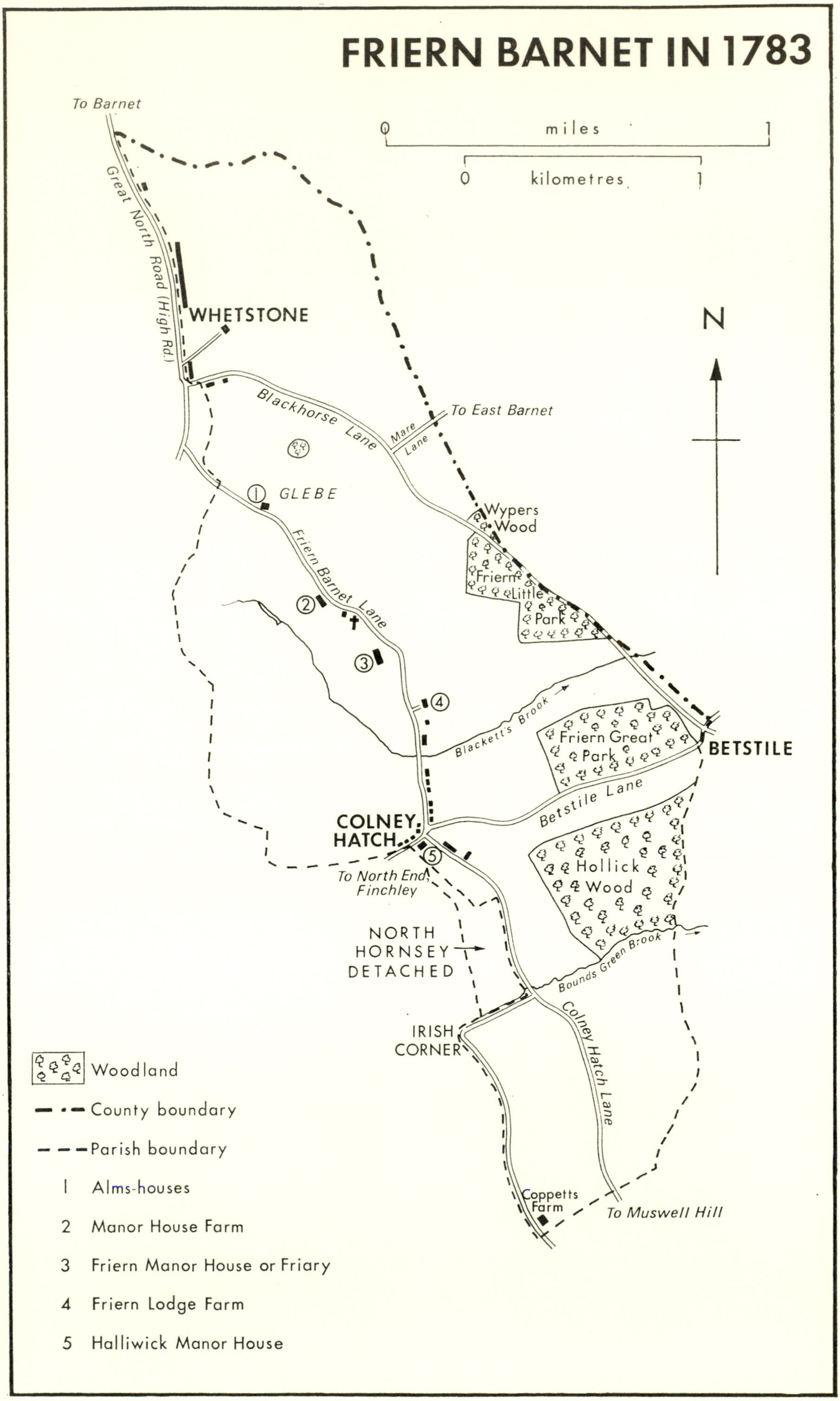
FRIERN BARNET IN 1783
To Barnet
0 miles 1
0 kilometres 1
N
Great North Road (High Rd.)
WHETSTONE
Blackhorse Lane
Mare Lane
To East Barnet
GLEBE
Wypers Wood
Friern Little Park
Friern Barnet Lane
Blackett's Brook
Friern Great Park
BETSTILE
Betstile Lane
COLNEY HATCH
Hollick Wood
To North End, Finchley
NORTH HORNSEY DETACHED
Bounds Green Brook
IRISH CORNER
Colney Hatch Lane
Coppetts Farm
To Muswell Hill
Woodland
County boundary
Parish boundary
1 Alms-houses
2 Manor House Farm
3 Friern Manor House or Friary
4 Friern Lodge Farm
5 Halliwick Manor House

(Pinkham Way) after 1929.[59] In 1975 a fly-over was built over it to carry Colney Hatch Lane.

In 1754 Whetstone High Road was turnpiked in spite of local opposition and after 1810, when it was managed by the Whetstone and Highgate turnpike trust, it was said to be one of the best roads in the country.[60] In 1856 the Compagnie Générale des Omnibus de Londres employed two omnibuses on the London–Barnet route via Whetstone[61] and *c.* 1870 the journey from Whetstone to the City took 1¾ hour.[62] In 1901 Middlesex C.C. and the Metropolitan Tramways and Omnibus Co. obtained light railway powers for routes from Highgate to Whetstone and from Tottenham via Southgate to Friern Barnet.[63] The first route was completed in 1905 and in 1906 workmen's trams left regularly from 5 a.m.[64] The second reached Oakleigh Road in 1906,[65] permitting travel to Wood Green and thence to Enfield or Finsbury,[66] but was not extended along Woodhouse and Friern Barnet roads until 1909.[67] In 1914 there were combined Underground and motor-bus tickets from London via Highgate to Colney Hatch Lane.[68] In 1933 a motor-bus ran from Friern Barnet across London[69] and in 1936 Oakleigh Road was served by so many buses from Palmers Green to Whetstone that Friern Barnet U.D.C. considered pruning the services.[70] There were good communications with all neighbouring parishes *c.* 1948: trolley-buses ran from Finchley via Colney Hatch to Holborn and regular motor-buses from Potters Bar via Friern Barnet Lane to Victoria station. Motor-buses in the east part of the parish and trolley-buses in the centre served stations on the Piccadilly line,[71] probably Bounds Green and Arnos Grove as in 1958, when there were also motor-buses to the City and west end of London.[72] An omnibus garage at no. 165 Sydney Road was opened *c.* 1931 by the London Passenger Transport Board, later London Transport.[73]

In 1845 the Great Northern Railway's line to York was planned to skirt the eastern edge of Friern Barnet.[74] It was built slightly farther west, through the eastern end of Hollick wood,[75] and helped to determine the choice of an adjoining site for the county lunatic asylum. In 1850 the G.N.R. agreed in principle to a station, after requests from the Middlesex justices, who insisted on a train's stopping daily.[76] The station was built next to the asylum, with a siding which connected by a tramway to the stores depot in the grounds.[77] There was one train hourly to Hatfield in the north and to Hornsey and King's Cross in the south in 1860, when the journey to King's Cross took 18 minutes.[78] Trains still ran hourly in 1975. Access to the City was eased by the opening of the Metropolitan Railway in 1863.[79] Colney Hatch station initially stood in Edmonton parish[80] but was moved in 1889–90 farther north to a position over the tracks.[81] It was renamed Southgate and Colney Hatch in 1855, New Southgate and Colney Hatch in 1876, and New Southgate and Friern Barnet in 1923.[82] The line was bridged for Friern Barnet and Oakleigh roads and tunnelled between Oakleigh Park and Brunswick Park. Oakleigh Park station, opened in 1873[83] between Colney Hatch and New Barnet stations, was in Hertfordshire.

Residents in the western and north-western parts of the parish could use stations beyond the boundary at Woodside Park and at Totteridge and Whetstone, on the branch line to High Barnet opened by the G.N.R. in 1872. The branch ran from Finchley Central on the line to Edgware from Finsbury Park, whence trains ran to King's Cross[84] and, from 1904, along the Great Northern and City Railway to Moorgate.[85] In 1940 the line to High Barnet became part of the Northern line, with Underground trains to the City and west end of London.[86]

The Freehold was served by Muswell Hill station on the G.N.R.'s branch line from Highgate to the Alexandra Palace. The line, opened in 1873, finally closed in 1954.[87]

GROWTH. The original settlement may have bordered Friern Barnet Lane near the church, but the manor-house built soon after 1551 and two farm-houses existing by the mid 17th century were the only residences near by in 1754.[88] The surrounding area, in the centre of the parish, consisted entirely of demesne late in the 15th century and was still mainly wood in 1544.[89] By 1488 there were two areas of copyhold land, one at Colney Hatch and the other north-east and south-east of Whetstone.[90] There were two chief pledges for Whetstone and one for Colney Hatch,[91] and copyhold tenements such as Sayers, Newmans, Cuckolds, and Tromers[92] were named after former holders, implying that the pattern of settlement was several generations old.

Whetstone village may have grown in the 14th century, when the diversion of the Great North Road made it an important road junction.[93] The

59 R. Hunter and I. Macalpine, *Psychiatry for the Poor* (1974), 152.
60 *Mdx. & Herts. N. & Q.* iv. 92.
61 V. Sommerfield, *London's Buses* (1933), 20.
62 *Hist. Lond. Transport*, i. 170.
63 Ibid. ii. 30.
64 Robbins, *Mdx.* 222.
65 *Barnet Press*, 11 May 1907; *Kelly's Dir. Barnet* (1906).
66 *Kelly's Dir. Barnet* (1906).
67 Robbins, *Mdx.* 222.
68 *Hist. Lond. Transport*, ii. 185.
69 Sommerfield, *London's Buses*, 86.
70 *Barnet Press*, 13 Feb. 1936.
71 M.R.O., D.R.O. 12/I/H/8a: copy of Friern Barnet U.D. *Official Guide* [*c.* 1948], 10.
72 M.R.O., D.R.O. 12/I/H/8b: copy of Friern Barnet U.D. *Official Guide* [1958], 15.
73 *Kelly's Dir. Finchley* (1930, 1932).
74 M.R.O., MR/UP254.
75 Hunter and Macalpine, *Psychiatry for the Poor*, 22.
76 M.R.O., Acc. 1038/1A (governors' min. bk.); 2A, pp. 40, 141, 181.
77 M.R.O., Acc. 1038/4A, p. 59; Hunter and Macalpine, *Psychiatry for the Poor*, 161; O.S. Map 6″, Mdx. VII. SW. (1897 edn.).
78 M.R.O., Acc. 1038/13.
79 G. R. Grinling, *Hist. of Gt. Northern Rly.* (1966), 201.
80 O.S. Map 6″, Mdx. VII. SW. (1863–6 edn.).
81 Ex inf. Mr. H. V. Borley.
82 J. E. Connor and B. L. Halford, *Forgotten Stations of Gtr. Lond.* (1972), 6, 11, 13.
83 M.R.O., MJ/SR 5322/84; ex inf. Mr. H. V. Borley.
84 Grinling, *G.N.R.* 234, 280; see below, p. 42.
85 *Hist. Lond. Transport*, ii. 49–50.
86 C. E. Lee, *60 Yrs. of the Northern* (1968), 26.
87 *V.C.H. Mdx.* v. 312–13; see below, p. 106.
88 Rocque, *Map of Mdx.* (1754).
89 See p. 21.
90 St. Paul's MSS., box B 17; box A 62. See also Guildhall Libr., map case 247; B.L.H.L., Acc. 9381/1 (photocopy of key to map *penes* Church Com.).
91 See p. 25.
92 St. Paul's MSS., box B 17; box A 62.
93 See above.

bell at the Bell House summoned people from Whetstone to Friern Barnet church,[94] thought to be conveniently located in 1650.[95] By 1677 settlement was concentrated on both the Finchley and Friern Barnet sides of the Great North Road,[96] and in 1754 it adjoined the entrances to Oakleigh Road and Friern Barnet Lane.[97] Probably most of the five offenders against the assize of ale in 1492 lived in Whetstone,[98] where inns were always numerous. The Lion, one of two mentioned in 1636,[99] existed by 1521[1] and may have been the same as the Red Lion,[2] later becoming the Green Man.[3] The Green Dragon existed by 1662,[4] the Bell House soon after,[5] and the Griffin by 1697.[6] There may have been seven public houses on the Friern Barnet side of the road in 1716[7] and by 1800 five of the parish's six inns were at Whetstone: the Griffin, Green Man, King's Head, Blue Anchor, and Black Bull.[8] In 1876 and 1882 the inns catered for waggoners and stage coaches, as did forges and coach-houses.[9] Travellers have often stopped where the road widens in front of the Griffin, a red-brick Georgian building of two storeys, rebuilt *c.* 1929 and abutting on a plain two-storeyed late-18th-century house.[10] The imposing Green Man, rebuilt in 1830, is of red brick in three narrow storeys and has been turned into a garage. In 1851 68 houses, with 367 inhabitants, were on the Friern Barnet side of the road,[11] where in 1876 buildings straggled for a considerable distance.[12] Apart from public houses, the village in 1882 consisted of shops and nondescript terraces,[13] many of them old-fashioned and poor.[14]

Colney Hatch was a hamlet in 1409.[15] Although on the edge of the manors of Whetstone and Halliwick and at the junction of Friern Barnet and Colney Hatch lanes with Friern Barnet Road, it lacked commercial importance. In 1795 it was estimated to have only twelve of the 78 houses in the parish[16] and those mostly belonged to gentlemen. Halliwick manor-house stood north of some cottages and on the south-west corner of the broad junction. The White House and the Orange Tree inn stood on the north-west, a little below Brook House, the Priory on the north-east, with the Woodlands, Greenbank, and Springfield farther north,[17] and the Hermitage and several cottages on the south-west by 1783.[18] Until rebuilt *c.* 1923[19] the Orange Tree consisted of two red-brick buildings: that to the south was cramped and later disfigured by hoardings but the northern one remained an elegant 18th-century building, of three storeys and two bays. Each had a large garden. There was very little change in the 19th century before the construction of the county lunatic asylum, and in 1882 Colney Hatch was described as a village which had sprung up to serve the staff.[20]

South of Bounds Green brook there was only Coppetts Farm between 1783 and 1846.[21] At the eastern end of Friern Barnet Road was the hamlet of Betstile. Before 1815 most of the houses lay in Hertfordshire or Edmonton, apart from Betstile House on the corner of Friern Barnet and Oakleigh roads,[22] but by 1846 others stood north of the road, on the site of the former Friern great park, and the former Friern little park in Oakleigh Road had been divided into plots with cottages.[23] Since the mid 19th century Betstile has been better known as New Southgate.

Growth was uneven from the mid 19th century. In 1801 there were 56 inhabited houses in Whetstone, 55 in Friern Barnet, and 33 in Colney Hatch, and by 1841 the population had doubled over forty years.[24] After 1852 several schemes for the central area were abandoned or only partially carried out: 35 new houses were inhabited there by 1883,[25] when it contrasted with the built-up periphery of the parish,[26] and no estate was completed before 1914. Until that date most houses were built for labourers and clerks in the Avenue, Freehold, and Holly Park districts, although all parts experienced some growth. In 1909 there were 971 dwellings in the south, 722 in the central, and 403 in the north wards, when it was proposed that the south ward should elect 5, the central ward 4, and the north ward only 3 members to the U.D.C.[27] After 1920 there was little building in the south ward but the centre and north were steadily covered. The U.D.C. was a leading builder from 1919, until in 1953 there were 674 council houses in a total of 8,162.[28]

In 1828 new roads were proposed for central Friern Barnet,[29] where early plans were made for access to the Great North Road rather than Friern Barnet Lane. In 1852 Finsbury Road (later Finchley Park), a cul-de-sac from the Great North Road into Friern Barnet with two southern spurs, had been laid out as the Finsbury estate in at least 36 plots.[30] There were a few houses in 1865[31] but the estate was not completed until after 1900.[32] It was bordered on the north by Goslings and

[94] *Finchley Press*, 14 Jan. 1949.
[95] *Home Cnties. Mag.* i. 57.
[96] Ogilby, *Map of Mdx.* (*c.* 1677).
[97] Rocque, *Map of Mdx.* (1754).
[98] St. Paul's MSS., box B 17, m. 2.
[99] *Mdx. & Herts. N. & Q.* iv. 78.
[1] St. Paul's MSS., box B 17, m. 14.
[2] Ibid. box B 15, m. 6d.
[3] Guildhall MS. 14223/3, pp. 1, 9, 23.
[4] St. Paul's MSS., box B 16, m. 1.
[5] *Finchley Press*, 14 Jan. 1949.
[6] M.R.O., Acc. 410/19.
[7] M.R.O., MR/LV3/3.
[8] Ibid. 10/87.
[9] Thorne, *Environs*, 693; Walford, *Gtr. Lond.* i. 336.
[10] Barnet Mus. 1056, 1060 (postcards).
[11] H.O. 107/1701/1A ff. 309–19.
[12] Thorne, *Environs*, 693.
[13] Walford, *Gtr. Lond.* i. 336. See below, plate facing p. 32.
[14] Thorne, *Environs*, 693.
[15] *Sel. Cases in K.B.* vii (Selden Soc. lxxxviii), pp. 186–7. There is no evidence that a decayed town lay in Hollick wood, as stated in Norden, *Spec. Brit.* 20.
[16] Lysons, *Environs*, ii. 21–5.
[17] Sales parts. in B.L.H.L.
[18] Guildhall Libr., map case 247.
[19] Barnet Mus. 1304, 1144.
[20] Walford, *Gtr. Lond.* i. 342.
[21] Guildhall Libr., map case 247; M.R.O., TA/FRI.
[22] M.R.O., EA/FIN.
[23] M.R.O., TA/FRI.
[24] *Census*, 1801, 1841. Figures for later yrs. exclude the occupants of the asylum.
[25] Nat. Soc. file; M.R.O., D.R.O. 12/I/K1/1 (par. mag., June 1883).
[26] *Barnet Press*, 13 Oct. 1883.
[27] Ibid. 19 June, 26 June 1909; B.L.H.L., Friern Barnet U.D., min. bk. (1908–11), p. 146.
[28] Barnet Mus. 2163: copy of Friern Barnet U.D. *Petit. for Incorp. as Municip. Boro.* (1953), 7.
[29] M.R.O., MA/AJ3/19.
[30] B.L.H.L., Acc. 9888 (deeds).
[31] O.S. Map 6″, Mdx. VI. SE. (1863–6 edn.).
[32] Ibid. (1897 edn.).

Dovescroft of $13\frac{1}{2}$ a., which in 1853 were acquired by Morgan Godbold and Co.,[33] who laid out the Finchley freehold estate of 114 allotments. Opposite the Swan with Two Necks in the Great North Road, Britannia Road stretched to the edge of John Miles's estates and was to form a square with other streets. Presumably there was little demand for housing, as by 1857 Miles had purchased almost the whole, redeeming certain lots from other buyers.[34] Only the west end of Britannia Road was constructed. A little farther south Torrington Park and Friary Road were laid out on Thomas Bensley's former estate between Friern Barnet Lane and the Great North Road by 1865,[35] where between 1866 and 1868 the land was sold by H. D. Holden. Some lots were incorporated in the estate of John Miles, later the North Middlesex golf course,[36] but most were sold to the Planet Building Society, which planned a road south-westward from Friern Barnet Lane across Torrington Park to the Great North Road.[37] The western stretch, intended to join Friern Park, was laid out as Torrington Road in the Finchley estate of the Middlesex Freehold Land Association on land that had not belonged to Bensley.[38] It was hardly built on by 1865 and was not finished until after 1897,[39] while the eastern end was never developed. Edmund William Richardson, secretary of the building society, bought most of the plots between Friary Road and Torrington Park as his garden,[40] in 1975 Friary park, and others were retained for agriculture by George Knights Smith.[41] There were a few houses between the roads by 1897 but the whole area was built over only between the World Wars.[42] It contained the Friern Watch estate of Newcombe Estates, which consisted of the avenues between High Road, Finchley Park, and Friary and Torrington roads.[43] Central Friern Barnet grew slowly as transport improved and was mainly farm-land until after the First World War. In 1883 it contained only 90 houses.[44]

The opening of Colney Hatch asylum and station brought new residents to the area east of the railway. In 1854 G. K. Smith was letting cottages in Carlisle Place and in 1864 Cornwall Terrace, Ely Place, and Railway Cottages had been built in Oakleigh Road South and Southgate Cottages in Friern Barnet Road.[45] Betstile House had been replaced by terraced cottages before 1888,[46] when Smith sold 8 a. between the two roads for further building.[47] Better known as the Avenue, the land was sold in 1890 to the United Estates & Investment Co.[48] St. Paul's, Holmesdale, and Stanhope roads, the Avenue, and Carlisle Place, with small houses close together, were laid out.[49] There were 185 houses with 925 occupants in 1883, when only the Freehold had a lower rateable value,[50] and in 1891 the district was considered one of the roughest in the northern suburbs.[51] Houses of similar type, such as Rathbone Cottages, were erected *c.* 1865 north of the Brunswick railway bridge.[52]

The Freehold's roads were defined in 1863,[53] probably by the Westminster Freehold Land Society,[54] and by 1867 they had *c.* 130 houses, with *c.* 1,000 inhabitants.[55] The influx was of labourers employed on the Alexandra Palace in Wood Green, whom the parish could not immediately absorb. In 1866 the roads, drains, and water supply were considered as bad as the moral condition of the newcomers,[56] many of whom left the district[57] when the first palace was burnt down.[58] Seven occupants per house was considered a modest estimate in 1867,[59] only two families kept servants in 1877,[60] and there were 870 inhabitants in 174 houses in 1883.[61] The rented houses, neglected and difficult to keep sanitary in 1893,[62] accommodated many young, poor, and abnormally large families in 1904.[63] As late as 1920 the inhabitants were mainly artisans and casual labourers.[64] In spite of such expansion, land east of Colney Hatch Lane was still being farmed in 1902 and was not built on until the 1930s.[65] The Albion Estates Co. had laid out half of its Halliwick Manor estate west of Colney Hatch Lane for 800 houses *c.* 1899[66] and there was land for 500–700 houses, with four miles of road frontage, in 1901.[67] The houses were intended for sale.[68] In 1909 4,537 people lived in 971 houses in the south ward.[69]

Holly Park, the district north of Friern Barnet Road and so called after 1871, attracted the first commuters after the opening of Colney Hatch station.[70] In 1904 they were mainly London clerks, keeping up appearances on small incomes.[71] They lived in small semi-detached houses, described as smart villas in 1876,[72] or in superior terraced houses with bay windows, such as Edith, Glen, and Thorne villas and Cyprus and Clydesdale terraces in Glenthorne Road.[73] The Holly Park estate of 33 a.

33 M.L.R. 1857/8/31; B.L.H.L., Acc. 9888 (deeds).
34 B.L.H.L., Acc. 9888.
35 O.S. Map 6″, Mdx. VI. SE. (1863–6 edn.).
36 See p. 25.
37 B.L.H.L., Acc. 9888.
38 M.R.O., Acc. 410/32; D.R.O. 12/I/B4/1.
39 O.S. Maps 6″, Mdx. VI. SE. (1863–6 and 1897 edns.).
40 B.L.H.L., Acc. 9888.
41 M.R.O., D.R.O. 12/I/B4/1.
42 O.S. Maps 6″, Mdx. VI. SE. (1863–6 and later edns.).
43 Sales parts. in B.L.H.L.
44 *Barnet Press*, 13 Oct. 1883.
45 O.S. Map 6″, Mdx. VII. SW. (1863–4 edn.); M.R.O., D.R.O. 12/I/F1/4, p. 42.
46 M.R.O., Acc. 410/85a; O.S. Map 6″, Mdx. VII. SW. (1863–4 edn.).
47 M.R.O., D.R.O. 12/I/G10/2.
48 Ibid.
49 *Kelly's Dir. Barnet* (1889 and later edns.); Friern Barnet U.D. *Ann. Rep. of M.O.H.* (1892).
50 *Barnet Press*, 13 Oct. 1883.
51 Ibid. 21 Feb. 1891.
52 O.S. Map 6″, Mdx. VII. SW. (1863–4 edn.); Barnet Mus. 78, 75.
53 O.S. Map 6″, Mdx. XII. NW. (1863–9 edn.).
54 They held the land in 1860: B.L. Add. MS. 31323 BBB.
55 M.R.O., D.R.O. 12/I/K2/2 (ann. rep. for 1867).
56 Ibid. (1866).
57 Nat. Soc. file; M.R.O., D.R.O. 12/I/G5/2, pp. 40, 76.
58 M.R.O., D.R.O. 12/I/G5/1; G5/2, p. 31.
59 Ibid. K2/1 (1867).
60 Nat. Soc. files.
61 *Barnet Press*, 13 Oct. 1883.
62 Friern Barnet U.D. *Ann. Rep. of M.O.H.*
63 Nat. Soc. files.
64 Friern Barnet U.D. *Ann. Rep. of M.O.H.*
65 M.R.O., Acc. 525/2–3.
66 M.R.O., D.R.O. 12/III/1/2.
67 Nat. Soc. files.
68 M.R.O., D.R.O. 12/III/1/2.
69 *Barnet Press*, 20 June 1909.
70 Building had not begun in 1871: R.G. 10/1334 ff. 60–110.
71 Nat. Soc. file.
72 Thorne, *Environs*, 115.
73 *P.O. Dir. N. Suburbs* (1888); *Kelly's Dir. Barnet* (1889).

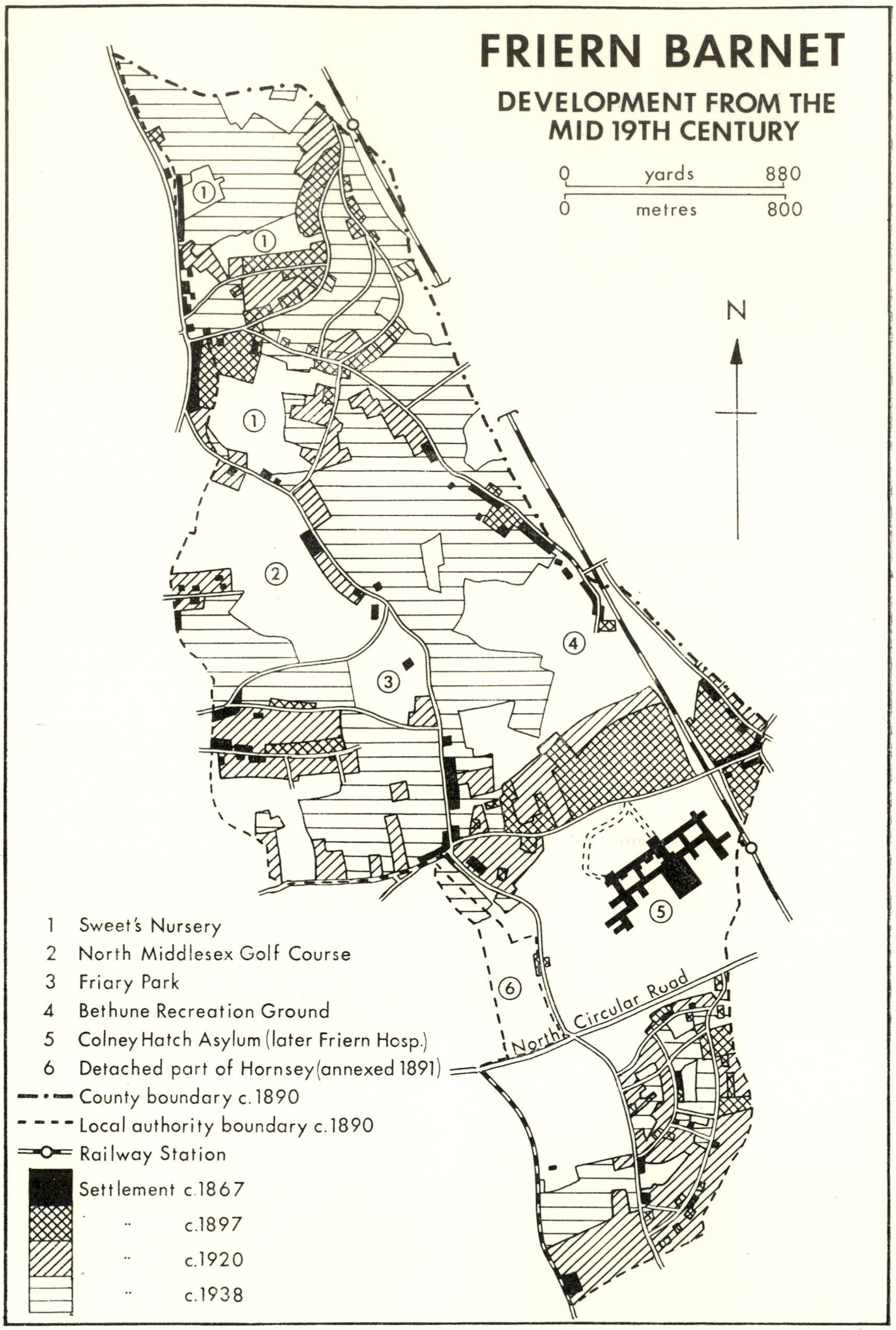
FRIERN BARNET
DEVELOPMENT FROM THE MID 19TH CENTURY
0 yards 880
0 metres 800
N
North Circular Road
1 Sweet's Nursery
2 North Middlesex Golf Course
3 Friary Park
4 Bethune Recreation Ground
5 Colney Hatch Asylum (later Friern Hosp.)
6 Detached part of Hornsey (annexed 1891)
County boundary c. 1890
Local authority boundary c. 1890
Railway Station
Settlement c. 1867
" c. 1897
" c. 1920
" c. 1938

adjoined the railway, with a frontage on Friern Barnet Road. It was laid out in 424 plots in 1879, when Beaconsfield, Glenthorne, and intervening roads were said to have been sewered, although only 47 plots on the main road had then been sold[74] and the roads were mere tracks in 1910.[75] By 1883 there were 198 houses with 900 occupants[76] and in 1889 Glenthorne Road contained 66 and Holly Park Road 74 houses.[77] The estate was virtually complete by 1897.[78]

Southgate Park, an estate of 24 a. which bounded Holly Park on the west,[79] included the Priory and fronted Friern Barnet Lane and Road. Still fields in 1889,[80] it had been divided into 314 plots around Stanford, Ramsden, Hartland, and two unnamed roads before the bankruptcy of the London Land Co. in 1887,[81] when 200 plots were put up for sale.[82] There were only 12 houses in Macdonald Road and 15 in Stanford Road in 1896,[83] and some of the estate was incomplete in 1920,[84] although the whole of the north side of Friern Barnet Road had been finished by 1900.[85] Building was mainly by local firms, notably Brown & Sweetland.[86]

North of Southgate and Holly parks Frenchman's farm, extending from Friern Barnet Lane to the railway, was offered for sale before 1879.[87] As the Bethune Park Garden estate of 110 a., it was intended to be the 'prettiest garden suburb to London', with a network of roads from Friern Barnet Lane to Oakleigh Road and with access to Friern Barnet Road via Holly Park. The plots had wide frontages and the quality of building was to be controlled on the whole estate, which would include Friern Barnet Garden Village on the Ridgeway. The Crescent was lined with expensive houses in 1910, when the area between it and Holly Park Road had been built over and the Ridgeway and Bethune Avenue had been constructed,[88] but little more was done before 1920.[89]

The Hollyfield estate, in the south corner of Friern Barnet Road and Colney Hatch Lane and previously part of Hillside farm, was laid out for building in 1903 by E. C. Day. St. John's and Hollyfield roads were to have houses and the frontages to the main roads were to have shops,[90] most of which had been built by 1912.[91]

West of Friern Barnet Lane and north of Woodhouse Road the White House estate of *c.* 55 a. of Frederick Crisp was acquired in 1908 by the British Land Co.[92] By 1911 Ashurst, Petworth, Bramber, Warnham, and Buxted roads had been laid out between Woodhouse Road and Friern Park and the first two had been built up.[93] Lewes Road was later inserted and Horsham Road was constructed across the grounds of Brook House, but contained little housing in 1920.[94]

The northern part of the parish had no houses in 1866 except in Whetstone High Street.[95] East of it and north of Oakleigh Road lay the district that became known as Oakleigh Park. The Whetstone Freehold Estate Co. had acquired land formerly of the Haughton Clarke family known as Matthews farm by 1869, when it diverted footpaths to lead to Oakleigh Park station.[96] In 1871, apart from the cottages in Beldhams Place, the whole area contained only six large houses.[97] The estate included long frontages in Oakleigh Road, which attracted buyers in 1875, when 25 large houses were occupied and other plots were for sale.[98] Demand persisted in 1888, when 40 such houses were occupied, some with tennis courts and stabling and many described as genteel villas.[99] In spite of building the area in 1882 was thought to be prettily timbered and undulating, with extensive rural views.[1] In 1883 the whole district of All Saints, which included Whetstone High Road, contained 271 houses with 1,255 inhabitants and had the highest rateable value in the parish.[2] In 1889 only 33 houses stood in Oakleigh Park North, 13 in Oakleigh Park South, and 10 in Athenaeum Road, which was lined with sports grounds.[3] By 1920 Oakleigh Gardens was partly built up but Oakleigh Avenue,[4] laid out as All Saints' Road in 1905,[5] was still an empty track.[6] The former estate of the duke of Buckingham and Chandos was sold in 1892[7] but Chandos Avenue alone had been constructed by 1920, when its eastern end was lined with houses.[8]

Myddelton Park, a short cul-de-sac from Oakleigh Road opposite the entrance to Oakleigh Park South, was built by John Miles before 1882, when he erected All Saints' church and Vicarage near by.[9] In 1903 the whole of his estate between Friern Barnet Lane and Oakleigh Road was acquired by the National Land Corporation which planned freehold houses for prosperous commuters and extended Myddelton Park to Friern Barnet Lane along an existing path, Loring and Pollard roads, and Queen's Avenue.[10] Initially 86 plots, fronting Oakleigh Road and in the part of Myddelton Park where there was roadway, were offered for

[74] M.R.O., D.R.O. 12/I/G7/1.
[75] M.R.O., Acc. 410/53.
[76] *Barnet Press*, 13 Oct. 1883.
[77] *Kelly's Dir. Barnet* (1889).
[78] O.S. Map 6", Mdx. VII. SW. (1897 edn.).
[79] M.R.O., D.R.O. 12/I/G7/3; G10/1.
[80] Ibid. G10/1.
[81] Ibid. G7/3.
[82] *Barnet Press*, 18 June 1887.
[83] *Kelly's Dir. Barnet* (1896).
[84] O.S. Map 6", Mdx. VII. SW. (1920 edn.).
[85] *Kelly's Dir. Barnet* (1900).
[86] *Barnet Press*, 6 Jan. 1883; M.R.O., Acc. 387/95–7.
[87] M.R.O., D.R.O. 12/I/A12/2.
[88] M.R.O., Acc. 410/53 (sales parts.); M.R.O., D.R.O. 12/I/H/9b (prospectus).
[89] O.S. Map 6", Mdx. VII. SW. (1920 edn.).
[90] M.R.O., D.R.O. 12/I/A12/17, 18; B.L.H.L., Friern Barnet U.D., min. bk. (1908–11), p. 111.
[91] *Kelly's Dir. Barnet* (1912).
[92] M.R.O., D.R.O. 12/I/B4/1. Planning permission had been given for new roads in 1903: B.L.H.L., Friern Barnet U.D., min. bk. (1900–3), p. 246.
[93] Sales parts. in B.L.H.L.
[94] O.S. Map 6", Mdx. VII. SW. (1920 edn.).
[95] Ibid. VI. SE. (1863–6 edn.).
[96] M.R.O., MJ/SR 5322/84; D.R.O. 12/I/C1/4 (printed notice).
[97] R.G. 10/1334 ff. 99–100.
[98] *Barnet Press*, 9 Jan. 1875.
[99] Barnet Mus. 99; Thorne, *Environs*, 693.
[1] Walford, *Gtr. Lond.* i. 335; see also panorama in Potter Colln. 20/116.
[2] *Barnet Press*, 13 Oct. 1883.
[3] *Kelly's Dir. Barnet* (1889 and later edns.).
[4] O.S. Map 6", Mdx. VI. SE. (1920 edn.).
[5] Barnet Mus. 110.
[6] O.S. Map 6", Mdx. VI. SE. (1920 edn.).
[7] Guildhall MS. 14223/8, pp. 15–18.
[8] O.S. Map 6", Mdx. VI. SE. (1920 edn.).
[9] W. G. Cameron, *75 Years of All Saints', Friern Barnet* (1957), 16 (commem. bklet.).
[10] Barnet Mus. 110; M.R.O., D.R.O. 12/I/A12/5, 7.

sale.[11] Successive sales followed, including those of 58 plots in 1905, when Loring and Pollard roads were still projected,[12] but there were only *c.* 50 houses by 1920: the frontage to Friern Barnet Lane was built up but not that to Oakleigh Road, and houses formed isolated groups elsewhere in the estate.[13]

In 1921 the population outside the lunatic asylum was 14,821, of whom 2,419 lived in All Saints' district including Whetstone, 4,598 in the Freehold, and 5,512 in the parish of St. James, which included Holly Park and Colney Hatch.[14] By 1920 most of the Freehold east of Colney Hatch Lane and south of Albion Avenue farther west was covered with building, as were the Avenue, Holly Park, and the Hollyfield estate. Housing was less concentrated in the north-west part of the parish, in Myddelton Park and Oakleigh Park, and large areas were almost rural.[15] In 1920 the population density in the north ward was 5·26 per acre, compared with 19·1 in the central and 26 in the south wards,[16] but only 448 a. or a third of the total land was built up.[17] Most of the remainder was built on between the World Wars.[18]

After the First World War the council was a major builder, following a scheme of 1919 by two projects for 100 houses each in 1925 and 1926. There were two main sites, the western part of the Freehold and 36 a. north of Oakleigh Road,[19] on the second of which houses were built along Russell Lane, Road, and Gardens, Simmons Close and Way, Miles Way, and Barfield Avenue. Under the initial scheme Russell Road was finished in 1921,[20] and by the end of 1926 73 houses had been built on the northern site and 38 on the southern. Nonetheless in that year, when the council was particularly active, it was responsible for only 78 of 266 houses under construction.[21] The schemes were complete in 1928.[22]

The southern and western parts of the Bethune estate were built as planned, although considerable space was left along the Crescent. Most of the northern part was acquired by the council for allotments and a recreation ground, cutting off Holly Park from the Church farm estate, which, on the completion of Myddelton Park, was laid out to the south by Church Farm Estates Ltd. between Friern Barnet Lane and Oakleigh Road North.[23] The first roads were Oakleigh Crescent, Church Way and Crescent, St. James's Avenue, and Friary Avenue, and building was still in progress in York Way in 1935.[24] The estate contained uniform semi-detached housing and blocks of flats, built to prescribed densities.[25] Building likewise occurred west of Friern Barnet Lane, where a network of roads linked the existing cul-de-sacs. The sites of large older houses were also used: on the death of Sydney Simmons's widow in 1935 her house Okehampton was demolished and a private road (Okehampton Close) between Torrington and Friern parks and two- and three-storeyed flats were approved for the site.[26] Similar building was carried out in Oakleigh Park, where only sports grounds were left. Even the Freehold provided space for high density blocks[27] and new roads, such as Bedford Close off Colney Hatch Lane in 1936.[28] The Orange Tree and White House at Colney Hatch were rebuilt *c.* 1923,[29] and the site of Halliwick manor-house was acquired in 1932 by Oldham Estates, who originally planned five new roads, 218 houses, and 57 shops.[30] In 1931 27·7 per cent of the population was considered to belong to the two highest social classes and only 14·5 per cent to the two lowest.[31]

After the Second World War the council was the only large-scale builder. It used few new sites, since little land not reserved as open space was left, although 215 a. were available for new schools.[32] The Freehold estate was extended westward before 1969 by the construction of Halliwick Road, George Crescent, and the west frontage of Colney Hatch Lane,[33] as planned in 1949.[34] Gardens in Oakleigh Park were appropriated between 1951 and 1957.[35] Wellington House, the Hollies, a large brick and concrete range of flats with flat roof and balconies on the corner of Oakleigh Road North and Oakleigh Park South, won a design award in 1953.[36] Since 1969 Sweet's Way has replaced the former nursery at Whetstone: it consists of small houses grouped in cul-de-sacs around lawns. By 1969[37] Friern Lodge north of the golf course had been replaced by Friern Court, a block of flats. The site of Derwent Lodge west of the links was built on in the 1950s[38] and Haldane Close was constructed on the former Cromwell recreation ground by 1975. Houses built before 1900 were considered worn out in 1930[39] but it was not until 1958 that the first slums were demolished at nos. 16–22 East Road, nos. 1–10 Lilly Villas, and nos. 1–21 Ada Villas.[40] The adjoining Link Road crossed the north-east corner of Bethune recreation ground by 1969. The near-by Avenue district was cleared after 1969;[41] by 1975, when there were still vacant patches, the Avenue itself, Stewards Holte Walk, Coppies

[11] M.R.O., D.R.O. 12/I/A12/6.
[12] Barnet Mus. 110.
[13] O.S. Map 6", Mdx. VI. SE. (1920 edn.).
[14] *Census*, 1921.
[15] O.S. Maps 6", Mdx. VI. SE., NE.; VII. SW.; XII. NW. (1920 edn.); Friern Barnet U.D. *Ann. Rep. of M.O.H.* (1924). In 1928 the parish was losing its semi-rural character: ibid. (1928).
[16] Friern Barnet U.D. *Ann. Rep. of M.O.H.* (1920).
[17] Ibid. (1921).
[18] O.S. Maps 6", Mdx. VI. NE.; VII. SW. (1938 edn.); O.S. Map 1/2,500, XII. 1. (1935 edn.).
[19] Friern Barnet U.D. *Ann. Rep. of M.O.H.* (1926); B.L.H.L., Friern Barnet U.D., min. bk. (1927–8), pp. 56, 83.
[20] Cameron, *All Saints', Friern Barnet*, 17.
[21] Friern Barnet U.D. *Ann. Rep. of M.O.H.* (1926).
[22] B.L.H.L., Friern Barnet U.D., min. bk. (1927–8), p. 277.
[23] M.R.O., Acc. 410/33.
[24] M.R.O., D.R.O. 12/I/A6/1; B.L.H.L., Friern Barnet U.D., min. bk. (1935), p. 7.
[25] B.L.H.L., Friern Barnet U.D., min. bk. (1935), p. 7.
[26] Ibid. p. 205; M.R.O., Acc. 410/85a (cutting).
[27] B.L.H.L., Friern Barnet U.D., min. bk. (1935), p. 6.
[28] M.R.O., Acc. 525/2, 3.
[29] Barnet Mus. 1144, 1304.
[30] *Evening Standard*, 29 Oct. 1932; *Barnet Press*, 5 Nov. 1932; M.R.O., Acc. 410/6a, ff. 7742–3.
[31] *Census*, 1931.
[32] Friern Barnet U.D., educ. cttee. min. bk. (1946–9).
[33] O.S. Maps 1/25,000, TQ 29 (1969 edn.).
[34] Ibid. (1949 edn.).
[35] Cameron, *All Saints', Friern Barnet*, 17.
[36] Plaque on bldg.
[37] O.S. Map 1/25,000, TQ 29 (1969 edn.).
[38] B.L.H.L., Acc. 9888 (corresp. with golf club).
[39] Friern Barnet U.D. *Ann. Rep. of M.O.H.* (1930).
[40] Ibid. (1956, 1958).
[41] O.S. Map 1/25,000, TQ 29 (1969 edn.).

Grove, and flats called Holmesdale and Stanhope had been built. Slum clearance had been proposed for the Freehold as early as 1933,[42] and in 1975 flats were being put up on the north frontage to Hampden Road. Four new schools included two in Bethune Park between the Crescent and Hemington Avenue.

Private building since 1945 has also been mainly on old sites, for flats. At Oxford Gardens, off Athenaeum Road, a cul-de-sac of town houses was partly finished by 1968.[43] In Stanford Road on the site of St. John's school (closed in 1968) a block of flats has been called Gilmore Court after the rector. Others stand in Whetstone High Road on either side of Friern Mount Drive, and Torrington Court, in the town-house style, occupies a single plot in Torrington Park. Wide frontages in Oakleigh Park have permitted the piecemeal construction of new houses. No part of the parish is without in-filling.

In 1975 Friern Barnet was still divided by the asylum and a large empty tract on either side of the North Circular Road. To the south the Freehold was orientated towards Muswell Hill, with buildings along Colney Hatch Lane straggling into north Hornsey. To the east terraces were interspersed with small corner shops, little changed since 1909 and concealing factories, some of them large employers. Many slums had been replaced and the west Freehold built up, except its extreme south part and the playing fields and recreation ground in the north.

In the north half of the parish only the eastern section from the Avenue to Russell Lane, dominated by council estates, is like the Freehold. Although parts remain waste, the Avenue has been rebuilt and the terraces in East and Oakleigh roads are being cleared. As in 1882 the largest shopping area is Whetstone High Road, with several blocks of shops, including multiple stores, public houses, and offices, most of them modern. It is not rivalled by Colney Hatch, New Southgate, or Oakleigh Road North, where small shops serve a local clientele. The rest of the parish is covered mainly by commuters' semi-detached houses. Some of the Victorian and Edwardian terraces in Holly Park are decaying and others are divided into flats, but most are structurally sound. Friern Barnet Lane, bordered by Friary park and the golf course, is the least populous part; with grass verges, it still seems rural, despite the felling of trees in the churchyard and in front of the alms-houses. After insertions and some rebuilding Oakleigh Park, with its winding roads lined with mature trees, preserves a distinct character. Apart from the alms-houses and an 18th-century building beside the Griffin, there are no buildings earlier than 1850.

There were 80 communicants in Friern Barnet in 1544[44] and 84 adult males took the protestation oath in 1642.[45] The population rose steadily from 432 in 1801 to 974 in 1851 and 3,344, including 2,009 in the lunatic asylum, in 1861. The rate of growth then accelerated to reach a total of 6,424 in 1881, 14,994 in 1911, 17,375 in 1921, and 23,101 in 1931; the figures include 2,351 in the asylum in 1881, 2,452 in 1911, 2,854 in 1921, and 2,880 in 1931. From a peak of 29,163 in 1951, numbers fell slightly to 28,813 in 1961. Friern Barnet ward, covering 313 hectares and about three-fifths of the size of the former U.D., had 15,112 persons in 1971.[46]

MANORS. The manor of *WHETSTONE* or *FRIERN BARNET* was held in 1336 by the knights of the Hospital of St. John of Jerusalem.[47] It was probably among the lands between Barnet and London taken from the abbey of St. Albans by William I,[48] who may have given it to the bishop of London. Lands in Barnet were held in fee of the bishop in 1196, when John Picot released those to which he had a hereditary claim.[49] John or his ancestor was the Picot the Lombard whose lands had been granted by 1199 to the Hospitallers by Bishops Gilbert Foliot (d. 1187) and Richard Fitzneal (d. 1198) and the chapter of St. Paul's.[50]

In 1338 the manor was a member of the bailiwick of Gings.[51] On the dissolution of the Hospitallers in England in 1540[52] it passed to the Crown and in 1544 it was granted in exchange to the chapter of St. Paul's.[53] The chapter sold the demesne lands in 1800[54] and the lordship later passed to the Ecclesiastical Commissioners.[55] Perquisites of court, royalties, and rents of assize and copyhold lands were excluded from leases of the demesne after 1519 and collected by the farmer as bailiff.[56] The rights were sequestrated during the Interregnum and in 1649 were sold to Richard Utber, draper of London,[57] whose arbitrary fines were resisted by copyholders in 1659.[58]

There was no manor-house in 1551, when Richard Clark was required to build a mansion within three years on a site chosen by the chapter. It was to contain a hall, parlour, and chambers,[59] and was eventually built by his son William (d. 1586).[60] Described as the Friary or Friern House in the late 18th and early 19th centuries[61] but never as the manor-house, it has been confused with Manor or Manor House Farm (later called the Manor House). It stood west of Friern Barnet Lane and south of St. James's church, with which it was connected by an avenue in 1783, when the extensive grounds were bounded to the west by ponds and Blackett's brook.[62] The house contained seventeen hearths in 1664, when it was unoccupied.[63] In 1797 the main east front of five bays with two wings was in an early-18th-century style but the

42 Friern Barnet U.D. *Ann. Rep. of M.O.H.* (1933).
43 Ex inf. Mrs. J. Corden.
44 E 301/34 no. 137.
45 H.L., Mdx. Protestation Returns.
46 *Census*, 1801–1971.
47 *Cal. Pat.* 1334–38, 352–3.
48 Walsingham, *Gesta Abbatum* (Rolls Ser.), i. 50.
49 *Feet of Fines, 1196–7* (P.R.S. xx), no. 37.
50 *Rot. Chart.* (Rec. Com.), 16.
51 *Knights Hospitallers in Eng.* (Camd. Soc. [1st ser.] lxv), 95.
52 *V.C.H. Mdx.* i. 196.
53 E 305/D7.
54 B.L.H.L., Acc. 9888 (loose).
55 Guildhall MSS. 14223/7, pp. 23, 224; 14223/8.
56 B.L. Cott. MS. Claud. E. vi, ff. 189v.–90.
57 C 54/3540 mm. 25–27 no. 10; St. Paul's MSS., box A 58.
58 C 10/51/58.
59 St. Paul's MS. C (lease bk.) Sampson, f. 227.
60 *Finchley Press*, 31 Dec. 1948.
61 M.L.R. 1790/10/90, 334.
62 Guildhall Libr., map case 247.
63 M.R.O., MR/TH/1.

core of an older house survived with piecemeal additions,[64] probably including a hall of *c.* 1660.[65] When occupied in 1797 by John Bacon, the house contained family portraits and a bust of Handel by Roubiliac.[66] It was always leased out with the demesne but sometimes was sub-let: in 1593 it was inhabited by Sir John Popham (d. 1607), Chief Justice of the King's Bench,[67] and in 1671–3 by Sir John Cropley.[68] Dr. King, said to have received Queen Anne there,[69] was still resident in 1728.[70] Bacon's seat had probably been demolished by 1828[71] but 23 a. south of Friary Road were renamed Friary park, where a house was built by Edmund William Richardson by 1871.[72] In 1909 the land was bought from his executors by Sydney Simmons and Middlesex C.C. as a public park.[73]

The manor of *HALLIWICK* was first mentioned between 1278 and 1285[74] and from 1810 to 1815 was incorrectly described as the manor of Colney Hatch.[75] Jurors were ignorant of the title in 1402.[76] Halliwick in 1537 was thought to be held of the honor of Boulogne by knight service and a pair of gilt spurs on coronation day.[77] The copyholds that existed between 1409 and 1600[78] had disappeared by 1810, when the tenure was revived for wastelands bordering the roads.[79] Often called a reputed manor in the 17th and 18th centuries,[80] its status was challenged *c.* 1835 because it had no demesne, copyhold tenure, services, or tenants.[81] In 1837 the lord took legal advice about his right to exploit the waste himself.[82] The manor extended along the south side of Friern Barnet Road from the Finchley boundary to Betstile and into Edmonton *c.* 1810, when it consisted of *c.* 350 a.[83] The lord still held *c.* 240 a. in 1801,[84] when the remainder was parcelled in freehold estates.[85]

The manor probably gave its name to the family of John de Halliwick, who sued Henry de Audley for a virgate in Little Barnet in 1234.[86] Audley appointed Henry de Halewyc as his attorney and called to warranty Walter de Morton,[87] from whom he had acquired his right by 1226.[88] Morton called to warranty John de Neville and Margery de Rivers, to whom John de Halewyc quitclaimed the lands in 1237.[89] The king had confirmed Audley's title in 1226 and on the same day[90] granted the lands to the earl of Chester,[91] apparently without effect. They descended in 1246 to Audley's son James, who gave them to Alice, wife of Robert de Beauchamp, before his death in 1272, when seisin was granted to his son James, from whom Alice recovered them in 1273.[92] By 1285 she had granted the lands to her son James and his heirs.[93]

Halliwick was held by Richard of Hackney (d. 1342–3),[94] draper of London, whose daughter Isabel and her husband William Olney settled it on their heirs.[95] William died before 1375[96] and in 1377 it was settled on Isabel (d. 1400) and her second husband John Wade for life, with remainder to her children by Olney. Isabel's heir was her son John Olney but Wade's trustees conveyed the manor to the judge John Cockayn (d. 1438),[97] who held it in 1409[98] and to whom John Durham quitclaimed his right as kinsman of John Olney's daughter Isabel in 1415.[99] In 1439 the manor was granted in remainder to Joan, granddaughter of John Cockayn,[1] and in 1455 Joan and her husband Robert Burley alienated it to John Wetwang.[2] In the years 1535–8 it was claimed by William Markham and Frances his wife, daughter of Humphrey Cockayn, apparently without success.[3]

Thomas Slade in 1530 settled Halliwick on his son Francis (d. 1537),[4] whose five daughters partitioned the manor.[5] Elizabeth and her husband Humphrey Cholmley sold their moiety in 1548 to Thomas Perse,[6] who in 1565 sold a moiety of the manor *c.* 250 a. to Rose Trott of London, widow (d. 1573).[7] In 1570 another daughter Wiburga, wife of Richard Wymark, conveyed her share to Rose Trott,[8] who presumably bought out the other coheirs. Rose left the manor to her son John (d. 1602),[9] from whom it descended to her great-grandson the childless William Trott (d. *c.* 1657). On William's marriage in 1645 to Sarah, widow of the second Lawrence Campe, the manor was conveyed to Sir John Reade, Bt. (d. 1694), and others to her use. In 1650 the reversion was settled on the heirs of Trott's body, with remainders to his wife's daughters and her son the third Lawrence Campe. A mortgage of Trott's life interest in 1647 was redeemed by Reade, who in 1652 was to retain the manor on Trott's death.[10] Alienations[11] had reduced

[64] H. Hunter, *Hist. of Lond. and its Environs* (1811), facing p. 87; below, plate facing p. 33; Brewer, *Beauties of Eng. and Wales*, x (5), 357.
[65] Hunter, *Lond. and its Environs*, 87.
[66] Lysons, *Environs*, ii. 22.
[67] Norden, *Spec. Brit.* 20; *D.N.B.*
[68] M.R.O., MR/TH/9; St. Paul's MSS., box A 58.
[69] Hunter, *Lond. and its Environs*, 87.
[70] *18th Rep. Com. Char.* H.C. 62, p. 382 (1828), xx.
[71] Barnet Mus. 104A (sales parts.); M.R.O., MA/AJ3/19.
[72] R.G. 10/1334 f. 72.
[73] M.R.O., Hist. notes 30/10/1967; sales parts. (1908) in B.L.H.L.; Friern Barnet U.D. *Opening of Friary Pk.* (pamphlet, 1909), 9.
[74] *Cat. Anct. D.* i, C 1497.
[75] M.R.O., Acc. 262/5A/1.
[76] C 137/32/5/2.
[77] C 142/59/48.
[78] *Sel. Cases in K.B.* vii (Selden Soc. lxxxviii), pp. 186–7.
[79] M.R.O., Acc. 262/5A/1; 5B.
[80] Ibid. 5B; 6A.
[81] Ibid. 5B.
[82] Ibid. 5B; 62/1, p. 82; 5A/1 (plan).
[83] Ibid. 61/14.
[84] See below; B.L.H.L., Acc. 9779.
[85] M.R.O., Acc. 262/5B; see below.
[86] *Cur. Reg. R.* xv, no. 983.
[87] Ibid. nos. 983, 1659.
[88] E 326/12466.
[89] *Cur. Reg. R.* xv, no. 1659; C.P. 25(1)/146/11/154.
[90] E 326/12466.
[91] *Cal. Chart. R.* 1226–57, 37.
[92] C.P. 40/3 rot. 28d.
[93] *Cat. Anct. D.* i, C 1497.
[94] C.P. 40/618, protectiones, rot. 3d.
[95] C 137/32/5/2; *Cal. Close*, 1374–7, 266.
[96] *Cal. Close*, 1374–7, 266.
[97] C 137/32/5/2.
[98] *Sel. Cases in K.B.* vii (Selden Soc. lxxxviii), pp. 186–7.
[99] C.P. 40/618, protectiones, rot. 3d.; B.L. MS. Lansd. 863, f. 178v.
[1] C.P. 25(1)/152/91/85.
[2] C.P. 25(1)/152/94/167.
[3] C 1/852/36.
[4] C 142/59/48.
[5] Ibid.; C.P. 25(2)/52/381/38 Hen. VIII East.; Wards 9/129 f. 249.
[6] C.P. 25(2)/61/473/2 Edw. VI Hil.
[7] C 54/790 mm. 24–26d.
[8] E 368/383 mm. 45d. et seq.
[9] M.R.O., Acc. 410/6, f. 7722; C 142/171/68; Prob. 11/57 (P.C.C. 1 Pickering).
[10] M.R.O., Acc. 262/6A.
[11] See p. 19.

the lands to 202 a. by the period 1657–62, when Reade bought out all the other claims.[12] In 1673 he was assessed for poor-rate more highly than anyone else in the parish.[13] The manor descended to his son and then to his grandson Sir John (d. 1712), who left four sisters as coheirs.[14] It was assigned to Anne and her husband Robert Middleton of Chirk (Denb.),[15] who in 1721 sold it and *c.* 180 a. to John Nicholl the elder (d. 1731).[16] In 1731 Nicholl settled the manor on his son John Nicholl (d. 1747) and the heirs of his body.[17] In 1747 it passed to Margaret Nicholl, later marchioness of Carnarvon, and on her death in 1768 to her husband James Brydges, later duke of Chandos (d. 1789), and then to her stepdaughter Anna Elizabeth, who married Earl Temple, later duke of Buckingham and Chandos. Earl Temple sold 115 a. of the demesne to George Curtis in 1801[18] and retained 83 a., which were sold in 1848 to George Knights Smith.[19]

Leases of the manor were held before 1567 by Robert Hayne[20] and in 1600 by Robert Sanny of Colney Hatch, yeoman,[21] of a family prominent in the parish from the 15th century[22] and the third largest copyholder of Whetstone manor in 1588,[23] who left it to his son. The manor was normally leased out from the late 17th century.[24]

Rose Trott's house in 1573 had formerly been three tenements.[25] The manor-house was new in 1602, when John Trott left it to his son and namesake.[26] It was sold with *c.* 88 a. by John Trott the younger in 1628[27] and thereafter descended as a separate estate.[28]

The reputed manor of *SARNERS BARNET*, said in 1316 to be held by the bishop of London with Finchley and Harringay for ¼ knight's fee,[29] was probably the subinfeudated manor of Whetstone. In 1297 × 1302, however, a jury of Ossulstone hundred declared that Finchley alone was held for ¼ knight's fee.[30] The name Sarners Barnet was applied to the church in 1341[31] and probably also to the parish.

OTHER ESTATES. In 1627 the demesne of Whetstone was said to consist of the site of the manor-house, six houses, a dovecot, six gardens, 40 a. of land, 100 a. meadow, 100 a. pasture, and 200 a. woodland.[32] There were 627 a. in 1799,[33] covering nearly half the parish and mainly south of the modern Oakleigh Road and north of Friern Barnet Road. The Friary, Manor farm, and Friern Lodge (later Frenchman's farm) existed by 1661[34] and in 1783 their dependent estates were 70 a., 176 a., and 234 a. respectively.[35]

The demesne lessee in 1519 was William Ward,[36] followed by John Spencer, clerk, and Francis Galliardietto in 1528,[37] by Galliardietto alone in 1531,[38] and later by Richard Clark,[39] whose term was extended in 1551[40] and whose son William obtained a 99-year lease in 1564.[41] William Clark left the reversion to his stepson William Pert, whose mother's third husband John Povey tried unsuccessfully to convert her life estate to fee simple.[42] William Pert was succeeded in 1608 by his son Tindal,[43] whose son William in 1627 left the remainder of the term to William Gilley.[44] It was held by Alderman Sir Hugh Perry from 1628 until his death in 1635 and later by Andrew Perry,[45] but *c.* 1647 was conveyed by Sir Hugh's daughters to William (later Sir William) Domville and Ellen, wife of Sir Heneage Proby. Domville was assigned the manor-house, Manor farm-house, and 192 a., Lady Proby received Friern Lodge farm-house and most of the lands, and the reversions were settled on their respective heirs *c.* 1651. In 1649, however, Friern Lodge and 352 a. were sold to Sir Heneage Proby[46] and Domville's share passed in trust to a Mr. Johnson. At the Restoration Lady Proby and Domville resumed possession and in 1662 a backdated lease was made for them in trust.[47] In 1663 Sir Heneage left the lease to his widow with successive remainders to his sons Sir Thomas Proby, Bt., of Elton Hall (Hunts.), John, and Heneage.[48] As attorney-general of Ireland, Domville was non-resident in 1664.[49] In 1684 he conveyed 12 a. to John Proby[50] and in 1687 the lease was renewed for Sir Thomas and John Proby.[51] After Sir Thomas's death in 1689 John assigned the lease to Edward Jennings, who held it until 1718.[52] It was held by Samuel Strode, his widow Anne, and William Strode until 1783,[53] when it was sold to John Bacon (d. 1816),[54] editor of Ecton's *Thesaurus Rerum Ecclesiasticarum*.[55] Bacon leased the

[12] M.R.O., Acc. 262/5A/1; 5B; 6A.
[13] St. Paul's MSS., box A 58.
[14] G.E.C. *Baronetage*, ii. 165; B.L.H.L., Acc. 9888.
[15] M.R.O., Acc. 262/5B.
[16] Ibid.; M.L.R. 1722/6/178–80.
[17] M.R.O., Acc. 262/47/66.
[18] *Complete Peerage*, iii. 132–3; M.L.R. 1801/2/50; B.L.H.L., Acc. 9888.
[19] M.R.O., D/A2/loose, t. 19.
[20] M.R.O., Acc. 410/24, quoting Guildhall MS. 9171/15, f. 184.
[21] St. Paul's MSS., F. Reg. Wills C, ff. 16v.–17v
[22] Ibid. box B 17.
[23] Ibid. box B 15, m. 19d.
[24] M.R.O., Acc. 262/5A/1, 2; TA/FRI.
[25] Prob. 11/57 (P.C.C. 1 Pickering).
[26] Prob. 11/97 (P.C.C. 24 Woodhall).
[27] C 54/2777 mm. 15–16, no. 16.
[28] See p. 19.
[29] *Feud. Aids*, iii. 374.
[30] E 315/45/77.
[31] *Inq. Non.* (Rec. Com.), 200.
[32] C.P. 25(2)/457/3 Chas. I Trin.; 25(2)/457/3 Chas. I Mich.
[33] B.L.H.L., Acc. 9381/2.
[34] St. Paul's MSS., box A 58.
[35] B.L.H.L., Acc. 9381/1.
[36] B.L. Cott. MS. Claud. E. vi, f. 189.
[37] L.R. 2/62 ff. 7d.–8.
[38] L.R. 2/62 ff. 94–5.
[39] L.R. 2/62 ff. 138–9.
[40] St. Paul's MS. C (Sampson), ff. 226v.–227v. (lease bk.).
[41] Ibid. (Nowell I), f. 120v.
[42] C 2/Eliz. I/P7/59; C 2/Eliz. I/P9/45; C 2/Eliz. I/P16/36; *Finchley Press*, 14 Jan. 1949.
[43] C 2/Jas. I/B35/36.
[44] C.P. 25(2)/457/3 Chas. I Trin.; C.P. 25(2)/457/3 Chas. I Mich.
[45] St. Paul's MS. W.C. 37; for what follows, see St. Paul's MSS., box A 58.
[46] C 54/3543/16.
[47] St. Paul's MS. C (Barwick), no. 53.
[48] Prob. 11/310 (P.C.C. 38 Juxon).
[49] M.R.O., MR/TH/5.
[50] C.P. 25(2)/786/36 Chas. II Trin.
[51] St. Paul's MS. C (Tillotson and Sherlock), ff. 36–38v.; see also Guildhall MS. 14217/2, f. 72v.
[52] St. Paul's MS. C (Godolphin III), f. 205v.; but see M.L.R. 1727/426.
[53] St. Paul's MSS. C (Godolphin III), f. 205v.; (Cornwallis), ff. 57v.–60v.; (Pretyman I), ff. 74v.–77v.
[54] Ibid.; *Gent. Mag.* lxxxvi (1), 276.
[55] *D.N.B.*

demesne until 1800,[56] when he sold it to the chapter of St. Paul's.[57]

All holders of the demesne were also copyholders. In 1815 John Bacon held 651 a. in the parish, of which 139 a. were in his own hands, 182 a. were held by his son John William, who lived at Manor Farm, 138 a. were leased to William Gaywood, and the rest distributed between eleven tenants.[58] John Bacon left his property to his sons John William and Francis Darcy Bacon, to hold a third each in their own right and a third in trust for their sister Maria, wife of Sir William Johnston, Bt. (d. 1844), for division among her children. Land was alienated from 1819 to meet John Bacon's debts[59] and in 1822 Chancery decreed the partition, which was ratified by a private Act[60] and which divided the estate into three broad bands stretching from Finchley eastward to the modern Oakleigh Road. Lady Johnston received the southern part, consisting of Friern Lodge Farm and 234 a., J. W. Bacon was assigned the Friary, Manor Farm, and 213 a., and F. D. Bacon *c.* 70 a. Both brothers also received land in Finchley.[61]

On his bankruptcy J. W. Bacon's estates were sold in 1824.[62] Thomas Bensley (d. 1835),[63] who bought 81 a., planned a lunatic asylum and laid out roads,[64] which eventually were built up between 1846 and 1865.[65] After Bensley's bankruptcy the Friern Park estate was assigned to J. D. Holden and J. Lewin, who had lent him money held in trust under the will of Joseph Holden (d. 1820) for his daughter Sarah Gibson and her heirs.[66] The estate, 87 a. in 1846,[67] was sold for building in 1866 and 1868 on behalf of Mrs. Gibson's heirs. The Friary park of 23 a. was bought in several lots by E. W. Richardson (d. 1909).[68] The rest of Bensley's land, 48 a. east of Friern Barnet Lane,[69] had passed by 1846 to Mrs. Bethune,[70] probably because he could not pay off a mortgage by John Bacon.[71]

Manor farm of *c.* 29 a. was sold in turn to John Easthope, Charles William Allen in 1832, and Edmund Walker, who lived there.[72] Walker bought other lands and owned 57 a. in 1846.[73] Shortly before his death in 1851, he sold the house and 29 a. to John Miles the younger,[74] who was also resident. Miles made further purchases from the trustee of the Friern Park estate and others, leaving 117 a. at his death in 1886. On his widow's death in 1902[75] 35 a. were sold to the National Land Corporation and built up as the Myddelton Park estate.[76] The remaining 81 a. passed to the North Middlesex Golf Co.[77]

The farm-house was mentioned in 1661[78] and was large in 1777, when several rooms were sublet to the rector.[79] In 1851 there was a lodge and the main building housed five people.[80] A coachman's dwelling had been added in 1871, when John Miles's seat housed 17 people, including 10 servants.[81] The existing club-house, white and of three storeys with dormers, was probably built by him. It was screened from the west by trees but in 1975 had westward views; the farm buildings were then in decay but the lodge was inhabited and a shop for the club had been added.

Church farm originated in 73 a. between Friern Barnet Lane and Oakleigh Road, bought by William Radford from J. W. and F. D. Bacon in 1824.[82] It comprised 69 a. in 1846, when a farm-house and buildings existed,[83] and survived until the 1930s.[84]

The Friern Lodge estate was sold on Lady Johnston's death in 1847, on behalf of her children. The largest portion, Frenchman's farm, consisted of 86 a.[85] It was considered in 1875 as the site of a sewage farm[86] and before 1879 as that of a housing estate.[87] It was held by Thomas Sketchley in 1889 and 1893,[88] by John Jones in 1896–7,[89] and by Frederick Crisp in 1900–1.[90] The farm-house was first mentioned in 1605 and was a small two-storeyed building of brick and weatherboarding with adjacent barns, all derelict, in 1897.[91] Another 43 a. with frontages on Friern Barnet Road and 30 a. behind the Orange Tree were sold to G. K. Smith.[92]

Members of the Goodere family were active in Friern Barnet by 1417.[93] In 1540–1 they held the largest and in 1588 the second largest copyhold estate,[94] most of which was once Goodyers grove.[95] From 1486 until 1537 there were two branches of the family. In 1499 John Goodere settled a house, a cottage, 27 a. of land, and 30½ a. of wood on his son Richard Goodere of St. Albans,[96] whose son Albany in 1537 granted them in reversion to Francis Goodere,[97] grandson of another John Goodere who held 3 a. in 1486.[98] Francis was succeeded in turn by Henry Goodere, his son William (d. 1577), and his grandson Sir Henry Goodere of Hatfield (Herts.),[99] who sold the whole estate of 95 a. to James Woodford of Totteridge

56 St. Paul's MS. C (Pretyman III), ff. 136v.–9.
57 B.L.H.L., Acc. 9888 (loose); M.L.R. 1807/2/471.
58 M.R.O., D.R.O. 12/I/H/7.
59 M.R.O., Acc. 260/1.
60 3 Geo. IV, c. 22 (Priv. Act). There are copies in M.R.O., Acc. 260/1; B.L.H.L., Acc. 9888.
61 M.R.O., Acc. 260/1; *P.O. Dir. N. Suburbs* (1880).
62 Barnet Mus. 1040A.
63 B.L.H.L., Acc. 9888; M.L.R. 1825/8/501–2.
64 M.R.O., MA/AJ3/19.
65 M.R.O., TA/FRI; O.S. Map 6″, Mdx. VI. SE. (1863–6 edn.).
66 M.L.R. 1825/8/502; B.L.H.L., Acc. 9888 (Chancery case, Wilkinson *v.* Gibson, on which the para. is based).
67 M.R.O., TA/FRI.
68 See p. 16.
69 M.L.R. 1825/9/47.
70 M.R.O., TA/FRI.
71 B.L.H.L., Acc. 9888 (Wilkinson *v.* Gibson).
72 Ibid. (deeds).
73 M.R.O., TA/FRI.
74 B.L.H.L., Acc. 9888.
75 Ibid.
76 Barnet Mus. 110; M.R.O., D.R.O. 12/I/A12/3, 4.
77 See p. 25.
78 St. Paul's MSS., box A 58.
79 E 126/31 Trin. 1778.
80 H.O. 107/179 f. 337.
81 R.G. 10/1334 f. 70.
82 M.L.R. 1824/10/308–9.
83 M.R.O., TA/FRI.
84 See p. 14.
85 B.L.H.L., Acc. 9888 (sales parts.).
86 *Barnet Press*, 10 Apr. 1875.
87 See p. 13.
88 *Kelly's Dir. Barnet* (1889, 1892–3).
89 Ibid. (1896–7).
90 Ibid. (1900–1).
91 M.R.O., Pr. 13/29; *Finchley Press*, 31 Dec. 1948.
92 See p. 20.
93 *Cal. Close*, 1413–19, 438.
94 St. Paul's MSS., box B 15, m. 19d.; S.C. 6/Hen. VIII/2402 m. 7.
95 See p. 22.
96 St. Paul's MSS., box B 17, m. 5.
97 Ibid. m. 15.
98 Ibid. mm. 11, 14.
99 C 6/136/41; C 9/22/83.

(Herts.) in 1628–9.[1] Woodford conveyed 29 a. to Richard Orme, tailor of London,[2] who left them in 1664 to his son Edward, with remainder to his daughter Mary and her husband Jeremy Becket the elder.[3] After their deaths Jeremy Becket the younger sold the land in 1669 to Oliver Wallis (d. 1700),[4] who was succeeded by his son John. Woodford's other lands in 1668 were settled in remainder on his daughter Judith, her husband Oliver Wallis, and their heirs.[5] John Wallis was admitted in 1725[6] and left the whole estate in 1751 to his nephew Thomas Jackson,[7] who left it in 1762 to his three daughters.[8] Their shares were settled in 1772 on Mary Jackson (d. 1812) on her marriage to William Tash (d. 1818).[9] Tash held 86 a. in 1815[10] and left the estate to Nicholson, Robert, Charles, and Walter Calvert,[11] who sold it to Sir Simon Haughton Clarke, Bt. (d. 1833), in 1821.[12]

Sir Simon Haughton Clarke also bought lands including 26 a. from Richardson Harrison in 1820,[13] 19 a. from J. W. Bacon in 1821,[14] and 19 a. formerly of the demesne.[15] In 1846 his family owned 135 a., mainly in Whetstone between Hertfordshire and Oakleigh Road on both sides of Russell Lane.[16] Since legacies could not be met by his sons Sir Simon (d. 1849) and Sir Philip Haughton Clarke,[17] the estate was broken up in 1857,[18] 86 a. in Whetstone being sold to John Nillson.[19] He sold it before 1869 to the Whetstone Freehold Estate Co.,[20] which built on it as the Oakleigh estate.[21] Sir Philip retained 20 a., which he sold in 1860.[22]

John Nicholl the younger (d. 1747) bought piecemeal a block of *c.* 90 a. of copyhold land at Whetstone,[23] which passed to his daughter Margaret (d. 1768),[24] later marchioness of Carnarvon. On her husband's death in 1789 it descended to his daughter Anna Elizabeth and so to the dukes of Buckingham and Chandos.[25] Following the sale of *c.* 7 a. in 1837,[26] it consisted of 85 a. in 1846.[27] From 1868 it was held in trust by Henry John Smith,[28] who enfranchised it in 1892 before its sale.[29]

Halliwick manor-house and *c.* 88 a.[30] were sold in 1628 by John Trott the younger to his mother Susan and her second husband Edmund Underwood, grocer of London.[31] The lands, which they held in chief,[32] were settled jointly in 1637 on Underwood and his wife Isabel, who surrendered her rights to permit a mortgage. The mortgage was redeemed by Edward Nevett the elder (d. 1671–2), alderman of London, who took possession on Underwood's death in spite of Isabel's resistance.[33] In 1655 he bought from the third Lawrence Campe 12 a. and the house called Mayfield,[34] newly built in 1600 when it was enfranchised and granted by John Trott the elder to his son-in-law the first Lawrence Campe (d. 1613).[35] Coppetts farm of 64 a. was sold to John Rawlinson and Eleanor his wife,[36] probably before 1672 when the rest of the estate was settled on Edward Nevett the younger and Theodora his wife.[37] They mortgaged Mayfield and 12 a. to John Nicholl of St. Andrew Holborn (d. 1688)[38] and their son John released his right to another John Nicholl of St. Andrew Holborn in 1697.[39] The manor-house and remains of the estate were sold in 1694 by John Nevett to John Cleeve, soap-maker of London,[40] descending in 1725 to his son and namesake and in 1748 to the younger Cleeve's nephew Henry Neale, on whose bankruptcy they were sold in 1772 to George Power.[41] Power sold the house and *c.* 5 a. to Neale's son-in-law Richard Down (d. 1814),[42] who bought the rest from Power's heirs in 1790[43] and, in 1800, bought Coppetts farm from the Rawlinson family.[44] Richard Down left the estate to his second son Edward subject to the life interest of his wife,[45] who held 86 a. in 1815.[46] In 1826 she and Edward Down conveyed it to the Bank of England,[47] which mortgaged or sold it,[48] but in 1846 the whole estate was held by George Smith (d. 1847), owner of 119 a. in the parish.[49] The manor-house passed to his son Henry John Smith (d. 1868), from whose family it was bought in 1891 by Constance Hill.[50] The Hill family ran a ladies' school there in 1884 and 1900. It was acquired in 1918 as a furniture store by William Jelks,[51] who sold it in 1932 to the Oldham Estates Co.,[52] which demolished it. Coppetts farm may have descended in the same way until 1898, when it

1 Barnet Mus., Pandora box I, P.B. 15/151, 155.
2 Ibid. 156.
3 Ibid. 159.
4 Ibid. 163, 168, 170.
5 Ibid. 160.
6 Ibid. 174.
7 Guildhall MS. 14223/3, p. 7.
8 Ibid. pp. 67–8.
9 Ibid. p. 182; 4, pp. 146, 212.
10 M.R.O., D.R.O. 12/I/H/7.
11 Guildhall MS. 14223/4, p. 247.
12 Ibid. pp. 268–75.
13 Ibid. p. 259.
14 B.L.H.L., Acc. 9888; M.L.R. 1822/10/45.
15 M.L.R. 1822/10/46; 1825/1/8; B.L.H.L., Acc. 9888.
16 M.R.O., TA/FRI.
17 M.L.R. 1857/3/294; B.L.H.L., Acc. 9888; Guildhall MS. 14223/6, pp. 167–75.
18 M.R.O., Acc. 410/48b.
19 Guildhall MS. 14223/6, pp. 169–75.
20 M.R.O., MJ/SR 5322/84.
21 Barnet Mus. 99.
22 Guildhall MS. 14223/6, p. 211.
23 M.R.O., Acc. 262/5A/1 (will).
24 Guildhall MS. 14223/3, p. 152; B.L.H.L., Acc. 9888.
25 *Complete Peerage*, iii. 132–3.
26 M.R.O., Acc. 262/5A/1; 62/1, p. 133.
27 M.R.O., TA/FRI.
28 Guildhall MS. 14223/6, p. 319.
29 Ibid. 8, pp. 15–18.
30 See p. 17.
31 C 54/2777 mm. 15–16 no. 19, but see M.R.O., D.R.O. 20/H/68.
32 C 66/2718, no. 96.
33 C 5/395/238; C 10/93/14; C.P. 25(2)/575/1659 Hil.
34 M.R.O., Acc. 262/5B; B.L.H.L., Acc. 9888.
35 M.R.O., Acc. 262/5B.
36 M.L.R. 1721/3/81.
37 M.R.O., Acc. 262/5B.
38 Ibid. 5A/2.
39 B.L.H.L., Acc. 9888.
40 C 54/47775 m. 6.
41 M.L.R. 1772/6/114.
42 M.L.R. 1778/2/20.
43 M.L.R. 1790/10/90.
44 M.L.R. 1800/2/392.
45 M.R.O., EA/FIN; M.R.O., D.R.O. 12/I/H/7; Guildhall MS. 10465/130, pp. 169–74.
46 M.L.R. 1833/2/157.
47 M.L.R. 1826/1/74.
48 M.L.R. 1833/2/160.
49 M.R.O., TA/FRI.
50 M.R.O., Acc. 410/6a, f. 7787.
51 B.L.H.L., Friern Barnet loc. bd., min. bk. (1884–6), p. 77; *P.O. Dir. N. Suburbs* (1888); M.R.O., Acc. 410/6a, ff. 7742–3.
52 *Evening Standard*, 29 Oct. 1932.

was sold for building by H. J. Smith's trustees.[53] The farm-house of 1670 was occupied in 1907 by the Friern Manor Dairy Co.[54]

Halliwick manor-house, new in 1602,[55] stood on the corner of Woodhouse Road and Colney Hatch Lane. It was thought a handsome villa in 1850.[56] In 1897 it was an L-shaped building with one wing of two storeys and another of three, each probably 18th-century,[57] and had 46 rooms, besides outbuildings and additions which included a gymnasium.[58] The grounds, stretching into Finchley and Hornsey, comprised 22 a. in 1909.[59] They contained a lake in the south-west part in 1850, many fine trees, and a garden celebrated for its vines.[60] Some trees had been felled by 1932, when the house had long stood empty.[61]

The lands of George Smith (d. 1847) north of Woodhouse Road passed to his son George Knights Smith (d. 1886),[62] who also acquired 30 a. of the Johnston estate there in 1850.[63] With further purchases from the Planet Building Society, Middlesex Freehold Land Association, and others, he built up the White House estate of *c.* 60 a. between Woodhouse Road, Torrington Park, and Friern Barnet Lane. After his death it was bought by Frederick Crisp of Holloway, later of the White House, who was planning building at his death in 1907.[64] G. K. Smith acquired a further 43 a. of the Johnston estate with frontages on Friern Barnet Road,[65] on part of which he built.[66] He sold 8 a. to James Ward in 1878[67] and a further 33 a. by 1879, when it was laid out as the Holly Park estate.[68] He also acquired 12 a. adjoining the asylum from the duke of Buckingham and Chandos and still held them in 1882.[69]

At Colney Hatch 115 a. of the demesne of Halliwick were sold in 1801 by Earl Temple and his wife to George Curtis,[70] from whom they passed to Alderman Sir William Curtis, Bt. (d. 1829), who also acquired Muswell Hill farm.[71] They descended to his son Sir William (d. 1847) and consisted of 194 a. in 1846.[72] His widow Mary Anne and her son Sir William sold 8 a. between 1847 and 1849 to the G.N.R. and 119 a. to the Middlesex justices of the peace for a lunatic asylum,[73] the site being chosen for its position and proximity to the railway.[74] Colney Hatch asylum (Colney Hatch mental hospital in 1930, Friern mental hospital in 1937, and Friern hospital from 1959) was the largest asylum in Europe when opened in 1851. It served the eastern division of Middlesex until 1889, when it was transferred to the L.C.C., and from 1970 has served Islington, Haringey, and Camden L.B.s. Designed for 1,250 patients, it was extended to take 2,000 between 1857 and 1859, held a maximum of 2,700 in 1937, and contained 1,500 in 1974; additions after 1857 included seven villas between 1903 and 1913 and Halliwick House in 1958. The early buildings have been extensively modernized. In 1903 a temporary annexe was burnt down, causing 51 deaths in England's worst asylum disaster, and in 1941 five villas were bombed. The grounds were gradually extended to 165 a. by 1929, when 7 a. were cut off by the new North Circular Road and assigned to the L.C.C. as a playground. The estate included gardens, a farm of 75 a. later disused, a cemetery in use until 1873, and a chapel. The early buildings had 6 miles of corridor and a north front 1,884 ft. long, designed by S. W. Dawkes in an Italianate style, with ventilation towers and a central cupola. Once a household name, Colney Hatch asylum was often mentioned in literature.[75]

ECONOMIC HISTORY. AGRARIAN HISTORY. More than half of the working population was engaged in agriculture in 1831[76] and 67 per cent of the area was still farm-land in 1887.[77] Little more than a third of the parish was wooded by 1544 and 94 per cent of the land had been cleared by 1846.[78] Farm-land dwindled to 990 a. in 1887 and 905 a. in 1897. By 1917 that amount had been halved, in 1937 it was 115 a., and in 1957 there was no agricultural land apart from allotments.[79]

Common fields probably never existed in Whetstone manor. In 1519 the demesne consisted only of large inclosures,[80] numbering 15 by 1531[81] and forming a compact block. The copyhold estates were concentrated in the north part of the parish and consisted of small groves and closes,[82] the latter apparently taken from the woods.[83] As assarting continued, the number of copyhold tenants rose from 10 in 1506[84] to 15 in 1541–2 and 1564[85] and to 18 in 1588.[86] Halliwick manor was already inclosed by the early 17th century.[87]

53 M.R.O., D.R.O. 12/III/1/3.
54 J. C. Marriott, 'Hist. Hornsey' (TS. in Bruce Castle Mus.).
55 See p. 17.
56 W. Keane, *Beauties of Mdx.* (1850), 160–1.
57 B.L.H.L., Banks Colln. (photo.).
58 B.L.H.L., Friern Barnet loc. bd., min. bk. (1884–6), p. 77.
59 Friern Barnet U.D. *Opening of Friary Pk.*; see also sales parts. (1905) in B.L.H.L.
60 Keane, *Beauties of Mdx.* 160–1.
61 *Barnet Press*, 1 Oct. 1932.
62 M.R.O., D.R.O. 12/I/B4/1.
63 Ibid. B4/1; G10/2; B.L.H.L., Acc. 9888 (sales parts.).
64 M.R.O., D.R.O. 12/I/K2/4 (ann. rep. for 1907); B4/1; *Barnet Press*, 27 July 1907.
65 B.L.H.L., Acc. 9888; M.R.O., D.R.O. 12/I/G10/2.
66 See p. 11.
67 M.R.O., D.R.O. 12/I/G10/2.
68 Ibid. G7/1.
69 M.R.O., D/A2/loose, t. 19.
70 M.L.R. 1801/2/150.
71 M.R.O., EA/FIN; M.R.O., D.R.O. 12/I/H/7.
72 M.R.O., TA/FRI.
73 M.R.O., Acc. 1038/1A, pp. 46–50 (min. bks.).
74 Ibid. p. 11; see above, p. 9. Except where otherwise stated, the rest of the para. is based on Hunter and Macalpine, *Psychiatry for the Poor.*
75 e.g. *Leaves from the Note-Bks. of Lady Dorothy Nevill*, ed. R. Nevill (1907), 75; G. K. Chesterton, *The Man Who Was Thursday* (1908), 28; P. G. Wodehouse, *The Code of the Woosters* (1938), 273; C. S. Lewis, *The Magician's Nephew* (1955). See below, plate facing p. 32.
76 M.A.F. 68/2815.
77 *Census*, 1831.
78 M.R.O., TA/FRI.
79 M.A.F. 68/1105; M.A.F. 68/1675; M.A.F. 68/2815; M.A.F. 68/3837.
80 St. Paul's MSS., box B 15, m. 19.
81 L.R. 2/62 ff. 94v.–95.
82 S.C. 6/Hen. VIII/2402 m. 7.
83 See p. 22.
84 St. Paul's MSS., box A 62(x).
85 S.C. 6/Hen. VIII/2402 m. 7; St. Paul's MSS., box B 15, m. 2.
86 B.L. Cott. MS. Claud. E. vi, f. 189.
87 B.L.H.L., Acc. 9888; C 54/2777 mm. 15–16, no. 19.

Apart from cartage, which was commuted, copyholders of Whetstone manor owed a common fine and rendered 11 days' work and 99 days' boon reaping in 1506.[88] In 1783 pasture was four times as extensive as arable[89] but by 1815 arable made up 42 per cent of the farm-land, including 110 a. in Manor farm,[90] perhaps resulting from improvements said to have been introduced by John Bacon.[91] Leases of the Chandos estate in the 18th and 19th centuries penalized conversion to tillage.[92] The parish as a whole was mainly meadow in 1795.[93] Arable fell from 36 per cent of agricultural land in 1815[94] to 24 per cent in 1846,[95] 5 per cent in 1887,[96] and 4 per cent in 1897.[97] By 1937 there were no draught horses.[98]

Hay, probably for London, was made on 74 per cent of the 940 a. of pasture in 1887, when only the remaining 233 a. were used for grazing;[99] 18 a. in Myddelton Park produced hay in 1887 and the whole of Frenchman's farm in 1891.[1] School children in the late 19th century were given a fortnight's holiday for haymaking.[2] There were 240 dairy cattle in 1897 but only 69 in 1937,[3] perhaps mainly on the asylum's farm. In 1920 all Friern Barnet's milk was said to be brought in by railway and in 1923 there was a single herd of 11 cows, probably those for which Friern Watch Dairy had difficulty in finding pasture in 1924 and which were ageing in 1930.[4] Sheep had been the chief stock on John Nicholl's Colney Hatch estate in 1747,[5] but there were only 59 in the parish in 1887[6] and by 1917 there was none.[7] Rights to pannage had figured in early leases.[8] Between 1887 and 1937 the number of pigs rose from 310 to 380;[9] probably some were kept in gardens, as in 1895 in Cromwell Road.[10] Three piggeries existed in 1954 but none in 1955.[11]

A nursery bordered Oakleigh Road in 1871.[12] There were several others near by in the late 19th and early 20th centuries but most had been built over by 1939.[13] The largest lay between Oakleigh Road, Friern Barnet Lane, and Whetstone High Road, and was extended around a small nursery by J. Sweet, who moved from Leyton (Essex) in 1862. By 1898 20 a. out of 29½ a. were under glass, and expansion was planned. Sweet, using glass-houses with larger panes and lighter frames, was described as 'the father of the modern hothouse nursery business'.[14] The land was requisitioned during the Second World War by the army, which controlled 33 a. in 1946.[15] In 1969 it became the site for Sweet's Way.

Several tenants of Whetstone manor paid more than 6*s.* rent in 1540–1 but Henry Goodere owed as much as 21*s.* 5*d.*[16] In 1588 Goodyers was one of three leading tenements, the others belonging to Richard Smith and Robert Sanny, who owed at least 14*s.* 10*d.*[17] or about three times that of anyone else. In 1664 and 1671 the parish contained 59 and 61 houses respectively, several of them vacant, and in 1664 only three had ten or more hearths, while 15 with one or two hearths were not taxed.[18] Thirty-seven houses were assessed for poor-rate in 1673: one at £140, ten at £50 to £100, and fourteen at less than £10.[19] There were few outstanding landowners in the late 17th or the early 19th centuries. Seven farms had over 50 a. in 1815 and 1846 but by the latter date only two exceeded 100 a., compared with five in 1815. On both occasions there was one farm of over 200 a.[20] Of the 84 people employed in agriculture in 1831, 71 worked on eight farms and the others as small-holders.[21] By 1917, when there were only two farms of over 50 a., there were still eleven small-holders.[22] In 1937 as many as 94 people were employed full-time and 112 part-time, probably in market gardening. There was one farm of 50–100 a., presumably the asylum's, and one of 20–50 a., which may have been Sweet's nursery.[23]

Woods. Probably the whole of the east part of the parish was once wooded. There were other woods in the south-west part and the centre, as well as Friern wood bordering Finchley common. In 1544 probably more than 450 a.[24] were woodland but by *c.* 1700 two-thirds of that had been felled. Friern wood had gone and the western half of the parish was farm-land before 1814, when the inhabitants were assigned allotments on Finchley common.[25] There were 127 a. of woodland in 1815,[26] 69 a. in 1846,[27] and only 8 a. after the clearance of Hollick wood by 1852.[28]

The demesne of Whetstone contained *c.* 200 a. of woodland in 1544.[29] Until 1574 woods were excluded from leases of the demesne by the Hospitallers and the chapter of St. Paul's.[30] Supplies of timber from Whetstone were often guaranteed when the Hospitallers leased other properties.[31]

88 St. Paul's MSS., box A 62; *V.C.H. Mdx.* ii. 77.
89 B.L.H.L., Acc. 9381/1.
90 M.R.O., D.R.O. 12/I/H/7.
91 *Gent. Mag.* lxxvi (1), 276.
92 M.R.O., Acc. 262/5A/1; 60/95.
93 Lysons, *Environs*, ii. 21.
94 M.R.O., D.R.O. 12/I/H/7.
95 M.R.O., TA/FRI.
96 M.A.F. 68/1105.
97 M.A.F. 68/1675.
98 M.A.F. 68/3837.
99 Ibid.
1 *Barnet Press*, 25 June 1887; 13 June 1891.
2 M.R.O., D.R.O. 12/I/G1/1, 5–6.
3 M.A.F. 68/1675; M.A.F. 68/3837.
4 Friern Barnet U.D. *Ann. Reps. of M.O.H.*
5 M.R.O., Acc. 262/5A/1.
6 M.A.F. 68/1675.
7 M.A.F. 68/2815.
8 B.L. Cott. MS. Claud. E. vi, f. 189v.
9 M.A.F. 68/1105; M.A.F. 68/3837.
10 *Barnet Press*, 23 Mar. 1895.
11 Friern Barnet U.D. *Ann. Reps. of M.O.H.*
12 R.G. 10/1334.
13 *Kelly's Dir. Barnet* (1895, 1912–13); *Kelly's Dir. Finchley* (1939).
14 *Jnl. Roy. Agric. Soc.* ser. 3, ix.
15 Friern Barnet U.D., educ. cttee. min. bk. (1946–9).
16 S.C. 6/Hen. VIII/2402 m. 7.
17 St. Paul's MSS., box B 15, m. 19.
18 M.R.O., MR/TH/1, 9.
19 St. Paul's MSS., box A 58.
20 M.R.O., D.R.O. 12/I/H/7; TA/FRI.
21 *Census*, 1831.
22 M.A.F. 68/2815.
23 M.A.F. 68/3837.
24 The para. is based on the section below.
25 M.R.O., EA/FIN.
26 M.R.O., D.R.O. 12/I/H/7.
27 M.R.O., TA/FRI.
28 Ibid.; see below, p. 22.
29 E 305/D7.
30 e.g. B.L. Cott. MS. Claud. E. vi, ff. 189v.–90; St. Paul's MS. C (Sampson) f. 227.
31 e.g. B.L. Cott. MS. Claud. E. vi, ff. 221–v.; L.R. 2/62 f. 14v.

In 1506 the heaviest services due from the copyholders, equal in value to their rent, concerned the cartage of timber.[32] The woods were fenced, Friern wood gate being mentioned in 1545 and Woodgate in 1577,[33] and in 1549 Robert Standish received custody of the key to the lord's park.[34] There was a woodward between 1528 and 1564.[35] Clauses restricting the lessees' rights were not closely observed but there were still *c.* 60 a. of woodland in 1783[36] and valuable standing trees in 1799.[37] The woods survived the tenure of John Bacon but consisted of only *c.* 5 a. in 1846.[38]

Friern wood of 88 a. was the largest wood in 1544,[39] probably stretching to the Finchley boundary from Friern Barnet Lane and perhaps bounded on the south by Blackett's brook.[40] It sheltered the manor-house[41] and consisted mainly of oaks in 1563, when the lessee had felled some without licence.[42] It was being wasted *c.* 1581[43] and still covered *c.* 21 a. in 1661,[44] but by 1783 no trace remained.[45]

Damsells grove, 5 a. in 1544[46] and adjoining Friern little park on the east,[47] had been cleared by 1649.[48] Friern little park faced the south end of Oakleigh Road and was bounded on the north by Blackett's brook in 1512–13.[49] It covered 28 a. in 1544,[50] 30 a. in 1649,[51] 23 a. in 1815, [52] and 19½ a. in 1825, when it was sold to James Wood,[53] who had divided it into plots with cottages by 1846.[54] Friern great park, north of Friern Barnet Road, probably adjoined Betstile grove to the west and was once separated from the little park only by Blackett's brook.[55] It comprised 54 a. in 1544,[56] 46 a. in 1649,[57] and 38 a. in 1815,[58] but had been divided into fields by 1846.[59]

The area north of Oakleigh Road may once have been wholly wooded. Much of it had been cleared by 1544 when, apart from Luckins grove of 9 a., Priests coppice of 1½ a.,[60] and Wypers wood, there were many copyhold groves. Most of them were small: five groves held by John Goodere in 1498–9 amounted to only 22½ a.[61] Much the largest was Goodyers grove on the boundary with Hertfordshire. Totalling 67 a., it was divided into seven closes by 1628[62] but had still contained 30½ a. of woodland in 1499[63] and 20 a. in 1537.[64] There were frequent references to fields formerly woods.[65] Little Wypers wood of 4 a. survived in 1783,[66] the others probably having been cleared by the mid 17th century.

Hollick and Tottenham woods were joined in 1623, when the king asked that gates be provided between them for his hunting.[67] In 1689 Hollick wood adjoined Muswell Hill Lane[68] and probably extended to the junction with Friern Barnet Road, where a hatch gate stood in 1810.[69] It consisted of 160 a. in 1652[70] but only *c.* 60 a. in 1716,[71] when several fields had been carved out of it. In 1783 they separated it from the roads to the north and west and it was bordered on the south by Bounds Green brook.[72] The wood still covered 61 a. in 1846[73] but had been cleared for Colney Hatch asylum by 1852.[74] In the 18th century large numbers of oaks had been felled annually.[75] James de Audley had been granted free warren in 1252[76] and the lord continued to take game during the 18th and 19th centuries.[77]

There was woodland on the site of Coppetts farm before 1565.[78] In 1628 two fields of 10 a. and 12 a. were called Small Harts wood and Deadmans Pitt heath.[79] The second had been cut down by 1565.[80] William Trott had a wood on the corner of Friern Barnet Lane and Friern Barnet Road in 1649.[81] The location of other coppices and woods is uncertain.

TRADE AND INDUSTRY. From 1488 there were several brewers, mainly on the highway at Whetstone. Many inns had fields attached to them and so served drovers' herds as well as wayfarers: in the late 17th century the lessee of the Green Dragon invested £120 to improve his land for travellers' cattle and sheep[82] and in 1851 the landlord of the Black Bull employed most of his servants on the land.[83] Innkeepers at Whetstone, also employing ostlers and domestic servants, supported 34 people in 1851. Travellers also accounted for the presence of wheelwrights, carriers, blacksmiths,[84] and in 1882 a veterinary surgeon.[85]

Trade at first was concentrated at Whetstone.

32 St. Paul's MSS., box A 62(2).
33 St. Paul's MSS., boxes B 15, m. 10; B 17, m. 16d.
34 Ibid. B 15, m. 2c.
35 L.R. 2/62 ff. 51v.–52; E 315/98 pp. 114–15; St. Paul's MS. C (Nowell), f. 86v.
36 Guildhall Libr., map case 247; B.L.H.L., Acc. 9781/1.
37 B.L.H.L., Acc. 9381/2.
38 TA/FRI.
39 E 305/D7.
40 B.L.H.L., Acc. 9381/1; St. Paul's MSS., box B 17, m. 16d.
41 Ibid. box A 58; C 2/Eliz. I/P16/36 m. 1.
42 St. Paul's MSS., box B 15, m. 3.
43 C 2/Eliz. I/P16/36 m. 1.
44 St. Paul's MSS., box B 15, m. 3.
45 B.L.H.L., Acc. 9781/1; Guildhall Libr., map case 247.
46 E 305/D7.
47 M.L.R. 1825/9/147.
48 C 54/3543/16.
49 St. Paul's MSS., box B 17, m. 11.
50 E 305/D7.
51 C 54/3543/16.
52 M.R.O., D.R.O. 12/I/H/7.
53 Barnet Mus. 1281.
54 M.R.O., TA/FRI.
55 Rocque, *Map of Mdx.* (1754).
56 E 305/D7.
57 C 54/3543/16.
58 M.R.O., D.R.O. 12/I/H/7.
59 M.R.O., TA/FRI.
60 E 305/D7.
61 St. Paul's MSS., box B 17, m. 4.
62 Barnet Mus., Pandora box I, P.B. 15/151.
63 See p. 18.
64 C.P. 25(2)/51/370/38.
65 St. Paul's MSS., boxes B 15, 17.
66 Guildhall Libr., map case 247.
67 *Cal. S.P. Dom.* 1619–23, 612.
68 M.R.O., Acc. 262/5A/2.
69 Ibid. 61/14.
70 Ibid. 5A/1.
71 B.L.H.L., Acc. 9888.
72 Guildhall Libr., map case 247.
73 M.R.O., TA/FRI.
74 Guildhall Libr., map case 247.
75 M.R.O., Acc. 262/5A/1, /2.
76 *Cal. Chart. R.* 1226–57, 409.
77 M.R.O., Acc. 262/6A.
78 C 54/790 mm. 24–26d.
79 C 54/2777 mm. 15–16 no. 19.
80 C 54/790 mm. 24 sqq.
81 C 54/3543/6.
82 C 5/581/7 mm. 1–3.
83 H.O. 107/1701 f. 310.
84 Ibid. ff. 309–19.
85 Walford, *Gtr. Lond.* i. 336.

In 1831 there were 48 families chiefly occupied in trade or manufacture, the second largest form of employment, 8 carpenters or professional men, and 14 non-agricultural labourers.[86] Most common trades were practised at Whetstone in 1851[87] but, probably because of the opening of the asylum, there were also many artisans at the Avenue in 1871 and at the Freehold, where women worked in occupations such as dress- or bonnet-making. Everywhere there was a considerable rise in the number of unskilled labourers.[88] Colney Hatch was becoming a shopping and service area by 1888[89] and was the main retail district *c.* 1948, when the absence of a shopping centre was attributed to municipal policy.[90] In 1911 there were 39 shops, in 1959 there were 312,[91] and in 1975 the only large departmental stores were at Whetstone. There were five laundries in 1893 and a dry-cleaning works was among the largest employers in 1954.[92]

Brickearth could be dug by the manorial lessee in 1551.[93] The soil in the central area was found suitable for bricks in 1828[94] and the asylum was largely built from bricks made locally.[95] Gravel ballast was used for road repairs[96] and in 1848 much of that north of Friern Barnet Road had been extracted.[97] There was a brickworks at Betstile in 1851, when a bricklayer with 12 employees lived at Whetstone.[98] Eleven householders at the Freehold in 1871 were bricklayers, six were carpenters, three were builders, and four were plasterers.[99] The construction industry prospered as the parish was built up.

In 1893 there were dairies, a bakehouse, and two slaughter houses. Only one workshop was visited under the Factories Act, probably the creosote works that emitted black smoke.[1] In 1911 there were four factories[2] and in 1920 there was a factory making boxes, another leather goods, and a third electrical instruments, probably Cambridge & Paul.[3] In 1924 there were said to be very few factories and workshops but eleven were listed in 1925, when there was no heavy industry except Biggs Wall & Co. and another unnamed engineering works.[4] An independent survey in 1933 considered that there were no factories in Friern Barnet.[5] There were said to be 74, mostly small, in 1954 and 84 by 1959. The five largest in 1954 included an electricity depot, a motor-bus garage, and the dry-cleaning works, and only the Cambridge Instrument Co. and Priory Handbag Co. were engaged in manufacture.[6]

In 1897 Robert Paul acquired land in Sydney Road in the Freehold for a film studio, alleged to be the first of its kind in Europe. In 1900 he moved his instrument workshop from Hatton Garden and in 1903 produced a galvanometer and later his prototype of the pulsator, a forerunner of the iron lung. From 1912, when Paul disposed of his rights, the firm made mainly measuring instruments, notably thermometers in the period between the World Wars. The premises were extended in 1937–9, 1959–61, and from 1963, but in 1975 production in Sydney Road and at another factory, in Finchley, together employing 750 people, was transferred to St. Neot's (Hunts.). In 1920 the firm amalgamated with the Cambridge Scientific Instrument Co. to form Cambridge & Paul, after 1924 the Cambridge Instrument Co. It merged in 1968 with George Kent and in 1971 with Foster Instrument Co., another subsidiary of the George Kent Group, to form Foster Cambridge. In 1974 it was taken over by the Swiss firm of Brown Boveri.[7]

The Priory Handbag Co., founded in Kilburn in 1942 to make ladies' handbags, moved to premises erected *c.* 1925 for a sawmill at Roman Road, the Freehold, in 1950. It produced footwear from *c.* 1971, changing its name to Priory Footwear, and in 1975 it employed 75–100 people.[8]

H. M. Creek began making tape-recorders *c.* 1950 at the rear of a radio shop and developed into the Magnetic Recording Co., leading the limited field of British tape-recorders. By 1958 it had been incorporated as the Wyndsor Recording Co. and occupied a model factory in Bellevue Road, Colney Hatch, where it produced *c.* 200 machines weekly in 1975.[9]

In 1951, 10,089 residents comprising 35 per cent of the total population worked outside the parish, 4,527 of them in central London. On the other hand 4,042 people who did not live in Friern Barnet worked there,[10] many of them presumably in offices at Whetstone.

SOCIAL AND CULTURAL ACTIVITIES. Inns were often used by the vestry in the 18th century[11] and it was claimed in 1883 that the sole place for meetings was a public house. Room was therefore provided in the new Congregational lecture hall[12] and in 1883 the ratepayers of New Southgate determined on their own hall.[13] Various buildings were used but none was satisfactory until the opening of the hall at Holly Park school.[14]

The Congregational elders intended their hall for purposes such as temperance meetings.[15] Temperance never obtained a strong following, although the local branch of the British Women's Temperance Association was a regular user by 1895.[16] In 1887 total abstinence was favoured by only one member of the Friern Barnet and New Southgate Mutual Improvement Society,[17] which

[86] *Census*, 1831.
[87] H.O. 107/1701 ff. 309–19.
[88] R.G. 10/1334 ff. 57–end.
[89] *P.O. Dir. N. Suburbs* (1888).
[90] Friern Barnet U.D. *Official Guide* [*c.* 1948], 12.
[91] *Census*, 1911; Friern Barnet U.D. *Ann. Rep. of M.O.H.* (1959).
[92] Friern Barnet U.D. *Ann. Reps. of M.O.H.*
[93] St. Paul's MS. C (Sampson), f. 227v.
[94] M.R.O., MA/AJ3/19.
[95] M.R.O., Acc. 1038/1A, 2A.
[96] B.L.H.L., Acc. 9888 (highway surveyors' accts.).
[97] Ibid. (sales parts.).
[98] H.O. 107/1701 ff. 309–19, 331–4.
[99] R.G. 10/1334 ff. 57–68.
[1] Friern Barnet U.D. *Ann. Rep. of M.O.H.* (1893).
[2] *Census*, 1911.
[3] Friern Barnet U.D. *Ann. Reps. of M.O.H.* (1920).
[4] Ibid. (1924, 1925).
[5] Smith, *Ind. of Gtr. Lond.* 73.
[6] Friern Barnet U.D. *Ann. Reps. of M.O.H.* (1953–4, 1959).
[7] Ex inf. Foster Cambridge Ltd.
[8] Ex inf. Priory Footwear Ltd.
[9] Friern Barnet U.D. *Official Guide* [*c.* 1958], 17, 19.
[10] *Census*, 1951.
[11] M.R.O., D.R.O. 12/I/C/1; D1/1.
[12] *Barnet Press*, 25 Aug. 1883.
[13] Ibid. 10 Mar. 1883.
[14] Ibid. 9 Jan. 1909.
[15] Ibid. 25 Aug. 1883.
[16] Ibid. 19 Jan. 1895.
[17] Ibid. 19 Mar. 1887.

produced a magazine.[18] In 1887 scandalized parishioners were assured that St. Peter's mission hall offered educational opportunities for the 'young roughs' who openly gambled in the Freehold.[19] Clergy of all denominations assisted parishioners in educating themselves: several parish rooms were opened at public demand, including St. Peter's mission hall in 1887 and one at Finchley Park in 1896,[20] and the Congregationalists' hall had a room where working men could study newspapers.[21] Evening classes were provided thrice a week at Friern Barnet and Colney Hatch in 1891–2,[22] and when many labourers were temporarily employed in 1886, a representative of the Navvy Mission Society ministered to them.[23]

The proximity of Colney Hatch asylum was not welcome to all residents. The Revd. Henry Hawkins, chaplain to the hospital 1867–1900, founded an association to help with aftercare, later part of the National Association for Mental Help,[24] and a Guild of Friends of the Insane at Colney Hatch, which lapsed. A league of friends of the hospital had only recently been established in 1974.[25]

Clothing was given to the charity school children[26] and a fund organized in 1850, to help the poor save for coal and clothing, survived in 1932.[27] In 1883 the rector had been encouraging a C. of E. working men's club for 12 years.[28] St. John's working men's club was at no. 61 Holly Park Road by 1889[29] and subscriptions were raised for a Conservative working men's club in 1891.[30] All Saints' working men's club existed by 1883[31] and from 1912–13 had premises at Oakleigh Road North beside the school.[32] An institute in the Freehold and a youth club active in 1887[33] may have been precursors of the Freehold social institute in Pembroke Road which existed by 1912–13.[34] The Revd. George Hennessy promoted a co-operative society in 1894 at the Freehold, which was said to have a tradition of mutual assistance[35] and whose ratepayers' association was a formidable pressure group immediately after the formation of the local board.[36]

Although previous ratepayers' meetings had been only occasional,[37] the first local elections were dominated by ratepayers' associations in spite of the councillors' alleged membership of the Conservative club.[38] The Conservatives opened the Constitutional club in 1895[39] and a New Southgate and Friern Barnet Conservative association had offices at Holly Park in 1900,[40] with branches in each ward by 1926.[41] Friern Barnet and New Southgate Liberal association dissolved itself in 1889 on the election of a new committee as a branch of the Central Liberal and Radical Committee.[42] A Liberal and Radical club was established in 1895[43] at Carlisle Place and had premises there from 1904 until 1932, when it housed the Betstyle hall and social club.[44] A central ward Liberal club existed in 1926,[45] a Muswell Hill Socialist society by 1907,[46] and a Friern Barnet branch of the Communist party in 1945.[47]

A bowling green at Halliwick manor-house was disused in 1628.[48] The Orange Tree inn was recommended in 1817 to sportsmen in pursuit of the plentiful wildfowl at Colney Hatch.[49] There was a cricket field at Friern Barnet Road by 1862[50] and a football club for Holly Park by 1875.[51] At first sport was played mainly in Oakleigh Park, where there were cricket and lawn tennis clubs in 1889.[52] From 1899 there was a private lawn tennis club in Athenaeum Road,[53] where the Congregational cricket club had a ground in 1900.[54] New Southgate and Friern Barnet lawn tennis club existed by 1895, when Friern Barnet cricket and lawn tennis club was founded,[55] and used grounds between the asylum and Colney Hatch Lane before acquiring its own field in Woodhouse Road by 1906.[56] By 1922 the railway clearing house acquired a field off Friern Barnet Lane and adjoining the glebe,[57] which was used as playing fields by the grammar school until 1939.[58] The Kennard lawn tennis club had courts in Colney Hatch from 1922,[59] when a rifle club was established there. The L.C.C. took over sports fields cut off from the asylum after the construction of the North Circular Road.[60] Some of the grounds were built upon but in 1939 there were new tennis clubs at Torrington Park and Wetherill and Wilton roads.[61] In 1964 the largest non-municipal playing fields were the L.C.C.'s (later the I.L.E.A.'s) 7 a., the railway clearance ground of 6 a. and glebe of 2 a., and the grounds off Chandos Avenue of 6 a. and between there and Athenaeum Road of *c.* 10 a.[62] The railway

18 *Barnet Press*, 12 Mar. 1887.
19 Ibid. 11 June 1887.
20 M.R.O., D.R.O. 12/I/K2/3 (1896); *Barnet Press*, 11 June 1887.
21 *Barnet Press*, 25 Aug. 1883.
22 M.R.O., D.R.O. 12/I/K1/2 (Oct. 1891); *Barnet Press*, 17 Jan. 1891.
23 M.R.O., D.R.O. 12/I/K2/2 (1886).
24 Walford, *Gtr. Lond.* i. 344; Hunter and Macalpine, *Psychiatry for the Poor*, 67.
25 Hunter and Macalpine, *Psychiatry for the Poor*, 67–8.
26 M.R.O., D.R.O. 12/I/G1/3.
27 Ibid. K2/1–6(1850–1932).
28 *Barnet Press*, 3 Feb. 1883.
29 *Kelly's Dir. Barnet* (1889).
30 *Barnet Press*, 12 Jan. 1895.
31 Ibid. 24 Feb. 1893.
32 *Kelly's Dir. Barnet* (1912–13).
33 *Barnet Press*, 11 June 1887.
34 *Kelly's Dir. Barnet* (1917–18).
35 *Barnet Press*, 12 June 1895.
36 See p. 27.
37 *Barnet Press*, 23 June 1883.
38 See p. 27.
39 *Barnet Press*, Jan. 1895.
40 *Kelly's Dir. Barnet* (1900–1).
41 *Barnet Press*, 20 Mar. 1926.
42 Ibid. 23 Apr. 1889.
43 Ibid. 9 Feb. 1845.
44 *Kelly's Dir. Barnet* (1904 and later edns.); *Finchley* (1926 and later edns.).
45 *Barnet Press*, 20 Feb. 1926.
46 Ibid. 19 Jan. 1907.
47 *Barnet Press*, 25 Mar. 1926; B.L.H.L., Friern Barnet U.D., min. bk. (1945–6), p. 38.
48 C 54/2777 mm. 15–16 no. 19.
49 J. Hassell, *Picturesque Rides and Walks* (1817), i. 194.
50 M.R.O., D.R.O. 12/I/C1/4.
51 *Barnet Press*, 30 Jan. 1875.
52 *Kelly's Dir. Barnet* (1889).
53 Ibid. (1899).
54 Ibid. (1900).
55 *Barnet Press*, 9 Mar., 13 Apr., 20 Apr. 1895.
56 *Kelly's Dir. Barnet* (1899–1901, 1906); *Barnet Press*, 9 Mar. 1895; M.R.O., D.R.O. 12/I/B/1 (plan, 1908).
57 *Kelly's Dir. Finchley* (1922).
58 M.R.O., D.R.O. 12/I/G8/2, p. 59.
59 *Kelly's Dir. Finchley* (1922).
60 Hunter and Macalpine, *Psychiatry for the Poor*, 152.
61 *Kelly's Dir. Finchley* (1939).
62 B.L.H.L., Acc. 9888; Friern Barnet U.D., educ. cttee. min. bk. (1946–9).

clearance ground and glebe also provided the site for Queenswell school.[63]

Brunswick recreation ground in Oakleigh Road South, East Barnet (Herts.), was opened in 1892 and Friern Barnet U.D.C. contributed towards its maintenance from 1895.[64] It included cricket pitches and tennis courts in 1909[65] but in 1895 was too distant to benefit Holly Park.[66] Friary park was acquired in 1909, when it was equipped with a bowling green,[67] and had tennis courts and a putting green *c.* 1948.[68] In 1924 the council acquired 33½ a., which became Bethune recreation ground in 1926; parts were devoted to allotments,[69] to a 9-hole golf course,[70] and, after levelling, to a cricket pitch and running track.[71] Halliwick recreation ground, 5½ a. adjoining Coppetts Road, was probably purchased with the near-by allotments in 1927[72] and included tennis courts *c.* 1948.[73] All municipal open spaces in 1935 were much used by sports clubs and schools lacking their own grounds.[74]

After the break-up of John Miles's estate in 1902,[75] 81 a. were bought in 1906 by Ernest Arthur Lazarus and passed in 1907 to the North Middlesex Golf Co. Outlying parts were sold and 74 a. settled in trust for use as a golf course.[76] The council acquired the land as an open space in 1928[77] and thereafter leased it to the North Middlesex Golf Club (1928) Ltd., whose course covered 60 a. in 1946.[78]

Friary park consists mainly of formal gardens and has a children's bathing pool and playground. By *c.* 1948 there were playgrounds at Halliwick and Cromwell recreation grounds, the second of which covered 1 a. and was solely for children.[79] In 1975 there was also a playground at Sweet's Way, Whetstone. Until the early 20th century there were pleasure grounds at the Green Man, Whetstone,[80] the Orange Tree, Colney Hatch, and the Railway hotel, New Southgate.[81] Private gardens were used for childrens' treats by 1880[82] and church fêtes and concerts were regularly organized.[83] The Railway hotel was licensed for music and dancing in 1855,[84] Whetstone coffee tavern in 1885,[85] and the Freehold social institute by 1913.[86] Entertainments by sports clubs and schools[87] were often held in schoolrooms,[88] at the Congregational lecture hall,[89] and from 1930 at the church hall. In 1883 musicians and gymnasts performed at the Athenaeum, Oakleigh Park,[90] but by 1887 bookings had declined. The building survived as photographers' studios in 1906.[91] By 1926 plays were produced by the Friern Strollers and there was an orchestral society.[92]

LOCAL GOVERNMENT. Friern Barnet Road divided the medieval parish between the manors of Whetstone and Halliwick.[93] There are no court rolls for Halliwick before 1810, by which date copyhold tenure had long been extinct. In 1488 a chief pledge for Colney Hatch as well as two for Whetstone was appointed annually in the Whetstone manorial court.[94] Tenants were to display distinguishing marks in the form of double crosses over their doorways[95] and in 1515, by long established custom, were to maintain the double crosses marking the boundaries of the manor with Finchley and Hertfordshire.[96] A cross at Betstile was mentioned in 1504[97] and one at Muswell Hill in 1399.[98] The court, which met on the Friday in Whitsuntide, consisted of a view of frankpledge and a court, known after 1557 as a court baron.[99]

A constable, three chief pledges or headboroughs, and an ale-taster were appointed for Whetstone in 1488.[1] After experiments with 4 or 5 headboroughs between 1497 and 1499[2] only one constable and one headborough were appointed until 1773,[3] when responsibility for their appointment passed to the vestry. There was a single ale-taster until 1550, when there were three,[4] and thereafter one until 1721.[5] In 1584 oaths of office were to be sworn in court.[6]

The court regulated the assize of ale and in 1598 ordered that the ale-taster should have a book of measures according to statute.[7] In 1616 a scold was ducked on the stool[8] ordained by the court in 1593[9] and in 1752 it was decided to provide stocks.[10] In 1577 anyone harbouring paupers was to promise to exonerate the vill from all expense.[11] Until 1612

63 See p. 36.
64 *Barnet Press*, 23 Feb., 1 Jan. 1895.
65 Friern Barnet U.D. *Opening of Friary Pk.*
66 *Barnet Press*, 9 Mar. 1895.
67 Friern Barnet U.D. *Opening of Friary Pk.*
68 Friern Barnet U.D. *Official Guide* [*c.* 1948], 15.
69 Friern Barnet U.D. *Ann. Rep. of M.O.H.*; *Petit. for Incorp. as Municip. Boro.* (1953), 8–9 (list of by-laws).
70 O.S. Map 6″, Mdx. VII. SW. (1938 edn.).
71 Friern Barnet U.D. *Official Guide* [*c.* 1948], 15–18.
72 B.L.H.L., Friern Barnet U.D., educ. cttee. min. bk. (1946–9); *Kelly's Dir. Finchley* (1927).
73 Friern Barnet U.D. *Official Guide* [*c.* 1948], 18.
74 B.L.H.L., Friern Barnet U.D., min. bk. (1935–6), pp. 66–7.
75 See p. 18.
76 B.L.H.L., Acc. 9888.
77 Ibid., Friern Barnet U.D., min. bk. (1927–8), pp. 38, 91 sqq.
78 Friern Barnet U.D. *Official Guide* [*c.* 1948], 13; B.L.H.L., Acc. 9888.
79 Friern Barnet U.D. *Official Guide* [*c.* 1948], 15–18.
80 M.R.O., Acc. 410/19.
81 O.S. Map 6″, Mdx. VII. SW. (1863 edn.).
82 e.g. M.R.O., D.R.O. 12/I/G5/1.
83 M.R.O., MR/M and D 25/4.
84 M.R.O., D.R.O. 12/II/B1/11; I/K1/4 (par. mag. Aug. 1894).
85 M.R.O., MCC/M and D 5/50 a–b.
86 Ibid. 11/15.
87 *Barnet Press*, 20 Apr. 1895.
88 Ibid. 19 June 1895.
89 Ibid. 20 Apr. 1895.
90 Ibid. 31 Mar., 21 July, 18 Aug. 1883.
91 *Kelly's Dir. Barnet* (1906).
92 *Barnet Press*, 17 Apr. 1926.
93 M.R.O., Acc. 262/5A/1; 5B.
94 St. Paul's MSS., box B 17, m. 1.
95 Ibid. m. 8d.
96 Ibid. m. 12d.
97 Ibid.
98 *Pub. Works in Med. Law*, ii (Selden Soc. xl), p. 38.
99 St. Paul's MSS., box B 17, mm. 23–4. At St. Paul's cath. libr. there are ct. rolls for 1488–1672, except for 1524–44 and 1642–60: St. Paul's MSS., boxes B 15–18, 98. Ct. rolls for 1528–32 are in M.R.O., Acc. 528. There are ct. bks. for 1668–1933: Guildhall MSS. 14717/2; 14223/1–9.
1 St. Paul's MSS., box B 17, m. 1.
2 Ibid. m. 4d.
3 Guildhall MS. 14223/3, p. 185.
4 St. Paul's MSS., box B 15, m. 23.
5 Guildhall MS. 14223/1, p. 110.
6 St. Paul's MSS., box B 15, m. 17.
7 Ibid. m. 29d.
8 *Mdx. Sess. Rec.* iii. 126.
9 St. Paul's MSS., box B 15, m. 24.
10 Guildhall MS. 14223/3, p. 8.
11 St. Paul's MSS., box B 15, m. 23d.

householders were fined for keeping inmates contrary to the Cottagers Act.[12]

Churchwardens held office in 1541–2[13] and overseers of the poor in 1598.[14] There was a salaried vestry clerk by 1761.[15] The constable and headborough, who were paid from 1786,[16] continued to be appointed by the vestry[17] until 1862, although the parish was included in the Metropolitan Police District in 1840.[18] Four surveyors of the highways were appointed annually from 1765[19] and ten after 1779,[20] when there was a northern or Whetstone division and a southern or Colney Hatch division.[21] By 1870 there was one surveyor for the whole parish.[22] The office of aleconner was revived in 1812[23] and a sexton was employed from 1822.[24] The offices of vestry clerk and assistant overseer were first combined in 1831[25] and were later held by the clerk to the local board and U.D.[26]

Between 1762 and 1766 an average of three vestries met annually in a public house or the church. Attendance fluctuated from 4 to 11, occasionally including the rector.[27] In 1778 it was expected that there would be only four annual vestries[28] but next year it was resolved to hold them at the alms-houses on the first Monday of every month.[29] Between 1780 and 1818 there was a normal attendance of 4 to 8, including the rector,[30] who presided by 1870.[31] There were seven vestries a year in 1818–19[32] compared with two in the 1870s, when there were several sub-committees.[33] Meetings were usually in the vestry-room after its construction at the church in 1807.[34]

A church house was rented by the churchwardens in 1541–2.[35] The overseers kept livestock for the poor in 1598,[36] when 40*s.* was left to augment it.[37] The poor had customary grazing rights on Finchley common and were awarded 1 a. at its inclosure in 1814.[38] The number of overseers was increased from two to four in 1781[39] and to six in 1909,[40] and there was an assistant overseer by 1831.[41] In 1781 the vestry decided to review the alms-houses four times a year[42] and by 1828 parish officers had long accommodated the poor there.[43] A doctor was retained for the poor in 1786[44] but in 1809 he was not to visit them without permission.[45] There was no workhouse: in 1779 the parish farmed the poor to the keeper of Enfield workhouse[46] and after joining Barnet union in 1835 was entitled to use Barnet workhouse.[47] The poor-rate was 1*s.* 2*d.* in the £ in 1776–7, when it brought in £82,[48] 9*d.* to 1*s.* in 1778–80, when it produced £153, and increased to 3*s.* in 1811, when it realized £596.[49] The yield varied around £400 between 1816 and 1841.[50]

Under the Sanitary Act of 1866 the vestry appointed a sanitary committee in 1866, to which in 1870 it gave all the powers that it could delegate except over finance.[51] The parish successfully resisted partial inclusion in the East Barnet and Edmonton local board areas between 1873 and 1875[52] and in 1874 was incorporated in Barnet rural sanitary authority,[53] which decided to enforce a sanitary scheme in 1883.[54] Friern Barnet's ratepayers then petitioned for a local board,[55] which was established in 1884.[56]

The clerk and nine members of the vestry, alleged to be Conservatives, supported one another in the first election,[57] which was contested by some 20 others.[58] John Miles (d. 1886), chairman of the vestry, became chairman of the local board, which was dominated by the vestry's candidates.[59] The board undertook an expensive scheme, which necessitated the sewering of private roads. With doubtful legality, instead of compensating landowners and charging them the costs of laying sewers, compensation was waived and sewers were laid free of charge.[60] Rates rose to 3*s.* in 1886[61] and in 1887 the 7*s.* rate was an election issue.[62] From 1886 the ratepayers' association opposed the free sewering of private roads and the board was evenly divided.[63] Certain members refused to sign cheques[64] and an appeal, later withdrawn,

[12] St. Paul's MSS., box B 18, m. 43; box B 15, m. 27, quoting 31 Eliz. I, c. 7.

[13] S.C. 6/Hen. VIII/2402 m. 7.

[14] St. Paul's MSS., F (Reg. Wills) C, f. 48v.

[15] M.R.O., D.R.O. 12/I/C/1. There are churchwardens' accts. for 1819–1919, ibid. B1/1, and vestry min. bks. for 1743–1954, ibid. C1/1–4.

[16] Ibid. C1/1.

[17] Ibid.

[18] Ibid. 4; *Lond. Gaz.* 13 Oct. 1840, p. 2250.

[19] M.R.O., D.R.O. 12/I/C1/1.

[20] Ibid.

[21] Ibid. Highway rate bks. for 1795–6 and acct. bks. for 1783–7 and 1793–5 are in B.L.H.L., Acc. 9888.

[22] M.R.O., D.R.O. 12/I/C1/3.

[23] Ibid. C1/1.

[24] Ibid. C1/2.

[25] Ibid.

[26] *Barnet Press*, 16 Apr. 1887.

[27] M.R.O., D.R.O. 12/I/C1/1.

[28] Ibid.

[29] Ibid.

[30] Ibid.

[31] Ibid. C1/3.

[32] Ibid. C1/1.

[33] Ibid. C1/3.

[34] Ibid. C1/1–3.

[35] S.C. 6/Hen. VIII/2402 m. 7.

[36] M.R.O., D.R.O. 12/I/C1/1–2.

[37] St. Paul's MSS., F (Reg. Wills) C, f. 48v. There are overseers' acct. bks. for 1743–1819, 1818, and 1836–70, an assessment for 1673, and rate bks. for 1792–4, 1786–7, and 1792: M.R.O., D.R.O. 12/I/D1/1; Acc. 1027; B.L.H.L., Acc. 9888; St. Paul's MSS., box A 58.

[38] M.R.O., EA/FIN.

[39] M.R.O., D.R.O. 12/I/C1/1.

[40] Ibid.

[41] Ibid. C1/2.

[42] M.R.O., D.R.O. 12/I/C1/1.

[43] *18th Rep. Com. Char.* H.C. 62, p. 382 (1828), xx.

[44] M.R.O., D.R.O. 12/I/C1/1.

[45] Ibid.

[46] Ibid.

[47] *1st Ann. Rep. of Poor Law Com.* H.C. 500, p. 250 (1835), App. D.

[48] M.R.O., D.R.O. 12/I/D1/1.

[49] Ibid. C1/1.

[50] *Rep. from Sel. Cttee. on Poor Law Returns*, H.C. 334, p. 357 (1825), iv; *Poor Law Com. 1st Rep.* 250; *Poor Law Returns*, H.C. 63, p. 98 (1844), xl.

[51] M.R.O., D.R.O. 12/I/C1/3, 4.

[52] *Barnet Press*, 14 July 1883.

[53] *Lond. Gaz.* 22 Sept. 1874, p. 4465.

[54] *Barnet Press*, 28 Apr. 1883.

[55] Ibid. 6 Oct. 1883.

[56] B.L.H.L., Friern Barnet loc. bd., min. bk. (1884–6), p. 1. All min. bks. of the loc. bd. and U.D. 1884–1965 are in the colln.

[57] *Barnet Press*, 13 Oct., 20 Oct. 1883.

[58] Ibid. 27 Oct. 1883 *et seq.*

[59] B.L.H.L., Friern Barnet loc. bd., min. bk. (1884–6), p. 1.

[60] *Barnet Press*, 15 Jan., 19 Mar., 21 May 1887.

[61] Ibid. 1 Jan. 1887.

[62] Ibid. 9 Apr. 1887.

[63] Ibid. 1 Jan., 15 Jan. 1887.

[64] Ibid. 21 May 1887.

was made against the rate.[65] Elections in 1887 did not resolve the deadlock[66] and at an inquiry over the refusal of the Local Government Board to sanction loans for sewering private roads, the board could not agree on its attitude.[67] Accounts were also challenged at the district audit.[68] Meanwhile the Freehold ratepayers' association claimed that private roads were neglected in the most populous but least represented area.[69] The problems apparently declined with the completion of the sewage works and the creation of wards.[70] In 1907 it was said that the election was more vigorously contested than any since the early days of the local board.[71]

Friern Barnet local board became a U.D.C. in 1895[72] and had nine members, elected by the whole parish rather than by wards as the ratepayers had wished.[73] In 1888 three wards, each with three members, were created:[74] the south ward consisted of the area east of the railway and south of Friern Barnet Road, the north ward stretched north of Friary Road and Holly Park, and the central ward covered the remainder.[75] The division gave greater weight to the Freehold, which tried unsuccessfully to partition the south ward in 1895[76] and to secure relatively more members in 1909,[77] when the number of councillors was increased to four for each ward.[78] In 1945 there were five wards, each returning three members, and five aldermen.[79] A third of the board was elected annually until 1895, when all members were to be elected triennially.[80] Meetings were twice a month in 1885[81] and monthly in 1909.[82] There were four committees in 1884,[83] seven in 1909,[84] nine by 1935,[85] and ten in 1953.[86] In 1888 the board had a clerk and a medical officer, and the functions of surveyor, engineer, collector, and assistant overseer were combined.[87] Friern Barnet escaped inclusion in Finchley M.B. in 1935[88] and failed to secure incorporation in 1953.[89] In 1965, under the London Government Act of 1963, it was included in Barnet L.B.[90]

The local board first met in St. James's schoolroom,[91] before leasing temporary offices at Parkhurst House, Friern Barnet Road, in 1884.[92] It moved to Tudor House, no. 18 Beaconsfield Road, in 1887,[93] and acquired the 200-year-old Priory, on the corner of Friern Barnet Road and Friern Barnet Lane, in 1906.[94] It remained there until 1939, when work began on a new building on the same site. Designed by Sir John Brown and Henson and opened in 1941,[95] the town hall was red-brick and of two storeys, with a central cupola and a concave front towards the road.[96] In 1975 it housed Barnet L.B.'s education and children's departments.

URBAN DISTRICT OF FRIERN BARNET. *Vert, a pale argent, on a chief dancetté or three fleurs-de-lys azure*
[Granted 1938]

PUBLIC SERVICES. Pymme's brook in Southgate was thought capable of poisoning the whole neighbourhood with sewage received from its tributary Bounds Green brook, until in 1856 public pressure secured a proper sewerage system for Colney Hatch asylum.[97] There was still some leakage from the asylum in 1875, when the streams were otherwise barely polluted.[98] After complaints by the Lee Conservancy Board in 1869 over sewage from the Avenue area, a tank was built at Ely Place and by 1873–4 there was no discharge into Hertfordshire. In 1873 the vestry regarded Friern Barnet as a rural parish with only minor problems and considered that earth closets were adequate for the thinly populated Oakleigh estate. On grounds of expense the parish wanted no part in schemes for East Barnet in 1873–4[99] or Finchley in 1875, and candidates for election as guardians at Barnet rural sanitary authority regarded demands for a sewage farm as 'humbug'.[1] By 1883 sewerage was out of control in several areas and improvements including an additional tank at Ely Place were inadequate.[2] Edmonton was unwilling to take the parish's sewage[3] and the rural sanitary authority was sued for polluting Pymme's brook.[4] Accordingly the authority, which had already laid some pipes,[5] decided to carry out an expensive scheme,[6]

65 Ibid. 1 Jan. 1887.
66 Ibid. 9 Apr. 1887.
67 Ibid. 15 Jan. 1887.
68 Ibid. 21 May 1887.
69 Ibid. 15 June, 19 Mar., 2 Apr. 1887.
70 See below.
71 *Barnet Press*, 2 Mar., 30 Mar. 1907.
72 M.R.O., *Reps. of Local Inqs.* (1889–1912).
73 Ibid.; *Barnet Press*, 6 Oct. 1883.
74 Ibid. 10 Dec. 1887; M.R.O., *Reps. of Local Inqs.* (1889–1912).
75 Friern Barnet U.D. *Ann. Rep. of M.O.H.* (1920).
76 *Barnet Press*, 1 June, 15 June 1895.
77 Ibid. 19 June 1909.
78 M.R.O., *Reps. of Local Inqs.* (1889–1912).
79 Barnet Mus. 2163: copy of Friern Barnet U.D. *Petit. for Incorp. as Municip. Boro.* (1953), 9.
80 *Barnet Press*, 19 Jan. 1895; M.R.O., *Reps. of Local Inqs.* (1889–1912).
81 *P.O. Dir. N. Suburbs* (1888).
82 M.R.O., *Reps. of Local Inqs.* (1889–1912).
83 B.L.H.L., Friern Barnet U.D., min. bk. (1894–6), p. 2.
84 M.R.O., *Reps. of Local Inqs.* (1889–1912).
85 B.L.H.L., Friern Barnet U.D., min. bk. (1935), p. 254.
86 Friern Barnet U.D. *Petit. for Incorp.* (1953), 9.
87 *P.O. Dir. N. Suburbs* (1888).
88 B.L.H.L., Friern Barnet U.D., min. bk. (1935), p. 103; Briggs, *Mdx. Old and New*, 120; *The Times*, 3 Jan. 1936.
89 Friern Barnet U.D. *Petit. for Incorp.* (1953); but see Royal Com. on Govt. of Gtr. Lond. *Mins. of Evidence* (1959), 21.
90 Barnet L.B. *Official Guide* [1967].
91 B.L.H.L., Friern Barnet loc. bd., min. bk. (1884–6), p. 1.
92 Ibid. p. 20.
93 Ibid. (1886–9), pp. 16–17.
94 M.L.R. 1906/13/523; M.R.O., Acc. 410 (newspaper cutting).
95 Friern Barnet U.D. *Official Guide* [*c.* 1947], 12.
96 Pevsner, *Mdx.* 57; Robbins, *Mdx.* 203.
97 Hunter and Macalpine, *Psychiatry for the Poor*, 32.
98 *Barnet Press*, 23 Jan. 1875.
99 M.R.O., D.R.O. 12/I/C1/3, 4.
1 *Barnet Press*, 10 Apr. 1875.
2 Ibid. 14 July 1883.
3 Ibid. 28 Apr. 1883.
4 Ibid. 30 June 1883.
5 Ibid. 21 May 1887.
6 Ibid. 14 July 1883.

whereupon Friern Barnet obtained its own local board of health.[7]

The sewage farm was on 30 a. in Wood Green and Edmonton, adjoining Cromwell Road in the Freehold,[8] as only there could the parish process its own sewage.[9] Able to serve 30,000 people and discharging a purified effluent into the brook, it was regarded in 1891 as a great credit to the designer, Baldwin Latham.[10] The surplus land was used for rubbish and allotments.[11] The asylum's pipes were connected to it in 1898[12] and in 1932 it was altered to make room for the North Circular Road. There were six houses with an inadequate supply of water to their closets in 1892–3 but only two in 1925.[13] From 1963 Friern Barnet's sewage was processed at Deepham's works, Edmonton, and the Cromwell Road works became redundant.[14]

Three brooks and surface wells supplied water until *c.* 1866. A conduit house adjoining the residence of John Cleeve the elder was to be freely used by all in 1718[15] and a public well at Whetstone was demolished in 1820.[16] Queen Elizabeth's well near Friern Barnet Lane was insanitary in the early 20th century[17] and in 1925 a drinking fountain was erected on the site. The New River Co. erected a pumping station at Colney Hatch by 1876,[18] when the vestry was told that water would be supplied under even pressure to New Southgate and that hydrants must be adapted.[19] The New River Co., from 1904 the Metropolitan Water Board, supplied less of the parish than did the Barnet District Gas and Water Co., later the Barnet Water Co., from 1892 to 1950.[20] The water from Barnet was excellent but insufficient.[21] Although Barnet was found to have an unlimited supply in 1893,[22] pressure in 1899 was still too low for a mechanical fire-engine.[23] Except for the inhabitants of the Freehold, who feared the expense of changing all their fittings, the whole parish wanted and in 1887 the board demanded a constant supply.[24] Part of the parish was receiving it in 1907,[25] when fittings in the remainder were being adapted.[26]

The Southgate and Colney Hatch Gas Light and Coke Co. was incorporated in 1858 and was supplying Friern Barnet from a gas-works in Edmonton, adjoining Colney Hatch station, by 1866. It was then reconstituted as the Colney Hatch Gas Co. and the whole parish was included in its sector.[27] Mains were extended from Colney Hatch to the Great North Road in 1862 but there was no main to the parish church in 1868–72, when the East Barnet Gas Co. was supplying it. Both companies had mains at Oakleigh Park in 1877 and the Colney Hatch Gas Co. had mains in Athenaeum Road in 1882.[28] There was still no gas supply in the Freehold in 1887.[29] In 1883 the vestry adopted the lighting provisions of the Lighting and Watching Act (1834). There were 42 street lamps in 1884, when plans were agreed with the gas company,[30] a further 45 were erected in 1885,[31] and others followed in response to local pressure.[32] The company was taken over by the Tottenham and Edmonton Gas Light and Coke Co. in 1938 and later by the Eastern Gas Board.[33]

In 1889 the local board considered using power from the manure engine at the sewage farm for electricity but instead sought expert opinion.[34] In 1901 Friern Barnet U.D.C. was authorized to supply electric lighting to the whole of the U.D., including private roads, and to lay mains in Station and Friern Barnet roads.[35] The order was revoked in 1907,[36] when the cost of electric lighting was an issue at the elections.[37] In 1909 responsibility for the parish passed to the North Metropolitan Power Supply Co.[38] It established an outside department at Friern Barnet Road, New Southgate, by 1923,[39] later the London Electricity Board (Northmet Sub-Area) central stores and meter-testing department.

In 1875 it was a matter for congratulation when the fire brigade from Finchley arrived within 30 minutes of an outbreak.[40] Ratepayers at New Southgate in 1883 resolved to establish a fire station in the Avenue area[41] but it is unlikely that it was done. There was a fire committee of the U.D.C. by 1907, when the formation of a volunteer fire brigade was an election issue, and it proposed to purchase a manual engine as water pressure was inadequate for a mechanical one.[42] By 1912–13 there was a fire station near the sewage farm, another beside the council offices, and a third near All Saints' church.[43] In 1936 tenders were invited for a new fire station and mechanical fire pump.[44] The central fire station by the town hall was the M.C.C.'s Fire and Ambulance Service Depot in 1960 and closed in 1968–9.[45]

The first allotments provided under the Allotments Act (1887) were on land not needed for the sewage farm in 1894. In 1909 encroachments were

[7] *Barnet Press*, 28 Apr., 2 Apr. 1883.
[8] Ibid. 28 Apr. 1883; 22 Aug. 1891.
[9] Ibid. 28 Apr. 1883.
[10] Ibid. 22 Aug. 1891.
[11] Friern Barnet U.D. *Ann. Rep. of M.O.H.* (1893; see below.
[12] Hunter and Macalpine, *Psychiatry for the Poor*, 33.
[13] Friern Barnet U.D. *Ann. Reps. of M.O.H.*
[14] Ex inf. works manager, Deepham's sewerage treatment works.
[15] M.R.O., Acc. 262/5A/1.
[16] *Home Cnties. Mag.* vi. 218.
[17] Friern Barnet U.D. *Ann. Reps. of M.O.H.*
[18] Thorne, *Environs*, 115.
[19] M.R.O., D.R.O. 12/I/C1/3.
[20] Friern Barnet U.D. *Ann. Rep. of M.O.H.* (1892, 1954).
[21] Ibid. (1892).
[22] Ibid.
[23] *Barnet Press*, 13 Mar. 1909.
[24] Ibid. 17 Sept., 31 Sept. 1887.
[25] Ibid. 28 Mar. 1891.
[26] Ibid. 12 Jan. 1907.
[27] 29 & 30 Vic. c. 82 (Local Act).
[28] M.R.O., Acc. 1153/II/196–7.
[29] *Barnet Press*, 21 May 1887.
[30] B.L.H.L., Friern Barnet loc. bd., min. bk. (1884–6), pp. 102, 104, 135–6.
[31] Ibid. pp. 284–5.
[32] Ibid. p. 330; (1886–9), pp. 20 sqq.
[33] *V.C.H. Mdx.* v. 181.
[34] B.L.H.L., Friern Barnet loc. bd., min. bk. (1886–9), pp. 447, 456.
[35] 1 Edw. VII, c. 174 (Local Act).
[36] *Barnet Press*, 2 Mar. 1907.
[37] Ibid. 30 Mar. 1907.
[38] 9 Edw. VII, c. 12 (Local Act).
[39] *Kelly's Dir. Finchley* (1923).
[40] *Barnet Press*, 20 July 1895.
[41] Ibid. 10 Mar. 1883.
[42] Ibid. 23 Mar., 20 Apr. 1907; 13 Mar. 1909.
[43] *Kelly's Dir. Barnet* (1912–13).
[44] *Barnet Press*, 13 Feb. 1936.
[45] *P.O. Dir. Lond.* (1960 and later edns.).

made by the farm[46] but the number of allotments increased with the spread of council housing in the 1920s.[47] There were 5 a. of permanent allotments by 1934 and 51 a. by 1946.[48]

Parochial lending libraries were provided by the church from before 1850 until at least 1907.[49] A branch of the county library existed at St. Peter's school by 1926, when new branches were opened at St. James's schools and the Priory for the north and central wards.[50] The existing library in Friern Barnet Road was built in 1933–4[51] and the South Friern branch library in Colney Hatch Lane in 1963–4.[52]

Friern Barnet had no hospital of its own. In 1894 the vaccination Acts were executed by the guardians of Barnet union and from 1935 the area came under the jurisdiction of the Hornsey, Finchley and Wood Green hospital committee and its successors.[53]

CHURCHES. The parish remained undivided until 1873, when the district chapelry of St. Paul, New Southgate, was assigned that portion of Friern Barnet east of the G.N.R. line.[54] In 1882 the northern part of the parish was assigned to the new district chapelry of All Saints, Oakleigh Park, whose boundary ran parallel to Oakleigh Road and *c.* 300 yd. to the south-west.[55] The district chapelry of St. Peter-le-Poer, Muswell Hill, from 1911 covered most of the parish south of the North Circular Road.[56]

A church mentioned in 1187[57] was probably the church of St. James, which was originally built in the later 12th century. The bishop of London gave it to the knights of St. John together with Whetstone manor,[58] of which it was an appendage. Although not mentioned by name the advowson was included in the Crown's grant of the manor to the chapter of St. Paul's in 1544[59] and it was specifically excluded from leases of the demesne from the 16th century.[60] The chapter was still patron in 1976.[61] Until late in the 17th century the church was often described as a chapel.[62] In 1519 the prior of St. John's stated that Friern Barnet lay in Finchley parish,[63] yet the incumbent was entitled to tithes in 1535[64] and probably as early as 1340.[65] No medieval institutions were recorded but there was a parish priest in 1486[66] and his rights were safeguarded in 1496.[67] Before the Reformation the church was exempt from episcopal intervention and afterwards it was subject to the chapter of St. Paul's as ordinary.[68] The incumbent was described as a vicar in 1544[69] and curate in 1545.[70] From 1549 the church has usually been regarded as a rectory.[71]

In 1772 the rector was entitled to both great and little tithes.[72] Tithes were valued at 13*s.* 4*d.* in 1340[73] and at 12*s.* in 1535.[74] There were disputes over them in 1772[75] and from 1698 to 1704, when they were farmed for £100 a year.[76] The rector customarily took a composition of 1*s.* 6*d.* or 2*s.* per acre in 1806,[77] when John Bacon ceased paying tithes for the Whetstone demesne, having discovered that it had belonged to an exempt order before the Fourth Lateran Council (1215).[78] In 1846 tithes were commuted for a rent-charge of £271.[79] The glebe, which lay east of the almshouses in Friern Barnet Lane, consisted in 1650 of 2 a. worth 30*s.* annually, which had been assigned by the committee for plundered ministers.[80] It was farmed for £9 between 1794 and 1815.[81] It was still being exploited in 1911,[82] was used as playing fields for the grammar school between the two World Wars,[83] then as allotments,[84] and became the site of Queenswell school *c.* 1957.[85] The priest's grove, 1 a. of copyhold land in Whetstone,[86] was occupied by successive incumbents from at least 1507.[87] At the inclosure of Finchley common in 1814[88] the rector was allotted 45 a., which were sold in 1888.[89] The living was exempt from royal taxation in 1428[90] and was worth £78 in 1650.[91] The rector received *c.* £310 between 1794 and 1805 and *c.* £240 after Bacon's retraction of tithes in 1808.[92] The income of £255 in 1849[93] increased to £360 in 1882[94] but had fallen to *c.* £200 in 1904.[95]

Both before and after 1574 rectors occupied the

[46] *Barnet Press*, 14 Aug. 1909.
[47] *Kelly's Dir. Finchley* (1927); see above, p. 14.
[48] Briggs, *Mdx. Old and New*, 120; B.L.H.L., Friern Barnet educ. cttee., min. bk. (1946–9).
[49] M.R.O., D.R.O. 12/I/K2/1 (ann. rep. for 1850); K1/9 (par. mag. Jan. 1907).
[50] *Barnet Press*, 15 May 1926.
[51] M.R.O., D.R.O., 12/I/K1/26 (par. mag. Jan. 1934); plaque on bldg.
[52] *P.O. Dir. Lond.* (1963, 1964).
[53] Friern Barnet U.D. *Ann. Reps. of M.O.H.*
[54] *V.C.H. Mdx.* v. 185; *Lond. Gaz.* 21 Nov. 1873, p. 5135.
[55] Hennessy, *Novum Rep.* 158–9.
[56] *Lond. Gaz.* 24 Jan. 1911, pp. 580–1.
[57] *Rot. Chart.* (Rec. Com.), 16. Bishop Foliot died in 1187.
[58] *Rot. Chart.* (Rec. Com.), 16.
[59] E 305/D7.
[60] St. Paul's MSS. C (Nowell), f. 120; (Pretyman III), f. 137v.
[61] *Crockford* (1975–6).
[62] e.g. *Valor Eccl.* (Rec. Com.), i. 434; St. Paul's MS. W.C. 45, ff. 12, 49.
[63] B.L. Cott. MS. Claud. E. vi, f. 189.
[64] *Valor Eccl.* (Rec. Com.), i. 434.
[65] *Inq. Non.* (Rec. Com.), 200.
[66] Phillips, *Sht. Hist. Friern Barnet*, 7.
[67] St. Paul's MSS., box B 17, m. 4d.
[68] Lysons, *Environs*, ii. 25.
[69] E 301/34 no. 137.
[70] St. Paul's MSS., F (Reg. Wills) A, f. 36.
[71] *Cal. Pat.* 1549–51, 171. But see Swiss Cottage libr. MS. J. Caley, *Hist. Feud. Mdx.* i, no. 41.
[72] E 126/132 Easter 1779.
[73] *Inq. Non.* (Rec. Com.), 200.
[74] *Valor Eccl.* (Rec. Com.), i. 434.
[75] E 126/132 Easter 1779.
[76] C 10/371/24.
[77] Caley, *Hist. Feud. Mdx.* i, no. 41.
[78] Ibid.; M.R.O., D.R.O. 12/I/A11/68.
[79] M.R.O., TA/FRI.
[80] *Home Cnties. Mag.* i. 57.
[81] M.R.O., D.R.O. 12/I/A11/68–87.
[82] Ibid. A12/8.
[83] Ibid. G8/2, p. 59.
[84] Ibid.
[85] Ex inf. the head teacher.
[86] St. Paul's MS. C (Nowell), f. 120.
[87] *Finchley Press*, 14 Jan. 1949.
[88] M.R.O., EA/FIN.
[89] Ibid.; M.R.O., D.R.O. 12/I/A12/1.
[90] *Feud. Aids*, iii. 380.
[91] *Home Cnties. Mag.* i. 57.
[92] M.R.O., D.R.O. 12/I/A11/68–87.
[93] S. Lewis, *Topogr. Dict.* 151.
[94] Nat. Soc. file.
[95] M.R.O., D.R.O. 12/I/K2/3 (ann. rep. for 1904).

Priest's House or Bell House in Whetstone High Road. Worth 40*s*. in 1650, it was burnt down *c*. 1662 and rebuilt as a public house.[96] A copyhold tenement in Friern Barnet Lane, acquired in 1682,[97] was used as a parsonage until 1772.[98] In 1851, 1871, and 1888 the rectors resided in private houses in Friern Park, Colney Hatch, and North Finchley, but a new rectory next to St. John's church was occupied from 1890.[99] Called Church-house, in 1975 it was the residence of assistant clergy and was used for parochial functions. A rectory at no. 147 Friern Barnet Lane was acquired in 1960–1.[1]

A lamp in the church was endowed with four cattle in perpetuity before 1544.[2] In 1495 John Copwood had built a chapel on common land adjoining the king's highway by Stockwell weir.[3] In 1498 he was licensed to keep the chapel, then dedicated to St. Catherine, together with a small plot, for a fixed annual rent and entry fine.[4] In 1530 the hermit was paid to say mass at the chapel, which was intended for the poor,[5] but by 1548–9 it was little used.[6] The site, often called the Hermitage in the 16th century,[7] eventually supported only a dwelling-house. It was probably the Hermitage house, from 1887 a school and by 1912 the London Female Preventive and Reformatory Institution, which survived in 1939.[8]

The benefice was held by three generations of the North family in the 16th century, by John and Edmund Duncon from 1663 to 1673, and by Frederick and Edward Gage Hall between 1882 and 1940.[9] George Smith, rector 1689–1724, was also vicar of Sarratt (Herts.), where he lived,[10] Thomas Roberts, rector 1795–8, was vicar of Tottenham,[11] and Samuel Brook, rector 1772–1794, was non-resident.[12] A. J. Trillo, rector 1950–5, was appointed bishop of Chelmsford in 1971.[13] An assistant curate was licensed from 1814[14] and from the 1860s there were normally at least two.[15]

Morning and evening service was attended by a total of 345 worshippers in 1851.[16] Communion was held on the first Sunday in the month.[17] The average Sunday attendance had fallen to 134 in 1903,[18] by which date there were four other Anglican places of worship in the parish. There were still private pews in 1892.[19] Robert Morris, rector 1850–82, introduced an annual report in 1850[20] and from 1883 a parish magazine was published.[21]

The church of *ST. JAMES THE GREAT* is on the corner of Friern Barnet Lane and Friary Road. It is built of flint with stone dressings and consists of a nave, chancel, south aisle and porch, north vestry, and south-west tower with shingled spire. The original structure consisted of a diminutive Norman nave and chancel, a wooden tower at the west end, and a south porch.[22] A vestry was added north of the nave in 1807[23] and the tower was rebuilt on a smaller scale in 1812.[24] West and south galleries had been added by 1705[25] and in 1819 a further west gallery was added for the charity children.[26] In 1819, 1828, and 1848 attempts were made to increase the seating,[27] but in 1853 there were pews for only 200. To provide 300 extra seats,[28] the church was enlarged by W. G. and E. Habershon in 1853.[29] Although materials may have been re-used, only the extensively restored Norman south doorway of the original structure was preserved.[30] The new church was built in the Early English style, and was considered to be in the 'very best taste'.[31] The spire fell in 1930 and was rebuilt to the same plan.[32] An octagonal parish room adjoining the north side of the church was under construction in 1977.

The church contains a relief of the children of Richard Down (1804) by John Bacon the younger (d. 1859),[33] and a classical wall monument to John Cleeve (d. 1725) and family. Other monuments, dating from 1668, are in the church and churchyard, which was enlarged several times in the 18th and 19th centuries.[34] The mature trees that made the setting attractive to visitors[35] were felled in 1974. In 1530 12*d*. a year was left for repairs to the bells.[36] A single bell by Thomas Mears, 1811,[37] replaced three bells in 1812.[38] The silver plate includes a flagon date-marked 1655, a cup and paten date-marked 1691, and a cup inscribed as having been the gift of John Nicholl in 1709.[39] There are registers of births from 1674, of marriages from 1812, and of burials from 1742.[40]

To meet a growing population, a church seating 360 was erected in Ely Place, Oakleigh Road South, in 1860. The land was given by George Knights Smith, who was the leading subscriber. The rector also subscribed and the London Diocesan Church

96 *Finchley Press*, 14 Jan. 1949; *Home Cnties. Mag.* i. 57.
97 Guildhall MSS. 14217/2, ff. 55–v.; 14223/2, p. 130.
98 It was held by another: Guildhall MS. 14223/3, f. 226; E 126/31 Trin. 1778.
99 M.R.O., D.R.O. 12/A12/14; B2/1; K2/2 (1882, 1887); H.O. 107/1701 f. 338; R.G. 10/1334 f. 69.
1 *P.O. Dir. Lond.* (1960–1).
2 E 301/34 no. 137.
3 St. Paul's MSS., box B 17, m. 3.
4 Ibid. m. 4d.
5 Guildhall MS. 9171/10 f. 142v.
6 St. Paul's MSS., box B 17, m. 20.
7 Ibid. box B 15, m. 5d.
8 B.L.H.L., Friern Barnet loc. bd., min. bk. (1886–9), p. 121; *Kelly's Dir. Barnet* (1912–13); *Finchley* (1939).
9 Hennessy, *Novum Rep.* 158; *Crockford* (1940–1).
10 Guildhall MS. 9550; M.R.O., Acc. 410/12 f. 37.
11 M.R.O., Acc. 410/12 f. 37.
12 E 126/132 Easter 1779.
13 *Crockford* (1971–2).
14 St. Paul's MS. W.C. 49 ff. 125v., 142.
15 M.R.O., D.R.O. 12/I/K2/2 (ann. rep. for 1883); K2/3 (1893).
16 H.O. 129/136/3/1/1.
17 Phillips, *Sht. Hist. Friern Barnet*, 17.
18 Mudie-Smith, *Rel. Life*, 411.
19 M.R.O., D.R.O. 12/I/K1/2 (par. mag. Dec. 1892).
20 Ibid. K2/1.
21 Ibid. K1/1.
22 Guildhall Libr., grangerized copy of Lysons, *Environs*, ii(1), 50, 52. See below, plate facing p. 33.
23 M.R.O., D.R.O. 12/I/C1; D1/1; H/3.
24 St. Paul's MS. W.C. 9, ff. 98–9.
25 M.R.O., D.R.O. 12/I/H/5; M.L.R. 1772/2/30.
26 M.R.O., D.R.O. 12/I/C1/1.
27 Ibid. H/4.
28 Ibid. B2/3.
29 Phillips, *Sht. Hist. Friern Barnet*, 17.
30 Hist. Mon. Com. *Mdx.* 27.
31 *Illus. Lond. News*, 26 Nov. 1853.
32 Barnet Mus. 2163.
33 R. Gunnis, *Dict. of Brit. Sculptors*, 28, 30.
34 M.R.O., D.R.O. 12/I/B3/1–31.
35 e.g. J. H. Sperling, *Church Walks in Mdx.* (1849), 113.
36 Guildhall MS. 9171/10 f. 142v.
37 *T.L.M.A.S.* xix. 57.
38 M.R.O., D.R.O. 12/I/C1/1.
39 Freshfield, *Communion Plate*, 18.
40 M.R.O., D.R.O. 12/I/A1/1; *T.L.M.A.S.* xviii(2), no. 73.

Building Society contributed towards both the building and its fittings. Intended for adaptation as a school, it was known as the school-church. In spite of pew-rents attendance was so satisfactory[41] that a curate was appointed in 1864.[42] The school-church was entrusted to the vicar of Southgate in 1871[43] and became St. Paul's National school[44] when the church of St. Paul was erected in Edmonton parish in 1873 on land probably given by Smith.[45] After 1893 it became the Liberal and Radical Club.[46]

The church of *ST. PETER-LE-POER* originated in 1866 in a mission to serve Muswell Hill.[47] It operated from the Cromwell Road schoolroom[48] and then from an adjoining iron building, which was rebuilt or extended in 1886–7[40] and still stood in 1908.[50] In 1884 the temporary iron church of St. Peter was erected on the corner of Sydney and Hampden roads.[51] Further land was acquired from the U.D.C. in 1895[52] but a site given in 1884 for a permanent church later reverted to the donor.[53] In 1899 1 a. for a church, vicarage, and mission hall was acquired from the Albion Estates Co. on the corner of Colney Hatch Lane and Carnforth Road (later Albion Avenue),[54] where a temporary church was erected in 1904. The older building was retained as a hall until some date before the sale of the land in 1935.[55] In 1909 work started on a permanent church, built with money from the sale of the redundant church of St. Peter-le-Poer in the City of London.[56] The new church is in the gift of the chapter of St. Paul's and was assigned a district chapelry in 1911.[57] In 1976 presentations to the benefice were suspended.[58] The Revd. George Hennessy, the ecclesiastical historian and for 18 years member of Friern Barnet local board and U.D.C., was curate and priest-in-charge from 1884 to 1903.[59]

The church was designed by W. D. Caroë and Passmore[60] in a debased Gothic style. A large red-brick building, it comprises sanctuary, north vestry, south chapel, aisled nave with a west gallery for the choir, and a west tower which houses the organ. The site falls away sharply to the car park in the west. On the north-west side is the single-storeyed, prefabricated church hall, built in 1964 to replace the temporary church of 1904.[61] The vicarage and garden adjoin the church to the north. The church contains many furnishings from old St. Peter-le-Poer, including the pulpit, bells, organ, stone mensa, font, server's seat, choir stalls, and duplicate sets of silver-gilt chalices, patens, flagons, and alms-dishes of 1561–2, beautified in 1792.[62]

In 1882 a chapelry in the northern part of the parish was assigned to the church of *ALL SAINTS*, Oakleigh Park.[63] John Miles, who gave the site and paid for the church,[64] was first patron. His son Henry Stewart Miles, the first vicar, gave the patronage to the bishop of London in 1902 but reserved the next presentation, which he made in 1932 after an incumbency of 50 years. From the foundation there has normally been an assistant curate.[65] H. S. Miles was an ardent Tractarian, who made communion the centrepiece of worship.[66] In 1888, in addition to an early communion, there were services in the morning, afternoon, and evening.[67] The church was designed to seat 520[68] and in 1903 its average Sunday congregation of 627[69] was the largest in the parish.

All Saints' church stands at the corner of Myddelton Park and Oakleigh Road North. Designed in an Early English style by J. Clarke,[70] it was built of flint with stone dressings and comprised an apsidal chancel and south vestry, aisled and clerestoreyed nave entered from north-west tower and spire, and a south porch. The vestry was converted into a chapel in 1907, when a new vestry was added.[71] Inside the walls and roofs are decorated throughout.

After 1882 the old parish church no longer served the most populous areas.[72] In 1887 the church of *ST. JOHN THE EVANGELIST*, Colney Hatch, although only a chapel of ease, was viewed as the future centre of the parish.[73] By 1903, before its completion, congregations at the Sunday morning and evening services averaged 188 and 304,[74] exceeding those at the parish church. The chapel originated in 1883 as a temporary iron building on the north side of Friern Barnet Road,[75] known as the school-church of St. John.[76] In 1888–90 it was replaced by an iron nave on the opposite side of the road on land given by G. K. Smith,[77] who, with his son Charles William Smith, contributed substantially towards building costs.[78] Other plots were later added to it. The chancel was consecrated in 1892,[79] but building was delayed by lack of funds and the extension of the church schools,[80] the nave

[41] M.R.O., D.R.O. 12/I/K2/1 (1860); C 54/15553 no. 12.
[42] M.R.O., D.R.O. 12/I/K2/1 (1864).
[43] Ibid. (1871).
[44] Ibid. (1873).
[45] *V.C.H. Mdx.* v. 185.
[46] *Barnet Press*, 8 June, 29 June 1895.
[47] M.R.O., D.R.O. 12/I/K2/1 (1860).
[48] Ibid. G5/1.
[49] *Barnet Press*, 11 June 1887; B.L.H.L., Friern Barnet loc. bd., min. bk. (1884–6), p. 451.
[50] M.R.O., Acc. 410/52.
[51] M.R.O., D.R.O. 12/III/1/4; Hennessy, *Novum Rep.* 159.
[52] B.L.H.L., Friern Barnet U.D., min. bk. (1894–6), pp. 304–5.
[53] M.R.O., D.R.O. 12/III/1/2.
[54] Ibid. 12/I/K2/3.
[55] Ibid. K1/6 (par. mag. Aug. 1904); B.L.H.L., Friern Barnet U.D., min. bk. (1935–6), pp. 53, 75.
[56] M.R.O., D.R.O. 12/I/K2/4 (1907); *Barnet Press*, 14 Aug. 1909; *The Times*, 5 Jan. 1909; M.R.O., D.R.O. 12/III/3/2.
[57] *Lond. Dioc. Bk.* (1911), 250.
[58] Ex inf. the priest-in-charge.
[59] Hennessy, *Novum Rep.* 159; *Crockford* (1907); *Barnet Press*, 12 June 1907.
[60] *T.L.M.A.S.* xviii(2), no. 76.
[61] Ex inf. the vicar and churchwardens.
[62] *St. Peter-le-Poer, Friern Barnet, 1910–60* (jubilee booklet), 5; Victoria and Albert Mus. *Ch. Plate of Brit. Isles and Eng. Monumental Brasses* (cat., n.d.).
[63] *Lond. Gaz.* 22 Dec. 1882, p. 6513.
[64] Hennessy, *Novum Rep.* 159.
[65] W. G. Cameron, *75 Yrs. of All Saints', Friern Barnet* (1957), 11, 25.
[66] Ibid. 8.
[67] *P.O. Dir. N. Suburbs* (1888).
[68] Cameron, *All Saints', Friern Barnet*, 18.
[69] Mudie-Smith, *Rel. Life*, 411.
[70] Cameron, *All Saints', Friern Barnet*, 18.
[71] Ibid. 21. See below, illus. facing p. 49.
[72] M.R.O., D.R.O. 12/I/K1/1 (June 1883).
[73] Ibid. K2/2 (1887).
[74] Mudie-Smith, *Rel. Life*, 411.
[75] Hennessy, *Novum Rep.* 159; M.R.O., D.R.O. 12/I/A12/14.
[76] M.R.O., D.R.O. 12/I/K2/2 (1883).
[77] Ibid. A12/14; Phillips, *Sht. Hist. Friern Barnet*, 19.
[78] M.R.O., D.R.O. 12/I/K2/3 (1900).
[79] Ibid. 12/II/B1/11.
[80] Ibid. 12/I/K2/3 (1899).

being built in two stages and consecrated in 1911.[81]

Constructed entirely of stone to an elaborate plan by J. L. Pearson,[82] the church is modelled on a Rhineland chapel.[83] It consists of an apsidal chancel with ambulatory and south chapel, two north vestries, an aisled and clerestoreyed nave, and a western narthex or baptistery of one bay. In an early Gothic style, it is vaulted throughout and seats 500 with ease. As a projected tower and spire[84] on the north were not built, the church is unimpressive from without.[85] The darkness inside at ground level was considered conducive to solemnity.[86]

The school-church of St. John was renamed the parish room after the erection of the iron nave[87] and was used for Sunday school and children's services until 1934.[88] It also served as a church hall and school for middle-class boys.[89] There were several other parish rooms and reading rooms[90] and most of the parochial schools were used for missions or Sunday schools.[91] It was not until 1921 that a permanent site was acquired at the foot of Friern Barnet Lane for a church hall,[92] which was erected in 1929.[95]

ROMAN CATHOLICISM. In 1866 Mr. Childe of Laburnum Villa, Oakleigh Road, built on his own property the temporary chapel of St. George, which was served from Barnet.[94] The chapel was closed *c.* 1880, perhaps because it was sold,[95] and from 1890 the congregation was served at Finchley.[96] In 1924 mass was celebrated at Harper's tea rooms in Whetstone High Road and then at Buffaloes' hall attached to the Black Bull.[97]

The chapel of St. Mary Magdalene, Athenaeum Road, was in use in 1925 and was administered by the Fathers of Sion until *c.* 1973.[98] In 1930 a larger temporary church of St. Mary Magdalene was built in Athenaeum Road[99] and the older building became the church hall,[1] which survived in 1975. A modern church on the same site was consecrated in 1958.[2] It is of red brick, with a chancel, nave, and west tower.

PROTESTANT NONCONFORMITY. There were apparently no dissenters in the 17th century and only short-lived congregations before the establishment in 1883–4 of the first surviving nonconformist church.[3] Methodists had a small chapel in Colney Hatch Lane from 1836,[4] with attendances of 25 in the morning and 38 in the evening on census Sunday 1851.[5] They later worshipped at a boarding school at no. 1 Torrington Park from 1852 to 1866,[6] and in Friern Barnet Lane until *c.* 1889.[7]

By 1903 an average of 813 nonconformists worshipped each Sunday, compared with 1,475 Anglicans. There were 567 Congregationalists, 37 Brethren, and 209 who attended the Railway Mission,[8] which was the most successful of the missions, many of which were ignored in the survey. Methodist churches were established in 1904 and *c.* 1930. There were seven nonconformist places of worship in 1911[9] and two Congregationalist, two Methodist, a Baptist, and two Brethren's places of worship in 1975. The more successful establishments were made north of Friern Barnet Road. Small mission halls of more radical denominations proliferated in the poorer Avenue and Freehold districts but most were not purpose-built and had closed by 1975.

Christ Church United Reformed church stands at the corner of Friern Barnet and Bellevue roads. The original Congregationalist lecture hall of 1883–4[10] is a red-brick building with stone dressings in an Early English style. It contained committee rooms, a common room, and a hall for 300,[11] which was used for services and had an average Sunday congregation of 225 in 1903.[12] A permanent church was built in front in 1910 to the design of George Baines & Co.[13] on a north–south axis. Also of red brick with stone dressings, it is square with an east transept and a low south-west tower and spire. It has a capacity of 600.[14] The first minister, Benjamin Waugh, 1883–7, was founder of the N.S.P.C.C.[15]

Oakleigh Park United Reformed church originated in 1887, when the Congregational school and chapel at Totteridge were too small and a site was chosen midway between Totteridge and Oakleigh Park stations, in the angle of Oakleigh Road North and Oakleigh Park North. The building was to be of two storeys, with a chapel or school hall on the first floor and a vestry and smaller rooms below. Built in 1888 of yellow brick with stone dressings[16] in the simplest early Gothic style, it was used as a hall in 1975. The permanent church was erected in 1900 in an idiosyncratic Gothic style by E. F. Knight.[17] It is of red brick and consists of a rectangular nave, polygonal east end, and two low western turrets. It seats 350.[18] In 1903 an average

[81] M.R.O., D.R.O. 12/II/B1/11.
[82] Ibid. B1/18; 12/I/K1/2 (Feb. 1891).
[83] Ibid. 12/II/B1/36.
[84] Ibid. B1/11.
[85] Pevsner, *Mdx.* 57.
[86] M.R.O., D.R.O. 12/II/B1/36.
[87] Ibid. 12/I/K1/1 (Feb. 1891).
[88] Ibid. K1/26 (Oct. 1934).
[89] Ibid. K2/2 (1883); 5 (1913).
[90] See p. 29.
[91] e.g. Cromwell Rd. sch., see p. 31.
[92] M.R.O., D.R.O. 12/I/B4/3.
[93] Ibid. 4, 6; Char. Com. files.
[94] *Finchley Cath. Rec.* July 1926, p. 6 (*penes* Mr. E. D. Luscombe).
[95] Ibid. July 1928, p. 13.
[96] Ibid. July 1926, p. 6.
[97] Ibid.
[98] Ibid. p. 7; ex inf. Mr. E. D. Luscombe.
[99] G.R.O. Worship Reg. no. 52937; *Finchley Cath. Rec.* Nov. 1930, p. 10.

[1] *Kelly's Dir. Finchley* (1934).
[2] Datestone on bldg.
[3] See below.
[4] Guildhall MS. 9580/7, p. 222; G.R.O. Worship Returns, iii, no. 1905.
[5] H.O. 129/136/3/2/5; H.O. 107/1701/136/3/2a f. 357.
[6] G.R.O. Worship Reg. no. 401.
[7] *Kelly's Dir. Barnet* (1889); O.S. Maps 6", Mdx. VI. SE. (1867–73, 1897 edns.).
[8] Mudie-Smith, *Rel. Life*, 411.
[9] *Census*, 1911.
[10] Ex inf. Mr. F. Nind; *Barnet Press*, 26 Aug. 1883.
[11] Ex inf. Mr. F. Nind.
[12] Mudie-Smith, *Rel. Life*, 411.
[13] Ex inf. Mr. F. Nind.
[14] Ibid.
[15] *D.N.B.*
[16] *Barnet Press*, 22 Nov. 1887.
[17] Pevsner, *Mdx.* 172.
[18] *Cong. Yr. Bk.* (1951), 213.

Whetstone High Road from the south *c.* 1900. The buildings on the left are in Finchley parish

Friern Hospital (formerly Colney Hatch Asylum) from the west. The railway line from King's Cross to Hatfield crosses the North Circular Road in the background

FRIERN BARNET

Friern Barnet: Campe's Alms-houses

Muswell Hill: Mr. Porker's House

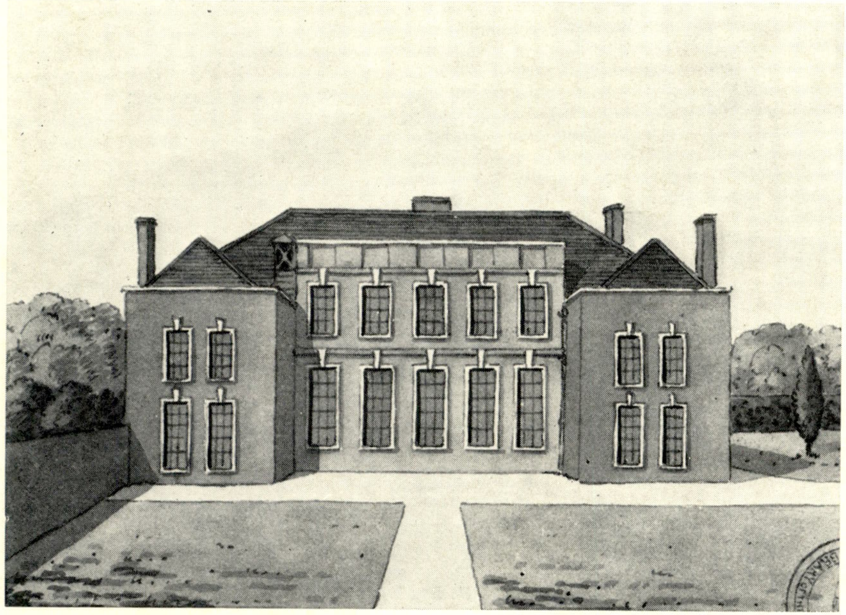
Friern Barnet: Manor House

Friern Barnet: St. James's Church

FRIERN BARNET AND MUSWELL HILL *c.* 1800

of 190 attended the morning and 152 the evening services on Sundays.[19]

Pembroke Road Methodist church, in the Freehold, was founded in 1904 by the main Muswell Hill Methodist church as a Wesleyan mission hall.[20] In 1922 it moved to the Freehold mission hall in Sydney Road,[21] which was replaced in 1954 by a new church in Pembroke Road.[22] In 1975 a small red-brick church seated 150 and shared a minister with Manor Drive Methodist church.[23]

Manor Drive Methodist church, planned in 1930 for Torrington Park[24] and temporarily established on the corner with Friern Barnet Lane by 1935,[25] opened on the corner of Manor Drive and York Way in 1938.[26] An imposing red-brick building in a modern style, it consists of a nave with shallow aisles, transepts, a low lantern tower, a polygonal chancel with adjoining vestries, and a narthex connecting the nave to the single-storeyed hall added in 1956.[27] It has seating for *c.* 300.[28]

Baptists from 1865 probably attended New Southgate Baptist church, sometimes described as in Colney Hatch.[29] Before 1887 it founded a mission hall at Pembroke Road,[30] known as the Pembroke Baptist mission room in 1902[31] and renamed the United mission hall *c.* 1922 when joined by seceders from the Freehold mission in Sydney Road. Although still governed by a trust deed held by the mother church, the congregation managed its own affairs in 1975. The original timber-framed and corrugated iron hut was then used for Sunday school and other activities but wooden huts of *c.* 1918 at the rear had been replaced *c.* 1968 by a brick building, containing a church for 75–100.[32]

In 1905 the Ebenezer Baptist chapel was registered in a house at no. 15 Beaconsfield Road, New Southgate, by Old Baptists.[33] It was described as the Old Baptist Union training house in 1906[34] and was disused by 1954.[35]

Christian Brethren from Highgate began to worship in Athenaeum Road, Whetstone, *c.* 1884. They met in a converted house with a capacity of *c.* 25,[36] probably the Christians' meeting-room recorded between 1889 and 1925,[37] until in 1926 they moved to a new brick hall in Oakleigh Road North, which seated 100. Oakleigh hall was enlarged in 1954, renamed Oakleigh chapel shortly afterwards,[38] and still used in 1975.

Christian Brethren from St. James's Lane, Muswell Hill,[39] acquired a small site on the corner of Wilton and Coppetts roads *c.* 1949. Wilton chapel, a low red-brick hall, was opened in 1952 and completed a few years later.[40]

The New Southgate branch of the Railway Mission was established *c.* 1883.[41] Between 1891[42] and 1899 it acquired a site north of Friern Barnet Road beside the railway,[43] where a tin chapel was erected. In 1903 there was an average attendance of 90 at morning service and 209 at evening service every Sunday.[44] The mission hall was still open in 1939[45] but later was used by the G.P.O.[46] and in 1975 as a builder's store.

The Bethel Full Gospel church in Cromwell Road, Muswell Hill, which was registered by the Assemblies of God in 1939, was disused by 1954.[47] It may have replaced the Bethel mission hall which was at Carlisle Place, New Southgate, between 1889 and 1939.[48]

The Freehold mission hall in Sydney Road, Muswell Hill, was built by 1901[49] for a congregation that had met in a shop. Described as interdenominational, it had close links with the Pembroke Baptist mission hall, to which some members seceded in 1922.[50] The brick chapel survives as the depot of the Hobart Manufacturing Co.

A meeting-room in Athenaeum road between 1889 and 1897 had disappeared by 1900[51] and a Gospel hall there in 1925 was disused by 1930.[52]

EDUCATION. A schoolmaster taught at the Bell House at Whetstone until it was burnt down shortly before 1662,[53] and a charity school existed from 1809 to 1853. As early as 1832 a National school had been proposed for Friern Barnet and the chapelry of Whetstone but it was not until 1853 that one was built. In 1859 an infants' school was established at Whetstone to serve both districts. Schools for New Southgate in 1860 and the Freehold in 1866 were followed by infants' schools for All Saints' in 1883 and St. John's in 1886, both of which soon took junior girls.[54] Ten extensions to schools between 1881 and 1901[55] enabled the Church to cater for the growth in numbers of pupils from *c.* 80 in 1853 to *c.* 240 in 1860 and 1,139 in 1905.[56] Friern Barnet was anxious to avoid a school board[57] and engaged in a constant struggle to raise funds, in which the ecclesiastical districts stood together. St. Paul's schools, which were annexed to St. Paul's, New Southgate,[58] were situated in a poor

19 Mudie-Smith, *Rel. Life*, 411.
20 G.R.O. Worship Reg. no. 40565.
21 Ibid. 48669.
22 Ibid. 64280.
23 Ex inf. the minister.
24 B.L.H.L., Friern Barnet U.D., min. bk. (1930–1), p. 3.
25 Ex inf. the minister.
26 G.R.O. Worship Reg. no. 57843.
27 Ex inf. the minister; *Muswell Hill Rec.* 23 Sept. 1955.
28 Ex inf. the minister.
29 Thorne, *Environs*, 115; *V.C.H. Mdx.* v. 193.
30 *New Southgate Bapt. Ch. 1865–1965* (centenary booklet); B.L.H.L., Friern Barnet loc. bd., min. bk. (1886–9).
31 *Kelly's Dir. N. Suburbs* (1902).
32 Ex inf. Mr. L. G. Dixon.
33 G.R.O. Worship Reg. no. 41210.
34 *Kelly's Dir. Barnet* (1906).
35 G.R.O. Worship Reg. no. 41210.
36 Ex inf. Mr. H. Andrews. Brethren worshipped at a sch. in 'Oakleigh Rd.' in 1885: G.R.O. Worship Reg. no. 27839.
37 *Kelly's Dir. Barnet* (1889); *Finchley* (1925).
38 Ex inf. Mr. H. Andrews.
39 See p. 187.
40 Ex inf. Mr. J. E. Small.
41 *Barnet Press*, 20 July 1895.
42 Ibid. 28 Nov. 1891.
43 *Kelly's Dir. Barnet* (1899).
44 Mudie-Smith, *Rel. Life*, 411.
45 *Kelly's Dir. Finchley* (1939).
46 Ex inf. the vicar of St. Paul's, New Southgate.
47 G.R.O. Worship Reg. no. 58878.
48 *Kelly's Dir. Barnet* (1889); *Finchley* (1939).
49 *Kelly's Dir. Barnet* (1901).
50 Ex inf. Mr. L. G. Dixon.
51 *Kelly's Dir. Barnet* (1889 and later edns.).
52 *Kelly's Dir. Finchley* (1925, 1930).
53 *Finchley Press*, 14 Jan. 1949.
54 See below.
55 Nat. Soc. files.
56 Ibid.; M.R.O., D.R.O. 12/I/K2/1 (1860); G7/22. In 1905 the average attendance was 872.
57 M.R.O., D.R.O. 12/I/K2/3 (1899).
58 Nat. Soc. files.

area and supported chiefly by the parish church and All Saints. A school board was suggested in 1877, when both St. James's and St. Peter's schools required extension,[59] and averted in 1883 by extensive repairs to St. Paul's schools,[60] towards whose rebuilding in 1893 New Southgate contributed only one-fifth of the cost.[61] Heavy running costs[62] were alleviated by the Education Act of 1902,[63] although responsibility for St. Peter's school was not transferred to the vicar and churchwardens of St. Peter-le-Poer until 1936.[64]

Under the Education Act of 1902, elementary education in Friern Barnet was controlled by Middlesex C.C.[65] In 1906 the education committee opened an infants' school and in 1908 founded a junior mixed and infants' school in Holly Park.[66] By 1927 those two schools received more than half the pupils in the parish[67] and in 1928 Oakleigh infants' school was founded.[68]

Following the Hadow Report, St. Peter's and Holly Park schools were reorganized as senior schools and pupils were to be transferred between church and council schools.[69] The agreements were breaking down in 1938, when St. Peter's school was condemned and Holly Park again admitted juniors,[70] but were retained at the outbreak of the Second World War. Although there were more places than pupils, in 1936 there was a campaign for a new secondary school. At that time 265 children attended schools outside the parish, especially Woodhouse grammar school in Finchley.[71]

Under the Education Act of 1944, Friern Barnet was controlled by a district education subcommittee.[72] A county secondary school was opened in 1960–1 and Holly Park again became a primary school. Two new primary schools were opened in 1950 and 1954 and three Church of England schools moved into new premises from 1969, while St. James's and Oakleigh infants' schools closed.

Maintained schools. In 1809 the vestry established a charity school for boys aged 5–9 and girls aged 6–13, to be financed by voluntary subscriptions and the sale of the children's work.[73] By 1819 there was also interest from £150 which had been saved.[74] All the children were to learn to read and the girls were also to be taught needlework. They were to attend morning and evening classes on weekdays and three services on Sundays, with holidays for Christmas and haymaking.[75] Classes met in the prayer room of the alms-houses,[76] where the teacher or teachers lived.[77] Intended for 10 boys and 10 girls,[78] by 1819 the school was failing to serve all the poor.[79] There were 65 children in 1847,[80] when George Smith left £100 in trust to the school,[81] and there was no longer room for them in 1853.[82]

St. James's Church of England primary school, formerly Friern Barnet National school, replaced the charity school in 1853.[83] Adjoining the alms-houses to the north and originally planned for 80 pupils, the accommodation was increased to 120 at the government's request.[84] It was attended by 133 boys and girls in 1865–6[85] and numbers increased steadily to 208 in 1884,[86] when the infants moved.[87] From 1889 it catered only for boys.[88] It received bad reports between 1887 and 1893, but in 1900 was thought an admirable village school.[89] Numbers were halved to *c.* 100 in 1909 by the exclusion of Finchley children[90] but recovered from 1926, reaching 168 by 1938.[91] Classrooms were added in 1877 and 1935[92] and in the 1940s extensions were proposed on the glebe at the rear.[93] The school was planned to close when the new All Saints' school was founded in 1969 and did so in 1975,[94] from which date the premises were used for nursery education.

In 1859 an infants' school was formed as an offshoot of Friern Barnet National school.[95] The site, given by John Miles, fronted Friern Barnet Lane and lay just outside the parish.[96] It was intended for children from both Friern Barnet parish and Whetstone chapelry.[97] The average attendance rose steadily from *c.* 56 in 1860.[98] In 1884 it was sold to the chapelry of St. John, Whetstone, as most of the pupils lived there.[99]

St. John's infants' school in Glenthorne Road, Colney Hatch, was founded with the proceeds from the sale of 1884,[1] replacing a temporary school for *c.* 80 children at no. 65 Holly Park Road in 1888.[2] In 1890 St. John's National school for 72 girls was founded on a neighbouring site.[3] It was mixed from 1898 until 1908 and thereafter catered only for juniors.[4] Although interdependent, the schools had separate headmistresses until 1930.[5]

59 Nat. Soc. files.
60 Cameron, *All Saints', Friern Barnet*, 7–8; M.R.O., D.R.O. 12/I/K2/2 (1883); Nat. Soc. files.
61 M.R.O., D.R.O. 12/I/G10/4.
62 Nat. Soc. files.
63 M.R.O., D.R.O. 12/I/K2/3 (1902).
64 Ibid. G7/22.
65 Mdx. C.C. *Primary and Secondary Educ. in Mdx. 1900–65*, 31.
66 See p. 35.
67 *Bd. of Educ., List 21, 1927* (H.M.S.O.).
68 See p. 35.
69 M.R.O., D.R.O. 12/I/K1/30 (Sept. 1938).
70 See p. 35.
71 *Barnet Press*, 25 Apr. 1936.
72 Mdx. C.C. educ. cttee. *List of Schs. 1957*. The rest of the para. is based on the section below.
73 M.R.O., D.R.O. 12/I/G1/3.
74 *Educ. of Poor Digest*, 558.
75 M.R.O., D.R.O. 12/I/G1/1; G1/3.
76 Ibid.; K2/1 (ann. rep. for 1853).
77 Ibid.; G1/1.
78 Ibid.
79 *Educ. of Poor Digest*, 558.
80 Nat. Soc. *Church Schs. Enquiry, 1846–7*, Mdx. 2–3.
81 M.R.O., D.R.O. 12/I/C1/4.
82 *Illus. Lond. News*, 26 Nov. 1853.
83 See above.
84 Nat. Soc. files.
85 *Rep. of Educ. Cttee. of Council, 1865–6* [3666], p. 554, H.C. (1866), xxvii.
86 Ibid. *1886* [C. 5123–1], p. 562, H.C. (1887), xxviii.
87 See below.
88 See p. 35.
89 M.R.O., D.R.O. 12/I/G3/15, pp. 19, 55, 74; G3/16, p. 7; G3/8.
90 Ibid. G3/14, p. 29; G3/8 (1908); K2/4 (1909).
91 Ibid. G3/14, p. 81; *Bd. of Educ., List 21, 1938* (H.M.S.O.).
92 Nat. Soc. files; M.R.O., D.R.O. 12/I/G3/11.
93 Ibid. G11/3.
94 *Barnet Press*, 15 June 1973.
95 Ed. 7/86.
96 M.R.O., D.R.O. 12/I/G4/1 (cover); Nat. Soc. files.
97 M.R.O., D.R.O. 12/I/K2/2 (1859).
98 Ed. 7/86.
99 M.R.O., D.R.O. 12/I/K2/2 (1884).
1 Nat. Soc. files.
2 M.R.O., D.R.O. 12/I/K2/2 (1888); Nat. Soc. files.
3 M.R.O., D.R.O. 12/I/K2/2 (1890).
4 Ibid. G7/17, pp. 160, 355.
5 Ibid. G7/16, p. 353.

An average combined attendance of 130 in 1894 increased to 234 in 1914,[6] but fluctuated from 130 to 180 between the World Wars.[7] New classrooms were added in 1898 and 1911.[8] Rebuilding was essential in 1960[9] and the school moved to new premises at no. 280 Crescent Road in 1969,[10] when it was called St. John's Church of England junior girls' and infants' school.[11] In 1975 there were 250 pupils on the roll.[12]

St. Paul's school, New Southgate, originated in 1857 as an infants' school in rented rooms,[13] which were extended in 1866.[14] There were *c.* 40 pupils in 1860.[15] There was no government grant until 1874, when it became St. Paul's National school for boys, girls, and infants and moved to the former school-church in Ely Place.[16] In 1887, when there were 186 pupils, the school was noted for absenteeism.[17] It closed for extensive repairs in 1883[18] and a classroom was added in 1889.[19] After being condemned in 1893,[20] it was completely rebuilt with 302 places close to the railway line and had an average attendance of 237.[21] There were more pupils than places in 1905,[22] 201 pupils in 1914,[23] and 130–40 in 1975, when it was again overcrowded. By then a neighbouring site had been acquired for a new school.[24]

Cromwell Road National, later St. Peter's, school opened in the Freehold in 1866[25] and was so called after moving to new premises fronting Sydney Road in 1868.[26] It served a poor neighbourhood and until *c.* 1879 standards were very low.[27] In 1920 the school again received a bad report.[28] Since the number of boys and girls rose from 50 in 1869 to 425 in 1914,[29] it remained overcrowded in spite of the addition of classrooms in 1877,[30] 1897, and 1907[31] and the removal of the infants in 1906. There was a slight fall in numbers until *c.* 1930[32] when it was designated a senior mixed school for 200.[33] In 1938 the Middlesex education committee declared that it must be rebuilt.[34] It was bombed in the war and not reopened.

All Saints' National school for infants was founded next to the church in 1883, on land given by John Miles.[35] It owed its establishment partly to a projected dissenting school, which had led to plans for an Anglican school in Blackhorse Lane in 1870.[36] A classroom was added in 1889 for girls from St. James's school[37] and the premises were extended in 1904.[38] From 56 in 1886 and 126 in 1893 average attendances grew to 146 in 1908,[39] when they began to decline until after 1922.[40] Despite the transfer of the infants to a council school in 1928,[41] there was an average attendance of 131 in 1938.[42] In 1969 the school took over the former Oakleigh infants' school for the girls and added classrooms for the infants, whereupon the old building became redundant. The new All Saints' Church of England primary school had a roll of *c.* 250 in 1975.[43]

Sydney Road council school was established in 1906 for infants from St. Peter's school.[44] It moved to permanent premises in 1907 with accommodation for 312[45] and by 1914 had 299 pupils.[46] Under the Hadow Report it became a junior mixed and infants' school and was extended in two stages to provide 524 places in 1936.[47] There were 377 pupils in 1938, when it had been renamed Hollickwood school.[48] The original building was demolished in 1974 and there was a roll of 224 in 1975.[49]

Holly Park council school was opened in 1908 for 300 mixed juniors and extended in 1915 to take infants.[50] Accommodation was reduced from 752 to 676 by 1932, when it became a senior mixed and infants' school.[51] There were 441 pupils in 1938,[52] when it began to admit juniors again,[53] but it still had a senior department in 1964.[54] The infants' extension closed in 1965 and was demolished in 1969, when a new building for infants was erected. In 1975, when it was a junior mixed and infants' school, with nursery classes there were 326 full-time and 51 part-time children on the roll.[55]

Oakleigh infants' school was founded in 1928 as All Saints' council school and renamed between 1932 and 1936.[56] Initially catering for infants from All Saints' school, the numbers rapidly increased to 223 in 1938.[57] In 1969 it was closed and handed over to All Saints' school.[58]

Queenswell primary school was established in

6 *Returns Relating to Elem. Educ.* [C. 7592], pp. 420–1, H.C. (1894), lxv; M.R.O., D.R.O. 12/I/G9/1.
7 *Bd. of Educ., List 21, 1919, 1927, 1936* (H.M.S.O.).
8 M.R.O., D.R.O. 12/I/K1/4 (Dec. 1899); G7/11.
9 Ibid. 21, p. 501.
10 *Barnet Press*, 11 Oct. 1968.
11 M.R.O., D.R.O. 12/I/G7/13.
12 Ex inf. the headmistress.
13 M.R.O., D.R.O. 12/I/K2/1 (1857).
14 Ibid. (1866).
15 Ibid. (1860).
16 Ibid. (1866); Ed. 7/86. See above, p. 31.
17 *Rep. of Educ. Cttee. of Council, 1887* [C. 547–1], p. 614, H.C. (1888), xxviii.
18 M.R.O., D.R.O. 12/I/K2/2 (1883).
19 Ibid. K2/3 (1893–5).
20 Ibid. F10/4; *Barnet Press*, 31 Jan. 1891.
21 *Rep. of Educ. Cttee. of Council, 1893* [C. 7437–1], p. 910, H.C. (1894), xxix.
22 M.R.O., D.R.O. 12/I/G7/22.
23 Ibid. G9/1.
24 Ex inf. the headmistress.
25 M.R.O., D.R.O. 12/I/K2/1 (1866, 1868).
26 C 54/16742 no. 3; Ed. 7/86.
27 Govt. inspectors' reps. in M.R.O., D.R.O. 12/I/G5/1, 2.
28 Ibid. G7/22, p. 83.
29 Ed. 7/86; M.R.O., D.R.O. 12/I/G9/1.
30 Nat. Soc. files; M.R.O., D.R.O. 12/I/K2/1 (1877).
31 Ibid. K1/4 (Nov. 1897); K2/4 (1907).
32 Ibid. G9/1, p. 53.
33 Ibid. G7/22, p. 102 (attached).
34 Ibid. K1/30 (Sept. 1938).
35 Ed. 7/86.
36 Nat. Soc. files.
37 Ed. 7/86; Cameron, *All Saints', Friern Barnet*, 30.
38 Nat. Soc. files.
39 *Rep. of Educ. Cttee. of Council, 1886* [C. 5123–1], p. 562, H.C. (1887), xxviii; *1893*, p. 910; *Pub. Elem. Schs., 1907* [Cd. 390], H.C. (1908), lxxxiv.
40 M.R.O., D.R.O. 12/I/G9/1; *Bd. of Educ., List 21 1922, 1927* (H.M.S.O.).
41 Cameron, *All Saints', Friern Barnet*, 30.
42 *Bd. of Educ., List 21, 1938* (H.M.S.O.).
43 Ex inf. the headmaster.
44 *Pub. Elem. Schs., 1906* [Cd. 3510], p. 447, H.C. (1907), lxiii.
45 Ed. 7/86.
46 M.R.O., D.R.O. 12/I/G9/1.
47 *Bd. of Educ., List 21, 1932, 1936* (H.M.S.O.).
48 Ibid. *1938*.
49 Ex inf. the headmistress.
50 M.R.O., D.R.O. 12/I/G7/22, p. 27; Ed. 7/86.
51 *Bd. of Educ., List 21, 1919, 1932* (H.M.S.O.).
52 Ibid. *1938*.
53 M.R.O., D.R.O. 12/I/G7/12.
54 Mdx. C.C. educ. cttee. *List of Educ. Services and Establishments* (1964), 55.
55 Ex inf. Mr. F. J. Maxwell.
56 *Bd. of Educ., List 21, 1932, 1936* (H.M.S.O.).
57 Ibid. *1938*; see above.
58 See above.

1950. It was built partly on the glebe east of Friern Barnet Lane and used temporary huts erected as the railway clearing house during the Second World War. The first stage in replacing the huts was completed in 1974. The school had a roll of *c.* 450 in 1975.[59]

Friern Barnet county school stands on a 3½-a. site between Hemington Avenue and Crescent Road. The main buildings were erected in 1960–1 in two stages and an arts' department and third laboratory have since been added. Pupils were transferred from Holly Park school before the official opening in 1961, when they numbered 500. In 1975 there were 600 pupils and it was still a secondary modern school, as schemes to become comprehensive had been rejected.[60]

Coppetts Wood primary school was founded in 1954 for infants and juniors. Numbers grew from 130 to 380 and in 1975 there were 330 juniors and infants and two nursery classes of 60. A mobile classroom was added in 1973.[61]

Private schools. The dissenting school at Whetstone in 1859 for *c.* 160 children aged over three was probably in Finchley. By 1883 there was a school for boys and girls at Oakleigh Park which had been proposed in 1870 by Brethren and Baptists.[62]

In 1884 the rector, Frederick Hall, founded a middle-class school for boys in Colney Hatch.[63] Known as St. John's high school for boys and after *c.* 1890 as Friern Barnet grammar school,[64] it had its own preparatory school from 1904.[65] A trust deed of 1900 permitted its use for Sunday school and parochial purposes and vested the management in a committee chaired by the rector.[66] Initial losses were borne by Hall[67] and fees of eight guineas a year in 1887 were later raised.[68] Originally housed in St. John's school-church,[69] later replaced by a one-storeyed building, the school was enlarged in the 1950s and replaced by a two-storeyed block in 1973.[70] There were high standards in 1892 and 1904[71] and in 1936 it was said that the school, although small, was the pride of the district and made a county secondary school unnecessary.[72] Numbers grew from 73 to 112 between 1882 and 1912,[73] reached *c.* 150 in 1937, and then declined. There were 175 pupils in 1975, when it provided grammar school education up to 'O' level.[74]

When the boys' high school became solvent in 1891, the rector founded a high school for middle-class girls, for which he detected even greater need, at the Firs, Friern Barnet Road.[75] Although an educational success, the school had only 33 pupils from kindergarten age upwards in 1892[76] and was never self-supporting. It closed in 1900.[77] In response to public demand, the Revd. E. G. Hall revived it in 1912 as Friern Barnet grammar school for girls, at Edenbrae[78] and later Friarshill, Torrington Avenue.[79] Catering for girls aged 11 and above,[80] the school had 76 pupils by 1918,[81] but in 1926 the rector leased the premises to Mrs. D. M. Roberts.[82] Friarshill school had closed by 1941.[83]

The Sisters of the Sacred Heart taught children aged 5–14 in a private house in Oakleigh Park South from 1936. Numbers rapidly grew to 120 in 1939 and 220 in 1945. During the Second World War two other houses were acquired and the seniors, juniors, and infants were housed separately. Additions consisted of a hall and dining facilities in 1956, a three-storeyed teaching block in 1961, and an administration building in 1971. Mobile classrooms for the infants were needed in 1962, but from 1967, when the school became Voluntary Aided, the seniors were phased out. The number of pupils increased from 300 in 1967 to 412 in 1975, almost all of them Roman Catholics.[84]

CHARITIES FOR THE POOR. In 1610 Lawrence Campe (d. 1613) gave a rent-charge in the City of London, from which £1 a year was to be divided equally among eight poor people of Friern Barnet.[85] In 1612 he gave a rent-charge of £8 6*s.* 8*d.* on land in Hertfordshire: £7 16*s.* was to be disbursed at the rate of 1*s.* monthly to twelve inmates of the alms-houses that he had erected in Friern Barnet, £1 6*s.* 8*d.* was for repairs, and the churchwardens were to keep the remaining 4*s.*[86] The total endowment of £9 6*s.* 8*d.* was paid in 1902 by the London Parochial Charities.[87] Campe's widow married Thomas Tooke (d. 1670), who assigned £3 a year to the poor from lands at Wormley (Herts.).[88] His gift may have been the so-called turnpike bond, first mentioned in 1729. Payment was due from John Nicholl the younger (d. 1747), whose son-in-law the duke of Chandos (d. 1789) paid the interest, until in 1785 the principal was exacted to meet repairs.[89]

Campe's six alms-houses were built on 1½ a. of copyhold land called Tromers,[90] and included two communal rooms for prayer and for washing, baking, or brewing. The founder's detailed statutes were largely ignored in the 18th century. After repairs in 1728 a seventh tenement was substituted

59 Ex inf. the headmaster.
60 Ex inf. the headmaster.
61 Ex inf. the headmistress.
62 Nat. Soc. files.
63 M.R.O., D.R.O. 12/I/K2/2 (1883); K1/4 (Oct. 1897).
64 Ibid. G8/4.
65 Ibid. K1/6 (Jan. 1904); K2/4 (1903).
66 M.R.O., D.R.O. 12/I/G8/4; copy *penes* Char. Com.
67 M.R.O., D.R.O. 12/I/K2/2 (1884).
68 Ibid. G8/2/63; Friern Barnet, *Official Guide* [1958], advert.; *Barnet Press*, 25 June 1887 (advert.); ex inf. Canon N. Gilmore.
69 M.R.O., D.R.O. 12/I/K2/2 (1883).
70 Ex inf. Mr. A. Heaps.
71 M.R.O., D.R.O. 12/I/K1/2, K1/6 (Jan. 1892, Feb. 1904).
72 *Barnet Press*, 25 Apr. 1936, 2 May 1936, 26 Dec. 1936.
73 M.R.O., D.R.O. 12/I/K2/2 (1892); K1/14 (Oct. 1912).
74 Ex inf. Mr. A. Heaps.
75 M.R.O., D.R.O. 12/I/K1/2 (Jan. 1892); K2/2 (1891).
76 Ibid. K2/2 (1892); K1/2 (Feb. 1892).
77 Ibid. K2/3 (1900).
78 Ibid. K2/4 (1912), 4; K1/14 (Aug. 1912).
79 Ibid. K1/25 (Jan. 1926).
80 Ibid. K1/18 (Mar. 1916).
81 Ibid. (May 1918).
82 Ibid. K1/25 (Apr. 1927); G8/12a–b, 15.
83 Ibid. G8/2.
84 Ex inf. the headmaster.
85 *18th Rep. Com. Char.* H.C. 62, p. 383 (1828), xx.
86 Ibid. pp. 382–3.
87 M.R.O., D.R.O. 12/I/F1/3.
88 C 2/403/52; Prob. 11/334 (P.C.C. 41 Duke).
89 *18th Rep. Com. Char.* 383; M.R.O., D.R.O. 12/I/B2/15, C1/1.
90 M.R.O., TA/FRI; Phillips, *Hist. Friern Barnet*, 11.

for the communal rooms and by 1828 prayers were no longer said.[91] Although restored in 1854,[92] prayers had again ceased by 1883[93] and in 1889 it was claimed that alms-people were chosen without regard for religious beliefs. In 1778 one tenement was vacant and the others had nineteen occupants, including two families. Eight inmates were then considered unsuitable[94] and in 1828 they included a woman of evil reputation and natives of other parishes.[95] The alms-houses were used as a school between 1809 and 1853,[96] housing the schoolmaster and schoolmistress in 1828[97] and the sexton in 1838.[98] There were 21 inhabitants in 1851, including 8 old people and, in two of the tenements, the families of the schoolmaster and schoolmistress and the parish clerk.[99] The inmates numbered 16 in 1871, 17 in 1897, and 7 in 1938.[1] In 1903 they had to be aged over 70, of twenty years' residence in Friern Barnet, with an annual income of not less than £31, and not in receipt of poor-relief.[2] Weekly pensions had been appropriated to other uses by 1795[3] but were restored in 1837[4] and finally withdrawn in 1961.[5]

The alms-houses were largely rebuilt in 1728 after a fire,[6] with help from a gift from Mrs. King of Friern House, and repaired in 1785–6,[7] 1809,[8] and 1843.[9] In 1855 John Miles subscribed £100 to augment the endowment and annual collections were started,[10] and in 1868 George Knights Smith gave the ground rents of nos. 1–7 Carlisle Place, worth £14.[11] Nevertheless the income was only £28 in 1867–8, including rent of £6 from 1 a. which had been allotted to the poor of Friern Barnet at the inclosure of Finchley common.[12] The sale of that land in 1889 brought £845,[13] and a Diamond Jubilee appeal raised over £600 for improvements to the fabric.[14] A Scheme of 1896 vested the alms-houses and the money raised by the sale of the Finchley allotment, collectively known as the Consolidated Almshouse Charity of Lawrence Campe, in the rector, churchwardens, and three representatives of Friern Barnet U.D.C.[15] Income rose to £169 in 1898[16] but had fallen to £118 by 1920–1, when there was a deficit.[17] The council requisitioned the alms-houses[18] and restored three tenements *c.* 1946[19] and the others after 1956,[20] partly at the trustees' expense.[21] After the leases of Carlisle Place had expired in 1953, some land was sold for £1,196 to the Eastern Electricity Board in 1962 and for £800 to Friern Barnet U.D.C. in 1964.[22] From 1959 the houses in Carlisle Place were unlet, depriving the charity of rent and in 1961 causing the pensions to be stopped. In 1962 an income of £175 from increased investments was sufficient to maintain the building[23] and between 1971 and 1974 the income was *c.* £1,000.[24] Further grants were made by Barnet L.B., and a Scheme of 1976 provided that inmates should contribute towards running costs.[25]

The alms-houses,[26] on the east side of Friern Barnet Lane, are of brick with stone dressings and tiled roofs. No trace remains of the stucco added in 1843.[27] The doorways of 1612 have four-centred tops and the low windows have three lights on the ground floor and two on the first.[28] The row faces south-west and was separated from the road by a short garden with trees[29] which had disappeared by 1957.

The alms-houses received several further endowments. Samuel Dorman (d. 1892) left £500, invested on the death of his widow in 1932.[30] Miss Sarah Anne Wilson in 1920 left the residue of her estate, £504.[31] In 1926–7 £200 was received from a fund known as the Holden bequest.[32] Sydney Simmons left sums totalling £1,320, paid over between 1926 and 1929;[33] a further £134 was paid on the death of his wife in 1936.[34] Henry Broadway Barnes (d. 1934) left £1,000.[35] He and Simmons were commemorated by a plaque inside the building.[36]

91 *18th Rep. Com. Char.* 381–3.
92 M.R.O., D.R.O. 12/I/K2/1 (ann. rep. for 1854).
93 Ibid. III/1/1.
94 Ibid. I/C1/1.
95 *18th Rep. Com. Char.* 382.
96 See p. 34.
97 *18th Rep. Com. Char.* 382.
98 M.R.O., D.R.O. 12/I/H/S.
99 H.O. 107/1701/1B f. 337.
1 M.R.O., D.R.O. 12/I/F1/3; Acc. 410/94h (cutting); R.G. 10/1334 ff. 71–2.
2 M.R.O., D.R.O. 12/I/F1/3.
3 *Gent. Mag.* lxv(1), 633.
4 M.R.O., D.R.O. 12/I/C1/2.
5 Char. Com. files.
6 *18th Rep. Com. Char.* 382.
7 M.R.O., D.R.O. 12/I/C1/1.
8 Ibid. G1/2.
9 Thorne, *Environs*, 32.
10 M.R.O., D.R.O. 12/I/K2/1 (1855).
11 Ibid. K2/1 (1868).
12 *General Digest of Endowed Chars.* H.C. 433(11), pp. 4–5 (1867–8), lii(1).
13 Char. Com. files; M.R.O., D.R.O. 12/I/C1/3.
14 M.R.O., D.R.O. 12/I/K2/3 (1898).
15 Char. Com. files.
16 M.R.O., D.R.O. 12/I/K2/3.
17 Ibid. F1/3.
18 Ibid. F1/4, p. 93.
19 Ibid. pp. 93–4.
20 Ibid. p. 213.
21 Ibid.; Friern Barnet U.D. *Official Guide* [*c.* 1948], 20.
22 M.R.O., D.R.O. 12/I/F1/4, pp. 109, 126, 144; Char. Com. files.
23 Char. Com. files.
24 Char. Com. files; M.R.O., D.R.O. 12/I/F1/4, pp. 158 sqq.; F1/5.
25 Char. Com. files.
26 See plate facing p. 33.
27 Thorne, *Environs*, 32.
28 Pevsner, *Mdx.* 57; Hist. Mon. Com. *Mdx.* 27–8 and plate 66.
29 Thorne, *Environs*, 32.
30 Char. Com. files; M.R.O., D.R.O. 12/I/F1/4, p. 40.
31 M.R.O., D.R.O. 12/I/F1/3.
32 Ibid. F1/5.
33 Ibid. F1/4, p. 18; F1/5.
34 Ibid. F1/4, p. 71; F1/5; Char. Com. files.
35 M.R.O., D.R.O. 12/I/F1/4, p. 55; Char. Com. files.
36 M.R.O., D.R.O. 12/I/F1/4, p. 57.

FINCHLEY

FINCHLEY,[1] whose shape has been compared to a leg of mutton[2] with its narrow end to the north at Whetstone, lay between Hertfordshire on the north and north-west, Hendon on the west, Hendon and Hampstead on the south, and Hornsey and Friern Barnet on the east. It contained 3,384 a. in 1871 and 3,475 a. from 1933, when boundary changes accompanying the creation of Finchley M.B. transferred 29 a. to Friern Barnet U.D., 9 a. to Hendon M.B., and 37 a. to Hornsey M.B. but added 18 a., 107 a., and 41 a. from those administrative areas respectively.[3] The boundary with Hertfordshire was narrow and remained fixed. Until 1933 the western boundary followed Dollis brook to its junction with Mutton brook, which formed the south-west boundary from the point where it left the bishop of London's demesne lands. Elsewhere field boundaries delimited the parish.[4] The southern boundary through the bishop's demesne lands in Finchley and Hornsey was fixed by 1738[5] but the eastern one was not finally settled until the inclosure of Finchley common in 1816. The road which came to be known as the Great North Road, bisecting the parish, passes the 6-, 7-, and 8-mile stones from London in its course through Finchley. The civil parish corresponded to Finchley U.D., created in 1895, and, after the boundary changes mentioned above, to Finchley M.B. in 1933. In 1965 it became part of Barnet L.B.[6]

Most of the area is covered by glacial deposits: boulder clay fringed by glacial gravel overlying London Clay, which has been exposed by the action of streams. There is a narrow band of alluvium along Dollis brook. At the southern end of the parish are Claygate Beds, Bagshot Sands, and a little pebble gravel at the Spaniards inn.[7] The resulting soil is a strong marly clay or gravel.[8] In 1871 Finchley became briefly remarkable when excavations for the railway at Church End revealed glacial fossil shells in the boulder clay.[9] Most of the land over 200 ft. corresponds with the boulder clay. At Whetstone, at East End, and in the south part the land rises to over 300 ft., reaching 401 ft. at the Spaniards inn on the edge of Hampstead Heath.[10]

The parish lies on a watershed separating Dollis or Brent brook (called Tateburn between 1216 and 1272)[11] and its tributaries on the west from the eastward-flowing tributaries of Pymme's brook, of which the most important was Strawberry Vale brook. Mutton brook flows westward from its source in Dirthouse (Cherry Tree) wood to join Dollis brook at the south-western corner of the parish, many southward-flowing tributaries joining it from the glacial gravel south of East End Road.[12]

Finchley, probably denoting Finch's clearing, is a late Anglo-Saxon name but was recorded only from the early 13th century.[13] The common along the parish's eastern side was a remnant of the woodland which once covered most of northern Middlesex and southern Hertfordshire;[14] known as Finchley wood until the 17th century[15] and later notorious for its highwaymen, it still contained more than a quarter of the parish in 1816.[16] The earliest settlement was probably in the south-west quarter of the parish at Church End, where people were living by the 13th century. East End and Parkgate, mentioned respectively in 1365 and 1375,[17] together formed a scattered hamlet where the later East End Road met the Great North Road at the exit from Hornsey park. The Great North Road also accounted for the growth in the north part of the parish of Whetstone, called 'le Weston' in 1398, 'Wheston' in 1417, and 'Whetestonestret' in 1439.[18] Its name, too early to have been connected with a large whetstone allegedly used before the battle of Barnet,[19] probably meant western settlement, in relation to Friern Barnet. North End, first recorded in 1462 to distinguish one of the many branches of the Shepherd family,[20] was another hamlet on the edge of the common, lying north in relation to Church End and East End.

Whetstone and North End together were more populous than Church End in the 17th century, as was East End. Whetstone, however, existed largely to serve travellers and had few wealthy residents either then or in the 18th and early 19th centuries. Most building took place around the old centres until transport began to improve with the coming of the railway in 1867, whereupon North End was transformed into the suburb of North Finchley. By 1920 Church End had been joined to both North End and East End by building, although the eastern edge of the parish was largely kept open by the establishment of cemeteries. The southern part was built up mainly after the First World War, forming an extension of Hampstead Garden Suburb and a wealthy area, cut off from the rest of Finchley by the North Circular Road. West Finchley dated only from the 1930s, when elsewhere in the parish large houses were giving way to smaller ones and flats, and when offices began to be opened in Whetstone.

1 The article was written in 1976–7; any references to later yrs. are dated. The help of Mrs. J. M. Corden in commenting on the article is gratefully acknowledged.
2 Robbins, *Mdx.* 253.
3 *Census*, 1831–1961.
4 O.S. Maps 6″, Mdx. VI. SE., VII. SW., XI. NE., SE., XII. NW. (1867 edn.).
5 Guildhall MS. 12417.
6 See p. 79.
7 Geol. Survey Map 6″, Mdx. XI. NE., SE. (1920 edn.).
8 *T.L.M.A.S.* xix. 48.
9 *The Times*, 24 Oct. 1871; H. Walker, *Glacial Drifts of Muswell Hill and Finchley* (1874).
10 O.S. Maps 6″, Mdx. VI. SE., VII. SW., XI. NE., SE., XII. NW. (1867 edn.).
11 C 146/5437.
12 Geol. Survey Map 6″, Mdx. XI. NE., SE. (1920 edn.).
13 St. Paul's MS. A 41/1523; *P.N. Mdx.* (E.P.N.S.), 92–3.
14 Cf. place-names ending in 'ley' and Barnet, above, p. 6.
15 S.C. 2/191/4.
16 M.R.O., EA/FIN.
17 W.A.M. 4818; St. Paul's MS. A 62/2.
18 S.C. 2/188/67 m. 12; S.C. 2/188/72 m. 5d.; Guildhall MS. 10312/73; *Cal. Close*, 1413–19, 438.
19 *P.N. Mdx.* (E.P.N.S.), 100–1. The stone survives outside the Griffin.
20 S.C. 2/188/81 m. 4.

Most of Finchley's distinguished residents are named elsewhere in the article.[21] Natives included Vice-Admiral Sir William Johnstone Hope (1766–1831), the judge Sir William Shee (1804–68), the opera director Frederick Gye (1810–78), Sir John Bridge (1824–1900), police magistrate, Osbert Salvin (1835–98), naturalist and son of the architect Anthony Salvin, Philip Stanhope Worsley (1835–66), poet, and Oliver Madox Brown (1855–74), author and painter. Those buried in Finchley included Tom Payne (d. 1799), bookseller, John Cartwright (d. 1824), political reformer,[22] James Thomson (d. 1883), architect, and Mathilde Blind (d. 1896), poet. Rudolph Ackermann (d. 1834), the book- and print-seller, lived at Brownswell and William Bernard Tegetmeier (d. 1912), the natural historian, lived for a time in North Finchley.[23]

COMMUNICATIONS. The road from London which came to be known as the Great North Road played an important part in Finchley's history. Norden's belief that the ancient highway to Barnet followed the line of Friern Barnet Lane[24] was perhaps correct, since Finchley wood originally presented a barrier to travellers and Finchley's earliest settlement was not on the line of the later Great North Road.

The change probably took place during the late 13th century or the 14th.[25] The hamlet of East End grew up during the 14th century at the exit of the road from Hornsey park but it is uncertain whether the route then passed directly northward across the common, as it did by Norden's time, or whether it followed East End Road through Church End and along Ballards Lane to Whetstone. Pavage was granted to the townsmen of Barnet in 1347 on the road from St. Albans to Finchley wood[26] and to two Highgate men in 1354 for the road from Highgate to the two crosses at Finchley, extended in 1359 to St. Albans.[27] The highway from Barnet to the two crosses was mentioned in 1374 and a watercourse at the two crosses was obstructed in 1385.[28] There were several crosses in Finchley: one next to the church,[29] another near Bibbesworth on East End Road,[30] the fair cross at Ballards Reding,[31] and probably one at Whetstone.[32] The southern portion of the road, from Hornsey park to East End, was called Newgate Lane by 1395[33] and the northernmost was Whetstone Street by 1439.[34] The intermediate stretch across the common was usually known as the Barnet Road and later as the Great North Road or High Road, its course probably following the highest and best-drained land.

Two routes from the south ran to Church End: Hendon Lane in the south-west, called Finchley Hill in 1659 and 1814[35] and probably identical with the medieval Alcockes Lane,[36] and Ducksetters Street or Lane, mentioned from 1475,[31] which ran from Golders Green a little west of the modern Regent's Park Road. The two roads joined just south of Church End, where in 1365 the road was called Church Street.[38] The road continued north to Finchley common as Ballards or Barrow Lane, so named in 1424,[39] probably from the Ballard family of *c.* 1300.[40] It was probably 'le Overstreet', so named in 1365 presumably because it ran parallel with Nether Street, to the west. Both streets were described in 1365 as the 'two old streets'.[41] In 1756 a raised way was built from the last house in Ballards Lane to the Great North Road at North End.[42] Nether Street, so called in 1365 and 'le lower street' in 1622, was an access road to houses and fields,[43] linked at both ends to Ballards Lane. Coles or Boles Lane, mentioned in 1393 and 1476,[44] may have been the southern link.[45] About 1867 the northern section was named Mosshall Lane.[46]

East End Road, linking East End and the southern section of the Great North Road with Church End, was the main east–west road. Although apparently not so named until the late 19th century,[47] it probably dated from the 14th-century growth of East End. Hunts Green, mid-way along the road, was mentioned in 1437[48] and Piryton Lane, named in 1423 and 1485, may have been the western section of the road near Church End.[49] Long Lane, named in 1719, ran from Ballards Lane to Bulls Lane at East End[50] and was probably the medieval Ferrours Lane.[51] The eastern section was called Broad Lane in 1814.[52] A short lane led from Bibbesworth manor-house to the church by 1657 and was called the Avenue by 1897.[53] Several roads linked Long Lane with East End Road. The most westerly was Squires, formerly Place, Lane, which ran north from Bibbesworth

21 Except where otherwise stated, the following para. is based on *D.N.B.*
22 Thorne, *Environs*, 217.
23 Finchley Soc. *Newsletter*, Sept. 1975.
24 Norden, *Spec. Brit.* 15.
25 See p. 103.
26 *Cal. Pat.* 1345–8, 334.
27 Ibid. 1350–4, 538; 1358–61, 132.
28 *Cal. of Wills in Ct. of Husting, Lond. 1258–1688*, ed. R. R. Sharpe, ii. 170; S.C. 2/188/65 m. 6 and d.
29 B.L.H.L., Banks Colln., Finchley ch., p. 00745 (will of Wm. Shepherd, 1539).
30 Cf. Crossfield: M.R.O., TA/FIN, nos. 21, 32.
31 St. Paul's MS. C (Sampson), f. 109v.; Guildhall MS. 9171/8, f. 17.
32 The large stone at the Griffin may have been the base of a cross: B.L.H.L., Banks Colln. xxxiii, St. Mary at Finchley.
33 S.C. 2/188/66 m. 15; Rocque, *Map of Mdx.* (1754).
34 S.C. 2/188/72 m. 5d. See also Guildhall MS. 10312/80, m. 8d.; S.C. 2/191/4; S.C. 2/191/7.
35 S.C. 2/191/12; M.R.O., EA/FIN. Finchley Hill, mentioned in 1498 and 1546, was probably a topographical feature: B.L.H.L., Acc. 6416/1; M.R.O., Acc. 1226/1.
36 S.C. 2/188/67 m. 5 (1396); S.C. 2/188/72 m. 2 (1436); S.C. 2/191/12 (1657). Field-names support the identification. And cf. Alkokkes (1365): W.A.M. 4818.
37 Dukcytyrstret: Guildhall MS. 10312/80, m. 3; Rocque, *Map of Mdx.* (1754). Walter Duk had land in Finchley before 1365: W.A.M. 4818.
38 W.A.M. 4818.
39 Guildhall MS. 10312/66.
40 B.L.H.L., Banks Colln. iv. 4144; x. 7067.
41 W.A.M. 4818.
42 *Mdx. & Herts. N. & Q.* iii. 35.
43 W.A.M. 4818; S.C. 2/191/7.
44 Guildhall MSS. 10312/62; 80, m. 8d.
45 Cf. Colefield: M.R.O., TA/FIN, no. 153.
46 O.S. Map 6", Mdx. VI. SE. (1867 edn.).
47 Ibid. XI. NE. (1897 edn.). It was described as the way to East End from Bibbesworth in 1616: Prob. 11/133 (P.C.C. 40 Parker, will of Alex. King).
48 S.C. 2/188/72 m. 4; M.R.O., Acc. 1140.
49 Guildhall MS. 10312/66; S.C. 2/189/6 m. 3.
50 M.R.O., Acc. 351/276; Rocque, *Map of Mdx.* (1754).
51 S.C. 2/188/73 m. 1d. (1440); S.C. 2/189/5 m. 3 (1484).
52 M.R.O., EA/FIN.
53 S.C. 2/191/12; Rocque, *Map of Mdx.* (1754); O.S. Map 6", Mdx. XI. NE. (1897 edn.).

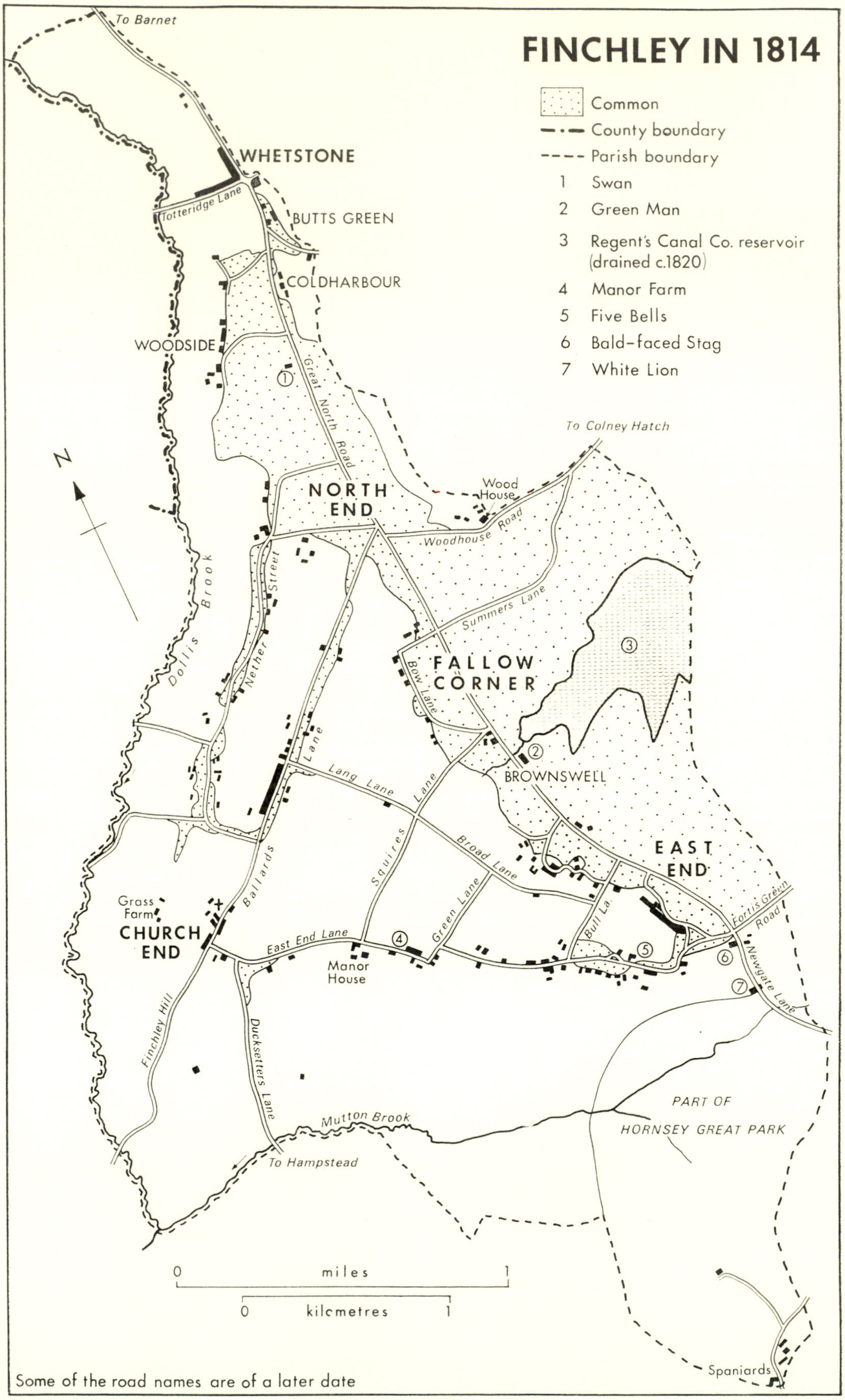
FINCHLEY IN 1814
Common
County boundary
Parish boundary
1 Swan
2 Green Man
3 Regent's Canal Co. reservoir (drained c.1820)
4 Manor Farm
5 Five Bells
6 Bald-faced Stag
7 White Lion
To Barnet
WHETSTONE
Totteridge Lane
BUTTS GREEN
COLDHARBOUR
WOODSIDE
Great North Road
To Colney Hatch
N
NORTH END
Wood House
Woodhouse Road
Dollis Brook
Nether Street
Summers Lane
FALLOW CORNER
Bow Lane
BROWNSWELL
Lane
Long Lane
Lane
Squires Lane
Broad Lane
EAST END
Ballards
Grass Farm
CHURCH END
East End Lane
Manor House
Green Lane
Bull La.
Fortis Green Road
Newgate Lane
Finchley Hill
Ducksetters Lane
Mutton Brook
To Hampstead
PART OF HORNSEY GREAT PARK
0 miles 1
0 kilometres 1
Spaniards
Some of the road names are of a later date

manor-house and continued across Long Lane to the common and eventually to the Great North Road.[54] Its northern section, Short Lane in 1657 and *c.* 1867,[55] was probably the Heybourne Lane mentioned in the 1380s.[56] Green *alias* Philips Lane joined the central portion of East End Road to Long Lane.[57] Bulls Lane, which after the building of Holy Trinity church in 1846 was called Church Lane, ran from the eastern section of East End Road across Long Lane to the common and the Great North Road.[58]

Friern Barnet Lane entered Whetstone at Butts Green and was still important in 1814.[59] An east-west route across the northern part of Whetstone existed by the early 18th century, the portion from Totteridge (Herts.) to Whetstone being called Totteridge Lane by 1651 and occasionally Brick Lane in the early 19th century.[60] It continued eastward across Friern Barnet along the line of the modern Oakleigh Road[61] to Betstile, where it was joined by another road running east from the Great North Road near Tally Ho Corner across the northern boundary of Finchley common, called Woodhouse Road by 1897.[62] Just west of Colney Hatch the later Woodhouse Road by 1754 was joined by Summers Lane, a more southerly route across the common from the Great North Road.[63] In 1814 the two roads were called North and South Colney Hatch Road respectively.[64] The only other easterly road from the parish, called Park Gate in 1754,[65] Muswell Hill Road in 1814, and Fortis Green Road by 1920, ran from the Newgate Lane stretch of the Great North Road by High Redings into Hornsey.[66]

In the west part of Finchley, Dollis Road or Lane joined the southern part of Nether Street with Hendon by 1488, although its name did not occur until much later.[67] A little to the north Love or Lovers Walk, mentioned in 1800, led to Hendon from Nether Street but was probably always a minor lane or path.[68]

In the south part of Finchley there were two lanes in 1754: Hampstead Lane, which crossed the southern tip of the parish on its way from Highgate to Hampstead, and George Lane, which ran north from Hampstead Lane to Spaniards Farm and thence, by field paths, to East End Road.[69]

Minor roads grew up along the edge of the common. Bow Lane, named from its shape, existed at Fallow Corner south of East End by 1814.[70] Farther south there was a settlement at Cuckolds Haven by 1678, linked by causeways before 1814,[71] the respective roads being named Red Lion Hill by 1821, Oak Lane by *c.* 1867, and King Street by 1920.[72] Farther south the Hogmarket developed into Market Place, so named by 1897, and Park Road, named by 1920,[73] while Prospect Place was built in 1825 to link the settlement with East End Road.[74] In Whetstone similarly, Swan, Woodside, and Lodge lanes all existed along the edge of the common by 1780. A footpath then led from Woodside Lane to Totteridge and a church path joined Whetstone to the northern part of Nether Street.[75] Unidentified roads included Smiths Lane or Way (1422),[76] Tromer Street (1424 and 1484),[77] Merelfield Street (1429),[78] Woodsend Lane (1436),[79] Procession Lane (1452),[80] Croftlethe Street (1457),[81] Cowperes Lane (1463),[82] and Bush Lane (1484).[83]

The road from St. Marylebone to the Great North Road was turnpiked under an Act of 1825,[84] Ducksetters Lane being replaced by a new road, Regent's Park Road, to the east and Ballards Lane being extended to a new junction with the Great North Road. The Finchley vestry had tried to resist the imposition of tolls, at least on existing roads, citing King John's charter.[85] In 1845 parishioners complained that for nearly 20 years they had been oppressed by tolls which were perhaps the heaviest near London. In 1847 the commissioners for the metropolitan turnpike roads intended taking over the St. Marylebone and Finchley turnpike road.[86] A vestry committee wished to abolish the tolls in 1851[87] but Highgate and Whetstone turnpike trust was not ended until 1862. Toll-gates survived at Whetstone until 1863 and by the White Lion in East End until 1901.[88]

The road pattern survived the spread of 19th- and 20th-century housing, the only major new

[54] Rocque, *Map of Mdx.* (1754). And see M.R.O., Acc. 1140.
[55] S.C. 2/191/12; O.S. Map 6″, Mdx. XI. NE. (1867 edn.).
[56] S.C. 2/188/65 m. 17d.; S.C. 2/189/5 m. 3.
[57] M.R.O., Acc. 1140. Phyppes Lane: S.C. 2/188/70 m. 3 (1435); Philpottes Lane: Guildhall MS. 10312/72 (1443).
[58] M.R.O., Acc. 1140; Acc. 351/461.
[59] M.R.O., EA/FIN.
[60] St. Paul's MS. B 68; Guildhall MS. 10465/139, p. 393.
[61] See p. 7.
[62] Rocque, *Map of Mdx.* (1754); O.S. Map 6″, Mdx. VI. SE. (1897 edn.).
[63] Rocque, *Map of Mdx.* (1754).
[64] M.R.O., EA/FIN.
[65] Rocque, *Map of Mdx.* (1754). Parkynesgate, mentioned in 1410, was not necessarily a road: S.C. 2/188/68 m. 2.
[66] M.R.O., EA/FIN; O.S. Maps 6″, Mdx. XI. NE., XII. NW. (1920 edn.). Fortes common was mentioned in 1558: St. Paul's MS. C (Sampson), f. 373.
[67] Guildhall MS. 10312/81, m. 2; Rocque, *Map of Mdx.* (1754); B.L.H.L., P.A.F. 3/1 (1815).
[68] *Mdx. & Herts. N. & Q.* iii. 147; M.R.O., EA/FIN; O.S. Maps 6″, Mdx. XI. NE. (1867, 1897 edns.).
[69] Rocque, *Map of Mdx.* (1754); Guildhall MS. 12407.
[70] M.R.O., EA/FIN. The beginnings of the road were apparent in 1780: M.R.O., Acc. 262/4/44.
[71] Guildhall MS. 10312/113; Rocque, *Map of Mdx.* (1754); M.R.O., EA/FIN; O.S. Maps 6″, Mdx. XI. NE. (1867 edn.); *Mdx. & Herts. N. & Q.* iii. 147.
[72] M.R.O., Acc. 262/4/13–14; O.S. Maps 6″, Mdx. XI. NE. (1867, 1920 edns.).
[73] M.R.O., Acc. 351/276; Rocque, *Map of Mdx.* (1754); M.R.O., EA/FIN; O.S. Maps 6″, Mdx. XI. NE. (1897, 1920 edns.).
[74] M.R.O., Acc. 262/4/39–40.
[75] M.R.O., Acc. 262/4/44; O.S. Map 6″, Mdx. VI. SE. (1867 edn.).
[76] Next Church field. There were, however, two Church fields (glebe and Bibbesworth demesne): S.C. 2/188/69 m. 11d.; S.C. 2/188/72 m. 5d.
[77] Guildhall MS. 10312/66; S.C. 2/189/5 m. 3.
[78] S.C. 2/188/70 m. 1d. Merrall field lay on the w. side of the par.: B.L.H.L., Acc. 8667/1.
[79] Probably in Whetstone: S.C. 2/188/72 m. 2.
[80] Probably near the ch.: Guildhall MS. 10312/74.
[81] S.C. 2/188/79 m. 3.
[82] Guildhall MS. 10312/76.
[83] S.C. 2/189/5 m. 3.
[84] 7 Geo. IV, c. 90; B.L.H.L., P.A.F. 1/6.
[85] M.R.O., EA/FIN; TA/FIN; Acc. 351/324; B.L.H.L., P.A.F. 1/5, 6. For the charter, see p. 66.
[86] B.L.H.L., P.A.F.
[87] Ibid. 1/8.
[88] *Mdx. & Herts. N. & Q.* iv. 125; *Barnet Press*, 7 Oct. 1933.

route being the North Circular Road, driven south-westward across the widest part of the parish in the 1920s.[89]

In 1826[90] there were three bridges or fords over Dollis brook and three culverts where tributaries of Pymmes brook crossed the Great North Road. Dollis brook was bridged by Hendon Lane at Finchley or Brent bridge, mentioned in 1438 and in disrepair in 1623.[91] A three-arched brick bridge, 16 ft. high and 13 ft. wide, was built in 1777 by Mrs. Aislabie of Hendon Place, who also dammed the stream to form a lake, and in 1826 the bridge was said to be of inconvenient height. Finchley inhabitants were indicted for neglecting to repair the bridge in 1623 and Middlesex inhabitants in 1820. It was repaired in 1844[92] and had been rebuilt by 1934.[93]

Totteridge Lane crossed Dollis brook from Whetstone by 1754 and Finchley and Totteridge shared the cost of maintaining a bridge there by 1787.[94] It was probably the footbridge which in 1826 lay south of a great ford there. A larger bridge, built in 1843 by John Hey Puget, continued to be maintained by both parishes[95] and was widened in 1939.[96] In 1826 Dollis Lane crossed Dollis brook by means of a deep ford flanked by two footbridges. A footbridge existed there by 1659[97] and Finchley paid half the cost of repairs in 1879.[98] Mutton brook, although not mentioned in 1826, was probably culverted by that date. Dirt House bridge, in 1444 the 'bridge in the highway at Harringay park', carried the Great North Road across Mutton brook.[99] It was the responsibility of the bishop of London in 1444 and 1455 but in 1577 the inhabitants of Finchley offered to repair it if he would provide the necessary timber.[1] It still existed in 1792.[2]

A daily coach left London for Finchley in 1817 at 4.0 p.m.[3] and in 1826–7 one left the Queen's Head, Church End, for London at 8.20 a.m., returning in the evening.[4] By the late 1830s one daily coach left the Queen's Head for the Bank and another left the Torrington Arms, while an omnibus ran from the Five Bells in East End Road to Charing Cross.[5] In 1845 there were three omnibuses a day from the Five Bells and in the 1860s three from Church End, besides two or three which passed through Finchley from Barnet.[6] Coaches from London to the north provided additional services: nineteen were said to pass daily to Birmingham in 1829[7] and the fact that Finchley lay on their route was one of the reasons why the architect Anthony Salvin (1799–1881) moved there in 1833.[8] In 1835 over 90 stage coaches passed daily through Whetstone[9] and in the 1860s the coach journey from Whetstone to London took about 1¾ hour.[10]

In 1867 the Great Northern Railway opened a line to Mill Hill (later Mill Hill East) and Edgware with stations at East Finchley and Finchley (later Finchley Central). A branch from Finchley to High Barnet, with stations at Woodside Park and Whetstone (called Totteridge and Whetstone) opened in 1872. West Finchley station at Nether Street, south of Woodside Park, was added in 1933. The railway greatly increased accessibility from London. In 1870 the journey from Church End took ½ hour and during the 1890s a return ticket on a workmen's train from Finchley cost 4*d.* There were 20 daily trains each way in 1870, 36 in 1876, 45 in 1884, 51 in 1889, and 60 in 1902. The railway became part of the London Passenger Transport Board's Northern line, which was electrified to East Finchley in 1939, to High Barnet in 1940, and to Mill Hill East in 1941.[11]

Intermediate or east–west journeys were less easy. Trams had been suggested in 1880 but it was not until 1898 that the Metropolitan Tramways and Omnibus Co. seriously proposed to introduce them to Finchley[12] and only in 1905 that a route was opened by Metropolitan Electric Tramways (the M.E.T.) between Highgate and Whetstone.[13] It was extended to the Hertfordshire boundary in 1906 and to Barnet in 1907 and was crossed by one from New Southgate to North Finchley and Golders Green from 1909.[14] A tramway depot opened just off the Great North Road near Tally Ho Corner by 1908 became the focus of the M.E.T.'s system before it was superseded by trolley-buses in 1938.[15]

Omnibuses still ran thrice daily between the Torrington Arms and Oxford Circus in 1890.[16] More horse-drawn omnibuses linked Church End, Whetstone, and Barnet from 1898[17] and another service opened in 1899 to run every 15 minutes between the Bald-faced Stag at East End and Euston Road. In 1900 there were several omnibuses, including one between Charing Cross and North Finchley, and in 1902 the London General Omnibus Co. opened a service between London Bridge and Finchley. The Associated Motor Omnibus Co. started a service between St. Martin's Lane and

[89] M.R.O., P.R. 163/35; M. S. Briggs, *Mdx. Old and New* (1934), 124.
[90] Except where otherwise stated, the para. is based on *Rep. on Bridges in Mdx.* 149.
[91] Guildhall MS. 10312/71, m. 2; *Mdx. Cnty. Rec.* ii. 238.
[92] M.R.O., MJ/SPB 125–9; MA/D/Br./25; Misc. P 45.
[93] Briggs, *Mdx. Old and New*, 132.
[94] Rocque, *Map of Mdx.* (1754); B.L.H.L., P.A.F. 3/1.
[95] P. G. Dawson, *Puget Family in Eng.* (pamphlet, 1976), 34; B.L.H.L., P.A.F. 1/7, 4/2.
[96] *The Times*, 8 Apr. 1939.
[97] S.C. 2/191/12.
[98] Finchley local bd., min. bk. i. 117–18 in Hendon town hall.
[99] Guildhall MS. 12396; S.C. 2/188/74 m. 2.
[1] S.C. 2/188/74 m. 2; S.C. 2/188/77 m. 3; Guildhall MS. 10312/92, m. 6.
[2] Guildhall MS. 10465/107, p. 165.
[3] J. Hassell, *Picturesque Rides and Walks* (1817), i. 184–6.
[4] *Pigot's Dir.* (1826–7).
[5] Ibid. (1839); *Hist. Lond. Transport*, i. 397.
[6] *Home Cnties. Dir.* (1845); *Hist. Lond. Transport*, i. 170.
[7] Robbins, *Mdx.* 74.
[8] B.L.H.L., Acc. 6787/7.
[9] *Home Cnties. Mag.* vi. 220. For the part played by Finchley and Whetstone in the coach trade, see below, p. 72.
[10] *Hist. Lond. Transport*, i. 170.
[11] Ibid. i. 129, 170, 215–16; ii. 244–5; M.R.O., Acc. 410/45a.
[12] Finchley local bd., min. bk. ii. 74–5; Potter Colln. 28/13–14; B.L.H.L., Map 7363/16.
[13] *Barnet Press*, 7 Oct. 1933.
[14] *Hist. Lond. Transport*, ii. 100–1.
[15] *Kelly's Dir. Mdx.* (1908); O.S. Map 6", Mdx. VI. SE. (1920 edn.); Finchley Soc. *Newsletter*, Sept. 1976; *Barnet Press*, 5, 12 Mar. 1938.
[16] *Kelly's Dir. Mdx.* (1890).
[17] *Barnet Press*, 7 Oct. 1933.

the Bald-faced Stag in 1905.[18] By 1908 motor-buses ran every 12 minutes from North Finchley to Oxford Circus.[19] Trolley-buses ran between Cricklewood and North Finchley from 1936 and between North Finchley and Barnet or Wood Green from 1938.[20] There were ten motor-bus and trolley-bus routes in 1955[21] but all trolley-buses disappeared between 1959 and 1962. In 1959 and 1964 the deficiencies of London Transport buses were such that Finchley B.C. considered running its own.[22]

Growth before the mid 19th century. Finchley's earliest settlement[23] grew up around the church on the edge of the boulder clay at *Church End*, where there was well-water and the land (282 ft. at the church) was far enough from Dollis brook to be safe from flooding. Houses were mentioned in the earliest records, from the 13th century. Conveyances often involved land in Hendon and Finchley, and settlement may have spread northward from Hendon along Hendon and Ballards lanes. The absence of ancient copyhold reinforces the impression that, while woodmen may have worked there earlier, agricultural exploitation began with assarting at the edge of Finchley wood in the 12th or early 13th centuries. Meadow land along Dollis brook bordered arable, although probably not open-field, land.

Settlement was not strongly nucleated. There were a few houses near the church, including the rectory and, by the late Middle Ages, the church- and clerk's houses. To the west, on the edge of the gravel, was the medieval Grotes farm. To the east at some distance from the main hamlet stood Bibbesworth manor-house. Ballards Lane and Nether Street, each with its medieval houses, carried the settlement northward. Early houses[24] included Kentesgarden (1398),[25] Warren's Gift (1489),[26] the church-house (1547) and clerk's house (1561),[27] and the 'ancient' Holly Cottage,[28] all in Church End. The house of the Barnvilles, who lived in Finchley by 1429,[29] was associated with one called Huddes in Nether Street.[30] Also in Nether Street were Rodbardes (1466),[31] Gibbs (*c.* 1509),[32] Sellars Hall (1602),[33] and Flints and Sawyers (17th century).[34] A house was built at Abbottesgarden in Ballards Lane between 1467 and 1498.[35] Others in Ballards Lane included Bakers (1501),[36] perhaps the later White or Grove House which Henry Stephens, inventor of the ink and father of Henry Charles Stephens, bought in 1844.[37] Little Angells (1633),[38] and Critchendell House (17th century)[39] were also in Ballards Lane.

In 1614 28 people in Church End, Ballards Lane, and Nether Street were assessed for poor-rates.[40] In 1664 31 were assessed for hearth tax in Church End and Nether Street, the largest houses being those of Richard Utber (17 hearths) and widow Hayton (11). Ballards Lane was assessed with Whetstone.[41]

Much building or rebuilding took place from the 17th century. In Nether Street a cottage at Little Bushells was described as newly built in 1635,[42] as was a house in Ballards Lane in 1646.[43] Sellars Hall was pulled down in 1680 and rebuilt soon afterwards,[44] and Gibbs was described as newly built in 1690.[45] The church-house had been licensed as the Queen's Head by 1718[46] and waste between it and the rectory was granted for building in 1727 to a bricklayer.[47] He may have divided the clerk's house, which by 1767 consisted of two tenements, one a chandler's shop. The cottage of Warren's Gift was rebuilt as two cottages in 1771 and had become three by 1776.[48] Park House opposite Gravel Hill, one of the few surviving old buildings, dates from 1739 although it probably occupies an older site.[49] Nether Street contained Elm Grange, formerly Elm Villa, by 1720[50] and two tenements on charity land by 1754. They were demolished in 1810 and replaced by Brent Lodge, a large rambling house, later the home of Francis A. Hamilton, Finchley's benefactor, between 1817 and 1824.[51] Elm Place, at the south end of Nether Street, existed by 1754.[52] In Ballards Lane the Red Lion had been built by 1717, Finchley Hall by 1719,[53] and Willow Lodge in 1727.[54] The King of Prussia, formerly the King's Head, was licensed by 1731.[55] A new house and coach-house stood on the site of a cottage in Ballards Lane in 1765[56] and Cornwell House was built on the site of Critchendell House in 1795.[57] Wentworth Lodge replaced an earlier house in the early 19th century.[58]

18 Potter Colln. 20/13.
19 *Kelly's Dir. Mdx.* (1908).
20 *Hist. Lond. Transport*, ii. 300–1.
21 Finchley Boro. *Official Handbk.* (1955).
22 *Hist. Lond. Transport*, ii. 351; *The Times*, 24 Nov. 1958; 1 Jan., 23 Nov. 1959; 27 July 1964.
23 See p. 38.
24 Dates refer to the earliest record of the names.
25 S.C. 2/188/67 m. 12d. John le Kent fl. 1365: W.A.M. 4818.
26 See p. 97.
27 See p. 76.
28 B.L.H.L., Banks Colln. xii; B.L.H.L., S/C (1908).
29 S.C. 2/188/70 m. 1d.
30 B.L.H.L., Acc. 6416/8; Acc. 9131.
31 B.L.H.L., Banks Colln. xii. 5025.
32 B.L.H.L., Acc. 9131.
33 C 9/28/91; C 9/28/99.
34 M.R.O., Acc. 351/277.
35 Potter Colln. 28/30–31.
36 Guildhall MS. 9171/8, f. 240.
37 M.L.R. 1844/8/270; B.L.H.L., Banks Colln., biog. Stephens.
38 S.C. 2/191/9.
39 M.R.O., Acc. 351/277.
40 M.R.O., Acc. 351/150, f. 1. The church-ho. and another ho. held of the parish in Church End were assessed separately.
41 M.R.O., MR/TH/1, ff. 34v.–35.
42 B.L.H.L., Acc. 9131.
43 C 54/3341.
44 C 8/340/101; *Mdx. Monthly*, i. 14–15.
45 C 54/4716 m. 13.
46 J. R. Biggers, *Finchley and Neighbourhood* (1903), 14; M.R.O., MR/LV3/97.
47 M.R.O., Acc. 351/276.
48 B.L.H.L., Banks Colln. viii. 1003, 1021; plans of char. estates (1776) in Finchley ch.
49 Min. of Town and Country Planning, List of Bldgs. (1948); B.L.H.L., Banks Colln. viii. 1002; *N. & Q.* 12th ser. xii. 172–3.
50 B.L.H.L., Banks Colln. xii. 5034.
51 Ibid. 5048; plans of char. estates (1776); Rocque, *Map of Mdx.* (1754); C. R. Smith, *Finchley As It Was*, 17. See below, p. 99.
52 Rocque, *Map of Mdx.* (1754); B.L.H.L., Banks Colln. xii. 5034.
53 M.L.R. 1719/4/244; 1720/1/98–9.
54 M.R.O., Acc. 351/277; B.L.H.L., Banks Colln. x.
55 M.R.O., MR/LV3/97; MR/LV8/40.
56 M.L.R. 1765/3/15.
57 Finchley Soc. *Newsletter*, May 1974; B.L.H.L., Prints 9071.
58 B.L.H.L., Banks Colln. xi. 7043.

Londoners had been attracted to Finchley since the Middle Ages, to invest in land and also as residents. In 1625 a citizen moved there to avoid the plague[59] and there were many like Sir Thomas Harris who lived in Ballards Lane in 1775.[60] About the time of inclosure Finchley was described as small but respectable, with many detached buildings, and also as a straggling village.[61] There were many elms, especially around Nether Street, and weatherboarded cottages alternated with more substantial brick and stuccoed houses.[62]

The building of Regent's Park Road and the turnpiking of Ballards Lane in 1826 brought changes. In 1849 the land within the triangle formed by Hendon Lane, Regent's Park Road, and Gravel Hill was for sale in fourteen lots and within eleven years it was covered with buildings, mostly houses[63] but including the bizarre Christ's College with its tower, which thereafter dominated the skyline and dwarfed the church.[64] More land was offered in 1848 for the building of villas 'so much in request by merchants and professional gentlemen preferring a location distant from London, undisturbed by railway excitement'.[65]

During the 19th century some of the larger houses became private schools, accounting, with St. Mary's National school, for the 12 teachers living at Church End in 1841, more than half the total in the parish. There were also more servants, 24 men and 58 women, than in other districts, but only 33 agricultural labourers. A clergyman, a solicitor, and a stockbroker lived there, as did 5 farmers and the usual tradesmen.[66] By 1851 there were 162 houses and cottages in the district of St. Mary's, corresponding in the main with the old hamlet of Church End.[67] Ballards Lane, with 56 houses and 7 under construction, was the most populous area, while Church End itself, which probably included Regent's Park Road, had 33. Nether Street had 17 houses, including Elm Place, Sellars Hall, Brent Lodge, Long Lodge, and Courthouse Farm, and housed 2 fund-holders, 2 members of the stock exchange, and 2 solicitors. There were many other residents of independent means, especially in Ballards Lane, which also had two private schools. Tradesmen lived mainly in the centre of Church End.

Whetstone hamlet, recorded in 1398, grew up along the Great North Road, the north-eastern part being in Friern Barnet and the rest in Finchley. There was only a narrow band of arable between the road and Dollis brook, probably too little to support the houses which by *c.* 1677 stood close together on both sides of the road.[68] Some of Whetstone's inhabitants followed occupations based on the abundant woodland, as charcoal-burners, tanners, or sawyers. Others catered for travellers, as carters, stable-keepers, brewers, and innkeepers.

There were many inns.[69] The George, one of the ancient freehold tenements and so named by 1474, was still an inn in 1692 but had been demolished by 1761.[70] Other inns included the King's Arms (*c.* 1683–1728),[71] and the Mare or Black Horse, built on the waste by Robert Odell in 1655 and used as an inn by 1713; it had been converted into three houses by 1741 but one was still licensed in 1779.[72] The Windmill, a public house by 1723, may have occupied either the windmill built in the 17th century by Basings ponds west of the Great North Road or a near-by house.[73] It was called the Windmill and Fighting Cocks by 1751 and the Swan or Swan with Two Necks by 1765.[74] A second Swan, also called the Swan with Two Necks by 1790, existed by 1731 just north of the lane to which it gave its name.[75] The Bull and Butcher, licensed in 1765 and probably the Butcher and Conjuror which was licensed in 1731, stood north of the junction with Totteridge Lane.[76] Other public houses included the Cock in the Tree (before 1760) and, in Coleharbour, the White Horse (before 1790) and the Dog or Queen's Head (before 1794).[77]

Newly built tenements at Whetstone existed in 1489.[78] By 1614 21 people in Whetstone and Woodside paid poor-rate and in 1664 46 people in North End, Whetstone, and Woodside were assessed for hearth tax and another 36 were not charged.[79] A cottage stood in Totteridge Lane by 1651 and five cottages by 1763.[80] The Limes on the west side of the Great North Road, north of Totteridge Lane, was built by 1734, a brown-brick two-storeyed building with later additions.[81] There were houses at Woodside (*costa bosc'*) by 1365.[82] Woodside House, so named in 1699, may have been the medieval Runtings.[83] By 1754 houses along the edge of the common at Woodside formed a distinct hamlet.[84] On the Friern Barnet border three tenements called the Woodhouses existed by 1655.[85] One of them was called Wood House by 1754[86] and a mansion was built there between 1784 and 1798,[87] becoming the centre of an estate created at

59 *Mdx. Cnty. Rec.* iii. 16.
60 M.R.O., Acc. 351/276.
61 Brewer, *Beauties of Eng. & Wales,* x(5), 355; Hassell, *Rides and Walks*, i. 184.
62 e.g. cf. B.L.H.L., Prints 6500; Smith, *Finchley As It Was*, 7–8, 11.
63 B.L.H.L., S/C (Church End, 1849); B.L.H.L., Acc. 6109/3–9, 24, 27–28.
64 Smith, *Finchley As It Was*, 3–4.
65 B.L.H.L., S/C (Church End, 1848).
66 G. R. P. Lawrence, *Village Into Boro.* (1964), 27.
67 It also included the area east of Ballards Lane, embracing Fallow Corner, Colney Hatch Rd., and a small section of the Gt. North Rd., besides a few hos. at the west end of East End Rd.: H.O. 107/1701/136/3/2a ff. 388–413.
68 Ogilby, *Map of Mdx.* [*c.* 1677].
69 For inns on the east side of the road, see p. 10.
70 S.C. 2/189/2 m. 3; C 8/346/4; B.L.H.L., Banks Colln. vii. 1823.
71 M.R.O., Acc. 276/284; M.L.R. 1728/2/207.
72 B.L.H.L., Banks Colln. i. 2801; M.R.O., MR/LV9/86.
73 M.R.O., MR/LV3/97; Guildhall MSS. 10465/40; 111, p. 93; M.R.O., TA/FIN, no. 482. See p. 70.
74 M.R.O., MR/LV7/8; MR/LV8/40.
75 M.R.O., MR/LV6/4; MR/LV9/185; M.R.O., TA/FIN, no. 454.
76 M.R.O., MR/LV6/4; MR/LV8/40; M.R.O., TA/FIN, no. 411.
77 M.L.R. 1760/2/215; 1796/5/595; C 108/238.
78 S.C. 2/189/8 m. 3.
79 M.R.O., Acc. 351/150, f. 1; M.R.O., MR/TH/1, ff. 35d.–36.
80 St. Paul's MS. B 68; M.L.R. 1764/3/20–2.
81 Date on rainwater head: Finchley Soc. *Ann. Rep.* (1976); Min. of Town and Country Planning, List of Bldgs. (1948).
82 W.A.M. 4818.
83 C 54/4848/30; Guildhall MS. 9171/8, f. 66.
84 Rocque, *Map of Mdx.* (1754).
85 Prob. 11/253 (P.C.C. 91 Berkeley, will of Allen Brent).
86 Rocque, *Map of Mdx.* (1754).
87 The rateable value jumped from £26 to £50: B.L.H.L., Acc. 6140/1. The mansion was referred to in 1813: D. Hughson, *London: the Brit. Metropolis*, vi. 428.

inclosure.[88] The existing two-storeyed building, a school, is mid-19th-century and consists of a central portion of five bays with an Ionic portico and two wings, one dating from the 1920s.[89]

Whetstone had few large houses. Friern Watch, on the Friern Barnet border, is early-18th-century and from 1848 was the home of Ebenezer Homan, a local benefactor.[90] Joseph Baxendale, who described himself as deputy lieutenant, magistrate, and carrier,[91] had built Woodside House by 1841.[92] It was described in 1850 as a beautiful villa with a pretty conservatory, in a setting of lawns, groves, and a lake.[93] St. John's church was built at the southern end of the estate in 1832[94] and the Torrington Arms at the corner of the Great North Road and Lodge Lane by the late 1830s.[95] Most building in the 19th century as in earlier times was of cottages. Charles Jaques built 21 in Lodge Lane in 1824[96] and another 17 by 1847.[97] Richard Attfield built 10 cottages on former common land at Whetstone by 1825[98] and others stood at Woodside by 1824 and in Swan Lane by 1847.[99]

Paupers were probably always numerous at Whetstone, where the percentage of people not assessed for hearth tax in 1664 was much higher than in other districts.[1] Whetstone provided a typical case of witchcraft by *maleficium* in that of Agnes Miller, a widow who was acquitted of the charge in 1619: she and her husband had been maintained at Finchley's expense in Friern Barnet's alms-houses and she had later been condemned as a common scold.[2] Her alleged offence was of causing death by witchcraft, as was that of another Finchley widow and pauper, who received a monthly contribution from the parish in 1614 and was hanged in 1615.[3] The Great North Road brought beggars on their way to and from London, many of whom died of the plague at Whetstone during the late 16th and early 17th centuries.[4] Villagers threatened to fire on men journeying from London in the plague of 1665[5] and in 1754 they drove off a surveyor and his labourers with pitchforks.[6] In the late 18th and early 19th centuries Whetstone was a centre of dissent[7] but in the mid 19th century it was noted for drunkenness and brawling.[8]

Inhabitants in 1841 included 2 clergymen, 3 teachers, 4 solicitors, 2 surgeons, and some tradesmen and craftsmen. Of the 226 people with occupations stated, 100 were labourers and 39 were female servants.[9] There were 255 labourers by 1851, many of them lodgers in cottages that were probably overcrowded.[10]

Settlement along the roads at the exit from Hornsey park can be traced to the Middle Ages. John Manypeny, who left tenements by will dated 1349, probably gave his name to the house in *East End* called Manny Pennys in the 18th century.[11] Porters, which included a house by 1583, was named in 1440.[12] Knightons, a house on the south side of East End Road by 1598–9, took its name from a family recorded in 1406.[13] Good Robins at Parkgate, mentioned in 1577 and certainly a house by 1732,[14] was probably named from the Robin family of the 14th and 15th centuries.[15] Worthy House, on the north side of East End Road at Hunters Green, existed in 1530 and Worthy field was much older.[16] Redings was a tenement in East End by 1548 and part of the Onyon estates by 1718.[17] Robert Osborne lived in 1557 at a house which may be identifiable with the Park Gate, later Park Lodge, in Market Place which was the home of the Odells and Jordans.[18] East End House on the north side of East End Road, later part of John Bacon's estates, may have been a new tenement mentioned in 1579.[19] On the south side of the road Old House and Elm House, later Elmshurst, may have dated from the late 16th century and been extended in the 17th; a fire-place in Old House was dated 1649.[20]

Twenty-seven people at East End and Parkgate were assessed for the poor in 1614,[21] and 41 houses were assessed for hearth tax in 1664, when none except Bibbesworth manor-house was very large.[22] Growth continued during the 17th and 18th centuries. In 1686 Cromwell Hall, on the south side of East End Road and east of the existing houses, was conveyed to Thomas Pengelly (d. 1696), a Shoreditch merchant. Its name derived from the Lord Protector's son Richard Cromwell, Pengelly's friend, who was said to have lived there for most of his life after returning from exile.[23] Droving and especially the trade in pigs stimulated the growth of the hamlet, which spread unevenly along the edge of the common, at Cuckolds Haven (by

[88] Thos. Collins bought the allotments of Ld. Buckingham and Sir Wm. Curtis; see p. 68.
[89] See p. 96
[90] Finchley Soc. *Newsletter*, Jan. 1977.
[91] H.O. 107/1701/136/3/2a f. 351.
[92] M.R.O., TA/FIN.
[93] W. Keane, *Beauties of Mdx.* (1850), 58–60. See illus. in W. B. Passmore, 'Finchley Par. Rec.' (MS. *penes* Finchley chars.), i. 196.
[94] See p. 85.
[95] See p. 42.
[96] Finchley Soc. *Newsletter*, Jan 1977. Banks (Index 1 *sub* Lodge La.) dates them 1836.
[97] B.L.H.L., Church-rates (1840, 1847).
[98] M.R.O., Acc. 1050.
[99] M.R.O., Acc. 830/1; B.L.H.L., Acc. 6123/1.
[1] M.R.O., MR/TH/1, ff. 35d.–36.
[2] *Mdx. Cnty. Rec.* ii. 121, 143; *Mdx. Sess. Rec.* ii. 33.
[3] *Mdx. Cnty. Rec.* ii. 108; M.R.O., Acc. 351/150.
[4] Finchley par. regs.
[5] D. Defoe, *Jnl. of the Plague Yr.* ed. L. Landa, 123.
[6] C. G. Harper, *Gt. North Road* (1922), i. 73.
[7] See p. 87.
[8] *Finchley Common Cong. Ch. 1864*, *N. Finchley Cong. Ch. 1964* (pamphlet).
[9] Lawrence, *Village Into Boro.* 27. Whetstone approximated to dists. 6 and 7.
[10] H.O. 107/1701/136/3/2a ff. 339–87.
[11] *Cal. of Wills in Ct. of Husting*, i. 527; M.R.O., Acc. 351/277.
[12] S.C. 2/188/73 m. 1d.; B.L.H.L., Banks Colln. ix. 4385.
[13] St. Paul's MS. A 62; C 2/Jas. I/S22/4.
[14] Guildhall MS. 10312/92; M.L.R. 1732/1/224–5.
[15] e.g. W.A.M. 4818; C 1/41/4; S.C. 2/188/66 m. 5.
[16] Guildhall MS. 9171/10, f. 155; M.R.O., Acc. 1140; S.C. 2/188/71 m. 2d.
[17] Consistory Ct. of Lond., Wymesley p. 14 (will of Geo. Burte); M.L.R. 1718/2/185–6.
[18] Guildhall MS. 9171/14, ff. 23v.–24v.; ibid. 12408; B.L.H.L., Banks Colln., biog. Jordan.
[19] B.L.H.L., Banks Colln. ix. 4321–4.
[20] *Finchley Press*, 23 Oct. 1953; B.L.H.L., Acc. 6787/7.
[21] M.R.O., Acc. 350/150, f. 1.
[22] M.R.O., MR/TH/1, f. 34v. Hos. not chargeable were listed with those in Church End.
[23] B.L.H.L., Banks Colln. ix. 4385. Cromwell as Mr. Clark lived at the Pengelly ho. in Cheshunt (Herts.), not in Finchley. Mrs. Pengelly sold the Finchley ho. in 1702: B.L. Add. MS. 32456; Hist. MSS. Com. 6, *7th Rep.*, *Webb*, p. 681.

c. 1677)[24] and the Hogmarket (by 1709). Several cottages were built on the waste at Bush Causey at the eastern end of East End Road in 1716 and two at the Bull Lane end of Long Lane in 1726. The latter, which had become five cottages, were conveyed in 1776 to a bricklayer, who presumably was to carry out more building.[25] Prospect House was built in 1721[26] and Oak Lodge in Oak Lane existed as three tenements in 1749, united by 1766 and probably rebuilt by 1780.[27]

Many inns appeared during the 18th century:[28] the George in the Hogmarket (from 1716), the Flower de Lis, later the Dirthouse, and White Lion on the west side of the Great North Road at Newgate Lane (1716 to *c.* 1902),[29] the Hog Driver, later the Sow and Pigs (1716–1800), the Bell at Parkgate (1722–65),[30] the Three Horseshoes in the Hogmarket (1722–79), the Five Bells in East End Road (from 1751),[31] and the Bald-faced Stag, licensed from 1790 but probably an inn from 1738.[32] The Spaniards inn, on the Hampstead boundary, was licensed to Francis Porero, the eponymous Spaniard, in 1721.[33] It stood at the south-west exit from Hornsey park, where a gate was marked in 1754 but where there is no evidence of a toll-lodge.[34] The building itself may be 17th-century, although it has been extensively altered and refaced.[35] It was there that the mob at the time of the Gordon Riots in 1780 was halted on its way to destroy Lord Mansfield's house at Kenwood.[36] Set on wooded heights, the inn attracted excursions from London; a visit to its tea-gardens was described by Dickens in the *Pickwick Papers*.[37]

A view of East End at the Bald-faced Stag in 1812 shows mainly open country.[38] Building, however, had begun near by on the east side of the Great North Road. High Reding, sold by the bishop in 1800, was leased to a builder, and by 1809 four villas stood on the south side of Fortis Green Road, then called Park Place. In 1822 nos. 3 and 4 were joined as Park Hall.[39] Anthony Salvin had designed two Italianate villas in Fortis Green Road by 1838.[40] Belle Vue was built west of Cromwell Hall by 1802[41] and Verandah House or Bow-Window House, later the home of the Grisewood family, horsedealers and saddlers, in Park Road in 1803.[42] Many houses, including the Old House, East End House, and Elmshurst, were rebuilt.[43] The 'innumerable' villas along East End Road were a feature of the parish in 1817[44] and were occupied in the 1830s by men like T. B. Herring, a 'rich retired tradesman', Salvin, and the Rews and the Butlers of Cromwell Hall.[45]

East End itself was a poor area, appalling near-by middle-class residents with its drunkards, 'godless persons', and general lack of moral restraint.[46] Prospect Place linked the Hogmarket to East End Road from 1825 and cottages had been built along it by 1841; there were 20 by 1869.[47] Ten cottages were built on an allotment near the White Lion between 1824 and 1844 and another four in 1846.[48] Many terraces sprawled haphazardly over former common land. New roads included Chapel Street, from 1853,[49] and Holy Trinity church and school were built to serve the growing community.[50] The cottages in the Hogmarket, Chapel Row, and Red Lion Hill in 1851 housed tradesmen, craftsmen, and many labourers.[51] In 1860 Finchley's increase in population was said to be concentrated in North End and East End, with East End as the most populous part.[52]

There was a marlpit at the *North End* of Ballards Lane by 1398, on which a house had been built by 1548.[53] Moss Hall fronted the more northerly of the two east–west portions of Nether Street by 1754[54] and was later owned by Thomas Harrison Andrew (d. 1824).[55] Its name may have come from the Mosse family, one of whom received land in 1463 on condition that he built a mansion house there.[56]

Other houses included Courthouse (later Court House) or Coathouse at the north-west corner of Nether Street, the seat of the Peacocks which was assessed for fourteen hearths in 1664.[57] To the north stood Finchley Lodge or Lodge House, built by 1667 on the edge of the common whence it was later reached by Lodge Lane.[58] It may be identifiable with Pigensland, a cottage built on the waste in 1564.[59] Two-Chimney House near Finchley Lodge existed by 1794 and probably by 1754.[60]

Fallow or Follow Corner was a locality on the edge of the common east of Ballards Lane, between North End and East End, by 1429.[61] At least one

24 J. Ogilby, *Map of Mdx.* [*c.* 1677].
25 M.R.O., Acc. 351/276–7.
26 B.L.H.L., Banks Colln., Index 1.
27 Finchley Soc. *Newsletter*, Sept. 1974.
28 Except where otherwise stated, the para. is based on M.R.O., MR/LV3/3 (1716); MR/LV3/97 (1722); MR/LV6/4 (1731); MR/LV7/8 (1751); MR/LV8/40 (1765); MR/LV9/86 (1779); MR/LV9/185 (1790); MR/LV10/87 (1800); MR/LV20/2 (1820).
29 Smith, *Finchley As It Was*, 29.
30 Described in 1774 as formerly three messuages: M.L.R. 1774/1/341.
31 See Smith, *Finchley As It Was*, 27.
32 B.L.H.L., Banks Colln. xxxvi.
33 M.R.O., MR/LV3/93.
34 M.R.O., Hist. Notes 3/1/61; Rocque, *Map of Mdx.* (1754).
35 Hist. Mon. Com. *Mdx.* 27.
36 Biggers, *Finchley*, 47.
37 A. L. Hayward, *Dickens Encyclopaedia* (1969), 146.
38 Potter Colln. 28/8.
39 M.R.O., Acc. 262/4/58–9; B.L.H.L., Banks Colln. iii. 5070.
40 Ex inf. Dr. Jill Allibone.
41 B.L.H.L., S/C (Belle Vue 1902).
42 B.L.H.L., Banks Colln., biog. Grisewood.
43 Min. of Town and Country Planning, List of Bldgs. (1948); B.L.H.L., Acc. 6787/7.
44 Hassell, *Rides and Walks*, i. 184.
45 B.L.H.L., Acc. 6787/7.
46 Ibid.
47 M.R.O., Acc. 262/4/39–40; B.L.H.L., Acc. 6416/32; M.R.O., TA/FIN; B.L.H.L., P.A.F. 3/3.
48 Guildhall MS. 10465/159, pp. 145–6; B.L.H.L., P.A.F. 1/7.
49 M.R.O., MJ/SR 4701/81; 4921/80; 4930/89a; B.L.H.L., P.A.F. 1/8 (1858).
50 See pp. 85, 94.
51 H.O. 107/1701/136/3/2a ff. 414–64.
52 B.L.H.L., P.A.F. 1/8.
53 S.C. 2/188/67 m. 12; Guildhall MS. 10312/66; Consistory Ct. of Lond., Wymesley, p. 14 (will of Geo. Burte).
54 Rocque, *Map of Mdx.* (1754). The later Moss Hall had a different site: M.R.O., Acc. 262/4/4–5.
55 B.L.H.L., Banks Colln. v. 3316.
56 Guildhall MS. 10312/76.
57 See p. 61.
58 B.L.H.L., Banks Colln. v. 3357 (18th-cent. letter by vestry clerk).
59 S.C. 2/191/8; B.L.H.L., Banks Colln. v. 3354.
60 M.R.O., Acc. 830/1. See Rocque, *Map of Mdx.* (1754).
61 S.C. 2/188/70 m. 1d.
62 C 10/173/71; Rocque, *Map of Mdx.* (1754).

house stood there by the mid 17th century and there were three or four by 1754.[62] The chief property was Fallow or Cobley's farm, part of the Peacock estates, at whose farm-house Charles Dickens was said to have written *Martin Chuzzlewit* in 1843.[63] The cottage leased to the clown Joseph Grimaldi (d. 1837) from 1806 to *c.* 1815 has been identified as Fallow Cottage; Grimaldi chose it for the country air and used to drive there after his performances in London.[64]

Inclosure and the new turnpike road brought some changes to North End. Tally Ho Corner, the junction between the new road and the Great North Road, acted as a staging post on the route from London to the north; stabling for sixteen horses was provided in expectation of increased traffic but proved an 'unfortunate speculation' and was abandoned in 1837.[65] Orchard House had been built there by 1841 and a few cottages had been added at the northern part of Ballards Lane and at Fallow Corner by 1851.[66] North End had not yet, however, become known as North Finchley.

The size of *Finchley Common* was estimated at anything between 500 a. and 1,600 a.[67] but at inclosure in 1816 it consisted of some 900 a.[68] Until Hornsey park was fenced off in the 13th century, Finchley wood was indistinguishable from the demesne woods and the division between the two long remained confused.

Herbage rights existed in Finchley wood by 1410[69] and in 1504 it was described as 'a common called Finchley wood'.[70] Felling and removing timber, however, was forbidden as on the demesne estates.[71] During the 16th century there was a direct conflict between the pasture rights of the inhabitants and the timber rights of the lord. In 1533 Finchley men asserted their traditional right to 'cooltes' for swine in Finchley wood, which they said had been destroyed by the bishop's woodward, who had also taken away their hedging bills.[72] In 1562 they defended their claim to common of pasture 'from time immemorial' against the lord's proposal to divide and separate a quarter of his woods.[73] Judgement was given for the bishop, in accordance with the Act of 1543 for the preservation of woods.[74] Possibly Great Colefall (later Coldfall) was the quarter so inclosed: when it was leased in 1645 with the other demesne woods it was called 'the wood in Finchley common'.[75] The inhabitants of Hornsey were within their rights under the Act of 1543 in claiming common within Great Coldfall, but it was treated as demesne rather than common in 1815.[76]

Conflict also arose during the 16th century between the parishes bordering the common. In the mid 16th century the right of tenants from Friern Barnet to intercommon was refused, Robert Sanny and others being amerced for pasturing sheep.[77] Presentments of Friern Barnet people were frequent in the early 17th century[78] and fines of £5 and £10 were respectively imposed in 1648 and 1650.[79] The two parishes went to court in the 1690s and, although the outcome is not known, presentments of Friern Barnet tenants ceased after that time.[80] The inclosure award of 1816, largely instigated by John Bacon of Friern Barnet, did not allot any of the common to Friern Barnet parish but made allotments to copyholders of Friern Barnet manor and a large one to Bacon himself.[81]

A survey of 1647 upheld the joint rights of the freeholders, copyholders, and leaseholders of Finchley and Hornsey to all commons and wastes within their two parishes.[82] An incloser of waste at Muswell Hill in 1671 was ordered by the Finchley court to open it because Finchley tenants had rights there.[83] A Hornsey man was presented in 1688 for sheep on Finchley common but his offence lay in overstocking and not, as in the case of Friern Barnet offenders, in merely keeping animals there.[84] At inclosure, however, none of Finchley common, except Great Coldfall, was allotted to Hornsey men, probably because their parish lacked an advocate like John Bacon.

Timber from Finchley wood was sold by the bishop during the 15th and 16th centuries[85] and the keepers of the woods complained in 1545, when timber was taken for the Tower of London, Westminster Palace, and the new ordnance house.[86] In 1645 the bishop reserved all timber in the woods and on Finchley common, when leasing out coppices and springs in Finchley and Hornsey.[87] In 1647 there was a great store of oak and hornbeam on the common worth £230, compared with trees worth £650 in the demesne woods.[88] Cutting or selling wood in Finchley wood was forbidden in 1604[89] and there were presentments for taking wood in 1609, 1615, 1616, 1623, 1652, and 1655.[90] During that period the wood came to be called Finchley common, an area of furze dotted with trees. There were still several thousand hornbeam and oak pollards in 1798 but they were being grubbed up and not replaced.[91]

63 H. Whiddon, *One Hundred Yrs. of Playing the Game* (Hillside Publishing Co.), 54; Hayward, *Dickens Encyclopaedia*, 62. See below, p. 61.

64 *Memoirs of Jos. Grimaldi*, ed. Boz (1838), ii. 39–40; *Memoirs of Jos. Grimaldi by Chas. Dickens*, ed. R. Findlater (1968), 187; B.L.H.L., Banks Colln. xvi (land tax 1815). Cf. Potter Colln. 28/11.

65 Guildhall MS. 12418.

66 M.R.O., TA/FIN; H.O. 107/1701/136/3/2a ff. 400, 406–8.

67 e.g. 500–600 a. (1647): Guildhall MS. 10464A, p. 85; 600 a. (1801): H.O. 67/16; 1,010 a. (1795): Lysons, *Environs*, ii. 335–43; 1,240 a. (1798): Middleton, *View*, 98; 1,600 a. (1717): *T.L.M.A.S.* xix. 48.

68 M.R.O., EA/FIN.

69 S.C. 2/188/68 m. 8d.

70 C.P. 40/970 carte rot. 1d.

71 S.C. 2/188/68 m. 8d.; S.C. 2/189/10 m. 2d.

72 *L. & P. Hen. VIII*, vi, p. 129.

73 M.R.O., MJ/SR 113/21.

74 35 Hen. VIII, c. 17.

75 Guildhall MS. 12395.

76 Ibid. 12418. See p. 154.

77 S.C. 6/Ph. & Mary/193 m. 13; S.C. 6/Eliz./1458–9.

78 S.C. 2/191/4; S.C. 2/191/7; S.C. 2/191/11; S.C. 2/191/12.

79 St. Paul's MS. B 68.

80 M.R.O., D.R.O. 12/1/C1/1.

81 M.R.O., EA/FIN. Bacon's land in Finchley did not justify his large allotment.

82 Guildhall MS. 10464A, p. 115.

83 St. Paul's MS. B 70.

84 Guildhall MS. 10464/3.

85 S.C. 6/1138/17; S.C. 6/1140/24 m. 4d.

86 *L. & P. Hen. VIII*, xx(1), p. 430; *Acts of P.C.* 1542–7, p. 178.

87 Guildhall MS. 12395.

88 Ibid. 10464A, pp. 85, 109.

89 S.C. 2/191/4.

90 Guildhall MS. 10312/22, m. 4; S.C. 2/191/6; S.C. 2/191/7; S.C. 2/191/12.

91 Middleton, *View*, 100.

The woodland cover was reduced by animals, who grazed in increasing numbers from the 16th century. Two people were presented for fattening pigs in 1632[92] and three in 1705.[93] A pigcot was among unauthorized buildings in 1716.[94] Cattle were grazed in 1650[95] but most 17th-century presentments were for sheep, kept in excessive numbers or by people who had no rights in Finchley.[96] In addition to the many offenders from Friern Barnet, there was one in 1626 from Kentish Town.[97] Finchley men also pastured outsiders' animals and in 1604 servants and others who did not pay scot and lot within the parish were reminded that they had no right of common.[98]

Regulations were issued in 1657, 1665, and, in more detail, in 1672, requiring that animals being driven to London should not stray from the road.[99] From 1664 only householders could keep cattle on the common.[1] There were pounds for north and for east Finchley, one being mentioned in 1652 when a man sawed through the rails to rescue his sheep.[2] The pound in North End needed repair in 1685[3] and both pounds were dilapidated in 1826 when the one at the northernmost point of the common, in Whetstone, needed complete rebuilding.[4] The southern pound seems to have been on Bibbesworth land; between Long Lane and the Manor House in 1815, it was moved in 1880 by H. C. Stephens of Avenue House.[5] Haywards were appointed at the manor court in 1662. Initially one each for North End and East End, they were increased to four in 1665, when they were to receive half of the fine imposed on drovers who did not keep to the roads.[6] By 1680, however, haywards were no longer appointed[7] and it was not until 1786 that a common driver was elected at the manor court, with a salary paid by the vestry from 1793 to 1798.[8] A driver was again appointed in 1802, whereupon the Bibbesworth court felt that its own rights might be threatened.[9] At first the office of common driver was combined with other parish duties but from 1804 a driver was elected at the bishop's manor court and paid by the vestry.[10]

In the late 18th century the larger landowners feared that their animals might suffer from contact with inferior beasts on the common. In 1798 the common was 'much poached by cattle' and supported a large stock, mostly of sheep, until after the hay harvest.[11] In 1801 the rector complained of bad sheep and unprofitable ponies.[12] The vestry tried to enforce the regulations, threatening landless people who pastured animals or anyone who surcharged the common.[13] Fines on all straying hogs and cattle and double fines on all belonging to outsiders were ordered in 1816.[14] A second driver was appointed in 1818 and two drivers were still being elected by the manor court in 1824; their salaries, however, were discontinued in 1820 and elections had ceased by 1834.[15] After inclosure straying animals continued to be impounded.[16]

Removal of bushes and furze was a frequent offence, especially during the 17th century by Friern Barnet men.[17] The manor court forbade cutting of bushes or young trees in 1604, carting away of furze in 1664, and cutting of furze between September and May and fern between April and the end of August in 1672.[18] Fines were imposed, the orders were repeated in 1673 and 1682,[19] sales to 'outtownsmen' were added to the amerciable offences in 1683, and penalties were increased in 1691.[20] Fines persisted in the mid 18th century, although offences were not then so frequent.[21]

Turf, leaf-mould, loam, sand, and gravel were also taken. When the sea-coal trade was disrupted by the Scots in 1640, turf from Finchley common was used by Londoners.[22] In 1680 the manor court allowed the inhabitants of Finchley to make ditches on the common and carry away the compost, provided that the ditches were 5 ft. wide.[23] Generally the court disapproved of anything being removed, particularly if it was sent outside the parish. The taking of gravel from the parish incurred fines in 1683[24] and as many as 80 loads were dug in 1652 and 50 in 1721,[25] whereupon the bishop successfully prosecuted one man for removing 'several thousand' loads.[26] Fines were also imposed for removing turf, mould, and compost and in 1751 were paid by ten offenders.[27] The homagers and vestry were probably less concerned to preserve the topsoil than to profit from it: in 1771 an East Barnet man paid to take 150 loads of sand from near the Three Horseshoes.[28]

'One or two' cottages had been built on the common by 1647,[29] three more in 1651, nine in 1652, and 25 cottages and barns in 1655.[30] A carpenter from East Barnet had built a cottage on the waste

92 S.C. 2/191/9.
93 Guildhall MS. 10465/20.
94 M.R.O., Acc. 351/271. Cf. swine 'cooltes' of 1533, above.
95 St. Paul's MS. B 68.
96 S.C. 2/191/4; S.C. 2/191/5; S.C. 2/191/7; S.C. 2/191/10; S.C. 2/191/12.
97 S.C. 2/191/8.
98 S.C. 2/191/4.
99 S.C. 2/191/12; Guildhall MSS. 10312/101, m. 14; 107.
1 Guildhall MS. 10312/100, m. 13.
2 S.C. 2/191/12.
3 Guildhall MS. 10832/3.
4 Guildhall MSS. 10245, pp. 49–50; 12416; M.L.R. 1844/8/641. It was disused by 1888: Finchley local bd., min. bk. vii. 52.
5 B.L.H.L., P.A.F. 3/1; Finchley local bd., min. bk. ii. 21.
6 Guildhall MSS. 10312/98, m. 16; 100, m. 13; 101, m. 14.
7 Ibid. 115.
8 Ibid. 10465/101, p. 123; B.L.H.L., P.A.F. 1/2, 3.
9 M.R.O., Acc. 351/276.
10 B.L.H.L., P.A.F. 1/3.
11 Middleton, *View*, 100.
12 H.O. 67/16.
13 B.L.H.L., P.A.F. 1/3.
14 Ibid. 1/5.
15 Ibid.; Guildhall MSS. 10465/139, p. 306; 149, p. 179.
16 B.L.H.L., P.A.F. 1/7.
17 S.C. 2/191/4; S.C. 2/191/5; S.C. 2/191/6; St. Paul's MS. B 68; Guildhall MS. 10312/111.
18 S.C. 2/191/4; Guildhall MSS. 10312/100, m. 13; 107.
19 Guildhall MSS. 10312/108, 117.
20 Ibid. 10465/1, 6.
21 e.g. in 1725: Guildhall MS. 10465/40; in 1754: ibid. 69, p. 87.
22 Robbins, *Mdx*. 52.
23 Guildhall MS. 10312/115; a marginal note added that such permission ought not to have been recorded.
24 Ibid. 10465/1.
25 S.C. 2/191/12; S.C. 2/191/16.
26 Cutting in B.L.H.L., Banks Colln., Finchley common file.
27 Guildhall MS. 10465/66, p. 213. And see ibid. 42 (1727), 62 (1747).
28 B.L.H.L., P.A.F. 1/1.
29 Guildhall MS. 10464A, p. 85. One had been built in 1635: S.C. 2/191/7.
30 St. Paul's MS. B 68; S.C. 2/191/12.

Highgate: no. 28 Wood Lane

Finchley: no. 1 St. Mary's Avenue

Finchley: Glenroy, Seymour Road

SUBURBAN HOUSES

Finchley: St. Mary's Church in 1798

Finchley: St. Mary's Church in 1979

Friern Barnet: All Saints' Church, Oakleigh Park

at night in 1668.[31] Encroachments were very often presented at both the bishop's and Bibbesworth manor courts during the 18th century, but in most cases only a little land was taken, from the edge of the common. Squatting was less frequent, although gypsies were driven off in 1797.[32]

Cleared of its woodland cover, the common was ideal for the massing of troops. An old man *c.* 1678 predicted that the English and French would fight on Finchley common,[33] which figured in most national emergencies. General Monck drew up his army there at the Restoration in 1660, there were encampments of *c.* 5,000 soldiers during the Jacobite alarm in 1745,[34] and of several regiments after the Gordon Riots in 1780.[35] Military reviews and manoeuvres were also held, since wide ditches and other obstacles offered an excellent training ground, with 'every difficulty that can possibly be met with to impede the progress of an army'.[36] Duels[37] and, in the 1730s, horse-races also took place. Shuttlecock was played between gentlemen of the western and northern counties in 1766, and there was a pigeon-shooting match in 1809.[38]

The common's main claim to fame was as a haunt of highwaymen. It featured in literature from *Tom Jones* to Lord Lytton's *Paul Clifford* and in the mostly fabulous exploits of Jack Sheppard and Dick Turpin. Sheppard was captured in 1724 at a farm-house and brought to an alehouse on the common which may have been the George at the Hog-market or the Hog Driver.[39] Turpin's oak, which was supposed to have sheltered Turpin, gave its name to Oak Lane. Coach drivers used to shoot at it to deter any robber but there is no evidence to connect Turpin himself with Finchley.[40]

A Londoner was robbed in Finchley wood in 1468,[41] and there was a highway robbery in Finchley in 1572 and a murder in Colefall in 1599.[42] Whetstone people were involved in theft or robberies in 1613, 1614, and 1616.[43] A gentleman of Finchley robbed a man on the highway in 1673[44] and nineteen drovers were robbed by one man between London and Barnet in 1686.[45] Crimes became more blatant during the 18th century: in 1725 one highwayman sued another for cheating him of his share of the spoils from their partnership on Finchley common and elsewhere.[46] Several robberies were the work of armed footpads, as in 1762,[47] but more were committed by horsemen.[48] Lady Ann Irwin had a narrow escape on the common in 1730, both the York coach 40 yards ahead and the stage coach 100 yards behind having been robbed.[49] One highwayman held up seven coaches in 10 minutes,[50] Scots M.P.s journeyed by sea rather than risk the road across Finchley common,[51] and Sir Gilbert Elliot in 1790 would not trust his throat there in the dark.[52] Assailants themselves were sometimes killed[53] and there were many indictments in the 1780s all for robbery on the common.[54] Gibbets included one near the 6-mile stone at the southern edge of the common, where crowds in 1772 saw two men hanged in chains[55] and in 1789 the parish officers were paid to attend an execution.[56] Mounted patrols set up in 1805 to police the major roads around London reduced the robberies and by 1807 the highwaymen were already a legend.[57] The end, for highway robbery as for so many activities associated with the common, came with inclosure in 1816.[58]

The only settlement away from the edges of the common was at Brownswell beside the Great North Road, where a well had been 'late re-edified' for travellers in 1593.[59] By 1718 it contained a newly repaired conduit[60] and during the 18th century it was maintained by the charity estates.[61] A cottage stood there by 1623 and the Huntsman, by 1731 called the Green Man, by 1718.[62] In 1754 there were some three buildings at Brownswell.[63]

Meadow land fronting the common was advertised in 1796 as a delightful situation for building.[64] A lease of land on the common was granted in 1805, for the building of substantial brick cottages.[65] By 1814 a few buildings stood on the west side of the Great North Road, north of the Green Man, and a few more on

[31] M.R.O., S. R. Dowdell, p. 82.
[32] B.L.H.L., P.A.F. 1/3.
[33] *Cal. S.P. Dom.* 1678, pp. 613–14.
[34] *V.C.H. Mdx.* ii. 54; Hist. MSS. Com. 4, *5th Rep., Field*, p. 401; ibid. 20, *11th Rep. V*, p. 329.
[35] M.R.O., Acc. 262/4/44. Over 100 victims of dysentery from the camp were buried at Finchley: *Mdx. & Herts. N. & Q.* iii. 203. Firearms dug up near by may date from that event: *Mdx. Monthly*, i (Mar. 1953), 14–15.
[36] Cutting of 1804 in B.L.H.L., Banks Colln., Finchley common file. See also *Lond. Daily Advertiser*, 8 Nov. 1751; *Brit. Chron.* 15–18 Oct. 1762 (cuttings in B.L.H.L., Banks Colln. vi. 7043).
[37] John, Ld. Bourke of Connell, was said to have been killed there in 1592 (Potter Colln. 28/45), although he died on Hounslow Heath: *Complete Peerage*, ii. 255.
[38] Cuttings of 1736, 1738, and 1766 in B.L.H.L., Banks Colln., Finchley common file; Potter Colln. 28/45.
[39] [Daniel Defoe], *Hist. of Remarkable Life of John Sheppard* (1724) in H. Bleackley, *Jack Sheppard* (1933), 147; M.R.O., MR/LV3/97.
[40] The Finchley tradition is considered fabulous in *D.N.B.*; B.L.H.L., Acc. 6787/7. Pistol balls were later extracted from the tree: E. Walford, *Gtr. Lond.* [1882], i. 341.
[41] C 88/159 no. 32; *Cal. Pat.* 1467–77, 50, 331.
[42] *Cal. Pat.* 1569–72, 372; *Mdx. Cnty. Rec.* i. 253.
[43] *Mdx. Cnty. Rec.* i. 261; ii. 162; *Mdx. Sess. Rec.* i. 58; ii. 160, 248; iii. 133, 304.
[44] *Mdx. Cnty. Rec.* iv. 38.
[45] A. Smith, *Hist. of Lives and Robberies of Highwaymen* (1719), ii. 169.
[46] *Gent. Mag.* lxxxii (1), 610–14.
[47] *Lond. Daily Advertiser*, 12 Dec. 1751; *Brit. Chron.* 15–18 Oct. 1762 (cuttings in B.L.H.L., Banks Colln. vi. 7043); *The Observer*, 17 Nov. 1805 (cutting in ibid., note bk. no. 3, p. 47).
[48] *Fog's Jnl.* no. 22, Feb. 1729; no. 58, 1 Nov. 1729 (cuttings in B.L.H.L., Acc. 10111).
[49] Hist. MSS. Com. 42, *15th Rep. VI*, pp. 72, 93; *Fog's Jnl.* no. 83, 25 Apr. 1730 (cutting in B.L.H.L., Acc. 10111).
[50] Undated cutting in B.L.H.L., Banks Colln., Finchley common file.
[51] Walford, *Gtr. Lond.* i. 336.
[52] Quoted in ibid. i. 341.
[53] Biggers, *Finchley*, 34; *European Mag.* Feb. 1797 in Potter Colln. 28/45.
[54] M.R.O., OB/SP 1783 Dec. /32; 1786 Aug. /30, /62; 1787 Oct. /49; 1789 /Dec. 83; M.R.O., Hist. Notes 9/5/61.
[55] See 1760, 1772 cuttings in B.L.H.L., Banks Colln., Finchley common file; Biggers, *Finchley*, 34.
[56] B.L.H.L., P.A.F. 1/2.
[57] *Ambulator*, 10th edn. (1807); 11th edn. (1811); 12th edn. (1820).
[58] For the common after inclosure, see pp. 36, 68.
[59] Norden, *Spec. Brit.* 16.
[60] *T.L.M.A.S.* xix. 48.
[61] Passmore, 'Finchley Par. Rec.' i, p. 45 (1762); *Mdx. & Herts. N. & Q.* iii. 65.
[62] S.C. 2/191/7; Guildhall MS. 10465/55; M.R.O., MR/LV3/97; MR/LV6/4.
[63] Rocque, *Map of Mdx.* (1754).
[64] C 108/238.
[65] B.L.H.L., Acc. 6416/26.

the east side, nearer East End.[66] Inclosure did not lead to a sudden spread of building. Some houses were built at Strawberry Vale east of the road near Brownswell by James Frost, who acquired an estate there in 1816,[67] and by 1851 villas and cottages were dotted on either side of the Great North Road between East End and North End.[68]

The parish had 118 chargeable and 84 non-chargeable houses in 1664[69] and was estimated to have 170 houses in 1717 and 250 in 1795.[70] There were 256 inhabited and 25 uninhabited houses in 1801. Fewer houses were recorded in 1811, when the census was apparently defective, and in 1821 the numbers were 359 and 11 respectively. Thereafter they rose steadily, to 540 and 49 in 1831, 640 and 41 in 1841, and 755 and 49 in 1851.[71]

There were 280 communicants in 1547.[72] Ninety-three ratepayers contributed to 20 poor people in 1614[73] and 244 adult males took the protestation oath in 1641.[74] The population, estimated in 1717 as 400,[75] had reached 1,503 by 1801, 3,210 by 1831, and 4,120 by 1851.[76]

GROWTH FROM THE MID 19TH CENTURY. Until the mid 19th century building took place in old settlements along existing roads. Thereafter, especially following the arrival of the railway, whole estates were sold for speculative building and growth accelerated. The number of houses rose from 991 in 1861 to 1,884 in 1881, 3,132 in 1891, 4,366 in 1901, and 7,622 in 1911. By 1911 there were also 240 flats and 379 inhabited shops.[77]

At Church End one of the earliest estates to result from the opening of a railway station in 1867 was Wentworth, adjoining Wentworth Lodge in Ballards Lane, where the Conservative Land Society offered building lots in 1868.[78] Lichfield Grove near the station was built on former Bibbesworth land in 1869.[79]

North End, increasingly called North Finchley, and Woodside were the areas which grew most rapidly until 1914, stimulated by the opening of Woodside Park station in 1872 and the introduction of trams in 1905.[80] Cottages fronting Ballards Lane were built on parts of Fallow Lodge estate by 1871 and large houses planned for the rest in 1872, although few were built until the next century.[81] In 1874 Christ Church parish in northern Finchley contained 350 households, most of them too poor to subscribe to the National Society.[82] Building near by, however, was increasingly for the middle class, which gave the church valuable support.[83] By 1905 North Finchley was said to be covered with pretty, well-built villas.[84]

Among estates in the centre of the parish was that of Fallow farm, 80 a. between Ballards, Long, Squires, and Bow lanes, where houses in 1878 included Saxonhurst (formerly Sussex Lodge), Fairlea, and Etchingham Lodge. In 1880 part of the estate was leased to Frederick Wheeler to build substantial brick houses facing Ballards Lane and Etchingham Park Road. Thirty-four acres had been let by 1886, when the rest was offered as building land.[85] Most of it was not built on by 1897[86] but by 1904 five-bedroom leasehold houses overlooking Victoria recreation ground were advertised as in one of London's most charming suburbs, with a rural setting and good transport services.[87] Large semi-detached houses were designed by C. J. G. Pawley in Seymour Road and Etchingham Park Road, and most of the land between Squires Lane and Bow Lane had been built on by 1907.[88] Finchley U.D.C. built 60 cottages in Squires Lane in 1902.[89] North of Etchingham Park the possible introduction of electric trams led to building on the Fallow Corner estate, formerly Ballards Reding. The Wimbush family's house and 12 a. were offered for sale in 1901 and part had been built on by 1902, when the rest was divided into 126 freehold plots, most of which had been built on by 1908.[90] Fallow Lodge or Holdenhurst at Fallow Corner was sold in 1904 with 13 a., 101 plots were laid out in 1905, and building was finished before 1920.[91] To the east the county school was built in 1903 and the cottage hospital in 1908.[92]

North-west of Ballards Lane the Moss Hall estate, which had been unsuccessfully offered for sale in 1830, was laid out from 1867, mostly for middle-class housing, as in Moss Hall Crescent.[93] To the north building leases of Dale Grove and Hutton Grove were granted from 1873.[94] Torrington Park, part of Henry Holden's Friern Park estate lying east of the Great North Road, was already being built up by 1872, when his land on the western boundary of the parish was misleadingly advertised as 'Torrington Park', a freehold building estate.[95] Most of the same estate (34 a.) was offered again in 1900 after Holden's death, by which time most of his land east of Holden Road had been built up.[96] 'Artistic villas' were under construction in Westbury Road to the south in 1910[97] and land in Woodside Avenue was offered for good-class housing in 1914.[98] St. Alban's

[66] M.R.O., EA/FIN.
[67] See p. 71.
[68] H.O. 107/1701/136/3/2a ff. 408–9, 434–7.
[69] M.R.O., MR/TH/1, ff. 34d.–36.
[70] *T.L.M.A.S.* xix. 48; Lysons, *Environs*, ii. 341.
[71] *Census*, 1801–51.
[72] E 301/34 no. 157.
[73] M.R.O., Acc. 351/150, ff. 1–4.
[74] H.L., Mdx. Protestation Returns.
[75] Probably an underestimate: *T.L.M.A.S.* xix. 48.
[76] *Census*, 1801–51.
[77] *Census*, 1861–1911.
[78] B.L.H.L., S/C (Wentworth estate); B.L.H.L., P.A.F. 1/9.
[79] B.L.H.L., S/C (The Laurels, 1913).
[80] See p. 42.
[81] B.L.H.L., Acc. 9838; B.L.H.L., P.A.F. 3/3.
[82] Nat. Soc. files.
[83] *Christ Ch. Centenary Celebrations, 1867–1967* (pamphlet).
[84] Potter Colln. 28/66.
[85] M.R.O., Acc. 1077; B.L.H.L., S/C (Etchingham Pk. estate).
[86] O.S. Map 6″, Mdx. XI. NE. (1897 edn.).
[87] Potter Colln. 28/66.
[88] B.L.H.L., S/C (Etchingham Pk. estate).
[89] *Finchley Press*, 6 Oct. 1933.
[90] B.L.H.L., S/C (Fallow Corner estate, 1901, 1902, 1903).
[91] Ibid. (Fallow Lodge, 1904; Holdenhurst, 1905); O.S. Map 6″, Mdx. XI. NE. (1920).
[92] See pp. 80, 96.
[93] B.L.H.L., S/C (Moss Hall, 1830; Moss Hall estate); M.R.O., Acc. 840/2.
[94] B.L.H.L., S/C (Dale and Hutton groves).
[95] M.R.O., Acc. 830/2.
[96] B.L.H.L., S/C (Woodside Pk.).
[97] *Muswell Hill Rec.* 9 Sept. 1910.
[98] B.L.H.L., S/C (Woodside Pk.).

church was opened in 1909 in the northern part of Nether Street, a 'rapidly growing' district.[99] It included the Court House estate between the railway and Nether Street, where 61 freehold plots for detached and semi-detached houses were for sale in 1909.[1] Most of the area was built up by 1920.[2]

East of the Great North Road the Churchfield estate, next to Christ Church, was divided for 50 medium-sized houses in 1900.[3] The Woodhouse estate on both sides of Woodhouse Road, stretching from the Great North Road into Friern Barnet, had already been offered in building lots. By 1900 roads had been laid out in the north-west corner and 46 a. of the rest were again offered as building land, in the heart of a rapidly growing suburb which was easily accessible from the City and the west end of London. A strip of land between Woodhouse Road and Summers Lane had been sold by 1909 and Woodgrange Avenue was built on it soon afterwards.[4] The U.D.C. bought most of the estate (36 a.) in 1915, building some 100 houses then and starting another 200 in 1919.[5] North Finchley by 1876 had good shops, inns, and many private houses.[6] Said *c.* 1885 to have lately sprung into existence, it then had several 'respectable' shops and residences.[7] By 1909 shop fronts there along the Great North Road were continuous.[8]

Church End, which meanwhile had lost its primacy to North Finchley, was in 1876 rambling and well wooded, with country lanes merging into the village street, although building was gaining ground.[9] Early attempts to build up Olders Hill in the south-west corner of the parish proved abortive. The National Standard Land Mortgage and Investment Co. bought the estate in 1880 but few lots had been built on by 1897.[10] Part of Grass farm, which adjoined Olders Hill to the north, was offered for building along Hendon Lane with similar lack of success in 1894.[11] In 1901 that part of Finchley, while providing excellent sites, was thought to be undeveloped because of poor transport, which would be improved by trams.[12] After the arrival of trams in 1905 housing spread quickly. There was building in 1906 on Grass Farm estate in Dollis Avenue, where Woodway Lodge, designed by Messrs. Bennet & Richardson, was one of several detached houses.[13] Near by at Elm Park west of Nether Street, where building had started in 1882, land was offered in 1900 for good-class villas which were said to be in great demand.[14] By 1908 housing was continuous up to Brent Lodge, which was offered with 26 a. for immediate building.[15] Finchley Co-Partnership Society was then formed to lay out a garden village like Hampstead Garden Suburb for the 'less wealthy middle classes'. In 1910 it decided to preserve Brent Lodge and to develop the 24-a. estate on a co-operative system.[16] Land of Bibbesworth demesne was among the first to be taken for housing, the land at Church End north of Gravel Hill being sold from the 1840s.[17] Building spread southward from Gravel Hill on the College farm estate, where Cyprus and Bibsworth roads existed by 1897, and by 1920 had reached the farm-house itself.[18]

East of Church End and Regent's Park Road, land north of East End Road was leased for building from 1864.[19] Avenue House was built there in 1867 and its freehold sold in 1874 to H. C. Stephens, who rebuilt it in the 1880s as a 40-bedroom pile in a 'reactionary Italianate' style.[20] Hertford Lodge, also large, was built next to it in 1869.[21] The area south of East End Road, mostly Bibbesworth demesne but including part of the glebe, began to be built up in the 1890s. James Vaughan bought land in 1891 and Ernest Vaughan was constructing roads there in 1892–3. About 70 'superior semi-detached' houses, designed by W. Barnaby Pinhey, had been built by *c.* 1900 and 120 by 1904 and were served by a shopping parade in Regent's Park Road and St. Luke's church in Mountfield Road.[22] Apart from the land opposite Avenue House, which had been bought by Stephens, the whole district had been built up by 1920.[23] Moat estate, 13 a. of Bibbesworth land between the railway and Manor farm, was offered for building in 1905 and Briarfield Avenue stood there by 1920.[24]

Typical of many large houses of that time in North Finchley and Church End was Glenroy in Seymour Road, designed by F. W. Poley and built by 1907.[25] Most houses were in a Gothic or Tudor style, much embellished. There was a revival of pargeting, the plaster designs displaying a great variety of patterns, still visible at the junction of Whetstone High Street with Woodside Lane, at Claverley Grove, Fallowcourt Avenue, and in the shopping arcades at the northern end of Hendon Lane.[26] The houses were intended for professional men and merchants from the City or west end of London,[27] whose arrival stimulated the hot-house industry and especially the growing of flowers.[28] Owners of big London stores included William Pearce Jones and Alfred Gamage at the Manor House, William Whiteley at Manor Farm, and John Harris Heal at Grass Farm. Frederick Goodyear

99 *The Times*, 12 Oct. 1908; 17 May 1909.
1 B.L.H.L., S/C (Court Ho. estate, 1909).
2 O.S. Map 6″, Mdx. VI. SE. (1920 edn.).
3 B.L.H.L., S/C (Churchfield estate, 1900).
4 M.R.O., Acc. 410/43–47; B.L.H.L., S/C (Woodhouse estate).
5 *The Times*, 3 Mar., 1 June 1914; 29 Jan. 1915; *Finchley Press*, 6 Oct. 1933; Nat. Soc. files.
6 Thorne, *Environs*, 218.
7 Walford, *Gtr. Lond.* i. 340.
8 B.L.H.L., S/C (High St., N. Finchley, 1909).
9 Thorne, *Environs*, 216–17.
10 B.L.H.L., S/C (Olders Hill estate, 1882, 1884); O.S. Map 6″, Mdx. XI. NE. (1897 edn.).
11 B.L.H.L., S/C (Grass Farm estate).
12 *The Times*, 18 June 1901.
13 B.L.H.L., S/C (Grass Pk. estate; Woodway Lodge); M.R.O., MJ/SB 2507/52–3.
14 B.L.H.L., S/C (Eversleigh Rd.). See p. 89.
15 Ibid. (Brent Lodge).
16 *The Times*, 20 Oct. 1908; 11, 18 Aug. 1910; B.L.H.L., Poor-rate (1911).
17 See above.
18 O.S. Maps 6″, Mdx. XI. NE. (1897, 1920 edns.).
19 M.R.O., Acc. 351/404.
20 Ibid.; B.L.H.L., Banks Colln., biog. Stephens; Pevsner, *Mdx.* 56. See below, p. 78.
21 M.R.O., Acc. 351/404; B.L.H.L., P.A.F. 1/9 (1871).
22 Potter Colln. 28/67; B.L.H.L., S/C (Finchley Manor estate, 1904); Finchley local bd., min. bk. xi. 181, 403.
23 B.L.H.L., Banks Colln., biog. Stephens; O.S. Map 6″, Mdx. XI. NE. (1920 edn.).
24 B.L.H.L., S/C (Moat estate, 1905); B.L.H.L., Acc. 8682; O.S. Map 6″, Mdx. XI. NE. (1920 edn.).
25 B.L.H.L., S/C (Glenroy, Seymour Rd., 1907). See plate facing p. 48.
26 Finchley Soc. *Newsletter*, July 1972.
27 B.L.H.L., S/C (Hertford Lodge, 1900).
28 *Jnl. of Royal Agric. Soc.* 3rd ser., ix. 512–38.

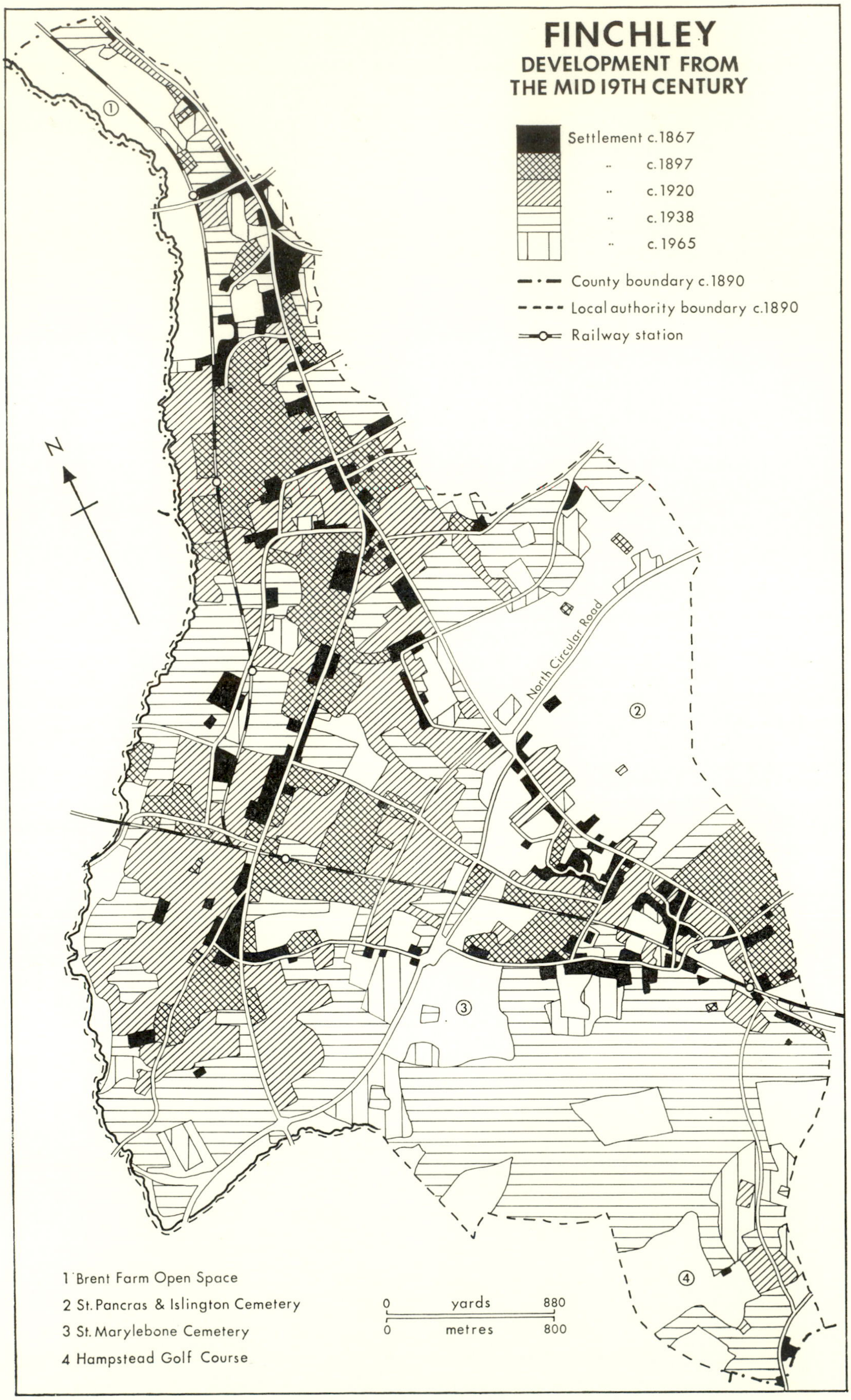
FINCHLEY
DEVELOPMENT FROM
THE MID 19TH CENTURY
Settlement c.1867
" c.1897
" c.1920
" c.1938
" c.1965
County boundary c.1890
Local authority boundary c.1890
Railway station
N
North Circular Road
1 Brent Farm Open Space
2 St. Pancras & Islington Cemetery
3 St. Marylebone Cemetery
4 Hampstead Golf Course
0 yards 880
0 metres 800

(d. 1937), who came to Finchley in 1849 and was active in local politics, lived at Fallow Lodge and was a straw-hat manufacturer.[29] Also active were Benjamin Todd (d. 1937) of Elm Grange, Nether Street, a button manufacturer,[30] and H. C. Stephens (d. 1919), a rich man as the result of his father's invention.[31] Other local benefactors included James Henry Lermitte (d. 1901) of Knightons, who prospered on the stock exchange, and Ebenezer Homan of Friern Watch (d. 1909), a boot manufacturer.[32] Samuel Pulham (d. 1938) of Elmshurst owned a butcher's business with 17 branches in and around Finchley.[33]

In contrast to North Finchley and Church End, Whetstone and East End remained predominantly working-class in the late 19th century. The Baxendales had left Whetstone by 1890 and vainly tried to sell their land for building *c.* 1901.[34] There were some 'genteel villas' at Oakleigh Park[35] but most building was still of cottages or terraced houses, like the 29 planned behind the Swan in 1871.[36] In 1876 Whetstone consisted of straggling groups of houses, some of them old and many poor,[37] and in 1884 the vicar estimated that three-quarters of the inhabitants were working-class. Very few were well-to-do in 1904 and by the 1920s most were artisans or lower-middle-class.[38]

East End grew rapidly after the Ecclesiastical Commissioners granted 99-year building leases from 1878.[39] In 1881 hundreds of cottages were 'new building',[40] in 1882 more were expected on Park Hall and the charity estates,[41] and in 1899 17 a. at Fortis Green Road were built over.[42] The large houses along East End Road began to disappear: in 1901 Sedgemere was sold and by 1920 it had been replaced by Sedgemere Avenue.[43] Housing none the less failed to keep pace with the rising population, the birth rate being higher there than in the rest of the parish[44] and the vicar of Holy Trinity complaining in 1905 that East End was becoming the receptacle for the poor of neighbouring parishes.[45] Many houses were divided into lodgings which were often insanitary.[46] Richer families made way for 'struggling clerks, small tradesmen, and artisans', many in casual work.[47] In 1899 the vicar, who had experience of East London, had 'rarely seen the Finchley boy equalled for profanity and rudeness'.[48]

While building linked East End along the Great North Road to North End and along the railway to Church End by 1920, it was limited near the eastern boundary by cemeteries. In 1854 87 a. allotted at inclosure to Bibbesworth were sold to the St. Pancras burial board, which sold 30 a. to that of St. Mary, Islington. Chapels were built by Messrs. Barnett and Birch and in 1855 St. Marylebone opened a cemetery on 26 a. of farm-land south of East End Road, between the demesne lands of Bibbesworth and Bibwell.[49] The St. Pancras and Islington burial grounds were enlarged in 1876 by the purchase of the Strawberry Vale estate (109 a.), which had also been created at inclosure and which the Regent's Canal Co. had sold in 1816 to James Frost, who had built some houses there and sold the rest as a farm to James Morison (d. 1840), founder of the British College of Health.[50] Although the cemeteries provided open space, Finchley local board in 1893 unsuccessfully objected to an extension of the St. Marylebone one on the grounds that it prevented better houses being built. The London parishes paid only nominal rates to Finchley but the 10,000 corpses a year caused serious health problems.[51] The cemeteries brought bizarre funeral processions, custom to the Bald-faced Stag, a boom in the work of ornamental stone-masons, and much wear and tear to the Great North Road and East End Road.[52]

As transport improved, residents increasingly worked outside the parish. Clerks and those engaged in commerce and insurance, most of them in London, formed a rising proportion of the work force. Of the men, clerks formed 8 per cent in 1901 and 1911, 14 per cent in 1921, and 17 per cent in 1931, while banking and insurance accounted for 11 per cent in 1911, 19 per cent in 1921, and 21 per cent in 1931. More women than men worked locally, mostly in domestic service, which employed 55 per cent of the female work force in 1901 and 49 per cent in 1911. Seventeen per cent were typists by 1921, when 43 per cent were still in domestic service, and 23 per cent were typists by 1931 and 38 per cent by 1961. In 1921 38 per cent of a total work force of 20,701 worked in Finchley and 39 per cent in London.[53] Most building ceased during the First World War and by 1919 houses were in short supply.[54] The council continued building at Woodhouse Road and provided another 50 houses in 1928 and 72 in 1930.[55] All building in the 1930s accorded with the council's town planning scheme of 12 houses to an acre where the site fronted a main road and 10 to the acre elsewhere.[56] There were 13,461 inhabited buildings by 1931 and 18,855 by 1951.[57]

After the First World War the main change was in

[29] *Barnet Press*, 23 Jan. 1937.
[30] *Finchley Press*, 15 Jan. 1937.
[31] H. C. Stephens left £297,000: B.L.H.L., Banks Colln. xiii. See below, p. 78.
[32] They left £197,000 and £324,803 respectively: B.L.H.L., Banks Colln. xiii. 5937–8.
[33] *Finchley Review*, 19 Mar. 1938; *Barnet Press*, 19 Mar. 1938.
[34] *Kelly's Dir. Mdx.* (1890); B.L.H.L., S/C (Whetstone bldg. land); O.S. Map 6″, Mdx. VI. SE. (1920 edn.).
[35] Thorne, *Environs*, 693; B.L.H.L., S/C (Highlands, 1905).
[36] B.L.H.L., P.A.F. 3/3.
[37] Thorne, *Environs*, 693.
[38] Nat. Soc. files.
[39] Guildhall MS. 12411.
[40] Nat. Soc. files.
[41] B.L.H.L., Acc. 9835 (Finchley sch. bd., min. bk. i. 280).
[42] *The Times*, 14 July 1899.
[43] B.L.H.L., S/C (Sedgemere, 1901).
[44] Finchley local bd. *Ann. Rep. of M.O.H.* (1892).
[45] Nat. Soc. files.
[46] *Ann. Rep. of M.O.H.* (1893).
[47] Nat. Soc. files.
[48] B.L.H.L., Banks Colln. xiii. 5913.
[49] *Illus. Lond. News*, 29 July 1854, 17 Mar. 1855; O.S. Map 6″, Mdx. XI. NE. (1867 edn.); Potter Colln. 28/9; *Finchley Press*, 10 Jan. 1930; J. S. Curl, *Victorian Celebration of Death* (1972), 147. See below, plate facing p. 176.
[50] M.R.O., EA/FIN; M.L.R. 1819/7/629; B.L.H.L., Banks Colln., biog. Morison; M.R.O., Hist. Notes 21/7/70.
[51] *Daily Chron.* 21 July, 16 Aug. 1893.
[52] Potter Colln. 28/6.
[53] *Census*, 1901–61.
[54] *The Times*, 23 Sept. 1919.
[55] *Finchley Press*, 6 Oct. 1933. Nos. of council hos. are available only up to 1930.
[56] B.L.H.L., S/C (Maple Ho. and Elm Ho., 1943; Elmshurst, 1939).
[57] *Census*, 1931, 1951.

the south part of the parish, where the former demesne farms and woods became an extension of Hampstead Garden Suburb.[58] The Bishop's Avenue from Bishop's wood to East End Road was constructed *c.* 1887 for expensive houses. Plots were let on 99-year and, more rarely, 999-year building leases[59] and in 1894 building began. Most leases were to single individuals but William Mattocks Dabbs, a builder from Stamford Hill, took 5 a. in 1898 and the National Hospital for the Paralysed and Epileptic took land at the northern end in 1895. Rich lessees included George Sainsbury, the provision merchant, in 1898 and Christian Carl Lorenzen, a chronometer manufacturer, in 1901. Twelve houses with large grounds existed by 1906. Residents, however, were often disturbed by horsemen who used the road as a galloping ground and later by noise from sports grounds which had opened by 1920. The woods attracted tramps and were used as rubbish tips; assaults forced the council to provide gas lamps,[60] but the road was still unmade in 1935.[61]

Apart from land leased to Hampstead golf club,[62] all the area west and north of the Bishop's Avenue was leased for building to Hampstead Garden Suburb Trust and to the Co-Partnership Tenants in 1909 and 1911. Houses in Falloden Way and some roads off it were built to the designs of G. L. Sutcliffe and C. G. Butler before the First World War. Most building, however, took place during the 1920s and 1930s, when other architects included C. M. Crickmer, J. A. Bateman, and J. C. S. Soutar.[63] The North Circular Road left the parish in the hitherto empty south-west corner. At the junction of the North Circular and Regent's Park roads, the statue *La Délivrance* was unveiled as a war memorial in 1927.[64] Houses and blocks of flats were built near by in the 1930s.[65]

Elsewhere small villas were built at Woodside, between Woodside House and the railway, after 1923.[66] Detached houses for the professional classes at East End Road, opposite Avenue House and adjoining the Woodhouse estate on the Great North Road, were built by Vernon Smith in the early 1930s,[67] Halliwick estate on the Friern Barnet boundary adjoining the Woodhouse estate existed by 1933,[68] and Essex Park and Wentworth Park west of Ballards Lane were built in 1934.[69] The new suburb of West Finchley was created between Dollis brook and the railway, with its own station from 1933.[70] By the 1930s most farm-land had been taken for housing. Large old houses in their own grounds were increasingly bought as building sites, while new offices and shop-fronts appeared in the village centres.

Whetstone began to lose its working-class character and in 1924 its transformation with office blocks was said to be imminent.[71] Some Edwardian houses had been built along the northern stretch of the Great North Road and smaller semi-detached houses were built in Walfield Avenue near the county boundary in the 1920s.[72]

North Finchley in contrast became less exclusive, especially along the Great North Road and Ballards Lane, where by 1934 there was a 'vulgar line of hoardings, petrol stations, blatant shops, and muddle of all kinds'.[73] Orchard Lodge was demolished in 1927 and Kingsway driven through its site in 1934.[74] Moss Hall was also demolished, in 1927.[75] Many blocks of flats were built, Etchingham Court dating from 1935[76] and Fallow Cottage being sold in 1939 to Wood & Wallers, who built flats on its site.[77] Willow Lodge on the east side of Ballards Lane was pulled down in 1929.[78] On the opposite side Maple House and Elm House were for sale in 1934 and made way for the flats of Finchley Court in 1935.[79] Bay Tree Cottage, already set among shops in Ballards Lane, was offered in 1936 and replacedby Woolworth's in 1938.[80] Court House at the northern corner of Nether Street was sold in 1936 and flats were built there a year later.[81] Rocklands, next to Dollis brook, was offered for sale in an area 'ripe for development' in 1938.[82]

In East End Road the large houses either became convents, like East End House (1864), Manor House (1919), and Knightons (1921),[83] or were sold for building. Cromwell Hall was demolished in 1934 and Elmshurst, set in 10 a., was sold to builders in 1939 on Samuel Pulham's death.[84] Prospect House was demolished in 1929[85] and eighteen blocks providing 318 flats were planned near the Red Lion in 1938.[86] During work in 1934, ten old cottages in Red Lion Hill were set alight to enable the fire service to give a demonstration.[87]

After the Second World War, housing was again in demand. In 1951 there were 18,430 separate dwellings, with a population density greatest in St. Paul's (Long Lane) ward (26·1 persons per acre) and Moss Hall ward (24·9) and least in the Bishop's ward (14·7). By 1961 the number of dwellings had risen to 20,883, although the population had fallen slightly, reducing the density in

58 i.e. the Bishop's Ave.: Finchley local bd., min. bk. v. 111; Church Com. file 39824. See also p. 63.
59 Except where otherwise stated, the para. is based on Guildhall MS. 12409.
60 Church Com. file 39824.
61 *The Times*, 13 Feb. 1935.
62 See pp. 63, 74.
63 Church Com. file 85003; [Hampstead Gdn. Suburb Residents' Assoc.], *Illus. Hist. of Hampstead Gdn. Suburb* [1954]; *The Times*, 5 Mar. 1930. See also *V.C.H. Mdx.* v. 13–14.
64 M.R.O., P.R. 13/148.
65 M.R.O., MJ/2523/129.
66 B.L.H.L., S/C (Birley Rd. estate, 1923).
67 Advert. in *Finchley Press*, 6 Oct. 1933.
68 *The Times*, 6 Sept. 1933.
69 B.L.H.L., S/C (Maple Ho. and Elm Ho., 1934).
70 Lawrence, *Village Into Boro.* 30; O.S. Map 6″, Mdx. XI. NE. (1938 edn.); see above, p. 42.
71 B.L.H.L., S/C (Arlington Cottages, 1924).
72 O.S. Maps 6″, Mdx. VI. SE. (1920, 1938 edns.).
73 Briggs, *Mdx. Old and New*, 128.
74 B.L.H.L., Banks Colln., Index 1 *sub* Orchard Lodge.
75 B.L.H.L., S/C (Moss Hall estate).
76 Ibid. (Etchingham Pk. estate).
77 B.L.H.L., Banks Colln. iv. 4125.
78 Ibid. x.
79 B.L.H.L., S/C (Maple Ho. and Elm Ho., 1934); Banks Colln. xi.
80 B.L.H.L., S/C (Bay Tree Cottage, 1936); Banks Colln. xi. 7029.
81 B.L.H.L., Banks Colln. v. 3346.
82 B.L.H.L., S/C (Rocklands, 1938).
83 See p. 87.
84 B.L.H.L., S/C (Elmshurst, 1939); *Barnet Press*, 19 Mar. 1938; *Finchley Press*, 20 Jan., 18 Feb. 1939.
85 B.L.H.L., Banks Colln., Index 1 *sub* Prospect Ho.
86 *The Times*, 10 Oct. 1938.
87 B.L.H.L., Banks Colln., Finchley common file.

St. Paul's ward to 24·4. About 54 per cent of the dwellings were then owner-occupied, 29 per cent privately rented unfurnished, and 10 per cent rented from the council.[88]

In the badly bombed East End tightly packed cottages between the Great North Road and the railway, around the George inn, were to be replaced by eleven-storeyed flats in 1954.[89] Building was under way in 1955, although many inhabitants regretted the disappearance of family shops and an older way of life.[90] A municipal estate of 274 flats was built at Vale farm near the Great North Road in East Finchley in 1975, replacing older houses,[91] as did 109 dwellings in Holden Road, under construction in 1977.[92] Some large houses were divided into flats[93] but most were rebuilt. Wentworth Lodge in Ballards Lane disappeared in 1945[94] and Wimbush's house at Fallow Corner was sold in 1955.[95] The Swan with Two Necks was destroyed in 1962.[96] Brent Lodge was divided into flats in the 1960s and demolished in 1971–2.[97] Much older property was replaced by houses and maisonettes in Woodside Avenue. Office blocks were built on the site of the Railway hotel and New Bohemia cinema in Church End, at the junction of Queensway and High Road in North Finchley, and at several sites in Whetstone, including one near the Swan.[98]

By 1977 the building of large blocks of offices and smaller blocks of flats had taken away most of the character of the old centres. Church End was still dominated by Christ's College on one side and the more restrained tower of the church on the other. The early-18th-century Park House survived in Hendon Lane and some fine mid-19th-century houses in Regent's Park Road stood derelict.[99] Most of the area to the south and westward to Dollis brook was covered by houses of the 1920s and 1930s, with more recent flats, although grass and trees bordered the brook.

Ballards Lane, a collection of Victorian and Edwardian houses, modern flats, used-car depots, chapels, and foreign restaurants, leads to North Finchley, centred on the bleak Tally Ho Corner. Much remains of Woodside, the late-19th- and early-20th-century suburb of 'large spiky houses and heavy foliage',[1] and of the older terraces on the eastern side of North Finchley. Woodhouse Road retains its large mid-Victorian house, a school, with municipal and other housing of the 1920s to the south.

Whetstone, except near North Finchley, is no longer working-class.[2] Some early-19th-century farm cottages survive in Lodge Lane but shops, middle-class houses, and office blocks line High Road. There are a few elegant mid-19th-century houses and, on high ground farther north, expensive detached and semi-detached houses built before and after the First World War overlooking the grassland along Dollis brook on the west.

The Great North Road links Whetstone, North Finchley, and East End, where infilling has left no boundary between the old districts. Between the garages and works there are shopping parades, some with dates on their elaborate façades, as at East End (1912). As in Church End and North Finchley, there are many foreign restaurants and provision shops.

At East End modern flats have recently destroyed even the street pattern of the old village. The rebuilt George inn and Holy Trinity church and school remain, however, and community feeling is stronger than in many parts of Finchley.[3] A few of the old houses survive in East End Road, notably those which are convents.[4]

The area south-east of the North Circular Road has more affinity with Hampstead Garden Suburb, of which it is an extension, than with the rest of Finchley. Expensive houses remain in the Bishop's Avenue, heavily protected,[5] although even there some have been divided or rebuilt. In 1977 there were plans to replace the Towers, former home of the singer Gracie Fields, with 'Europe's most luxurious home', for an Arab buyer.[6]

Finchley's population grew from 4,937 in 1861 to 11,191 in 1881, 22,126 in 1901, and 46,716 in 1921. It was 58,964 in 1931, reached its height of 69,991 in 1951, and fell slightly to 69,370 by 1961.[7]

MANORS. In 1294 the bishop of London claimed that his predecessors had exercised rights over Finchley as a member of Fulham 'time out of mind'.[8] Although not mentioned in the Domesday survey, *FINCHLEY* manor probably formed part of the 50 hides in Fulham and elsewhere which Tyrhtel, bishop of Hereford, granted to Wealdheri, bishop of London, *c.* 704.[9] No evidence supports the tradition that St. Albans abbey had owned land 'between Barnet and London stone', which was seized by William I.[10] Although Finchley was called a manor in 1374,[11] it continued to be treated as part of Fulham until its transfer to the bishop's lordship of Hornsey in 1491.[12] About the period 1297–1302 Finchley was said to be held by the

88 *Census*, 1951–71.
89 *Finchley Press*, 14 May 1954.
90 e.g. chickens and pigs were kept in yards: *Finchley Press*, 7 Oct. 1955.
91 *Finchley Press*, 31 Oct. 1975; *The Times*, 9 Sept. 1975.
92 Hoarding on site.
93 e.g. a ho. in Claverley Grove in 1951: B.L.H.L., S/C (no. 21 Claverley Grove).
94 B.L.H.L., Banks Colln. xi. 7043.
95 Ibid. biog. Wimbush.
96 *Focus on Finchley*, Sept. 1962 in B.L.H.L.
97 Char. Com. files.
98 Lawrence, *Village Into Boro.* 32.
99 From 1965 their site was intended for a civic centre. In 1977 it was to be turned over to private builders: *Evening Standard*, 21 Oct. 1977.
1 Robbins, *Mdx.* 254. See also Finchley Soc. *Newsletter*, Jan. 1977.
2 Finchley Soc. *Newsletter*, Jan. 1977.
3 *Finchley Press*, 29 Aug. 1975.
4 i.e. Manor Ho., Good Shepherd, and Nazareth Ho. convents.
5 The high gates and barred windows make some of the hos. resemble prisons.
6 *Daily Telegraph*, 26 Nov. 1977.
7 *Census*, 1861–1961.
8 *Plac. de Quo Warr.* (Rec. Com.), 475.
9 P. H. Sawyer, *Anglo-Saxon Charters*, no. 1785; *Eng. Hist. Docs.* i, ed. D. Whitelock, p. 449; *V.C.H. Mdx.* i. 106.
10 Thos. Walsingham, *Gesta Abbatum* (Rolls Ser.), ed. H. T. Riley, i. 50; L. F. Rushbrook Williams, *Hist. of Abbey of St. Albans*, 33–6. But cf. *V.C.H. Mdx.* v. 96, 105.
11 *Cal. Pat.* 1370–4, 462–3.
12 S.C. 2/189/10 m. 2d.

bishop of London of the honor of Stortford for ¼ knight's fee.[13] Except during the Interregnum, when the manor was held from 1649 by Sir John Wollaston (d. 1658), alderman of London, and his widow Rebecca,[14] the bishops remained lords until their rights were vested in the Ecclesiastical Commissioners.[15] The last manorial rights were extinguished in 1938.[16]

Demesne estates had been created out of the woodland by 1298.[17] In 1318 Lordsfield and Little Redings, two 20-a. arable clearings on the edge of Hornsey park, were administered as part of the Harringay demesne, as was the pannage of Finchley tenants.[18] Other demesne estates were High or Rote Redings, recorded from 1395, mainly in Hornsey but extending across the Finchley boundary to Newgate Lane,[19] Ballards Reding, on the edge of Finchley wood at the northern end of Ballards Lane by 1425,[20] and Bibwell, between Hornsey park and Bibbesworth, in 1434 'a certain close in Finchley'.[21] Apart from the bishop's hunting lodge within Hornsey park, on the parish boundary,[22] there was no grange or other administrative building in Finchley.[23]

The demesne was farmed in 1298, exploited directly in 1318, and leased out again from the 15th century,[24] when new demesne estates were created within Hornsey park, which extended deep into Finchley. Oxleas, an estate comprising meadow land and part of the herbage of the park in 1540, had become three closes by 1576.[25] The woodland remained in hand until 1645, when it was leased out, and was progressively grubbed up until in 1820 it consisted of 178 a. of farm-land and 88 a. of woodland in Finchley and 124 a. of farm-land and 306 a. of woodland, including Great Coldfall wood (116 a.) in Hornsey. Except Great Coldfall wood the woodland estate, including Bishop's wood (92 a.) of which two-thirds lay in Finchley, was within Hornsey park.

Most of the 113 a. allotted to the bishop at inclosure was added to the leasehold demesne estates but one block of 40 a. formed a new demesne estate which was leased separately. From the 17th to the mid 19th centuries the bishop's control was slight and the demesne estates were held on long and often hereditary leases for lives. Ballards Reding was sold in 1855 and the inclosure allotment in 1865. During the late 19th century the Ecclesiastical Commissioners, seeing the potential value of building land, bought out the remaining interests of the lessees at considerable expense, acquiring parts of Oxleas in 1873 and 1878, the woodlands in 1885, and Bibwell in 1902.

About 1900 the whole of south-eastern Finchley was in the hands of the commissioners, who let building plots on either side of the Bishop's Avenue from 1894. In addition they owned *c.* 629 a. of farm- and park-land in Finchley, divided into Park, Lodge, Spaniards, and Manor farms and Hampstead and Highgate golf courses.[26] Over 400 a. of farm-land were leased for building in 1911, the freehold being sold in 1958 and 1959. In 1977 the Church Commissioners owned the freeholds of only the convalescent home and no. 46 the Bishop's Avenue.[27]

The sub-manor of Finchley or *BIBBESWORTH*, first called a manor in 1319,[28] may have originated in 12th-century subinfeudations by the bishops.[29] There is no evidence that it was held for anything other than rent.[30] The Finchley family, which included a canon of St. Paul's, was active in the early 13th century[31] and in 1248–9 Richard, son of Richard of Finchley, granted 80 a. in Finchley to Michael Tovy, first of the many important Londoners connected with Bibbesworth.[32] Tovy, who already possessed property in Finchley in 1245–6,[33] acquired another 100 a. in 1248–9 from Hamon FitzAlan.[34] He sold the estate, apparently a manor, in 1252–3 to Adam de Basing,[35] who made further purchases in the 1250s.[36] One grant of 40 a. by Thomas of London was held of Hernicus the tailor[37] but any mesne interest between the bishop and Bibbesworth soon withered away.

Adam de Basing (d. 1262) was succeeded by his son Thomas (d. 1275), a minor, and then by his daughters Avice and Joan, wives respectively of William de Hadestok (d. 1296) and Henry le Waleys (d. 1301).[38] By 1299 Hadestok's daughter Joan and her husband Adam de Bedyk were in possession,[39] although they had earlier lost a suit against Waleys.[40] Adam was dead by 1302[41] and his son Henry Bedyk, who also had property in Hendon and Totteridge, conveyed the manor to

[13] E 315/45/77.
[14] St. Paul's MS. B 68; S.C. 2/191/12.
[15] *Lond. Gaz.* 6 July 1855, pp. 2593–4; see below, p. 140.
[16] Guildhall MS. 10465/228, p. 140.
[17] E 352/36 rot. 5.
[18] St. Paul's MS. A 62. The deed, an acct. made for the chapter of St. Paul's during a vacancy in the see, is dated 12 Ed., usually interpreted as 12 Ed. I (1283–4). No vacancy occurred then but there was one in 1318, 12 Ed. II.
[19] S.C. 2/188/66 m. 15.
[20] Guildhall MS. 10312, m. 3d.
[21] St. Paul's MS. A 86.
[22] O.S. Map 6", Mdx. XI. NE. (1867 edn.). See p. 140.
[23] The grange at Finchley, mentioned in *Acct. of Executors of Ric., Bp. of Lond. 1303* (Camden Soc. N.S. x), 98, was probably part of the bp.'s personal rather than his episcopal estate: P. J. Taylor, 'Estates of Bishopric of Lond. from 7th to early 16th cents.' (Lond. Univ. Ph.D. thesis, 1976), 353–5.
[24] E 352/36 rot. 5; St. Paul's MS. A 62. For the leasehold estates, see below, pp. 61–4.
[25] St. Paul's MS. C (Sampson), f. 109v.; (II Nowell), ff. 453 and v.
[26] B.L.H.L., Rate bk. (1911); Guildhall MS. 12409. Manor Dairy farm-ho. lay just outside Finchley. Most of Highgate golf course was in Hornsey.
[27] Ex inf. Church Com. For the convalescent home, see p. 80.
[28] B.L.H.L., Acc. 9132/14.
[29] Taylor, 'Estates of Bishopric of Lond.' 104 sqq.
[30] It was held of the bp. for £2 2*s.* *c.* 1500: M.R.O., Acc. 351/260.
[31] St. Paul's MS. A 41/1523; C.P. 25(1)/146/7/72; *Cur. Reg. R.* x, p. 521; Le Neve, *Fasti, 1066–1300, St. Paul's*, 60, 94–5.
[32] C.P. 25(1)/147/16/291. For the Lond. connexion, see p. 65.
[33] J.I. 1/538 m. 20.
[34] C.P. 25(1)/147/16/284.
[35] i.e. a ho., carucate, and appurtenances including demesnes, homage, service, and rents: C.P. 25(1)/147/18/333.
[36] C.P. 25(1)/147/20/388; C.P. 25(1)/147/21/411.
[37] Described as 'capital lord of the fee': C.P. 25(1)/147/21/413.
[38] G. A. Williams, *Medieval Lond. from Commune to Capital* (1963), 333–5.
[39] C.P. 40/27 rot. 4.
[40] C.P. 40/78 rot. 84.
[41] *Cal. Close*, 1296–1302, 609; C. O. Banks, *Romances of Finchley Man.*

uses in 1319.[42] Accordingly, after Henry's death in 1335, two-thirds of the estate was held in trust with reversion to his son Thomas, while Henry's widow Joan, who married Ernald de Mounteney, had dower rights in the rest.[43]

In 1352–3 Sir Thomas Bedyk sold the manor to Simon Francis, who in 1357 left property in four counties to his son Thomas.[44] The latter sold Finchley manor in 1358–9 to Richard of Piriton and Richard of Haversham, clerks,[45] who in 1360 granted it to William Palmer and Richard Rook,[46] to whom Sir Thomas Bedyk's mother Joan sold her dower rights in 1360–1.[47] Palmer and Rook exercised patronage of the manor chantry in 1361 and 1363[48] and Rook, acting for the abbot of Westminster, held courts in 1364 and 1365.[49] In 1366 Rook conveyed the manor to Richard of Stoke and others, who in 1386, on behalf of Westminster, enfeoffed John Flete. From 1392–6 Flete owed suit of court for the holding once Thomas Bedyk's.[50]

In 1400 the manor was conveyed by Flete to trustees[51] and by 1401 it was held by Drew Barentyn, in 1412 the richest landowner in Finchley with property worth £6 13*s.* 4*d.*[52] Barentyn died in 1415 and his nephew Reynold conveyed the manor by 1418 to Edmund Bibbesworth (d. 1443), who left it to his wife Godith for life.[53] In 1448–9 his son John Bibbesworth sold the manor, then described as six houses, 550 a. of land and woodland, and rent in Finchley and Hendon, to John Pontrell and others.[54]

At about that time the lords of Bibbesworth also acquired the so-called manor of *MARCHES* or *NORMANS*. In 1397 Sir William March died seised of 'the manor of Finchley' and 80 a., held of Philip Pelytot for 1 lb. of pepper a year, and 20 a., held of the bishop for rent. March was said to have been enfeoffed, with others, by William Creswick and John Berveyr.[55] The estate may have been a house, 158 a., and a mill in Finchley and Hendon, which had been held by Robert Kersebroke in 1313–14 and which Walter Kersebroke granted to Creswick, Berveyr, and others in 1378.[56] It may also have included land which had belonged to John atte Pole (d. 1361) and which was conveyed by his trustees to John Barnes, a Londoner like most of the others.[57] During the minority of Sir William March's son Thomas the estate was granted to Thomas Chipstead, who in 1412 was the second richest landowner in Finchley.[58] Chipstead still held it in 1435 but in 1439 trustees sold 'the manor called Marches', a house, 262 a., and rent in Finchley and Hendon to John Norman.[59] From 1442 to 1445 Norman was presented for lands once Chipstead's but by 1448 some had passed to the tenants of Bibbesworth and some to John Holtoft.[60] By 1453 all were in the hands of John Pontrell, lord of Bibbesworth.[61]

Pontrell and his fellow trustees conveyed the manor and combined estates to William Chester and others in 1461–2 and by 1464 they were held by John Plomer or Leynham (d. 1479), who left them to his widow Margaret and his nephew's son Richard Fisher.[62] They sold them almost immediately to William Hastings, Lord Hastings (d. 1483), whose widow Catherine (d. *c.* 1503) held the manor during the minority of her son Edward[63] and apparently was still in control in 1490.[64] Edward, Lord Hastings, held the manor in 1502 and after his death in 1506 it was held by his widow Mary during the minority of their son George, who came of age in 1509. George, heavily in debt, sold the manor in 1527 to Sir William Compton (d. 1528).[65] The Crown held it during the minority of Sir William's son Peter (d. 1539),[66] whose widow Anne (d. 1588), later countess of Pembroke, held it as dower and in 1577 settled it on her son Henry, Lord Compton (d. 1589), with remainder to Henry's second son Thomas.[67] In 1594 Thomas with his elder brother William, Lord Compton, sold Bibbesworth and Normans to Alexander King, auditor of the Exchequer.[68] King died childless in 1618, leaving Bibbesworth to his widow Elizabeth (d. 1622),[69] whose executors were to sell it to raise legacies.[70]

Edward Allen, a London alderman, bought the manor in 1622[71] and other small properties in East End. He was succeeded in 1625[72] by his son, later Sir Thomas Allen, who in 1627 married Mary, daughter of Sir John Weld of Arnolds in Southgate.[73] In 1674 Sir Thomas settled his extensive Middlesex estates, including Bibbesworth, in tail male. On his death in 1681 the estate descended to his son Edward and on Edward's death childless in 1692 it passed to Thomas, son of Edward's brother James (d. 1690).[74] Thomas (d. 1764)

42 B.L.H.L., Acc. 9132/14.
43 St. Paul's MS. A 66/25; C 135/65/12; *Cal. of Wills in Ct. of Husting*, i. 404–5; C.P. 25(1)/150/68/382.
44 C.P. 25(1)/150/65/301; *Cal. Inq. p.m.* x, p. 349.
45 C.P. 25(1)/150/67/360. Piriton was later a prebendary of St. Paul's and archdeacon of Colchester: Le Neve, *Fasti, 1300–1541, St. Paul's*, 13, 32.
46 M.R.O., Acc. 351/445.
47 C.P. 25(1)/150/68/382.
48 *Reg. Sudbury* (Cant. & York Soc.), i. 228, 235.
49 M.R.O., Acc. 351/445; W.A.M. 4818, 19589; B. Harvey, *Westm. Abbey Estates*, 351, 395. Rook was steward of Westm. and held the neighbouring man. of Frith in Hendon: F. Hitchin Kemp, 'Notes on Messeder's Survey of Hendon' (TS. in B.L.H.L.), 75.
50 M.R.O., Acc. 351/445; W.A.M. 19875; S.C. 2/188/66 mm. 4d., 6d.; S.C. 2/188/67 m. 6. Flete may have been Bedyk's son-in-law: Banks, *Romances of Finchley Man.*
51 M.R.O., Acc. 351/445.
52 Guildhall MS. 10312/63; *Feud. Aids*, vi. 490.
53 S.C. 2/188/69 mm. 4, 7; B.L.H.L., Acc. 9131; Prob. 11/1 (P.C.C. 15 Rous).
54 C.P. 25(1)/152/93/144.
55 C 136/100/41.
56 C.P. 25(1)/149/44/135; *Cal. Close*, 1377–81, 216.
57 C.P. 25(1)/150/68/396; B.L. Add. Ch. 40515–17, 40520.
58 Hist. MSS. Com. 78, *Hastings*, i, p. 215; *Feud. Aids*, vi. 490.
59 S.C. 2/188/70 m. 3.
60 S.C. 2/188/73 m. 3d.; S.C. 2/188/74 mm. 2, 5; S.C. 2/188/75 m. 2; Guildhall MS. 10312/72.
61 St. Paul's MS. B 80.
62 C.P. 25(1)/294/77/1; Guildhall MS. 10312/77; C 140/73/74.
63 S.C. 2/189/5 m. 3.
64 S.C. 2/189/9 m. 2.
65 E 210/9773; M.R.O., Acc. 351/213; B.L.H.L., Acc. 9131. For the story that Sir Wm. intrigued on the king's behalf with Hastings's wife Ann, see *L. & P. Hen. VIII*, i(1), p. 286.
66 C 142/147/64; E 326/9202.
67 M.R.O., Acc. 351/208; C 66/1153, 3rd pt. m. 19 (23); *V.C.H. Mdx.* v. 326; *Complete Peerage*, s.v. Compton.
68 M.R.O., Acc. 351/209.
69 M.R.O., Acc. 351/11.
70 Ibid. 12.
71 Ibid. 249.
72 C 142/429/125.
73 M.R.O., Acc. 351/258.
74 Prob. 11/411 (P.C.C. 179 Fane); M.R.O., Acc. 351/266.

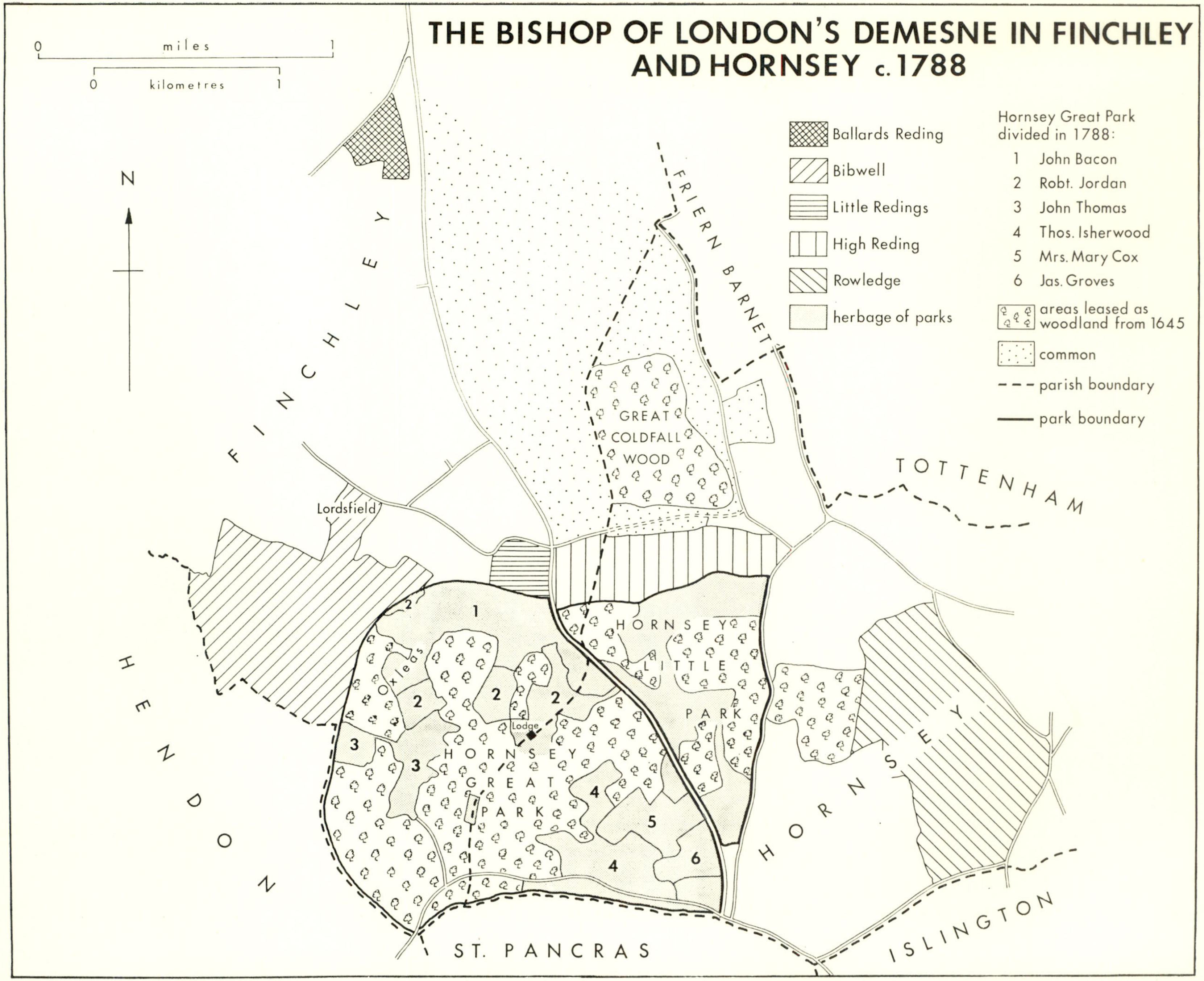
THE BISHOP OF LONDON'S DEMESNE IN FINCHLEY AND HORNSEY c.1788
0 miles 1
0 kilometres 1
N
Ballards Reding
Bibwell
Little Redings
High Reding
Rowledge
herbage of parks
Hornsey Great Park divided in 1788:
1 John Bacon
2 Robt. Jordan
3 John Thomas
4 Thos. Isherwood
5 Mrs. Mary Cox
6 Jas. Groves
areas leased as woodland from 1645
common
parish boundary
park boundary
FINCHLEY
FRIERN BARNET
TOTTENHAM
HENDON
HORNSEY
ST. PANCRAS
ISLINGTON
GREAT COLDFALL WOOD
HORNSEY LITTLE PARK
HORNSEY GREAT PARK
Lordsfield
Oxleas
Lodge

added to the estate and was succeeded by his son Edward (d. 1774)[75] who broke the entail in 1764 and left it in trust for life to his brother Thomas. Thomas, who until 1774 bore the surname Greenhalgh,[76] by will proved 1780 conveyed the manor in trust for life to his son Thomas,[77] who died childless in 1830. The title was then disputed between the Revd. Edward Cooper,[78] under the will of Edward Allen (d. 1774), and descendants of Edward Allen (d. 1692),[79] under the will of Thomas Allen (d. 1780). In 1832 Cooper's title passed to his son the Revd. Edward Philip Cooper (d. 1864), who bought out the other claimants[80] and settled his Finchley estates on his daughters Edith Cassandra (d. 1888) and Sophia Mary Leigh (d. 1888), the wife of Frederick A. H. Fitzgerald. On their deaths Bibbesworth manor passed to Albert Henry Arden (d. 1897), son of their father's sister. A. H. Arden was succeeded by his son Edward Cooper Arden,[81] who held the last court in 1936.[82]

The Bibbesworth estate remained encumbered in the 19th century. Churchfield, already divided by Regent's Park Road, was sold from 1849[83] and sales of other portions continued until 1909, when E. C. Arden sold most of the remaining land for building.[84] William Gamage bought the house with 29 a. at about that time and sold it in 1919 to the convent of Marie Auxiliatrice, which still owned it in 1977.[85] The Express Dairy bought Sheephouse or College farm in 1909. The farm-house and a small part of the land were conveyed to the Department of Transport in 1974, after most of the surrounding fields had been sold for building.[86]

In 1376 Richard of Stoke and others leased Bibbesworth manor to Lawrence of Allerthorpe[87] and in 1502 Edward, Lord Hastings, leased it to Sir Thomas Frowyk, whom he made steward and bailiff.[88] After Frowyk's death in 1506 the lease was held by his widow Elizabeth, who by 1508 had married Thomas Jakes.[89] In 1515 Elizabeth surrendered the lease to Lord Hastings[90] and in 1530, during the minority of Peter Compton, the manor was leased by the Crown to Sir William Brereton,[91] who sold some of the land.[92] After Brereton's execution in 1536 his widow Elizabeth, who resumed her former husband's name of Savage, petitioned Cromwell for Bibbesworth,[93] which in 1537 was leased to her 'cousin' Urian Brereton, still the lessee in 1547–8.[94] The manor was never again leased in its entirety.

Bibbesworth manor-house stood at the centre of the estate, south of East End Road and between Church End and East End. The manor-house, mentioned in 1335,[95] existed by 1253 and may have been the house of Michael Tovy where two people were burnt to death in 1245–6.[96] The house was probably rebuilt or extended by the Bibbesworth or Hastings families. In the early 16th century it was the 'great place of Bibbesworth' and in 1502 it comprised a chief messuage, orchard, and building within the moat and a great barn and long stable outside the moat.[97] It was the largest house in the parish in 1664, being assessed at nineteen hearths,[98] and by 1692, when it figured in a dispute between two Elizabeth Allens, respective widows of Edward and James, it apparently already had the distinctive fishponds on the northern side of East End Road and extensive pleasure gardens.[99]

After the Allens ceased to live in Finchley, Bibbesworth manor-house was leased as a boys' school to William Fanning (1819–37) and Dr. Henry Worsley (1838–57).[1] Miss Lucy Worsley was in occupation in 1859 and Miss H. Legeyt, who ran it as a girls' school, in 1862.[2] In 1863 it was leased with 23 a. to George Plucknett, a magistrate who often heard cases in the hall of the house.[3] Between 1882 and 1887 the lease passed to William Pearce Jones, who surrendered it *c.* 1906.[4]

The existing house was built for Thomas Allen *c.* 1723 north of the earlier seat.[5] It is a large plain building, seven bays by three and with three storeys above a basement. The interior, which has an unusual plan with four internal chimney stacks, retains the original oak staircase and much panelling.[6] Later fittings include fire-places and panelling of the late 18th century and many features in the 18th-century style but probably of *c.* 1900, at about which time a billiards room was added to the north-west. Since 1919 a chapel and classrooms have been built on the north-west and an attic has been added to the old part. An Ionic garden temple was removed to Surrey *c.* 1970.[7]

OTHER ESTATES. Matthew of Ditton (? Ryfton) granted 40 a. and a house in Hendon and Finchley

75 M.R.O., Acc. 351/271–3, 565.
76 Ibid. 35.
77 Ibid. 61, 572.
78 The Coopers were descended from Ann Noel, aunt of Edw. Allen (d. 1774): M.R.O., Acc. 351/5.
79 Ibid. 582.
80 Ibid. 565, 572.
81 B.L.H.L., Acc. 8682; Acc. 9132/9; M.R.O., Acc. 351/85, 202, 483, 494.
82 M.R.O., Acc. 351/375.
83 B.L.H.L., Acc. 9132/9, 11; Acc. 6109/1–32; S/C (Church End).
84 M.R.O., Acc. 1368/64; M.L.R. 1874/14/979; B.L. H.L., S/C (Hertford Lodge; Olders Hill; Finchley Man. estate; Moat estate); Acc. 8682; Potter Colln. 28/67.
85 B.L.H.L., Poor-rate bk. (1911); M.R.O., Hist. Notes 2/7/1957. See below, pp. 87, 97.
86 Ex inf. Dept. of Transport.
87 M.R.O., Acc. 351/445.
88 E 210/9773; E 210/9863; E 210/9922; C.P. 40/976 carte rot. 6.
89 C 142/20/4; E 326/12771; C 1/326/26.
90 M.R.O., Acc. 351/445; C 142/119/114.
91 E 326/9069; E 326/9202.
92 E 326/10676.
93 She sent a gelding as a bribe: *L. & P. Hen. VIII*, x, p. 364; xi, p. 414; xii(1), p. 537.
94 Ibid. xiv(1), p. 444; S.C. 6/Hen. VIII/5879; S.C. 6/Ed. VI/750 m. 2d.
95 St. Paul's MS. A 66/25.
96 C.P. 25(1)/147/18/333; J.I. 1/538 m. 20.
97 M.R.O., Acc. 351/260; E 210/9773.
98 M.R.O., MR/TH/1, f. 34v.
99 C 6/329/8; C 8/436/1; M.R.O., Acc. 351/551.
1 M.R.O., Acc. 351/299–300; M.R.O., TA/FIN; B.L.H.L., Acc. 6140/2.
2 B.L.H.L., Church-rate (1859); *Kelly's Dir. Mdx.* (1862).
3 M.R.O., Acc. 351/404; Walford, *Gtr. Lond.* i. 338.
4 *Kelly's Dir. Mdx.* (1882, 1908); B.L.H.L., Poor-rate (1887).
5 Date and Allen's crest on rain-water heads; M.R.O., Acc. 1140.
6 Thorne, *Environs*, 216, says that the hall is panelled in oak but in 1977 it had been painted.
7 Photographs *penes* the community and ex inf. Sister Kelland.

to the Knights Templars in 1243.[8] The estate presumably passed on the Templars' suppression to the Knights Hospitallers, who in 1364 held Temple Croft of Bibbesworth manor.[9] After the Dissolution it was granted by the Crown in 1544 to Sir John and Ralph Allen and Sir John Champnez,[10] whose title seems to have lapsed. In 1526 the Hospitallers had leased Temple Croft, with other land probably in Hendon, to Henry Barker, smith of Hendon, and in 1571 John Barker leased it for 99 years to Simon Scudamore (d. 1609), goldsmith of London.[11] In 1620 Scudamore's widow Jane leased it to Nicholas Luke, who assigned it in 1621 to John Ore, to whom Thomas Barker quitclaimed in 1623.[12] By will proved 1630 Ore bequeathed his interest to his daughter Elizabeth, wife of William Rolfe, who assigned it in 1640 to Joseph Devereux, from whom it passed in 1666 to Samuel Neale.[13] In 1668 the Rolfes quitclaimed to Neale, who in 1675 claimed that he held by inheritance, not by lease;[14] Neale's title was confirmed and in 1690 he conveyed Temple Croft to Thomas Ingram, who in 1732 sold it to Thomas Allen,[15] in whose Bibbesworth estate it was absorbed. It lay on East End Road near Church End,[16] and Avenue House, the home of H. C. Stephens, was later built there.[17]

About 1528 the abbot of Westminster held a field of Bibbesworth manor, probably in Hendon, although Westminster had sold the manor in 1386.[18]

Among property inherited by John Ore's daughter Elizabeth was Gibbs, 8 a. in East End which she and William Rolfe conveyed to Christopher Sutton in 1642.[19] By will proved 1660, Sutton devised it to his son Richard, who in 1717 conveyed it to John Lyons, from whom in 1718 it passed to Christ's Hospital, still the owner in 1887.[20]

The largest medieval freehold estate apart from the manors was Grotes or Grass farm, between Church End and the Hendon boundary. It was held of the bishop for rent and was probably the house, 86 a., and rent conveyed by Agnes, widow of William atte Welle, to Thomas of Blechenham and his wife Olive in 1315.[21] Olive and her second husband Edmund Laner were in possession in 1336–7 and tenants of Laner were fined at the bishop's court in 1393.[22] Roger Grote, in possession in 1394, had property in Finchley worth £3 6*s*. 8*d*. in 1412[23] and was succeeded by Andrew Grote between 1427 and 1429.[24] Andrew, pardoned for outlawry for debt in 1468, lost his estate between 1462 and 1467 to John Alfrey. Grotes was held by John Plomer[25] and thereafter descended with Bibbesworth and Normans until 1602, when Thomas Compton sold it to Sir James Altham, baron of the Exchequer, who in 1615 settled it on his wife Helen.[26] On her death in 1639 the estate was divided between Lady Ann Astley (d. 1662) and Charles Tryon, her daughters' children. After the Astley line had died out in 1688,[27] all the lands were held by Charles Tryon, who in 1724 conveyed them to Thomas Inwen, merchant of Southwark;[28] his daughter Sarah (d. 1776) married successively Henry Howard, earl of Suffolk (d. 1745), and Lucius Charles Cary, Viscount Falkland (d. 1785).[29] In 1794 Francis M. Austin, devisee under Lady Falkland's will, sold Grotes to John Peter Hankey, a banker whose widow Isabel purchased more land in 1819 and owned 118 a. in 1841.[30] In 1856 Sir William Hankey sold it to John Harris Heal, grandson of the founder of the furniture firm, who in 1861 also bought Sabin, 65 a. later called Furzby farm, from Philip S. Worsley.[31] After Heal's death in 1876 his widow Annie held the estate until her death in 1890.[32] Frank Heal then lived at the house and still owned some of the land in 1900, although the rest had been sold in 1894 to James Williamson of Elm Grange, who had built on it by 1906.[33] In 1911 the farm was owned and occupied by Edward Wormald.[34]

A house formed part of the estate in 1315 and Grotes farm-house stood within an ancient moated site in the centre of its land, a little west of the main Church End settlement.[35] An old house there, assessed for six hearths in 1664 and 1674, was demolished in 1923.[36] From *c*. 1610 until 1762 the farm was leased to the Nicholl family.[37]

During the 16th century a branch of the Peacock family of Redbourn (Herts.) acquired freehold land in northern Finchley and Woodside as part of an extensive estate embracing Totteridge manor (Herts.), Frith manor in Hendon, and land in South Mimms.[38] Richard Peacock, a younger son of Walter Peacock of Redbourn, had property in Finchley by 1577 and bought other estates, originally belonging to the Bigmore or Bekmore family, the Smiths, and the Copwoods.[39] In 1589 and 1598 Richard was assessed for tax at £30 on land, the

8 C.P. 25(1)/147/13/204. See *V.C.H. Mdx.* v. 21.
9 W.A.M. 4818.
10 *L. & P. Hen. VIII*, xix(2), p. 77.
11 B.L. Cott. MS. Claud. E. vi, f. 288; M.R.O., Acc. 351/207; Prob. 11/113 (P.C.C. 50 Dorset).
12 M.R.O., Acc. 351/499, 531.
13 Ibid. 14, 503, 531.
14 Ibid. 504; C 8/240/12.
15 M.R.O., Acc. 351/505–6, 513–14.
16 M.R.O., TA/FIN, no. 26.
17 O.S. Map 6", Mdx. XI. NE. (1867 and 1897 edns.).
18 E 315/410 f. 62; see p. 57.
19 B.L.H.L., Acc. 8668.
20 Prob. 11/302 (P.C.C. 275 Nabbs); B.L.H.L., Banks Colln. iii; B.L.H.L., Poor-rate bk. (1887).
21 C.P. 25(1)/149/45/160.
22 C.P. 25(1)/150/57/108; S.C. 2/188/66 m. 6d.
23 S.C. 2/188/66 m. 11d.; *Feud. Aids*, vi. 490.
24 Guildhall MS. 10312/69, m. 1d.; S.C. 2/188/70 m. 1d.
25 *Cal. Pat.* 1467–77, 82; S.C. 2/188/81 m. 4; S.C. 2/189/2 m. 3; Guildhall MS. 10302/78.
26 C.P. 25(2)/Mich. 44 Eliz. I; Wards 2/34/127/1.
27 S.C. 2/191/10; *Complete Peerage*, s.v. Astley; P. Morants, *Hist. Essex* (1768), ii. 60.
28 M.L.R. 1724/4/103–4.
29 *Illus. Lond. News*, 17 Mar. 1855.
30 M.L.R. 1794/5/499–50; M.R.O., Acc. 351/170–3; M.R.O., TA/FIN.
31 B.L.H.L., Acc. 10111; Finchley local bd., min. bk. v. 348.
32 B.L.H.L., F/728; *Hendon & Finchley Times*, 4 Apr. 1890.
33 *Kelly's Dir. Mdx.* (1890); B.L.H.L., Poor-rate bk. (1900); B.L.H.L., S/C (Grass Fm. estate (1894); Grass Pk. estate (1906); Woodway Lodge (1906); B.L.H.L., Banks Colln. viii. 1098.
34 B.L.H.L., Poor-rate bk. (1911).
35 C.P. 25(1)/149/45/160; Rocque, *Map of Mdx.* (1754).
36 M.R.O., MR/TH/1, f. 34v.; E 179/143/370 m. 7d.; B.L.H.L., Banks Colln., biog. Hastings.
37 B.L.H.L., Banks Colln., Wills s.v. Nicoll; Guildhall MS. 10312/122, m. 6.
38 *Mdx. Pedigrees* (Harl. Soc. lxv), 52–3; *V.C.H. Mdx.* v. 19.
39 Guildhall MS. 10312/92, m. 6; C.P. 25(2)/66/545/7; M.R.O., Acc. 351/132, 209; B.L.H.L., Banks Colln. v. 3331 sqq.

highest amount in Finchley. A separate estate was held there by his nephew Sir Edward Peacock (d. 1605), marshal in the King's Bench.[40] After Richard's death in 1615 another of his nephews, William Peacock, was accepted as his heir[41] and in 1623 was succeeded by his son Richard (d. 1671), who devised the estate to his widow Rechord for life with remainder to his sons in tail male.[42] One son, William, was in control at Finchley in 1673 but his mother had regained the property by 1674.[43] Rechord outlived all her sons and in 1689 was succeeded by her daughters' descendants, Rechord Wilson, Mary Williams, and Dorothy Walker, who between 1710 and 1718 sold the estate to Sir John Lade, Bt., a brewer.[44] Then including nine houses besides the main seat and 212 a. in Finchley, the estate was devised by Lade in 1740 to his brother's grandson, John Inskip, who was to take the surname Lade.[45] Inskip, who became Sir John Lade, Bt., in 1758, in 1759 left a posthumous son, another Sir John Lade, Bt., gambler and friend of the Prince Regent.[46] During the 1790s he sold the heavily mortgaged estate, Crockford's farm (80 a.) at Woodside in 1794 to John Bacon, Cobley's farm (68 a.) at Fallow Corner in 1796 to William Clulow, and Court House and 21 a. in 1797 to William Leader.[47]

The Peacocks' mansion, assessed on fourteen hearths in 1664,[48] was probably the farm-house at the northern end of Nether Street, called Court House possibly because the courts of Frith manor were held there.[49] It was the main house on the estate until Frith manor-house was built in Hendon in 1790.[50] When William Leader died in 1829, the house and surrounding lands passed to his son John Temple Leader, who conveyed them in 1886 to Mrs. Ethel W. Burridge, who sold them for building in 1936. The farm-house, a red-brick building, was extended in 1863 by the tenant Samuel Wimbush and demolished in 1936.[51] In the late 1880s it was leased to Jersey Farm Dairies, forming part of a 200-a. farm.[52]

Fallow or Cobley's farm, so called after its 18th- and 19th-century lessees, descended on the death of William Clulow in 1822 to his son William Whitaker Clulow and then to George and Francis William Child, children of his daughters Elizabeth and Martha. Francis was declared insane in 1865 and his portion passed to his brother Charles. The estate, by that time called Etchingham Park after the Clulow home in Sussex, was sold on building leases from 1880.[53] The farm, still owned by the Child family in 1900, disappeared soon afterwards and the farm-house made way for suburban housing in the 1920s.[54]

Woodside farm, for a while part of the extensive Bacon estates, was sold by John Bacon (d. 1816) to Joseph (d. 1820) and Joseph Douglas Holden, who held it in 1841.[55] Henry Holden, to whom mortgage interests in the Bacon estate were conveyed in 1877, began to build on Woodside in the 1880s and the rest was put up for sale by his executrix in 1900.[56]

Richard Utber in 1647 began to build up an estate on either side of Ballards Lane by the purchase from Bartholomew Clerk of a house and 20 a., including Frithfield which had belonged to Bibbesworth. Thomas Compton had sold Frithfield in 1594 to George Shepherd, whose son John sold it in 1600 to Stephen Haughton; thereafter it had been sold to Robert Marsh in 1623, to Robert Nicholl, and in 1641–2 to Robert Alden, who had conveyed it to Clerk in 1646.[57] Alden had acquired a house and Crossfield in Ballards Lane from Thomas Banks in 1626 and Colefield, south of the junction with Nether Street, from William Sherman in 1638.[58] Alden built a new house in Ballards Lane which in 1664 was assessed for seventeen hearths, the largest in Finchley after Bibbesworth,[59] and in 1669 Richard Utber sold it, with other houses and 21 a., to John Searle (d. 1682), who had made his fortune from a sugar plantation and who left his estate to his widow Anne.[60] Searle and his widow, who married Sir William Hedges, alderman of London and former governor of Bengal, acquired more land in Finchley in 1673, 1682, 1683, and 1690.[61] Anne (d. 1724) and her sons John and Charles Hedges bought out the interests of her daughters by her first marriage, Elizabeth, wife of Thomas, Lord Trevor of Bromham (d. 1730), and Hester, wife of Sir James Bateman.[62] Administration of Charles Hedges's estate was granted to his brother John in 1784 and Charles's grandson Hugh Bisshopp, son of his daughter Susan, had control by 1800.[63] In 1841 Bisshopp had 69 a. of old inclosure and 13 a. of allotted land mostly at Ballards Lane.[64] The estate was offered for sale as building land in 1848.[65]

The demesne lands of both the bishop's and Bibbesworth manors formed beneficial leasehold estates from an early period. Bibwell, west of

[40] E 179/269/41; E 179/142/239 m. 10d.
[41] Wm. was the s. or grands. of Ric.'s eldest brother Thos. and Sir Edw. was the s. of Edw. another brother. C 2/Jas. I/P14/31; Sta. Cha. 8/248/10; Wards 5/30/657; C.P. 43/129 mm. 2–3; Prob. 11/126 (P.C.C. 81 Rudd); M.R.O., Acc. 351/150.
[42] Prob. 11/142 (P.C.C. 72 Swann, will of Wm. Peacock); Prob. 11/337 (P.C.C. 127 Duke, will of Ric. Peacock); C 142/473/51.
[43] C 10/163/88; R. Blome, *Britannia* (1673), 403; E 179/143/370 m. 7.
[44] C 6/258/84; *V.C.H. Herts.* iii. 149; B.L.H.L., Acc. 8707; M.L.R. 1711/5/46; 2/36; 1717/2/96–7; 1719/1/12; E 214/1200.
[45] B.L.H.L., Acc. 3805.
[46] B.L.H.L., Banks Colln., biog. Lade.
[47] M.L.R. 1794/2/553; 1796/6/176; 1797/2/414; 1798/1 565.
[48] M.R.O., MR/TH/1, f. 35d.
[49] O.S. Map 6", Mdx. VI. SE. (1867–73 edn.).
[50] *V.C.H. Mdx.* v. 19.
[51] B.L.H.L., Banks Colln. v. 3346 sqq.
[52] [Jersey Farm Dairies], *Memento of Finchley* in B.L.H.L.
[53] B.L.H.L., Banks Colln., Wills (P.C.C. 511 Herschell, will of Wm. Clulow); M.R.O., Acc. 1077.
[54] B.L.H.L., Poor-rate bk. (1900); B.L.H.L., Banks Colln. iv. 4163 sqq.
[55] M.R.O., TA/FIN. And see p. 18.
[56] M.R.O., Acc. 830/1; B.L.H.L., S/C (Woodside Pk., Woodside Hall).
[57] B.L.H.L., Acc. 9131; G.L.R.O., Harben Deeds C 237.
[58] B.L.H.L., Acc. 9131.
[59] M.R.O., MR/TH/1, f. 39v.
[60] G.L.R.O., Harben Deeds C 230; Prob. 11/370 (P.C.C. 102 Cottle).
[61] B.L.H.L., Acc. 6416/9; Acc. 9131; C 54/4716 m. 13.
[62] M.L.R. 1714/3/25; 1726/2/4–5, 60; Prob. 11/600 (P.C.C. 247 Bolton, will of Anne Hedges).
[63] B.L.H.L., Banks Colln., will of Chas. Hedges; Banks Colln. xvi (land tax, 1800); *Complete Peerage*, s.v. Zouche.
[64] M.R.O., EA/FIN; TA/FIN.
[65] B.L.H.L., S/C (Church End).

Hornsey great park and amounting to 170 a. in 1647,[66] was leased in 1434 by the bishop to John Sanny for 40 years.[67] Thomas Sanny was lessee in 1489[68] and Robert Shepherd leased Bibwell for 46 years in 1497.[69] At about that time Lordsfield, to the north, and Little Redings, to the east at Parkgate, became part of the Bibwell estate; they later amounted to 13 a. and 15 a. respectively. Little Redings had been leased out by 1447[70] and in 1464–5 William Osborne leased both Little Redings and Lordsfield from the bishop,[71] as did John Osborne in 1476 and Robert Shepherd in 1514–15.[72] In Henry VIII's reign both Robert Rolfe and Robert Lister claimed to have derived a title from Robert Shepherd.[73] In 1537 the bishop confirmed the lease of Bibwell for 46 years to John Kellet, who was dead within the year and whose widow Joan, who married Thomas Walker, merchant tailor of London, was granted the lease on the same terms.[74] Lordsfield and Little Redings were leased to Robert Rolfe for life in 1542 and to Agnes his widow in 1547.[75]

In 1570 the bishop leased Bibwell, Lordsfield, and Little Redings to William Kirton, gentleman of London, and his sons Israel and John for three lives.[76] The estate was leased to Henry Kerry of Southwark for 21 years in 1588 and to John Stone, haberdasher of London, for the lives of Anne Kerry and her cousins in 1592.[77] Bishop Juxon leased it in 1639 to his kinsman John Juxon of London for three lives and thereafter such leases continued until 1902. Leases were made to Sir William Juxon, Bt., of Little Compton (Warws.) in 1710[78] and to trustees for his widow Susannah in 1755. Susannah married Charles Fane, Viscount Fane (d. 1766), and on her death in 1792 devised the lease to the Revd. Henry Jerome de Salis.[79] Alexander Murray of Elm Place became lessee in 1810, under an agreement with de Salis of 1799,[80] and sold the lease in 1821 to Lewis Loyd (d. 1858), a City banker, from whom it descended to his son Samuel Jones Loyd, Lord Overstone (d. 1883), and granddaughter Harriet Sarah Loyd-Lindsay, Lady Wantage. In 1902 the trustees appointed under Lord Overstone's will sold their interest to the Ecclesiastical Commissioners.[81] In 1874 the estate was called Park Farm, after the freehold farm-house near by in East End Road.[82] By 1905 Park Farm had been leased by the Ecclesiastical Commissioners to the circus proprietor Lord George Sanger, who was murdered there in 1911.[83]

Ballards Reding, a small area of demesne cleared from Finchley wood at Ballards Lane, was leased out by 1447,[84] and from 1540 was leased with Hornsey great park[85] until William Strode, lessee of the whole estate, split it up in 1788. It consisted of 22 a. in 1811, when John Bacon sold it to Thomas Harrison Andrew (d. 1824) of Moss Hall, whose devisees conveyed it to Samuel Wimbush.[86] In 1854 Wimbush's sons Samuel, Joshua, and Henry inherited the leasehold as tenants in common, buying the bishop's remaining interest in 1855.[87] In 1841 the Wimbush estate, centred on Fallow Corner, consisted of 45 a. of freehold and 113 a. of leasehold land.[88] It remained with the family until 1901, when Barnes Wimbush sold it to E. L. Perry.[89]

Much of Hornsey great park, including Oxleas, meadow land in its north part, lay within Finchley. Oxleas was leased with Ballards Reding and the herbage of the park from 1540 until 1788,[90] when William Strode sold the largest portion, 117 a. mostly in Finchley and containing Ballards Reding (22 a.)[91] and most of Oxleas, to John Bacon. Robert Jordan bought 56 a. of Oxleas and John Thomas 35 a. The other 115 a. of the great park lay within Hornsey parish.[92] In 1811 Bacon sold 111 a., including most of Oxleas, to Elizabeth Adamson, whose heir in 1815 was Margaret, wife of the Revd. John Harrison.[93] Harrison and Ann Bassindale held 90 a. in 1841,[94] and their lease had been sold back to the Ecclesiastical Commissioners by 1887.[95]

The 56 a. of Oxleas purchased in 1788 by Robert Jordan and held by his family as under-lessees at least since 1756 were known by 1810 as Park Gate. It descended from Robert (d. 1797) to his brother Edward (d. 1797) and to Edward's son Edward, who by will proved 1810 devised the estate to his mother Sarah (d. 1835), with remainder to the child of his sister Mary, wife of John George Graeff. Mary's son John George Graeff sold it in 1838 to Anthony Salvin, who in 1878 sold his leasehold to the Ecclesiastical Commissioners.[96] Fothergills, the 35 a. of Oxleas purchased by John Thomas in 1788, had been held by him as under-lessee at least since 1781.[97] By will proved 1797 he devised it to his daughter Sarah Smith and her heirs, in 1817 it passed to Sarah's son John (d. 1847), and in 1873 John's son John sold his interest to the Ecclesiastical Commissioners.[98]

Hornsey woods, including 266 a. in Finchley, were leased from 1645 until 1885, when the leasehold was surrendered to the Ecclesiastical Commissioners.[99]

A new demesne estate was created at inclosure

[66] Guildhall MS. 10464A, p. 85.
[67] St. Paul's MS. A 86.
[68] S.C. 2/189/8 m. 3.
[69] Req. 2/5/290.
[70] Guildhall MSS. 10312/73, m. 2; 10464A; 12401.
[71] S.C. 6/1140/24 m. 4d.
[72] Guildhall MSS. 10312/80, m. 8d.; 10123/1, f. 9v.
[73] Req. 2/5/290.
[74] St. Paul's MS. C (Sampson), ff. 42v.–3, 61 and v.
[75] Ibid. (Sampson), ff. 137 and v., 182v.
[76] Ibid. (I Nowell), ff. 334v.–5.
[77] Ibid. (II Nowell), ff. 269 and v.; (III Nowell), ff. 5 and v.
[78] Guildhall MSS. 12401; 10234/1, pp. 545–6.
[79] Ibid. 10234/5, pp. 309–10; 7, pp. 321–5; 10242, p. 128.
[80] M.R.O., Acc. 190/1; Guildhall MS. 10234/9, pp. 55–9.
[81] Guildhall MS. 12401.
[82] *Kelly's Dir. Mdx.* (1867); B.L.H.L., Highway-rate bk. (1879).
[83] Potter Colln. 28/25.
[84] Guildhall MS. 10312/73. For later lessees see S.C. 2/188/75 m. 4; S.C. 2/188/77 m. 2d.; S.C. 6/1140/24 m. 4d.; Guildhall MSS. 10123/1, f. 25v.; 2, f. 46; 3, f. 26.
[85] See p. 141.
[86] Guildhall MSS. 12405; 12406; 10234/9, pp. 259–63; 10, pp. 213–17.
[87] Guildhall MS. 10234/13, pp. 328–33.
[88] M.R.O., TA/FIN.
[89] B.L.H.L., Banks Colln., biog. s.v. Wimbush.
[90] See p. 141.
[91] See above.
[92] Guildhall MSS. 10242, pp. 130–1; 12418.
[93] Ibid. 10234/9, pp. 253–8; 12405; 10245, pp. 125–6.
[94] M.R.O., TA/FIN.
[95] B.L.H.L., Rate-bk. (1887).
[96] Guildhall MSS. 12396; 12405; B.L.H.L., Banks Colln. xvi (rate and land tax bks.).
[97] Guildhall MSS. 10242, pp. 130–1; B.L.H.L., Banks Colln. xvi (rate and land tax bks.).
[98] Guildhall MSS. 12405; 12407.
[99] For the descent of Hornsey woods, see p. 153. And see p. 56.

when 40 a., formerly part of Finchley common between the Great North Road and Coldfall wood, was let on 21-year leases.[1] In 1813 it was leased to John Honywood Randolph of Fulham, who sold his interest in 1828 to Lewis Loyd, who assigned it in the same year to Isaac Sutton Cooper.[2] Cooper, in 1855 of Park Hall, Finchley, bought the bishop's reversionary interest in 1865.

Oxleas was sub-leased by 1576 and in 1647 Hornsey park, Oxleas, and Ballards Reding were divided among six under-tenants.[3] By *c.* 1788 there were twelve under-tenants on the Hornsey park and Oxleas estate and another ten on the Hornsey woods estate,[4] holding small amounts of land but sometimes the nucleus of a farm. The largest of the Oxleas under-leased estates consisted of 78 a. held from the mid 18th century until *c.* 1811 by the Ecken family, *c.* 1815 by Thomas Goodson,[5] and from *c.* 1841 to 1859 by Benjamin Briers.[6] By 1871 Lodge Farm had been built on the northern edge of the estate and occupied by John Cotton,[7] who was there in 1887. The lessee in 1900 was James Woodward and in 1911 Thomas Ewers.[8] Spaniards farm-house had been built at the southern part of Fothergills by 1814, when the estate, with adjoining woodland, was sub-leased to John Norbury.[9] The farm was sub-leased to Charles Hicks in 1859 and to James Doughty in 1880.[10]

The Hornsey wood estate, once entirely woodland within Hornsey park, had gradually been cleared until by *c.* 1788 it consisted of 273 a. of farm-land and 400 a. of woodland. The lessee, the earl of Mansfield, retained most of the woodland in hand.[11] After the Ecclesiastical Commissioners had bought out the mesne interest in the demesne estates, there was a rearrangement of boundaries, although the under-tenant sometimes continued as lessee. Spaniards farm had been increased by 11 a. from Salvin's estate in 1880 and by 120 a. of woodland *c.* 1885. Charles Bourn, who leased it in 1882, was ejected in 1890 and the farm, reduced to 83 a., was leased to George Medcalf (d. 1910) while Bishop's and Turners woods (109 a.) were kept in hand. In 1894 Hampstead golf club leased 38 a. of Spaniards farm-land and Medcalf received a new lease of 71 a., consisting of the rest of Spaniards and 23 a. from Manor farm. The golf club increased its area to 44 a. in 1907 and in 1930 bought the freehold. Medcalf's family still held the lease in 1931 when 15 a., including the farm-house site, were leased to Hampstead Garden Suburb Trust.[12]

Most of the former Hornsey park and Hornsey woods east of the Bishop's Avenue formed part of Manor farm, which in 1883 consisted of 466 a. in Finchley and Hornsey administered from the farm-house next to the Great North Road, just outside the Finchley boundary. It was leased from the mid 1870s to Joseph Wilmington Lane (d. 1903) and as Manor Farm Dairies continued to be leased to his family until 1932, although the acreage contracted with building and with leasing to Highgate golf club and other sports clubs. In 1926 some fields were sold to the Metropolitan Water Board.[13]

The main motive of the Ecclesiastical Commissioners in buying out the long leasehold interests in the demesne estates was to profit from building. Land at the Bishop's Avenue in the heart of Hornsey park was offered on building leases from 1894.[14] In 1909 the Commissioners granted a 999-year building lease of 112 a., forming the southern portion of Bibwell or Park farm, to Hampstead Garden Suburb Trust. In 1911 300 a., comprising the rest of Park farm and the north-west portion of Hornsey park, were leased on the same terms to Co-Partnership Tenants Ltd. Building was not completed until the mid 1930s and Park farm-house continued to be sub-leased until after the First World War.[15] Portions of Spaniards farm, totalling 50 a., were leased on 999-year building leases to Hampstead Garden Suburb Trust in 1914, 1931, and 1934.[16]

From the mid 16th until the mid 18th century the Bibbesworth estate was divided, some portions being small. There were at least five lessees *c.* 1530,[17] and nine in 1623 and 1708.[18] Lessees frequently held land at opposite ends of the estate and even Normans, the forerunner of Manor farm and identifiable from the Middle Ages, had different fields in 1594 from those in 1598.[19] In 1708 Thomas Allen kept 56 a. in hand, mostly former woodland in the south-west part. Bibbesworth's largest leasehold estate then consisted of 130 a., mostly in the west, which were leased to Richard Bradford and in 1682 had been leased to Thomas Barnett. Thomas Sanny had leased 80 a. in the north-west part since 1691; Thomas Bradford had leased 49 a. south of the manor-house and Worthy House in East End since 1707; John Williams had leased 47 a. in the north-east part and Cotes Croft since 1705. Five other lessees included Daniel and Richard Clewin, who leased 17 a. and a house, which may have been Normans.[20]

Normans or Manor farm had emerged as the main leasehold estate by 1764, when Daniel Clewin leased 138 a. in four blocks.[21] Clewin, well known as a wealthy farmer, was robbed in his farm house in 1778 by a band led by 'Gentleman Harry'.[22] His son Richard succeeded in 1780 and by 1786 Manor farm formed a compact 150 a. on the eastern borders of the Bibbesworth lands.[23] After

1 M.R.O., EA/FIN; except where otherwise stated, the para. is based on Guildhall MS. 12402.

2 Guildhall MSS. 10234/10, pp. 610–17, 635–43.

3 St. Paul's MS. C (I Nowell), f. 453 and v.; Guildhall MS. 10464A, p. 85.

4 Guildhall MS. 10242, pp. 122–3, 130–1.

5 Guildhall MSS. 10234/9, pp. 253–8; 12405; B.L.H.L., Banks Colln. xvi (rate and land tax bks.).

6 B.L.H.L., Rate bks. (1841, 1859).

7 B.L.H.L., P.A.F. 1/9.

8 B.L.H.L., Poor-rate bks. (1887, 1900, 1911).

9 M.R.O., EA/FIN; B.L.H.L., Banks Colln. xvi (rate and land tax bks.).

10 B.L.H.L., Church-rate bk. (1859); Church Com. file 50263.

11 Guildhall MS. 10242, pp. 122–3; M.R.O., TA/FIN.

12 Church Com. files 50263; 92372.

13 Ibid. 39824; 55543; 64346; *Kelly's Dir. Hornsey* (1932, 1933); ex inf. Unigate.

14 See p. 54.

15 Church Com. file 85003.

16 Ibid. files 39824, 92372.

17 E 315/410 ff. 62–64v.

18 M.R.O., Acc. 351/257; 272–3.

19 Ibid. 209; 479–80.

20 Ibid. 372–3; B.L.H.L., Acc. 9131.

21 M.L.R. 1764/3/535.

22 Potter Colln. 28/43; B.L.H.L., Banks Colln., biog. s.v. Clewin.

23 B.L.H.L., Banks Colln., Finchley Manor file (18th- and 19th-cent. notes on farms).

Richard's death in 1788 the bulk of his estate was held by Mrs. Sarah Clewin (d. 1795) and then by Thomas Verrall. William Fanning leased it from 1819, holding 175 a. in 1834 and 153 a. in 1841.[24] The lease passed in 1843 to Bruce Johnson, who held it in 1871.[25] From 1879 to 1897 Manor farm, then 204 a., was leased to William Whiteley.[26] It was held by George E. Arden in 1900 and James Scott in 1911, when all but 68 a. had been sold off for building.[27] The farm was later held by Deards, originally farmers who became haulage contractors. In 1956, after their move to eastern Finchley, the council acquired the site and demolished the old farm-house.[28]

Sheephouse (later College) farm originated in the leasehold estate held in 1708 by Richard Bradford, who was not a Finchley man[29] and may have subleased or sold his interest to John Odell (d. 1762), a hog farmer with property in Church and East End and lessee of much of Bibbesworth in 1756. John Jones, Odell's brother-in-law, leased 105 a. of Bibbesworth land in 1764 in three blocks, mostly in the south-east part. By 1774 they were divided into two, the larger being held by Edward Jordan and the smaller by Ann Jones until 1777, when they passed to James Bindley (d. 1818), the book collector, who was Odell's nephew.[30] By 1815 both portions were united in a block of 168 a. leased to Richard Claridge.[31] A building existed on the estate by 1814[32] but may have been only a barn or sheephouse. In 1842 97 a., described as Hendon Lane farm, were assigned to one Hamilton, who acquired the rest from Claridge in 1843.[33] From *c.* 1857 to 1866 the farm, called Sheephouse farm, was leased to John Tanqueray.[34] In 1868 it was leased to George Barham of the Express Dairy Co., who renamed it College farm and employed Frederic Chancellor to build a model dairy on the site of the old farm buildings in 1882.[35] Although most of the land was sold for building, the farm-house and some fields continued to be leased to the company until it bought the freehold in 1909.[36]

Most of the north-west part of Bibbesworth which had been held in 1708 by Thomas Sanny was in 1764 leased to Mrs. Claridge.[37] It passed from John Claridge to Richard Carpenter in 1821 and at that date formed a block of 108 a., which was leased to John Caleb Simmonds in 1838 and to John Tomlin in 1843.[38] Most of the estate disappeared in the sales of 1849, some of the rest being incorporated into Manor farm.[39]

ECONOMIC HISTORY. AGRARIAN HISTORY. Finchley was not mentioned in the Domesday survey and in 1086 was probably included in the woodland for 1,000 pigs which formed part of Fulham manor.[40] Clearance of the woodland, which covered much of the parish until the 18th century, may have begun from Hendon during the land hunger of the 12th and 13th centuries. In spite of one reference in 1668 to land in a 'common field',[41] it is unlikely that there were regular open fields. The villagers, who were mostly freemen, probably collaborated in clearance and divided the assarts among themselves.[42] In the 13th century there was land 'in a field called le Reding', a name given to many such clearings in the parish.[43] Land described as a *cultura* belonged to tenants of Bibbesworth in 1365[44] and some fields were still shared *c.* 1500[45] but most were consolidated into closes, held severally. By the end of the Middle Ages farm-land, although still interspersed with woodland and surrounded by thick hedges, covered the western side of the parish, between Dollis brook and Ballards Lane and Whetstone Street, and stretched eastward along Mutton brook to the palings of Hornsey park.

In 1341 half of the 120-a. Bibbesworth estate was sown in winter or spring and half was fallow, indicating a two-course rotation.[46] On the bishop's demesne lands in 1318, however, all the arable, Lordsfield (20 a.), Little Redings (20 a.), and Sorfield (8 a.), was apparently sown.[47] Continuous exploitation would have exhausted the soil and the fields when next mentioned were used for pasture.[48]

Most farm-land until the late 15th century was arable.[49] In 1297 arable was valued at 3*d.* an acre, compared with 2*d.* an acre at Hendon.[50] In 1303 at the bishop's grange in Finchley oats (34 qr.) were by far the largest crop, compared with rye (2 qr.), barley (2 bu.), beans (2 qr.), and peas and vetch (4 qr.).[51] Oats were sown on a small estate in 1380[52] and rye was bought for winter and spring sowing on the bishop's demesne *c.* 1404.[53]

Pannage for pigs formed part of the demesne revenues[54] and herbage within the park became increasingly important among the demesne estates.

[24] B.L.H.L., Acc. 6140/1–2; B.L.H.L., Banks Colln. xvi (rate and land tax bks.); M.R.O., Acc. 351/299–300; M.R.O., TA/FIN.
[25] M.R.O., Acc. 351/404.
[26] B.L.H.L., rate bks. (1879–97).
[27] Ibid. (1900, 1911).
[28] B.L.H.L., Prints Colln. 9908–12; ex inf. Barnet L.B. Estates Officer.
[29] He was a Westm. victualler: Guildhall MS. 12401.
[30] B.L.H.L., Banks Colln. xvi (poor-rate bk. 1756); Banks Colln., Wills s.v. Odell; Potter Colln. 28/41; M.L.R. 1764/3/535; B.L.H.L., Banks Colln., Finchley Manor file; B.L.H.L., Acc. 9130; *D.N.B.*
[31] B.L.H.L., Banks Colln. xvi (poor-rate bk. 1815).
[32] M.R.O., EA/FIN.
[33] M.R.O., Acc. 351/299.
[34] B.L.H.L., P.A.F. 1/9; B.L.H.L., Church-rate bk. (1859). Tanqueray, who purchased the neighbouring Decoy fm. in Hendon in 1854, purchased Quagg field, part of Sheephouse, in 1857: M.R.O., Acc. 1368/17, 64.
[35] M.R.O., Acc. 351/183–7; B.L.H.L., F/728; Finchley Soc. *Newsletter*, Sept. 1974; May 1975.
[36] See above, p. 59.
[37] M.L.R. 1764/3/535.
[38] B.L.H.L., Banks Colln. xvi (poor-rate and land tax bks.); B.L.H.L., Acc. 6140/1–2; M.R.O., Acc. 351/299, 404; M.R.O., TA/FIN.
[39] See p. 59.
[40] *V.C.H. Mdx.* i. 121.
[41] Guildhall MS. 10312/104.
[42] Cf. the system in western Edmonton, a similarly wooded region: *V.C.H. Mdx.* v. 166.
[43] Hist. MSS. Com. 78, *Hastings*, i, p. 214.
[44] W.A.M. 4818.
[45] e.g. Agnesfield: B.L.H.L., Acc. 6416/1; Amyetts: C.P. 40/970 carte rot. 1d.
[46] C 135/65/12.
[47] St. Paul's MS. A 62.
[48] See p. 62.
[49] Cf. descriptions in ft. of fines: 'land' is predominant in the early ones, meadow and pasture predominate from late 15th cent.
[50] C 133/79/5.
[51] *Acct. of Executors of Ric., Bp. of Lond. 1303* (Camd. Soc. N.S. x), 98.
[52] Guildhall MS. 9171/1, f. 72v.
[53] St. Paul's MS. B 78/43.
[54] St. Paul's MS. A 62; S.C. 6/1138/17; S.C. 6/1140/24 m. 4d.

The name 'Somerlese', which was part of the Bibwell estate in 1464, indicates some form of transhumance[55] and place-names like Hogmansherne and Pigensland record pigs, especially on the edges of Finchley wood.[56] Stray animals were mainly pigs and cattle.[57] Sheep were mentioned in 1393[58] and 1447[59] but there is no evidence for the theory that wool-merchants raised them on their Finchley lands.[60] Wills of the 14th and 15th centuries indicate that farming was mixed, most peasant farmers growing grain and hay, pasturing pigs and cattle, and using oxen and horses as draught animals.[61] A few sheep were kept for domestic use[62] and cows were owned even by the carpenter and wheelwright.[63]

Apart from a reference to bond land leased in 1393,[64] there is no evidence for any ancient customary tenements held of the bishop. There were some twelve ancient freehold tenements upon which reliefs and fines of alienation were payable.[65] In 1647 it was stated that there were no copyholds except for a few cottages on the waste,[66] the earliest of which had been granted in 1463.[67] Some copyhold tenements were held from Bibbesworth manor in 1365, and autumn carting works and reliefs, but not heriots, were owed by freehold and copyhold tenants alike.[68]

The lordship of Finchley brought the bishop little profit. Perquisites of court were rarely more than £1 in the Middle Ages,[69] while assised rents rose from some £3 5*s.* a year in 1318 to £4 4*s.* in 1404–5, £4 5*s.* 7¼*d.* in 1509–10, and £5 10*s.* 11¼*d.* in 1555–6.[70] By 1647 they yielded £6 1*s.* 6*d.*[71] From *c.* 1681 to 1711 the yield was £7 10*s.* 2*d.*[72] but by the late 18th century there was no regular rental and the bishop received only fixed admission fines 'of no great account'.[73] The direct exploitation of Finchley wood and the woodland within Hornsey park was, for a time, very profitable.[74] Timber, usually faggots or underwood, from Finchley wood was sold for £22 19*s.* 2*d.* in 1406, £31 6*s.* 4*d.* in 1436–7, and £4 7*s.* in 1464–5.[75] Deforestation was particularly destructive in the 16th century, £360 being obtained for wood and underwood from 120 a. in the years 1577 to 1579.[76]

Cultivation of the demesne on both Finchley and Bibbesworth manors drew little on customary services, a fact which may have encouraged the early and widespread practice of leasing. The rent for Bibwell, leased for £3 6*s.* 8*d.* in 1434, had risen to £5 6*s.* 8*d.* in 1538.[77] Little Redings and Lordsfield were leased for £1 2*s.* in 1464–5 and £2 in 1542[78] and from 1570 the rent for Bibwell, Little Redings, and Lordsfield remained £7 6*s.* 8*d.* until the 19th century.[79] Ballards Reding, leased for 10*s.* in 1464–5,[80] was from 1540 leased with Oxleas and herbage in Hornsey park for £13 18*s.* 8*d.*[81] With the leasing of the woodland within Hornsey park from 1645, all the demesne was farmed out. Bibbesworth, for most of the Middle Ages held by London merchants, was also apparently farmed mainly by lessees.

Londoners' connexions with Finchley,[82] apparent from the 13th century, were most obvious in the history of Bibbesworth. Both the goldsmith Michael Tovy and the draper Adam de Basing were mayors of London. Adam's son Thomas was a leading wool-merchant, who died young, whereupon his property was disputed between his executor Richard de Ashwy, a mercer and alderman, and his sisters' husbands William de Hadestok, alderman, and the cordwainer Henry le Waleys, who was twice mayor. Hadestok's son-in-law Adam de Bedyk was a merchant tailor, whose son Henry was collector of customs for Middlesex and appointed John de Pulteney, a draper and alderman, as his son Thomas's guardian. Simon Francis was a mercer and alderman, as was John Shadworth, trustee in 1400, and many other late-14th-century trustees were probably also Londoners. Drew Barentyn was a goldsmith and twice mayor, William Chester a skinner and merchant of the staple, and John Plomer or Leynham a grocer and alderman.

Marches estate, too, was associated with Londoners: John Barnes, alderman and mayor, Walter Kersebroke, sherman, William Creswick, grocer and alderman, John Bestchurch, barber, and John Norman, draper and mayor. Other citizens with interests in Finchley were Richard de Manehale, chandler (1362–3), John Horwood (*c.* 1365–81), Thomas atte Welle, Richard French (1400–1), Thomas Brown, grocer (1412), and one Mancell, butcher (1489).

Londoners probably were mainly interested in drawing rents or using property as security in business transactions. Some lords of Bibbesworth, notably the Bedyks and possibly also the Basings, Tovy, Barentyn, and Plomer, may have stayed at the manor-house. Apart from the Bedyks, whose

55 S.C. 6/1140/24 m. 4d.
56 M.R.O., Acc. 262/3/1; S.C. 2/189/2; S.C. 2/191/8.
57 e.g. a boar, cow, and calf in 1393: S.C. 6/188/66; 16 hogs and a heifer in 1450: S.C. 2/188/75 m. 4; steer in 1491: S.C. 2/189/10 m. 2d.
58 S.C. 2/188/66.
59 Guildhall MS. 10312/73.
60 e.g. C. O. Banks in *Finchley Press*, 29 Mar. 1957.
61 e.g. Guildhall MSS. 9171/1, f. 72v.; 3, ff. 57, 373v.; 4, ff. 177, 268; 6, f. 228v.; 9, f. 129v.
62 e.g. in 1379: Guildhall MS. 9171/1, f. 68v.
63 Guildhall MSS. 9171/5, f. 307; 9, f. 85.
64 S.C. 2/188/66 m. 6d.
65 S.C. 2/189/6 m. 3; Guildhall MS. 10312/63; St. Paul's MS. A 62.
66 Guildhall MS. 10464A, p. 85.
67 Ibid. 10312/76.
68 W.A.M. 4818. Cf. M.R.O., Acc. 351/162.
69 e.g. 12*s.* 8*d.* in 1404–5: St. Paul's MS. B 78/43; 15*s.* 2*d.* in 1438–9: S.C. 6/1138/7; 19*s.* 11*d.* in 1464–5: S.C. 6/1140/24 m. 5d.; £1 6*s.* 9*d.* in 1516–17: Guildhall MS. 10123/1, f. 20.
70 St. Paul's MSS. A 62; B 76/7; B 78/43; S.C. 6/Hen. VIII/2109; S.C. 6/Ph. & Mary/193 m. 13.
71 Guildhall MS. 10464A, p. 85.
72 Guildhall MSS. 10124/1, 31.
73 Guildhall MS. 10242, pp. 140–1.
74 For Hornsey park, which included part of Finchley, see p. 153.
75 St. Paul's MSS. B 91, 94; S.C. 6/1140/24 mm. 4d.–6.
76 S.P. 12/137 f. 16.
77 St. Paul's MS. A 86; St. Paul's MS. C (Sampson), ff. 61 and v.
78 S.C. 2/1140/24 m. 4d.; St. Paul's MS. C (Sampson), ff. 137 and v.
79 St. Paul's MS. C (I Nowell), ff. 334v.–335; Guildhall MS. 12401.
80 S.C. 6/1140/24 mm. 4d.–6.
81 St. Paul's MS. C (Sampson), f. 109v.; Guildhall MS. 12400.
82 Information about Londoners is based upon A. B. Beaven, *Aldermen of City of Lond.* i–ii (1908, 1913); G. A. Williams, *Medieval Lond.*; Sylvia Thrupp, *Merchant Class of Medieval Lond.* (1948); Ruth Bird, *Turbulent Lond. of Ric. II* (1949).

three generations in the male line ended in Sir Thomas, more a country gentleman than a merchant, Londoners did not found dynasties. That was due largely to high mortality of children in London,[83] to the continuing attraction of the city itself, and to the need to pay debts at death. When heirs inherited, as did Thomas Francis in 1357, Reynold Barentyn in 1415, or Margaret Plomer and Richard Fisher in 1479, they often sold the estate.

In contrast the local families which worked the land, as small freeholders or as lessees, were often both prolific and long-lived, with names that survived for centuries. Such families[84] were Bigmore or Bekmore (*c.* 1270–1616),[85] Blakewell (*c.* 1270–*c.* 1473),[86] Pratt (1297–1679),[87] Goodyer or Godzer (1321–1657),[88] Shepherd (1365–1669),[89] Warren (1365–1488),[90] Sanny (1375–1804),[91] Heybourn (1377–1474),[92] Martin (1384–1498),[93] Osborne (1392–1779),[94] Luce (1393–1531),[95] Noke (1401–1576),[96] Haynes or Heyne (1405–1616),[97] Nicholl or Nicoll (1445–1762),[98] Copwood (1453–1577),[99] and Rolfe (1473–1664).[1]

The Tudor period brought changes, notably the growing dominance of London, which had effects upon the land market, agriculture, and the appearance of the countryside. Some of the medieval London merchants had financial links with the Crown and there were also men like Hugh Cressingham, clerk of the Exchequer and treasurer of Scotland (d. 1297),[2] and Thomas Aldenham, surgeon to Henry VI (d. 1431),[3] who held land in Finchley. It was during the 16th century, however, that men connected with the court became prominent among the local landowners. Both the Hastings and Compton families, which held Bibbesworth, were closely associated with the king, as was William Brereton, gentleman of the Privy Chamber, who was executed with Anne Boleyn. Sir Thomas Frowyk (d. 1506), Chief Justice of the Common Pleas, was first connected with Finchley through his wife Elizabeth Barnville[4] and was often visited at Bibbesworth by his clients.[5] By 1508 his widow had married Thomas Jakes, keeper of the records of the Common Bench, more commonly described as 'clerk of Hell'.[6]

The bishop's demesne, at first leased to natives like the Sannys, Shepherds, Osbornes, and Rolfes, from the 16th century was leased to outsiders like Robert Lister (d. 1547), an Exchequer official 'well friended and allied', who intimidated the inhabitants.[7] From that time most of the demesne lessees were Londoners who sub-leased to local farmers: both Alexander King and Sir James Altham, who bought parts of Thomas Compton's large estate, were Exchequer officials. The descendants of Edward Allen, the alderman who bought Bibbesworth in 1622, remained squires of Finchley until 1830. Increasingly other freehold estates passed to outsiders, many of whom retired to Finchley as 'gentlemen'. Such were John Dorchester, clothworker (d. 1604),[8] Simon Scudamore, goldsmith (d. 1609),[9] Thomas White, grocer and holder of East India stock (d. 1610),[10] James Middleton, clothworker (d. 1654),[11] and Robert Fluellin, tallow-chandler (d. 1680).[12] Finchley boys were apprenticed to Londoners,[13] and some of the citizens who held land in Finchley may have come from there, including William Heybourn, clothworker (fl. 1557),[14] Walter Osborne, leather-seller (d. 1636),[15] William Rolfe, chandler (d. 1649),[16] and William Rolfe, barber-surgeon (fl. 1637–68).[17] Farming and local government continued to be dominated by the old Finchley families. Among new names were Somerton (1504–89),[18] Page (1545–1777),[19] Odell (1641–1762),[20] Clewin (1649–1793),[21] Roberts (1705–1800),[22] Jordan (1725–1835),[23] Claridge (1756–1842),[24] and Cobley (1798–1881).[25]

In 1199 King John exempted the bishop of London and his men from tallage and all other exactions within and outside cities and towns.[26] The charter was confirmed in 1564, with specific reference to the bishop's men within Finchley manor,[27] and again in 1627.[28] After it had been successfully 'tried' against the lord mayor of London,[29] the charter became the basis of Finchley's

83 See Thrupp, op. cit. 191 sqq.
84 The dates refer to the first and last mention of a name.
85 Hist. MSS. Com. 78, *Hastings*, i, p. 214; S.C. 2/191/6.
86 Hist. MSS. Com. 78, *Hastings*, i, p. 214; C.P. 25(1)/152/97/44.
87 C 133/79/5; Guildhall MS. 10312/114.
88 C.P. 25(1)/149/50/393; C 6/136/41. Later Gooderes owned land in Finchley but probably did not live there.
89 W.A.M. 4818; Prob. 11/331 (P.C.C. 146 Coke).
90 W.A.M. 4818; M.R.O., Acc. 351/134.
91 St. Paul's MS. A 62/2; *Mdx. & Herts. N. & Q.* iii. 148.
92 E 179/141/23/12; S.C. 2/189/2 m. 3.
93 Guildhall MSS. 10312/61, m. 3; 9171/8, f. 17.
94 S.C. 2/188/66 m. 4d.; Guildhall MS. 10475/3.
95 S.C. 2/188/66 m. 5; Guildhall MS. 9171/10, f. 176.
96 Guildhall MS. 10312/63; Req. 2/74/100.
97 St. Paul's MS. A 62; S.C. 2/191/6.
98 C.P. 25(1)/293/71/305; B.L.H.L., Banks Colln., Wills (Mrs. Abigail Nicoll 1762).
99 St. Paul's MS. B 80; Guildhall MS. 10123/8, ff. 17–18.
1 C.P. 25(1)/152/97/44; M.R.O., MR/TH 1, ff. 34d., 35 and d.
2 *T.L.M.A.S.* xv. 221–35; C 133/79/5; *D.N.B.*
3 Norden, *Spec. Brit.* 20.
4 S.C. 2/188/78 m. 3; M.R.O., Acc. 262/4/63.
5 Hist. MSS. Com. 8, *9th Rep., Canterbury Corporation*, p. 147.
6 *L. & P. Hen. VIII*, i(1), p. 206.
7 Req. 2/5/290.
8 C 9/28/97; B.L.H.L., Acc. 9131.
9 B.L.H.L., Acc. 6416/6; Prob. 11/113 (P.C.C. 50 Dorset).
10 Prob. 11/117 (P.C.C. 11 Wood).
11 Prob. 11/253 (P.C.C. 76 Berkeley).
12 Prob. 11/366 (P.C.C. 58 North).
13 e.g. 1646 Finchley boy apprenticed to shoemaker of St. Sepulchre's: M.R.O., MJ/SBB 54, p. 19. In 1793 five boys from the poorho. were apprenticed to Londoners: B.L.H.L., P.A.F. 1/2.
14 C.P. 25(2)/74/630/49.
15 S.C. 2/191/4; S.C. 2/191/10.
16 C 7/293/64.
17 M.R.O., Acc. 351/501, 504.
18 C.P. 40/970 carte rot. 1d.; E 179/269/41.
19 E 179/141/138; Guildhall MS. 10475/3.
20 H.L., Mdx. Protestation Rets.; B.L.H.L., Banks Colln., Wills.
21 C 7/447/75; M.R.O., Acc. 351/276.
22 Guildhall MSS. 10465/20; 12408.
23 Ibid. 10465/40; 12396.
24 B.L.H.L., Banks Colln. xvi, Poor-rate bk. (1756); M.R.O., TA/FIN.
25 B.L.H.L., Acc. 6140/1; M.R.O., Acc. 1077. The fam. still existed, though not in Finchley, in 1926: B.L.H.L., Banks Colln. iv. 5014.
26 M. Gibbs, *Early Charters of Cath. Ch. of St. Paul, Lond.* (Camd. 3rd ser. lviii), 36–7.
27 *Cal. Pat.* 1563–6, p. 5.
28 B.L.H.L., Acc. 8786; B.L.H.L., P.A.F. 1/6 (vestry mins. 26 Feb. 1826).
29 In 1717 the case had happened 'some years since': *T.L.M.A.S.* xix. 48.

fight to avoid paying tolls at London markets. Finchley lost a suit brought by the chamberlain of the City of London between 1776 and 1778[30] but farmers taking hay to Smithfield still invoked the charter in 1826, usually with success, and sometimes gained exemption elsewhere.[31] The charter did not, however, protect Finchley's inhabitants against turnpike tolls.[32] The Victorian King John's Cottages in Long Lane and King John's House in King Street were probably named in commemoration of the charter and not, as local tradition had it, because they marked the site of a royal hunting lodge.[33]

During the 16th and 17th centuries subsistence farming gave way to an agriculture based on the needs of London. Mixed farming continued on most estates, wheat, oats, and hay being grown and pigs, cattle, horses, oxen, and, increasingly, sheep being raised.[34] There was a pinfold on the bishopric demesne by 1514–15,[35] sheep were stolen from one of the Bibbesworth lessees in 1699,[36] and there were sheep-houses on the Nicholl estate in 1702[37] and John Odell's estate at Church End in 1762.[38] Field-names indicate others at Oxleas by 1788[39] and Bibwell by 1799,[40] while Mutton brook was supposedly so called because it was used for sheep-washing.

Arable accounted for 15 per cent of the 544-a. estate of the Comptons *c.* 1530.[41] Wheat and oats were grown as part of a three-course rotation on Bibbesworth in 1623[42] but by 1834 there was 'scarcely any' arable on the manor.[43] The parish in 1801 contained only 69 a. of arable, consisting of 40 a. which had yielded an abundant wheat crop, 24 a. of peas, and 5 a. of potatoes.[44]

Woodland, too, was converted to meadow and pasture. On the Compton estate *c.* 1530 pasture and meadow accounted for 55 per cent and woodland for 30 per cent. On the Bibbesworth portion of the estate woodland was reduced from 34 per cent *c.* 1530[45] to 30 per cent in 1590[46] and 23 per cent, 100 a., in 1623.[47] By 1694 it had shrunk to 41 a., mainly in the south-west part,[48] and by 1708 most had been grubbed up.[49]

Apart from individual woods and groves, bands of woodland and hedgerows surrounded the fields which had been created by assarting.[50] The fields expanded as hedgerows were grubbed up and animals ate the young trees, until by 1810 hedges had been reduced to a few pollarded trees.[51] On the bishop's demesne High Reding, 52 a. in 1640, grew to 76 a. by 1647 and 85 a. by 1792,[52] while Ballards Reding doubled from 12 a. in 1647 to 23 a. in 1815.[53] Early leases of Bibwell reserved the timber but from 1570 the woods were leased with the rest and, despite a clause to preserve young trees,[54] the estate grew from 185 a. in 1647 to 246 a. in 1810, of which 10 per cent, mostly in the south-west part, was woodland.[55] By 1647 meadow land within the park amounted to 235 a., most of it in Finchley. At that date woodland still covered some 75 per cent of the area bounded by the park[56] but by 1841, of the 433 a. of the park in Finchley parish, only 88 a., mostly in Bishop's wood, was woodland.[57] Similarly 46 per cent of the 103-a. Grotes estate was wooded *c.* 1530, when the rest was equally divided between arable and pasture.[58] The woods were sold off separately *c.* 1530[59] and one survived in 1754 but all had disappeared by 1841.[60] In 1795 outside the common there were *c.* 150 a. of woodland, 100 a. of arable, and 1,950 a. of grassland.[61] In 1841, of 2,032 a. subject to tithe, 1,769 a. or 87 per cent were meadow or pasture, 124 a. were woodland, and 86 a. were arable; there were also 46 a. of garden and 7 a. of orchard.[62]

Grass, used at first as pasture, was later grown for hay to feed London's horses. In 1794 there were large hay barns in the Finchley district[63] and in 1834 farming was said to be almost exclusively devoted to hay for the London market.[64] It is thought that Dirthouse, later the White Lion, was so called because 18th-century hay waggons stopped there on their return from London, laden with soot and manure.[65]

The common became increasingly important in the economy during the two centuries before its inclosure, as animals were turned on to it to preserve the hay and as the woodland cover was cleared. Many owners pastured animals on their own land only after the hay crop had been gathered. Pig-farmers were especially dependent on the common, those presented for fattening pigs in 1705 including Jonathan Roberts of East End and Thomas Odell,[66] whose son John (d. 1762) was one of the leading hog-dealers in England. Most of Odell's property,

30 B.L.H.L., P.A.F. 1/1; Biggers, *Finchley*, 3.
31 B.L.H.L., P.A.F. 1/6.
32 See p. 41.
33 B.L.H.L., Prints Colln. 6647–8, 6714.
34 B.L.H.L., Acc. 6416/8; Guildhall MSS. 9171/10, f. 270; 14, ff. 6, 11; Prob. 11/48 (P.C.C. 32 Crymes, will of Ric. Aps); Prob. 11/102 (P.C.C. 108 Bolein, will of Thos. Sanny).
35 Guildhall MS. 10123/1, f. 7v.
36 M.R.O., MJ/SP/Dec. 1699/55; B.L.H.L., Acc. 9131.
37 M.R.O., Acc. 262/3/51–2.
38 B.L.H.L., Banks Colln., Wills (John Odell).
39 Guildhall MS. 12396.
40 M.R.O., Acc. 190/1.
41 M.R.O., Acc. 351/163–5.
42 Ibid. 257.
43 Ibid. 300.
44 H.O. 67/16.
45 M.R.O., Acc. 351/163–5. Pasture was valued at 10*s.* an a., compared with 8*s.* for arable and 6*s.* for wood.
46 M.R.O., Acc. 351/144.
47 Ibid. 155.
48 Ibid. 267.
49 Ibid. 272–3.
50 Cf. 16th-cent. maps of Kingsbury and Hendon: All Souls Coll., Oxford, Hovenden maps, portfolio II, nos. 9–15.
51 Guildhall MS. 12418.
52 Guildhall MSS. 10237, p. 65; 10234/7, pp. 331 sqq.; 10464A, pp. 109, 115; 12398.
53 Guildhall MSS. 10234/9, pp. 259–63; 10464A, pp. 85, 115.
54 St. Paul's MSS. C (Sampson), ff. 42v.–3; (I Nowell), ff. 344v.–5.
55 Guildhall MSS. 10234/9, pp. 55–9; 10464A, pp. 85, 115.
56 Guildhall MS. 10464A, pp. 85, 109.
57 M.R.O., TA/FIN.
58 M.R.O., Acc. 351/164.
59 E 326/9202.
60 Rocque, *Map of Mdx.* (1754); M.R.O., TA/FIN.
61 Lysons, *Environs*, ii. 335.
62 M.R.O., TA/FIN.
63 P. Foot, *Gen. View of Agric. of Mdx.* (1794), 57.
64 M.R.O., Acc. 351/300.
65 *N. & Q.* 6th ser. iii. 289, 471; Guildhall MS. 10465/102, p. 147.
66 Guildhall MS. 10465/20.

including a Bibbesworth farm, was leasehold but his wealth lay in his pigs, as shown by the cluster of his buildings around the Hogmarket. He left £4,350 in legacies, besides gifts to the poor.[67] A hog-butcher from London acquired property on the edge of the common in 1747[68] and another Finchley pig-dealer, Thomas Wattnall, acquired property at Brownswell from Jonathan Roberts's heir in 1775.[69]

Agitation for inclosure began in 1805.[70] The Act, affecting Friern Barnet and Hornsey as well as Finchley, was not passed until 1811,[71] the plan being drawn in 1814 and the award published in 1816.[72] Inclosure was mainly concerned with Finchley common, since there were no open fields and the other wastes were little more than roadside verges. The whole of the common (*c.* 900 a.) was placed in Finchley parish, although Friern Barnet freeholders and copyholders were granted allotments. The lords of Finchley and Bibbesworth received shares equivalent to 1/18th of the acreage of their manors, giving the bishop 40 a. and Thomas Allen 97 a.; Hornsey was excluded and manorial rights over the common were denied to Friern Barnet manor. The rector of Finchley received 116 a. in lieu of glebe and tithe, 139 a. were sold to defray expenses, and the rest was divided proportionately among the freeholders, copyholders, and lessees of the bishopric demesne. The largest allotments were to John Bacon (94 a.), the marquess of Buckingham (45 a.), and Sir William Curtis (39 a.), holders of the demesne lands of Friern Barnet and Halliwick manors, Alexander Murray as lessee of Bibwell (25 a.), and the earl of Mansfield as lessee of the demesne woods (20 a.).

Inclosure of the common had an immediate effect upon agriculture. The rector's belief that it would lead to great crops of corn[73] was apparently justified, most of the former common lands being in a 'high state of cultivation' in 1817.[74] Without careful husbandry, however, the soil became exhausted and in 1834 one lessee decided to drain and fallow his arable and then lay it down to grass.[75] The former common was excluded from a survey made for tithe commutation in 1841.[76] Much of the former common was later sold for cemeteries and other municipal enterprises.

For the small man, with little or no pasture of his own, economic hardship may have been made worse by inclosure. In 1819 a few sheep apparently were still kept on the common by such people but most of the hedges were probably already established. Begging seems to have been a growing problem and allotments for the poor were provided by the parish. In 1823 there were many out of employment.[77]

Inclosure also affected the farmers who had pastured their animals on the common while concentrating on growing hay. Turnpiking and the construction of the Paddington (1801) and Regent's canals made hay less profitable, since horse-feed could be brought from much farther afield and Middlesex lost its advantage. Oats replaced dearer hay as the favoured feed and in 1848 London was said to offer the cheapest market for hay in England. In 1834 the valuer of the Bibbesworth estate recommended a change from hay to livestock, with fodder crops and straw to supplement grass. The tenant at Bibwell went over to grazing and asked permission in 1848 to convert 42 a. to arable.[78] Beef-cattle and sheep were raised at Salvin's farm at Fortis Green in 1849.[79] On Henry Stephens's farm at Grove House in 1850 there were bullocks and Welsh sheep bought at Barnet fair, horses, and pigs, fed on grain from the brewers; rabbits and ducks were kept and both hay and beans were grown.[80] Sheep were stolen from Bibbesworth Manor farm in 1865[81] but it was at Sheephouse, the other Bibbesworth farm, that they were especially important: there was a sheep-house by 1834[82] and flocks of more than 1,000 were kept before 1868.[83] By 1867 out of 2,968 a. of farm-land, 2,494 a. (84 per cent) were permanently under grass and 383 a. (13 per cent) were arable, producing mainly vegetable and fodder crops (163 a.), wheat (114 a.), and oats (84 a.).[84] Sheep (1,897) were by far the most numerous animals, followed by pigs (463), dairy cows (312), and cattle (196); horses were not recorded. Sixty-nine of the 106 farmers possessed land and livestock, 36 had only land, and one kept only livestock.

The amount of farm-land contracted steadily from 2,968 a. in 1867 to 109 a. in 1937, with sharp drops in the 1880s and 1900s reflecting the growth of North Finchley and again from 1917 to 1937 reflecting suburban building, particularly on the demesne farms of Hampstead Garden Suburb. The Second World War brought more land (262 a.) into cultivation but by 1957 the area had dwindled again, to 155 a. Permanent grass and hay never formed less than 86 per cent of the total farm-land until the Second World War. They were grown mainly to support livestock, aided by small but important fodder crops. Grain covered only 17 a. in 1887 and thereafter had no significance except during the Second World War, when it took up 54 per cent of the total farm-land. Animal farming reached its peak *c.* 1887, when there were 738

[67] B.L.H.L., Banks Colln., Wills (John Odell); *Brit. Chron.* 9–11 Aug. 1762 (quoted in B.L.H.L., Banks Colln. xiv. 1564); B.L.H.L., Banks Colln. xvi, Poor-rate bk. (1756).
[68] Guildhall MS. 10465/62.
[69] M.L.R. 1776/1/145–6.
[70] B.L.H.L., P.A.F. 1/3; J. Caley, 'Hist. Feud. Mdx.' nos. 36, 38, 41 in Swiss Cottage libr. And see pp. 47–8.
[71] 51 Geo. III, c. 23.
[72] Except where otherwise stated, the following paras. are based on M.R.O., EA/FIN.
[73] H.O. 67/16.
[74] Hassell, *Rides and Walks*, i. 184–6. See also J. Dugdale, *New Brit. Traveller* (1819), iii. 487.
[75] Guildhall MS. 12418.
[76] M.R.O., TA/FIN.
[77] B.L.H.L., P.A.F. 1/5.
[78] M.R.O., Acc. 351/300; Guildhall MS. 12401.
[79] B.L.H.L., Acc. 6787/6.
[80] B.L.H.L., Banks Colln., biog. H. C. Stephens (extracts from notebk. of farm bailiff, Evans). Stock in 1850 included 44 ewes, 2 rams, 39 lambs, and 60 lb. of Welsh and 113 lb. of English wool.
[81] B.L.H.L., P.A.F. 1/9.
[82] M.R.O., Acc. 351/300.
[83] B.L.H.L., Banks Colln., biog. H. C. Stephens (quoting shepherd on farm).
[84] Except where otherwise stated, the following paras. are based on decennial agricultural returns 1867–1957 and 1962: M.A.F. 68/535; M.A.F. 68/1105; M.A.F. 68/1675; M.A.F. 68/2245; M.A.F. 68/2815; M.A.F. 68/3358; M.A.F. 68/3837; M.A.F. 68/4206; M.A.F. 68/4575; M.A.F. 68/4777.

pigs, 649 sheep, 188 cattle, 335 dairy cows, and 107 horses. In 1897 there were 328 pigs and by 1917 only 76, when many farmers kept a few[85] and some were kept in back yards; in 1955 25 pigs and 200 fowls were kept in a yard at Prospect Place, near the 18th-century hogmarket.[86] There were still 434 sheep in 1927 but they disappeared soon afterwards, while beef cattle fell from 141 in 1897 to 59 in 1907 and remained at about that figure thereafter. The number of horses varied between 100 and 200 until 1917 but by 1927 was only 47.

The main change in the late 19th century, as suburban building spread, was towards dairy farming. In 1851 there were 16 farmers and 4 cow-keepers, in 1878 9 farms and 9 dairies, in 1890 6 farms and 11 dairies, and by 1920 only a poultry farm and a goat farm but 17 dairies. Many dairies were short-lived and several were absorbed into Manor Farm Dairies and its successor United Dairies.[87]

At College farm George Barham, founder of the Express Dairy Co., changed from sheep to dairy herds, stocked Guernsey, Shorthorn, and Kerry cows and a few goats, and built a model dairy. Although the herd was small and most Express Dairy milk came from much farther afield, College farm was a showplace, used for exhibitions and training courses. New developments were tried out, as in 1921 when the first tuberculin-tested dairy was opened there. The farm was therefore retained, on a reduced scale, long after other farms near London had been abandoned.[88] In 1977, when the company had finally left, it was still used for grazing cattle and a few horses.[89]

The larger Jersey Farm Dairies, with more than 100 cows, was established between Nether Street and Dollis brook *c.* 1887. Like College farm it prided itself on its products and was open to the public. The owners may have been succeeded by Dollis Park Dairy Co., which had 28 a. at Nether Street in 1911. Part of the Jersey farm buildings still existed in 1920 but disappeared soon afterwards.[90] Manor Farm Dairies[91] were founded *c.* 1875 by Joseph Wilmington Lane and joined in the 1920s with United Dairies, which had been founded in 1917. Although the company's Manor Farm, Highgate, and Oakleigh Park Farm, Whetstone, were both outside Finchley, much of their land lay within it, while the head offices were in High Street, Whetstone, and later in High Road, East Finchley.[92] Manor farm survived until 1932.[93] Dairying also featured on the Woodhouse estate in 1902[94] and on Park farm (Bibwell) for many years before 1918[95] until the fields were sold for building.[96]

Market-gardening also accompanied suburban growth. A single nurseryman existed in 1845 and 1851[97] and three nurserymen and two florists in 1867 and 1878, by which date there were 4½ a. of orchards and 9¼ a. of nurseries. They had increased to 19½ a. and 28 a. respectively by 1887 and 19¼ a. of orchard and 39¼ a. of soft fruit in 1897. Eleven people had nurseries and commercial greenhouses in 1900, mostly in Whetstone and North Finchley, and seven in 1920. Most had gone before the Second World War but there were four in 1964, when 5¼ a. were under glass and 3 a. were orchard.[98]

The earliest and most important nursery was that of Peter Kay, who by 1845 leased an acre in Ballards Lane for flowers and fruit.[99] In 1878 it was owned by Peter and Susan Kay[1] and a second nursery, called Claigmar, had been started in 1874 in Long Lane by Peter Edmund Kay. During the 1890s the Ballards Lane nursery closed and Claigmar was extended until in 1899 Kay had 18½ a. under glass and 161 greenhouses, producing 100 tons each of grapes and tomatoes and 240,000 cucumbers a year.[2] Equally large nurseries were opened east of Squires Lane until at their greatest extent the Kay nurseries, between Long Lane and the High Barnet railway line, stretched from Duke Street eastward to Green Lane.[3] Peter Kay was probably dead by 1930 and his grounds soon afterwards were built over.[4]

Other nurseries were smaller and short-lived, except those of the Clementses and of James Cutbush, who leased 6 a. of Bibbesworth land from 1864. By 1909 William Cutbush & Son, the Highgate firm, had Plant Farm, which survived in 1938, south of East End Road, next to the St. Marylebone cemetery.[5] William Clements was a florist who came from Colchester (Essex) in 1874 and built a nursery at the junction of Regent's Park Road and Hendon Lane, which he sold in 1911 on moving to Salisbury Avenue farther south. George Clements was there in 1920[6] and there was still a florist's, Clements's of Finchley, in 1977.[7] William Batho, a nurseryman of Nether Street, started business in 1895 and went bankrupt in 1902, although he had over 40 a. (Furzby farm).[8] Vegetables and poultry

[85] e.g. Manor Ho. farm in 1890s: Finchley local bd., min. bks. ix. 165; xv. 229; e.g. Wm. Batho of Furzby farm in 1900; B.L.H.L., Poor-rate bk. (1900).
[86] B.L.H.L., Acc. 10111.
[87] H.O. 107/1701/136/3/2a; *Kelly's Dir. Mdx.* (1878, 1890); *Kelly's Dir. Finchley* (1920, 1930, 1939, 1950).
[88] B. Morgan, *Express Journey, 1864–1964*, 29, 33, 38, 62, 114; B.L.H.L., F/728. And see above, p. 59.
[89] Ex inf. Dept. of Transport.
[90] [Jersey Farm Dairies], *Memento of Finchley*, pamphlet in B.L.H.L.; B.L.H.L., Poor-rate book (1911); O.S. Map 6″, Mdx. VI. SE. (1897, 1920 edns.).
[91] Not to be confused with Manor (Bibbesworth) farm.
[92] Church Com. files 55543, 64346; B.L.H.L., Poor-rate bks. (1900, 1911); Morgan, *Express Jny.* 48; information from Unigate Ltd.
[93] *Kelly's Dir. Hornsey* (1932, 1933).
[94] M.R.O., Acc. 410/45a.
[95] Church Com. file 85003.
[96] See p. 54.
[97] *Home Cnties. Dir.* (1845); H.O. 107/1701/136/3/2a f. 391v.
[98] M.A.F. 68. Cf. above; *Kelly's Dir. Mdx.* (1878); *Kelly's Dir. Finchley* (1920, 1930, 1939); Barnet L.B. *Dir.* (1964–5), ii, Finchley Boro.; B.L.H.L., Poor-rate bk. (1900).
[99] *Home Cnties. Dir.* (1845); B.L.H.L., S/C (Church End, 1848); H.O. 107/1701/136/3/2a f. 391v.
[1] *Kelly's Dir. Mdx.* (1878).
[2] *Kelly's Dir. Barnet* (1889–90, 1900–1); O.S. Map 6″, Mdx. XI. NE. (1897 edn.); Finchley Soc. *Newsletter*, Mar. 1972.
[3] O.S. Map 6″, Mdx. XI. NE. (1920 edn.).
[4] Mrs. Kay was at Claigmar in 1930 but it was not described as a nursery: *Kelly's Dir. Finchley* (1930); O.S. Map 6″, Mdx. XI. NE. (1938 edn.).
[5] M.R.O., Acc. 351/404; *Kelly's Dir. Barnet* (1909–10); O.S. Maps 6″, Mdx. XI. NE. (1920, 1938 edns.).
[6] B.L.H.L., Banks Colln., Index 1, s.v. Clements; Smith, *Finchley As It Was*, 5; *Kelly's Dir. Mdx.* (1890); *Kelly's Dir. Finchley* (1920).
[7] In Regent's Park Rd.
[8] *The Times*, 22 Feb. 1902; B.L.H.L., Poor-rate bk. (1900).

from William Whiteley's Bibbesworth Manor farm supplied his London stores.[9] There were water-cress beds along Mutton brook in 1895 and 1920.[10]

In 1801 183 people earned their living in agriculture, compared with 56 in trade, craft, or manufacture, and in 1811 and 1831 35 per cent of families were dependent on it.[11] In 1831 there were 14 farmer employers and 256 agricultural labourers and in 1851 some 18 per cent of people with occupations worked on the land,[12] including 12 farmers, 76 gardeners, and at least 194 agricultural labourers; in addition, many of the 162 men described simply as 'labourer' may have been farm workers. In the late 19th century those owning or occupying land dwindled from 116 in 1877 to 77 in 1897 and 49 in 1907. In 1901 the 515 men employed in agriculture formed only 5 per cent of the work force and by 1921 621 were so employed out of a work force of 13,253. Numbers fell still further until in 1962 there were six holdings, four of 1–5 a. and two of 50–100 a., employing 17 men and 1 woman.

MILLS. Hugh of Arderne and his wife Alice quitclaimed a windmill in Finchley to Simon le Ferour in 1310–11.[13] A mill, possibly the same one, was conveyed with land in Finchley and Hendon in 1314–15 by Robert Kersebroke to Simon the marshal and his wife Alice.[14] A mill also featured in an estate in Finchley and Hendon conveyed by William the tailor to Eve of Boltby in 1346–7.[15] Mill fields, part of Bibbesworth manor from 1365 until the break-up of the estate in the late 16th century, indicate that at least one of the mills stood on the edge of the common, east of Ballards Lane.[16] A water-mill on Dollis or Mutton brook, near their junction, is suggested by closes called Millfields in 1764 in the south-west corner of Finchley, bounded by Dollis brook, Hendon Lane, and Bibbesworth demesne lands.[17] Either of the Millfields could be identified with the Millcroft mentioned in 1430.[18]

In 1627 a piece of waste next to Basings pond west of the road to Whetstone was granted to Thomas Rawson to build a windmill and miller's house. Rawson, described as a miller of Hornsey, surrendered the mill in 1628 to the use of Richard Turvin of Paddington, who surrendered it to the use of Michael Grigg of London in 1635.[19] By 1654 it was held by Edward Crane (d. 1663), who also owned a windmill at Bushey Heath in Harrow. The mill was held by Crane's widow Eleanor and, after her death, probably in 1676, by their son George. In 1676 the mill-house passed to George's sister Ellen or Eleanor (Cropper), who surrendered it in 1691,[20] and by 1722 it was the Windmill public house, later the Swan with Two Necks.[21] The windmill itself was recorded *c.* 1677[22] and probably in 1734,[23] but apparently it had gone by 1754.[24]

MARKETS AND FAIRS. There was no charter for Finchley's pig market, which grew up at East End on the edge of the common where drovers rested. Several pig-dealers lived near by, often maintaining public houses like the George and the Hog Driver or Sow and Pigs.[25] By 1717 a customary market was held on Wednesdays and Thursdays for pigs brought from most parts of England and Wales.[26] At the Hogmarket[27] at the end of the 18th century hogs from Shropshire were sold to butchers to be fattened on the offal of the London distilling industry.[28]

When the common was inclosed a small piece of land was allotted to the bishop for occasional use as a pig market,[29] most of the animals being kept in piggeries surrounding the George inn.[30] During the 19th century housing crowded around the market[31] and there were problems over drainage and slaughter-houses.[32] The market, still much frequented by London butchers, was held on Mondays in 1845 but was extinct by 1869.[33]

TRADE AND INDUSTRY. People not employed in agriculture included a bottle-maker in 1393, a wheelwright who left a shop and implements in 1518, and a wheelwright at Whetstone in 1614.[34] There were tailors in 1599 and 1615, a linen-weaver in 1614, two glovers in Whetstone in 1617,[35] and an optical instrument-maker at Whetstone in 1813.[36] In 1801 56 people were employed in trade, craft, or manufacturing,[37] which supported 80 families in 1811, 101 in 1821, and 176 in 1831. Retail trade and handicrafts employed 200 people in 1831. By 1841 the commonest occupation of the 1,161 employed people, apart from agriculture, was

[9] Finchley local bd., min. bk. xiv. 119; O.S. Map 6", Mdx. XI. NE. (1920 edn.).

[10] R. S. Lambert, *Universal Provider*, 101; ex inf. the archivist, B.L.H.L.

[11] Except where otherwise stated, the para. is based on *Census*, 1801–1961; M.A.F. 68, see above, p. 68 n. 84.

[12] i.e. excluding housewives and dependents: H.O. 107/1701/136/3/2a.

[13] C.P. 25(1)/149/41/60.

[14] C.P. 25(1)/149/44/135.

[15] C.P. 25(1)/150/61/220.

[16] W.A.M. 4818; M.R.O., Acc. 351/147, 209.

[17] B.L.H.L., Acc. 8665; M.R.O., Acc. 1368/2.

[18] S.C. 2/188/71 m. 4d. See glebe land: M.R.O., TA/FIN.

[19] S.C. 2/191/9.

[20] Prob. 11/312 (P.C.C. 113 Juxon); St. Paul's MS. B 68; Guildhall MSS. 10312/101, m. 18d.; 111; 10465/6.

[21] M.R.O., MR/LV3/97.

[22] Ogilby, *Map of Mdx.* [*c.* 1677].

[23] *Fog's Weekly Jnl.* 20 July 1734, quoted in B.L.H.L., Banks Colln., Index 1 *sub* Windmill. Jos. Remington murdered Wm. Wells at his ho., the Windmill. The Windmill inn was at that time licensed to Edw. Hartell: Guildhall MS. 10465/57.

[24] Rocque, *Map of Mdx.* (1754).

[25] e.g. Jonathan Roberts, licensee of Hog Driver in 1716: M.R.O., MR/LV3/3, 97. See p. 67.

[26] *T.L.M.A.S.* xix. 48.

[27] M.R.O., Acc. 351/277.

[28] Middleton, *View*, 375; J. C. Clutterbuck, 'The Farming of Mdx.', *Jnl. of Royal Soc. of Eng.* 2nd ser. v (1869), 40 n. 3.

[29] M.R.O., EA/FIN; Guildhall MS. 12402.

[30] M.R.O., Acc. 262/4/15.

[31] See photo. of Hogmarket *c.* 1902: Smith, *Finchley As It Was*, 25.

[32] e.g. 1832: B.L.H.L., P.A.F. 1/7; 1857: B.L.H.L., Acc. 10111.

[33] *Home Cnties. Dir.* (1845); *Jnl. Royal Soc.* 2nd ser. (1869), 40 n. 3.

[34] S.C. 2/188/66 m. 6d.; Guildhall MS. 9171/9, f. 85; *Cal. Mdx. Sess. Rec.* i (1612–14), 378.

[35] *Mdx. Cnty. Rec.* i. 253; *Cal. Mdx. Sess. Rec.* i. 455; iii. 91; iv. 165.

[36] M.L.R., 1813/5/4.

[37] Except where otherwise stated, the following section is based on *Census*, 1801–1961.

domestic service (346); there were 58 craftsmen and 45 shopkeepers.[38]

Retail trade in 1851 was represented by greengrocers, fishmongers, hairdressers, stationers, and booksellers, besides the more numerous bakers, butchers, and grocers. There were several suppliers of shoes and clothing, and most crafts were available locally.[39] Finchley had nearly 40 kinds of shopkeeper by 1886 and retail trade remained important, in spite of fears that better transport would lead to shopping in London.[40] There were 537 shops in Finchley in 1911.

Local industry began to grow *c.* 1900: there were 73 workshops in 1902 and 88 in 1903,[41] and 39 factories by 1911. Building was still the largest industry in 1911, with 12 per cent of the male work force. Transport employed 1,428, 10 per cent of the male work force, in 1921, when there 841 men in metal-working, 253 in electrical works, and 335 in carpentry and furniture-making but when building employed only 594, compared with 1,343 in 1911. In 1931 transport, with 1,795 men, still employed 9 per cent of the male work force; building employed 981, metal-working 1,078, electrical working 421, and wood-working 776. By 1961 11 per cent (2,380) of the male work force was in engineering and 42 per cent, mostly working outside Finchley, had professional, commercial, or clerical jobs.

Apart from the land itself, Finchley's main economic resources were wood, brickearth, and the Great North Road. Charcoal-burning may have been widespread in the Middle Ages, although evidence survives mainly from the 16th and 17th centuries. Henry Downer (d. 1558) left 'bush coal' and John Nicholl, who lived at the George in Whetstone before 1575, was a collier.[42] Two Finchley colliers were indicted for selling defective measures of coal in 1614,[43] charcoal-burning caused a fire in the bishop's woods in 1727,[44] and three colliers received poor-relief in 1787.[45]

A tanner was drowned in Finchley *c.* 1274 when his horse, laden with bullocks' hides, slipped into a ditch.[46] By the 17th century tanning was found throughout the parish, at Woodside, East End, and Nether Street.[47] The bishop apparently exploited the bark for tanning before he leased the woods out in 1645. Timothy Taylor, tanner in 1627, was one of his lessees, Tanners scrubs had been created by 1662,[48] and the bark continued to be reserved after the rest of the woodland was leased out. Tanning, hereditary in the Rolfes and some other families, died out in the early 18th century as woodland contracted.[49]

Sawyers and carpenters were recorded from the 14th and 15th centuries, when the Shepherd family included carpenters,[50] and a saw-pit in Whetstone obstructed the highway between 1616 and 1619.[51] In 1851 there were 60 carpenters, who were outnumbered only by servants, labourers, and gardeners.[52] A cabinet-maker worked in Whetstone in 1813[53] and several, mostly in North Finchley and Whetstone, in the late 19th and early 20th centuries.[54] The Joyce family had saw-mills in eastern Finchley by 1887 and, as P. O. Joyce Ltd., timber merchants, still traded in 1975.[55]

The underlying boulder clay could be used for brick-making. A tile-house, later called a tile-kiln, existed in the west side of the parish, probably at Whetstone, in 1547,[56] and bricklayers were recorded from 1604 and brick-makers from 1615.[57] A Brick field lay at the junction of Long Lane and Squires Lane in 1727,[58] the field diagonally opposite was called 'Old Brickfield' *c.* 1867, and there was another 'Old Brickfield' between Hendon Lane and Regent's Park Road.[59] Totteridge Lane in Whetstone was called Brick Lane in 1817.[60] There were 58 bricklayers in 1851, some of whom probably worked for the 7 brick-makers,[61] and 241 brick-makers in 1911.[62]

Brick-makers included William Woods in High Road (*c.* 1840–7), William and Adam Wright in East End (*c.* 1847–1851), George Pymm in Long Lane (*c.* 1859), Frederick Goodyear (*c.* 1879), Samuel Lenney (*c.* 1879), and John Lawford in Summers Lane (*c.* 1879–1900).[63] The long-established family firm of Plowman & Co.[64] may have originated with Charles Plowman, a carpenter at Ballards Lane before 1790. About 1825 Mark Plowman established a building firm at East End. He collaborated with James Frost, the cement manufacturer who bought land at Strawberry Vale in 1816 and began to build there in the 1820s with the yellow bricks characteristic of Plowman's brick-field.[65] Plowman also worked with Anthony Salvin and was responsible for much building in the 1840s and 1850s, including Holy Trinity church and school, St. Mary's school, the clerk's house, and the rebuilt George inn. By 1851 he employed 15 men and 3 boys at East End Road, his three sons

38 Lawrence, *Village into Boro.*, p. 27.
39 H.O. 107/1701/136/3/2a.
40 Lawrence, op. cit. 29.
41 Finchley U.D. *Ann. Health Reps.* (1902, 1903).
42 Guildhall MS. 9171/14, f. 59; B.L.H.L., Banks Colln. vii, s.v. Woodside.
43 M.R.O., S.R. 528/121–2; S. Reg. ii, p. 72.
44 Guildhall MS. 10242, p. 498.
45 B.L.H.L., P.A.F. 1/2.
46 J.I. 1/543 rot. 59.
47 E 214/1200; B.L.H.L., Banks Colln. ix. 4385; xii. 5025.
48 B.L.H.L., Banks Colln. ix. 4385; Guildhall MS. 10234/1, pp. 248 sqq.
49 E 214/120; B.L.H.L., Acc. 8667/2; M.L.R., 1718/4/93–4; S.C. 2/191/16 m. 20.
50 S.C. 2/188/66 m. 5; S.C. 2/188/76 m. 2; S.C. 2/189/3 m. 4; S.C. 2/189/10 m. 2d.
51 S.C. 2/191/6; S.C. 2/191/7.
52 H.O. 107/1701/136/3/2a.
53 M.L.R. 1813/5/4.
54 *Kelly's Dir. Mdx.* (1867, 1890, 1908); *Kelly's Dir. Finchley* (1920).
55 B.L.H.L., Poor-rate bks. (1887); *Kelly's Dir. Lond.* (1975).
56 C 54/454 m. 24; B.L.H.L., Banks Colln. v. 3331.
57 *Mdx. Cnty. Rec.* ii. 5; *Cal. Mdx. Sess. Rec.* iii. 102; iv. 198; *Cal. Mdx. Sess. Bks.* (1689–1709), 259; M.R.O., Acc. 351/276.
58 M.R.O., Acc. 1140.
59 O.S. Map 6″, Mdx. XI. NE. (1867 edn.); Geol. Survey Map, Mdx. XI. NE. (1920 edn.).
60 Guildhall MS. 10465/139, p. 393.
61 H.O. 107/1701/136/3/2a.
62 *Census*, 1911.
63 B.L.H.L., Church-rate bks. (1840, 1847, 1859); Highway-rate bk. (1879); Poor-rate bks. (1887, 1900); *Home Cnties. Dir.* (1845); H.O. 107/1701/136/3/2a; B.L.H.L., Acc. 6109/35; O.S. Map 6″, Mdx. XI. NE. (1897 edn.).
64 Except where otherwise stated, the information is based on B.L.H.L., Banks Colln., biog. Plowman.
65 M.L.R. 1819/7/629; B.L.H.L., Acc. 6416/29; M.R.O., Hist. Notes 21/7/70.

being a builder, a carpenter, and a plumber's apprentice. Thomas Plowman of the Hogmarket, perhaps Mark's brother, in 1851 employed 8 men[66] and in 1855 carried on an 'extensive manufacture' at his own brick-field.[67] Legg & Plowman existed as a firm of brick-makers in 1867,[68] by which date Mark's son Charles, formerly a carpenter, seems to have taken over his father's firm. In 1873 as 'builder, of Ballards Lane', Charles helped to restore the church and by the end of the 1870s he had entered local politics and taken over the brick-field of Legg & Plowman.[69] After his death in 1906 Chas. Plowman Ltd. abandoned brick-making to concentrate on joinery.[70] The firm was taken over *c.* 1952 by David Gomim, who retained the old name, built a new timber-mill, and in 1956 had some 50 employees making fittings for schools and council flats.[71] The mill closed between 1975 and 1977.[72]

There were nine masons in 1851[73] and after 1854 firms in eastern Finchley like Joslin[74] or Bower of High Road provided elaborate monuments for the three cemeteries.[75]

The Great North Road from an early date stimulated the brewing industry. The many medieval offences concerning ale included brewing against the assize, regrating, selling by cup rather than measure, failing to send for the ale-taster or to display a sign, and, in 1484, placing hops in the ale 'to the great damage and danger of the king's lieges'.[76] The number of offenders, 10 brewers in 1436 and 14 regrators in 1475, suggests that much ale was brewed for travellers.[77] Many of the inns were along the high street in Whetstone.[78] Five of the twelve public houses in 1841 lay along the Great North Road[79] and at least another two grew up there on the edge of the common.[80] The White Lion, where the road left Hornsey park and prominent throughout the 18th century, had by 1841 apparently ceased to be a public house.

Large stables were needed at the inns and from the 16th century Finchley men benefited from the droves of animals and waggons journeying to London. Between 1613 and 1617 a mealman and nine others from Finchley and Whetstone were licensed as badgers and kidders.[81] Horse-dealing, although not horse-breeding, became profitable in Whetstone and in the 18th century Coleharbour was an important centre. William Castle (d. 1775),[82] horse-dealer, was probably the father of William Castle of Coleharbour (fl. 1784).[83] In 1790 Coleharbour was sold to John Kendrick, a dealer from Kilburn who exported to France and who leased the premises, which included stabling for 45 horses, to another dealer, John Shaw of Finchley.[84] Mark Lemon, a stable-keeper from Oxford Street, bought land in Finchley *c.* 1800[85] and Samuel Wimbush and his sons, job-masters of Oxford Street, trained horses for the royal family.[86]

Pickford's, the carriers, from their earliest days used the Great North Road.[87] Joseph Baxendale, a native of Lancashire who worked for the cotton trade in London, began investing in Pickford's in 1817 and soon controlled it. Having purchased property at Whetstone in the 1820s, including some from Francis H. Choppin, a bankrupt horse-dealer,[88] and built a country residence, he established a hospital for 100 sick horses, with fields for 200 more. His sons and grandson maintained the connexion with Whetstone until horses gave way to mechanized transport.[89]

In 1936 Pickford's took over Chaplin and Horne, their rivals for over a century. Benjamin Worthy Horne, who had stables at the White Lion, and William Chaplin, with more than 82 stables at the Swan and Pyramids in Whetstone in 1840, were London coach-masters who in the 1830s had joined forces in the carrying business. At the height of his prosperity Chaplin had 2,000 horses and 27 mail-coaches leaving London every night, many of which used the Great North Road but most of which were superseded by the railways.[90] In 1851 there were still 7 horse- or stable-keepers, 4 horse-dealers, 17 grooms and a jockey, 19 smiths, and 2 harness-makers. There were 16 coachmen, some employed privately and others by the 2 coach proprietors, 13 carriers, and 3 carmen. Inns and beer-houses employed 31 people.[91]

William Onyon and his son Thomas were coach-makers in 1735[92] and there was coach-building in Church End at the end of the 18th century.[93] Bicycles were made, usually in small workshops, from the late 19th century and after the First World War there were several firms connected with motor cars, in 1920 including Blaker Motor & Welding Co. at Manor works in East End Road, the East Finchley Motor Engineering Co. in High Road, East Finchley, and De Dion Bouton (1907) at

66 H.O. 107/1701/136/3/2a ff. 418, 449.
67 B.L.H.L., P.A.F. 1/8.
68 Guildhall MS. 10465/172, p. 530; B.L.H.L., Church-rate bk. (1859); *Kelly's Dir. Mdx.* (1867).
69 B.L.H.L., P.A.F. 1/9; Finchley local bd., min. bk. i; B.L.H.L., Highway-rate bk. (1879); M.R.O., Acc. 351/404.
70 *Barnet Press*, 7 Oct. 1933.
71 *Finchley Press*, 15 June 1956.
72 *Kelly's Dir. Lond.* (1975).
73 H.O. 107/1701/136/3/2a.
74 Joslin still existed in High Rd. in 1977.
75 B.L.H.L., Rate bks. (1879, 1887); *Kelly's Dir. Mdx.* (1890, 1908).
76 S.C. 2/188/66 m. 4d.; S.C. 2/188/72 m. 2; S.C. 2/188/79 m. 3; S.C. 2/189/5 m. 3; Guildhall MSS. 10312/44, 66.
77 S.C. 2/188/72 m. 2; Guildhall MS. 10312/80, m. 3.
78 See p. 44.
79 i.e. the Bull and Butcher, Whetstone, the Swan, the South Swan, the Green Man at Brownswell, and the Stag (Bald-faced Stag) at East End: M.R.O., TA/FIN.
80 i.e. the George and Red Lion, both in East End.
81 *Cal. Mdx. Sess. Rec.* i. 26, 82, 256, 449; ii. 122, 293; iii. 68–9, 237; iv. 26, 159, 285–6.
82 B.L.H.L., Banks Colln., Wills (Wm. Castle).
83 B.L.H.L., P.A.F. 1/2.
84 C 108/238.
85 M.R.O., Acc. 262/3/18.
86 Guildhall MS. 10234/13, pp. 328–33; B.L.H.L., Banks Colln. xvi (land tax 1816); Whiddon, *One Hundred Yrs. of Playing the Game*, 54.
87 Except where otherwise stated, the following two paras. are based on *Transport Saga, 1646–1947* (anon. hist. of Pickford's); *World's Carriers & Contractors' Review*, 15 Oct. 1904 (supplied by sec., Nat. Freight Corp.).
88 Guildhall MSS. 10465/139, p. 393; 166, p. 350.
89 Pickford's were still at Whetstone in 1920: *Kelly's Dir. Finchley* (1920). See drawing of Baxendale's ho. in Passmore, 'Finchley Par. Rec.' i.
90 Chaplin sold most of his coaches and horses to invest in rlys.: *Transport Saga*, 25–6; Harper, *Gt. North Rd.* i. 16, 65 sqq., 73; B.L.H.L., Banks Colln., biog. Chaplin.
91 H.O. 107/1701/136/3/2a.
92 Guildhall MS. 12401; B.L.H.L., Banks Colln., Wills s.v. Onyon.
93 M.L.R. 1806/6/660.

Woodside works in High Road, North Finchley.[94] The Finchley branch of Mann Egerton & Co. originated after the First World War, when J. Sherwood began selling surplus army vehicles in Totteridge Lane. He purchased a body-repair department in Ballards Lane, calling it Great Northern Motors, and left Totteridge Lane for Whetstone and North Finchley, where show-rooms were built on the Great North Road, in 1936. In 1945 the company was sold to H. A. Saunders, who expanded it to 13 branches and sold it in 1969 to Mann Egerton & Co., employers of some 130 people in Finchley and Whetstone in 1977.[95]

In 1977 there were several firms connected with motor cars, especially along the Great North Road in North Finchley. The most important was CAV Ltd. at East Finchley, where Frederick Simms, a pioneer in the field of motor mechanics, had bought the Grange and 6 a. at Oak Lane and founded Simms Motor Units (1920). The factory closed between 1921 and 1926 but thereafter production rose and *c.* 1935 the company acquired a new headquarters in East Finchley. New buildings, including laboratories and an instruction school, were added until in 1960 there was no room for expansion. Subsidiary companies were taken over from the 1950s, in 1968 Simms itself was acquired by CAV Ltd., part of Lucas Industries, and in 1973 the name was changed to CAV Ltd. Rising petrol prices from 1973 stimulated the production of diesel engines and in 1975 major changes were begun, involving rebuilding and the lease of an adjacent site. By 1977 the company employed some 1,960 people in East Finchley.[96]

Most industry has been small, short-lived, and varied. Among the larger and older firms are Clark's Bakeries, which moved from Upper Holloway and opened in 1927 as Burton's Bakeries on the site of an old house in the Walks, Park Road. The name was changed to Merry Miller Bakeries in the early 1930s and, after Rank's had taken it over in 1961, to Clark's Bakeries in 1963. The premises were extended in 1934 and 1961 and 200 people were employed there in 1977.[97] Advance Cleaners & Launderers (London), founded in 1928 by the amalgamation of fourteen laundries, employed *c.* 176 people in 1977.[98]

One of the biggest employers in 1977 was Ever Ready Co. (GB), with *c.* 500 in offices at Ever Ready House, which opened in 1966 at the corner of Totteridge Lane and the Great North Road.[99] Others included Commercial Union Assurance with 180 employees,[1] and O. C. Summers, which moved its administration to Britannia House in Whetstone from Camden Town in 1963, Aluminium Supply Co., which moved to Whetstone from Hendon in 1966, and the Anglo Continental Clock Co., which moved to North Finchley from Hatton Garden in 1970, each of which employed some 60 people.[2]

SOCIAL AND CULTURAL ACTIVITIES.[3] Hunting, fishing, and hawking were restricted to the bishop as lord of the manor and leased out from 1662.[4] Partridges were said to have been taken in the lord's warren in 1393 and a man was indicted for taking them in 1618.[5] In 1577 bowls had been played contrary to the statutes and in 1615 a Whetstone man was accused of 'cozenage at decoy at cards'.[6]

Sport often centred on the inns. There was a cock yard at the Five Bells in 1776, prize fights were held there in the 1840s,[7] and a man was killed at a boxing match at the Red Lion in 1825.[8] There was a skittle ground in the 1850s at the Queen's Head in Church End[9] and a bowling green *c.* 1860 at the Bald-faced Stag, which was advertised as possessing a restaurant suitable for visitors to the neighbouring cemeteries.[10] Finchley had seven friendly societies, which usually met at inns, between 1814 and 1868.[11]

In the 1840s East End was the scene of much drunkenness and of foot-races and steeplechases which alarmed the middle-class inhabitants.[12] Races were also held from 1869 until 1872, when they were abandoned as a public nuisance.[13]

Entertainment at middle-class homes during the 19th century included skating and firework parties, dances, and concerts.[14] The tenor John Braham[15] sang at a concert at a villa in Finchley in 1822[16] and large houses were later used for garden parties, like those held at Hamilton House *c.* 1900, or for fêtes such as that opened by Queen Amélie of Portugal at Manor House in 1921.[17]

Finchley literary society of 1879 may have been the same as North Finchley literary society, which closed in 1892.[18] Finchley had a brass band by 1891, a choral society from 1903, and an orchestral society by 1907.[19] Finchley children's music group, founded *c.* 1959, by 1965 had attained a national reputation and commissioned an opera by Malcolm Williamson and Geoffrey Dunn.[20] Finchley society of arts was founded in 1960 and became Finchley arts council in 1963.[21] Finchley record society, founded by the

[94] *Kelly's Dir. Mdx.* (1890, 1908); *Kelly's Dir. Barnet* (1889, 1900); *Kelly's Dir. Finchley* (1920); *The Times*, 12 Feb. 1917.
[95] Ex inf. Mann Egerton & Co. Ltd.
[96] St. John C. Nixon, *The Simms Story* [*c.* 1953]; B. Morgan, *The Simms Story*, 1891–1964; ex inf. CAV Ltd.
[97] Ex inf. Clark's Bakeries.
[98] Ex inf. Advance Cleaners & Launderers (London) Ltd.
[99] Ex inf. Ever Ready Co.
[1] Ex inf. Commercial Union Assurance.
[2] Ex inf. O. C. Summers Ltd.; Aluminium Supply Co.; Anglo Continental Clock Co. Ltd.
[3] For the part played by the common in social life, see p. 49.
[4] Guildhall MS. 12394.
[5] S.C. 2/188/66 m. 6d.; *Mdx. Sess. Rec.* iv. 317.
[6] Guildhall MS. 10312/92, m. 6; *Mdx. Sess. Rec.* ii. 295.
[7] Plan of char. estates in Finchley ch.; B.L.H.L., Acc. 6787/7.
[8] *The Times*, 13 July 1825.
[9] B.H.L.H., Acc. 6109/9–14.
[10] Potter Colln. 28/6.
[11] F.S. 2/7/1477; F.S. 2/7/1484; F.S. 2/7/3103; F.S. 2/7/3181; F.S. 2/7/4366; F.S. 2/7/4537; F.S. 2/7/ 4675.
[12] B.L.H.L., Acc. 6787/7.
[13] Walford, *Gtr. Lond.* i. 339.
[14] B.L.H.L., Acc. 6787/4.
[15] *D.N.B.*
[16] B.L.H.L. Print. Colln. 6625.
[17] *Mdx. Pictorial*, no. 3, May–June 1960, pp. 4–5; *The Times*, 28 June 1921.
[18] B.L.H.L., Banks Colln., Finchley common file; *Barnet Press*, 7 Oct. 1933.
[19] *Barnet Press*, 7 Oct. 1933; *Finchley Festival of Arts Programme* (1963) in B.L.H.L.; *Finchley Press*, 5 Sept. 1947.
[20] *The Times*, 6 Dec. 1965.
[21] *Finchley Festival of Arts Programme* (1963) in B.L.H.L.

local historian C. O. Banks, flourished from 1925 to 1939.[22] The Finchley society, founded in 1971, produces a monthly newsletter.

Finchley cricket club existed in 1832 and Finchley Amateurs and Whetstone or Woodside club, which had been founded by Joseph Baxendale in the grounds of his house, by 1869. The three clubs were merged in 1872 and had absorbed others, such as Torrington Park (1890), by 1894.[23] Said to be one of the best in north London by 1905,[24] Finchley cricket club played at Ballards Lane and Long Lane until it acquired its pitch at East End Road by 1908.[25] Other cricket clubs included East Finchley (1889), Thursday Club (1896), and West Finchley (1935), which had all disappeared by 1955.[26] Middlesex county cricket club acquired 20 a. in Finchley for playing fields in 1938 but was prevented from using them by the war.[27] In 1956 Middlesex county cricket school moved from the Alexandra Palace to a new building on the site of Manor Lodge, where it remained in 1977.[28]

Finchley football club was founded in 1874 and played on rented pitches in Long Lane, Whetstone, and Fallow Corner before acquiring part of the Glebeland sports field in 1932.[29] Finchley and District football league existed by 1935 and two other football clubs by 1955.[30] Nicholas Lane Jackson, known as 'Pa', who had founded the football club and revived the cricket club, started Finchley rugby club in 1875. It was re-formed in 1895 and 1925 and acquired a pitch at Glebeland in 1932, where a new club-house was opened in 1968.[31]

North Finchley tennis club in Nether Street existed by 1887 and there were still courts near by in 1936, although they were built over soon afterwards.[32] Finchley tennis club started *c.* 1928 and still existed in 1977. Other sports clubs included Finchley boxing club, founded by 'Pa' Jackson in 1879,[33] Finchley Harriers, also founded in 1879, which provided members of the Olympic team in 1908,[34] Shaftesbury Harriers, founded in 1890, and Victoria bowling club, which existed by 1935.[35]

The Finchley sports federation between 1925, when fifteen clubs were affiliated to it, and 1953 pressed the council to provide more grounds and, specifically, a running track.[36] The federation may have been alarmed because the many athletics grounds which were leased from the Ecclesiastical Commissioners near the Bishop's Avenue were taken for building.[37] By the mid 1930s, however, there were, in addition to the sports complex at Glebeland, grounds bordering Dollis brook and in East End Road, playing fields in Whetstone, three bowling greens, and five tennis courts.[38] A 'magnificent' skating rink was opened at High Road, North Finchley, in 1910 but it had been replaced by a motor works by 1935.[39]

Finchley golf club, one of the earliest in Middlesex, was founded in 1892 and opened a small course with a club-house across the Hendon boundary in 1903.[40] It was refounded in 1930 by the council, with the original course and adjoining land, which after 1933 lay within Finchley.[41] Hampstead golf club, which was founded in 1893, leased and in 1930 bought land within Finchley from the Ecclesiastical Commissioners.[42]

The churches supported many clubs. In the late 19th and 20th centuries Christ Church had a library and cricket club[43] and St. Mary's a temperance band of hope.[44] North Finchley Baptist church ran lawn tennis and bowling clubs[45] and Church End Congregational church ran tennis courts, a library, a literary and social union, and a music circle founded in 1917.[46] An acting group was founded at Ballards Lane Methodist church in 1946.[47]

Woodside hall and assembly rooms were built in 1885 by Henry Holden, the proprietor of Woodside Park estate. Of red brick with a slate roof in the 'Elizabethan' style and enlarged in 1898, the building housed the Woodside club from 1886 to 1951. Facilities included tennis and billiards, and members numbered 114 by 1906. The hall was licensed for plays and music, mostly performed by Woodside Park musical society,[48] and became a synagogue in 1950.[49]

A working men's institute, called Whetstone club in 1887, existed in Totteridge Lane by 1864,[50] had moved to Friern Barnet Lane by 1900, and survived in 1935.[51] There was an institute at East End by 1871, perhaps the working men's institute in Bull Lane in 1890.[52] In Church End, Hamilton hall opened in 1899 and a working men's club was founded by the vicar by 1900.[53] Finchley allotment holders' exhibition society was founded in 1892 to encourage thrift among the working class,[54] East Finchley constitutional club had its own premises in

22 *Barnet Press*, 9 Mar. 1947. The Banks Colln. is in B.L.H.L.
23 Whiddon, *One Hundred Yrs. of Playing the Game*, 230.
24 Potter Colln. 28/66.
25 Whiddon, *Playing the Game*, 230; *Kelly's Dir. Mdx.* (1908).
26 B.L.H.L., Prints Colln. 7170; B.L.H.L., Acc. 8689; Finchley Boro. *Official Handbk.* (1955).
27 B.L.H.L., Acc. 8689.
28 Ex inf. Mdx. Cnty. Cricket Sch.; *Finchley Press*, 29 Sept. 1956.
29 Whiddon, *Playing the Game*, 9, 40, 54, 93.
30 B.L.H.L., Acc. 8689; Finchley Boro. *Official Handbk.* (1955).
31 Whiddon, *Playing the Game*, 9–10, 37, 119.
32 B.L.H.L., Poor-rate bks. (1887, 1900); O.S. Map 1/2,500, Mdx. XI. 4 (1936 edn.).
33 Whiddon, *Playing the Game*, 10, 104.
34 *V.C.H. Mdx.* ii. 297, 302.
35 B.L.H.L., Acc. 8689.
36 Ibid.
37 Guildhall MS. 12410; O.S. Map 6", Mdx. XI. SE. (1920 edn.); Church Com. file 55543.
38 O.S. Maps 1/2,500, Mdx. VI. 12, 16; XI. 3, 4, 8 (1935, 1936 edns.).
39 M.R.O., Acc. 410/85a; O.S. Maps 1/2,500, Mdx. VI. 16 (1913, 1935 edns.).
40 *V.C.H. Mdx.* ii. 278, 280.
41 Ex inf. the sec.; *V.C.H. Mdx.* v. 29.
42 *V.C.H. Mdx.* ii. 278; see p. 63.
43 *Christ Ch. Centenary Celebrations, 1867–1967* (pamphlet), p. 14; *Kelly's Dir. Mdx.* (1908).
44 *Finchley Press*, 31 Oct. 1975.
45 *N. Finchley Baptist Ch. 1868–1968* (pamphlet).
46 B.L.H.L., Acc. 9987/36.
47 *Finchley Festival of Arts Programme* (1963) in B.L.H.L.
48 *Kelly's Dir. Mdx.* (1890, 1908); B.L.H.L., Acc. 9175; B.L.H.L., S/C (Woodside hall, 1905).
49 See p. 91. A Woodside Park club existed in 1977 but lay outside Finchley and had no connexion with the earlier club: ex inf. the sec.
50 O.S. Map 1/2,500, Mdx. VI. 12 (1864 edn.); B.L.H.L., Poor-rate bk. (1887).
51 B.L.H.L., Poor-rate bk. (1900); O.S. Map 1/2,500, Mdx. VI. 12 (1935 edn.).
52 B.L.H.L., P.A.F. 3/3; *Kelly's Dir. Mdx.* (1890).
53 Datestone on bldg.; B.L.H.L., Poor-rate bk. (1900); B.L.H.L., Banks Colln. xiv; O.S. Map 1/2,500, Mdx. XI. 3 (1936 edn.).
54 *Finchley Press*, 5 Sept. 1947.

Market Place by 1908,[55] and Finchley boys' club met at St. Mary's school during the 1930s.[56]

There were assembly rooms in Church End in the 1880s.[57] Halls licensed for music and dancing included King Edward's and the Grand hall in North Finchley[58] in 1913, when the former Methodist chapel in Stanhope Road was converted from a theatre into a cinema.[59] Finchley Theatre Co. was wound up in 1932.[60] There were five cinemas by 1913: the Empire and the Picturedrome in Great North Road, East Finchley, the Rink and the Stanhope in North Finchley, and the Alcazar, later renamed the Bohemia.[61] The Stanhope, an iron hall, was put up for sale in 1916 as a lecture hall or factory.[62] The Bohemia, in Ballards Lane, became a factory and a second Bohemia later made way for the municipal Gateway House.[63] In 1919 there were protests against a proposed cinema in Church End, probably the one in Regent's Park Road, north of Arcadia Avenue.[64] The Grand Hall cinema, which was presumably the successor of the Rink, was replaced in 1939 by the Odeon, later the Gaumont, at the junction of Great North Road with Kingsway.[65] It survived in 1977,[66] when the only other cinema was the Phoenix, formerly the Rex, which had opened in Great North Road, East End, by 1935.[67]

The *Barnet Press and General Advertiser* was founded in 1859 as a weekly newspaper for a wide area, including Finchley and Whetstone,[68] and survived in 1978 as the *Finchley Press, Friern Barnet Chronicle and Muswell Hill Press*.[69] The *Finchley Press*, a member of the Barnet Press group, was founded in 1893,[70] and still published weekly in 1978.[71]

LOCAL GOVERNMENT. MANORIAL GOVERNMENT. In 1294 a jury upheld the bishop of London's claim to view of frankpledge, assizes of bread and ale, infangthief, outfangthief, felons' goods, and gallows over his men in Finchley as members of his manor of Fulham.[72] Freeholders owed suit of court every three weeks at Fulham although it is improbable that courts met so frequently.[73] By 1384 a view of frankpledge and court leet was held for the bishop's Finchley tenants annually at Fulham on the Sunday after Hokeday. In 1491 it was moved to Highgate, where it was held on Monday in the fifth week after Easter.[74] Occasionally a second court was held, as on 9 Oct. 1396,[75] and from the 18th century extra courts authorized land transfers.[76] The common fine of 6*s.* 8*d.* was paid at the main court each year until 1840.[77] From 1792 the parish made an additional payment of £1 a year, raised in 1828 to £3 3*s.*[78]

Only freeholders, who numbered 10 in 1406 and at least 21 in 1612, owed suit of court. Most paid fines rather than attend and many more inhabitants, 63 in 1612, were amerced for not being in tithing.[79] Perquisites of court, which included the common fine, varied between 12*s.* 8*d.* in 1404–5 and £9 13*s.* 4*d.* in 1606.[80]

Early courts were mostly concerned with enforcing the assizes of bread and ale and with ditches, encroachments on the waste, strays, and occasionally with affrays. There were stocks by 1577.[81] From the 17th century abuse of the common became a major concern and land transactions, including the granting of waste as copyhold, became increasingly important. Enfranchisements took place from 1843 to 1938.[82]

Officers elected at the Finchley court included two ale-tasters (until 1681), two headboroughs, and two constables (from 1423).[83] A constable existed by 1377.[84] The court elected a beadle during the 14th and early 15th centuries. In 1396 it named three, possibly for the bishop to make a final choice.[85] From the mid 15th century the beadle's function, which was mainly to collect rents and fines, was exercised by the bailiff, an appointed official, or one of the demesne lessees.[86] Officers were sometimes reprimanded, presentments of ale-tasters being very common in early court rolls. The beadle was presented in 1396 for not having a rod in his hand, a constable was fined in 1654 for non-attendance,[87] and the surveyors of the highways were presented in 1659 for not rendering their accounts.[88] No officers were elected at the court after 1840; the last view of frankpledge was held in 1848 and the last court in 1938.[89] With occasional gaps, the court rolls and books are extant from 1384 except for the period 1492–1602, which is represented by a single roll for 1577.[90] Some of the rolls may have been lost during

55 *Kelly's Dir. Mdx.* (1908).
56 Char. Com. files.
57 B.L.H.L., Acc. 9987/36; *Crouch End & Hornsey Weekly News*, 12 May 1888.
58 M.R.O., M.C.C., M. & D. 6/38; M. & D. 8/95.
59 O.S. Map 1/2,500, Mdx. VI. 16 (1913 edn.). See p. 89.
60 *The Times*, 8 Nov. 1932.
61 M.R.O., M.C.C., M. & D. 8/96–7, 100–1, 103; ex inf. Mr. G. H. Musgrove. The picture theatre shown in 1913 and 1935 as in Great North Rd., south of its junction with Castle Rd., was probably the Rink: O.S. Map 1/2,500, Mdx. VI. 16 (1913, 1935 edns.).
62 B.L.H.L., S/C (Stanhope Rd.).
63 O.S. Map 1/2,500, Mdx. XI. 4 (1914 edn.); M.R.O., M.C.C., M. & D. 10/717–21; *The Times*, 29 Dec. 1925; B.L.H.L., Banks Colln. xiii. 5963; ex inf. Mr. G. H. Musgrove.
64 *The Times*, 23 Sept. 1919; O.S. Map 1/2,500, Mdx. XI. 4 (1936 edn.).
65 *Finchley Press*, 18 Feb. 1939.
66 'Public Services in Finchley' (leaflet, 1961) in B.L.H.L.
67 O.S. Map 1/2,500, Mdx. XI. 8 (1935 edn.).
68 B.L.H.L., Banks Colln. xiii. 5983.
69 *Willing's Press Guide* (1978).
70 Ex inf. *Finchley Press* (1977). For *Finchley Mail*, see *V.C.H. Mdx.* v. 28.
71 *Willing's Press Guide* (1978).
72 *Plac. de Quo Warr.* (Rec. Com.), p. 475.
73 St. Paul's MS. A 62; C 135/140/6.
74 S.C. 2/188/66 m. 5; S.C. 2/189/10 m. 2d.
75 S.C. 2/188/67 m. 7.
76 Guildhall MSS. 10465/55; 118, p. 372.
77 St. Paul's MS. B 80; Guildhall MSS. 10465/155, p. 217; 156, p. 177.
78 B.L.H.L., P.A.F. 1/2, 6.
79 St. Paul's MS. A 62; S.C. 2/191/5.
80 St. Paul's MS. B 78/43; S.C. 2/189/9 m. 2; Guildhall MSS. 10312/76, 79.
81 Guildhall MS. 10312/92, m. 6.
82 Church Com., S3 survey, pp. 57 sqq.; M.A.F. 9/169.
83 Guildhall MSS. 10312/116, 66.
84 E 179/141/23/13.
85 S.C. 2/188/67 m. 5.
86 e.g. S.C. 6/1140/24 m. 5d.; S.C. 6/Hen. VIII/2109; Guildhall MSS. 10123/1–18.
87 S.C. 2/188/67 m. 5; St. Paul's MS. B 68.
88 S.C. 2/191/12.
89 Guildhall MSS. 10465/156, p. 177; 164, pp. 194–8; 228, p. 140.
90 The ct. rolls are divided, with no apparent logic, among the P.R.O. (S.C. 2/188/65–81; S.C. 2/189/270; S.C. 2/191/4–12, 16); the Guildhall Libr. (MSS. 10312/61–117) and St. Paul's Cathedral (MSS. A 62; B 68, 80). The ct. bks. (MSS. 10465/1–228) and indexes (MSS. 10475/1–12; 10465/230–1) are in the Guildhall Libr.

the stewardship of Hugh Stewdley in the mid 16th century.[91]

For Bibbesworth manor, whose tenants were subject to the Finchley leet, a single court roll, listing tenants and their rents and services, survives for 1364–5. There is also a record of a court held in 1597 which was concerned with breaking hedges and cutting wood.[92] Court books exist for the years 1716 to 1830 and 1847 to 1936 and mostly record encroachments and admissions.[93] Courts baron were held usually once a year but often less frequently, with occasional special courts, at the Queen's Head in Church End and in 1869 at the Railway tavern.

PARISH GOVERNMENT TO 1837. The parish emerged early as the unit of government. The churchwardens already had charge of property on behalf of the parish in 1488[94] and the clerk, mentioned in 1379 as the rector's clerk, was in 1536 associated with the rector in the administration of money.[95] The church house was said in 1547 to have been built by the parishioners and to be used for their common assembly 'for matters of the king as for the church and parish'.[96] By 1561 the church and clerk's houses had become part of the charity estates, which in turn were closely associated with the parish government and officers.[97] The parish may have been divided about that time into two wards, called Finchley and Whetstone in 1577, East and North later.[98]

Overseers, mentioned in 1586, assisted the churchwardens in dealing with the poor by 1614 and four surveyors of the highways existed by 1659.[99] Parishioners, acting in concert, appointed two of their own number as attorneys in a dispute over the quartering of Parliamentary troops in 1644.[1] A general vestry mentioned in 1648 apparently consisted only of the charity estates' feoffees, headed by Sir Thomas Allen. The parishioners gained more financial powers during the Interregnum: in 1656 they were invited to see the charity accounts and in 1659 they were supposed to inspect the surveyors' accounts at the church house.[2]

The first extant vestry minute book begins in 1768 and is marked 'no. 6',[3] earlier records probably having been lost in a fire of 1836 which destroyed the Queen's Head.[4] Meetings in theory were held once a month, from 1796 on the last Wednesday in the morning and from 1798 on the last Sunday after evening service, but were usually more frequent, varying from 8 a year in 1838 to 63 in 1835. They took place in the vestry room at the church, at the church house, which from 1718 was the Queen's Head, or, if business concerned East End, at the Five Bells. A new room was built at the church in 1841 but could not accommodate the large meetings of the 1850s, which often adjourned to the National school.

In addition to nominating and supervising the parish officers, and dealing with church-, highway-, and poor-rates, repairs to the church, drainage, and policing, the vestry was also concerned with the common and grants of waste. In 1803 it provided eight militia men. In 1818 it set up a savings bank and in 1819 it began to enforce temperance, ensuring that public houses did not open during Sunday services. During the 18th century the vestry was dominated by the lessee farmers but by *c.* 1819 the rector usually took the chair. In 1832 a committee of fifteen was set up to make by-laws, although the rector denied that the parish had a select vestry.[5]

The vestry usually chose the churchwardens and overseers in March or April and the surveyors of the highways in September. From 1794 the rector appointed one of the churchwardens. From 1804 anyone refusing to serve in those offices had to pay £10 to the parish. Although constables and headboroughs continued to be elected at the manor court until 1840, control gradually passed to the vestry, which paid them. When there was a dispute or an unsuitable appointment, the vestry had to settle it or make a new appointment, as it did in 1773, 1774, 1794, and 1818. In 1811 a constable refused to serve and was prosecuted by the vestry. There was one constable for each of the two wards, and a special constable was named in 1803 in anticipation of a French invasion. Other officers appointed by the vestry included a common driver,[6] vestry clerk, beadle, sexton, parish doctor (1782), organist (1801), apothecary (1804), church clerk (1812), and collector of the poor-rates (1813), who were all salaried, and a pew opener, who in 1796 was to wear a greatcoat and hat.

The issues of property left to the parish in the 15th and 16th centuries were administered by the churchwardens before they became vested in the feoffees of the charity estates.[7] Another source of income was the rent roll, half the rent from grants of waste from 1588[8], which by 1776 brought in £16 17*s.* a year.[9] Quarterly contributions for the poor were levied in 1614[10] and 67 people were indicted for not fulfilling their statutory obligations to mend the highways in 1616.[11] In 1690 justices returning from meetings of the charity feoffees became stuck in the mud,[12] and in 1694 the surveyors petitioned for an assessment to be made because statute labour was insufficient to keep the main road in repair.[13] A highway-rate was levied by 1703[14] and a composition in lieu of statute labour was levied in the late 18th century, with an occasional highway-rate, usually of 4*d.* or 6*d.* in

[91] C 2/Eliz. I/L11/18.
[92] W.A.M. 4818; M.R.O., Acc. 351/146.
[93] M.R.O., Acc. 351/276, 375.
[94] Guildhall MS. 10312/81, m. 2.
[95] Guildhall MS. 9171/1, f. 68v.; B.L.H.L., Acc. 6416/8.
[96] E 301/34 m. 30d., no. 157.
[97] *10th Rep. Com. Char.* H.C. 103, pp. 318 sqq. (1824), xiii; see below, p. 98.
[98] Guildhall MS. 10312/92, m. 6.
[99] Guildhall MS. 9537/6, f. 4; M.R.O., Acc. 351/150, f. 4; S.C. 2/191/12.
[1] *Cal. S.P. Dom.* 1644, p. 119.
[2] B.L.H.L., Acc. 9131 (notes from the 'church bk.', since lost); S.C. 2/191/12.
[3] Except where otherwise stated, the following paras. are based on the vestry mins. 1768–1873: B.L.H.L., P.A.F. 1/1–9. Minutes for 1769–70, 1798–9, and 1825–6, together with a table of rates and mtgs. 1780–1841, are printed as App. to H. C. Stephens, *Parochial Self-Govt. in Rural Dists.* (1893).
[4] Stephens, op. cit. 65; *Home Cnties. Mag.* v. 269–72.
[5] *Rep. from Commrs. on Poor Laws*, H.C. 44 (1834), xxxv, App. B 2, pt. 1, p. 95 *f.*
[6] For the common driver, see p. 48.
[7] See p. 97.
[8] S.C. 2/191/9. The other half went to the lord both on the bishop's and on Bibbesworth man.
[9] B.L.H.L., Banks Colln. xvi (rent roll 1776).
[10] M.R.O., Acc. 351/150.
[11] *Mdx. Sess. Rec.* iv. 32–4.
[12] Passmore, 'Finchley Par. Rec.' i, f. 37.
[13] *Mdx. Cnty. Rec. Sess. Bks, 1689–1709*, 113.
[14] *Mdx. Cnty. Rec. Sess. Bks. 1689–1709*, 263.

the £.[15] Poor-rates were levied between one and three times a year, varying between 6*d.* and 5*s.* for the period 1768 to 1836[16] and raising usually under £500 a year before the 1790s, between £1,000 and £2,000 from 1800 to 1830, and over £2,000 by 1836.[17] In 1684 the overseers applied to the justices for an inquiry, alleging that a considerable sum assessed for poor-relief had been mis-spent by a previous overseer,[18] and in 1705 another overseer took the money for his own use.[19] Seven leading farmers appealed against the poor-rates in 1753,[20] and in 1831 the assessment was reduced because of the great depreciation of property. By that date many officers had business interests in London and in 1832 a salaried assistant overseer, John Tattam, was appointed. The parish was *c.* £600 in debt in 1833 and solvent by 1838 but again in trouble in 1840, when Tattam was dismissed for misapplying funds.

In 1614 £31 18*s.* 6*d.* was spent on monthly contributions to sixteen poor people and quarterly contributions to another four.[21] Pensions continued to be paid to paupers: 14 in 1768, 27 in 1785, 36 in 1796, and 28 in 1819. By 1834 the parish supported 15 bastards and relieved 36 labourers.[22] The vestry also made *ad hoc* payments, for clothing girls in service in 1768, to send a man to the East Indies in 1820, and for clothes, medical expenses, food, or fuel. In 1796 recipients of parish relief were to be badged. Pauper children were apprenticed, in 1793 in London, in 1796 to cotton- and calico-printing factories in Lancashire, and in 1804 in Derbyshire. In the 16th century many paupers who had used the Great North Road were buried in Finchley and in the early 17th century strangers often had to be removed.[23] In 1656 the headborough complained that he had spent 50*s.* in conveying vagrants and cripples along the road from London to the north of England[24] and in 1681 the magistrates answered a complaint from Finchley by ordering the Highgate constable to pass his vagrants northward directly to Whetstone and not through Finchley town.[25] There were similar disputes with Friern Barnet at the end of the 17th century,[26] when the Finchley constables were paying between £8 and £14 a year in conveying vagrants through the parish.[27] Numbers rose during the Napoleonic wars: in two days in March 1798 134 soldiers' wives and 447 children were relieved and given passes.

In 1614 Finchley paid 30*s.* a year to keep a man and his wife in Friern Barnet's alms-houses.[28] From 1684 Finchley's alms-houses accommodated some paupers[29] and the parish bought or leased poor-houses for others. One such in Blackhorse Lane, Whetstone, was leased by the parish at least from 1773 to 1803.[30] Another was a wooden cowhouse on the common, which was bought by the vestry in 1797.[31] There were two parish cottages by 1817, for which rent was charged in 1822.

A workhouse existed in 1768, when four adults and four children occupied a leased building near Fallow Corner. Said in 1777 to accommodate eighteen people,[32] it was two-storeyed in 1782 and presumably had a garden, since vegetable seeds were bought in 1796. The workhouse held 25 inmates in 1785 and was so full in 1788 that consideration was given to 'putting out' some of them. When the lease expired the vestry took a 21 years' lease of the Five Bells in East End Road from the feoffees of the charity estates. Two rooms for the sick were added in 1805 but in 1808 the vestry, which had suggested that the inmates could receive weekly out-relief or be moved into the small poorhouse purchased in 1797, leased a house in Green Lane as a new workhouse. In 1813 regulations forbade 'spiritous liquor', except for medicinal purposes, and substituted coffee for beer. Further regulations in 1825 enjoined sobriety and attendance at Sunday service and required that inmates be in the house by 7.0 in winter and 8.0 in summer. The workhouse usually held between 10 and 12.[33] Despite proposals to build a larger one in 1833, it remained until it was superseded by the Barnet union workhouse.

The poor were farmed from 1768 to 1816. Initially £160 a year, the cost rose to £280 a year in 1788, 3*s.* 9*d.* (a week) a head in 1798, and 5*s.* a head in 1806. In 1774 the farmer was to live in the workhouse and keep the poor employed. Care was transferred from the farmer to the overseers in 1816 and salaried managers or matrons attended the workhouse from 1822.

The two decades following the Napoleonic wars saw a rising number of unemployed and a tightening of regulations on poor-relief in an attempt to control expenditure. In 1818 the able-bodied poor were set to work by the overseers on the 17 a. allotted to the parish at inclosure.[34] During 1831 27 a. were leased out as allotments and the large number of unemployed were paid a daily wage to cultivate them, the crops being sold. In 1832 Finchley set up a rudimentary employment exchange, urging parishioners to employ the poor of their own parish. The vestry, led by John Verrall, tried to curb drunkenness. In 1819 a list of those receiving out-relief was sent to all the public houses with instructions to refuse to serve them, in 1820 a pauper was committed to the cage

[15] B.L.H.L., P.A.F. 3/1 (surveyors' acct., 1780–1840).
[16] A rate bk. for 1756, giving £87 as the rate raised by 6*d.* in the £, was found in New York by Ald. V. Wells and still in his possession in 1938. There is a copy in B.L.H.L., Banks Colln. xvi.
[17] B.L.H.L., Acc. 6140/1–2 (Poor-rate bks. 1784–1830); *Rep. from Sel. Cttee. on Poor Rate Returns*, H.C. 556, p. 99 (1822); H.C. 334, p. 133 (1825); *2nd Rep. of Poor Law Commrs.* H.C. 595–II, p. 213 (1836), xxix. See Stephens, *Parochial Self-Govt.* 183 sqq. for assessments.
[18] M.R.O., MJ/SBB 416, p. 46.
[19] C 8/367/27; *Mdx. Cnty. Rec. Sess. Bks. 1689–1709*, 309.
[20] M.R.O., MJ/SBB 1098/34.
[21] M.R.O., Acc. 351/150.
[22] *Rep. from Commrs. on Poor Laws*, H.C. 44 (1834), xxxvi, App. B 2, pt. iii, pp. 95*h*, *k*.
[23] B.L.H.L., Banks Colln. xvii (Finchley par. regs.); S.C. 2/191/4; Guildhall MS. 10312/122.
[24] M.R.O., MJ/SBB 159, p. 17.
[25] Ibid. 387, p. 46.
[26] *Mdx. Cnty. Rec. Sess. Bks. 1689–1709*, 19, 177.
[27] Ibid. 69, 81, 97, 112–13, 115, 121.
[28] *Mdx. Sess. Rec.* ii. 33.
[29] See pp. 98–9.
[30] It was used as a chapel in 1830: M.L.R. 1773/4/291–2; M.L.R. 1830/1/528.
[31] Except where otherwise stated, the following paras. are based on vestry mins.: B.L.H.L., P.A.F. 1/1–9; *Rep. from Commrs. on Poor Laws*, H.C. 44 (1834), xxxv–xxxvi, App. B 2.
[32] *Abs. of Returns made by Overseers of Poor* (1777), p. 100.
[33] e.g. 3 sick women and 1 old woman, 1 old and 1 idiot man, and 4 children in 1833.
[34] M.R.O., EA/FIN, nos. 40, 117.

for applying for relief while drunk and 'grossly insulting' the vestry, and in 1826 a drunkard was ejected from the vestry. Relief was refused to anyone who kept a dog in 1825.

LOCAL GOVERNMENT AFTER 1837. Under the Poor Law Amendment Act of 1834 Finchley became part of Barnet union. A meeting of the ratepayers in 1836 condemned the Act as 'an atrocious Whig measure'[35] and the parish, considering its representation inadequate, refused until 1837 to nominate its guardian of the poor, to the astonishment of the Poor Law Commissioners. A second guardian was appointed in 1839 and a third in 1855. The parish continued to resist the union, refusing proposals to sell the two cottages leased to paupers in 1827 and to set up a fund to aid emigration in 1849.

The parish and vestry clerks and the sexton received their salaries from the churchwardens until 1857, and a parish constable was still being elected in 1863.[36] A salaried collector of the highway-rate was appointed in 1840 and a salaried surveyor in 1856. Elected surveyors were increased from two to four in 1865 and six in 1870, reflecting the importance of highways in the work of the vestry. Church-rates were abolished in 1863.[37]

As general meetings became larger during the 1850s, the vestry began to appoint committees: on roads, charities and bequests, nuisances, closing the churchyard, assessment for rates, and audit. A committee was appointed in 1866 to undertake the duties of the Sewage and Sanitary Acts of 1865 and 1866 but it was dissolved in the same year, as the vestry waited to see what neighbouring parishes were doing, and again formed in 1868. The six surveyors of the highway were described as a highway board in 1871, although a regular highway board was not appointed until 1874. In 1872, fearful that it would completely lose control of its affairs to Barnet, the vestry decided to adopt the Local Government Act of 1858 which it had hitherto opposed on the grounds of expense. From 1873 until under the Act a local board of health was formed in 1878, Barnet rural sanitary authority exercised powers in Finchley.

Finchley local board[38] consisted of twelve members and first met in 1878, when it elected Edward Sayer (d. 1897), a local landowner, as chairman and appointed a salaried clerk.[39] The board set up highways, sanitary, and finance and general purposes committees and appointed a medical officer of health. A works committee had been added by 1881 and legal and fire committees by 1890. Other salaried officers by 1884 included a surveyor and an inspector. Sewerage proved controversial and featured in a conflict between Fredrick Goodyear of North Finchley and H. C. Stephens of Church End. Stephens, described by Goodyear as 'the uncrowned king of Finchley', was never chairman of the board but enjoyed considerable influence. He was elected Conservative M.P. for Hornsey in 1887 and advocated ratepayers' control, seeking in 1893 to introduce a Bill to restore 18th-century parish govenment and citing Finchley vestry minutes as evidence.[40] Stephens was probably behind the resistance to union with Friern Barnet in 1881.[41] His opponents objected that government was in the hands of the ratepayers of Church End, who could command more property and voting power than those in northern and eastern Finchley.

After the local board became an urban district council in 1895, with Goodyear as chairman, the opposition began to gain strength.[42] Finchley ratepayers' association, which had been formed in 1882, had pressed unsuccessfully in 1890 and 1894 for a division into wards, in an attempt to break the control of Church End. There were similar applications by five ratepayers' associations in 1896 and by the Whetstone ratepayers and the U.D.C. itself in 1897, when an inquiry led to the division of the district in 1898 into approximately equal East, North, and West wards, each with four councillors.[43]

The U.D.C. met every third Monday at offices in Bibbesworth House, Church End,[44] until in 1902 it moved to Finchley Hall, built after 1836 on the site of the church house.[45] At first the committees of the local board were retained and expenditure was mainly on highways and sanitation. After acquiring responsibilities in other fields, the council and its committees held 206 meetings during 1902.[46] In 1921 control of finance passed from the clerk to a new department and by the end of the 1920s housing had become the chief expense, followed by electric lighting.

In 1909 the council decided to set up a distress committee for the unemployed and offered work on the sewage farm and private roads.[47] In 1914, when the road employees were dismissed, there was uproar in the council chamber and the police were called.[48] Controversy was also caused in 1914 by a town-planning scheme for Finchley and part of Totteridge and by the proposed building of council houses at Woodhouse. Finchley continued to oppose outside bodies, clashing with Finchley Electric Light Co. over cables and with Barnet District Gas & Water Co. over the water-rate in 1901 and with the Post Office over the installation of telephones in 1913.[49] H. C. Stephens provoked further controversy by his bequest of Avenue House, whose grounds were opened to the public in 1918; no endowment was left for the house itself,[50] which Church End ratepayers' association resolved to retain in 1923 and

35 *The Times*, 29 Apr. 1836.
36 *Lond. Gaz.* 7 July 1857, p. 2376.
37 *Finchley Press*, 6 Oct. 1933.
38 Except where otherwise stated, the information is based on Finchley local bd., min. bks. i–xiv (1878–1894) in Hendon town hall; B.L.H.L., Banks Colln. xiii (press cuttings on local govt.). Cf. also B.L.H.L., P.A.F. 4/1 (Sanitary inspectors' rep. bk. 1889–93); P.A.F. 4/2 (acct. bk. 1881–4).
39 B.L.H.L., Banks Colln., biog. s.v. Sayer.
40 Stephens, *Parochial Self-Govt.* The Bill was not introduced probably because it was overtaken by the Local Govt. Act, 1894. Stephens played an active part in the debates on that measure.
41 B.L.H.L., Acc. 10111.
42 U.D.C. records until 1923 in Hendon town hall, after 1923 at B.L.H.L.
43 M.R.O., *Reps. of Local Inqs.* (1889–97), 175–87, 189–216; (1895–1907), unpag.; Biggers, *Finchley*, 19–20.
44 Not the manor-ho.
45 *Kelly's Dir. Mdx.* (1908); *Barnet Press*, 7 Oct. 1933; see below, p. 98.
46 M.R.O., *Reps. of Local Inqs.* (1895–1907), 1903 inquiry.
47 *The Times*, 8, 31 Dec. 1909.
48 B.L.H.L., Acc. 10111.
49 *The Times*, 17 Oct., 19 Dec. 1901; 8 Jan. 1913.
50 Ibid. 11 Sept. 1918.

which was opened to the public and used for the housing department in 1928.[51]

Although a charter of incorporation was sought in 1926, when the council feared threats to its identity from Middlesex C.C. and the L.C.C.,[52] it was not until 1933 that Finchley became a municipal borough.[53] The borough was divided into the three wards of the old U.D., each with six councillors.[54] By 1951 there were eight wards (Glebe, Manor, Moss Hall, St. Mary's, St. Paul's, the Bishop's, Tudor, and Whetstone), each with three councillors,[55] who elected eight aldermen and a mayor. Administration was by the departments of the town clerk, treasurer, surveyor, medical officer of health, education officer, housing officer, and librarian.[56]

BOROUGH OF FINCHLEY. *Vert, on a chevron raguly, between in chief two bugle horns stringed or and in base a mitre argent garnished or, a rose gules surmounted by another argent.*
[Granted 1933]

In 1965, under the London Government Act of 1963, Finchley became part of Barnet L.B. Four of Barnet's 20 wards (Finchley, East Finchley, St. Paul's, and Woodhouse) lay within the old parish, the eleven departments being housed in the former council offices of the constituent authorities.[57]

LONDON BOROUGH OF BARNET. *Azure, a paschal lamb proper standing upon a grassy mount; on a chief per pale argent and gules a Saxon crown or between two roses counterchanged barbed and seeded proper.*
[Granted 1965]

The offices at Finchley Hall were extended in the 1930s.[58] Avenue House became the chief municipal office after Finchley was bombed in 1940 but by the 1950s there were also departments in Hertford Lodge, next to Avenue House in East End Road, and Regent's Park Road.[59] New council offices were built at Gateway House in Regent's Park Road in 1974.[60]

The borough council was predominantly Conservative before the Second World War and again, after a period of control by Independents, from 1949.[61] Finchley became a separate parliamentary constituency in 1919 and has usually returned Conservative members,[62] including, since 1959, Mrs. Margaret Thatcher.

PUBLIC SERVICES. The 'fine spring water' of many wells was noted as a feature of the parish as a whole in 1717 and of individual houses in the 19th century.[63] Wells were supplemented by numerous ponds and by rainwater tanks.[64] Public wells included Brownswell, which was used by travellers across the common and repaired by the feoffees of the charity estates.[65] In 1717 the conduit had recently been mended.[66] The feoffees also maintained wells at Church End in 1791, abandoned in 1792 after it had fallen in, and in Nether Street from 1793 until after 1844.[67] The town well at Whetstone was ordered to be opened in 1819, whereupon the encloser brought an action against the parish officers in 1820. The vestry had to pay damages but the inhabitants' right to use the well was upheld.[68]

The Regent's Canal Co. acquired land for a reservoir at Strawberry Vale in 1811 but the scheme was abandoned and the site drained *c.* 1820.[69] There were water works in High Road and Hampstead Lane belonging to the New River Co. in 1859.[70] In 1866, when considering the problems of drainage and sewerage, the vestry declared that it was not necessary to do anything about the water supply but by 1871 the East Barnet Water Co. was supplying cottages at Whetstone.[71] In the 1880s water was still drawn from wells, many of which were contaminated by sewage.[72] By 1890 the East Barnet Water Co. was the Barnet District Gas & Water Co., which in 1901 defended itself against the U.D.C.'s charge that the water-rate was too high by claiming that deep boring had been necessary.[73] The company, called the Barnet District Water Co. in 1955, was absorbed into the Lee Valley Water Co. in 1960.[74]

Sewerage, because of large-scale building, presented problems by 1867, when complaints to the Home Secretary led to an inquiry.[75] The inspector stated that he had long been worried by Finchley's sanitary condition: open pools and streams were polluted and many houses were being built without sewers. Cholera provided the necessary stimulus to spend money, which was borrowed to build sewers and tanks at Church End, East End, North End, and Whetstone. By 1868, however, the sewers were

[51] Ibid. 12 June 1925.
[52] Ibid. 15 June 1926.
[53] Barnet L.B. *Official Guide* [*c.* 1973].
[54] *Finchley Press*, 6 Oct., 7 Oct. 1933; *The Times*, 18 Sept. 1933.
[55] *Census*, 1951.
[56] Finchley Boro. *Official Handbk.* (1955).
[57] Barnet L.B. *Official Guide* [*c.* 1973].
[58] *The Times*, 30 Nov. 1932; 19 Dec. 1934; 29 Sept. 1936; 23 Feb., 19 June, 7 Aug. 1937.
[59] Finchley Boro. *Official Handbk.* (1955); B.L.H.L., Banks Colln. ix. 4376.
[60] Finchley Soc. *Newsletter*, Mar., Oct. 1973; *Evening Standard*, 21 Oct. 1977.
[61] Election results in *The Times*, e.g. 2 Nov. 1938, 14 May 1949, 12 May 1950.
[62] *Whitaker's Almanack* (1915 and later edns.).
[63] Geol. Surv. Map, Mdx. XI. NE., SE. (1920); M.R.O., Acc. 262/4/42; *T.L.M.A.S.* xix. 48. e.g. B.L.H.L., S/C (Moss Hall, 1830); M.R.O., Acc. 262/4/15–18; *Finchley Press*, 28 May 1954.
[64] e.g. B.L.H.L., S/C (Long Lodge, 1876).
[65] *Mdx. and Herts. N. & Q.* iii. 65.
[66] *T.L.M.A.S.* xix. 48.
[67] Passmore, 'Finchley Par. Rec.' i, ff. 62–4, 88, 92.
[68] B.L.H.L., P.A.F. 1/5.
[69] *Barnet Press*, 4 Sept. 1954; M.R.O., Hist. Notes 21/7/70.
[70] B.L.H.L., Church-rates (1859).
[71] B.L.H.L., P.A.F. 1/9, 3/3.
[72] B.L.H.L., Banks Colln. xiii.
[73] *Kelly's Dir. Mdx.* (1890); *The Times*, 19 Dec. 1901.
[74] Finchley Boro. *Official Handbk.* (1955); Barnet L.B. *Official Guide* [*c.* 1973]; *V.C.H. Mdx.* v. 297.
[75] Except where otherwise stated, information about sewerage is based on B.L.H.L., P.A.F. 1/9 (vestry mins. 1864–74).

full and other houses needed cesspools, especially in Whetstone. Privies were made compulsory for all houses in 1869. In 1870 the Lee Conservancy Board complained about sewage from Bounds Green brook, while East Finchley's sewerage flowed through St. Pancras cemetery, where it was further polluted by the shallow graves of paupers. A special vestry meeting vetoed plans to draw up a drainage scheme for the whole parish, and a committee, unable to find a panacea 'any more than they have discovered the Philosophers' stone', decided that the existing system of six outfalls of sewage in the east was the cheapest. Finchley blamed Colney Hatch asylum for continued pollution of Bounds Green brook, open drains were still a nuisance in 1871,[76] and typhoid broke out at Whetstone in 1872. In 1874 Barnet rural sanitary authority drew Finchley's attention to the need for comprehensive drainage.

Sewerage was one of the main problems facing the new local board of health, whose medical officer in 1879 revealed that little had changed since 1867.[77] Finchley, after considering plans to co-operate with Friern Barnet and Edmonton,[78] acquired over 100 a. at Strawberry Vale[79] and built a complete system to serve 2,355 a. of the most populous part of the parish, with high- and low-level sewers discharging into works built at Summers Lane in 1885.[80] Later improvements included bacteriological treatment of the sewage from 1897 and works to deal with surface water draining into the near-by brooks in 1903.[81] Sewage was rerouted to Deepham, Edmonton, in 1963, the Summers Lane works being demolished.[82] A refuse destructor was built near the sewage farm in 1928 and demolished in 1965.[83]

Hospital provision had been foreshadowed by the addition of two rooms to the workhouse in 1805.[84] In 1831, expecting cholera, the vestry set up a committee which issued instructions for cleanliness and took the opportunity to warn that in cases of insobriety the disease was 'most peculiarly fatal'.[85] The outbreak was less severe than had been feared.[86] Poor sanitary conditions, especially in Whetstone and East End, made diseases like typhoid common throughout the 19th century,[87] although in 1880 Finchley was said to have less tuberculosis than most areas.[88]

During a smallpox epidemic in 1881 St. Pancras put up temporary tents on its land in Finchley in spite of opposition from the local board, which sent its own smallpox victims to Barnet union workhouse or to Highgate.[89] In 1889 the board built its own hospital for infectious diseases, unsuitably sited near the sewage farm in Summers Lane.[90] It accommodated 24 in 1913 but was superseded by Coppetts Wood hospital in Hornsey, with whose council Finchley and Wood Green agreed to share costs in 1922.[91]

Finchley cottage hospital, built mostly by subscription on a site at Fallow Corner given by Ebenezer Homan,[92] opened with 18 beds in 1908 and was renamed Finchley Memorial hospital and extended to 46 beds in 1922. A private wing was opened in 1933 and there were 124 beds by 1977.[93]

A convalescent home belonging to the National Hospital for Diseases of the Nervous System, Bloomsbury, had opened in East End Road in 1870 and had 16 female patients by 1881. It moved to the Bishop's Avenue in 1895, where it had 36 beds in 1931 and 25 in 1961. A rehabilitation building was opened in 1967.[94]

Woodside Home for incurable and infirm women moved in 1888 from Great Ormond Street to Whetstone, where H. Lloyd Baxendale gave it a house and grounds.[95] It had 44 patients in 1891[96] and 54 beds in 1931 but closed between 1937 and 1941.[97] The Grange, a private lunatic asylum, had opened by 1901, when it had seven inmates and twice as many staff.[98] St. Elizabeth's, a female geriatric hospital, opened in 1953 in Friern Watch, Ebenezer Homan's home on the Friern Barnet border at Whetstone, and had 40 beds by 1975.[99]

A cage on the waste near the church, with stocks near by, was to be built in 1784 on the magistrates' recommendation.[1] In 1801 the parish contributed towards Highgate cage[2] but in 1806 a bricklayer was to repair a cage which presumably stood in Finchley.[3] In 1812 Finchley and Friern Barnet failed to agree on a joint plan to build a cage aginst the toll-house at Whetstone.[4] In 1815 the vestry asserted that a place of confinement was absolutely necessary and again planned cages at Whetstone and near the stocks at Church End, suggesting that the earlier cage was no longer in use. There was still no agreement with Friern Barnet but a brick cage was built at Church End close to the Queen's Head.[5] Pupils of the National school had to pass the cage and in 1860

76 B.L.H.L., P.A.F. 3/3.
77 *Finchley Press*, 6 Oct. 1933; Finchley local bd., min. bk. i. 56–8.
78 Finchley local bd., min. bk. i. 79–80; ii. 117–18; *Finchley Press*, 16 Nov. 1928.
79 Finchley U.D.C. *Ann. Rep. of M.O.H.* (1907); Finchley local bd., min. bk. ii. 262; *N. Mdx. Chron.* 19 Nov. 1881.
80 Finchley local bd., min. bk. iii. 451; B.L.H.L., Banks Colln. xiii. 5947.
81 *Finchley Press*, 6 Oct. 1933; M.R.O., *Reps. of Local Inqs.* (1895–1907), 1903 inquiry.
82 B.L.H.L., Print Colln. 6717; ex inf. the works manager, Deephams sewerage works.
83 *Finchley Press*, 6 Oct. 1933; B.L.H.L., Print Colln. 6710.
84 B.L.H.L., P.A.F. 1/4.
85 Ibid. 1/6.
86 Ibid. 1/7.
87 e.g. the prevalence of 'fever' at East End in 1849: B.L.H.L., Acc. 6787/6; cholera in 1866: B.L.H.L., P.A.F. 1/9; typhoid at Whetstone in 1872: ibid. 3/3; typhoid and diphtheria in 1889: ibid. 4/1.
88 *N. Mdx. Chron.* 26 June 1880.
89 Finchley local bd., min. bk. ii. 135–8, 211, 300; M.R.O., P.R. 13/34 (illus. of temporary hosp.); B.L.H.L., P.A.F. 4/2.
90 Finchley local bd. of health, *Ann. Rep. of M.O.H.* (1892); O.S. Map 6", Mdx. XI. NE. (1897 edn.).
91 Finchley U.D.C. *Ann. Reps. of M.O.H.* (1913, 1923); see below, p. 171.
92 B.L.H.L., Banks Colln., biog. Homan.
93 Ex inf. Finchley Memorial hosp.; *The Times*, 8 Sept. 1922, 4 Mar. 1933; Finchley U.D.C. *Ann. Rep. of M.O.H.* (1923).
94 Ex inf. Nat. Hosp. for Nervous Diseases; *Census*, 1881; *Hospitals Yr. Bk.* (1931, 1961).
95 *Kelly's Dir. Mdx.* (1908).
96 *Census*, 1891.
97 *Hospitals Yr. Bk.* (1931, 1937, 1941).
98 *Census*, 1901.
99 Ex inf. Barnet area health authy. dist. administrator; *Hospitals Yr. Bk.* (1975).
1 B.L.H.L., P.A.F. 1/2.
2 Ibid. 1/3.
3 Ibid. 1/4.
4 Ibid.; M.R.O., D.R.O. 12/1/D1/1.
5 B.L.H.L., P.A.F. 1/4, 5.

HIGHGATE: ARCHWAY ROAD FROM THE NORTH-WEST
St. Augustine's Church and the Archway are in the background

FINCHLEY: PARK HOUSE, HENDON LANE

Friern Barnet: Goldsmith Road

Finchley: Lincoln Road

Muswell Hill: Rookfield Estate

Muswell Hill: Hillfield Park

TERRACED HOUSES

the prisoners' behaviour led the vestry to demand its closure, but the Metropolitan Police insisted on keeping it: 143 persons had been confined there during the last five years.[6] The cage was eventually removed in 1880.[7]

Three police forces operated in the mid 19th century: the parish constable,[8] the Metropolitan Police, and the Bow Street horse patrol.[9] The patrol, revived in 1805 to safeguard the turnpike roads out of London,[10] was first recorded in Finchley in 1818. By 1828 its third division operated as far as Whetstone and in 1836 four constables worked from Finchley and two from Whetstone. There was still a Bow Street horse patrol station on the Great North Road in 1851, with four men. There were then eleven other policemen, presumably from the metropolitan force, in the parish.[11] From 1840 Finchley was included in the Metropolitan Police District.[12] A police station was built at Whetstone, on the east side of the main road, in 1851 and was inadequate in 1911, when a new site was bought in Friern Barnet Lane. It was only in 1948, however, that the adjoining premises at the corner of High Road and Friern Barnet Lane were bought and in 1960 that the new station opened there and the old one closed.[13] In 1865 the vestry requested more police[14] and in 1873 a police station was opened in Church End, in a rented house. Wentworth Lodge in Ballards Lane was bought in 1886 and a station was opened on the site in 1889, closed in 1965, and rebuilt shortly afterwards.

A fire-engine had to be brought from Highgate in 1813 but by 1824 Finchley had its own,[15] which the churchwardens were responsible for repairing in 1845 and 1849.[16] A volunteer fire brigade was formed *c.* 1870;[17] composed mainly of traders, it kept a hose and cart in a shed opposite Woodhouse Road and later at the Queen's Head hotel in East End Road. A fire station opened in 1888 in a shop in Hendon Lane and later in adjoining shops.[18] In 1890 the brigade consisted of twelve men and five auxiliaries.[19] The local board had a fire committee by 1889 but decided against a new station on grounds of expense.[20] The new U.D.C. took over the voluntary brigade and in 1899 formed a professional force,[21] which in 1904 acquired one of the first motor-powered fire-engines.[22] A sub-station for North Finchley opened in 1890 at Tally Ho Corner, moved in 1902 to Torrington Park, and closed in 1930. Another for East End opened in 1895 near the Bald-faced Stag, moved to Church Lane and then to Chapel Street, and closed in 1931. Whetstone was served by a sub-station opened near the police station in 1896 and closed *c.* 1933.[23] In 1935 a combined fire and ambulance station opened at the junction of Long Lane and the North Circular Road, superseding the Church End station and the recently closed sub-stations.[24]

The Hornsey Gas Co. opened negotiations to light Finchley in 1861 but by 1863 decided that the hamlets were too scattered and withdrew in favour of the Southgate Gas Co.[25] The latter, as the Southgate and Colney Hatch Gas Light and Coke Co., tion, notified its intention to enter the parish in 1866, as did the East Barnet Gas and Water Co.[26] Meanwhile the Finchley Gas Co. had retired in 1863 in favour of the North Middlesex Gas Co., founded in 1862 to supply Finchley, Hendon, and Mill Hill.[27] The company began work in Hendon and in 1870 was permitted by the vestry to enter Finchley.[28] By 1879 the Southgate, the East Barnet, and the North Middlesex Gas companies had laid mains in Finchley, although none had gas-works there.[29] Street lighting was introduced in 1883.[30] The Southgate company was absorbed into the Tottenham and Edmonton Gas Light and Coke Co. in 1938 and on nationalization in 1948 became part of the Eastern Gas Board, which supplied northern Finchley in 1973. The other two companies in 1948 became part of the North Thames Gas Board, which in 1973 supplied the rest of the area.[31]

The West Middlesex Electric Lighting Co. unsuccessfully proposed to supply Finchley in 1882.[32] Finchley Electric Light Co., incorporated in 1900, installed a small gas-engine generating station near Mountfield Road but soon clashed with the U.D.C., which in 1897 began considering whether it should provide electricity itself. By 1899 the U.D.C. obtained a provisional order under the Electric Lighting Act of 1882 and in 1901 it started to cut the Finchley Electric Light Co.'s cables. Cutting was forbidden after litigation but in 1902 the U.D.C. drew up a scheme and in 1903 it opened a generating station, from which 130 houses were supplied by 1904. Some street lamps were then converted from gas to electricity and in 1905 the Finchley Electric Light Co. was bought by the U.D.C.[33] By 1955 control had passed to the Eastern Electricity Board.[34]

A voluntary public library opened at Seymour Terrace in High Street, North Finchley, in 1896.[35] Ratepayers pressed for libraries from 1912 but it was not until 1933 that the first municipal library opened at Avenue House. A second opened in

[6] Ibid. 1/8.
[7] Finchley local bd., min. bk. i. 213, 267.
[8] See p. 76.
[9] Except where otherwise stated, the following paras. are based on information from Police Constable L. Martin of Finchley police stn.
[10] A. Babington, *A House in Bow St.* 194.
[11] H.O. 107/1701/136/3/2a. The horse patrol was under the Metropolitan Police from 1836, although the old name was retained: Babington, *Bow St.* 234.
[12] *Lond. Gaz.* 13 Oct. 1840, p. 2250.
[13] O.S. Map 6″, Mdx. VI. SE. (1867–73 edn.); ex inf. New Scotland Yd. rec. officer.
[14] B.L.H.L., P.A.F. 1/9.
[15] Ibid. 1/4, 5.
[16] Ibid. 1/7.
[17] *Barnet Press*, 7 Oct. 1933.
[18] B.L.H.L., Banks Colln. xiii. 5948.
[19] *Kelly's Dir. Mdx.* (1890).
[20] Finchley local bd., min. bk. viii. 3, 119.
[21] B.L.H.L., Banks Colln. xiii. 5948.
[22] See illus. in Smith, *Finchley As It Was*, 6.
[23] B.L.H.L., Banks Colln. xiii. 5948.
[24] *Finchley Press*, 28 Dec. 1935.
[25] M.R.O., Acc. 880/46.
[26] B.L.H.L., P.A.F. 1/9.
[27] Ibid. 1/8; *Finchley Press*, 17 June 1932.
[28] B.L.H.L., P.A.F. 1/9; 34 & 35 Vic. c. 144.
[29] B.L.H.L., highway-rate (1879); *Kelly's Dir. Mdx.* (1890).
[30] *Barnet Press*, 7 Oct. 1933.
[31] *V.C.H. Mdx.* v. 181; Finchley Boro. *Official Handbk.* (1955); Barnet L.B. *Official Guide* [*c.* 1973]; ex inf. N. Thames Gas.
[32] Finchley local bd., min. bk. iii. 69.
[33] B.L.H.L., Banks Colln. xiii. 5945; *Finchley Press*, 6 Oct. 1933; *The Times*, 17 Oct. 1901.
[34] Finchley Boro. *Official Handbk.* (1955).
[35] *Barnet Press*, 7 Oct. 1933.

Ravensdale Avenue, North Finchley, in 1936 and a third in High Road, East Finchley, in 1938.[36] The library at Avenue House closed in 1939 and thereafter used temporary premises in Regent's Park Road and Hendon Lane.[37] A new library for Church End was opened in Hendon Lane in 1964.[38]

Victoria park (18 a.) was opened in 1902 to commemorate Queen Victoria's diamond jubilee.[39] It was still Finchley's only public pleasure ground in 1912, when Middlesex C.C. offered to meet a quarter of the cost of acquiring another 43 a.[40] In 1914 the U.D.C. finally bought Brook and Wyatts farms, 62 a. adjoining Dollis brook in Whetstone, and in 1915 it bought another 13 a., Cherry Tree wood on the Hornsey boundary, from the Ecclesiastical Commissioners.[41] The bequest of Avenue House by H. C. Stephens in 1918 included 10 a. of landscaped gardens.[42] In 1930 the U.D.C. drew up a town-planning scheme for Hampstead Garden Suburb which included Lyttelton playing fields (23 a.), Big (18 a.) and Little woods, and a walk alongside Mutton brook;[43] land was also being acquired along Dollis brook to create Brookside Walk. By 1932, after the acquisition of *c.* 90 a. of glebeland, once part of Finchley common, Finchley had some 412 a. of open space.[44] The glebeland, part of which was sold to the army in 1938, comprised 46 a. in 1955.[45]

Slipper and swimming baths were opened at Squires Lane in 1915. An open-air swimming pool was opened as part of a sports ground on the former glebeland in High Road, north of the junction with the North Circular Road, in 1931.[46]

CHURCHES. A church at Finchley was first recorded in 1274, although some of its fabric was probably older.[47] The benefice has always been a rectory in the patronage of the bishop of London except during the Interregnum when it was exercised by Sir John Wollaston.[48] Edward I presented *sede vacante* in 1274, Archbishop Chichele in 1425,[49] and Elizabeth I by royal prerogative in 1599.[50] Daughter churches were first established at Whetstone in 1832 and East End in 1846, and numbered six from 1904.[51]

The church was assessed at £8 in 1291 and the rectory including tithes was worth £22 a year in 1535[52] and £86 10*s.* in 1650.[53] The living was worth £150 a year in 1718, £494 in 1851,[54] and was still considered one of the richest in the diocese in 1928.[55] The glebe, said to be 43 a. in 1650 and 48 a. in 1778,[56] included one large field surrounding the church and parsonage and others, recorded from the 15th century, around Church End, mostly interspersed with the demesne lands of Bibbesworth manor.[57]

The rector received all tithes, valued at 8*s.* in 1362 and £2 in 1535.[57] Woods were said to be excluded from tithe assessment in 1647.[59] In 1718 Finchley was contrasted with its neighbours as being the only parish where the inhabitants, all freeholders, paid only 2*d.* an acre in tithe.[60] The modus was on grassland, no modus being payable on arable or for small tithes.[61] The rector in 1798 intended to take tithes in kind, [62] and at inclosure he received 116 a. in a block on either side of Summers Lane, mostly in lieu of tithes payable on Finchley common.[63] By an award published in 1841, all remaining tithes were commuted for a rent-charge of £100 a year.[64] In 1848 the rector mortgaged the glebe and rent-charges and in 1861 he sold part of the ancient glebe in south-west Finchley.[65] The Ecclesiastical Commissioners purchased 27 a. of the inclosure allotment in 1886 and most of the remaining glebeland was sold in 1892 and 1906.[66] In the late 1950s part of the glebe near the church was sold to the local authority and in 1977 the rest was sold to the Pewterers' Company's Housing Association, leaving only the Rectory and a small garden.[67]

The parsonage house, mentioned in 1476, stood near the church and in 1810 was chiefly built of timber, with roofs of slate and tiles.[68] Ralph Worsley, rector 1794–1848, went to live at Moss Hall in Nether Street, which his wife had inherited, whereupon the rectory house was leased.[69] One of the first actions of Thomas Reader White, rector 1848–77, was to replace the old house with one to the north, built in stock brick to the design of Anthony Salvin.[70] In 1974 a smaller rectory was built to the west and the Victorian one was demolished.[71]

By will proved 1296 William de Hadestok devised a rent-charge of six marks a year on property in London to support a chantry for the souls of himself

[36] *Finchley Press*, 13 Oct. 1933; 21 Jan., 7 Oct. 1938; *Finchley Review*, 3 Oct. 1938.
[37] *Finchley Press*, 15 Sept., 22 Dec. 1938; Finchley Boro. *Official Handbk.* (1955).
[38] Datestone.
[39] Biggers, *Finchley*, 19.
[40] *The Times*, 29 Nov. 1912.
[41] M.R.O., M.C.C. C/E & H 47.
[42] *The Times*, 11 Sept. 1918; see above, p. 78.
[43] *The Times*, 5 Mar. 1930.
[44] Ibid. 12 Mar., 23 Apr. 1932; Briggs, *Mdx. Old and New*, 126–7.
[45] *The Times*, 29 Jan., 18 Mar. 1938; Finchley Boro. *Official Handbk.* (1955).
[46] *Finchley Press*, 6 Oct. 1933.
[47] *Cal. Pat.* 1272–81, p. 41.
[48] *Calamy Revised*, ed. Matthews, 230–1.
[49] *Cal. Pat.* 1272–81, p. 41; *Reg. Chichele* (Cant. & York Soc.), i. 227.
[50] Hennessy, *Novum Rep.* 155 sqq.
[51] See below.
[52] *Tax. Eccl.* (Rec. Com.), p. 17; *Valor Eccl.* (Rec. Com.), i. 433.
[53] *Home Cnties. Mag.* i. 57.
[54] *T.L.M.A.S.* xix. 48; H.O. 129/136/3/2/3.
[55] Char. Com. files.
[56] *Home Cnties. Mag.* i. 57; survey of glebe (1778) in Finchley ch.
[57] S.C. 2/188/68 m. 6; S.C. 2/188/71 m. 4d.; S.C. 2/188/72 m. 5d.; S.C. 2/189/5 m. 3; Guildhall MSS. 10312/66; 67, m. 1d.; 80, m. 8d.; M.R.O., Acc. 1140.
[58] *Reg. Sudbury* (Cant. & York Soc.), i. 47; *Valor Eccl.* (Rec. Com.), i. 433.
[59] Guildhall MS. 10464A, p. 115.
[60] *T.L.M.A.S.* xix. 48. Copyholders in surrounding pars. paid 2*s.* 2*d.* an acre.
[61] Guildhall MS. 9628/5/3.
[62] B.L.H.L., P.A.F. 1/3.
[63] M.R.O., EA/FIN.
[64] M.R.O., TA/FIN.
[65] M.R.O., Acc. 1368/83.
[66] Church Com. file 67091; *44th Rep. Eccl. Com.* [C. 6616], p. 67, H.C. (1892), xxvii; *58th Rep.* [Cd. 2859], p. 90, H.C. (1906), xxvi.
[67] Ex inf. the rector.
[68] Guildhall MSS. 9171/6, f. 184v.; 9628/5/3; plan of rectory in 1778: survey of glebe in Finchley ch.
[69] B.L.H.L., P.A.F. 1/7; B.L.H.L., Church-rate (1840); B.L.H.L., Acc. 6787/7.
[70] M.R.O., Acc. 1368/83; ex inf. Dr. J. Allibone; H.O. 136/3/2/3.
[71] Ex inf. the rector.

and his ancestors. On the advice of Hadestok's successor Henry Bedyk, the bishop of London established the chantry at Finchley.[72] Bedyk, who in 1334 presented a priest to the Finchley chantry, by will dated 1335 devised a rent-charge to endow seven chantries for a year after his death, two of them to be in Finchley church.[73] A chantry chaplain from Finchley church exchanged benefices in 1356 and the lords of Bibbesworth exercised patronage of the chantry in 1361 and 1363, when it was described as 'Finchley chapel in the manor'.[74] In 1368 an inquest decided that Hadestok's chantry had never been established, perhaps because it was thought to be in London.[75] There is no evidence that priests in Finchley other than the rector were there because of the chantry, which had lapsed by 1535.[76]

Many Finchley inhabitants left small sums for lights and obits, including Thomas Noke (1476), John Smith (1484), and Agnes Martin (1498).[77] John Haynes left 6*s.* 8*d.* charged on land for an obit in 1536 and Thomas Dale, by will proved 1526, devised lands called Doves, which produced £2 a year, to maintain ornaments in the church and to establish an obit.[78] The land was sold to John Hulson and William Pendered in 1549.[79] The charities of Robert Warren (1489) and Thomas Sanny (1506) provided, *inter alia*, for ornaments for the church and 'certain superstitious purposes', presumably obits.[80]

William Vigorous, rector 1329–32, was also archdeacon of Essex and John Barville, 1454–70, and John Hill, 1492, later became prebendaries of St. Paul's, but pluralist rectors were not usual until the 16th century. Thereafter the following rectors also held prebends of St. Paul's or London benefices: Walter Preston, 1527–33, Hugh Baker, 1533–4, John Spendlove, 1534–54 and 1558–81, William Cotton, 1581–99, John Barkham, 1608–15, Thomas Worrall, 1626-39, Thomas Wykes, 1640–2, John Hall, 1666–1707, Nathaniel Marshall, 1707–29, John Marshall, 1730, William Crowe, 1731–43, Thomas Archer, 1743–67, James Waller, 1767–70, and Samuel Carr, 1770–94.[81]

William Vigorous was the bishop's confidant and administrator of his estates,[82] Stephen de Scaldeford, 1332–5, was a bishop's clerk,[83] and John Spendlove, John Bancroft, 1601–8, and James Waller were relatives of the bishops who presented them. William Cotton, later bishop of Exeter, spent his youth in Finchley and bought property there.[84] Thomas Latewar, rector 1599–1601, was a noted preacher and Latin poet. John Barkham was an antiquary, John Hall, 1666–1707, an author of theological tracts and prayers, and William Crowe, a Greek scholar and author of published sermons.[85]

A second priest was usual from the 14th century, at first perhaps to serve the chantry.[86] During the early 16th century in spite of the chantry's disappearance, there was invariably at least one priest other than the rector. In 1530 and 1531 there were two.[87] Such priests served as rector's or parish clerk, living in the clerk's house next to the churchyard[88] until after the Reformation, both Richard Fynch, 1558, and William Anderson or Sanderson, 1583–4, being priests and clerks.[89] Anderson was probably the last of the consecrated clerks, whose house was lost in the reorganization of the parish charities in 1561.[90] Assistant curates were recorded from 1590 to 1593, in 1612, and in 1639.[91] They were usual throughout the 18th century and included John Hall the younger in 1706, presumably the rector's son.[92]

In 1461 the pope confirmed the custom of blessing the Easter candle in Finchley church.[93] The main shrine in the chancel was dedicated to Our Lady, of whom there was a statue, clad in a velvet coat.[94] A crucifix, possibly made *c.* 1434, was attached to the rood beam[95] and lights burned before the altars or images of St. Margaret, St. Nicholas, St. Faith, and, in 1496, of St. Gregory in the new aisle.[96] There were vestments of gold, silver, and blue velvet and copes of velvet in 1552.[97]

John Spendlove, although a pluralist, served the cure himself and was largely responsible for converting the pre-Reformation charities to secular parochial uses.[98] He was ejected in 1554, when his immediate successor was John Feckenham or Howman, who resigned after a few months to become dean of St. Paul's and, in 1556, abbot of Westminster.[99] Spendlove was restored under Elizabeth I and was followed by William Cotton, an opponent of Puritanism. Doctrinal differences may have provoked the attack by William Anderson, Cotton's curate, upon a parishioner in the church in 1584.[1] There was fighting during the service in 1645 and

72 Corp. of Lond. Rec., husting roll 53/12.
73 *Reg. Baldock* (Cant. & York Soc.), 304; *Cal. of Wills in Ct. of Husting*, i. 404–5.
74 *Cal. Pat.* 1354–8, p. 343; *Reg. Sudbury* (Cant. & York Soc.), i. 228, 235.
75 *Cal. to Estreat R.* 1340–89, p. 139 (Corp. of Lond. Rec. m. 26).
76 *Valor Eccl.* (Rec. Com.), i. 433.
77 Guildhall MSS. 9171/6, f. 184v.; 8, f. 17; Prob. 11/7 (P.C.C. 9 Logge).
78 Guildhall MS. 9171/10, ff. 268v., 82; C 1/677/8; E 301/34 m. 30d. no. 157.
79 *Cal. Pat.* 1549–51, p. 130.
80 *10th Rep. Com. Char.* H.C. 103, pp. 318 sqq. (1824), xiii. See p. 98.
81 Dates refer to the Finchley incumbency: Hennessy, *Novum Rep.* 155 sqq.; Le Neve, *Fasti, 1300–1541, St. Paul's; Fasti, 1541–1857, St. Paul's.*
82 P. J. Taylor, 'Estates of Bpric. of Lond.' (Lond. Univ. Ph.D. thesis, 1976), 372.
83 *Reg. Baldock* (Cant. & York Soc.), 299, 306 n.
84 *D.N.B.*; B.L.H.L., Banks Colln., Finchley ch., p. 02036.
85 *D.N.B.*; *Home Cnties. Mag.* iii. 248.
86 See above. And e.g. Rob. Fauconer (1487); Wm. Rose (1500); Wm. Layfield (1501): Guildhall MSS. 9171/7, f. 88v.; 8, ff. 226, 240.
87 Guildhall MS. 9171/10, ff. 155, 164, 176.
88 e.g. Hen. Monkey (1536): Guildhall MS. 9171/10, f. 270.
89 Guildhall MS. 9171/14, ff. 39v., 59; B.L.H.L., Banks Colln., Wills (Wm. Gibb); *Mdx. Cnty. Rec.* i. 149.
90 See pp. 76, 98.
91 Hennessy, *Novum Rep.* 155 sqq.; par. regs.; B.L.H.L., Banks Colln., Finchley ch., p. 02036.
92 Guildhall MSS. 9800/2; 9537/30, f. 62; 9550; par. regs.; B.L.H.L., Banks Colln., xxxiii. 4727.
93 *Cal. Papal Reg.* xii, p. xxiv.
94 E 315/498 ff. 37d.–38; Guildhall MSS. 9171/1, f. 72v.; 5, f. 228.
95 Guildhall MSS. 9171/4, f. 268; 2, f. 29v.; 3, ff. 46v., 50, 373v.; 1, f. 72v.
96 Guildhall MSS. 9171/4, f. 268; 8, f. 120v.; Prob. 11/26 (P.C.C. 4 Hogen).
97 E 315/498 ff. 37d.–38.
98 E 301/34 no. 157. See pp. 76, 97–8.
99 *Home Cnties. Mag.* iii. 287–9; Le Neve, *Fasti, 1541–1857, St. Paul's*, 5, 25; B.L.H.L., Banks Colln. viii. 1042.
1 *D.N.B.* (Wm. Cotton); *Mdx. Cnty. Rec.* i. 149.

again in 1671.[2] Thomas Goulston, rector 1657–62, was ejected in 1662.[3]

About 1685 the bishop directed that the names of strangers who preached at Finchley should be recorded and also ordered new books and tables.[4] In the mid 18th century services were held twice on Sundays, and communion was administered at the three major festivals and once a month at other times.[5] A pair of organs had existed in 1552[6] and an organ was rebuilt in 1691. John Snetzler, the German-born organ-builder, was paid for a new organ in 1748,[7] which was replaced in 1877.[8] William Savage (d. 1789), a singer who had performed for Handel, was organist in Finchley church.[9]

Ralph Worsley, rector 1794–1848, was castigated by Eliza Anne Salvin as an incompetent and gouty old man, who enjoyed good dinners and preached the same sermon every Christmas. Believing that his only duties were to read the service and preach, he left parochial work to his curates, of whom Charles Worsley, master of Manor House school, was one.[10] The curates were responsible for the foundation of the first two daughter churches in 1832 and 1846.[11] Worsley was followed by T. R. White, young and probably evangelical, who demolished the old rectory and clerk's house, destroyed the piscina in the church, built a new National school, founded Christ's College, and involved himself in the affairs of the parish.[12] On census Sunday 1851 the church, with 600 sittings, was attended by 250 people in the morning and 200 in the afternoon.[13] On one Sunday in 1903 the respective numbers were 405 and 501, and the church was still the best attended in the ancient parish.[14] A parish hall was erected in 1885.[5] Stewart Bernays, 1924–41, like earlier rectors a prebendary of St. Paul's, founded St. Mary's men's club and, by co-operating with the Congregational minister, began the ecumenical movement in Finchley.[16]

The church of *ST. MARY*, so called by 1356,[17] is of ragstone rubble with freestone dressings and has a chancel with north chapel and north vestries, a clerestoreyed nave with north aisle, double south aisle, and porch, and a west tower. Fragments of carved 12th-century stonework are set into the west wall of the nave and the foundations of a smaller building are said to have been found beneath the floor in 1872.[18] The medieval parts of the existing building, however, all date from the late 15th or early 16th centuries and consist of the north wall, tower, and parts of the north arcade of the nave and chancel. At that period the nave had a clerestory but no south aisle. A north aisle, with a chantry chapel, existed in the 14th century but the aisle was described as 'new' in 1496.[19] The south porch had been built by 1484 and the clerestory was probably built *c.* 1487.[20] The doorway to the roof-loft, at the north-west corner of the chancel, was inserted in the early 16th century. A new chapel, mentioned in 1575,[21] was presumably that on the north side of the chancel which appears to be of the earlier 16th century.

A steeple was repaired in 1544 and 1654 but had disappeared by the late 18th century,[22] and a gallery was provided in 1594, with money from the charity estates.[23] In 1684 the rector claimed that in 1648 the parishioners undertook to repair the chancel in return for the erection of four pews there. There is no record that the rector paid for repairs, which were always financed by the charity estates or church-rates.[24] Pews were sold in 1804 to individuals who, with other 'opulent inhabitants', were asked for subscriptions in 1812.[25]

A west gallery, which may have replaced the Elizabethan one, was erected in 1729 and a gallery in the north aisle in 1804.[26] In 1778 weatherboarding at the west end of the chancel was taken down and the buttresses, tower battlements, and south windows were renewed.[27] In 1812 the tower and roof timbers were in a very bad state, whereupon the vestry decided to repair the roof and top part of the tower but not to render the exterior.[28] Anthony Salvin gave his services free in 1841, when a new vestry room was built and more repairs were made.[29] In enlargements in 1872 by Messrs. Newman & Billing, the chancel was extended eastward, a south arcade and aisle were added, the north gallery was removed, and the arches of the north arcade and the clerestory windows were rebuilt. The restoration uncovered portions of the old fabric, including the sedilia and piscina and a life-sized figure of St. George and the dragon.[30] During the incumbency of William St. Hill Bourne, 1900–24, plaster was removed to expose the original roof timbers.[31] Vestries were added in 1888[32] and a further south aisle and new vestries were built in the south side in 1932.[33] After bombing in 1940 the church lost all its windows and the east wall. The fabric was restored and the chancel extended in 1953.[34]

[2] *Mdx. Cnty. Rec.* iii. 180–1; *Mdx. & Herts. N. & Q.* iii. 32.
[3] *Calamy Revised*, ed. Matthews, pp. 230–1.
[4] Guildhall MS. 9537/20, p. 92.
[5] Ibid. 9550.
[6] E 315/498 ff. 37d.–38.
[7] B.L.H.L., Banks Colln., Ch. and hatchments.
[8] Notes from feoffees' accts. in Passmore, 'Finchley Par. Rec.' i; *V.C.H. Mdx.* ii. 190.
[9] *Gent. Mag.* lix (2), 765.
[10] Not a relative: B.L.H.L., Acc. 6787/6, 7; *Finchley Press*, 15 Apr. 1955.
[11] See below.
[12] B.L.H.L., Banks Colln., biog. T. R. White; *The Times*, 12 Dec. 1877.
[13] H.O. 129/136/3/2/3.
[14] Mudie-Smith, *Rel. Life*, 412.
[15] M.R.O., E.M.C. 120, D.R.O., D, E 1/3.
[16] B.L.H.L., Acc. 9987/36; B.L.H.L., Banks Colln. xiv.
[17] *Cal. Pat.* 1354–8, p. 343.
[18] *Home Cnties. Mag.* iii. 127–38.
[19] Guildhall MS. 9171/8, f. 120v. (will of Joan Pratt).
[20] Prob. 11/7 (P.C.C. 9 Logge, will of John Smith); Guildhall MS. 9171/7, f. 88v. (will of John Martyn).
[21] Prob. 11/57 (P.C.C. 57 Pyckering, will of Wm. Godolphin); *T.L.M.A.S.* xx. 2–16.
[22] Guildhall MS. 9171/41, f. 18; B.L.H.L., Acc. 9131 (notes from ch. bk.). There is no sign of a steeple in illus. of *c.* 1798: B.L.H.L., prints 8222, 8225. See also below, plate facing p. 89.
[23] B.L.H.L., Acc. 9131 (notes from ch. bk.).
[24] Ibid.; *Proc. of Lond. & Mdx. Archaeol. Soc.* (1871), 79–80; vestry mins., *passim*; Guildhall MS. 9628/5/3.
[25] B.L.H.L., P.A.F. 1/3, 4.
[26] *Proc. of Lond. & Mdx. Arch. Soc.* (1871), 79–80; B.L.H.L., P.A.F. 1/3; B.L.H.L., Prints 6574.
[27] B.L.H.L., P.A.F. 1/1.
[28] Ibid. 1/4.
[29] Ibid. 1/7.
[30] Ibid. 1/9; *Home Cnties. Mag.* iii. 127–38; *T.L.M.A.S.* xii. 662–8; *Proc. of Lond. & Mdx. Arch. Soc.* (1871), 79–80; Hist. Mon. Com. *Mdx.* 26.
[31] Finchley Soc. *Newsletter*, June 1972.
[32] *The Times*, 15 Mar. 1927; 9, 11, 25 June 1928; *T.L.M.A.S.* xii. 662–8.
[33] *The Times*, 8 Feb., 21 Nov. 1932.
[34] *Hendon & Finchley Times*, 11 Oct. 1940; *The Times*, 30 Sept. 1953.

The Purbeck marble bowl of an early-13th-century font, found in the rectory stables, was installed in 1911.[35] The church is rich in brasses and monuments.[36] Among the former are brasses for Richard Prate (Pratt) (1487) and his wife, for William Godolphin (1575), for Simon Scudamore (1609) and his wife, for Simon's daughter Elizabeth and her husband Nicholas Luke, and for Thomas White (1610) and his wives, and inscriptions for William Blakwell and his son Richard (*c.* 1500) and for the foundation of Thomas Sanny's charity (1509). There are marble effigies of Alexander King (d. 1618) and his wife and monuments to Sir Thomas Allen (d. 1681) and his wife, to Thomas Allen (d. 1780), his wife Ann (d. 1796), and son Thomas (d. 1830), to Lt. Col. John Searle (d. 1682), and to William Seward (d. 1799). Norden noted the marble tomb of Thomas Frowyk although the brass inscription had already been defaced.[37] In 1718 the tomb was described as sumptuous but as having been much defaced in the Civil War.[38] It stood between columns on the north side of the chancel and made way for new pews in 1760.[39]

Money was left by Thomas Marsh to purchase a bell in 1434 and by William Pepys for the casting of the 'great bell of Finchley' in 1535.[40] There were five bells and one small bell in 1552.[41] Bells were repaired in 1762, 1770 when new ones were ordered to make up a peal of six, 1806, 1847, and 1912–13.[42] There are six bells: (i-iii) and (v) by Pack & Chapman of London, 1770; (iv) by Thomas Mears, 1804; (vi) by C. & G. Mears, 1847.[43]

By will proved 1484 John Smith bequeathed his best mazer to Finchley church.[44] The silver plate consisted in 1552 of two chalices and a pyx and in 1685 of a bowl and one large and two smaller patens.[45] It was presumably the latter which, together with a silver communion cup and flagon, were stolen in 1789.[46] Two flagons, a chalice, a paten, and plates for bread and for collections were purchased in 1791 and stolen in 1818, but apparently recovered.[47] They were given to a colonial church and replaced in 1896 with silver plate donated by F. A. Hamilton,[48] which in turn was stolen in 1936.[49] In 1977 the church had a set of brass plate.

The registers, which in 1685 were not kept in a chest,[50] date from 1558 and are complete except for baptisms 1604, 1625, 1696–1700, marriages 1604, 1643–53, 1655–7, and burials 1604, 1643–52, 1679–1700.[51]

In 1832 Joseph Baxendale gave land in High Road, at the southern end of his Woodside House estate, as a site for a church to serve Whetstone. A chapel of ease, dedicated to *ST. JOHN THE APOSTLE*, was built there, financed by private subscription and endowed from Queen Anne's Bounty. The patronage, initially exercised by trustees, in 1835 was transferred to the bishop in return for a stipend for the perpetual curate.[52] A district chapelry was assigned in 1836, there was seating for 407 in 1851,[53] and on one Sunday in 1903 there were 120 worshippers in the morning and 122 in the evening.[54] The church, a small, plain building with polygonal turrets and a campanile, was extended when the chancel, designed by James Brooks, was added in 1879 and a vestry in 1898. The east window, by William Morris & Co., and the roof date from 1879. The church was restored in 1948.[55] Fittings include a modern statue of the Virgin and Child and other indications of High Church practice. A church hall was built in 1958.[56]

HOLY TRINITY[57] church was built in Church (formerly Bull) Lane in 1846 after Charles Worsley, Mrs. Salvin, and others had stressed the spiritual needs of the 'godless' hamlet of East End.[58] A district chapelry was assigned in 1846[59] and a vicarage created in 1872.[60] The bishop, who was the patron, endowed the living with £100 a year and gave the site of the parsonage in East End Road, at some distance from the church.[61] The Church Building Society and Queen Anne's Bounty made grants and local benefactors like the Lermitte family raised subscriptions.[62] The church, which possessed 437 sittings, was attended by 295 in the morning and 330 in the evening on census Sunday 1851.[63] Numbers had declined to 141 in the morning and 190 in the afternoon by one Sunday in 1903,[64] after the parish had been reduced by the creation of All Saints', East Finchley. It was further reduced after the opening of St. Jude's, Hampstead Garden Suburb, in 1932. Anthony Salvin, who was also churchwarden, designed both church and vicarage. The church, built of stone in the Early English style and consisting of chancel, nave, and west turret, was enlarged in 1860 by a south aisle and in 1866 by a north aisle, both provided for in the original design.[65] The clerestory windows were added in 1893. A red-brick hall was built next to the church in 1913.[66]

CHRIST CHURCH, North Finchley, originated in 1864 when the London Diocesan Home Mission

35 Note in ch.; Finchley Soc. *Newsletter*, June 1972.
36 Except where otherwise stated, the para. is based on *T.L.M.A.S.* xx. 2–16, and Hist. Mon. Com. *Mdx.* 26–7.
37 Norden, *Spec. Brit.* 20.
38 *T.L.M.A.S.* xix. 44–51.
39 *Home Cnties. Mag.* iii. 127–38.
40 Guildhall MSS. 9171/5, f. 29v.; 10, f. 266v.
41 E 315/498 ff. 37d.–38.
42 Notes from feoffees' accts. in Passmore, 'Finchley Par. Rec.' i; B.L.H.L., P.A.F. 1/1; St. Mary's ch., B 3/6–7.
43 *T.L.M.A.S.* xix. 57–9.
44 Prob. 11/7 (P.C.C. 9 Logge).
45 E 315/498 ff. 37d.–38; Guildhall MS. 9537/20, p. 92.
46 B.L.H.L., P.A.F. 1/2.
47 Ibid. 1/2, 4, 5.
48 Freshfield, *Communion Plate*, 15.
49 *The Times*, 5 Dec. 1936.
50 Guildhall MS. 9537/20, p. 92.
51 M.R.O., E.M.C. 120, D.R.O. A1/1–24; *Mdx. & Herts. N. & Q.* iv. 200–3. Marriages 1560–1837 are printed in Phillimore, *Mdx. Par. Regs.* vii. 1–42. There are bps.' transcripts of bapts., marriages, and burials 1800–34.
52 *Home Cnties. Mag.* vi. 215–20; Guildhall MS. 10234/11, pp. 539–48, 661–4; M.R.O., TA/FIN, no. 322; C. Hodgson, *Queen Anne's Bounty*, pp. ccxix, cccxiv.
53 *Lond. Gaz.* 2 Sept. 1836, pp. 1552–3; H.O. 129/136/3/2/2.
54 Mudie-Smith, *Rel. Life*, 412.
55 Walford, *Gtr. Lond.* i. 335; Pevsner, *Mdx.* 172; Biggers, *Finchley*, 60; *T.L.M.A.S.* xviii (2), no. 70.
56 Ex inf. the vicar.
57 Except where otherwise stated, the para. is based on Josephine Cashmore, *Holy Trinity, E. Finchley* (pamphlet).
58 B.L.H.L., Acc. 6787/7.
59 *Lond. Gaz.* 29 Dec. 1846, p. 6023.
60 *Crockford* (1872).
61 Guildhall MS 10234/12, pp. 581–6, 588–90.
62 M.R.O., Acc. 1083/3; Hennessy, *Novum Rep.* 158; Hodgson, *Queen Anne's Bounty*, p. lxix.
63 H.O. 129/136/3/2/4.
64 Mudie-Smith, *Rel. Life*, p. 412.
65 *T.L.M.A.S.* xviii (2), no. 68; ex inf. Dr. Jill Allibone.
66 Datestone.

sent Henry Stephens to open a mission for navvies working on the railway.[67] Services were held in an iron building in High Road until part of a permanent church was consecrated near by in 1869. A consolidated chapelry was assigned from the mother parish, St. John's, Whetstone, and Holy Trinity in 1872. The patronage was vested in trustees, including the rector, who had given glebeland for the site,[68] and later exercised by the Church Patronage Society.[69] Additions were made to the building as funds became available, especially from wealthy parishioners like the Hamiltons. On one Sunday in 1903, when there were 700 sittings, 237 people attended in the morning and 314 in the afternoon.[70] Christ Church always maintained an evangelical tradition. By 1899 two curates helped to run the memorial hall and library in High Road, which had been built in memory of Henry Stephens (d. 1898), an institute in Percy Road (*c.* 1899), and missions at Holden Road (1885–1909)[71] and Summers Lane (1906–60). In 1938 the Stephens memorial hall was sold and a new hall built behind the church. Designed by J. Norton, the church is of brick with stone facings in the early Gothic style. The foundation stone of the nave was laid in 1867. The north aisle was built in 1874, the south aisle in 1880, and the chancel, side chapel, and vestries were built in 1891. The large Victorian vicarage next to the church survived in 1977.

In 1885 Mrs. F. A. Hamilton of Brent Lodge laid the foundation stone of the church of *ST. PAUL*, Long Lane. Financed by private subscriptions and the Bishop of London's Fund, the church was built in 1886 and a parish was formed from Christ Church and St. Mary's.[72] The benefice was augmented from investments belonging to the rectory, and the first vicar was a former curate of Finchley.[73] Patronage was vested in the Simeon Trustees. Attendance on one Sunday in 1903 was second only to St. Mary's, with 301 in the morning and 324 in the evening.[74] The church, of stone in the Early English style and designed by John Ladds, consists of chancel, nave, aisles, transepts, and turret.[75] It contains a bell inscribed '*Beatus venter qui te portavit*' of *c.* 1380, probably made by John Langhorne of London (d. 1406) and brought from Hatford (Berks.).[76] A church hall was built in 1899.[77]

An iron mission church, dedicated to *ST. BARNABAS*,[78] was built in Holden Road in 1885 by Christ Church[79] to serve the growing population of Woodside Park. It was attended by 98 people on the morning of one Sunday in 1903.[80] In 1912 a permanent church was founded on the same site and in 1914 a parish was created, with the Church Patronage Society as patron.[81] The church, built of red brick with stone dressings in the Gothic style to the design of J. S. Alder, has a stone interior, a rounded apse, and wooden barrel roof. It consists of chancel, aisled and clerestoreyed nave, and south-east chapel. The iron building was moved to Gainsborough Road, where it served as the parish hall until its replacement by a larger hall, which was sold in 1969 to St. Alban's Roman Catholic church. The west end of the church has been altered to form a new hall.

ALL SAINTS'[82] church was built in 1891 in Durham Road, on the eastern border of East Finchley, on land given by the Ecclesiastical Commissioners. A consolidated chapelry was assigned in 1900 from Holy Trinity and St. James's, Muswell Hill,[83] and the Ecclesiastical Commissioners made further grants for building and endowment.[84] From 1900 the church was a vicarage in the patronage of the bishop of London.[85] There were 500 sittings and attendances on one Sunday in 1903 of 208 in the morning and 337 in the afternoon.[86] Built of brick with stone dressings in the Perpendicular style to designs by J. E. K. and J. P. Cutts, the church consists of clerestoreyed nave, aisles, south chapel, north-east organ chamber, and western narthex. The chancel was added in 1912. High Church fittings in 1977 included a rood and stations of the cross. An adjacent hall was built in the 1930s.[87]

A parish for the church of *ST. LUKE*, Mountfield Road, was created in 1904 from St. Mary's and St. Paul's. The Ecclesiastical Commissioners made grants towards the church but the largest sums were contributed by subscribers, in whom the patronage was vested[88] before it passed to the Church Patronage Society.[89] The church, built in 1905 to the design of W. D. Caroë, is of red brick with stone dressings and consists of chancel, nave, and north aisle.[90] A church hall was erected in 1937.[91]

ROMAN CATHOLICISM. Mary Talbot, countess of Shrewsbury, and Catherine Ewers, both widows of Finchley, were indicted as recusants in 1625.[92] In 1692 Elizabeth, widow of James Allen, denied that she had ever been a recusant[93] and in 1706 the curate reported that he could find no papists in the parish.[94]

67 Except where otherwise stated, the para. is based on *Christ Church, N. Finchley, Centenary Celebrations, 1867–1967* (booklet); *T.L.M.A.S.* xviii (2), no. 67; ex inf. the vicar.
68 *Lond. Gaz.* 31 May 1872, p. 2562; C 54/16386 no. 2.
69 *Lond. Dioc. Bk.* (1970).
70 Mudie-Smith, *Rel. Life*, 412.
71 *Kelly's Dir. Barnet* (1899–1900); *Kelly's Dir. Mdx.* (1908). The Holden Rd. mission became St. Barnabas ch.: see below.
72 Biggers, *Finchley*, 15.
73 *40th Rep. of Eccl. Com.* [C. 5330], p. 55, H.C. (1888), xxxiv; Hennessy, *Novum Rep.* 157.
74 Mudie-Smith, *Rel. Life*, 412.
75 *T.L.M.A.S.* xviii (2), no. 72.
76 *T.L.M.A.S.* xvi. 310–11.
77 Ex inf. the vicar.
78 Except where otherwise stated, the para. is based on information from the vicar.
79 See above.
80 Mudie-Smith, *Rel. Life*, 412.
81 *Lond. Dioc. Bk.* (1970); *Barnet Press*, 7 Oct. 1933.
82 Except where otherwise stated, the para. is based on information from the vicar and *Kelly's Dir. Mdx.* (1908).
83 *53rd Rep. of Eccl. Com.* [Cd. 497], p. 58, H.C. (1901), xviii.
84 *54th Rep. Eccl. Com.* [Cd. 1001], p. 33, H.C. (1902), xxii; *55th Rep.* [Cd. 1482], p. 32, H.C. (1903), xix; *65th Rep.* [Cd. 6653], p. 80, H.C. (1912–13), xxi.
85 *Crockford* (1901).
86 Mudie-Smith, *Rel. Life*, 412.
87 *T.L.M.A.S.* xviii (2), no. 66.
88 *56th Rep. Eccl. Com.* [Cd. 1966], pp. 34, 67, H.C. (1904), xviii; *57th Rep.* [Cd. 2411], pp. 27, 67, H.C. (1905), xxiii; *59th Rep.* [Cd. 3377], pp. 30, 67, H.C. (1907), xx.
89 *Lond. Dioc. Bk.* (1970).
90 Pevsner, *Mdx.* 55; *T.L.M.A.S.* xviii (2), no. 71.
91 Ex inf. the vicar; datestone.
92 *Mdx. Cnty. Rec.* iii. 5.
93 C 8/436/1.
94 Guildhall MS. 9800/2.

In 1893 priests from St. Andrew's institute, High Barnet, opened a mission in St. Gabriel's, a greenhouse belonging to a nursery on the Great North Road near Tally Ho Corner. In 1896 the mission moved to a laundry at Albert Villa, Fallow Corner, and in 1900 to a loft over a stable at no. 4 Percy Road,[95] which on one Sunday in 1903 was attended by 127 in the morning and 46 in the evening.[96] There was a permanent priest from 1903, when a room at the presbytery in Nether Street was registered.[97] A mission hall dedicated to St. Alban was opened in Nether Street in the same year and used for worship until St. Alban's church was opened in 1909.[98] Built of brick with stone dressings, the church is a simple basilica, with a tower at the west end.

At East End the former Congregational chapel in High Road was opened in 1898 as St. Mary's Roman Catholic church.[99] It had congregations of 188 and 56 at the morning and evening services on one Sunday in 1903.[1] The church was destroyed in 1940 and services were held from 1941 at no. 279 High Road,[2] where a church seating 400 was built in 1953. One of the earliest European churches to contain pre-cast concrete, it is a simple brick building with stone dressings, next to a hall built in 1959.[3]

At Church End the chapel of Manor House convent was used for public worship from 1919 until 1925, when the ground floor of Derwent House in Gravel Hill was converted into a chapel dedicated to St. Philip the Apostle.[4] St. Philip's hall, designed by T. H. B. Scott and built on the site by 1930, had by 1933 been transformed into the sacristies of a new church.[5] The church, of yellow brick in a simple basilican style, was enlarged in 1960. A parish centre was opened in 1968.[6]

Finchley, with its large houses and proximity to Hendon, where there were several Roman Catholic institutions,[7] attracted many religious orders from London or its inner suburbs. In 1864 the Sisters of the Good Shepherd bought East End House on the north side of East End Road, where until 1948 they maintained a refuge for distressed Roman Catholic women, including former prisoners. In 1900 they aided 180 'poor penitents' and 130 younger girls. New buildings on the site included a church in 1875 and a wing for the novitiate in 1886, when East End House became the provincial house for the order. After a fire in 1972 land was sold for housing and most of the buildings were demolished, although the original house remained.[8]

Sisters of the Poor Child Jesus established themselves in 1908 at the Grange in Nether Street, North Finchley, which they renamed St. Michael's convent and where they opened a school.[9] The French Society of Marie Auxiliatrice in 1919 turned the former billiards room at Bibbesworth manor-house into a chapel to serve Church End until the foundation of St. Philip's church and also opened a school.[10] Poor Sisters of Nazareth moved in 1921 from Chiswick to a large house on the south side of East End Road, where they cared for children and the aged. Extensions were built in 1928 and 1936, a new nursery was added in 1963, and the last children left Nazareth House in 1974. Mass, which is often attended by outsiders, has been celebrated in the convent chapel since 1921.[11] Other religious orders in 1976 included the Xaverian Missionary Fathers in Nether Street and the Sisters of Our Lady of the Cenacle, who had moved to Cyprus Road in 1974 from Whetstone, where they had opened a convent or retreat house in 1972.[12]

PROTESTANT NONCONFORMITY. Finchley common may have been a resort of nonconformists after the Conventicle Act of 1664 but no evidence supports the tradition that John Bunyan and Richard Baxter held meetings there, although Baxter lived in neighbouring Totteridge *c.* 1670.[13] In 1778 there were said to be a Methodist meeting-house at Whetstone and two or three dissenters in Finchley parish. In 1790 there were 'four or five Presbyterians' and the Methodists were not numerous, but by 1810 there were Methodist meeting-houses at both Whetstone and Finchley and dissent was increasing.[14] One of the Methodist chapels was described in 1813 as very well attended.[15]

Whetstone was considered a nucleus of dissent *c.* 1832.[16] By the mid 1830s there were well-filled Wesleyan and Independent chapels in East End, supported by the Mason family and, after the building of Holy Trinity church in 1846, engaged in rivalry with the Anglicans. By 1851 Finchley had two Independent chapels, at East End and North Finchley, and two Wesleyan, at East End and Whetstone. Of the 857 nonconformist worshippers on census Sunday in 1851, 667 were Independents and 190 Methodists; 552 attended services in East End, 242 in North Finchley, and 63 in Whetstone.[17]

Expansion was most rapid during the late 19th century. Primitive Methodists became active in Whetstone and on Finchley common in the 1850s and opened a chapel in East End in 1872. Wesleyans opened a chapel in North Finchley in 1879 and a mission in 1886, Baptists appeared first in North Finchley in 1868, building their own chapel in 1878

95 *Finchley Cath. Rec.* July 1928, p. 13; Apr. 1932, p. 14; *Cath. Dir.* (1900).
96 Mudie-Smith, *Rel. Life*, 413.
97 *Finchley Cath. Rec.* July 1928, p. 13; G.R.O. Worship Reg. no. 39906.
98 G.R.O. Worship Reg. nos. 40108, 44241; *The Times*, 12 Oct. 1908, 17 May 1909.
99 G.R.O. Worship Reg. no. 36804. For the chapel's previous history, see p. 88.
1 Mudie-Smith, *Rel. Life*, 413.
2 G.R.O. Worship Reg. no. 59851.
3 Ex inf. the par. priest; G.R.O. Worship Reg. no. 63922.
4 *Cath. Dir.* (1920); *Finchley Cath. Rec.* May 1926, p. 8; G.R.O. Worship Reg. no. 49807.
5 *Finchley Cath. Rec.* Aug. 1930; G.R.O. Worship Reg. no. 54622.
6 Ex inf. the par. priest.
7 *V.C.H. Mdx.* v. 38.
8 Ex inf. the Good Shepherd Provincialate; *Cath. Dir.* (1900). And see p. 97.
9 *Finchley Cath. Rec.* May 1926, p. 10; ex inf. the headmistress, St. Mic.'s grammar sch. See below, p. 97.
10 Ex inf. former headmistress, Manor Ho. sch., for which see below, p. 97.
11 Ex inf. the mother superior.
12 *Cath. Dir.* (1976); ex inf. the provincial superior.
13 B.L.H.L., Prints Colln. 6608; *Home Cnties. Mag.* i. 234–8; vi. 215–20; *Autobiog. of Ric. Baxter*, ed. J. M. Lloyd Thomas, 211.
14 Guildhall MSS. 9557, f. 21; 9558, f. 435.
15 Press cutting in B.L.H.L., Banks Colln., Finchley common file.
16 'Finchley Par. Rec.' i.
17 B.L.H.L., Acc. 6787/7 (Salvin diaries); H.O. 129/136/3/2/5–8.

and establishing congregations at East Finchley in 1877, Church End in 1892, and Whetstone in 1898. Meanwhile Quakers had appeared in North Finchley by 1882, the Salvation Army at North Finchley in 1886 and East Finchley in 1896, Brethren at North Finchley in 1893, and Presbyterians at Church End in 1894 and East Finchley in 1900.

In 1903 there were sixteen recorded nonconformist congregations and a total of 4,479 worshippers.[18] The Congregationalists were still the most numerous, with four groups[19] and 1,558 attendances. The Methodists had 1,267 attendances, the Baptists 794, the Presbyterians 550, the Salvation Army 254, and Brethren 56.[20] There were as many as 2,246 nonconformists in East Finchley, 1,260 in North Finchley, 924 in Church End, and 49 in Whetstone.

London traders supported the first Wesleyan and Independent chapels in East End[21] and wealthy individuals helped the Congregationalists of North Finchley and Church End. Established chapels quickly became centres of social life, maintaining not only missionary and temperance groups but many sporting and cultural activities.[22]

Growth continued in the early 20th century. A new Congregational church was founded at Church End in 1905 and a Strict Baptist chapel moved in 1916 from London to North Finchley, where Unitarians had appeared in 1911. Unspecified missions opened at Whetstone in 1904 and East End *c.* 1920, and Kensit Memorial Bible college at Church End in 1908.

Newcomers in the 1930s included the Elim Foursquare Gospel Alliance in 1934 and Christian Spiritualists in 1938. After the outbreak of the Second World War many chapels closed, although a Quaker group was founded in 1945 and a Swedenborgian church in 1952, besides some short-lived undenominational groups in the 1950s and 1970s. Closures were carried out between 1939 and 1949 by the Primitive Methodists, the Presbyterians, the Unitarians, and possibly the Salvation Army in North Finchley. Whetstone Baptist chapel had closed by 1954 and other denominations, like the East End Congregationalists, built smaller chapels. Contraction stimulated the ecumenical movement: there was co-operation between the rector of Finchley and Church End Congregationalists in 1924 and between the Congregational and Presbyterian churches at Church End in 1935. Finchley Council of Churches was formed in 1943, the merger of Church End Congregational[23] and Presbyterian churches in 1969 preceded the formation of the United Reformed Church in 1972, and the Elim Foursquare Gospel Alliance began to share East Finchley United Reformed church in 1974.

CONGREGATIONALISTS. The Methodist meeting-house at Whetstone in 1778 may have been Whetstone Congregational chapel for which registers exist from 1788.[24] James Mathews, the pastor, was described as a Methodist by his son, the actor Charles Mathews (1803–78), and registered a wooden building in Totteridge Lane for Independents in 1800.[25] It was probably the building once used as a poorhouse, which passed to Joseph Baxendale.[26] In 1827 the congregation moved to Totteridge Independent chapel, founded by Catherine Puget next to her school in Totteridge Lane.[27] Congregationalists met in 1830 at the house of Elizabeth Pride, described as in Colney Hatch, Finchley,[28] and J. H. Puget ran a mission at Whetstone, possibly in Sherwood Street.[29] Whetstone Congregationalists also attended Oakleigh Park church, Friern Barnet, from 1888,[30] and after 1908 there was a short-lived hall behind Whetstone Parade in High Road.[31]

East Finchley Congregational chapel originated with meetings of Independents,[32] encouraged by the Hoxton Itinerant Society, in various buildings in the Hogmarket, East End, from 1804.[33] They built a chapel on the edge of Finchley common, facing the Great North Road, in 1830 and enlarged it in 1846. On census Sunday 1851, when it was attended by 257 in the morning and 168 in the evening, it had 340 seats.[34] The building, further enlarged in 1861 and 1874, was restored as a lecture hall and Sunday school after a fire in 1875. An imposing stone chapel, designed in the Gothic style by J. Tarring & Son and accommodating 600, was opened at the junction of High Road and East End Road in 1878.[35] A new hall and Sunday school were built behind in 1895, whereupon the old chapel was sold.[36] There were 228 worshippers in the morning and 307 in the evening on one Sunday in 1903.[37] The chapel was extended in 1926 but demolished in 1965, when part of the site was sold. A smaller chapel and hall, each seating 150, were opened in 1970.[38]

North Finchley Congregational chapel[39] grew out of meetings held by Thomas Campion Newman in the 1830s at his schoolroom in Lodge Lane. In 1842 Newman, who lived at Orchard House near Tally Ho Corner, licensed a disused stable there as an Independent chapel.[40] Usually known as the 'cot-

[18] Mudie-Smith, *Rel. Life*, 412–13, 462.
[19] E. Finchley Sunday sch. or children's church was recorded as a separate congregation.
[20] The Quakers were not recorded.
[21] See list of trustees: C 54/10722 no. 2; C 54/10768 no. 8.
[22] e.g. Church End Cong. ch.: B.L.H.L., Acc. 9987/36; N. Finchley Baptist ch.: pamphlet hist.; see above, p. 74.
[23] From 1956 to 1961 Church End Cong. ch. allowed Finchley Central synagogue to use its Victoria hall: see below, p. 91.
[24] P.R.O., Census Rm., Reg. 4; Guildhall MS. 9558, f. 435.
[25] Guildhall MS. 9580/2; Mrs. [A.] Mathews, *Life and Correspondence of Chas. Mathews* (1860), 4.
[26] M.L.R. 1830/1/528.
[27] *V.C.H. Herts.* iii. 150; ex inf. Mr. P. G. Dawson; Dawson, *Puget Family*, 23.
[28] G.R.O. Worship Returns, iii, no. 1657.
[29] Dawson, *Puget Family*, 34; ex inf. Mr. P. G. Dawson.
[30] See p. 32.
[31] G.R.O. Worship Reg. no. 43240.
[32] Except where otherwise stated, the para. is based on information from the ch. sec.
[33] G.R.O. Worship Returns, iii, nos. 589, 615, 1626; M.L.R. 1822/7/182; Guildhall MSS. 9580/2; 6, pp. 237–8.
[34] G.R.O. Worship Returns, iii, no. 2082; H.O. 129/136/3/2/8; C 54/10768, no. 8; Guildhall MS. 9580/8, p. 92.
[35] G.R.O. Worship Reg. no. 23946.
[36] Ibid. 34861. To the 'dismay' of the Congregationalists, the chapel was bought by Rom. Catholics: see p. 87.
[37] Mudie-Smith, *Rel. Life*, 412.
[38] G.R.O. Worship Reg. no. 71991.
[39] Except where otherwise stated, the para. is based on *Finchley Common Cong. Ch. 1864*, *N. Finchley Cong. Ch. 1964* (pamphlet) and information from the minister.
[40] Guildhall MS. 9580/8, p. 146; G.R.O. Worship Returns, iii, no. 2136.

tagers' chapel', it seated 80 and was attended on census Sunday 1851 by 78 in the morning, 87 in the afternoon, and 77 in the evening.[41] In 1864 J. H. Puget offered a site in Nether Street,[42] where an imposing stone building was designed in the Gothic style by Messrs. Searle and opened in 1865,[43] the 'cottagers' chapel' being sold by Newman's widow to the Baptists in 1868.[44] Accommodation was increased in 1875-6 and enlargements in 1894 included a hall. The church maintained a mission room in High Road from 1869 until 1884, when it built a hall at the corner of Avenue Road. On one Sunday in 1903 the church was attended by 272 in the morning and 356 in the aftermoon.[45] An annexe was built in 1924 for the Sunday school and the mission hall was sold to pay for it in 1934.[46]

At Church End there was a brief attempt in 1799 to found an Independent church.[47] In 1882, when Elm Park estate was being built, land in Dollis Road was offered to the London Congregational Chapel Building Society[48] and from 1884 to 1886 services were held by the London Congregational Union in assembly rooms adjoining the Railway hotel. In 1905 the Dollis Road site, which had never been suitable, was sold and R. S. Griffin of Cyprus Hill Lodge bought a site in Victoria Avenue, near Ballards Lane. Until the church hall was opened there in 1907,[49] members worshipped at Hamilton hall in Hendon Lane. A memorial hall was built in 1919 and there was a very active social life during the first decade, although in 1923 some members resigned over the socialist views of the minister. In 1924 it was decided not to build the intended large church but to adapt the church hall, in 1929 the memorial hall was sold, and in 1970 a new hall was opened next to the church. From 1935 until 1955 and again in 1965 services were held jointly with St. Margaret's Presbyterian church and in 1969 the two bodies united as Union church, Finchley Central, from 1972 called St. Margaret's United Reformed church. Thereafter most services were at Victoria Avenue, although the halls of both former churches were used for other activities.

METHODISTS. East Finchley Methodist church originated in a Wesleyan congregation established by 1817 and probably by 1810.[50] John Freeman held prayer meetings in Lincoln Lodge, a cottage in High Road at the corner of Strawberry Vale, in 1820. A small chapel, attended mostly by labourers, opened in 1829 in King's Corner or Street,[51] providing 110 sittings and attended on census Sunday 1851 by 45 in the morning, 52 in the afternoon, and 30 in the evening.[52] It was replaced in 1868 by a building to hold 300,[53] which in turn was replaced in 1897 by a red-brick chapel built in the Gothic style on the corner of High Road and Park Road with 650 sittings.[54] It was attended on one Sunday in 1903 by 462 in the morning and 372 in the afternoon.[55] The building was again registered in 1915[56] and remained in use in 1977.

Primitive Methodists registered a building at Finchley common fron 1854 until 1866.[57] A Primitive Methodist chapel opened in East End Road in 1872,[58] moved to no. 142 High Road in 1905,[59] and closed between 1939 and 1949.[60]

Finchley Methodist church in Ballards Lane opened as Wentworth Park Wesleyan chapel in 1879.[61] Built of yellow brick with stone dressings to a design by Charles Bell,[62] it was attended by 169 in the morning and 211 in the afternoon on one Sunday in 1903.[63] A red-brick hall in a Gothic style was built in 1904 next to the church,[64] which survived in 1976.

A Wesleyan mission hall for 300 people[65] was registered in Stanhope Road, North Finchley, in 1886[66] and closed before 1913.[67]

BAPTISTS. North Finchley Baptist church[68] was founded in 1868 under the aegis of a student of J. A. Spurgeon. After a few weeks at a private house in the Great North Road, members moved into the former 'cottagers' chapel' near Ballards Lane, where there was room for 150.[69] After initial difficulties, numbers grew and in 1878 the foundation stone of the existing church was laid at the junction of Ballards Lane and Dale Grove. The church, opened in 1879 with seating for 400, was built in stone to a Gothic design by Morton M. Glover and registered by Calvinistic Baptists.[70] In 1903 it had the largest Baptist congregation in Finchley, with 147 on one Sunday morning and 187 in the evening,[71] and in 1908 transepts were added to accommodate another 260. The growth of the Sunday school and of church societies led to the acquisition of Dale Grove hall from the Congregationalists in 1894. Grenfall hall was built at the side of the church in 1922 and Carey hall behind Dale Grove hall in 1933.

East Finchley Baptist church was founded in 1877

[41] H.O. 129/136/3/2/7.
[42] C 54/16318 no. 1; Dawson, *Puget Family*, 37–8.
[43] G.R.O. Worship Reg. no. 16652; Thorne, *Environs*, 216–18.
[44] See below.
[45] Mudie-Smith, *Rel. Life*, 412.
[46] The hall was demolished in 1975.
[47] Guildhall MS. 9580/2.
[48] Except where otherwise stated, the hist. of Church End Cong. ch. is based on information from the ch. sec. and on ch. rec. in B.L.H.L., esp. Acc. 9987/36.
[49] Registered in 1909: G.R.O. Worship Reg. no. 43507.
[50] B.L.H.L., Acc. 6140/2 (rate bk. s.v. 1817, 1824, 1830); Guildhall MS. 9558, f. 435.
[51] Passmore, 'Finchley Par. Rec.' i; C 54/10722 no. 2.
[52] H.O. 129/136/3/2/6; O.S. Map 6", Mdx. XI. NE. (1867 edn.).
[53] Passmore, 'Finchley Par. Rec.' i; G.R.O. Worship Reg. no. 19666; Potter Colln. 28/18.
[54] G.R.O. Worship Reg. no. 35856; foundation stone dtd. 1896; *Kelly's Dir. Mdx.* (1908).
[55] Mudie-Smith, *Rel. Life*, 412.
[56] G.R.O. Worship Reg. no. 46665.
[57] Ibid. 6068.
[58] Ibid. 20551.
[59] Ibid. 40944.
[60] *Kelly's Dir. Finchley* (1939); *Finchley Dir.* (1949). In 1976 the bldg., roughcast in a Gothic style, was used as a youth hall.
[61] G.R.O. Worship Reg. no. 24640.
[62] Foundation stone.
[63] Mudie-Smith, *Rel. Life*, 412.
[64] G.R.O. Worship Reg. no. 55633; *Barnet Press*, 7 Oct. 1933.
[65] *Kelly's Dir. Mdx.* (1908).
[66] G.R.O. Worship Reg. no. 29728.
[67] *Kelly's Dir. Barnet* (1909–10); O.S. Map 1/2,500, Mdx. VI. 16 (1913 edn.).
[68] Except where otherwise stated, the para. is based on *N. Finchley Baptist Ch. 1868–1968* (pamphlet) and information from Mr. L. D. Edwards.
[69] For the 'cottagers' chapel' see above. The bldg. was demolished in 1891.
[70] G.R.O. Worship Reg. no. 24760.
[71] Mudie-Smith, *Rel. Life*, 412.

in Long Lane as a New Connexion church by J. Batey.[72] A church was built at the corner of High Road and Hertford Road in 1889 and registered in 1894.[73] A new church, of flint with stone dressings in an elaborate Gothic style, was built in Creighton Avenue in 1902[74] and attended on one Sunday in 1903 by 143 in the morning and 187 in the evening.[75] It became a hall when the existing church, of red brick with stone dressings in a Gothic style, was built in 1950.[76]

Church End or West Finchley Baptist church derives from services held in Queen's Terrace in 1892. An iron tabernacle was opened in Station Road in 1895,[77] although not registered until 1910,[78] and may have been the iron room attended on one Sunday in 1903 by 7 in the morning and 69 in the evening.[79] The existing church, a plain brick building with a hall and seating for 200, was opened in 1936 on the corner of East End Road and Stanhope Avenue.[80]

Whetstone Baptist church opened in Lyric House, High Road, in 1898[81] and was attended on one Sunday in 1903 by 18 in the morning and 31 in the afternoon.[82] It moved to Oakleigh Road in 1906[83] and back to High Road in 1945, where it closed before 1954.[84]

STRICT BAPTISTS. Soho Memorial chapel at the junction of High Road and Fallowcourt Avenue, North Finchley, originated in a group which met in Lincoln's Inn Fields in 1790. It moved several times and was reorganized at the Soho chapel in Oxford Street in 1818, later moving to Shaftesbury Avenue. In 1916 the church moved to North Finchley, opening a school chapel in 1918 and an adjacent chapel in 1925.[85] Both buildings, in yellow brick with red-brick dressings in a simple Gothic style, were still in use in 1976. The chapel benefited from the charities of Florence Alice Simpson (d. 1947) and Hannah Albertina Simpson (d. 1949).[86]

SOCIETY OF FRIENDS. A Quaker meeting-house in Ballards Lane from *c.* 1882 until *c.* 1909[87] was not registered. A constituent of the Hampstead monthly meeting met in Finchley from 1945 until 1950. Finchley particular meeting opened in 1952,[88] registering a room at no. 131 Nether Street in 1955,[89] and built a striking new meeting-house in 1967 at no. 58 Alexandra Grove.[90]

THE SALVATION ARMY. A barracks was opened at no. 4 Lodge Lane, North Finchley, in 1886 and was attended by 20 in the morning and 31 in the evening on one Sunday in 1903. It had probably closed long before 1954.[91]

A hall was opened in High Road, East Finchley, in 1896 and superseded in 1903[92] by a barracks, later designated a hall, in Hertford Road near High Road.[93] The small yellow- and red-brick hall, attended by 65 in the morning and 138 in the evening on one Sunday in 1903,[94] was still used in 1976.

A hall in Summers Lane near Friern Barnet was registered in 1934[95] and closed between 1939 and 1949.[96]

PRESBYTERIANS.[97] In 1891 the Presbyterian Church of England acquired land at the corner of Ballards Lane and Redbourne Avenue, where a hall was opened in 1893 and registered in 1894.[98] The church, of red brick with stone dressings in the Gothic style, was registered in 1895[99] and attended by 224 in both the morning and the evening on one Sunday in 1903.[1] Called St. Margaret's from 1932, the church joined Church End Congregational church in 1969 to form Union church, Finchley Central; after the formation of the United Reformed church in 1972, it was known as St. Margaret's United Reformed church. The old Presbyterian church hall was still used by the united congregation in 1976 but was demolished in 1977.

A Presbyterian mission started in Hamilton Road in 1898, moved to an iron hall in Brackenbury Road, East Finchley, in 1899,[2] and closed between 1939 and 1949.[3] The former Wesleyan chapel in King Street was used as a Presbyterian hall from *c.* 1930 until *c.* 1939.[4]

CHRISTIAN SPIRITUALISTS. A hut in Christchurch Avenue, North Finchley, was registered in 1934 by Christian Spiritualists,[5] who in 1943 moved to a tin hut in Woodbury Grove,[6] which they still occupied in 1978.

ELIM FOURSQUARE GOSPEL ALLIANCE. Elim hall in Christchurch Avenue, perhaps formerly used by the Christian Spiritualists, was registered by Elim Foursquare Gospel Alliance from 1938 until 1954.[7] The alliance then used the former Wesleyan chapel in King Street[8] until 1974, when it began sharing

[72] W. T. Whitley, *Baptists of Lond.* (1928), 220, 278.
[73] G.R.O. Worship Reg. no. 34427; Finchley local bd., min. bk. vi. 444.
[74] Datestone on bldg.; G.R.O. Worship Reg. nos. 39601, 53157.
[75] Mudie-Smith, *Rel. Life*, 412.
[76] Datestone.
[77] Whitley, *Baptists of Lond.* 245, 278.
[78] G.R.O. Worship Reg. no. 44264.
[79] The returns were sent in late and therefore not listed under denominations: Mudie-Smith, *Rel. Life*, 462.
[80] Ex inf. the minister; G.R.O. Worship Reg. no. 57615.
[81] G.R.O. Worship Reg. no. 37181.
[82] Mudie-Smith, *Rel. Life*, 412.
[83] Whitley, *Baptists of Lond.* 246, 278; G.R.O. Worship Reg. no. 49224.
[84] G.R.O. Worship Reg. no. 61141.
[85] Whitley, *Baptists of Lond.* 134, 279; G.R.O. Worship Reg. no. 47388.
[86] Char. Com. files.
[87] *Kelly's Dir. Mdx.* (1882); *Kelly's Dir. Barnet* (1909–10).
[88] Rec. of gen. monthly mtgs. in Friends' Ho., Lond.
[89] G.R.O. Worship Reg. no. 65044.
[90] Ibid. 71301; W. M. White, *Six Weeks Mtg. 1671–1971*, 90.
[91] G.R.O. Worship Reg. no. 29700; Mudie-Smith, *Rel. Life*, 413.
[92] G.R.O. Worship Reg. no. 35304.
[93] Ibid. 39582.
[94] Mudie-Smith, *Rel. Life*, 412.
[95] G.R.O. Worship Reg. no. 55183.
[96] *Kelly's Dir. Finchley* (1939); *Finchley Dir.* (1949).
[97] Except where otherwise stated, the para. is based on *St. Marg.'s Presb. Ch. of Eng. Finchley Jubilee Yr. Bk. 1893–1953* (pamphlet) and information from the sec., St. Marg.'s United Reformed ch.
[98] G.R.O. Worship Reg. no. 34218.
[99] Ibid. 34906.
[1] Mudie-Smith, *Rel. Life*, 413.
[2] G.R.O. Worship Reg. no. 37750; *St. Marg.'s Presb. Ch. 1893–1953*.
[3] *Kelly's Dir. Finchley* (1939); *Finchley Dir.* (1949).
[4] *Kelly's Dir. Finchley* (1930, 1939).
[5] G.R.O. Worship Reg. no. 55544.
[6] Ibid. 60503.
[7] Ibid. 58226.
[8] Ibid. 64448. See above.

East Finchley United Reformed church in East End Road.[9]

OTHER DENOMINATIONS AND UNSPECIFIED MISSIONS. Brethren had a meeting-house in Ballards Lane from 1893 until 1911,[10] where there were 10 worshippers in the morning and 46 in the evening on one Sunday in 1903.[11]

Unitarians registered Granville hall, Granville Road, in 1911[12] and remained there until between 1939 and 1949.[13]

The North Finchley Brotherhood met in Ballards Lane in the 1950s[14] and the Swedenborgian North Finchley New Christian church, founded at no. 71 Gainsborough Road in 1952,[15] survived in 1976. It was a beneficiary of several small charities regulated by a Scheme of 1957.[16]

The London City Mission ran an interdenominational mission at no. 8 St. John's Parade, Whetstone, from 1904 until 1925.[17]

Kensit Memorial college, originally for 'Evangelical Protestants' and later interdenominational, opened in Hendon Lane in 1908. Services took place in the college's conservatory until 1910, when an iron church was opened. New church and college buildings were opened in 1968.[18]

There was a gospel hall in East End Road, possibly the former Primitive Methodist chapel, from *c.* 1920 to *c.* 1939.[19] A group of 'Christians' met at no. 144 Ballards Lane in 1940, moving to no. 134 in 1941 and to no. 4 Granville Road in 1949.[20] It may have been the same group which registered no. 23a the Grove in 1954.[21] An undesignated congregation registered no. 197 East End Road in 1970[22] and a similar group, which first used no. 214 East End Road in 1971, still existed in 1976.[23]

ORTHODOX CHURCH. In 1948 Marian Fathers belonging to the Byelorussian Catholic Church acquired a large house in Holden Avenue, North Finchley. A chapel there, registered for public worship according to the Byzantine–Slavonic rite in 1952, contains an iconostasis featuring ancient icons from Byelorussia. Another house in Holden Avenue is used in mission work.[24]

JUDAISM. A Sephardi Jew, Moses Costa, lived in Finchley in 1756 but modern Judaism dates from the late 19th century.[25] Finchley synagogue, a constituent member of the United Synagogue, grew out of services begun in 1930 at no. 7 Crescent Road. A synagogue for 500 people opened in Kinloss Gardens near the North Circular Road in 1935 and was replaced in 1967 by one on an adjacent site, for 1,350.[26]

Hampstead Garden Suburb synagogue was built in 1934 by M. de Metz at Norrice Lea and registered in 1935. It is one of the largest constituents of the United Synagogue.[27]

Woodside Park Hebrew congregation, which from *c.* 1945 met at no. 3 Alexandra Grove,[28] registered the former Woodside hall in Woodside Park Road in 1950 and was renamed North Finchley and Woodside Park district synagogue. It is a district synagogue of the United Synagogue.[29]

A Liberal synagogue was founded in 1953,[30] meeting in North Finchley library and private houses and also using Christ Church, St. Mary's, and Moss Hall school until the existing synagogue was built in Hutton Grove in 1964. Called Finchley Progressive synagogue after 1971, the building holds 350.[31]

Garden Suburb Beth Hamedrash, a constituent member of the Union of Orthodox Hebrew Congregations, began in 1953 in North Way on the Hendon side of Hampstead Garden Suburb and moved to no. 5 the Bishop's Avenue in 1955.[32]

Finchley Central synagogue, a constituent of the Federation of Synagogues, first met in 1956 at the Congregational hall in Victoria Avenue. A synagogue to hold 325 was opened in 1961 in Redbourne Avenue.[33]

Finchley Reform synagogue was built in 1961 in Fallowcourt Avenue, North Finchley, and replaced in 1974 by a new synagogue on the same site and seating 220.[34]

EDUCATION. Sixteenth-century grammar schools at Highgate and Barnet served Finchley boys, although the places may not have been taken up.[35] In 1682 there was at least one schoolmaster at Whetstone.[36] Ann Orme (d. 1704), who lived in East End Road, was a schoolmistress.[37] A small charity school existed by 1719[38] until shortly after 1785[39] and may have been the 'academy' kept by William Smallbourn (d. by 1790) on the common in 1784.[40] In 1795 education was available only in the free school in

9 In 1976 the King St. chapel was no longer used for worship: ex inf. the sec., E. Finchley United Reformed ch.
10 G.R.O. Worship Reg. no. 33748.
11 Mudie-Smith, *Rel. Life*, 413.
12 G.R.O. Worship Reg. no. 45051.
13 *Kelly's Dir. Finchley* (1939); *Finchley Dir.* (1949).
14 *Finchley Dir.* (1951); Finchley Boro. *Official Handbk.* (1955).
15 G.R.O. Worship Reg. no. 63778; Char. Com. files.
16 Char. Com. files.
17 G.R.O. Worship Reg. no. 40393.
18 Ex inf. the coll. principal and minister; G.R.O. Worship Reg. nos. 52576, 71507; *The Times*, 8 Jan. 1931.
19 *Kelly's Dir. Finchley* (1920, 1930, 1939).
20 G.R.O. Worship Reg. nos. 59495, 59743, 62331.
21 Ibid. 64211.
22 Ibid. 72088.
23 Ex inf. Mr. G. W. Brown.
24 Ex inf. Bishop C. Sipovich; G.R.O. Worship Reg. no. 63602.
25 B.L.H.L., Banks Colln. xvi (1756 poor-rate).
26 Ex inf. the sec.; G.R.O. Worship Reg. nos. 53606, 56187.
27 G.R.O. Worship Reg. no. 56188; *Illus. Hist. Hampstead Gdn. Suburb* [1954].
28 *Jewish Yr. Bk.* (1945–6).
29 G.R.O. Worship Reg. no. 62863.
30 *Jewish Yr. Bk.* (1953).
31 Ex inf. the rabbi; G.R.O. Worship Reg. no. 68864.
32 G.R.O. Worship Reg. no. 67933; *Jewish Yr. Bk.* (1953–5).
33 Ex inf. the sec.; G.R.O. Worship Reg. no. 68203; *Jewish Yr. Bk.* (1956).
34 Ex inf. the sec.; G.R.O. Worship Reg. nos. 70445, 73817.
35 *Finchley Press*, 1 Mar. 1927.
36 Guildhall MS. 10116A/1. See also F. Davis in *Finchley Press*, 4 July 1975.
37 B.L.H.L., Banks Colln., Finchley ch.
38 M. G. Jones, *Char. Sch. Movement* (1938), 368; B.L.H.L., Banks Colln., wills (Dame Ann Hedges, 1724; Robt. Hopper, 1719).
39 B.L.H.L., P.A.F. 1/2, Finchley vestry mins. (1781–96), 4 May 1785.
40 B.L.H.L., Acc. 6140/1, poor-rate bk. (1784–90); Print Colln. 8409.

neighbouring Highgate[41] or in small, short-lived dame schools in Finchley. Schooling for pauper children, in the poorhouse[42] or in dame schools,[43] was provided by the vestry, which made payments to help individuals to start schools until well into the 19th century.[44]

There were abortive attempts in 1804[45] and 1809[46] to set up a parochial charity school. A 'villager' in 1813[47] commented that no parish within 300 miles of London had a greater proportion of its inhabitants 'in a more deplorable state of ignorance'. Methodists had opened a school at their chapel, where two young men came on Sundays from London to teach. In 1812 concern about dissenters' influence led the bishop to recommend that a church school should be established, whereupon the vestry proposed one school at Church End and another at Whetstone. The second was not opened until 1833 but a National school was founded at Church End in 1813 and, with 100 pupils from a population of nearly 1,300, was thought adequate in 1819 for all the poor who desired education.[48] By 1833 the two National schools had 135 places.[49]

Educational wants were 'considerable' in 1846[50] and the remaining hamlets, East End, and North Finchley, received National schools in 1847 and 1869. In both districts they were preceded by Congregationalist foundations in 1842 and 1864. At Whetstone Puget's schools, formally undenominational but connected with chapels, had started in 1825 and 1842. By 1870, with a population of 6,000, there were nearly 1,300 places in six maintained and four private schools.[51]

The 1870s saw Church and dissenters in dispute. Everyone desired more places, especially in East End,[52] but Anglicans vehemently opposed a board and in 1876 the vicar of Christ Church reported that they had 'beaten the life out of the school board movement'.[53] Congregationalists at East End and North Finchley, however, set up a joint committee to press for a board in 1877. The Church then found that it could not raise enough money to cater for the increasing population, partly because the newcomers were mainly lower-middle-class, replacing the wealthier patrons of the early Anglican schools.[54] A school board was established in 1881[55] and immediately was offered the use of the nonconformists' two schools as temporary board schools.[56] The Church continued its opposition, the rector complaining of heavy expenditure in 1882 and the vicar of Whetstone, whose parish adjoined the still boardless Friern Barnet, appealing in 1884 for funds to keep the school board at a distance.[57]

The board had built only two schools before its replacement under the Act of 1902 by the education committee of Finchley U.D.C.,[58] which opened elementary schools in 1906 and 1913. North Finchley, which in the 1880s had seen an outbreak of rowdiness in the schools,[59] in the 1890s and 1900s became an upper-middle-class suburb, where builders advertised not the maintained schools but Christ's College and many new private establishments for girls.[60] Roman Catholics also founded private schools and in 1926 opposed the U.D.C. when it proposed to build a large school on the Woodhouse site, as an alternative to which the Roman Catholics offered a much cheaper school of their own.[61] Both schools were opened and in 1931, when reorganization took place under the Hadow Report, Finchley accommodated 2,900 children in council schools and 1,700 in voluntary schools.[62]

Under the Hadow Report only the one Roman Catholic school remained an all-age mixed school. Christ Church was made a senior school, the three other church schools becoming junior schools. One council school, renamed Martin, was made a junior school and three others, renamed Manor (later Manorside), Alder, and Northside, were divided between seniors and juniors. Summerside, for juniors, was opened in 1933. Middlesex C.C. was responsible for Finchley county secondary school and for two grammar schools (Christ's College and Woodhouse). Under the Education Act of 1944 the county schools became grammar schools and the borough council's senior schools became secondary modern. Two Roman Catholic Voluntary Aided schools, Finchley Catholic grammar and St. Michael's convent, became grammar schools for boys and girls respectively. In 1956 Alder was reserved for boys and Manorside for girls, while Northside, renamed Hillside, moved. Four primary schools opened after the Second World War and a mixed secondary modern Roman Catholic school in 1963.

Barnet L.B. became the education authority in 1965 and introduced a modified comprehensive scheme in 1971. Two comprehensive schools were formed but other schools remained outside the scheme, partly because of the local M.P., Mrs. Margaret Thatcher, then secretary of state for Education and Science.[63] In 1975 Barnet approved a scheme for all the remaining schools except St. Michael's convent, making Woodhouse a sixth-form college and planning a comprehensive school at Brooklands to replace Alder and Christ's College in 1978. In 1977 Christ Church was planned as the upper and Friern Barnet county as the lower school of another comprehensive school.[64]

41 Lysons, *Environs*, ii. 343.
42 B.L.H.L., P.A.F. 1/2, vestry mins. 27 Apr. 1796; 1/3, vestry mins. 24 May 1798.
43 Ibid. 1/3, vestry mins. 27 Dec. 1797; 5 June 1799.
44 Ibid. 1/5, vestry mins. 22 Feb. 1826; 1/6, vestry mins. 6, 27 Mar., 3 Apr. 1834.
45 Ibid. 1/3, vestry mins. 18 Nov. 1804.
46 Lysons, *Environs* (Suppl.), 144.
47 B.L.H.L., Banks Colln., Finchley common (press cutting).
48 *Educ. of Poor Digest*, 536.
49 *Educ. Enquiry Abs.* 560.
50 Nat. Soc. *Church Schs. Enquiry*, *1846–7*, Mdx. 4–5.
51 *Returns relating to Elem. Educ.* H.C. 201, pp. 242–3 (1871), lv. The returns are incomplete: one maintained sch. made no return and the no. of priv. schs. (4) is too low.
52 *Rep. of Educ. Cttee. of Council*, *1878–9* [C. 2342–I], p. 746, H.C. (1878–9), xxiii.
53 Nat. Soc. files.
54 e.g. vicar of Holy Trinity's letter, 1894, in Nat. Soc. files.
55 *Lond. Gaz.* 7 Jan. 1881, p. 73.
56 B.L.H.L., Acc. 9835, Finchley sch. bd., min. bk. i (1881–3).
57 Nat. Soc. files.
58 B.L.H.L., Acc. 9835, Finchley sch. bd., min. bk. (1902–3), p. 292.
59 Ibid. i (1881–3), p. 211.
60 Sales parts. in B.L.H.L. For priv. schs., see below.
61 *Finchley Catholic Rec.* May 1926.
62 i.e. Our Lady of Lourdes with 224 places: B.L.H.L., Finchley educ. cttee., proc. xxviii (1930–1), pp. 76, 112.
63 *Hendon Times*, 4 Feb. 1972.
64 Barnet L.B. *Secondary Educ. in Barnet* (1977); town clerk's press statement, 10 Feb. 1975; *Finchley Press*, 22 Apr. 1977.

Elementary schools founded before 1881. St. Mary's or Finchley National school opened for 35 boys and 30 girls in 1813 in an old building in Hendon Lane leased from the charity estates; the building was extended in 1824.[65] In 1816 the school was united to the National Society, which made it a grant.[66] A small annual grant from the charities and school pence were also received but most income came from subscriptions.[67] In 1843–4 standards were very low[68] and although by 1846 they had much improved, the premises consisted only of two small classrooms for 67 boys and 32 girls.[69] The new rector, T. R. White, gave glebeland near the church in 1848, where a school-house was opened in 1853. The National Society refused a building grant because there were nonconformists on the school's management committee[70] but one was obtained from the education committee of the Council,[71] which made annual grants from 1865.[72] In 1878 the inspector viewed a lesson in digging and remarked that if the boys' arms were as well trained as their brains, 'Finchley ought to blossom as a rose'.[73] After a gradual rise, the average attendance increased sharply from 175 in 1880 to 258 in 1884.[74] Extra classrooms were built in 1897[75] but overcrowding continued as a result of suburban growth.[76] In 1905 an infants' school was built on adjoining glebeland, increasing the total accommodation from 379 to 534. The average attendance rose from 387 in 1906[77] to a peak of 463 in 1922, the infants' school being amalgamated with the juniors' in 1933.[78] More classrooms were added in 1949 and 1967 and St. Mary's primary school, then Voluntary Aided, had 415 children on the roll in 1975.[79]

Puget's schools originated in 1825 with a foundation by Mrs. Catherine Puget (d. 1842) of Poynters Grove on family land in Totteridge Lane, in Hertfordshire, midway between Totteridge and Whetstone. It contained 40 boys and girls in 1833.[80] Catherine's son J. H. Puget (d. 1897) built a school for girls and infants in Blackhorse Lane (later Oakleigh Road North), near the Great North Road and just within the Finchley boundary. The girls were taught plain needlework and the sole income was from pence until 1877, when Puget's son Lt.-Col. John Puget (d. 1894) applied for a parliamentary grant.[81] The school in Totteridge Lane closed *c.* 1883,[82] probably accounting for an increase in numbers at the Oakleigh Road school, then called Col. Puget's school, from 77 in 1880 to 119 in 1884.[83] Despite its name that school received less support from the colonel than it had from his evangelical father and by 1890 was controlled by the vicar, aided by 'a lady bountiful'. Although average attendance rose to 146 in 1901, lack of funds led to closure in 1904.[84]

St. John's National school, Whetstone, opened in 1833 in a building in Totteridge Lane belonging to Joseph Baxendale.[85] It was a Sunday school and day-school for 29 boys and 30 girls, supported by voluntary contributions, pence, and small grants from the charity estates and the National Society.[86] In 1863 a parliamentary building grant enabled a new school to be built in Britannia Road, on land bought by the minister of St. John's.[87] In 1869 the new incumbent closed the school, whose buildings were neglected until their reopening in 1874 and their enlargement, mainly at the expense of two local ladies.[88] Annual parliamentary grants were made from 1878–9, when 57 children attended.[89] In 1884 the vicar of Whetstone paid for another classroom and asked the National Society to help buy the small infants' school in Friern Barnet Lane which had been built as part of Friern Barnet National school in 1859.[90] The Friern Barnet Lane school received separate grants until 1888[91] but later closed, probably in 1905, when the accommodation in the main school was raised from 198 to 274, including 90 places for infants.[92] Average attendances at St. John's rose from 92 in 1881 to 149 in 1888 but dropped to 100 in 1899,[93] rising again to 265 in 1932 when the school was enlarged. A new school was built in Swan Lane in 1972 and was Voluntary Aided in 1976, when it had 254 children on the roll.[94]

65 Ed. 7/88; J. Dugdale, *New Brit. Traveller* (1819), iii. 487; M.R.O., TA/FIN, no. 119; *10th Rep. Com. Char.* H.C. 103, p. 320 (1824), xiii. See drawing in Passmore, 'Finchley Par. Rec.' i, f. 122. The bldg. was demolished in 1882.

66 Nat. Soc. *17th Annual Rep.* (1828), 54.

67 Ed. 7/88; *Analytical Digest of Reps. from 1832*, H.C. 115, pp. 420–1 (1835), xl. The bp. of Lond. was sarcastically said to have subscribed a pastoral letter: B.L.H.L., Banks Colln., Finchley common.

68 *Mins. of Educ. Cttee. of Council, 1843–4* [622], p. 57, H.C. (1845), xxxv.

69 Ibid. *1846* [787], p. 154, H.C. (1847), xlv.

70 Nat. Soc. files; B.L.H.L., Banks Colln., biog. T. R. White; Print Colln. 8647, 8921; *Illus. Lond. News*, 24 Nov. 1855, pp. 629–30.

71 *Mins. of Educ. Cttee. of Council, 1851–2* [1532], p. 150, H.C. (1852), xxxix.

72 *Rep. of Educ. Cttee. of Council, 1865–6* [3666], p. 554, H.C. (1866), xxvii.

73 Ibid. *1878–9*, p. 749.

74 Ibid. *1880–1* [C. 2948–I], p. 634, H.C. (1881), xxxii; *1884–5* [C. 4483–I], p. 592, H.C. (1885), xxiii.

75 Nat. Soc. files; ex inf. the headmaster.

76 See p. 51.

77 *Public Elem. Schs. 1906* [Cd. 3510], p. 456, H.C. (1907), lxiii; *Returns of Non-Provided Schs. 1906*, pp. 23, 28, H.C. 178 (1906), lxxxviii.

78 *Bd. of Educ., List 21, 1936* (H.M.S.O.).

79 Ex inf. the headmaster.

80 Listed under Whetstone in *Home Cnties. Dir.* (1845); Dawson, *Puget Family*, 23; *Educ. Enquiry Abs.* 366.

81 Dawson, *Puget Family*, 33; Ed. 7/87; O.S. Map 6", Mdx. VI. SE. (1867 edn.); M.L.R. 1858/9/125.

82 *Kelly's Dir. Mdx.* (1882); *Kelly's Dir. Barnet* (1889–90).

83 *Rep. of Educ. Cttee. of Council, 1880–1*, p. 644; ibid. *1884–5*, p. 590.

84 Dawson, *Puget Family*, 44; *Schs. under Admin. of Bd. 1901–2* [Cd. 1277], p. 168, H.C. (1902), lxxix.

85 Probably one of the three tenements belonging to Baxendale in 1841: M.R.O., TA/FIN, no. 326. According to the ch.-rate bk. of 1840 (B.L.H.L.) the sch. was in Blackhorse Lane but other evidence indicates Totteridge Lane: *Home Cnties. Dir.* (1840, 1845); H.O. 107/1701/136/3/2a f. 351.

86 Ed. 7/88; Nat. Soc. files; Nat. Soc. *Church Schs. Enquiry, 1846–7*, Mdx. 4–5.

87 C 54/15807 no. 7; Nat. Soc. files; *Rep. of Educ. Cttee. of Council, 1870–1* [C. 406], p. 496, H.C. (1871), xxii.

88 *Finchley Press*, 25 July 1975; Ed. 7/88.

89 *Rep. of Educ. Cttee. of Council, 1878–9*, p. 947.

90 Nat. Soc. files; C 54/15383 no. 1. See also p. 34.

91 *Rep. of Educ. Cttee. of Council, 1888–9* [C. 5804–I], p. 608, H.C. (1889), xxix.

92 *Public Elem. Schs. 1906* [Cd. 3182], p. 456, H.C. (1906), lxxxvi; Nat. Soc. files.

93 *Rep. of Educ. Cttee. of Council, 1880–1*, p. 644; ibid. *1888–9*, p. 608; *Schs. in receipt of Parl. Grants, 1898–9* [C. 9454], p. 168, H.C. (1899), lxxiv.

94 *Bd. of Educ., List 21, 1932* (H.M.S.O.); ex inf. the headmaster.

East End British,[95] also called Chapel Street, school opened for infants in a room behind the Congregational chapel in 1842. The education committee of the Council, in contrast to the British and Foreign Schools Society, made a building grant, although most of the money was raised privately.[96] Subscriptions enabled a second schoolroom to be built overhead for older children in 1850 and, with pence, maintained the school[97] until government grants were made from 1867. In 1875 the chapel and school, then attended by *c.* 66 children,[98] were burnt down. Although the building was restored, the chapel could not afford to reopen the school and in 1881 offered the premises as a board school. Adapted by the board, they accommodated 219 children and were attended by an average of 193 in 1884, when they were replaced by East Finchley board school.[99]

There was a small infants' school in Lodge Lane, North Finchley, by the 1830s.[1] It was run by T. C. Newman and was superseded by North Finchley Congregational schools.[2]

Holy Trinity or East End National or industrial school[3] was built in 1847 on demesne land of the bishop of London in East End Road near High Road. The architect was Anthony Salvin, one of the original managing committee, and the builder was Mark Plowman, also active in local affairs. The school accommodated 252 children, divided equally into boys', girls', and infants' departments.[4] Designed to give a vocational as well as an academic education to poor children of East End,[5] the school was one of the first to seek a grant under the resolution of the education committee of the Council in 1846,[6] although it was never an industrial school like those in the northern manufacturing towns. Boys were taught husbandry and animal-keeping and girls domestic service, in spacious buildings[7] whose grounds furnished boys with their own garden plots. Inspectors lavishly praised the importance of an experiment[8] which kept older boys at school.[9] Money was raised from the National Society, the charity estates, local endowments, contributions, and school pence[10] and there were several parliamentary building grants.[11] As the first wealthy subscribers left the district, they were replaced by tradesmen and clerks who wanted a conventional education for their children.[12] In 1877 the industrial section, no longer officially subsidized, was closed.[13] The school was enlarged in 1881, 1887, and 1898,[14] when it reached its maximum of 565 places,[15] although attendance was always well below 300. In 1976 there were 270 on the roll at a new building in Market Place to which Holy Trinity primary school, then Voluntary Aided, had moved in 1974, the older buildings being used by a private school of English.

North Finchley Congregational day-schools[16] were built in 1864 in Dale Grove on land given by J. H. Puget, who maintained them until his death in 1867, when a managing committee was set up by the church. The premises originally consisted of classrooms for 40 infants and 40 older children[17] and by 1870, when annual parliamentary grants were made, the average attendances were respectively 64 and 93.[18] From 1881 until 1884 North Finchley's building was a temporary board school.[19] Congregationalists used the buildings for a Sunday school until 1893, when they sold them to the Baptists.[20]

Christ Church National school opened in 1869 as a mixed school in the old Lodge Lane building belonging to Mrs. Newman. Supported by voluntary contributions and pence and also used as a Sunday school,[21] it was regarded as temporary. In 1874 the vicar asked the National Society for a grant to build a larger school, drawing attention to the well built Congregational school near by.[22] The new school opened in Stanhope Road in 1875, with places for 225 children of all ages. Parliamentary grants had been received since 1872, when the average attendance was 60.[23] By 1884 the average attendance of 161 at Christ Church was only 73 per cent, the lowest percentage in Finchley.[24] The inspector thought standards poor and in the 1890s the vicar, who personally supplied much of the finance, felt that he was competing unequally with the better equipped board school.[25] The school was enlarged in 1904 but council houses brought many extra children[26] and in 1932 average attendance was 421. In 1933 the National Society made a grant for two new classrooms, entitling Christ Church to recognition as a senior school under the Hadow Report.[27] It

[95] According to Miss K. M. Nichol, sec. of E. Finchley United Reformed ch., who supplied much information on the sch., it did not become a British sch. until 1867. It was, however, described as British in 1847: Nat. Soc. files.
[96] *Returns of List of Applics. for Grants for Educ. 1840–2*, H.C. 444, p. 34 (1843), xl; British and Foreign Schs. Soc. *36th Rep.* (1841), 28.
[97] Ed. 7/88.
[98] *Rep. of Educ. Cttee. of Council, 1873–4* [C. 1019–I], pp. 372–3, H.C. (1874), xviii.
[99] Ex inf. Miss K. M. Nichol; *Rep. of Educ. Cttee. of Council, 1884–5*, p. 592; Finchley sch. bd., min. bks. (1881–1903), pp. 18, 73.
[1] *Finchley Common Cong. Ch. 1864, N. Finchley Cong. Ch. 1964* (pamphlet); H.O. 107/1701/136/3/2a f. 384.
[2] Dawson, *Puget Family*, 37. The bldg. was then used by Christ Church sch.: see below.
[3] Except where otherwise stated, information on the sch. is from 'Holy Trinity Ch. of Eng. Sch. 1847–1974' (TS. pamphlet) and the headmaster.
[4] Nat. Soc. files; C 54/13559 no. 2.
[5] C 54/13559 no. 2.
[6] *Mins. of Educ. Cttee. of Council, 1846*, pp. 6–7.
[7] Ibid. *1852–3* [1623], p. 411, H.C. (1852–3), lxxix.
[8] Ibid. *1848–50* [1215], pp. 70, 79, H.C. (1858), xliii; ibid. *1850–1* [1358], p. 49, H.C. (1851), xliv.
[9] Ibid. *1852–3*, p. 411.
[10] Ed. 7/88; C 54/14578 no. 7.
[11] *Mins. of Educ. Cttee. of Council, 1854–5* [1926], p. 199, H.C. (1854–5), xlii.
[12] Nat. Soc. files.
[13] M. A. Morris, 'Rec. of Holy Trinity Sch., E. Finchley' (thesis, 1948, in B.L.H.L., schools file 370).
[14] Nat. Soc. files; *Kelly's Dir. Mdx.* (1908).
[15] *Schs. in receipt of Parl. Grants, 1898–9*, p. 168.
[16] Except where otherwise stated, the account of the sch. is based on information from Mr. P. G. Dawson, archivist, N. Finchley United Reformed ch.
[17] Ed 7/88.
[18] *Rep. of Educ. Cttee. of Council, 1870–1*, p. 496.
[19] Ed. 7/88; ex inf. Miss K. M. Nichol.
[20] *Finchley Common Cong. Ch. 1864, N. Finchley Cong. Ch. 1964.*
[21] Ed. 7/88. The bldg. was still owned by a Newman and leased to the Revd. H. Stephens in 1887: B.L.H.L., rate bk. (1887).
[22] Nat. Soc. files.
[23] Ed. 7/88; *Rep. of Educ. Cttee. of Council, 1872–3* [C. 812], p. 455, H.C. (1873), xxiv.
[24] B.L.H.L., Acc. 9835, Finchley sch. bd., min. bk. ii (1883–6), p. 267.
[25] Nat. Soc. files.
[26] Ibid.; *Kelly's Dir. Mdx.* (1908).
[27] Nat. Soc. files; *Bd. of Educ., List 21, 1934* (H.M.S.O.).

became a Voluntary Aided secondary modern school under the Act of 1944 and had 450 children on the roll in 1976, in a new building in Hilton Avenue to which pupils had moved in 1968.[28] It was proposed to make it part of a comprehensive school in 1977.[29]

Elementary schools founded 1881–1945. East Finchley board school, replacing the temporary Chapel Street premises, opened in 1884 in Long Lane for 500 boys and girls and 250 infants.[30] Average attendance rose to 603 in 1893,[31] the accommodation to 1,116 by 1898[32] and 1,200 in 1903,[33] and attendance to 1,101 in 1907.[34] Only 692 pupils, divided into mixed and infants' departments, attended in 1919 and the school was reorganized into senior mixed and infants' departments and renamed Alder council school in 1931.[35] It became a mixed secondary modern under the Act of 1944 and a boys' school in 1956. There were 300 boys on the roll in 1976, still using the yellow-brick board school building.[36] In 1977 a comprehensive school to replace Alder was being built at Brooklands.[37]

North Finchley board school in Percy Road, often called Albert Street school, in 1884 replaced the temporary board school in the Congregationalists' buildings.[38] The school could accommodate 750 in mixed and infants' departments,[39] was enlarged to take 930 in 1898,[40] and in 1922 had an average attendance of 784. In 1923 it was reorganized into senior and junior departments, with a total of 1,004 places. The name was changed to Northside in 1932[41] and the senior department under the Act of 1944 became a secondary modern school, renamed Hillside in 1955 and moving to Summers Lane in 1956.[42] The juniors stayed in Percy Road, where 470 children occupied Northside primary school in 1976.[43]

The first school built by Finchley U.D.C. was Squires Lane in Church End, which opened in 1906 with 600 places divided equally between mixed and infants' departments.[44] By 1919 there were senior, junior, and infants' departments with a total of 980 places and an average attendance of 817. In 1922 it was reorganized into boys', girls', and infants' and in 1932 into senior mixed and junior mixed and infants' departments, changing its name to Manor and by 1936 to Manorside council school.[45] The senior school became a mixed secondary modern school under the Act of 1944 and a girls' school from 1956.[46] After the girls merged into Manorhill school in 1971, Manorside junior and infants' schools remained in Squires Lane in 1976, with 253 and 123 children on their rolls.[47]

The Great North Road council school opened in 1913 in High Road, East End, where adjoining buildings accommodated 500 seniors and 500 juniors and infants. In 1931 the seniors moved to Long Lane, reducing the accommodation to 488, and by 1936 the name had been changed to Martin school.[48] After reorganization under the Act of 1944 the junior and infants' departments were regarded as separate schools,[49] which in 1976 had 270 and 241 children respectively.[50]

Our Lady of Lourdes Roman Catholic school, for 224 children of all ages, opened at Bow Lane in 1929. Extensions were built in 1956 and older children moved to the new Bishop Douglass school in 1963. In 1976 there were 335 children on the roll, some in temporary annexes at the school and in the grounds of Manorhill school.[51]

Summerside council school, with places for 450 juniors and infants, opened in 1933 at Crossway to serve the municipal estate in north-east Finchley. From 1939 a new building next to the original one housed the infants' department, which thereafter formed a separate school. After alterations and extensions in 1968–9 and 1973, there were 260 juniors and 130 infants on the rolls in 1976.[52]

Primary schools founded after 1945. Moss Hall school, built in Moss Hall Grove to serve the area between Church End and North Finchley, opened in 1952. There were 410 juniors and 305 infants in adjacent buildings in 1976.[53]

Tudor school opened as a combined junior and infants' school in Queen's Road, North Finchley, in 1952. An extension to the building was used by other schools[54] until 1975, when it became a nursery for Tudor school, which in 1976 had 260 children on the roll.[55]

Brookland schools for juniors and infants, established at Hill Top near the North Circular Road in 1954,[56] were the first council schools in the southern part of Finchley. There were 292 juniors on the roll in 1976.[57]

St. Theresa's Roman Catholic school, a Voluntary Aided school for juniors and infants, was built by the Sisters of Marie Auxiliatrice in the grounds of Manor convent to replace their independent school in 1966. There were 260 children on the roll in 1976.[58]

28 Ex inf. the headmaster.
29 Barnet L.B. *Secondary Educ. in Barnet* (1977).
30 Ed. 7/88.
31 *Returns relating to Elem. Educ.* [C. 7529], pp. 420–1, H.C. (1894), lxv.
32 *Schs. in receipt of Parl. Grants, 1898–9*, p. 168.
33 *Public Elem. Schs. 1906* [Cd. 3182], p. 456, H.C. (1906), lxxxvi.
34 Ibid. *1907* [Cd. 3901], p. 456, H.C. (1908), lxxxiv.
35 *Bd. of Educ., List 21, 1932* (H.M.S.O.); B.L.H.L., Finchley educ. cttee., proc. xxviii (1930–1), p. 112.
36 Finchley Boro. *Official Handbk.* (1955); ex inf. the headmaster.
37 Barnet L.B. *Secondary Educ. in Barnet* (1977).
38 B.L.H.L., Acc. 9835, Finchley sch. bd., min. bk. ii (1883–6), p. 193.
39 *Rep. of Educ. Cttee. of Council, 1885–6* [C. 4849–I], p. 556, H.C. (1886), xxiv.
40 *Schs. in receipt of Parl. Grants, 1898–9*, p. 168; *Kelly's Dir. Mdx.* (1908).
41 *Bd. of Educ., List 21, 1922–36* (H.M.S.O.).
42 Finchley Boro. *Official Handbk.* (1955).
43 Ex inf. the headmaster.
44 *Public Elem. Schs. 1907*, p. 456; Ed. 7/88.
45 *Bd. of Educ., List 21, 1919–38* (H.M.S.O.).
46 Finchley Boro. *Official Handbk.* (1955).
47 Ex inf. the head teachers.
48 Ed. 7/88; ex inf. the head teachers; *Bd. of Educ., List 21, 1932–6* (H.M.S.O.).
49 Finchley Boro. *Official Handbk.* (1955).
50 Ex inf. the head teachers.
51 Ex inf. the headmaster; *Bd. of Educ., List 21, 1932* (H.M.S.O.).
52 Ex inf. the head teachers.
53 Ex inf. the head teachers.
54 i.e. Manorside and Haynes schs.
55 Ex inf. the headmaster.
56 Finchley Boro. *Official Handbk.* (1955); M.R.O., P.R. 75/593601 (photos. and programme of official opening).
57 Ex inf. the headmaster.
58 Ex inf. the headmaster and Sister Mary Xavernie Kelland, former headmistress of Manor House sch.; and see below.

Secondary and senior schools founded before 1971. The earliest public secondary education in Finchley consisted of science classes in a laboratory built by the school board at Long Lane school in 1894. In 1896 60 pupils, aged 12 to 16, were taught in the evenings by the head of the board school. By 1900, although still in Long Lane, the classes were recognized as a higher elementary school, which in 1902 was attended by 101 pupils.[59]

Finchley county school originated in a new school, west of the Great North Road and more central than Long Lane, in 1903. It accommodated 330, thus qualifying for a regular parliamentary grant,[60] and in 1909 was acquired from the U.D.C. by Middlesex C.C., which administered it as a mixed secondary day-school.[61] After additions, Finchley county school had 400 pupils on the roll in 1971, when it was merged into Manorhill comprehensive school.[62]

Christ's College, an independent boys' school in Hendon Lane, ran into financial trouble[63] and in 1909 was taken over by Middlesex C.C. It became a county grammar school and in 1976 had 600 boys on the roll.[64] In 1978 there were plans to combine it with Alder in a boys' comprehensive school at Brooklands.[65]

Woodhouse school opened in the house of that name near the Friern Barnet border in 1922 as a mixed selective central school with 320 places. It became a grammar school in 1925 and in 1976 accommodated 632 pupils in the original building, to which laboratories had been added in 1921 and 1960.[66] In 1977 it was expected to become a sixth-form college.[67]

Finchley Catholic grammar school, originally an independent Roman Catholic school, became a direct grant school in 1939 and a Voluntary Aided grammar school for boys in 1945. It had 600 pupils in 1971, when it became part of the comprehensive Finchley Catholic high school.[68]

Hillside, a mixed secondary modern school, opened in 1956 in Summers Lane in north-east Finchley. It had *c.* 550 pupils on the roll in 1971, when it was merged into Manorhill school.[69]

St. Michael's convent grammar school was established in 1958 as a Voluntary Aided girls' school in a new building in Nether Street, where it had existed as an independent Roman Catholic school since 1908. The school expanded in 1964, 1971, and 1973, and in 1976 had *c.* 630 girls on the roll.[70]

Bishop Douglass, a mixed secondary modern Roman Catholic school, opened with Voluntary Aided status in Hamilton Road in 1963. In 1969 it merged with the independent Manor House convent school in the near-by East End Road, which thereafter housed the sixth form of the expanded school. New buildings were added in Hamilton Road in 1969, 1973, and 1976, when there were 1,140 pupils on the roll.[71]

Comprehensive schools founded after 1971. Finchley Catholic high school was formed in 1971, when Finchley Catholic grammar school merged with the independent Challoner school. There were 400 boys on the roll in 1976.[72]

Manorhill, a mixed school, for 1,200, was formed in 1971 by the amalgamation of Finchley county grammar with Hillside and Manorside secondary modern schools. The lower forms were housed on the old county school site in High Road and the upper in the former Hillside premises in Summers Lane, which later were extended.[73]

Special school. Oak Lodge, one of the earliest public special schools, opened in 1916 in a former private house in Oak Lane. Pupils, who were educationally sub-normal children from Finchley, Hornsey, and Wood Green, numbered 70 by 1918. Extensions were made until 1974, when the school, retaining its old name, moved to Heath View. In 1976 there were 130 children on the roll, from Barnet and Haringey L.B.s.[74]

Private schools.[75] Of 444 school-children in 1833, more than half were educated at their parents' expense, in six boarding and four day-schools.[76] Boarding schools were attended by 460 pupils in 1871[77] and private schools by 385, compared with 1,468 at maintained schools, in 1881, when another 253 children were taught at home.[78] There were eleven private schools in 1882, 20 in 1920, and *c.* 25 with 2,000 places *c.* 1933.[79] The number of schools later declined, especially after the Second World War. Some entered the state system but most were small and short-lived, in large houses such as Elm Tree Lodge, Falkland House, the Gables, Cambridge House, Court House, Yverden, and Glencairn.

Abraham Cousins (d. 1831) had a school in Ballards Lane by 1802. It passed to his son Frederick (d. 1841), by 1841 was called Union House academy with 42 boy boarders, and survived until the building up of the Moss Hall estate in 1879.[80]

William Fanning in 1819 opened a boarding school for young gentlemen at the Manor House in East End Road, which was taken over by Henry and Charles Worsley in 1838 and closed in the early 1860s.[81] Many of the boys went to the school opened by the rector in 1857 at Finchley Hall, later Christ's

59 B.L.H.L., Acc. 9837, Finchley educ. rec.
60 *Kelly's Dir. Mdx.* (1908); *Public Elem. Schs. 1906* [Cd. 3182], p. 456, H.C. (1906), lxxxvi.
61 B.L.H.L., Acc. 9836, Finchley U.D.C. educ. cttee., min. bk. (1908–10), 68, 77.
62 Ex inf. the headmaster of Manorhill; see below.
63 B.L.H.L., Acc. 9836, Finchley U.D.C. educ. cttee., min. bk. (1909–10), 77, 99. For the hist. of Christ's Coll., see *V.C.H. Mdx.* i. 290, and below.
64 Ex inf. the headmaster.
65 Barnet L.B. *Secondary Educ. in Barnet* (1977).
66 Ex inf. the headmaster; *Bd. of Educ., List 21, 1927* (H.M.S.O.); Ed. 7/88.
67 Barnet L.B. *Secondary Educ. in Barnet* (1977).
68 Ex inf. the sen. science master, Finchley Catholic high sch.
69 Ex inf. the headmaster of Manorhill.
70 Ex inf. the headmistress; and see below.
71 Ex inf. the headmaster. For Manor Ho. convent sch., see below.
72 Ex inf. the sen. science master.
73 Ex inf. the headmaster.
74 Ex inf. the headmaster.
75 Except where otherwise stated, the section is based on *Home Cnties. Dir.* (1845); *Kelly's Dir. Mdx.* (1862–82); ibid. *Barnet* (1889–1910); ibid. *Finchley* (1920–39); *Finchley Dir.* (1951); *Finchley Boro. Dir.* (1961).
76 *Educ. Enquiry Abs.* 560.
77 *Census*, 1871.
78 B.L.H.L., Acc. 9835, Finchley sch. bd., min. bk. i (1881–3), p. 229.
79 B.L.H.L., Banks Colln. xiii, p. 5942.
80 M.L.R. 1802/5/67; B.L.H.L., Banks Colln. St. Mary's memorial stones, *sub* Cousins; *Finchley Press*, 25 July 1975.
81 F. Davis in *Finchley Press*, 25 July 1975.

Shops in Crouch End Broadway and Tottenham Lane

Town Hall

HORNSEY

Verandah Cottages, North Hill

High Point, North Road

HIGHGATE

College.[82] East Finchley College in East End Road was opened by Edward Cox in 1861[83] and survived until 1890, when it was probably succeeded by East Finchley grammar school in High Road until 1930.

Girls' schools, more numerous although probably smaller than boys', included those run by Abraham Cousins's daughter Louisa Cousins (before 1845 to 1871), Miss Isabella Claridge (*c.* 1851–*c.* 1889), and Miss S. Pearce (*c.* 1874–*c.* 1920). Among those founded *c.* 1880 were Clydesdale (*c.* 1882–*c.* 1899), Alexandra House (*c.* 1882–*c.* 1909), which specialized in music and languages, and Saxonhurst, later at Hertford Lodge (*c.* 1882–*c.* 1939). Boys' schools of the same period included Allandale (*c.* 1882–*c.* 1930), Fern Bank (*c.* 1883–*c.* 1967),[84] Finchley high school, formerly Bellbrook (*c.* 1899–1939), and Holmewood (*c.* 1899), one of the few to survive in 1976. Preparatory schools and kindergartens were advertised from *c.* 1899. Some schools opened junior departments and new schools included Lamorna (*c.* 1909–*c.* 1939), Leas House, which moved from Golders Green to Kingsley Way in Hampstead Garden Suburb in 1934,[85] and Annemount, which opened in Holne Chase in 1936 and had 78 pupils in 1976.[86]

Religious orders opened several fee-paying schools, although there was no public Roman Catholic school until 1929. Apart from St. Margaret's industrial school for girls, which for a short time *c.* 1870 used the Good Shepherd convent in East End House although served from Hendon,[87] the first Roman Catholic school was opened in 1908 by the Sisters of the Poor Child Jesus. St. Michael's convent school in Nether Street took girls of all ages and small boys, until in the 1930s it was reorganized into girls' secondary and preparatory schools. The secondary school was a maintained school from 1958 but the junior school remained independent until its closure in 1964.[88]

In 1921 the Sisters of Marie Auxiliatrice opened a small day- and boarding-school at Manor House, the former Bibbesworth manor-house. The school, for girls of all ages, was extended in 1932 and accommodated 650 in the late 1950s. It was merged into Bishop Douglass school in 1969.[89]

Finchley grammar school opened in 1926 under the auspices of St. Alban's church and moved into Woodside Grange in 1927, later acquiring the adjoining houses. Originally for boys aged 8 to 18, it became a direct grant school in 1939 and Voluntary Aided in 1945, when an independent preparatory school, St. Albans, was founded next door. In 1949 the parish priest of St. Alban's founded Challoner school as an independent Roman Catholic school for senior boys who failed to enter the grammar school. Challoner was amalgamated with the grammar school in 1970, leaving the preparatory school as the only independent Roman Catholic school.[90]

St. Joseph's school for maladjusted senior girls opened in 1951 at the Good Shepherd convent, where the nuns had housed, although not formally educated, disturbed and destitute girls since the convent opened in 1864. The school closed after a fire in 1972.[91]

Jewish schools, mainly for children of nursery age but including a junior school at Norrice Lea, were founded in the 1950s and 1960s in connexion with several synagogues.[92]

CHARITIES FOR THE POOR.[93] From 1562 the same trustees managed all the charity estates originating in late-15th- and early-16th-century gifts and later including the alms-houses. In 1892 the estates were amalgamated with those distributive charities not administered by the parish, to form the Finchley Parochial Charities.

Charity estates. In 1488 Robert Warren of Finchley was demised a house, garden, and croft called Ryefield, held of Bibbesworth manor. He settled Ryefield in 1488[94] and the house and garden in 1489[95] in trust to provide ornaments for Finchley church and repair the church and highways, any residual income to be distributed among the poor on Mid Lent Sunday.[96] In 1547 6*s.* 8*d.* was given to the poor and £1 remained for other purposes.[97] Ryefield alias Barleyfield, known also as Warren's first gift, was *c.* 11 a. at Church End between Dollis brook and Nether Street. In 1757 it consisted of two tenements and Homefield and Great and Little John's fields.[98] It was let at £18 in 1682, £42 in 1794, and £67 12*s.* from 1815. The tenements were demolished before 1810 and replaced by Brent Lodge[99] between 1817 and 1824. The whole, known as the Brent Lodge estate, was alienated in 1854 for a rent-charge of £60,[1] which was still paid in 1976. Warren's second gift, the house and garden, became three tenements, which had been reduced to two by 1803, when they yielded £9 rent. One building was occupied from 1813 by St. Mary's National school, which held it at the preferential rent of £12 in 1824. The other was then a shoemaker's shop and was later let to paupers. Both cottages were let in 1882 on an 80-year building lease to William Royal, on whose bankruptcy nos. 1–3 Royal Terrace, later nos. 50–54 Hendon Lane, were incomplete. They were let by the charity for 70 years from 1890 and at £600 rent from 1960.

In 1506 Thomas Sanny enfeoffed trustees with property including a house and the crofts of Fore

[82] For Christ's Coll., see above and *V.C.H. Mdx.* i. 290.
[83] F. Davis in *Finchley Press*, 8 Aug. 1975.
[84] Barnet L.B., List of Independent Schs. (1967). The sch. had closed by 1976.
[85] Finchley Boro. *Official Handbk.* (1955).
[86] Ex inf. the proprietor.
[87] Cath. Dir. (1870); *Lond. Gaz.* 9 June 1871, p. 2700; and see *V.C.H. Mdx.* v. 47.
[88] Ex inf. the headmistress.
[89] Ex inf. the former headmistress of Manor House sch.
[90] Ex inf. the sen. science master, Finchley Cath. high sch.
[91] Ex inf. Sister E. Hills, the Good Shepherd convent.
[92] Barnet L.B., List of Independent Schs. (1967).
[93] Except where otherwise stated, the section is based on *10th Rep. Com. Char.*, H.C. 103, pp. 318–27 (1824), xiii; *Gen. Digest of Endowed Chars.* I, H.C. 433, pp. 16–17 (1867–8), lii (1); *Endowed Chars.* (*Mdx.*), H.C. 306, pp. 8–9 (1899), lxx; Char. Com. files; *Mdx. & Herts. N. & Q.* i. 134–8; ii. 17–19; iii. 31–5, 65–8, 147–9, 173–8; vi. 241–3; W. B. Passmore, 'Finchley Par. Rec.' i (MS. *penes* Finchley Chars.); Finchley Par. *Rep. of Cttee. on Chars.* (1887); ex inf. the clerk to Finchley Chars. The rec. of Finchley Chars. were not available for study.
[94] M.R.O., F. 97; Acc. 351/134.
[95] M.R.O., Acc. 351/135.
[96] Ibid. 136.
[97] E 301/34 no. 157.
[98] M.R.O., Acc. 262/4/25.
[99] M.R.O., Hist. Notes 14/4/67.
[1] C 54/14769 mm. 34–43 no. 5.

Ryders and Stukefield held of Bibbesworth manor for 1*s*. 3½*d*. rent. By will dated 1509 he left £2 a year from the house and Stukefield for the good of his soul and 6*s*. 8*d*. for the repair of his house and the highways and other charitable purposes.[2] The rent-charge, from which £1 18*s*. 8½*d*. remained for charitable purposes in 1547,[3] was forfeited under the Chantries Act and granted in 1549 to John Hulson and William Pendered, respectively a scrivener and a 'founder' of London,[4] who conveyed it to Hugh Losse.[5] Hugh's infant son Robert was found to be his heir in 1555,[6] but a second jury traversed the inquisition[7] and in 1561 the Court of Wards restored not merely the charge but the estate from which it arose to the charity trustees.

Sanny's gift consisted of a tenement fronting East End Road and fields behind stretching to the modern Market Place, East Finchley. The house had become the Five Bells inn by 1757, when the land formed Homefield and Poor Toms field.[8] There were also two cottages in 1803 when the inn was let as a workhouse to the parish, which sub-let it and in 1807 surrendered the lease. All the buildings were replaced in 1812 with the three Homefield Cottages, paid for largely by the sale of timber and let at £39 in 1824 and £59 in 1884.[9] The estate was divided by the G.N.R. in 1864, adjacent land opening into Market Place was bought in 1866,[10] and there were nine gardens and fields by 1884.[11] In 1890 leases were granted on the seven Stanley Villas facing East End Road. East of Stanley Road eight terraced houses were leased for 99 years in 1900; to the west lay allotments by 1896 and Homefield Cottages, one of which had become Homefield garage by 1951. The land north of the railway was sold piecemeal from 1929, Finchley council buying the last 1½ a. of Poor Toms field in 1964. Stanley Villas by 1977 had been replaced by eighteen town houses off Stanley Road. Homefield Cottages and garage had been demolished by 1972 and, with help from the Housing Corporation, two three-storeyed blocks of 38 alms-houses called Homefields were being built in 1977.

Sanny's feoffees also held four crofts and a meadow called Pointalls of Finchley manor for 4*s*. 4*d*. rent in 1525, when they settled them in trust with Sanny's gift. The terms of the trust were unknown in 1547, when the income of 9*s*. was spent on the poor.[12] The estate passed to the Crown with the chantries and in 1551 was granted to Henry Tanner and Thomas Butcher of London,[13] who immediately conveyed it to Hugh Losse, but in 1561, by decree of the Court of Wards, Pointalls was restored to the surviving trustees.

Four parish alms-houses had been built by 1614 on part of Pointalls meadow.[14] Customarily rent-free in 1723, they were condemned in 1739 and rebuilt as six double alms-houses mainly at the expense of Thomas Brandon (d. 1744). There were 16 inmates, 40 years' old and more, in 1805, 13 aged inmates in 1850, and 14 in 1886. Between 1803 and 1824 the alms-houses cost a total of only £85 in repairs and Christmas gifts to the inmates. In 1836 the trustees granted weekly pensions of 2*s*., which in 1876 were raised to 3*s*.; in 1886 the inmates' pensions ranged from 2*s*. 6*d*. to 10*s*., together amounting to £126 a year, and Christmas gifts were £2 17*s*. 6*d*. By 1860 most alms-people were receiving poor-relief. Although three widows who were constantly drunk had been replaced in 1817, evictions were said to be never necessary in 1886, when alms-people were chosen from aged paupers long resident in Finchley.

Administered with the other charity estates and lying between Long and Oak lanes and the modern North Circular Road, where it totalled 11 a. in 1757, Pointalls was often threatened with encroachment: *c*. 1823 ¾ a. had to be bought for £350 to restore its unity. In addition to the alms-houses built on Pointalls by 1614[15] there was a brick house by 1757;[16] the house was beyond repair in 1824, when the trustees vainly hoped to let the whole estate for building. From *c*. 1834 some and from *c*. 1900 most of Pointalls was let as allotments, which were resumed by Finchley Parochial Charities in 1967. In 1969 2 a. were let to Simms Motor Co. (later CAV Ltd.), in 1971 Barnet L.B. bought 108 a. of Pointalls and the trustees' allotment[17] for £441,000 and in 1972 a small plot was let for an electricity sub-station, 3½ a. being reserved for additional alms-houses.

In 1547 parishioners assembled at the church house, which they had built at their own expense near the churchyard and which they let for 8*s*., paid towards the church.[18] The house and garden, with the neighbouring clerk's house and various groves and hedgerows, were held from 1562 with the charity estates. The church house was let subject to reasonable access until 1718, when it became the Queen's Head inn. The rent rose steadily to £50 by 1824 and the inn was rebuilt after having been destroyed by arson in 1836. As Finchley Hall, the building was leased to the rector for a middle-class school, later Christ's College, in 1857 and to Finchley U.D.C. for municipal offices in 1902. After being bombed in 1944 the 2-a. site was used for temporary storage until 1959, when the council bought it for £4,000, later building a library there. The clerk's house, which was let at only £1 in 1674, was replaced by two timber houses before 1776.[19] In 1824 one was let to a poor widow and the other was a chandler's shop. One or both may have been rebuilt in 1849 and one was a brick house and the other a timber cottage unfit for habitation in 1879. Both were leased to the rector and churchwardens from 1884, one being replaced by the modern reading room. The other, described as the clerk's house, was dilapidated *c*. 1940, when it suffered bomb damage, but survived in 1977.

The Finchley inclosure award allotted the trustees *c*. 6 a.,[20] of which ½ a. was let with Sanny's gift and the rest formed a block between High and Sylvester

2 Brass in ch.
3 E 301/34 no. 157.
4 E 318/box 30/1718; *Cal. Pat.* 1549–51, 130, 133.
5 C 54/465 mm. 12–13 no. 14.
6 Wards 7/80.
7 C 43/4/28; C 43/6/13.
8 M.R.O., Acc. 262/4/25.
9 Finchley loc. bd., finance cttee. accts. (1884–7).
10 C 54/16615 mm. 5–9 no. 12.
11 Finchley loc. bd., finance cttee. accts. (1884–7).
12 E 301/34 no. 157.
13 *Cal. Pat.* 1548–9, 422.
14 S.C. 2/191/5 m. 8.
15 See below.
16 M.R.O., Acc. 262/4/25.
17 See below.
18 E 301/34 no. 157.
19 Plans of char. estates, 1776, f. 2, at Finchley ch.
20 M.R.O., MR/DE FIN.

roads and Oak Lane, separated from Pointalls by a footpath. The estate was neglected in 1823 when it was let on a 50-year lease, under which Oak and Edgell cottages were built fronting High Road by 1826[21] and Leicester House by 1851. The land at the rear was let as allotments from 1892. Oak and Edgell cottages were demolished between 1967 and 1970, when Leicester House remained, with allotments and nursery land behind. In 1971 the estate was sold with Pointalls to Barnet L.B.

Expenditure in the 16th century was left to the churchwardens and by the mid 17th century to the trustees or one of them acting as warden of the charities. In 1672 the warden's power to authorize expenditure was restricted to sums under £2 but an unsuccessful attempt to curb the trustees in 1684 left them free from parochial control but resulted in provision for approval of new trustees and audit by the justices. After 1857 the rector and parish officers were excluded from the annual audit, to which they had been admitted as observers since 1668. The trustees tried to resist encroachments on the lands, ordered surveys, repaired buildings, and apparently tried to enhance the estates' value with building leases from 1760. The income rose from £65 10*s*. in 1671 to £90 in 1740, £170 in 1805, £278 in 1824, £303 in 1868, and £526 in 1885; it sufficed for normal expenditure and permitted savings for rebuilding and special acts of charity.

In 1612 the charities' income was to provide £2 for bread on Mid Lent Sunday, the residue to be spent on the church, highways, poor-relief, and other charitable purposes. Maintenance of the alms-houses was also an object in 1684. Highways often involved major works and in 1824 the trustees helped to repair all ways leading to the church. Wells and pumps, with highways, cost £1,410 or almost a third of the total expenditure between 1803 and 1824. Over the same period £686 was spent on the church, including salaries of the organist, organ-blower, and clock-maker. Contributions were also made towards the adornment and repair of the church: £250 subscribed for a new gallery in 1805 was much criticized. In addition £413 was spent on coal and £224 on bread between 1803 and 1824, although only £2 was spent on bread in the three years before 1824. Barley loaves were given away in the famine years of 1697–8 and £75 was spent on bread in 1796 and £67 in 1800. In 1825, in preference to spending more on bread, the trustees assisted apprentices, as in 1675 and 1699, and from 1809 they contributed towards the National school. In 1824 several cottages were let at low rents to the poor, as had been done in 1675 in lieu of poor-relief. The feoffees also maintained the alms-houses, giving the inmates fuel and cloth and from 1836 pensioning them. Other pensions were paid by 1860 and nine outpensioners received a total of £2 5*s*. a week in 1886. Contributions to church paths and highways ceased in 1853 and 1866 but by 1848 gifts were made to new Anglican churches and schools. Land was also let as allotments.

While they often co-operated with the vestry, the trustees refused merely to relieve the rates, whether for the church in 1684 or the highways as in 1866. They were continually criticized from 1850: in 1857 a memorial sought more expenditure on the church, the highways, and the poor, and in 1859 the vestry claimed that gifts to district churches were illegal and that the trustees were unrepresentative. Dissension grew in the 1880s,[22] when successive vestries appointed committees to influence the trustees, until in 1892, after litigation, Chancery established a Scheme amalgamating the charity estates with several distributive charities.[23]

Finchley Parochial Charities. Under the Chancery Scheme of 1892 trustees would ultimately be single nominees of the Ecclesiastical Commissioners, the rector, and the churchwardens and overseers, four nominees of the vestry, and four co-opted trustees, although the Scheme was modified by the Local Government Act, 1894. All the fuel fund's land was to consist of allotments and other estates were to serve a similar purpose. In 1899 allotment-holders opposed plans to build on the land constituting Sanny's gift and in 1972 they defeated a planning application for the fuel land. The income from the fuel land was still to provide coal, of which £100 worth was distributed in 1919 and annually between 1968 and 1972, usually among the alms-people and pensioners; any surplus went to the Finchley District Nursing Association by 1939, when the trustees vainly sought confirmation of the practice. Finchley church was to receive £50 a year and the district churches were to share £100 until 1976, when a Scheme amended the sums to £700 and £1,400. Provision was also made in 1892 for the alms-houses, pensions, and a wide range of discretionary payments; the last were redefined in 1955 but of little importance in 1977.

The combined incomes of the charity estates and the distributive charities, which had totalled £679 in 1885, were augmented by bequests after 1892. Edwin Layton gave £25 for pensions to old people awaiting admission to the alms-houses in 1903 and F. A. Hamilton of Brent Lodge gave £500 for the same purpose in 1904. The trustees in 1904 received £64 stock left by Mrs. Sophia Low and later a further £25 bequeathed to her executor John Yates Paterson. By 1925 the sums had been consolidated as £637 stock known as the donation fund, yielding £14 a year.

Further bequests included £1,000, evidently given by one Laming to augment the pensions. William Alfred Taylor (d. 1941) left the residue of his estate after his wife's death to provide pensions of 7*s*. 6*d*. for poor residents of Finchley; £5,841 was ultimately received, most of it in 1955. Ellen Maria Hall bequeathed one-sixth of her residuary estate, amounting to £300 received in 1952. Finchley Charities' income was £823 in 1919 and £940 in 1922: of £580 spent in 1919, £150 was given to churches, £100 in fuel, and £300 to the alms-houses and pensioners. The income grew to £1,350 by 1954 and more rapidly thereafter. Although sales of land paid for additional alms-houses, the income reached £5,915 in 1969 and £40,931 in 1972. Much of the money from the sale of Pointalls was spent on building.

The alms-houses, under the Scheme of 1892, were to be rebuilt as twelve, for old inhabitants not receiving poor-relief. Pensions of 6*s*. were to be paid to inmates and 10*s*. 6*d*. to married couples. Pensions

[21] M.R.O., Acc. 262/4/26.
[22] *Daily News*, 12 Jan. 1891.
[23] See below.

of not more than £15 a year might be granted to non-residents and a ceiling of £270, later £300, was placed on all pensions combined. Plans for the new alms-houses were ready by 1893 and carried out soon afterwards. There were 18 alms-people, including 6 couples, in 1918, 14 in 1952, and 12 in 1954, shortly before a communal room was converted into an extra alms-house. Pensions were reduced by a Scheme of 1910 but temporary increases for inmates were allowed in 1918 and 1924. In 1918 the inmates received from 2*s.* 6*d.* to 10*s.* a week and eighteen others received 2*s.* 6*d.*, and in 1954 both alms-people and others received 6*s.* 6*d.* A Scheme of 1955 raised the ceiling on pensions to £400 and permitted new building. Four extra alms-houses were finished in 1958 and another eight by 1969, when the estate had been renamed Wilmot Close. A further 26 units for 30 old people and a steward's house were later built, providing a total of 50 units for 60 alms-people. Annual expenditure on Wilmot Close rose from £2,447 in 1968 to £3,383 in 1972, while pensions increased from £485 to £542. By a Scheme of 1976, ability to contribute towards the running costs of the alms-houses might be made a qualification for admittance.

Distributive charities. Thomas Cleave gave £50 to buy a rent-charge of £2 16*s.* to provide thirteen penny loaves for distribution among the poor of Finchley every Sunday. In 1636 a rent-charge was bought to supply the twelve poorest churchgoers, including the sexton, who also received the thirteenth loaf for administering the charity. In 1824 the net income was £2 10*s.* 10*d.* and distribution was normally to widows at the church, although the sexton had recently been told to make it to children at the National school.

Roger Hayton in 1663 gave a rent-charge of £2 12*s.* on a house for distribution of 1*s.* worth of bread every Sunday. The house had been demolished by 1729, when the charity was defunct.

Thomas Tickner in 1667 was granted land from Finchley common to enlarge the grounds of the later Lodge House, subject to perpetual payments of £2 to the poor and £2 to repair the church causeways. The charge was extinguished under the Finchley inclosure award.

William Haynes's and William Nicholl's bequests of rent-charges of £2 were recorded on a table of benefactions in 1734. Joseph Newton was then recorded as the payer of 12*s.* 6*d.* a year from Mill House.

William Norris by will dated 1809 left £300 in trust to pay for repairs to his family tomb, the residue to be distributed in bread or money; £270 was invested to yield £12 4*s.* 10*d.* in 1824, when any residue was spent on bread or occasionally distributed in money or coals. Meat and groceries were supplied in 1865.

John Orsley in 1810 left money in trust to provide bread. The income was spent on blankets in 1864–5 and amounted to £7 16*s.* 6*d.* in 1868.

Under the inclosure award 17 a. were allotted and let at £40, to provide coal for the poor. In 1824 every chosen family received a sack and the residue was divided according to need. After 1868 a plot was sold to the G.N.R. and *c.* 1875 2 a. were sold to Samuel Wimbush, the proceeds being invested. In 1885 there was an income of £46 from rents and £65 from dividends. Prolonged pressure led the trustees *c.* 1888 to convert the remaining 15½ a. to allotments, which were still used in 1977.

Alexander Murray in 1829 bequeathed £400 stock for the repair of his tomb and distribution of bread. The income was spent on groceries in 1864–5 and amounted to £12 in 1868.

Francis Matthews by codicil dated 1830 left £200 stock for the repair of his tomb and bread for the poor. In 1864–5 the income was spent on groceries and coal and in 1868 it amounted to £6.

Jane Andrews by will proved 1849 left £100 subject to repairs to her tomb for distribution in fuel. The income was spent on groceries in 1865 and yielded £2 17*s.* 9*d.* in 1868.

Mrs. Sharma Jemima Clarinda Morison in 1860 left £100 for distribution of fuel. The income was spent on coal in 1865 and yielded £3 3*s.* 7*d.* in 1868.

The charities of Cleave, Norris, Orsley, Murray, Andrews, and Morison, with the fuel fund established under the inclosure award, became part of Finchley Parochial Charities in 1892.

James Lermitte in 1858 gave £200 stock, half of the income to maintain his tombstone and be distributed among the poor and half to assist the National schools. In 1861 the transaction was completed by his executors and in 1905 the Charity Commission divided the stock into an educational and an eleemosynary charity, the latter to be devoted entirely to the poor of the chapelry. In 1965–6 the income of *c.* £2 7*s.* was distributed by the vicar of Holy Trinity.

John Anthonie Bradshaw (d. 1884) left £500 to provide annual distributions of groceries and coals to at least 60 poor parishioners. In 1965 the income of £11 4*s.* was added to a large balance and in 1966 only £5 was distributed by the rector, but from 1967 expenditure greatly exceeded income. Most payments were contributions of £1 5*s.* (£2 in 1971) towards fuel for between 7 and 24 people. From 1969 distribution was by the Finchley Guild of Social Service.

Ann Sims (d. 1942) left the residue of her estate totalling £2,536 towards a trust fund for distressed gentlefolk or other poor persons in Finchley. Trustees were established by a Scheme in 1948 and there was an income of £70 from 1965 to 1971. In 1965 £51 was distributed to the needy and £10 given to the Finchley Guild of Social Service towards chiropody and Christmas presents. In 1971 £45 was given to the needy, £12 10*s.* to the guild, and £10 to St. Elizabeth's Home.

HORNSEY

INCLUDING HIGHGATE

HORNSEY,[1] once remarkable for its low death-rate, lies between 3 and 6½ miles north-west of London. Longer from east to west than from north to south, the main part projects northward from the north-west corner between Finchley and Friern Barnet. A south-easterly projection covers the open space known from 1857 as Finsbury Park.[2] The present account excludes two southern detached parts of Hornsey ancient parish embedded in Stoke Newington parish, but includes a northern detached part, a triangular area stretching from the North Circular Road to Woodhouse Road, Colney Hatch. It also includes land at Muswell Hill which belonged to the priory of St. Mary, Clerkenwell, from *c.* 1160 until 1539 and thereafter formed a detached part of Clerkenwell parish until its transfer to Hornsey in 1901. Part of Highgate village which lay in St. Pancras is also treated in this article.[3]

Hornsey parish contained 2,978 a. in 1881. The northern detached part, *c.* 10 a.,[4] was transferred to Friern Barnet parish in 1891. The area called South Hornsey, which had its own local board of health from 1865, comprised a peninsula of 172 a. known as Brownswood Park lying immediately south-east of the open space of Finsbury Park and the two southern detached parts amounting to 60 a. In 1899 South Hornsey was transferred to Stoke Newington M.B. and the county of London. With those changes and the addition of the 61 a. of Clerkenwell detached, Hornsey in 1901 measured 2,875 a.[5] It had had a local board of health from 1867 and became a U.D. in 1894 and M.B. in 1903. In 1965 it joined Tottenham and Wood Green in Haringey L.B., while South Hornsey formed part of Hackney L.B.

The only natural boundary was Tottenham wood, east of Clerkenwell detached and north of Hornsey village. The east boundary with Tottenham and Stoke Newington lay along Green Lanes, running west of the road in the north and taking in 29 a. in Clissold Park east of the road at the south-east corner. From there to Highgate much of the boundary with Islington to the south-west and south followed roads and was disputed until the mid 19th century; for the stretch along Hornsey Lane it lay near the watershed. West of Highgate the southern boundary with St. Pancras and Hampstead ran parallel with but south of Hampstead Lane. Hornsey manor, like Finchley manor to the west, was held by the bishop of London, whose lodge apparently straddled the western boundary.[6] As woods in the south and commons in the north also stretched across it, the boundary was probably established relatively late. East of where the parish ends in a point it enfolds the Freehold, a promontory of Friern Barnet.

Until the 19th century the only important internal boundary was the 'northern hog's back',[7] the ridge between Crouch Hill and Harringay (West) station, which separated Brownswood manor to the south from Hornsey manor and its dependencies to the north. New roads created divisions in the 19th century. The first was Archway Road, which is treated in the present article as the boundary between Hornsey and Highgate. Seven Sisters Road was a local government boundary from 1965.

The parish is hilly. Most of the lower ground lies on London Clay of great thickness. The Boulder Clay with its edging of glacial gravel at Finchley skirts the north-western boundary and south of Creighton Avenue and north of Woodside Avenue protrudes in a broad tongue, roughly corresponding with the summit of Muswell Hill, to the Wood Green boundary. The northern heights from Hampstead to Crouch Hill lie on Claygate Beds, except the Upper Chalk summit of Highgate Hill. Clissold Park is on the edge of the brickearth to the south-east.[8]

From Friern Barnet and the North Circular Road the land rises from 200 ft. to Muswell Hill, reaching 340 ft. at the corner of Queen's Avenue and Fortis Green Road. The 300-ft. contour encompasses land between the Alexandra Palace in Wood Green, Fortis Green near the Finchley boundary, and the corner of Muswell Hill Road and Woodside Avenue. A ridge roughly along the line of Muswell Hill Road and Southwood Lane rises towards Highgate, which stands at 426 ft. at the corner of North Road and Hampstead Lane. From the ridge the land falls only slightly to the west; to the east it descends more sharply, most steeply at Muswell Hill in the north, while to the south two spurs protrude eastward. Shepherd's Hill, the more northerly, extends nearly to Crouch End, with sharp descents to north and east. The other, the 'northern hog's back', is an extension of the northern heights from Highgate. It follows Hornsey Lane, forms the summits of Crouch End and Crouch (Mount Pleasant) hills, and extends at 200 ft. almost to Harringay (West) station, where it falls abruptly to the east and north. The highest point to the north is Hornsey Hill (150 ft.), which overlooks Hornsey High Street; the area immediately to the north, called the Campsbourne after a stream, lies at less than 100 ft. Eastern Harringay is the lowest part of the parish at 75 ft. South of the hog's back, the highest point is the 150-ft. knoll in Finsbury Park; much of Brownswood Park is below 100 ft.

[1] Except where otherwise stated, the following paras. are based on the sections below and on O.S. Maps 6″, Mdx. XI. SE., XII (1873, 1894–6, and 1920 edns.). The article was written in 1976–7; any references to later yrs. are dated. The authors gratefully acknowledge the help of Mrs. Gwynydd Gosling, Dr. Joan Schwitzer, Sir James Brown, and the headmaster of Highgate School, who have commented on parts of the article.

[2] *P.N. Mdx.* (E.P.N.S.), 123. For the district called Finsbury Pk., see below, p. 114.

[3] For the boundaries of Highgate as treated below, see p. 122.

[4] *Early Rec. of Harringay alias Hornsey*, ed. S. J. Madge (1938), 56.

[5] *Census*, 1881, 1901.

[6] *Early Rec. of Harringay*, 46.

[7] Ibid. 43, 50, 52.

[8] Geol. Surv. Map 1″, drift, sheet 256 (1951 edn.).

There were four principal streams. Bounds Green or Strawberry Vale (1956)[9] brook, a tributary of Pymme's brook, flowed eastward from Finchley into Friern Barnet, touching Hornsey at Irish Corner and the southern edge of north Hornsey detached. Stroud Green brook flowed from Islington across the southern tip of Hornsey. In 1826 Mutton brook rose west of Muswell Hill, skirted Gravel Pit wood, and crossed Archway Road. The Moselle stream, which rose east of Muswell Hill, in 1826 crossed Park Road, where it sometimes flooded to a depth of 4½ ft., and three times crossed Priory Road, draining into a lake behind Campsbourne Lodge north of High Street.[10] From there it flowed northward into Tottenham. It was more usually known as the Campsbourne, a name used for adjoining fields in the 17th century,[11] and in 1958 was said to flood the basements of houses every year.[12]

The New River, completed in 1613 to carry water from Chadwell and Great Amwell (Herts.) to Islington,[13] entered the parish north of Hornsey village and flowed south and then east, crossing the Moselle once and Hornsey High Street three times. Thence it meandered southward through Harringay, entering Tottenham north of Seven Sisters Road. On returning to Hornsey south of Manor House it followed an S-like course, crossing Brownswood to the east, flowing southward along the parish boundary into Islington and eastward across Mountgrove Road into Hornsey again. Along that stretch it crossed Stroud Green brook by a wooden aqueduct, which gave it the name of the Boarded River and was replaced in 1776 by a raised bed of clay.[14] Still in Hornsey, it crossed Green Lanes into Clissold Park and flowed westward along the south-western edge of the parish before recrossing Green Lanes into Islington. As the boundary of estates and a source of fresh water, particularly for cattle,[15] the river became a local asset and in 1861 the parish opposed the New River Co.'s diversion of it.[16] Thenceforth it flowed from Wood Green at a point slightly west of the G.N.R. main line into filter beds in Brownswood Park, which were connected with a pumping station east of Green Lanes. As Hornsey came to be built up, most of the New River was enclosed in pipes.

Most of the parish was apparently wooded in the pre-Conquest era, when Haring or Hær's people made an enclosure, later called Harringay and ultimately corrupted into Hornsey.[17] Another early hamlet was Crouch End; it was so named by 1375, after a cross which was the customary place for certain manorial business[18] and which had existed before that date.[19] Muswell Hill was so named after its mossy spring or well by 1159, when there was also a chapel there.[20] The empty south-eastern corner of the parish was called Stroud, denoting marshy ground covered with brushwood, in 1407 and later Stroud Green.[21]

The main feature of Hornsey's history before 1850 was the clearance of woods and commons, which covered half of the total area *c.* 1390 and a third *c.* 1648, and the expansion of farm-land. The predominant role of grassland rather than arable from 1550 kept the parish thinly populated, with settlement mainly confined to Hornsey village, Crouch End, and, from the mid 14th century, Highgate. From *c.* 1600 Highgate, with aristocratic residents, became increasingly urban, while the rest of the parish remained rural. Farm-land contracted from the mid 19th century in the face of building, which between 1870 and 1914 transformed Hornsey into a residential suburb for commuters to London. Social decline, already noticeable in 1911, became marked after 1945, until in 1978 only Highgate remained select.

Several times in the late Middle Ages Hornsey was the scene of national events. It was there that in 1388 the future lords appellant assembled forces to overawe Richard II[22] and that in 1441 Roger Bolingbroke and Thomas Southwell, priests, allegedly practised treasonable sorcery in collusion with Eleanor Cobham, duchess of Gloucester (d. 1454).[23] Henry VII was met there by the citizens of London after the battle of Stoke in 1487.[24] Distinguished residents not mentioned elsewhere in this article included John Lightfoot (d. 1675), biblical critic and Hebraist.[25] The émigré Magdalene, duchess of Uzès (d. 1799), was buried in Hornsey churchyard but was removed to Uzès *c.* 1838.[26] W. B. Tegetmeier (d. 1912), natural historian, lived from 1858 at several addresses in Fortis Green and Muswell Hill, where he had a model apiary.[27] John Whitehead (1860–99), ornithologist, was born at Muswell Hill.[28] Patrick McDowell R.A. (d. 1870), sculptor, lived at no. 34 Wood Lane,[29] W. E. Henley (d. 1903), poet and critic, lived at Stanley Lodge, Tetherdown, Muswell Hill, between 1896 and 1899,[30] Frederic Harrison (1831–1923), jurist, historian, and positivist, spent his boyhood at Belle Vue, Muswell Hill,[31] Henry Vivian, inspirer of the co-partnership housing movement, died at his home in Crouch End in 1930,[32] and Arnold Bennett (d. 1931), novelist, lived at no. 46 Alexandra

[9] Hornsey Boro. *Ann. Rep. of M.O.H.* (1956). The para. is based on *Rep. on Bridges in Mdx.*

[10] Potter Colln. 20/99. Springs in Clerkenwell detached, which drained into Tottenham, apparently were unconnected with the Moselle: B.L. Add. MS. 31323 BBB.

[11] *Court Rolls of the Manor of Hornsey, 1603–1701*, ed. W. McB. and F. Marcham (1939), 22, 52.

[12] *Hornsey Jnl.* 22 Aug. 1958.

[13] *V.C.H. Mdx.* v. 131. For the para. see also *Rep. on Bridges in Mdx.*; M.R.O., MR/DE Hornsey.

[14] Lysons, *Environs*, iii. 52.

[15] Bruce Castle Mus., D/PH/2A/1 (1850).

[16] Ibid. 2A/2, pp. 23, 25–8, 29–33.

[17] S. J. Madge, *Origin of Name of Hornsey* (1936); *P.N. Mdx.* (E.P.N.S.), 121.

[18] St. Paul's MSS., box A 62.

[19] Ibid.; C 146/3364.

[20] Madge, *Early Rec. of Harringay*, 61–3, 73.

[21] *P.N. Mdx.* (E.P.N.S.), 124.

[22] *Rot. Parl.* (Rec. Com.), iii. 357.

[23] *Eng. Chron. 1377–1461* (Camd. Soc. [1st ser.], lxiv), 57–60.

[24] Leland, *Collectanea*, ed. T. Hearne (1770), iv. 207.

[25] *D.N.B.*

[26] M.R.O., D.R.O. 20/B2/4.

[27] F. W. M. Draper, *Muswell Hill Past and Present* (1936), 17–18; idem. *Literary Associations of Hornsey* (1948), 12; *Country Life*, clvi. 47.

[28] *D.N.B.*

[29] Plaque on ho.

[30] *D.N.B.*; Draper, *Muswell Hill*, 19–20.

[31] Draper, *Muswell Hill*, 15–16; idem. *Literary Assocs. of Hornsey*, 12.

[32] M. Tims, *Ealing Tenants Ltd.* (Ealing Loc. Hist. Soc. viii), 37.

Road, Hornsey, in 1890.[33] Bridget, the Irish wife of Alois, half-brother of Adolf Hitler, was summoned for non-payment of rates at Highgate in 1939.[34] Dr. S. J. Madge (d. 1961), historian and local antiquary, from 1896 taught for many years at schools in Stroud Green and South Harringay.[35]

COMMUNICATIONS. The hills of Hornsey obstructed communication to north and south until the late 19th century. None of the main Roman roads out of London passed through the parish but by the early Middle Ages it straddled the Great North Road. According to Norden,[36] the main road had formerly entered the parish south of Crouch End and run north-north-westward through Muswell Hill to Colney Hatch, but because it was so bad had been moved farther west to ascend Highgate Hill and cross the park of the bishop of London. The bishop was charging a toll in 1318.[37] By 1354 there was a road from Highgate to Finchley, and Highgate was so called, presumably from the hill-top gate at which the tolls were paid.[38] The road from the foot of Highgate Hill was part of the main highway north by 1380, when the inhabitants of Islington and St. Pancras were granted pavage to repair it,[39] as they had been several times before.[40] Pavage was granted for the stretch from Highgate to Finchley in 1354[41] and the road was later maintained by the hermits of Highgate.[42] In 1526–7 the bishop spent money on the road[43] and in 1558 it was called the bishop's highway.[44] Responsibility had devolved on the tenants of Hornsey manor by 1577, when they were ordered to repair the road.[45]

The road from Highgate northward passed to a turnpike trust, later the Highgate and Whetstone turnpike trust, in 1754 and was of high standard after 1810.[46] The road up Highgate Hill itself was unsatisfactory: the arch of the Gatehouse obstructed traffic,[47] the tolls were difficult to collect,[48] and the gradient was so steep that it caused accidents.[49] In 1798 it was estimated that an extra horse per team was needed to ascend the hill.[50]

It was the steepness of the road, rather than the tolls or the negligible saving in distance,[51] which led in 1809 to a project for a tunnel from Upper Holloway through which traffic would be diverted east and north of Highgate. Work by the Archway Road Co. was authorized in 1810[52] and after the collapse of the tunnel in 1812 the company built Archway Road in a deep cutting in 1813. Hornsey Lane crossed it on a bridge 36 ft. high and the old route was rejoined at the Wellington inn.[53] Although tolls were more expensive than on the old road,[54] Archway Road was regarded as the only tolerable route northward.[55] It was little used by natives of Hornsey, Finchley, and Friern Barnet, who outnumbered all other users of Highgate Hill in 1846, doubtless because they were exempt from toll.[56] The tolls on Archway Road were unpopular[57] and in 1865 were possibly a deterrent to traffic.[58] Tolls on both roads were abolished in 1876[59] and by 1884 use of Archway Road had increased enormously.[60] The Archway itself, railed from 1885 to deter suicides,[61] was replaced by a wider iron bridge on which work began in 1897 and which was officially opened in 1900.[62] Traffic in Archway Road increased steadily and from the 1920s there were various schemes, which aroused widespread local opposition and resulted in a major widening in the early 1970s.[63] Further works were the subject of an inquiry involving much controversy in 1977,[64] when rush-hour conditions were very bad and many frontages along Archway Road were decaying.

Apart from the road through Hornsey park there were three north–south routes. Green Lanes, which extended along the whole eastern edge of the parish towards Bush Hill, Enfield, was turnpiked in 1789 in spite of Hornsey's opposition.[65] At Clissold Park it diverged from Norden's old north road, of which the stretches northward to Crouch End are called Mountgrove Road (Gipsy Lane in 1872),[66] Blackstock Road (still called Boarded River Lane in 1849),[67] Stroud Green Road, and Crouch Hill, which together were known as Tallingdon Lane between 1593 and 1795.[68] In 1795 Tallingdon Lane had only recently been a rough track,[69] which Blackstock Road remained in 1832,[70] and in 1850 the railway was built across it. North of Crouch End, Park Road (called Maynard Street from at least 1503 until 1854)[71] led to Muswell Hill, whence Colney Hatch Lane (Hollick or Halliwick Street or Lane 1359–1815 and Muswell Hill Lane by 1814)[72] ran into Friern Barnet parish.

33 *D.N.B.*; *Hornsey Jnl.* 17 Apr. 1953.
34 *Evening Standard*, 20 Jan. 1939.
35 *Hornsey Jnl.* 10 Feb., 17 Feb. 1961.
36 Norden, *Spec. Brit.* 15, 22.
37 *Medieval Rec. of Harringay alias Hornsey*, ed. S. J. Madge (1939), 65, 68.
38 *Cal. Pat.* 1350–4, 538; see also Norden, *Spec. Brit.* 21. A gateway was mentioned in 1365: *Cal. Pat.* 1364–7, 180.
39 S.C. 8/51/2529.
40 *Cal. Pat.* 1361–4, 409; 1374–7, 476; 1364–7, 180.
41 Ibid. 1350–4, 538.
42 See p. 178.
43 Guildhall MS. 10123/3.
44 St. Paul's MS. C (Sampson), f. 375.
45 Guildhall MS. 10312/92, m. 7.
46 See p. 9.
47 Lysons, *Environs* (Suppl.), 200; see below, p. 128.
48 e.g. in 1751: Guildhall MS. 10243, p. 121.
49 *Home Cnties. Mag.* v. 197.
50 Middleton, *View*, 101.
51 See below; *The Times*, 9 Aug. 1810; Brewer, *Beauties of Eng. & Wales*, x (5), 223.
52 50 Geo. III, c. 88 (Local Act).
53 Brewer, *Beauties of Eng. & Wales*, x (5), 222–3.
54 *The Times*, 9 Aug. 1813; Met. Bd. of Wks. *Mins. of Proc.* (1865), i. 340; Guildhall MS. 123701.
55 Met. Bd. of Wks. *Mins. of Proc.* (1865), i. 340.
56 Guildhall MS. 123701.
57 e.g. *The Times*, 19 Nov. 1822, 9 Oct. 1866.
58 Met. Bd. of Wks. *Mins. of Proc.* (1865), i. 340.
59 *The Times*, 29 Apr. 1876.
60 Ibid. 8 Oct. 1884.
61 Ibid. 3 Nov. 1885.
62 M.R.O., Hist. Notes 10/D2; ex inf. Mr. H. V. Borley.
63 M. F. Collins and T. M. Pharaoh, *Transport Organisation in a Great City* (1974), 266–74; review in *Hornsey Hist. Soc. Bull.* ix (Dec. 1975).
64 *The Times*, 20 Apr. 1977.
65 D. O. Pam, *Stamford Hill, Green Lanes Turnpike Trust* (Edmonton Hund. Hist. Soc. N.S. ii), 20; M.R.O., D.R.O. 20/C1/1, ff. 139–40v., 150.
66 Guildhall MS., Church Com. 156978.
67 M.R.O., D.R.O. 20/H/1.
68 Norden, *Spec. Brit.* 15; Lysons, *Environs*, iii. 60; Marchams, *Ct. Rolls*, 77.
69 Lysons, *Environs*, iii. 60.
70 Photos. of watercolours in Stoke Newington ref. libr.
71 C 146/7069; Guildhall MS. 10465/168, 54–5.
72 *Pub. Wks. in Medieval Law*, ii (Selden Soc. xl), 38; Guildhall MS. 10465/129.

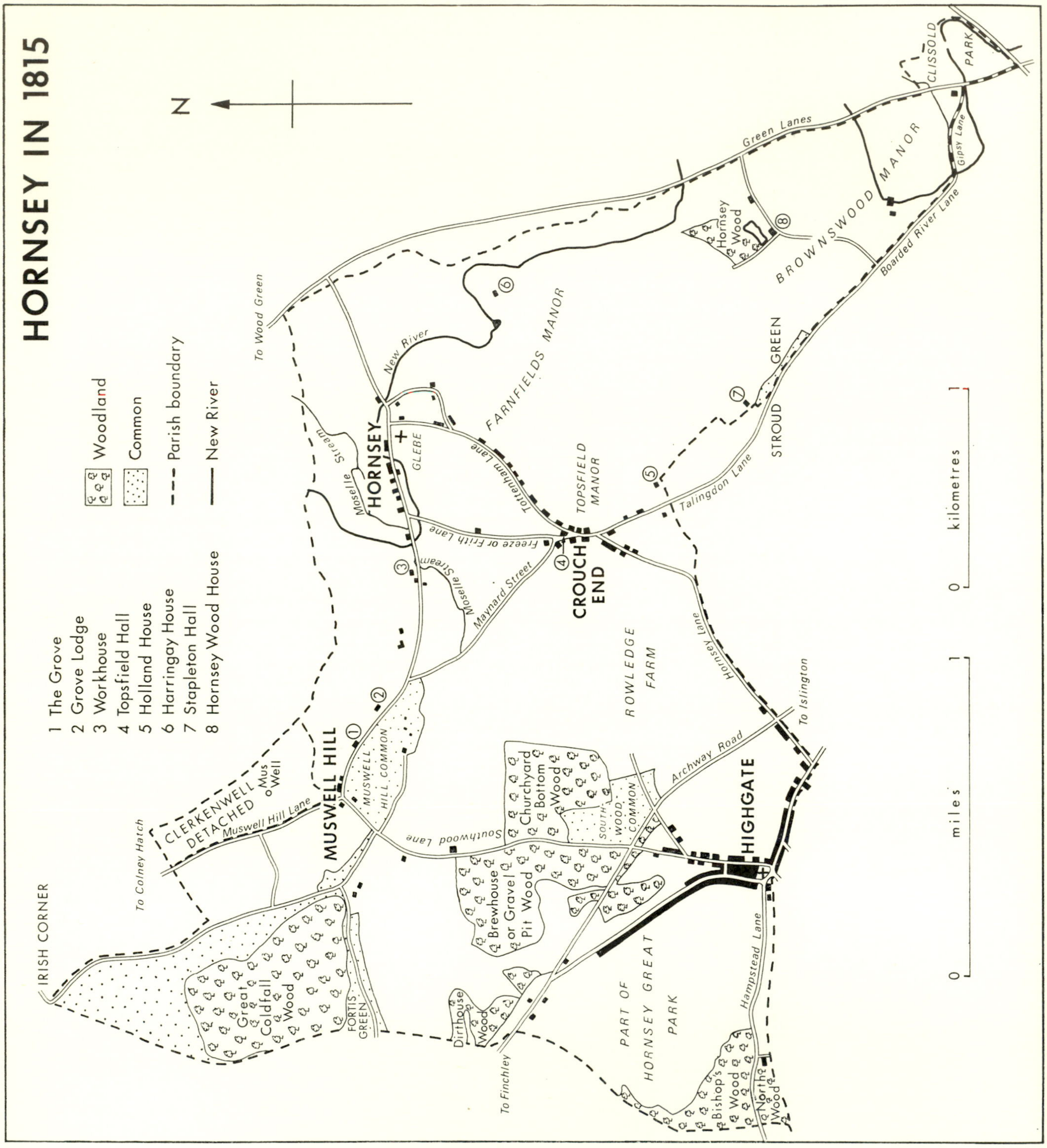

HORNSEY IN 1815
N
1 The Grove
2 Grove Lodge
3 Workhouse
4 Topsfield Hall
5 Holland House
6 Harringay House
7 Stapleton Hall
8 Hornsey Wood House
Woodland
Common
Parish boundary
New River
IRISH CORNER
To Colney Hatch
CLERKENWELL DETACHED
Mus Well
Muswell Hill Lane
MUSWELL HILL
MUSWELL HILL COMMON
Great Coldfall Wood
FORTIS GREEN
To Wood Green
Moselle Stream
HORNSEY
GLEBE
New River
FARNFIELDS MANOR
Tottenham Lane
Freeze or Frith Lane
Maynard Street
CROUCH END
TOPSFIELD MANOR
Talingdon Lane
STROUD GREEN
Hornsey Wood
BROWNSWOOD MANOR
Green Lanes
Gipsy Lane
Boarded River Lane
CLISSOLD PARK
ROWLEDGE FARM
Hornsey Lane
To Islington
Archway Road
HIGHGATE
Southwood Lane
Churchyard Bottom Wood
SOUTHWOOD COMMON
Brewhouse or Gravel Pit Wood
Dirthouse Wood
To Finchley
PART OF HORNSEY GREAT PARK
Hampstead Lane
Bishop's Wood
North Wood
miles
0
1
kilometres
0
1

Highgate was connected to Muswell Hill by Muswell Hill Road (the northern stretch of Southwood Lane from 1604 to 1898).[73] Coppetts Road, from Fortis Green via Irish Corner[74] to Colney Hatch, existed as a track in 1754.[75]

East–west communication was provided in the north by the road from Tottenham to Muswell Hill, later called in its various parts Turnpike Lane (Tottenham Lane in 1863), High Street, and Priory Road. From Muswell Hill, Fortis Green ran westward into Finchley. Along the southern boundary Hampstead Lane connected Hampstead and Highgate, and the latter was linked to Crouch End by Hornsey Lane, so called in 1604,[76] and Crouch End Hill (1619).[77] Other local roads included Tottenham Lane and Middle Lane (Frith or Freeze Lane from 1503 until 1810)[78] between Crouch End and the two ends of Hornsey High Street, Wood Lane which ran from Stroud Green Road to Green Lanes by 1577,[79] and Page's Lane, leading westward from Colney Hatch Lane and called in turn Jones's (1611) and Red House Lane.[80] In addition there were a few paths, notably Church Path from Tottenham Lane to Hornsey church, and various lanes were created leading to allotments under the inclosure award of 1815. The road system already existed by the 16th century.[81] Efforts to close the footpaths by the G.N.R., the Archway Road Co., and the New River Co. were vigorously resisted in the 1850s by the vestry's footpaths committee.[82]

In 1832 Seven Sisters turnpike road was built from Islington in a north-easterly direction across Stroud Green Road and Green Lanes;[83] it replaced Wood Lane *c.* 1866.[84] Some of the new streets built in the 19th century were important lines of communication: Endymion Road, built *c.* 1875 under the Finsbury Park Act of 1857, connected Stroud Green and Green Lanes north of Finsbury Park;[85] Ferme Park Road, *c.* 1885, joined Tottenham Lane and Stroud Green;[86] Shepherd's Hill and Wolseley roads were built by 1886 between Highgate and Crouch End;[87] Wood Lane, Highgate, was extended as Queenswood Road through Queen's wood to Park Road after 1896, and Wightman Road of *c.* 1885, parallel to Green Lanes, was intended as a major thoroughfare between Endymion Road and Turnpike Lane.[88] The northern tip of Hornsey touches the North Circular Road (1929). Within the parish communication is impeded by the railways, even those that are no longer in use; there is only one road-bridge over the main line between Stroud Green Road and Turnpike Lane.

In the 14th century Hornsey's roads were said to be impassable in winter,[89] although the Great North Road was maintained from pavage and bequests.[90] There were legacies towards Brokhersthill (perhaps Crouch Hill),[91] the way from Highgate to St. Mary's church, and other local byways.[92] Statute duty was often neglected in the 17th and 18th centuries, particularly in the period 1679 to 1686,[93] and in 1792 another attempt was made to exact labour rather than compositions.[94] Roads across the waste were liable to excavation,[95] especially in the 17th century, and in 1815 most of the roads were broad and ill defined.[96] The pond on top of Muswell Hill, which was a danger to travellers in 1820,[97] was filled in only in 1858, when the gradient was reduced,[98] and a large sum was spent in 1824 to make safe the Bank at Highgate.[99]

Maintenance also suffered because Hornsey shared the responsibility for many of its far-flung roads. Repairs to Stroud Green Road, remembered as bad in 1593,[1] or Hornsey Lane, the subject of indictments in 1736 and 1746,[2] were a frequent cause of dispute with Islington.[3] The part of Colney Hatch Lane bordering Clerkenwell detached was in disrepair in 1359 and 1399, when responsibility rested with the prioress of Clerkenwell.[4] Although Hornsey had never contributed to its repair before 1778,[5] the two parishes agreed in 1835 that each should maintain a stretch.[6] After long neglect the Clerkenwell section was repaired before 1891 but it remained bad[7] and in 1899 the whole road became Hornsey's responsibility. The roads dividing Hornsey detached from Islington, Stoke Newington, and Hackney were also disputed.[8] As Hornsey local board was uninterested in the repair or lighting of Seven Sisters Road (toll free from 1872), the boundary with South Hornsey was moved from the centre to the northern side of the road in 1874.[9]

Green Lanes in 1577 crossed Stroud Green brook by Stone, White, or Maiden bridge,[10] and the road between Crouch End and Muswell Hill crossed the Moselle in 1668 by two foot-bridges and two cart-bridges.[11] Under the Great

[73] Marchams, *Ct. Rolls*, 10; Guildhall MS. 12380.
[74] See p. 7.
[75] J. Rocque, *Map of Mdx.* (1754).
[76] Marchams, *Ct. Rolls*, 8.
[77] Ibid. 50, 108.
[78] C 146/7069; Guildhall MS. 10465/123.
[79] St. Paul's MS. C (II Nowell), f. 11; see also Rocque, *Map of Mdx.*
[80] Marchams, *Ct. Rolls*, 30 n.
[81] St. Paul's MSS. C (Sampson), ff. 100-1; (I Nowell), f. 129; (II Nowell), ff. 9v.–11, 151.
[82] Bruce Castle Mus., D/PH/2A/1.
[83] *V.C.H. Mdx.* v. 311.
[84] See below.
[85] 20 & 21 Vic. c. 150; 37 & 38 Vic. c. 97; 38 & 39 Vic. c. 179 (Local Acts).
[86] *Kelly's Dir. Hornsey* (1886).
[87] Ibid.; *P.O. Dir. Mdx.* (1882).
[88] M.R.O., Acc. 804.
[89] Norden, *Spec. Brit.* 15.
[90] Guildhall MS. 9171/5, ff. 91, 309.
[91] Ibid. 9171/2, f. 17; *Cat. Anct. D.* iii, C 3585.
[92] Guildhall MSS. 9171/2, ff. 156v., 201v.; 3, ff. 80v., 190, 223v.
[93] Cal. Mdx. Sess. Bks. 1644–52, 10; 1679–82, 24, 68, 75, 89; 1686–9, 2, 14, 82, 96; 1736–8, 30; D.R.O. 20/C1/1, f. 38.
[94] M.R.O., D.R.O. 20/C1/1, ff. 179–80v.
[95] Marchams, *Ct. Rolls*, 84.
[96] M.R.O., MR/DE Hornsey.
[97] M.R.O., D.R.O. 20/C1/4.
[98] Bruce Castle Mus., D/PH/4A/2, pp. 267 sqq.
[99] M.R.O., D.R.O. 20/C1/4.
[1] Norden, *Spec. Brit.* 15.
[2] M.R.O., D.R.O. 20/C1/1, f. 29; Cal. Mdx. Sess. Bks. 1736–8, 30.
[3] M.R.O., D.R.O. 20/C1/1, f. 169v.
[4] *Pub. Wks. in Med. Law*, ii. 38; K.B. 9/177/31.
[5] M.R.O., D.R.O. 20/C1/3; for its state see ibid. 20/H/1; 20/F3/1.
[6] Bruce Castle Mus., D/PH/2B/21.
[7] Ibid. D/PH/2B/40.
[8] M.R.O., D.R.O. 20/H/1, pp. 89–91.
[9] Shoreditch libr., HOR/2, pp. 226–8, 317, 334–5.
[10] St. Paul's MS. C (II Nowell), ff. 9v.–11. The rest of the para. is based on *Rep. on Bridges in Mdx.* and M.R.O., MR/DE Hornsey.
[11] M.R.O., D.R.O. 20/F1/1.

North Road, Mutton brook was culverted by 1826, when the Moselle also ran through culverts.

The coaches on the Great North Road which called at Highgate daily in the 18th century[12] were little used by local people. In 1816 three coaches ran to Holloway, Crouch End, Hornsey, and Muswell Hill from London and back daily but the earliest time of departure from Muswell Hill was 9 a.m.[13] In 1825 four coaches from Highgate and four from Hornsey made respectively ten and eight journeys to London every day.[14] In 1834 four coaches daily left the Globe, Moorgate Street, for Hornsey and three from Newgate and Tottenham Court Road for Highgate, but none was advertised to leave earlier than 11 a.m.[15]

In 1838–9 two omnibuses and a short-stage coach from Highgate and three omnibuses from Hornsey ran to the City daily.[16] By 1845 there was a regular service of nine omnibuses, the first leaving Highgate at 8.30 a.m.[17] Watkin's omnibuses conveyed people daily to their offices *c.* 1862,[18] by which date the Archway tavern at the foot of Highgate Hill had become the terminus for omnibuses from several parts of London.[19] In Southwood Lane in the 1870s Mary Kingsley observed pale-faced men with black bags passing morning and evening on their way to and from the City.[20] Hornsey village was served in 1845 by Baker's omnibuses and by Wilson's from Muswell Hill.[21] None the less the recommended way from London to Muswell Hill in 1846 was by the Finchley stage or omnibus and thence by cab.[22] Travellers from Fortis Green still depended on the Barnet mail omnibus along Finchley High Road in 1856.[23] In the 1840s the relatively few residents of Muswell Hill who worked daily in the City still travelled by four-horse carriage.[24] In the period 1851–5 the only omnibus between Hornsey and the City was that of Vass and Rogers, later of Rogers alone.[25] By 1862 it was no longer running owing to competition from the trains, although Wilson's omnibuses provided a ten-minute service from the Hanley Arms, Hornsey Road, Islington, until 1870[26] and others were running by 1874 from the Duke of St. Albans, Highgate Rise,[27] also just south of the parish.

The most important of the early railways in the parish was the Great Northern Railway, opened from Maiden Lane in 1850 (from King's Cross in 1852), with Hornsey as the first station from London.[28] Seven Sisters Road station, renamed Finsbury Park in 1869 and rebuilt in the 1870s, was opened in 1861 just across the boundary with Islington,[29] and a station at Harringay (West) in 1885.[30] Hornsey station was re-sited in 1866, when the old lines became sidings[31] and there were 16 trains a day to the City.[32] In 1875 the North London Railway started a service to and from Broad Street.[33] There were 54 trains a day from Hornsey to the City in 1885,[34] when they were very crowded during rush-hours,[35] and in 1904 the holders of season-tickets using the station each day numbered 3,500.[36] By 1884 there were cheap fares on workmen's trains.[37]

Under an Act of 1862 the Edgware, Highgate & London Railway Co., part of the G.N.R. from 1866,[38] opened a line from Finsbury Park to East Finchley, with stations at Crouch End and Highgate, in 1867.[39] Stroud Green station was opened in Stapleton Hall Road in 1881.[40] A branch line linked Highgate and the Alexandra Palace in 1873, was closed after the destruction of the palace in the same year, reopened in 1875 with a new station at Muswell Hill, and closed for varying periods on several occasions up to 1952. Cranley Gardens station, on the corner of Woodside Avenue and Muswell Hill Road, was opened in 1902.[41] In 1954 the whole of the line from Finsbury Park to Highgate and beyond was closed to passenger traffic; freight services continued to Muswell Hill until 1956 and to Highgate and Finchley until 1964, the track to the Alexandra Palace being taken up in 1958 and to Highgate in 1970.

From 1868 the Great Eastern Railway, and from 1870 the Midland Railway, ran passenger services to Fenchurch Street station along the Tottenham and Hampstead Junction Railway. There were stations called Crouch Hill from 1870 and at South Harringay, called Harringay Park (later Stadium), from 1880, each just outside Hornsey parish.[42] Although season-tickets to London were relatively cheap,[43] the line was more important as a link between the G.E.R. and the Midland Railway than as a commuters' route.[44]

An Underground line from Finsbury Park to Moorgate was built in 1904 by the Great Northern & City Railway Co.; it was taken over in 1913 by the Metropolitan Railway and in 1933 by the London Passenger Transport Board, becoming part of the Northern line in 1939, and was converted in 1975–6 for use by British Rail.[45] What was later part of the L.P.T.B.'s Piccadilly line

[12] *Home Cnties. Mag.* v. 197.
[13] J. Hassell, *Picturesque Rides and Walks* (1817), i. 37, 195.
[14] *Hist. Lond. Transport*, i. 391.
[15] *Pigot's Com. Dir.* (1834).
[16] *Hist. Lond. Transport*, i. 398.
[17] *P.O. Dir. Six Home Cnties.* (1845).
[18] *P.O. Dir. Mdx.* (1862); *The Times*, 15 Sept. 1934.
[19] *P.O. Dir. Mdx.* (1862).
[20] Draper, *Literary Assocs. of Hornsey*, 18.
[21] *P.O. Dir. Six Home Cnties.* (1845).
[22] Draper, *Muswell Hill*, 17.
[23] Nat. Freehold Land Soc. *Freeholders' Circular*, Mar. 1856.
[24] Draper, *Muswell Hill*, 16.
[25] *P.O. Dir. Six Home Cnties.* (1851, 1855).
[26] Ibid.; *P.O. Dir. Mdx.* (1862–70).
[27] *P.O. Dir. Mdx.* (1874).
[28] *Hist. Lond. Transport*, i. 47; G. H. Grinling, *Hist. of Gt. Northern Rly.* (1966), 90, 124.
[29] *Hist. Lond. Transport*, i. 129.
[30] M.R.O., Acc. 804; *Hornsey Hist. Soc. Bull.* v (1974).
[31] *Wonderful Lond.* ed. A. St. J. Adcock [1926–7], 524.
[32] R. O. Sherington, *Story of Hornsey* (1904), 32.
[33] Ex inf. Mr. H. V. Borley.
[34] M.R.O., Acc. 804.
[35] A. Bennett, *Hilda Lessways* (1911), 139.
[36] Sherington, *Story of Hornsey*, 38.
[37] *Hist. Lond. Transport*, i. 215.
[38] Grinling, *G.N.R.* 234.
[39] Except where otherwise stated, the para. is based on *Railway World*, xxviii (1967), 374–8, and information from G.N.R. and Brit. Rail rec. supplied by Mr. H. V. Borley.
[40] Sherington, *Story of Hornsey*, 38.
[41] Ibid. 37; Grinling, *G.N.R.* 455.
[42] *Hist. Lond. Transport*, i. 130–1, 349.
[43] *Finsbury Pk. Weathercock*, 26 Jan., 27 Apr. 1877.
[44] *V.C.H. Mdx.* v. 312.
[45] C. E. Lee, *60 Yrs. of the Northern* (1968), 10.

began in 1906 as the Great Northern, Piccadilly and Brompton Railway, was taken over by the London Electric Railway in 1910, and was extended to Arnos Grove in 1932, with stations close to the Hornsey boundary at Manor House and Turnpike Lane.[46] London Transport's Victoria line added another Underground route through Finsbury Park in 1968.[47]

What later became a part of the Northern line of the London Underground was opened in 1907 by the Charing Cross, Euston & Hampstead Railway Co. as a branch to Archway station (formerly called Highgate) at the bottom of Highgate Hill. It was absorbed by the L.E.R. in 1910 and by the L.P.T.B. in 1933, and was extended to Highgate, where a station was completed in 1941 beneath that of the G.N.R., and along the old G.N.R. tracks, converted for Underground use, to East Finchley.[48]

The North Metropolitan Tramways Co. began services from Moorgate to Finsbury Park and Green Lanes in 1872;[49] trams along Seven Sisters Road from 1885 provided a link with the line from London to Edmonton, and from 1887 the North London Tramways Co. also ran trams to Wood Green.[50] In 1905 the M.E.T. opened a route from Turnpike Lane via Hornsey High Street to the Alexandra Palace.[51] From the Archway tavern, linked by trams with the City by 1873 and with the west end of London by 1882,[52] a cable tramway, the first of its type, was taken up Highgate Hill in 1884,[53] making Highgate wood readily accessible.[54] The cable tramway was out of use from 1892 to 1897[55] and in disrepair in 1906–7, suffering from competition from the M.E.T.'s electric trams along Archway Road, started in 1905.[56] The cable tramway was closed in 1909 and reopened as an electric tramway in 1910.[57] Trolley-buses replaced tramcars in Archway Road and between the Alexandra Palace and Turnpike Lane in 1938,[58] but were withdrawn in the 1950s, as were the tramcars south from Manor House.[59]

Motor-buses were running from Muswell Hill to Finsbury Park in 1914 and 1926, and to Tottenham Hale via Crouch End in 1926.[60] In 1958 there were eleven motor-bus routes through the body of the parish and eight serving outlying parts.[61]

GROWTH BEFORE THE MID 19TH CENTURY.[62] Implements of the early Stone Age have been found in the three streams that cross northern, central, and southern Hornsey.[63] An early Bronze Age flint dagger of *c.* 1900 B.C. has also been found.[64] No Roman road in the parish is known but finds of coins at Highgate and Muswell Hill and a hoard at Cranley Gardens indicate settlement on the higher ground in the 3rd and 4th centuries A.D.[65] The hoard was hidden not far from where, in the north part of the modern Highgate wood, two kilns were operating in the late 1st century A.D.[66] As the sites of the discoveries were waste or woodland during the Middle Ages, it is unlikely that there was continuity of settlement between the Roman and early Saxon periods.

At an unknown date the parish was included in a grant of Stepney to the cathedral church of St. Paul and before 1066 it was divided between the bishop of London and the chapter,[67] represented then or later by a canon whose successors were prebendaries of Brownswood. The bishop's and prebendary's shares were divided by the watershed later marked roughly by Ridge and Dickenson roads. The enclosure which is indicated by the name Hornsey[68] was probably near where the church was built, at the corner of High Street and Church Lane. It was not far from the Moselle or from Green Lanes, perhaps already a major road.[69] As the village gave its name to the parish it was probably the earliest place to be inhabited. Later settlement may have extended westward and to the south, where glebe and copyhold lands lay, towards Crouch End.

Crouch End was the junction of four locally important roads, perhaps including the road from London to the north, and was the early centre of cultivation, where the farmsteads seem to have been grouped.[70] An estate of 1½ hide and 1 virgate in 1066 was apparently Topsfield, immediately to the east; farther east lay Farnfields, which was granted away by 1175, small open fields, and land cultivated by 1294 which was later part of the manor of Ducketts. To the west was Rowledge farm, the grange of the bishop, which was being exploited by 1318. A villein and 6 bordars dwelt near Crouch End as early as 1086.[71]

South of the northern hog's back Brownswood manor was on the low-lying area around Stroud Green, whose name was still apt in 1548, when bushes were to be cleared.[72] The high rent demanded for buildings may have contributed to their absence in 1577, when there were only three houses for the nine copyholders who together held 223 a.[73]

By 1406 there were 63 tenants of the manor of Hornsey, including such important local families as the atte Felds, atte Fryths, Mayhews, and

[46] C. E. Lee, *60 Yrs. of the Piccadilly* (1966), *passim*.
[47] *Hist. Lond. Transport*, ii. 347.
[48] Lee, *60 Yrs. of the Northern*, *passim*; see also *Railway World*, xxviii. 374–8.
[49] A. Aris, 'Urban development in Hornsey in the latter half of the 19th century', 15 (TS. in Bruce Castle Mus.).
[50] *V.C.H. Mdx.* v. 312.
[51] *Boro. of Hornsey, 1903–53*, ed. F. N. McDonald and W. B. Stevenson (1953), 9.
[52] *P.O. Dir. Mdx.* (1873, 1882).
[53] *Hornsey Boro. 1903–53*, 8.
[54] *The Times*, 11 Sept. 1884.
[55] Aris, 'Urban devel. in Hornsey', 16.
[56] Bruce Castle Mus., Hornsey Boro. *Min. Bk. 1906–7*, 408; ex inf. Mr. H. V. Borley. See above, p. 9.
[57] *Hornsey Boro. 1903–53*, 8.
[58] Ibid. 9.
[59] Stoke Newington M.B. *Official Guide* [1960]; Hornsey Boro. *Official Guide* [1961, 1963].
[60] *Hornsey Boro. 1903–53*, 9.
[61] Hornsey Boro. *Official Guide* [1958].
[62] Highgate village, in Hornsey and neighbouring pars., and the extension of Highgate into Hornsey, are described separately below.
[63] Madge, *Early Rec. of Harringay*, 15–17.
[64] Ibid. 17–18.
[65] Ibid. 21–4; see also *T.L.M.A.S.* xxiii. 165–9.
[66] *Camden Jnl.* iii. 100–1.
[67] *V.C.H. Mdx.* i. 120–1; Madge, *Early Rec. of Harringay*, 26, 35 sqq.
[68] S. J. Madge, *Origin of Name of Hornsey* (1936); *P.N. Mdx.* (E.P.N.S.), 121.
[69] *V.C.H. Mdx.* v. 309.
[70] The para. is based on the sections below.
[71] *V.C.H. Mdx.* i. 120; see below, pp. 140, 142–3, 150.
[72] St. Paul's MS. C (Sampson), f. 279v.
[73] Ibid. (II Nowell), ff. 9v.–11.

Maynards,[74] some of whose names were given to roads. Former tenements were already divided, in at least some cases into minute fragments. Wills of the 15th and early 16th centuries show local society dominated by resident priests and a few prominent tenants, among them Giles Eustace (d. 1495) and Geoffrey London (d. 1453) and his son John (d. 1461).[75] There was no resident lord whose household stimulated local supply, no known industry, and pilgrims to Muswell Hill, where there had been a chapel since at least 1159, were not economically significant.

Already by *c.* 1400 outsiders were acquiring land, especially Londoners like the Oughams and their successors as lords of Topsfield and aldermen John of Northampton (d. *c.* 1398), William Horne (d. 1496), and John Stokker (d. 1485).[76] In the 16th century Sir John Skeffington (d. 1525), alderman, Ranulph Cholmley (d. 1563), recorder, Sir William Rowe (d. 1593), lord mayor, and John Draper (d. 1576), brewer of London, all founded important local estates and the first three also built large houses. Other outsiders were Sir Julius Caesar (d. 1636), Master of the Rolls, who possessed the freehold mansion of Mattysons at Muswell Hill in 1619;[77] Sir Thomas Stapleton at Stroud Green;[78] and Alderman Nicholas Moseley (d. 1612) at Hornsey.[79] At least 90 Londoners held copyhold land of Hornsey in the 17th century, many of them at Highgate.[80]

In 1664, when Highgate contained 161 houses, there were only 62 in the rest of the parish (Hornsey Side).[81] The number had grown threefold by 1801 but in 1821 the proportions in Hornsey and Highgate sides had scarcely altered.[82] In Hornsey Side in 1664 there had been four houses with more than 20 hearths, eight with 10 or more, eighteen with more than 6, twenty-two with 3–5, and only eleven with 1 or 2. Nobody was too poor to be assessed.[83] In spite of such apparent prosperity there was considerable pressure of population, which resulted in overstocking of the commons and encroachment. Illegal cottages were a problem throughout the 17th century and as many as twelve were presented in 1654. Most formed an extension of Highgate over Southwood common but there were others at Muswell Hill common and at Fortis Green.[84] Between 1647 and 1815 the commons were much reduced and the woodland was halved.[85] In the fifteen years before 1795 *c.* 40 houses were built[86] and immediately before 1793, when the graveyard needed extension, there had been a substantial increase in population.[87] By 1791 the influx enabled landlords to raise the rents of cottages previously let to labourers, who were driven into the workhouse.[88] The newcomers, for whom the cottages were improved, may have been occupied in trade or handicrafts, which by 1821 and probably by 1801 employed more people than agriculture.[89]

In spite of the construction of the New River, no new settlements were established and immigrants were absorbed by existing communities, especially Hornsey village, which in 1795 was much larger than Crouch End.[90] In 1816 there were several big houses in Hornsey village but increasingly they came to be concentrated at Crouch End and at Muswell Hill,[91] where many of the largest had stood in 1664.[92] About 1773 it was a subject of satire that Londoners could retire to country seats in Hornsey and in 1782 businessmen retreated there for summer weekends.[93] In the early 19th century the parish was a place where the prosperous retired to comfortable villas, with which Hornsey was studded by 1858.[94] In 1834 42 gentry resided in Hornsey Side.[95]

In 1816 only Coldfall wood and wasteland lay north of Fortis Green and west of Coppetts Road.[96] Several houses stood near the junction of Fortis Green with Muswell Hill Road, where the scattered dwellings included the parish poorhouses and Upton Farm. The angle of Muswell Hill Road with Colney Hatch Lane was occupied by the Limes, a three-storeyed house with portico and two-storeyed wing, which was approached by a double carriage drive from impressive gateways. The large grounds extending to Tetherdown included a lake.[97] Opposite lay Muswell Hill pond, behind which a cluster of buildings included the stone-built Green Man inn[98] and Bath House academy, which was formerly the property of the Pulteneys. It also included the Elms, a squat three-storeyed house later improved by Thomas Cubitt (d. 1855) and with 11 a., part of which was to be laid out by Sir Joseph Paxton.[99] A short distance down the north side of Muswell Hill was the Grove, of three storeys and nine bays, with pedimented projections at each end.[1] It stood in 8 a., which contained a 200-yd. avenue of oaks, and by 1774 was occupied by Topham Beauclerk (1739–80), the friend of Dr. Johnson.[2] A little farther down stood Grove Lodge, also in wooded grounds.[3] Altogether eight seats in Muswell Hill were worthy of note in 1817.[4] Parallel with Muswell Hill a track known as St. James's Lane ran across a triangle of waste. Houses were already dispersed along it and at the foot was Lalla Rookh, a two-

74 St. Paul's MSS., box A 62.
75 Guildhall MSS. 9171/5, ff. 91, 309; 9171/8, f. 91v.
76 C 1/62/78–81; St. Paul's MS. C (II Nowell), f. 10.
77 W. Robinson, *Hist. Tottenham* (1841), i, map of 1619.
78 See p. 147.
79 Marchams, *Ct. Rolls*, 4 n.
80 Ibid. *passim.*
81 M.R.O., MR/TH/1.
82 *Census*, 1801, 1822; M.R.O., D.R.O. 20/E5/4/8.
83 M.R.O., MR/TH/1.
84 Marchams, *Ct. Rolls, passim.*
85 See pp. 151–3.
86 Lysons, *Environs*, iii. 57–8.
87 M.R.O., D.R.O. 20/C1/1, f. 191v.
88 M.R.O., D.R.O. 20/H/83; see p. 164.
89 *Census*, 1801, 1821; M.R.O., D.R.O. 20/E5/4/8.
90 Lysons, *Environs*, iii. 58.
91 M.R.O., MR/DE Hornsey.
92 M.R.O., MR/TH/1.
93 Guildhall libr., V/HOR, Satirical print 74; *Ambulator* (1782).
94 *Illus. News of the World*, 3 July 1858.
95 *Pigot's Com. Dir.* (1834).
96 For information relating to 1816 in the following paras. see M.R.O., MR/DE Hornsey.
97 J. Keane, *Beauties of Mdx.* (1850), 148–9; Hornsey libr., N. Mdx. Photo. Soc. no. 632.
98 Postcard in Hornsey libr.
99 B.L. Maps Dept., sales parts. (1880).
1 See plate facing p. 33.
2 Keane, *Beauties of Mdx.* 239–41; *Hornsey Hist. Soc. Bull.* Sept. 1975; M.L.R. 1779/5/494; M.R.O., MR/DE Hornsey; *Ambulator* (1787 and later edns.).
3 C. Nicholson, *Scraps of Hist. of a Nthern. Suburb of Lond.* (1879), 16; sales parts. (1939) in Hornsey libr.
4 Hassell, *Rides and Walks*, i. 194.

storeyed villa with wide verandah rented in 1817 by Thomas Moore, the poet.[5] Others were apparently cottages or huts, both single and in terraces.[6] The scattered village of Muswell Hill thus consisted mainly of detached villas in large gardens.[7] In 1787 it was said that nowhere within 100 miles of London was there a village so pleasant or with such varied views.[8]

Hornsey village in 1816 straggled along the later High Street and Priory Road. Building was mainly north of the road and more concentrated towards the east. West of Middle Lane there were only a few isolated houses, among them Jacob Warner's new red-brick seat of three storeys, which was considered too tall for its width. His family replaced it *c.* 1826 with a castellated Gothic mansion called the Priory.[9] Farther east the parish watch-house, school, and workhouse were grouped together and immediately beyond the first bridge over the New River stood two buildings, one of them apparently the Elms, a large single-storeyed villa that existed until 1939.[10] Beyond it in 1876, half-encircled by the Moselle, was the Rectory, shortly to be rebuilt. Farther on stood Campsbourne Lodge, with ten bedrooms and landscaped gardens, including a lake.[11] Beyond stood, as they still do, Eagle Court, a large four-storeyed house with a pedimented doorcase,[12] and the adjoining Eagle Cottage, a two-storeyed house of the early 18th century.[13] Manor House, with conservatory and large grounds,[14] evidently stood farther west, near a row of weatherboarded, two-storeyed shops. Archways led to Allen's and Preston's courts, where wooden three-storeyed cottages with mansard roofs were ranged around yards.[15] The fewer houses south of the road included the Three Compasses, a red-brick Georgian inn of three storeys with bay windows and a mansard roof.[16] Grove House stood back from the street, near Middle Lane, down which lay the large house later called Frieze House. St. Mary's church stood by itself on the corner of Church Lane, with the glebe to the south. Between the church and the houses to the north the street divided either side of a strip of waste, preserved in 1816 to maintain a rural appearance.[17]

In the early 19th century buildings were scattered along the east side of Tottenham Lane from near the junction with Church Lane to near the modern Ferme Park Road, where they became continuous. Harringay or Ferme farm-house was a stone building of two storeys and three bays, to which two bays had been added at one end and sheds at the other.[18] Since 1781 or earlier large houses had stood on the sites later occupied by Lightcliffe and Alresford houses. Beyond were Linslade House and Old Crouch Hall; the second, which already existed in 1681, was of brick with a thatched roof and had two storeys and dormers, mullioned windows, and a heavy oak doorcase. Next door, across the alley to Broadway chapel, was Lake Villa, a long low building with its upper storey weatherboarded and gable-end facing the street. Only Holland House stood beyond the junction with Crouch Hill. It was a three-storeyed bow-fronted villa erected after 1781.[19] In the angle of Crouch and Crouch End hills there was a jumble of shops and cottages with an inn and smithy. The cottages known as nos. 1–14 Wright's Buildings had probably already been built on the east side of Crouch End Hill and a further nine, later nos. 20–28, on the west.[20] There were houses on the west side of Crouch End Hill, including the King's Head, which abutted on Rowledge Farm, and farther north, opposite the corner of Tottenham and Middle lanes, Crouch End academy.[21] On the corner of Middle and Tottenham lanes Topsfield Hall was erected *c.* 1790 and another large house in 7 a. was on the corner of Park Road and Middle Lane.

There were no houses between Crouch End and Archway Road to the west and only the huge Harringay House between Crouch End and Green Lanes. To the south Stapleton Hall stood alone at Stroud Green, near the recently inclosed common and Hornsey Wood House, and several cottages were in Wood Lane. A path led south-west to a bridge over the New River. On the opposite side, facing Blackstock Road, had stood since before 1804 the old Eel-Pie house, later Highbury Sluice-House tavern, with riverside gardens by 1847 and the sluice-house itself immediately to the south.[22] Other than those and houses in South Hornsey detached, there was nothing south of the hog's back.

Much of the parish was empty in 1816. There was a density of 1·4 people per acre and the marked recent growth had been absorbed without difficulty by existing hamlets. The country houses were secluded in their grounds, the trees on the hills imparted a wild character,[23] and in Hornsey village the meandering New River enhanced the picturesque appearance fostered by the inhabitants. Rustic scenes were celebrated in art[24] and in verse.[25] Muswell Hill, too, was noted for its views[26] and the setting of Lalla Rookh was thought beautiful. In the east Harringay House, on a knoll in a curve of the New River, stood in a timbered park[27] and the

5 Thorne, *Environs*, 443–4.

6 Photos. (1935) in Hornsey libr.; Hornsey Boro. *Ann. Rep. of M.O.H.* (1930); see also Sherington, *Story of Hornsey*, 42.

7 Brewer, *Beauties of Eng. & Wales*, x (5), 213; *Ambulator* (1820).

8 *Ambulator* (1787).

9 Brewer, *Beauties of Eng. & Wales*, x (5), 211; Hassell, *Picturesque Rides and Walks*, i. 30; *Hornsey Jnl.* 12 Oct. 1933.

10 *Hornsey Jnl.* 2 Sept. 1939.

11 Keane, *Beauties of Mdx.* 254–5; British Land Co. *Reg. of Properties* (1867), 14.

12 *Hornsey Jnl.* 2 Nov. 1951.

13 Hist. Mon. Com. *Mdx.* (1937), 80.

14 See *Hornsey & Finsbury Pk. Jnl.* 14 July 1881; *Muswell Hill Rec.* 21 July 1881, 8 May 1905.

15 Hornsey libr., N. Mdx. Photo. Soc. nos. 598, 600, 602–5.

16 Potter Colln. 21/4–6.

17 M.R.O., D.R.O. 20/J/4.

18 Hornsey libr., N. Mdx. Photo. Soc. nos. 573–4. For the para. see also *T.L.M.A.S.* xiii. 393–407; M.R.O., Acc. 1289/2 (map).

19 Hassell, *Rides and Walks*, i, illus. facing p. 195.

20 They were erected in 1798–1829: M.R.O., Acc. 731/13; see also M.R.O., Acc. 1289/1/1.

21 Potter Colln. 20/52; see p. 196.

22 See p. 158.

23 Hunter, *Environs of Lond.* ii. 84.

24 Brewer, *Beauties of Eng. & Wales*, x (5), 210–11.

25 *Hornsey Hill, Middlesex; with other poems* (1841), v (copy in Hornsey libr.).

26 Brewer, *Beauties of Eng. & Wales*, x (5), 213; *Ambulator* (1820).

27 Keane, *Beauties of Mdx.* 48 sqq.; Hornsey libr., N. Mdx. Photo. Soc. no. 557.

enlarged Hornsey Wood House, where country pastimes were enjoyed, was apostrophized by poets.[28] Hill and woods separated the hamlets and even after the inclosure of the commons there remained 394 a. of wood, which was only halved over the ensuing century. Observers continued to stress the rural character of the parish: Hornsey itself was seen as a country village in 1876,[29] although by 1841 it had changed so much since 1802 that it might be considered almost part of London.[30] In 1848 it could be described as a metropolitan district,[31] although both in 1855 and 1889 it was excluded from the area of metropolitan government.

In 1821 there were 1,810 people living in 283 houses in Hornsey Side. By 1851 there were 3,925 in 661 houses, of whom 1,036 in 180 houses lived in South Hornsey detached.[32] Hitherto a relatively unimportant part of the parish, it was the closest to London and the first to be built up: building begun *c.* 1838 accelerated in the 1840s.[33] In the rest of the parish population was already growing in 1816 but may have been restrained by shortage of housing plots, a need satisfied at least in part by allotments inclosed from the commons.[34] James Wright the elder (d. 1828), carpenter of Crouch End, built the 'Victoria' and three cottages in Park Road on allotments at Muswell Hill by 1817,[35] and other houses were erected in Muswell Hill Road in 1818[36] and at Crouch End by 1820.[37] Most of the newcomers were probably poor, like those who arrived in large numbers between 1821 and 1831,[38] but there were also many new villas. In spite of the Brownswood Estate Acts of 1821 and 1826, which provided for building leases of the demesne,[39] Stroud Green remained empty. Only *c.* 1850 did speculative builders begin operations at Crouch End.

Fortis Green was still almost empty in 1816 but in 1851 there were 61 houses,[40] most of them on former wasteland between the road and Coldfall wood. The inhabitants were mainly labourers, who presumably erected the quaint wooden cottages.[41] Among large houses were the residence of the Haygarth family and the villa built for Benjamin Watson Jackson by Salvin, which was approached by an avenue of sycamores from Finchley High Road. Each had a park stretching to Highgate wood.[42] By 1851 there were 58 houses in St. James's Lane, many of them poor and 16 forming alleys at the foot of the hill.[43] Among the few large houses in Colney Hatch Lane the most substantial were North Lodge and Essex Lodge. Essex Lodge, built for a farmer, was a stuccoed detached villa on two floors with a pilastered porch.[44] Altogether 795 people lived north of St. James's Lane in 165 separate dwellings;[45] they were served by St. James's church, which stood by itself at the top of St. James's Lane, equidistant from the several settlements in the chapelry. In 1848 Muswell Hill was a place of elegant villas to which the wealthy retired, as in Thackeray's *Vanity Fair.*[46]

Just outside the St. James's district, cut off from it by woodland and from Highgate by Archway Road, part of what had been Southwood common had been laid out as Wood Lane. On either side small two-storeyed detached villas were constructed and near the eastern end the Priory was built *c.* 1848 for Dr. Henry Willmer.[47]

Hornsey had appeared ready for expansion in 1810, when a landowner had laid out roads on his estate between Middle Lane, Park Road, and High Street before offering it for sale.[48] Nothing had happened then and even in 1851 the most ambitious project consisted of the Nightingale tavern and 14 wooden cottages in Nightingale Place north of High Street.[49] The workhouse had been demolished, the Priory and Rectory rebuilt, and Manor Place, a three-storeyed terrace of eight weatherboard cottages with mansard roofs, stood west of Tottenham Lane;[50] there were probably other cottages. At Crouch End itself there were several new villas, among them Oakfield Villa in Crouch End Hill, a small two-storeyed house with a verandah at the rear,[51] the larger Oakfield House in Crouch Hill,[52] and Crouch Hall. The house in the angle of Middle Lane and Park Road was demolished between 1850 and 1854, when the 3-a. site was laid out as New Road and the narrow Back Lane, with 78 cottages, by Joshua Alexander and William Bradshaw. In 1847 they had acquired two smaller plots in Park Road, on which they had built the Maynard Arms by 1851 and 8 cottages by 1854.[53] James Wright the elder had erected 10 cottages on two plots, partly by building leases, between 1818 and 1829[54] and his son James (d. 1870) had erected 2 more by 1844.[55] The 12 cottages of Maynard Place, later Park Villas, were being built from 1846 under leases of Amelia Wright, widow.[56] There were also several smaller groups of cottages in 1851, when 41 houses stood in Park Road and another 45 were under construction:[57] there had been none in 1816. Even excluding Park Road, 1,048 people inhabited 167 houses in Tottenham Lane, Crouch End, and the area south and east of them.[58]

[28] Hone, *Everyday Bk.* (1838), i. 759–62; see below, p. 158.
[29] Thorne, *Environs*, 363.
[30] *Hornsey Hill*, v–vi.
[31] J. T. Smith, *Centralization or Representation?* (1848), iii.
[32] M.R.O., D.R.O. 20/E5/4/8; H/1 (loose, pp. 6–7); Bruce Castle Mus., D/PH/2A/1.
[33] Bruce Castle Mus., D/PH/2A/1.
[34] *Census*, 1821.
[35] M.R.O., Acc. 731/40.
[36] See p. 165.
[37] M.R.O., Acc. 1289/1/1.
[38] M.R.O., D.R.O. 20/E5/4/2B.
[39] See p. 145.
[40] H.O. 107/1702/1/2.
[41] H. B. Foley, *Our Lanes and Meadow Paths* (1887), 29.
[42] Keane, *Beauties of Mdx.* 201, 215–16.
[43] H.O. 107/1702/1/2; H.O. 107/1702/1/1.
[44] H.O. 107/1702/1/2; *Hornsey Jnl.* 1 Feb. 1952.
[45] H.O. 107/1702/1/2. It does not cover the area south of St. James's Lane.
[46] Draper, *Literary Assocs. of Hornsey*, 4.
[47] J. H. Lloyd, *Hist. Highgate* (1888), 278; Madge, *Early Rec. of Harringay*, 18.
[48] B.L. Add. MSS. 12545 d, e.
[49] H.O. 107/1702/1/1.
[50] H.O. 107/1702/1/3; cuttings in Hornsey libr.
[51] H.O. 107/1702/1/3; photos. in Hornsey libr.
[52] H.O. 107/1702/1/3.
[53] Guildhall MS. 10465/168, pp. 547–55; H.O. 107/1702/1/2; see also M.R.O., Acc. 1289/4 (plan, 1855).
[54] M.R.O., Acc. 731/8–10, 12, 20.
[55] M.R.O., Acc. 731/20.
[56] M.R.O., Acc. 731/49–54.
[57] H.O. 107/1702/1/2.
[58] H.O. 107/1702/1/2.

There were 160 communicants in Hornsey in 1547,[59] 119 adult males took the protestation oath in 1641,[60] and in 1801 there were 2,716 inhabitants. The population thereafter rose by nearly a quarter in each decade to 1851, when it numbered 7,135.[61]

GROWTH FROM THE MID 19TH CENTURY.[62] Modern Hornsey dates from the late 19th century. New building at first was confined to existing centres and was slow, perhaps partly because of poor sewerage,[63] until the 1860s. Country houses were being built until the 1880s but growth was such in 1875 that the 1871 census was no longer a reliable guide to population.[64] In the south part Brownswood Park was built up in the 1860s and 1870s and Stroud Green, begun in the 1860s, was almost complete in the 1870s. Harringay was a product of the 1880s, while Ferme Park and the Crouch Hall estate were partly built up by 1894. Eastern Hornsey and northern Crouch End were built up more slowly and western Hornsey, Muswell Hill, and Fortis Green had been little altered by 1891.

Attempts were made to establish select suburbs at Brownswood Park, Shepherd's Hill, and Muswell Hill, so that in 1904 Hornsey could be extravagantly compared with Kensington as North London's west end.[65] Elsewhere builders provided terraced and semi-detached houses for the poorer white-collared workers. The lack of local employment excluded the working class, except for domestic servants: in 1901 there were 7,852 people in service, of whom 6,598 worked indoors, 6,548 being female, and there were still 7,217 in 1931.[66] Hornsey attracted men from the metropolitan parishes who worked in the City[67] and in 1901 11 per cent of the population were clerks,[68] who needed to live near railway stations. Access to London was emphasized, as early as 1867 it was assumed that most men travelled thither by the G.N.R.,[69] and in 1886 Hornsey's seven stations were considered sufficient explanation for its expansion.[70] After 1873, when trains were running to all parts of the parish, building depended mainly on the availability of land. At Hornsey and Crouch End building was thwarted for decades by private landowners and Harringay's rapid growth took place only on the sale of a large estate. In the west the vast property of the Ecclesiastical Commissioners was not on the market until relatively late and much of it was preserved for recreation. The establishment of Finsbury Park as an open space ensured that Brownswood evolved independently from the rest of Hornsey. The high proportion of parkland partly explains why 'Healthy Hornsey' had the lowest death-rate on record in 1905 and the lowest of all large towns in 1906.[71] In 1906–7 the density of population was only 30·2 people per acre.[72]

The first public open spaces were Finsbury Park, opened in 1869, Highgate wood, opened in 1886, and Clissold and Waterlow parks, opened respectively in 1889 and 1891. All passed to the L.C.C. except Highgate wood, which remained with the City of London, and from 1899 Clissold Park lay within Stoke Newington.[73] Crouch End playing fields, bordering Park Road, were leased from the Ecclesiastical Commissioners by a company formed in 1892. Originally 18 a.,[74] they covered *c.* 40 a. by 1926[75] and 53 a., mostly serving private clubs, by 1956.[76] Hornsey recreation grounds originated in a plot of wasteland opposite the Rectory, acquired by the local board in 1887, and in *c.* 8 a. along Middle Lane, which were to be laid out as gardens in 1894.[77] A field beside Priory Road was also acquired in 1921–2[78] and, with a further 9 a. acquired in 1926, formed Priory Park.[79] Queen's wood, an eastern extension of Highgate wood, was so named on its acquisition by Hornsey U.D. in 1898.[80] By 1918 over 460 a. or 16 per cent of the borough consisted of open spaces; they included 17 a. of allotments, Highgate golf course, and 38 a. of Alexandra Park.[81] Coldfall wood was added in 1934[82] and on the north bordered Muswell Hill sports ground, a reclaimed rubbish tip, from 1962.[83]

Muswell Hill and Fortis Green were affected by the G.N.R.'s stations at Finchley (1867) and Muswell Hill (1872) and by the opening of Alexandra Park in 1872. The Alexandra Palace's workforce, however, was housed in Friern Barnet[84] and few visitors to the palace chose to settle. Near the western end of Fortis Green was the Woodlands, erected regardless of expense *c.* 1863 for Frederic Lehmann and visited by many leading literary and musical figures.[85] At Fortis Green 20 houses were built in the decade to 1861,[86] most of them probably on the estate south of the road acquired in 1852 by the National Freehold Land Society and called Haswell Park. Intended for superior villas,[87] it was divided into 180 plots facing Eastern, Western, and Southern roads and the paths later called Haswell Passage, Francis Road, and Shakespeare Gardens.[88] Some roads existed by 1855[89] and in 1856 it was claimed that all lots were fenced

59 E 301/34 no. 129.
60 H.L., Mdx. Protestation Rets.
61 *Census*, 1801–51.
62 Except where otherwise stated, the following paras. are based on sections below and on O.S. Maps 6″, Mdx. XI. SE., XII (1873, 1894–6, 1920 edns.). The growth of Highgate is treated separately below.
63 See p. 169.
64 Hornsey sch. bd. *Mins. 1875*, 4.
65 *Hornsey Jnl.* 30 Apr. 1904.
66 *Census*, 1901, 1931; see also Hornsey Housing Trust, *Chairman's Rep.* (1949).
67 *The Times*, 7 Dec. 1886.
68 *Census*, 1911.
69 *Hornsey Hornet*, 15 Jan. 1867.
70 *The Times*, 7 Dec. 1886.
71 Hornsey Boro. *Ann. Rep. of M.O.H.* (1905, 1906); see also ibid. (earlier and later edns.); Hornsey loc. bd. *Ann. Rep. of M.O.H.* (1892); *Hornsey Boro. 1903–53*, 31.
72 Hornsey Boro. *Min. Bk. 1906–7*, 456.
73 J. J. Sexby, *Munic. Pks. of Lond.* (1898), 311, 320, 577; *Kelly's Dir. Essex, Herts. and Mdx.* (1908).
74 Prospectus in Hornsey libr.
75 *Hornsey Jnl.* 9 May 1926.
76 Hornsey Boro. *Official Guide* [1956].
77 Hornsey Loc. Bd., 'Rep. of Property of Bd.', Bruce Castle Mus. O/H/3/6.
78 *Hornsey Jnl.* 9 Nov. 1928.
79 *Hornsey Boro. 1903–53*, 10; F. E. Cleary, *Beauty and the Boro.* (1904), 24.
80 See p. 154.
81 *Better Health*, May 1928.
82 *Hornsey Boro. 1903–53*, 25.
83 *Hornsey Jnl.* 30 Sept. 1960, 7 Sept. 1962.
84 See p. 11.
85 Draper, *Literary Assocs. of Hornsey*, 6–8.
86 R.G. 9/791/2.
87 Nat. Freehold Land Soc. *Freeholders' Circular*, Mar. 1852.
88 M.R.O., Acc. 525/5.
89 Bruce Castle Mus., D/PH/4A/1, pp. 299, 369.

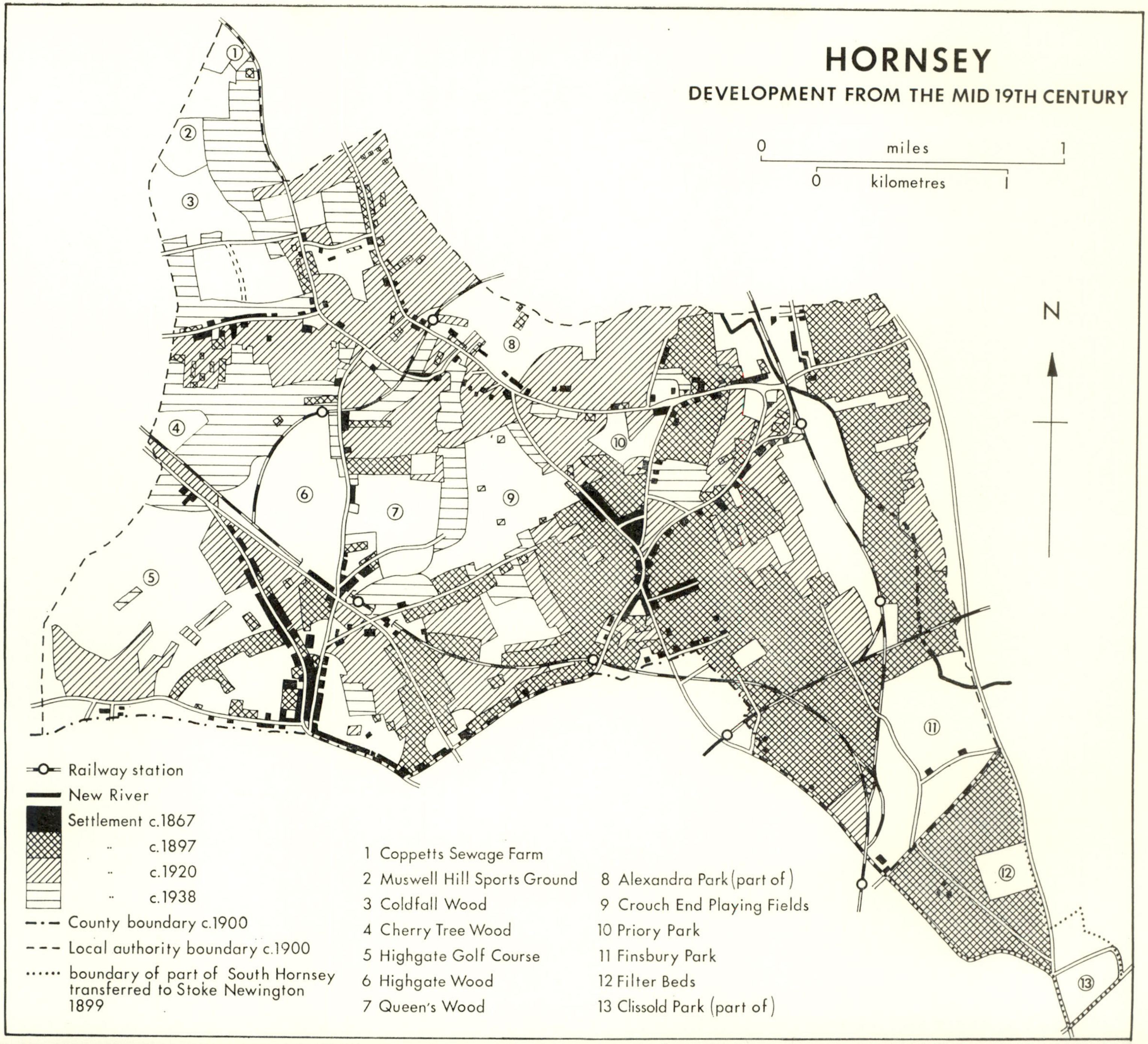

HORNSEY
DEVELOPMENT FROM THE MID 19TH CENTURY
0 miles 1
0 kilometres 1
N
Railway station
New River
Settlement c.1867
" c.1897
" c.1920
" c.1938
County boundary c.1900
Local authority boundary c.1900
boundary of part of South Hornsey transferred to Stoke Newington 1899
1 Coppetts Sewage Farm
2 Muswell Hill Sports Ground
3 Coldfall Wood
4 Cherry Tree Wood
5 Highgate Golf Course
6 Highgate Wood
7 Queen's Wood
8 Alexandra Park (part of)
9 Crouch End Playing Fields
10 Priory Park
11 Finsbury Park
12 Filter Beds
13 Clissold Park (part of)

and connected to main services.[90] In spite of auctions in 1852 and 1856[91] some lots were unsold in 1858;[92] there were only 28 houses in 1871,[93] vacant plots remained in 1896, and the southern part of the estate was never built on. The delay in building may have stemmed from poor communications via Finchley High Road.[94] In 1871 twelve houses, six built during 1867–8, stood north of Fortis Green[95] and in 1896 two large houses alone lay between Eastern and Muswell Hill roads. Building had spread up both sides of Tetherdown since 1871,[96] when eight houses stood in Page's Lane.[97]

At Muswell Hill itself Bath House and the Grove made way for Muswell Hill station,[98] and a three-storeyed terrace was erected facing the road by the Imperial Property Investment Co. as its Grove House estate.[99] Farther down the hill Grove Lodge was rebuilt in 1854 as a large two-storeyed stuccoed house.[1] The number of houses in Colney Hatch Lane grew slowly and in 1871 most were large detached villas like Carisbrooke Cottage, built by 1861, Wood Villa, Milford Lodge, and Laurel Bank Cottage.[2] In Clerkenwell detached 12 a. were laid out in small plots for building *c.* 1878. Two plots facing the main road were built on and four more houses were never finished.[3] It was probably on the same estate that *c.* 1879 plots were bought cheaply by people who squatted rate free in shanties until at least 1888.[4] Not all the 12 a. of *c.* 1878 had faced Colney Hatch Lane. About the same time land formerly part of Alexandra Park and stretching eastward into Wood Green was acquired by the London Financial Association. In 1884 Muswell Avenue and Muswell and Coniston roads had been laid out and the last 125 lots west of Muswell Avenue were auctioned. Only two houses had been erected and the company evidently had difficulty in selling plots.[5] In 1891 only 54 houses with 318 residents stood in Clerkenwell parish[6] and little change had occurred by 1896. Muswell Hill was still a place where the rich built seats.[7]

At Hornsey village, after the opening of Hornsey station, building in the late 1860s was proceeding as rapidly as land became available. By 1861 the village had spread east of the railway over the former Cocksfields.[8] In 1861 sixteen houses stood in Clarendon Road, where the gas-works was moved in 1867, and the first house fronting Turnpike Lane itself was let in 1860.[9] The Hornsey Park estate, which by 1881 comprised the later Hornsey Park, Alexandra, Ravenstone, and Brook roads, Malvern Parade, Park Ridings, and the Avenue in Hornsey and Tottenham,[10] was being laid out by 1869;[11] in 1879 it belonged to the Imperial Property Investment Co.[12] Six-roomed houses there were selling well in 1880,[13] and by 1896 the whole district was built over; Turnpike Lane was coming to be a major thoroughfare in the 1880s but even in 1900 it contained only 30–40 houses.[14] West of the G.N.R. the Birkbeck Freehold Land Co. had acquired the Grove House estate, on the corner of Middle Lane and High Street, by 1866 and had built up the frontages to Middle Lane and the new Grove House and Birkbeck roads.[15] The estate had been bounded on three sides in 1855 by the land of John Holland, which adjoined the Three Compasses inn.[16] In 1865 the National Freehold Land Society acquired his estate[17] on which Haringey, Lightfoot, St. Mary's, Westfield, Rectory, and Holland roads were constructed. By 1870 street lighting could be supplied to St. Mary's estate, perhaps the area known as Lister Park between High Street and Church and Tottenham lanes.[18] Campsbourne Lodge and 24 a. north of High Street were acquired in 1866 by the British Land Co.,[19] which laid out the Campsbourne estate of small terraced and semi-detached houses in the Campsbourne and in Newlands, Campsbourne, Boyton, and Myddelton roads. By 1871 1,294 houses, more than a quarter of them uninhabited, had been built at Hornsey, 117 were under construction, and the population had risen to 3,116.[20]

Despite near-by building the village had changed little in 1876 when viewed from High Street, which remained broad and tree-lined;[21] nothing had been built west of the Rectory and Middle Lane or south of the church on the glebe, which the rector refused to sell. Although he had started leasing land by 1881,[22] the glebe was only partly built up in 1896, when Middle Lane still marked the eastern limit of building. Farther south growth was halted by the grounds of the new Rokesley House, Hermiston Lodge, and Elm House.[23] In 1887 builders could not obtain freehold sites because all were held by one proprietor.[24] In Hornsey village there were 62 people to the acre in 1906–7.[25]

At Crouch End, where building strained the sewerage system, Christ Church replaced the

90 *Freeholders' Circular*, Mar. 1856.
91 Ibid. 92 Ibid. Sept. 1858. 93 R.G. 10/1336.
94 *Freeholders' Circular*, Mar. 1856.
95 H. Warner, *Acct. of Chars. of Par. of Hornsey* (1889), 13; R.G. 10/1336.
96 R.G. 10/1336; stone on bldg.
97 R.G. 10/1336.
98 Sherington, *Story of Hornsey*, 84.
99 Hornsey libr., sales parts.
1 Min. of Town and Country Planning, List of Bldgs. (1950).
2 R.G. 10/1336; R.G. 9/791/2; *N. Mdx. Chron.* 26 Jan. 1892; see also datestones 1881 and 1898 (the Firs).
3 *N. Mdx. Chron.* 1 Sept. 1888.
4 Hornsey libr., sales parts.
5 Sales parts. in Hornsey libr.; undated map in B.L., Maps Dept. Some plots were offered several times.
6 *Census*, 1891.
7 Draper, *Literary Assocs. of Hornsey*, 27.
8 Potter Colln. 20/3.
9 R.G. 9/791/1; M.R.O., Acc. 969/70.
10 Potter Colln. 20/3.
11 Bruce Castle Mus., O/H/1/1, pp. 60, 180.
12 Ibid. 1/5, pp. 74–5.
13 *Finsbury Pk., Crouch Hill & Hornsey Ho. and Property Reg.* 1 June 1880.
14 *N. Lond. Mercury*, 10 Feb. 1900.
15 Bruce Castle Mus., D/PH/2A/2, pp. 148–9; Potter Colln. 20/100.
16 Guildhall MS. 10465/170, pp. 450–4.
17 Bruce Castle Mus., D/PH/4A/4, p. 175; *Freeholders' Circular*, Apr. 1865.
18 M.R.O., Acc. 880/47, p. 360; *P.O. Dir. N. Suburbs* (1880).
19 J. C. Marriott, 'Hist. . . . of Hornsey' (1906), 517 (MS. in Bruce Castle Mus.); Potter Colln. 20/99; *Freeholders' Circular*, Sept. 1866.
20 *Census*, 1871.
21 Thorne, *Environs*, 363; Hornsey loc. bd. *Min. Bk. 1892–4*, 659.
22 *The Times*, 10 Sept. 1884.
23 For their hist. see *Hornsey Jnl.* 10 Aug. 1934; they did not exist in 1851: H.O. 107/1702/1/1.
24 J. R. Kellett, *Impact of Rlys. on Victorian Cities* (1969), 418 n.
25 Hornsey Boro. *Min. Bk. 1906–7*, 456.

smaller Broadway chapel in 1862 but itself needed a new aisle by 1866.[26] Both villas and labourers' cottages sprang up. In 1856 there were already 156 houses in Park Road, 29 in New Road, and 5 in Middle Lane.[27] Park Villas and Park Terrace, on either side of Park Road, and Richmond Villas, west of Middle Lane, extended north of New Road by 1871.[28] The ribbon of housing stretched little farther north in 1896, when it was barred by the Chestnuts in Middle Lane, but substantial terraces extended as far as Palace Road. As early as 1869 houses had been erected in the Grove[29] and 57 cottages had been built by Thomas Beall in the Grove, Willow Walk, and Park Road.[30] West of Tottenham Lane, north of the Topsfield Hall estate, the road was lined with shops and cottages as far as Holy Innocents' church (1877).[31] Likewise Crouch End Hill, where Christ Church stood by itself in 1869, was lined on both sides with humble shops of brick or weatherboard with mansard roofs as far as the church *c.* 1885.[32] Nevertheless Crouch End was still a pleasant, even rural, place in 1876.[33] Well-spaced houses extended along the eastern side of Tottenham Lane through Crouch End and up Crouch Hill, the newer ones in Crouch Hill including Amedee Villa, home of Ambrose Heal, and Cecile House.[34] At the summit but standing back from the road in 2 a. was Womersley House, apparently built for the London draper Peter Robinson, who lived there in 1871.[35] At right angles to Crouch Hill, Haringey Park had been laid out by 1855, with 15 large houses in 1861 and 25 in 1871.[36] Another large house, the Limes, stood by 1869 at the top of Crouch End Hill opposite Crouch End station. The opening of the station had contributed by 1871 to the transformation of Hornsey Lane, where 21 detached houses joined Hornsey Lane Farm, and to the construction of Crescent Road.[37]

In 1855 the Ecclesiastical Commissioners obtained possession of 156 a. of the Brownswood demesne. Bounded by Seven Sisters and Blackstock roads and by Green Lanes and wholly undeveloped, the land's accessibility from London made it ideal for building. The road system had been decided by 1861[38] and plots were let to individual builders. John Brookes Porter, later chairman of South Hornsey local board[39] and a bankrupt, built the earliest houses from 1862. Most of the frontages of Seven Sisters Road and Green Lanes were built up in the 1860s, the bulk of Queen's Road (later Drive) and King's Road (later Crescent) were completed by 1871,[40] and the remainder of the estate, except for Prince's (later Princess) Road, was built up in the 1870s. Green Lanes and Brownswood and King's Road were to contain detached or semi-detached houses and Queen's Road was to have terraces or semi-detached houses, but the builders were more lavish. Stressing the good communications and rural setting, Porter advertised four-storeyed terraced houses in both Queen's and King's roads;[41] houses in Green Lanes and Seven Sisters Road were even larger. Brownswood Park, as the district was called, was regarded as a particularly good part of a select suburb.[42] The copyhold land on the east became the Sluice-House estate,[43] with similar houses built, for the most part, by the same men. The first houses were completed in 1869 and at least 84 were ready in 1873.[44] In 1894, when the area had been built up for five years, there were 1,077 houses with 7,359 inhabitants in the 164 a. of Brownswood Park.[45]

Stapleton Hall was the only house in Hornsey between Crouch End and Seven Sisters Road as late as 1861[46] but the streets of Islington were approaching Stroud Green Road, along the east side of which stood several large houses. Rapid growth followed the opening of Seven Sisters, Crouch Hill, and Crouch End stations. In 1863 Joseph Lucas of Stapleton Hall leased land for building[47] and in 1868 Mount Pleasant Road had been built from the corner of Stapleton Hall and Stroud Green roads over the T. & H.J.R.[48] to meet Mountview Road, which already crossed the railway farther north. There were 25 houses in Mount Pleasant Road in 1871.[49] Stapleton Hall Road had been laid out by 1876 and Ferme Park Road was driven over the ridge towards Tottenham Lane in 1880.[50] To the south the grid of streets was already planned in 1868[51] and Osborne and Albert roads and Upper Tollington Park contained 49 houses in 1871,[52] by which time the roads in the angle of Stroud Green Road and the G.N.R. were largely built up.[53] In the 1870s they were considered to be in the ill-defined area called Finsbury Park, which included Brownswood Park and parts of Islington. By 1877 Finsbury Park was a growing neighbourhood[54] with a strong community feeling and its own newspaper[55] and was inhabited mainly by commuters with third- and second-class season tickets.[56]

26 M.R.O., D.R.O. 23/I/C1/1.
27 H. M. Ramsay, *Rep. on Hornsey Village Drainage* (1856) in Hornsey libr.
28 R.G. 10/1336.
29 *N. Mdx. Chron.* 30 Oct. 1869.
30 M.R.O., Acc. 949/4a. Most of the hos. were leased to the Elders in 1894: sales parts. in Hornsey libr.
31 *Hornsey Hist. Soc. Bull.* v (Dec. 1974); Potter Colln. 21/8 (photos.).
32 Photos. in Hornsey libr.
33 Thorne, *Environs*, 365; see also C. R. Watson, *Hundred Yrs. of Crouch End, 1862–1962* (1962), 11; Hornsey loc. bd. *Min. Bk. 1892–4*, 659.
34 Hornsey libr., sales parts.
35 R.G. 10/1336; see also *N. Mdx. Chron.* 30 June 1900; plan (1886) in Hornsey libr.
36 *P.O. Dir. Six Home Cnties.* (1855); R.G. 9/791/3; R.G. 10/1336.
37 R.G. 10/1336; see also M.R.O., Acc. 880/42, pp. 383, 402, 446.
38 R.G. 9/791/4.
39 The para. is based on Church Com. deeds at the Guildhall Libr.
40 Shoreditch libr., HOR/2, p. 460.
41 R.G. 10/1335.
42 Stoke Newington ref. libr., sales parts. (including illus.).
43 W. Macqueen-Pope, *Back Numbers* (1954), 25–34; 'Rep. on applic. for triennial retirement of cllrs.' in M.R.O., *Reps. of Local Inqs.* (1895–1907).
44 R.G. 10/1335; for what follows see Shoreditch libr., HOR/1–2.
45 'Rep. on div. betw. Hornsey and S. Hornsey dists. 1894', in M.R.O., *Reps. of Local Inqs.* (1889–1907).
46 R.G. 9/791/4.
47 M.R.O., Acc. 616/15.
48 M.R.O., Acc. 616/16, 16d.
49 R.G. 10/1335.
50 M.R.O., Acc. 237/2.
51 Bruce Castle Mus., O/H/1/1, p. 136.
52 R.G. 10/1335.
53 Ibid.
54 *Finsbury Pk. Weathercock*, 2 Feb. 1877; see also ibid. 15 Feb., 16 Oct. 1876.
55 Ibid. 15 Feb. 1876; 2 Feb., 9 Feb. 1877.
56 Ibid. 26 Jan. 1877.

When Hornsey was divided into wards in 1894 the southern part became Finsbury Park ward and the area farther north Stroud Green ward. Endymion, Lothair, and adjoining roads carved out of the park were completed in 1885 by the British Land Co.[57] All roads south of the ridge existed by 1880,[58] when Holy Trinity church was consecrated. Building continued as late as 1893 in Stapleton Hall Road[59] and in 1896 the area was virtually built up.

From 1840[60] the whole area between Green Lanes, Turnpike Lane, the G.N.R., and the T. & H.J.R., in both Hornsey and Tottenham, was attached to Harringay House. The land was undulating, wooded, and crossed by the meandering New River.[61] Both north of Turnpike Lane and south of the T. & H.J.R. sites were prepared by the British Land Co., which bought the whole estate during 1880–1.[62] The land was laid out on a grid between Green Lanes and the parallel Wightman Road, with a total of 23 streets, and was divided into Harringay Park estate in the south and Hornsey Station estate in the north. Only half was laid out in 1885 but the first auction of plots in the southern portion had been in 1881 and in the northern part in 1882. Sewerage was difficult because of the contours and the New River had to be diverted into tunnels. Advertising stressed access to London, in particular via Hornsey and Harringay (West) stations, the second of which was provided at the company's insistence. Uniform two-storeyed terraced or semi-detached houses were erected throughout and were inhabited mainly by clerks in 1901. By 1899, when building was completed, there were 1,016 houses in the north part and 1,400 in the south. South Harringay ward had 53 people to the acre in 1906–7 and North Harringay ward, which probably included the area north of Turnpike Lane, had 81 per acre.[63]

After the growth of Stroud Green and Harringay the fields north of the ridge, henceforth called Ferme Park, were soon taken for building. Of the roads across the ridge before 1883[64] the most important was Ferme Park Road itself, which had been laid across Farnfields manor from Tottenham Lane to Stapleton Hall Road by 1880.[65] By 1884 Weston Park, Bourne, Landrock, and Gladwell roads were laid out between it and the Elder estate to the west and in 1888 plots there were for sale.[66] Large semi-detached houses in Elder Avenue and Weston Park were ready in 1889 and Cecile Park was constructed by 1892.[67] Both Cecile and Weston parks were planned by J. Farrer, architect to the Elder family.[68] The whole district west of Ferme Park Road was built over by 1896 but progress farther east was slower. Hornsey Vale, said to have been the grounds of a house called Abyssinia facing Tottenham Lane, was laid out as Spencer, Gordon, Hanbury, Canon, Abyssinia, Enfield, and Montague roads by 1880, when over 200 terraced houses had been built.[69] Eastern Weston Park and the whole of Ridge and Oakworth (later Nelson) roads were built by 1884.[70] Some of Farnfields manor became the Ferme Park estate of the Streatham and Imperial Estate Co. by 1888, when it was selling plots in Nelson Road,[71] and the eastern part, with the grounds and house of Rathcoole facing Tottenham Lane, formed the Rathcoole estate of J. C. Hill stretching back to Ridge Road. Four three-storeyed shops in Milman Terrace, Tottenham Lane, were built in 1889[72] and in 1893 Hill constructed a three-storeyed terrace of shops near the junction with Church Lane.[73] Altogether he planned 257 houses in Rathcoole Avenue, Rathcoole Gardens, and Harvey and Uplands roads[74] but few were completed before 1896. Those built were terraced and cheaper than those on the Elder estate. Like Harringay, Stroud Green, and Finsbury Park, Ferme Park mainly housed commuters of moderate means, who were contrasted in 1888 with the richer residents of Shepherd's Hill.[75]

In 1856 Rowledge farm was divided between the Ecclesiastical Commissioners and C. S. Dickens: Dickens received 121 a. bounded by Shepherd's Hill, Hornsey Lane, Crouch End Hill, and an intended road, perhaps Stanhope Road; the commissioners were assigned 173 a. bounded by Churchyard Bottom wood, Shepherd's Hill, and Park Road.[76] They also owned Highgate wood, on which they probably hoped to build,[77] and even after surrendering it in 1885 they planned roads through Churchyard Bottom wood.[78] From 1870 they leased land for building in Stanhope Road.[79] Dickens had built large detached houses along Hornsey Lane and the new Crescent Road by 1871[80] and had laid out Coolhurst Road from Hornsey Lane to Shepherd's Hill by 1882, when the Imperial Property Investment Co. was his agent.[81] The company also acted for the commissioners from 1882,[82] when it acquired the leasehold rights of the Bird family in Crouch Hall,[83] treating all three estates as one.[84] On its own behalf the company bought *c.* 1885 as its Muswell Hill estate Upton farm, consisting of 42 a. bounded by Muswell Hill Road, St. James's Lane, Churchyard Bottom wood, and, in the east, land stretching to Park Road.[85] By 1896 it had acquired land farther east, called the whole Imperial Park, and apparently

57 M.R.O., Acc. 804.
58 *P.O. Dir. N. Suburbs* (1880).
59 Hornsey loc. bd. *Min. Bk. 1892–4*.
60 See p. 149.
61 See photo. (1882), N. Mdx. Photo. Soc. no. 557 in Hornsey libr.
62 For what follows see Aris, 'Urban devel. in Hornsey'; Bruce Castle Mus., O/H/3/7 (corresp. betw. surveyor and Hornsey loc. bd.); B.L. Maps 3465 (36), no. 11.
63 Hornsey Boro. *Min. Bk. 1906–7*, 456.
64 *The Times*, 10 Sept. 1883.
65 M.R.O., Acc. 237/2.
66 Sales parts. in Hornsey libr.; M.R.O., Acc. 1025.
67 *Hornsey & Mdx. Messenger*, 18 Jan. 1889; *Crouch End & Hornsey Weekly News*, 9 June 1888; Hornsey loc. bd. *Min. Bk. 1892–4*, 135.
68 *London*, 19 Mar. 1896.
69 M.R.O., Acc. 1025; cutting (9 Feb. 1880) in Hornsey libr.
70 M.R.O., Acc. 1025.
71 *Crouch End & Hornsey Weekly News*, 9 June 1888.
72 Stone on bldg.
73 Hornsey loc. bd. *Min. Bk. 1892–4*, 220.
74 Ibid. 302, 308.
75 *Crouch End & Hornsey Weekly News*, 12 May 1888.
76 Guildhall MS. 12386.
77 *The Times*, 10 Sept., 20 Nov. 1884.
78 Ibid. 17 Nov. 1886, 19 Sept. 1893.
79 Guildhall MS. 12382.
80 R.G. 10/1336.
81 *N. Mdx. Chron.* 11 Nov. 1882.
82 Ibid.
83 Ibid.; Potter Colln. 20/55; *The Times*, 16 Mar. 1886.
84 *N. Mdx. Chron.* 11 Nov. 1882; Hornsey libr., Heal Colln., sales parts.
85 Potter Colln. 20/66; sales parts. (1885) in Hornsey libr.

planned an integrated road system for over 350 a. Both Crouch End and Highgate were considered good residential areas, which all parties meant to preserve.[86] Building began in the east part of Coolhurst Road, where twelve roads for 588 houses had been laid out in 1882.[87] Detached Jacobean-style houses in Shepherd's Hill Road, three-storeyed and with nine bedrooms, were advertised *c.* 1885. In Wolseley, Coleridge, Coolhurst, and Crouch Hall roads smaller two-storeyed Queen Anne-style detached houses were available.[88] On the Muswell Hill estate three-storeyed eight-bedroomed detached houses were built.[89] Failure to sell some new houses in 1886[90] may partly explain why the company was reconstituted in 1894 and often sought improved terms from the Ecclesiastical Commissioners,[91] in spite of the district's rural attractions[92] and convenient railway services. Only the area near Crouch End and a strip of land along Shepherd's Hill Road, together containing 700 houses,[93] and part of Onslow and Cranley gardens had been built on by 1896. As late as 1920 much of the southern estate was vacant.

During the 1890s building spread over Muswell Hill, Fortis Green, and western Hornsey. The number of inhabited houses rose from 9,712 in 1891 to 12,571 in 1901 and 19,940 in 1911,[94] giving the parish its modern appearance. The hamlets survived much as they were in 1851 or even 1816 until, during the 1890s, the old centres of Crouch End, Muswell Hill, and, to a lesser extent, Hornsey itself, made way for municipal buildings and shopping parades. Meanwhile estates merged into a continuous suburb that extended into neighbouring parishes. Only a third of Hornsey was built over by 1894[95] and it was expected that the population would exceed the level it ultimately reached. Combined with relative prosperity and good public services, such confidence encouraged Hornsey's desire for borough and even county borough status.[96]

Building activity had slackened by 1914[97] in spite of a continuing demand and, by 1923, a shortage of houses.[98] There was a lack of sites as large areas remained open, notably Muswell Hill north of Creighton Avenue, Highgate wood, and Crouch End playing fields.[99] No more building was possible in Stroud Green or Harringay between 1901 and 1911, when their populations fell.[1] The declining size of families, however,[2] permitted multiple occupation of houses and the provision of blocks of flats, which were associated with lower standards as early as 1900.[3] Subdivision of houses caused concern by 1911, particularly in North and South Harringay and Stroud Green.[4] In 1921 1·35 families on average lived in each house,[5] the trend being especially marked in the south and east and in 1923 linked to working-class immigration from Islington and correlated with a recent increase in poor-law cases.[6] At Stroud Green houses were divided and the district was in decay *c.* 1925.[7] Hornsey council accordingly built its own working-class housing, providing 424 dwellings by 1913, including 248 in Hornsey Side, 634 by 1926, and 1,072 including 839 in Hornsey Side, by 1939.[8] From 1930 it concentrated on replacing obsolete houses[9] and from 1932 supported the Hornsey Housing Trust,[10] which by 1939 had divided 50 houses into 237 flats.[11] Nowhere did overcrowding exceed the legal limits in 1923 and there were no slums then or in 1932, although there were pockets of poverty in the Campsbourne and St. Mary's estates at Hornsey, at Hornsey Vale, and at St. James's Lane, Muswell Hill.[12] Only the last was concerned in the demolition of 148 houses between 1920 and 1938.[13] In 1923 it was recognized that as the wealthy moved farther out Hornsey's prosperity would decline.[14] The borough nevertheless consisted mainly of houses for the well-to-do in the 1920s[15] and many clerks still lived in Hornsey, Harringay, Crouch End, and Stroud Green in 1925.[16]

At Muswell Hill building was in progress on various sites before 1896, when it accelerated as land became available and when visitors were attracted to Tetherdown, scene of the notorious Muswell Hill murder.[17] Building was still proceeding on the Alexandra Park estate in 1900 when the Elms, north-east of Muswell Hill, was demolished and laid out in conjunction with James Edmondson & Son of Highbury as the Station estate.[18] The frontage became a terraced crescent of four-storeyed shops called Station Parade,[19] similar to Edmondsons' contemporary parade at Crouch End, and Station (later Duke's) Avenue and other roads were built between Muswell Hill and Wood Green.[20] Edmondsons were still building there in 1910.[21]

86 See Guildhall MSS. 12380, 12382.
87 *N. Mdx. Chron.* 11 Nov. 1882.
88 Sales parts. in Hornsey libr., Heal Colln.; see also *Crouch End & Hornsey Weekly News*, 28 Apr. 1888.
89 Potter Colln. 20/66. Hornsey libr., Heal Colln., sales parts.
90 *N. Mdx. Chron.* 4 Dec. 1886.
91 Guildhall MS. 12380.
92 Sales parts. in Hornsey libr., Heal Colln.
93 *London*, 19 Mar. 1896.
94 *Census*, 1901–11; the para. is based on the ensuing paras. and on O.S. Maps 6", Mdx. XII, XI. SE. (1920 edns.); 1/25,000, XII. 1, 5–6, 9–10, 14 (1935–6 edn.).
95 Hornsey loc. bd. *Min. Bk. 1892–4*, 659.
96 See p. 167.
97 'List of hos. built in Hornsey 1902–14' in Hornsey libr.
98 Hornsey Council of Soc. Welfare, *Hornsey Social Survey* (1923), 12.
99 See p. 111.
1 Hornsey Boro. *Ann. Rep. of M.O.H.* (1911).
2 Ibid. (1930).
3 Hornsey U.D. *Ann. Rep. of M.O.H.* (1900).
4 Hornsey Boro. *Ann. Rep. of M.O.H.* (1911, 1912).
5 *Hornsey Social Survey*, 13.
6 Ibid. 4; see also *Wonderful Lond.* i. 16.
7 *Wonderful Lond.* i. 16.
8 *Hornsey Social Survey*, 13–14; Hornsey Boro. *Abs. of Accts.* (1962–3); Cleary, *Beauty and the Boro.* (1949), 24–5; Hornsey Boro. *Official Guide* [1926].
9 Hornsey Boro. *Ann. Reps. of M.O.H.* (1934, 1938).
10 Ibid. (1932–4, 1938).
11 Hornsey Housing Trust *Chairman's Rep.* (1949); see below, p. 119.
12 *Hornsey Social Survey*, 4, 13; Hornsey Boro. *Ann. Rep. of M.O.H.* (1932).
13 Hornsey Boro. *Ann. Rep. of M.O.H.* (1934, 1938).
14 *Hornsey Social Survey*, 4.
15 Hornsey Boro. *Ann. Rep. of M.O.H.* (1922); *Official Guide* [1926].
16 *Official Guide*; *Wonderful Lond.* i. 16.
17 Except wh reeotherwise stated, the para. is based on Draper, *Muswell Hill.*
18 Cutting in Potter Colln. 20/94; *Hornsey & Finsbury Pk. Jnl.* 10 Feb. 1900. A similar proposal had been made in 1880: B.L. Maps Dept., sales parts.
19 *N. Lond. Mercury*, 10 Feb. 1900.
20 *Hornsey & Finsbury Pk. Jnl.* 10 Feb. 1900; see also *Muswell Hill Rec.* 15 Apr. 1910.
21 *Muswell Hill Rec.* 17 June 1910.

On the opposite side of Muswell Hill two large houses, Belle Vue and Summerlands, were replaced respectively by a dairy in 1900 and by the shops and flats called Summerlands Mansions by 1904.[22] Farther north, on the west of Colney Hatch Lane, North Lodge was replaced by Edmondsons' North Lodge estate, which included Woodberry Crescent.[23] By 1900 other builders had laid out the curved Creighton Avenue from Page's Lane to Coldfall wood and were selling houses in Eastwood Road;[24] in 1908 Burlington Road and the western frontage of Tetherdown were built up.[25] In 1896 Edmondsons bought the Limes, with grounds stretching to Fortis Green, and promptly laid out Queen's Avenue. Immediately to the south the triangle facing Fortis Green and Muswell Hill roads was sold soon after, probably to Edmondsons, who in 1900 built the shops and flats called St. James's Mansions fronting Fortis Green Road.[26] By 1900[27] W. J. Collins had laid out the area south of Fortis Green and west of Muswell Hill Road, previously the site of Midhurst, Fortismere, and the Firs, which were replaced before 1905 by six streets of tightly packed terraces running southward from Fortis Green to Grand Avenue.[28] South of Fortis Green Road, on opposite sides of Firs Avenue, flats in Birchwood Mansions and Firs Mansions were erected *c.* 1910 and *c.* 1907.[29] South of Fortis Green itself, Leaside Mansions and the Gables dated from *c.* 1907[30] and Midhurst Mansions, on the site of Midhurst itself, from 1902.[31] Farther west building was in progress in Lynmouth and Southern roads and Springcroft Avenue in 1908[32] and to the south large houses had been erected on the Hall estate by 1900.[33] East of Muswell Hill Road cottages fronting Queen's Road were replaced in 1898 by 27 three-storeyed semi-detached houses.[34] Immediately to the north, in Cranley Gardens, R. Metherill was building in Woodland Gardens and in 1900 houses were planned in Woodland Rise.[35] There was no direct connexion with Shepherd's Hill but Cranley Gardens was linked to the Rookfield estate on the lower slopes of Muswell Hill and St. James's Lane. The Rookfield Garden Village[36] of W. J. Collins contained two-storeyed semi-detached houses in short streets lined by trees. Building was in progress before 1910[37] and involved the demolition of Lalla Rookh, already threatened in 1898.[38] In 1934 26 cottages in St. James's Lane were replaced by Valette Court, a block of council flats.[39]

In 1896 Muswell Hill, with its natural advantages, seemed likely to achieve distinction.[40] To encourage the trend Edmondsons[41] built an Athenaeum and gave sites for chapels and a public library.[42] The broad streets were lined with shops, which in 1908 it was hoped would make Muswell Hill the finest shopping centre in London,[43] and flats and houses were built in quiet and accessible roads. In 1908 it was select[44] and in 1926 it still attracted the wealthy, although the residents were less eminent than some in Highgate. By 1911 Muswell Hill, with 11,391 inhabitants,[45] was joined to neighbouring suburbs.

By 1920 almost the whole area north of Crouch End playing fields, Queen's wood, and Woodside Avenue, and south of Coldfall wood and Page's Lane was built over. Many large houses were subdivided or replaced, particularly in Colney Hatch Lane. A small shopping centre had sprung up near the northern boundary by 1926 and on the western side a row of houses made way for four blocks of flats, Seymour Court *c.* 1936, and Barrington, St. Ivian, and Cedar courts *c.* 1937.[46] After 1920 building was possible only at the expense of the remaining open spaces, in Woodside Avenue and adjoining roads or over Coldfall wood, through which Creighton Avenue had been built. On land carved out of the wood facing Fortis Green several blocks of flats were erected: Woodside by 1921,[47] Long Ridges by 1930, and Twyford Court by 1933.[48] The other roads running northward were not constructed until after 1935. The original mission church of St. Matthew was established to serve the council's Coldfall estate, a grid of five roads of 412 terraced houses erected during 1924–6[49] between Coppetts Road and Coldfall wood. As the attenuated wood and open area to the north were preserved, Muswell Hill had attained its modern limits by 1939. Although much larger and more diverse than had been hoped, it was the newest and most prosperous part of Hornsey.

Hornsey village was considered quaint, partly old and partly new, in 1900.[50] Shortage of land delayed its spread westward until *c.* 1896 when the Priory estate, known as Priory Park, was sold.[51] The seven roads constructed across it from Priory Road northward to Alexandra Park contained mainly three-storeyed terraces. The Priory itself was demolished *c.* 1902.[52] Campsbourne, a field to the north-east adjoining Nightingale Lane, was acquired by Hornsey U.D.C. for its first working-class housing in 1897. By 1899 108 terraced cottages on 4½ a. had been erected in Northview and Southview

[22] Cutting in Potter Colln. 20/94; *Hornsey & Finsbury Pk. Jnl.* 10 Feb. 1900; inscr. on dairy (1900); Draper, *Literary Assocs. of Hornsey*, 12.
[23] *Muswell Hill Rec.* 3 Apr., 17 Apr. 1908, 21 Jan. 1910.
[24] Ibid. 26 May 1900.
[25] *Muswell Hill Rec.* 15, 29 May 1908.
[26] *N. Lond. Mercury*, 7 July 1900; stone on bldg.
[27] *N. Lond. Mercury*, 23 June, 10 Nov. 1900.
[28] *Kelly's Dir. Wood Green* (1907–8).
[29] Ibid. (1905–6 and later edns.).
[30] Ibid. (1905–8).
[31] Ibid. (1901–3).
[32] *Muswell Hill Rec.* 14 Feb., 17 Apr., 19 June 1908.
[33] *Hornsey & Finsbury Pk. Jnl.* 10 Feb. 1900.
[34] Char. Com. files.
[35] *N. Lond. Mercury*, 24 Feb., 23 June 1900.
[36] Cleary, *Beauty and the Boro.* 29; *Hornsey Hist. Soc. Bull.* v. 11.
[37] *Muswell Hill Rec.* 25 Nov., 2 Dec. 1910.
[38] *News of the World*, 28 Aug. 1898.
[39] Hornsey Boro. *Ann. Rep. of M.O.H.* (1932); *Abs. of Accts.* (1962–3).
[40] Except where otherwise stated, the para. is based on Hornsey Boro. *Official Guide* [1926]; *Wonderful Lond.* i. 16.
[41] *London*, 19 May 1898.
[42] See pp. 171, 186.
[43] *Muswell Hill Rec.* 3 Jan. 1908.
[44] Ibid.
[45] *Census*, 1911.
[46] *Kelly's Dir. Hornsey* (1936–8).
[47] *Kelly's Dir. Wood Green* (1921).
[48] *Kelly's Dir. Hornsey* (1930, 1933).
[49] Hornsey Boro. *Abs. of Accts.* (1962–3); *Hornsey Boro. 1903–53*, 22.
[50] *N. Lond. Mercury*, 17 Mar. 1900.
[51] *London*, 19 Mar. 1896.
[52] *Hornsey Jnl.* 2 Oct. 1953; *Hornsey Boro. 1903–53*, 10.

roads and in Nightingale Lane itself,[53] where older weatherboarded cottages had been demolished in 1896.[54] An enthusiastic observer compared the new terraced houses with villas.[55] A second scheme in 1904 consisted of 140 cottages in Hawthorne and Beechwood roads on 6 a. acquired in 1902.[56] Building to the west was halted by Alexandra Park and Grove Lodge but south of Priory Road only Park Road separated Muswell Hill's Rookfield estate from Hornsey after *c.* 1900. By then building had begun on the farm-land in the angle of Park and Priory roads. The weatherboarded Rose Cottage on the corner was pulled down in 1902 and Farrer Road and Park Avenue South were built.[57] The western sprawl of Hornsey village thus met the northward advance of Crouch End up Park Road.

East of Middle Lane and immediately south of Priory Park, created in 1926,[58] Chestnut Avenue replaced the Chestnuts, part of the 13½-a. Elm House estate of Leopold Keller (d. 1905), which was auctioned in 1909. It included Hermiston Lodge, Rokesley House, and Elm House, whose grounds, all stretching to Tottenham Lane, barred the spread of building between Hornsey and Crouch End, Hermiston Lodge, the northernmost, was replaced by Rokesley Avenue and Holy Innocents' Road (later part of Hermiston Avenue), but it was not until *c.* 1934 that the other two houses made way for Elmfield Avenue and the rest of Hermiston Avenue.[59] The latter joined Hillyfield Avenue and other roads on the former glebe where houses were under construction in 1896. The same builder remodelled that part of High Street[60] not already fronted with terraced shops. On its south side the Three Compasses was demolished in 1896[61] and the Pavement, a three-storeyed terrace of shops, was erected. To the north Campsbourne Parade was erected in 1908–9.[62] The old wooden shops and Preston's and Allen's courts made way for the council's bath- and wash-houses in 1920,[63] whereupon High Street took on its modern appearance. Only a few older houses were left: Elm Cottage; the Elms, which was pulled down *c.* 1939;[64] and the Rectory, which in 1928 was partly encircled to the west by Rectory Gardens council estate.[65] By 1920 most of the estates were built up and in 1926 the shops were mainly utilitarian,[66] reflecting near-by poverty, especially in the Campsbourne. Rebuilding there was contemplated[67] but only Newlands, municipal flats of 1930, dated from before the Second World War.[68]

Crouch End village was still recognizable in 1894, in spite of building on all sides and the disappearance of some large houses, notably Crouch Hall (1885), Crouch End academy (1882), Old Crouch Hall, and Linslade House (1888). At the southern end of Broadway the smithy and cottages, the Harringay Arms, and Park chapel, stretching a short way up Crouch Hill, formed part of the estate sold in 1894 on the death of Mrs. Sarah Elder. Topsfield Hall and its grounds were bought by Edmondsons, who demolished the house, laid out Rosebery Gardens and the continuation of Elder Avenue, and put up substantial terraces. Middle and Tottenham lanes were widened and on the frontage of the latter and the corner was built a four-storeyed parade of good shops. On the other side of Tottenham Lane J. C. Hill replaced houses with a similar parade[69] and constructed Felix Avenue and Fairfield Gardens through their long gardens. In front of where Topsfield Hall had stood the council erected Crouch End clock-tower, an ornate red-brick and stone memorial to Henry Reader Williams.[70] On the opposite corner of Broadway, Hill replaced the smithy with a bank and built shops up the west and probably the east of Crouch Hill as far as Haringey Park and Park chapel.[71] An opera house and assembly hall were also built.[72] In 1926 Crouch End was the main shopping centre for a wide area[73] and in 1935 it was chosen as the site for Hornsey town hall.[74]

Many of Crouch End's old buildings survived the 1890s. They included Broadway chapel until 1925 and Lake Villa,[75] both east of Broadway, terraced shops in Crouch End Hill and Tottenham Lane,[76] and large houses in Crouch Hill. East of Crouch Hill, Womersley and Crouch Hill houses remained in 1920, as did Oakfield House north of Haslemere Road and Oakfield Villa in Crouch End Hill. By then all the large houses in Tottenham Lane had disappeared and the fields to east and west were almost built up. More space could be found only by demolition, which began as early as 1908 in Haringey Park, where a house gave way to Ravensdale Mansions, three blocks of 47 flats.[77] Mountview automatic telephone exchange replaced Oakfield Villa[78] and the terraced shops east of Crouch End Hill, and Lake Villa made way for the town hall.[79] Oakfield House was replaced by 58 flats in Oakfield Court by 1937.[80] The terraced shops of Manor Place, Tottenham Lane, were pulled down in 1935,[81] when the town hall was opened amid streets which showed signs of decay.[82]

The Priory, Southwood Hall, and the houses in Wood Lane were the only houses between Shepherd's Hill, Muswell Hill Road, and Queen's wood in 1898.[83] In 1899 the Freehold and Leasehold Investment Co. acquired the Priory and its large

53 Hornsey Boro. *Partics. of Properties of Boro.* (1904).
54 S. J. Kitchener, 'Hist. of Hornsey: the Village' (TS. in Hornsey libr.).
55 Cutting in Hornsey libr.
56 Hornsey Boro. *Partics. of Properties of Boro.* (1904).
57 *Hornsey Boro. 1903–53*, 10–11.
58 See p. 111.
59 *Hornsey Jnl.* 10 Aug. 1934.
60 *London*, 19 Mar. 1896.
61 Kitchener, 'Hist. Hornsey: Village'.
62 Ibid.; *Hornsey & Finsbury Pk. Jnl.* 6 Jan. 1900.
63 Hornsey Boro. *Ann. Rep. of M.O.H.* (1938).
64 *Hornsey Jnl.* 2 Sept. 1939; *Hornsey Boro. 1903–53*, 10.
65 Hornsey Boro. *Abs. of Accts.* (1962–3).
66 Hornsey Boro. *Official Guide* [1926].
67 *Hornsey Boro. 1903–53*, 23.
68 Hornsey Boro. *Abs. of Accts.* (1962–3).
69 *London*, 19 Mar. 1896; see above, plate facing p. 96.
70 Hornsey loc. bd. *Min. Bk. 1892–4*, 712.
71 *London*, 19 Mar. 1896.
72 Sherington, *Story of Hornsey*, 72.
73 Hornsey Boro. *Official Guide* [1926].
74 See p. 167.
75 Photo. in *T.L.M.A.S.* xiii, facing p. 414.
76 Photos. in Hornsey libr. (1929, 1935).
77 *Kelly's Dir. Hornsey* (1907–9).
78 *Hornsey Boro. 1903–53*, 14; see also photo. (1935) in Hornsey libr.
79 *T.L.M.A.S.* xiii. 419.
80 *Kelly's Dir. Hornsey* (1937).
81 Cuttings in Hornsey libr.; *Hornsey Boro. 1903–53*, 11.
82 *The Times*, 2 May 1930; see above, plate facing p. 96.
83 Guildhall MS. 12380.

grounds[84] and by 1920 had laid out Priory Gardens. By 1935 the whole site was built over. Southwood Hall, on the corner of Wood Lane and Muswell Hill Road, was replaced by 1937 by red-brick blocks of flats.[85] Nine cottages, called Churchyard Bottom or Woodside Cottages, were demolished in 1930–1 by the council and replaced by Summersby Road, which contained eighteen flats.[86] A little farther south the frontage to Archway Road and the streets immediately to the east, including the three-storeyed terraced houses of 1873–4 in Holmesdale Road,[87] were built up by 1896. The whole area west of Archway Road, north of Hornsey Lane, and south of the G.N.R. was built over by 1920.

Hornsey was heavily bombed during the Second World War, when over 80 per cent of the houses suffered damage.[88] By 1945 131 houses had been destroyed and 611 required demolition[89] but only 256 were wholly rebuilt at the government's expense, most of them apparently in 1949–50.[90] Others provided sites for municipal housing. An acute shortage was alleviated when the council provided 82 temporary bungalows[91] and put up cheap dwellings, most of them model flats.[92] By 1951, when 1,005 dwellings were complete, 639 had been built by the council, many of them in Stroud Green.[93] The council remains the largest builder and has concentrated on redevelopment, particularly in Hornsey village. It had completed 930 post-war dwellings by 1956,[94] 1,164 by 1965,[95] and *c.* 1,900 by 1976. Of those built or under construction in 1965, 85·6 per cent were flats.[96] A further 972 flats were provided in Brownswood Park by Stoke Newington M.B. and Hackney L.B. and by 1976 Hornsey Housing Trust owned 50 houses, containing 260 flats and bed-sitting rooms, and three purpose-built blocks.[97] Private builders, relatively inactive during the 1950s, completed 91 dwellings in 1960, 167 in 1961, and 245 in 1964–5, when the 563 under construction (153 by the council)[98] was the highest yearly total since *c.* 1902. Consisting mainly of luxury flats, private building reached a peak *c.* 1970 and had resumed by 1976.[99]

Hornsey's increasingly working-class character was shown by the presence of only 1,657 domestic servants in 1951[1] and in its change from a safe Conservative parliamentary constituency in 1945 to a marginal one by 1974.[2] There was a very long waiting list for housing in 1964,[3] in spite of the departure to new towns of 1,000 people each year before 1959 and more thereafter.[4] Between 1959 and 1961 10,000 English-born people left Hornsey but the population fell by only 147: the newcomers included over 9,000 born outside the United Kingdom, among them 3,000 from Eire.[5] Over the same decade Hornsey was the only Middlesex borough where the number of rooms with 1·5 or more inhabitants increased, from 7·4 to 8·4 per cent of the total. The rise was particularly steep in the areas of immigration, Finsbury Park and Stroud Green wards, with percentages of 16·9 and 9·8, and at Harringay. It was 7·6 per cent in Hornsey, little less in Crouch End, and even in Highgate and Muswell Hill it was 6 and 5 per cent.[6] In 1960 the practice was growing of dividing three- or four-storeyed houses into ten or twelve bed-sitting rooms.[7] In 1961 it was believed that fewer houses would be converted, since larger ones would be replaced by purpose-built flats.[8] In 1976 that had happened only in the more prosperous western parts, while other areas became increasingly decayed towards London. In 1961 most working residents not only were employed elsewhere,[9] as in 1867, but were immigrants and peripatetic flat-dwellers. In 1976, when Hornsey had been submerged in a larger local government unit, the districts had a clearer identity than the old parish.

At Brownswood Park many of the original families had moved out by 1895 and others were being replaced by poorer people in 1913. Social decline continued[10] until in 1954 the district was inhabited mainly by students, foreigners, and the working class, with most houses containing four or five families and all in decay.[11] Until the Second World War only a few houses had been replaced and by 1959 the area was apparently seen as a potential slum.[12] In 1949, as part of Stoke Newington's Green Lanes development scheme, Lakeside Court was built in Gloucester Drive,[13] and by 1958 St. John's Court, three blocks with 121 flats, had been built in Princess Crescent. Between Portland Rise, Green Lanes, and Seven Sisters Road 123 flats had been erected by 1958, when others were going up;[14] the completed Portland Rise estate consists of 193 flats in eight blocks.[15] Between Green Lanes, King's Crescent, and Queen's Drive, Hackney L.B. built the King's Crescent estate. Apart from Sawbridge and Barkway courts, each a nineteen-storeyed tower of 114 flats, there are houses, eight smaller blocks, and a total of 634 dwellings.[16] In 1974 Brownswood Park was essentially a dormitory area[17] and in 1976 its main

[84] Ibid.; *Municipal Jnl.* 18 May 1900.
[85] *Kelly's Dir. Hornsey* (1937).
[86] Hornsey Boro. *Ann. Rep. of M.O.H.* (1934).
[87] Stone on bldg.
[88] *Hornsey Boro. 1903–53*, 19–21.
[89] Hornsey Boro. *Housing and Repair of War Damage* (1945).
[90] Hornsey Boro. *Final Rep. of Boro. Engineer on Postwar Hornsey Programme* (1965).
[91] Hornsey Boro. *Ann. Rep. of M.O.H.* (1951).
[92] *Financial Times*, 28 Sept. 1948; 'Opening of Mildura Ct.' (1951) in Hornsey libr.
[93] Hornsey Boro. *Ann. Rep. of M.O.H.* (1951).
[94] Hornsey Boro. *Official Guide* [1956].
[95] Hornsey Boro. *Final Rep. of Boro. Engineer* (1965).
[96] Ibid.
[97] Ex inf. the sec. and housing manager.
[98] *Hampstead and Highgate Express*, 4 Oct. 1964; *Hornsey Jnl.* 9 Sept. 1960; Hornsey Boro. *Final Rep. of Boro. Engineer* (1965).
[99] See p. 120.
[1] *Census*, 1951.
[2] *Whitaker's Almanack* (1946, 1976).
[3] *Evening Standard*, 13 Feb. 1964.
[4] Hornsey Boro. *Final Rep. of Boro. Engineer* (1965).
[5] *Hornsey Jnl.* 29 Nov. 1963.
[6] Ibid. 21 June 1963.
[7] Hornsey Boro. *Ann. Rep. of M.O.H.* (1960).
[8] *Hornsey Jnl.* 20 Jan. 1961.
[9] *Census*, 1961.
[10] W. G. Lewis, *St. John the Evangelist, Brownswood Park, 1874–1974* (Jubilee booklet), 10, 11, 13.
[11] Macqueen-Pope, *Back Numbers*, 51.
[12] Royal Com. on Loc. Govt. in Gtr. Lond. *Mins. of Evidence*, 318.
[13] Stoke Newington M.B. *Official Guide* [1950].
[14] Ibid. [1958].
[15] *Reg. of Electors* (1975).
[16] Map on site (1976); *Reg. of Electors* (1976).
[17] Lewis, *St. John's, Brownswood Pk.* 22.

frontages in Green Lanes and Seven Sisters Road still consisted of large houses, some derelict and others converted into offices or private hotels. Houses on the corner of Seven Sisters and Adolphus roads were pulled down in 1975 by Ferme Park Properties.[18] In the angle of Seven Sisters and Wilberforce roads was Park House, an eleven-storeyed block of flats, and on the corner with Queen's Drive the ten-storeyed Alexandra National hotel.

Hornsey council's first major post-war rebuilding was at Stroud Green, where most of the land between Victoria, Stroud Green, and Lorne roads and Upper Tollington Park was cleared. Facing the main road Wall Court, a balconied block much admired when new,[19] was completed in 1947, Lawson, Wiltshire, and Marquis courts and Brackenbury were built in Osborne Road in 1948, and flats in Nichols Close between 1948 and 1952. Wisbech and Fenstanton date from 1953, the flats and shops of Charter Court from 1954, and Hutton Court from 1960. In 1948 Ronaldshay and Wallace Lodge, on opposite corners of Florence and Wallace roads, and Ednam House facing them were built and in 1952 an extension to Ronaldshay was finished. Carlton Court, 64 flats in Carlton Road, dates from 1947. On opposite corners of Oakfield and Connaught roads Connaught Lodge and Churchill Court were completed in 1949 and on the corner of Oakfield and Stapleton Hall roads Norman Court was completed in 1947.[20] The cul-de-sac Osborne Grove was replaced by an old people's home by 1973.[21] In 1974 Ennis and Woodstock roads were reprieved from demolition[22] and in 1976 several yellow-brick terraced houses were being renovated.

In 1976 many of the modest houses of Ferme Park and Harringay were occupied by immigrants, Cypriots being prominent in Harringay[23] and coloured people on either side of Ridge Road.[24] Since housing is less dense and better preserved than in Stroud Green, large-scale rebuilding has been confined to Hornsey Vale, where 147 houses covered 7 a.[25] Council dwellings are scattered over the whole area, among them 84 flats in Fairfax Road built in 1948, 31 at Quernmore Court, Quernmore Road, of 1957, and 138 at Chettle Court, Ridge Road, of 1969.[26] Hornsey Housing Trust's Norah Clegg House was built at no. 49 Oakfield Road in 1965, a year when private firms built only 39 flats in the area, at Upper Tollington Park, Ridge Road, and Mountview Road. A few other blocks of private flats existed in 1976.

Private builders have concentrated on the area between Shepherd's Hill, Crouch Hill, and Hornsey Lane. In the late 1930s a few large houses made way for other buildings, including Northwood Hall, a seven-storeyed tower of 183 flats in Hornsey Lane, and in Shepherd's Hill itself the flats of Eton Court and the flat-roofed houses of Broughton Gardens.[27] Rebuilding was marked by 1960[28] and in 1976 there were at least twenty post-war developments in Shepherd's Hill, nine each in Avenue, Crescent, and Stanhope roads, six in Hornsey Lane, three in Waverley Road, two in Haslemere Road, and one each in Crouch Hall Road and Stanhope Gardens. Most are rectangular blocks of luxury flats, of at least three storeys and standing on one or more plots, often corner sites. As each was planned independently, they vary in appearance. Williams Court, on the corner of Coolhurst and Crescent roads, was erected by the council in 1948,[29] and Goldsmith Court replaced the bombed Coleridge Buildings in 1950.[30] Southview in Hornsey Lane, Alyn Bank and Alyn Court in Crescent Road, Stanhope and Hill courts in Stanhope Road, and Priory Court, Dale Lodge, and Highview in Shepherd's Hill, were all completed by 1955, when Crescent Court in Crescent Road was under construction. Thornhill Court, Crescent Road, and Tor House, Shepherd's Hill, were finished in 1956. Middlesex C.C.'s girls' hostel at no. 66 existed by 1964 and Altior Court was completed in 1965 by Overcourt, also the builders of Melior Court *c.* 1968 and Pastor Court.[31] The two-storeyed houses of Shepherd's Close were put up in 1965 on the steep gardens of nos. 8 and 10,[32] which have since been replaced by three-storeyed town houses. Highgate Heights, Panorama Court, Jameson Lodge, Mount Lodge, Fitzroy Court, and no. 55 were all built in 1967 and no. 64 by 1976. In 1976 an orange-brick block was being built at no. 24 and the corner with Montenotte Road had been cleared for houses by Michaelides & Son.

Building was equally rapid in the other roads; Avenue Hall in Avenue Road, Northern Heights in Crescent Road, and Alford House in Stanhope Road were built by 1964; Sandy Lodge in Avenue Road and Brook Lodge and Hurst Lodge in Coolhurst Road in 1965;[33] Lorelei, Christopher Lodge, and nos. 4 and 6 Avenue Road, David Court in Waverley Road, Cranleigh in Christ Church Road, Corrib Heights in Crescent Road, Midhurst Court in Haslemere Road, High London in Hornsey Lane, and no. 15 in Coolhurst Road by 1967; Wren View, Bridge House, Philip Court, and the Y.W.C.A.'s Roden Court in Hornsey Lane, Viewside Lodge in Stanhope Road, Melisa Court and Grenville Lodge in Avenue Road, and Highgate Spinney in Crescent Road, by 1968; Phoenix House in Waverley Road by 1970; Marbleford Court in Hornsey Lane and Kenilworth Court in Waverley Road by 1975; no. 5 Haslemere Road and Hillside in Crescent Road by 1976. Among blocks under construction in 1976 were two in Coolhurst Road and one in Stanhope Road;

[18] Notice on site.
[19] *Financial Times*, 28 Sept. 1948. For what follows see Hornsey Boro. *Final Rep. of Boro. Engineer* (1965); *Abs. of Accts.* (1962–3).
[20] See also 'Formal opening of Norman Ct.' (1947), in Hornsey libr.
[21] Haringey L.B. *Ann. Reps. of M.O.H.* (1967–9); ex inf. the municipal housing management offr.
[22] Haringey L.B. *Health in 1972* (1972).
[23] Aris, 'Urban devel. in Hornsey'.
[24] See p. 119.
[25] See also Haringey L.B. *Ann. Rep. of M.O.H.* (1966); *Hornsey Social Survey*, 13.
[26] Ex inf. the municipal housing management offr.
[27] *Kelly's Dir. Hornsey* (1937, 1939). Except where otherwise stated, the para. is based on *Kemp's Dir. Hornsey* (1955–67); *P.O. Dir. Lond.* (1958 and later edns.); *Reg. of Electors* (1975).
[28] *Hornsey Jnl.* 9 Sept. 1960; see also *Hampstead and Highgate Express*, 4 Oct. 1964.
[29] Hornsey Boro. *Abs. of Accts.* (1962–3).
[30] Hornsey Housing Trust *Chairman's Rep.* (1949); ex. inf. the sec. and housing manager.
[31] Ex inf. Druce & Co., estate agents; *Final Rep. of Boro. Engineer* (1965).
[32] *Final Rep. of Boro. Engineer* (1965).
[33] Ibid.

Overcourt were building Courtside, town houses behind Brook Lodge, Coolhurst Road, and Wychwood, terraced houses in Stanhope Road.[34] All the roads still consist mainly of old houses, although rebuilding is particularly marked in Crescent Road, Hornsey Lane, and Avenue Road. Many sound houses have been demolished because they were expensive to convert.[35] Other private flats have been erected east of Crouch Hill.

At Crouch End, apart from extensions to the Y.M.C.A. hostel (1958)[36] and central library (1965),[37] there has been little building since 1945. Imperial Buildings, west of Broadway, were replaced by a row of shops, and many other shops were refronted. Crouch End, which was considered fashionable in 1951,[38] thus remained an important shopping centre. The age of Broadway was apparent from the rear and the cottages between Middle Lane and Park Road, among the oldest in the parish, were decayed in 1976, when Topsfield Cottages, Back Lane, were being renovated. North of New Road were streets of small terraced and semi-detached houses. Council flats built since the Second World War included Clemence Court of 1951 in Lynton Road, Ramsey Court of 1952 and Veryan Court of 1953 facing Park Road, and Truro and Buckley courts of 1952 in Palace Road.[39] The Grove, on the north side of Lynton Road, was cleared in 1969[40] and in 1976 there were 48 dwellings in small red-brick blocks. Margaret Hill Court in Middle Lane was built in 1950 by Hornsey Housing Trust.[41]

Hornsey High Street itself has not changed much since 1945, except for the disappearance of St. George's church in the west and St. Mary's in the east, unlike the areas to the north and south. In addition to major schemes in the Campsbourne, St. Mary's estate, and Denmark Road, 30 municipal dwellings were built in Ashford Avenue south of High Street and flats in 1950 at Mildura Court, Church Lane, in Beechwood Avenue and South View Road, and in 1952 in Warner Road.[42]

In 1949 Hornsey council devised a master scheme[43] for the Campsbourne, which had been the poorest area in the borough in 1923[44] and contained many unsound and damp houses.[45] The first stage concerned Brook Road, 21 a. with 125 houses, mostly in two-storeyed terraces and sub-let, containing 488 dwellings.[46] Some flats were ready in 1952[47] and 105 of the proposed 469 dwellings were occupied by 1958[48] and 270 in 1965.[49] Most were finished by 1976, when terraced houses were being erected south of Eastfield Road, opposite a large empty site, and the only surviving rows of houses were in Newlands and Campsbourne roads. Amid established trees,[50] cul-de-sacs, and pedestrian areas the council built mainly three- and four-storeyed blocks in varying materials. The scheme also included shops and factories south of Pembroke Road. North of Myddelton Road the central council depot was rebuilt.

South of Hornsey High Street old housing had been condemned in 1923.[51] In 1963 21 a. with 563 dwellings were compulsorily purchased.[52] Demolition had begun by 1967[53] and by 1976 the whole area between High Street and Birkbeck, Westfield, and Lightfoot roads had been cleared. Lightfoot Road was extended northward along the former Westfield Road and yellow-brick three-storeyed terraces were built across the hill. They were connected by paths except at the foot, where a new road had been built behind High Street. Building was still in progress in the south-west and north. The London and Quadrant Housing Trust, formed in 1973 from the London Housing Trust and Quadrant Housing Association, built 71 of the 267 houses[54] and Haringey L.B. the remainder.

Between the G.N.R., Turnpike Lane, and Wightman Road were Haringey Grove and Denmark Road, a third area of rebuilding. Properties were compulsorily purchased in 1961, work began *c.* 1965,[55] and in 1976 Denmark Road was a cul-de-sac containing the sixteen-storeyed Dylan Thomas House of 90 flats, the smaller Hollam House, and 42 terraced houses. The flats were built by the council and the houses by the London and Quadrant Housing Trust.[56]

At Muswell Hill and Fortis Green almost the only new building sites after 1945 were those of Muswell and Cranley Gardens stations, which were taken for a school, Cranwood old people's home, and the terraced Holt Close which was under construction for Haringey L.B. in 1976.[57] The first municipal scheme was Keynes Close, old peoples' bungalows built in 1947 in conjunction with Hornsey Housing Trust.[58] Hornsey M.B. built Dale Court, Etheldene Avenue, in 1947 and Blaenavon, Fortis Green, in 1953, some houses in Coppetts Road in 1949, and more in Springfield Road in 1950. In 1976 Haringey L.B. was building houses on the north-west edge of the Coldfall estate and on the corner of Muswell Hill Place and Alexandra Gardens, as well as smaller ones in St. James's Lane beside Yeoman House, a four-storeyed office block. Private firms built Grosvenor Gardens,[59] the flats of Summerlands Grange where a cinema had stood,[60] and a

34 Sales parts.; ex inf. Druce & Co.
35 *Hampstead and Highgate Express*, 4 Oct. 1964.
36 Stone on bldg.
37 Stone on bldg.
38 H. P. Clunn, *Face of Lond.* (1951), 387.
39 'Opening of Ramsay Ct., Truro Ct., and Buckley Ct.' (1952) in Hornsey libr.; Hornsey Boro. *Abs. of Accts.* (1962–3).
40 Hornsey Boro. *Ann. Rep. of M.O.H.* (1969).
41 Ex inf. the sec. and housing manager.
42 Hornsey Boro. *Abs. of Accts.* (1962–3).
43 Hornsey Boro. *Ann. Rep. of M.O.H.* (1949).
44 *Hornsey Social Survey*, 13.
45 Hornsey Boro. *Ann. Rep. of M.O.H.* (1957).
46 Ibid. (1950).
47 Ibid. (1952).
48 *Hornsey Jnl.* 22 Aug. 1958.
49 Hornsey Boro. *Final Rep. of Boro. Engineer* (1965).
50 Hornsey Boro. *Official Guide* [1961]; *Hornsey Jnl.* 22 Aug. 1958.
51 *Hornsey Social Survey*, 13.
52 *Hornsey Jnl.* 22 Nov. 1963; Hornsey Boro. *Ann. Rep of M.O.H.* (1963); *Final Rep. of Boro. Engineer* (1965).
53 Hornsey Boro. *Ann. Rep. of M.O.H.* (1967).
54 Ex inf. Mr. Murphy, London & Quadrant Housing Trust.
55 Hornsey Boro. *Ann. Rep. of M.O.H.* (1961); Hornsey Boro. *Final Rep. of Boro. Engineer* (1965).
56 Ex inf. Mr. Murphy, London & Quadrant Housing Trust.
57 Haringey L.B. *Capital Budget* (1973–4). The para. is based on Hornsey Boro. *Abs. of Accts.* (1962–3); *Final Rep. of Boro. Engineer* (1965).
58 Hornsey Housing Trust *Chairman's Rep.* (1949).
59 *Hornsey Jnl.* 9 Sept. 1960.
60 Ex inf. a resident (1976).

block *c.* 1968 in place of Essex Lodge, Colney Hatch Lane,[61] but they have built mainly in Fortis Green. The Copse, a block of police flats, stood there in 1958, Lynton Grange by 1969, Coldfall Lodge by 1969, Priory Grange by 1970, and Chessing Court and Westside by 1975. There are other flats in Southern and Western roads.[62]

The roads and centres antedating Hornsey's growth survived in 1976, when Highgate wood, Queen's wood, and Crouch End playing fields still cut off most of the ancient parish from Highgate. Outside Highgate village very little remains from before 1850: Albion Lodge and Cottage at Fortis Green, Eagle Cottage, the adjoining house, and the tower of St. Mary's church at Hornsey village, Stapleton Hall at Stroud Green, and a row of detached villas built after inclosure along Wood Lane, Highgate. Old cottages still stand along Fortis Green, north of Haswell Park, and in the triangle between Park and New roads and Middle Lane, although both groups are decrepit. Since rebuilding has affected only a fraction of the total housing, Hornsey consists mainly of suburbs built between 1870 and 1914, in districts which are distinct. Large houses are disappearing but the smaller expensive ones of Muswell Hill have not yet been divided. In 1978 territorial divisions between social groups persisted, partly because Shepherd's Hill and Muswell Hill enjoyed high ground, open spaces, and good shops.

Hornsey's population rose to 11,082 in 1861, 19,357 in 1871, 37,078 in 1881, and 61,097 in 1891. In 1901, when South Hornsey had been transferred and Clerkenwell detached had been added, there were 72,056 people. Although the number had risen to 84,592 by 1911, the rate of growth had slackened. The peak recorded in 1951 was only 98,159 and by 1961 the population had fallen to 97,962. South Hornsey's population was 16,698 in 1901, reached 18,617 in 1921, and fell to 18,057 in 1931 and 15,063 in 1951.[63]

HIGHGATE.[64] For over 400 years Highgate has contained fine houses, for the rich and sometimes the famous, and a school established by Sir Roger Cholmley.[65] The centre, known as Highgate village, is remarkable for its many 17th- and 18th-century buildings and still attracts wealthy residents, while Cholmley's foundation has come to be well known as a public school.

Highgate has always straddled a boundary, formed by High Street and a line running west from the Gatehouse a few yards south of the present Hampstead Lane.[66] To the north and east lay the old parish and the bishop of London's manor of Hornsey, to the south and west St. Pancras parish and the St. Paul's prebendal manor of Cantlowes.[67] The south-western half was included in the county of London from 1889,[68] becoming part of St. Pancras M.B.,[69] and in Camden L.B. in 1965;[70] the north-eastern half remained in Middlesex until 1965, when, with the rest of Hornsey, it passed to Haringey L.B.[71] The slopes below Hornsey Lane and Dartmouth Park Hill, south of the old village and from the 19th century loosely described as part of Highgate, lay within Islington.

Although the Hornsey and St. Pancras halves acquired some special status within their respective parishes in the 16th century,[72] Highgate as a single unit was not delimited until the Lighting and Watching Act of 1774.[73] Ecclesiastical separation was first achieved only in 1834, when the consolidated chapelry of St. Michael was given wide boundaries stretching eastward and northward beyond Archway Road, westward to Finchley, and south-westward into St. Pancras as far as the later church of St. Anne, Brookfield.[74] The following account excludes Islington[75] and, on the St. Pancras side, covers only Highgate village: the houses at the top of Highgate Hill and along High Street, those in Pond Square, South Grove, and the Grove, and at the top of Highgate West Hill.[76] It also covers the Hornsey side of Highgate and its late-19th- and 20th-century extensions to Archway Road and the foot of North Hill, Highgate golf course, and the Finchley boundary.

Highgate is indebted to its elevated situation. Presumably its name derives from a hill-top gateway at the entrance into Hornsey park of the Great North Road from London to Finchley.[77] The bracing air and the fine views across London have been praised since John Norden's day[78] and an inscription inside the west doorway of St. Michael's church records that it is level with the top of the cross on the dome of St. Paul's. At the same time early building was hemmed in, between the demesne lands of Rowledge farm to the east, the common and woods of the bishop's park to the north and west, and steep slopes, an obstacle to traffic, to the south.[79]

The road pattern is therefore simple and, in the village, has changed little over four centuries. The village is centred on High Street, the stretch of the Great North Road approaching Hornsey park where the bishop was apparently levying tolls by 1318,[80] and on the adjoining area around the ponds known by 1490 as Highgate green.[81] The northward continuation of High Street beyond the Gatehouse was called North Road and North Hill only in the 19th century[82] but Highgate Hill

[61] *Kemp's Dir. Hornsey* (1967); *P.O. Dir. Lond.* (1968).
[62] *P.O. Dir. Lond.* (1918 and later edns.); *Kemp's Dir. Hornsey* (1955 and later edns.).
[63] *Census*, 1861–1961.
[64] The section was written in 1977. Any refs. to later years are dated.
[65] For the hist. of the sch., see *V.C.H. Mdx.* i. 302–4.
[66] Except where otherwise stated, the following two paras. are based on O.S. Maps 6″, Mdx. XII. SW. (1873 and later edns.).
[67] For the manorial recs. of Hornsey and Cantlowes, see pp. 162–3.
[68] Local Govt. Act, 1888, 51 & 52 Vic., c. 41.
[69] Local Govt. Act, 1899, 62 & 63 Vic., c. 14.
[70] Lond. Govt. Act (1963), c. 33.
[71] See p. 167.
[72] See p. 163.
[73] See p. 165.
[74] *Lond. Gaz.* 3 Oct. 1834, p. 1768.
[75] The leper hosp. of St. Anthony, Highgate, was in Islington: *V.C.H. Mdx.* i. 205–6.
[76] A similar area is covered in *L.C.C. Survey of Lond., Village of Highgate* (*St. Pancras, pt. 1*), xvii (1936). See map in ibid., facing p. 7.
[77] *P.N. Mdx.* (E.P.N.S.), 123.
[78] Norden, *Spec. Brit.* 22.
[79] See map on p. 58.
[80] See p. 103.
[81] W. McB. Marcham, 'Abs. of Ct. Rolls of Cantlowes, 1480–1632' (TS. in G.L.R.O.), 19.
[82] The names are in *P.O. Dir. Six Home Cnties.* (1845), although neither occurs on the O.S. 6″ map of 1873.

itself, to the south, was mentioned in 1565.[83] Four other ways up the hill were the present Dartmouth Park Hill (formerly Maiden Lane),[84] Swain's (occasionally Swine's) Lane, mentioned in 1481,[85] Bromwich Walk, a bridle path connecting the top of Highgate West Hill with the bottom of Swain's Lane in the 18th century but closed in 1904,[86] and Highgate West Hill. The last was of unknown origin but presumably medieval, since it was part of the route to Kentish Town which bounded the manor of Cantlowes; it, too, was known as Highgate Hill *c.* 1800[87] and later, until 1941, it was simply West Hill.[88] Hornsey Lane provided a link with Crouch End by 1604[89] but it ran south of Highgate village and perhaps was originally a north-easterly continuation of Maiden Lane.[90] Southwood Lane (in 1774 known also as Chapel Lane)[91] led past Southwood common to Muswell Hill and was so named by 1601.[92] Jackson's Lane (reputedly named after J. B. Jackson of Hillside) branched eastward from Southwood Lane and continued as a footpath to Crouch End before the construction of the road called Shepherd's Hill.[93] Hampstead Lane ran westward from the Gatehouse by *c.* 1677,[94] and perhaps was used much earlier as a way to the bishop's hunting lodge;[95] it was called Caen Wood Lane in 1774,[96] shortly before stretches were diverted a few yards farther north to avoid Fitzroy House and Kenwood House.[97] The construction of Archway Road in 1813 cut Highgate off from the rest of Hornsey parish, but new residential roads around the village were not laid out until the late 19th century.[98]

Although so named by 1354, Highgate in the 14th century was recorded only in connexion with the road to the gateway[99] or with the hermits who lived near by and repaired the road. Early growth was presumably due to general traffic and to the hermitage, which attracted pilgrims by 1464.[1]

From the mid 15th century residents often left money to the hermitage.[2] So too did John Green, a London butcher, who in 1463 held property in Highgate.[3] Thomas Combes of Clerkenwell also had land in Highgate in 1467.[4] Others with land there by 1480 were Richard Rawson,[5] alderman and master of the Mercers' Company of London,[6] Richard Lylborne, gentleman, of St. Botolph's Aldersgate,[7] and John Bridlington, saddler. A London stationer conveyed his cottage called Lightwells at Highgate green to a pinner or wire-drawer in 1490.[8] The Swan inn, mentioned in 1480, was acquired in 1482 by Richard Kemp and sold in 1502 by John Kemp.[9] Giles Eustace, mentioned in 1462[10] and an illicit brewer in 1480, acquired the Cornerhouse, beside High Street, in 1490.[11] Two houses stood there when he made his will in 1495[12] and a brew-house and horse-mill were leased by Thomas Eustace in 1525.[13] The site of the Cornerhouse was that later occupied by the Angel at the junction of South Grove with High Street.[14] There were also at least two houses at Dancok or Dancope (later Dampoipe) Hill, on Highgate West Hill, by 1481.[15] Tilers dug gravel at Dancok Hill from 1485, without licence, and sand and gravel were taken from Highgate green in 1515.[16] On the east side of the main road, where the hermit's chapel stood, there was probably building, since much of the gravel belonging to Cantlowes was carted into Hornsey manor.[17]

During the 16th century Highgate began to outstrip neighbouring settlements. At Cantlowes manor court a constable for Highgate was appointed in the 1530s[18] and at Hornsey there were separate officials for Hornsey Side and Highgate Side by 1577.[19] Highgate had five ale-houses in 1552, when Hornsey had three and Muswell Hill one.[20] Londoners increasingly acquired property in Highgate and some ambitious building was mentioned in the 1550s, when Richard Lylborne's cottage had been replaced by a fair mansion house at the expense of his brother-in-law Robert Whetnall.[21] Richard Hawkes, a gentleman with land on the slopes farther south in 1516, lived at Highgate in 1530. His sons sold the house in 1536 to Sir Roger Cholmley, serjeant-at-law (d. 1565),[22] whose property lay in both parts of Highgate and included a block bordering the green, apart from the Cornerhouse site, from the high road to Swain's Lane. Cholmley lived on the St. Pancras side, probably near the top of the hill on the site of Fairseat, and was Highgate's first known eminent resident[23] and the heaviest taxpayer in St. Pancras parish.[24] His endowment of a

83 *P.N. Mdx.* (E.P.N.S.), 122.
84 *Lond. Gaz.* 3 Oct. 1834, p. 1768.
85 Marcham, 'Cantlowes Ct. Rolls', 6–7.
86 *Survey of Lond.* xvii. 66. The top of Bromwich Walk was later moved from the side of South Grove Ho. to an exit by the garage of no. 79 Highgate West Hill: ex inf. Sir Jas. Brown.
87 Ibid. 1. The road was called Highgate Hill on a map of St. Pancras par. by John Tompson, 1804: ibid., plate 1. An undated copy of the map and a terrier bk. of 1804 are in Swiss Cottage libr.
88 *P.O. Dir. Lond.* (1941). Several ho. nos. were afterwards changed: see below, p. 137, n. 59.
89 See p. 105.
90 Lloyd, *Hist. Highgate*, 159.
91 Highgate Lighting and Watching Act, 15 Geo. III, c. 43.
92 Highgate Sch. rec., box 3, bdle. 1.
93 Lloyd, *Highgate*, 162, 277. Jackson's ho. was sold in 1827, on his death: M.R.O., Acc. 546.
94 J. Ogilby, *Map of Mdx.* [c. 1677].
95 F. Prickett, *Hist. Highgate* (1842), 74.
96 Highgate Lighting and Watching Act, 15 Geo. III, c. 43.
97 *Survey of Lond.* xvii. 104. Kenwood is reserved for treatment under St. Pancras, although the outbldgs. and part of the grounds north of the ho. lay within Hornsey.
98 See p. 131.
99 See p. 103.
1 See p. 178.
2 See pp. 178, 180.
3 Guildhall MS. 9171/5, f. 349r.
4 Ibid. 6, f. 10r.
5 Marcham, 'Cantlowes Ct. Rolls', 2.
6 A. E. Beaven, *Aldermen of Lond.* ii. 15.
7 Marcham, 'Cantlowes Ct. Rolls', 2; Guildhall MS. 9171/8, f. 233r.
8 Marcham, 'Cantlowes Ct. Rolls', 5, 19, 40.
9 Ibid. 2, 9, 49.
10 Guildhall MS. 9171/5, f. 334v.
11 Marcham, 'Cantlowes Ct. Rolls', 1, 19.
12 *Survey of Lond.* xvii. 138.
13 Marcham, 'Cantlowes Ct. Rolls', 87.
14 *Survey of Lond.* xvii. 138.
15 Marcham, 'Cantlowes Ct. Rolls', 6–7; *Survey of Lond.* xvii. 67.
16 Marcham, 'Cantlowes Ct. Rolls', 11, 41, 73.
17 Ibid. 20, 23.
18 Ibid. 100, 103; see below, p. 163.
19 See p. 163.
20 *Mdx. Cnty. Rec.* i. 11.
21 Marcham, 'Cantlowes Ct. Rolls', 43.
22 Ibid. 75, 98, 110; *L. & P. Hen. VIII*, xi, p. 52.
23 *Survey of Lond.* xvii. 5, 24; *D.N.B.*
24 E 179/142/193.

free school in 1565 led to the rebuilding of the former hermits' chapel, which served as the local church, and so compensated for the disappearance of the hermitage at the Reformation.[25]

From 1565 Londoners' interests in Highgate were demonstrated in the choice of governors of Cholmley's school: among the original six both Sir William Hewett and Sir Richard Martin were lord mayors.[26] Courtiers too began to acquire houses. Sir Roger Cholmley's estate was divided on his death[27] but John Dudley, 'servant' to the earl of Leicester, left property at Highgate in 1581.[28] Lord Henry Howard wrote from Highgate in 1581, as did Sir William Hatton in 1592[29] and Sir Thomas Cornwallis (1519–1604), formerly comptroller of the royal household,[30] in 1587.[31] Princess Elizabeth had lingered at Highgate, when being led by Cornwallis from Ashridge (Herts.) after Wyatt's rebellion in 1554.[32] Sir Thomas's son Sir William Cornwallis (d. ?1631)[33] bought a house and land by the green, west of Swain's Lane, in 1588.

Presumably William Cornwallis himself built the mansion later famous as Arundel House in 1588 and received Elizabeth I there in 1589, 1593, and 1594.[34] His house and its views were praised by Norden in 1593[35] and it was there that James I was entertained with the *Penates*, newly composed by Cornwallis's friend Ben Jonson, in 1604.[36] The countess of Huntingdon went to take the air at Highgate in 1595.[37] Norden, remarking that the hill offered 'most pleasant dwelling, yet not so pleasant as healthful',[38] was the first to record attractions which were making Highgate fashionable.

The restricted site and water supply were to lead to very cramped building, around Pond Square and in narrow yards off High Street, producing an almost urban appearance. In the early 17th century, however, there was still room in the centre of the village. Ponds on the green were known to Norden, who ascribed them to gravel-digging,[39] and an open stretch, 'the bank before the Elms', bordered the green and high road in 1619, when a cottage had been newly built there.[40] The gateway and the school and its chapel marked the northern limit of building, although by 1601 the school's land, the 1½-a. chapel field extending northward between the high road and Southwood Lane, had been divided among lessees. In 1601 a new windmill stood in the north part of the field but much of the rest may have been used for brickearth, since it was leased to a brickmaker who was to repair the school-house and chapel. In 1606 only low buildings of 1½ storey were to be permitted on part of the field.[41]

The forerunners of many large houses, in addition to Cornwallis's, existed by Norden's time. A residence on the site of Lauderdale House was occupied by Sir Richard Martin's son Richard, a goldsmith, and before 1599 by John Povey, both of whom married into a family of London haberdashers, the Bonds.[42] Thomas Throckmorton[43] lived in 1603 in a house by the green, apparently east of Cornwallis's and described as very old and large in 1715.[44] On the Hornsey side of the high road Anne Smith, widow of Robert, held a 10-a. pasture called High Reding with two new houses in 1603.[45] Near by, a building on the site of Cromwell House was sold in 1605 by George Crowther, a London vintner, to Robert Sprignell, son of Richard Sprignell, a barber-surgeon.[46] John Arundell of Lanherne (Cornw.), a recusant like Throckmorton, was confined to Highgate from *c.* 1599 to 1603.[47]

Grand houses multiplied in the early 17th century.[48] At Richard Martin's former seat in 1611 Sir William Bond received Lady Arabella Stuart and her guards on their way north. Mary, countess of Home (d. 1645), later bought the house and her son-in-law the earl of Lauderdale remodelled it. Immediately north stood a long low building of timber and plaster, apparently substantial in the 1660s; it came to be known, without good foundation, as 'Andrew Marvell's Cottage' and survived until 1868.[49] To the north-west on a site occupied since 1565 Bisham House was later owned successively by Sir Edward Gould,[50] the controversialist Joseph Mendham (d. 1856), and Capt. Peter Heywood (d. 1831),[51] a former midshipman in the *Bounty*. The grounds stretched from High Street to Swain's Lane and were built over in the 1880s.[52] Cornwallis's house on the green was sold in 1610 to Thomas Howard, earl of Arundel (d. 1646), the art collector, a lavish entertainer whose guests at Highgate included James I in 1624.[53] It was at Arundel House that Francis Bacon, Viscount St. Alban, died in 1626. The western part was on the site later covered by Old Hall, and farther west stood a banqueting house, presumably built by the earl. Arundel House, or possibly just the banqueting house, was depicted as a square, three-storeyed building with a central tower;[54] it was divided

25 See p. 178.
26 *Survey of Lond.* xvii. 141.
27 Ibid. 16, 24.
28 Prob. 11/63 (P.C.C. 15 Darcy).
29 *Cal. S.P. Dom.* 1581–90, 29; ibid. 1591–4, 219.
30 *D.N.B.*
31 Hist. MSS. Com. 9, *Hatfield Ho.* iii, p. 269.
32 *Acts and Monuments of John Foxe*, ed. S. R. Cattley, viii. 607.
33 *D.N.B.*
34 *Survey of Lond.* xvii. 48.
35 Norden, *Spec. Brit.* 22. Prickett's statement that Arundel Ho. stood on the Bank north of Cromwell Ho., repeated in later histories, was disproved by F. Marcham: *Survey of Lond.* xvii. 50. The ho. at Highgate is confused with one in the Strand in Mary F. S. Hervey, *Life of Thos. Howard, earl of Arundel* (1921).
36 *Survey of Lond.* xvii. 48.
37 Hist. MSS. Com. 77, *De L'Isle*, ii. 184.
38 Norden, *Spec. Brit.* 22.
39 Ibid.
40 *Survey of Lond.* xvii. 105; Marcham, 'Cantlowes Ct. Rolls', 16.
41 Highgate Sch. rec., box 3, bdle. 1.
42 *Survey of Lond.* xvii, 7, 9, 145.
43 Probably Thos. Throckmorton of Coughton (Warws.) (d. 1614): G.E.C. *Complete Baronetage*, ii. 197.
44 *Survey of Lond.* xvii. 41–2; Hist. MSS. Com. 9, *Hatfield Ho.* xii, p. 698. It is possible that Throckmorton was merely a tenant of Arundel Ho.
45 Marchams, *Ct. Rolls*, 2.
46 Ibid. 10; P. Norman, *Cromwell Ho.* (L.C.C. *Survey*, monograph xii), 21–3.
47 See p. 182.
48 Except where otherwise stated, the para. is based on *Survey of Lond.* xvii.
49 Illus. in ibid., plate 13; also in Potter Colln. 7/112–14, and Swiss Cottage libr., Heal Colln., A III, 81–5.
50 *Survey of Lond.* xvii. 22, 24.
51 *D.N.B.*
52 See p. 131.
53 *Cal. S.P. Dom.* 1623–5, 267.
54 The only known illus.: *Survey of Lond.* xvii, plate 36a.

between 1665 and 1674 and later largely demolished. Farther west a house was conveyed by William Cholmley to Sir James Harrington of Swakeleys, in Ickenham,[55] in 1656. Part of it survived in Hollyside, formerly no. 49 West Hill. Almost opposite stood the Blue House, between the later no. 1 the Grove and Witanhurst. John Warner the younger, whose father's estate had bordered the west side of the green and covered 38 a., conveyed the Blue House to Sir Robert Payne in 1620. Payne later acquired Arundel House and sold the Blue House to Henry Pierrepont, marquess of Dorchester (d. 1680), lord of Cantlowes manor during the Interregnum. The Blue House then became known as Dorchester House and was a three-storeyed mansion of brick with stone dressings, [56] designed by John Thorpe the elder or younger.[57] The gardens were on two levels, with a brick wall for the upper terrace which may have been the 'bulwarks' mentioned in 1688 and which is still visible from the garden of no. 7 the Grove.[58] Dorchester House, whose garden also covered the ground later taken for nos. 1–6 the Grove, was replaced by an 18th-century house, known by 1875 as Grove Bank. Two acres farther north, afterwards the site of nos. 7–12, were leased by the elder John Warner to Richard Lyllie, a builder who erected his own house there. The house passed to Sir Robert Payne and in 1651 to Thomas Collett (d. 1675) of the Middle Temple, who enlarged and embellished the grounds. It was later replaced by Grove House.[59]

Probably the most desirable sites were on the Cantlowes side, near the top of the hill and bordering the green, which commanded the finest prospects. The largest surviving 17th-century house, however, was built on the Hornsey side of the high road *c.* 1638 by Sir Richard Sprignell, Bt. (d. 1659). Later known as Cromwell House, it replaced the house conveyed to Richard's father Robert in 1605.[60] A still bigger house to the north, at the later corner of Cholmeley Park and High Street, was that of the lord mayor Sir John Wollaston (d. 1658), who bought the lordship of Hornsey manor in 1647.[61] Sir Thomas Abney (d. 1722), another lord mayor, was said to have been a later resident.[62] Abney's second wife Mary was perhaps related to Thomas Gunstone, who lived on the site of Fairseat in 1665.[63]

Sir Richard Sprignell, connected by marriage with the regicide Sir Michael Livesey, lived opposite Lauderdale House, which was held during the earl's sequestration by Sir John Ireton, lord mayor in 1658 and brother of Cromwell's son-in-law.[64] Ralph Harrison (d. 1656), father-in-law of the regicide Maj.-Gen. Thomas Harrison, also lived at Highgate, probably in a house which his widow leased from Wollaston in 1658.[65] Sir James Harrington, resident until *c.* 1643, was named to try Charles I and later served on the council of state.[66] Sprignell and Ireton witnessed each other's wills and, with Wollaston and the Harrisons, formed a powerful parliamentarian group. Royalists included the solicitor-general Sir Thomas Gardiner (d. 1652), Sir Robert Payne, to whom Gardiner sold Arundel House, Lord Dorchester, himself a nephew of the theologian Nicholas Ferrar, and, before his imprisonment in 1651, Lord Lauderdale. National divisions were reflected in the expulsions of Gardiner and, at the Restoration, of Ireton as governors of Cholmley's school[67] and in the vicissitudes of the schoolmaster and chapel reader.[68]

Meanwhile smaller buildings were multiplying along the road frontages. The first inclosure on the bank before the Elms, by 1619, covered the site of the later nos. 47, 49, and 51 High Street. The next, on the site of nos. 39–45, was made by a blacksmith in 1664 and led to the erection of a forge which stood at the corner of the high road and Pond Square, facing Angel Row, until 1896. A strip between the two inclosures remained open until 1685.[69] Beyond the school a house had replaced the windmill by 1641 and various buildings, presumably including Wollaston's alms-houses, stood on the old chapel field in 1657.[70] Inclosures were made from the green for cottages, gardens, and stables. Some twenty encroachments, including at least ten houses,[71] were presented in 1656 at Cantlowes manor court. Thomas Collett, steward of the manor, and Lord Dorchester were among those who had encroached on the green. In 1662 Collett was licensed to connect his house with the high road opposite the chapel by means of a tree-lined causeway across the green, which came to form an arm of South Grove and eventually formed the top of Highgate West Hill. Collett's new road cut off building land to the north-west from the area around the ponds, and, with the control of further encroachments, determined the future shape of the centre of Highgate.[72]

By the 1660s Highgate was much the largest centre of population in Hornsey and St. Pancras. The Hornsey part contained 49 houses assessed for hearth tax and 85 which were not chargeable in 1664,[73] when the St. Pancras side had 27, all chargeable.[74] The Hornsey side had grown rapidly since 1642[75] and was more populous presumably because poor families had congregated in the forerunners of Townsend's Yard and other alleys, which had been built off the east side of the high road without detriment to the green. By 1674 there were 80 chargeable houses in the Hornsey part[76] and 60 in the St. Pancras part. The largest was

[55] *V.C.H. Mdx.* iv. 103.

[56] Watercolour drawing, from painting of 1654, in Swiss Cottage libr., Heal Colln., A III, 74. It is also in Wm. Blake's bird's-eye view of Highgate *c.* 1688: *Survey of Lond.* xvii, plate 39.

[57] Plan, in Soane Mus., in *Survey of Lond.* xvii, plate 51b.

[58] Lysons, *Environs*, iii. 64; ex inf. Sir Jas. Brown.

[59] See also 'Thos. Collett' (MS. *penes* Sir Jas. Brown).

[60] Norman, *Cromwell Ho.* 36; see above, p. 124.

[61] Marchams, *Ct. Rolls*, xiv, xvii, 150, 195. For Wollaston, see also V. Pearl, *Lond. and the Outbreak of the Puritan Revolution* (1961), 328–31.

[62] Kitchener, *Old Highgate*, 12–13; *D.N.B.*

[63] *Genealogist*, v. 91; *Survey of Lond.* xvii. 139.

[64] See p. 136.

[65] Marchams, *Ct. Rolls*, 151.

[66] *Survey of Lond.* xvii. 69, 128; *D.N.B.*

[67] *Highgate Sch. Reg.* (5th edn. 1950), pp. xxii–xxiii; 'Thos. Collett', 28, 37–8.

[68] See p. 179.

[69] *Survey of Lond.* xvii. 105.

[70] Highgate Sch. rec., box 1, bdle. 2; box 3, bdle. 1.

[71] Guildhall MS. 14220/8. Part of the ct. roll is defective.

[72] *Survey of Lond.* xvii. 92; 'Thos. Collett', 17–22.

[73] M.R.O., MR/TH/1.

[74] M.R.O., MR/TH/2.

[75] See p. 135.

[76] The rest of the para. is based on *Survey of Lond.* xvii. 139–40 and Marchams, *Ct. Rolls*, xiii–xiv.

Dorchester House with 31 hearths, followed by Lauderdale House with 26, Cromwell House with 25, and Arundel House, with 23 in 1664. A forerunner of Winchester Hall had 19 hearths, the former home of Sir John Wollaston had 18, a house on the site of Fairseat had 15, and another ten houses, including Collett's, had 10 hearths or more.

Although Highgate grew up partly to serve the rich, it also catered for travellers. The Red Lion, in North Hill, had 9 hearths in 1664, when the Angel had 6 and the White Hart, in Highgate West Hill, had 7.[77] The Gatehouse, first mentioned as a dwelling in 1661, had 9 hearths *c.* 1674.[78] Between 1668 and 1670 tokens were issued by the landlords of the Gatehouse, the Angel, and the Red Lion, as well as an otherwise unknown establishment, the Sugar Loaf.[79] The 17th-century Angel may have occupied a different site from the existing inn of that name, which was recorded in 1725 as formerly having been the White Lion.[80] The Mermaid, with 10 hearths,[81] was mentioned from 1619 until 1679[82] and the popular ceremony of Swearing on the Horns, later associated with the Gatehouse and other inns, apparently dated from the same period.[83]

Despite the fines for encroachments growth continued in the late 17th century. Several of the large houses assessed in 1664 and 1674, in addition to Arundel House, were divided between those dates.[84] Near the top of West Hill the site of the Fox and Crown, inclosed in 1663, and adjoining inclosures contained 4 houses in 1665 and 7 in 1674.[85] Three-quarters of an acre lying west of the ponds had long served as a bowling green in 1672, when the lord conveyed it to trustees. It bordered some wasteland which was inclosed in 1663 and where there was a house, probably the forerunner of the Flask inn, by 1682.[86] More inclosures were permitted north-east of the bowling green and also beyond, where the causeway joined the high road opposite the Gatehouse, in 1692. A building stood on each site by 1739, one being the forerunner of Rock House and its neighbours, the other of a row to the north, later nos. 46–51 South Grove (in 1977 nos. 49–54 Highgate West Hill). Together with the buildings along High Street they came to form three sides of Pond Square, although only Rock House and others on the west, which faced inward, were thought to belong to the square (nos. 1–6).[87] The Gatehouse itself was extended southward after an inclosure from the green in 1670.[88]

The 1680s and 1690s saw new gentlemen's houses on the south and west sides of the green, where attractive sites had been monopolized by Arundel House and Dorchester House. The Arundel House estate was sold in 1670 by Sir Robert Payne's son William to Francis Blake, who divided the mansion and allowed his younger brother William to occupy the banqueting house farther west. Andrew Campion, a later purchaser, moved to a new residence, afterwards South Grove House, on the western part of his land in 1675. He sold the banqueting house itself to William Blake,[89] who adapted it for his ill-fated Ladies' Hospital.[90] William Blake made way in 1681 for his son Daniel, who soon conveyed the property to his father's creditor Sir William Ashurst, later lord mayor of London (d. 1720). Ashurst replaced the western part of Arundel House with Old Hall in the 1690s[91] and also chose the site of the banqueting house for a grander residence. Ashurst House, sometimes called the Mansion House, impressed Defoe.[92] It was a large square building set back from the green, at the end of an avenue later marked by the approach to St. Michael's church, and commanded formal gardens stretching much farther down the hill than those of its neighbours.[93] The house was sold by Sir William's grandson William Pritchard Ashurst to John Edwards (d. 1769) and leased by Edwards's descendants Sarah Cave and Sarah Otway Cave, whose tenants included the judge Sir Alan Chambré (d. 1823). After serving as a school, Ashurst House was bought as the site for a church in 1830.[94]

Along the west side of the green Thomas Collett's old house at the northern end was bought in 1678 by Sir Francis Pemberton (d. 1697), the future lord chief justice, who replaced it with Grove House. Pemberton's seat, approached by an avenue from the green, was bought in 1782 by Charles Fitzroy, Lord Southampton (d. 1797), and demolished before 1808, when George Fitzroy, Lord Southampton (d. 1810), incorporated most of the land in Fitzroy farm.[95] At the southern end Dorchester House was acquired briefly for the Ladies' Hospital by William Blake, who built three pairs of semi-detached houses in the garden (later nos. 1–6 the Grove). Pemberton, as mortgagee, acquired the whole property in 1683, pulling down Dorchester House between 1688 and 1699 but profiting from the new houses in the Grove, which by 1769 were known as Pemberton Row and by 1804 as Quality Walk.[96]

The last noble householders included Lord Dorchester's great-nephew Robert Pierrepont, earl of Kingston (later marquess of Dorchester and duke of Kingston) from 1694 to 1702, Lord Holles from 1694 to 1700, and the duke of Newcastle from 1702 until 1710.[97] Lord Holles was presumably John Holles, earl of Clare, created duke of

[77] M.R.O., MR/TH/2.
[78] M.R.O., MR/TH/66. The 'high gate' was 14th-cent. but no building was specified in early-17th-century leases of the tolls: Guildhall MS. 12371.
[79] Lloyd, *Highgate*, 416.
[80] *Survey of Lond.* xvii. 28.
[81] M.R.O., MR/TH/66.
[82] Marchams, *Ct. Rolls*, 51, 182.
[83] See p. 158.
[84] *Survey of Lond.* xvii. 139–40.
[85] Ibid. 74.
[86] Ibid. 111.
[87] Ibid. 107–10.
[88] Ibid. 104.
[89] Ibid. 52–3, 60–1, 65. The account in the *Survey* is amended from information supplied by Sir Jas. Brown. For South Grove Ho., see also below, p. 134.
[90] See p. 191.
[91] *Survey of Lond.* xvii. 53, 60–1.
[92] Daniel Defoe, *Tour through Eng. and Wales* (Everyman edn. 1928), ii. 3.
[93] Engraving by J. Kyp in *Britannia Illustrata* (1715), illus. in *Survey of Lond.* xvii, plate 41, and below, plate facing p. 128. Later sketches, suggesting that the n. side of the ho. was not so tall, are in *Survey of Lond.* xvii, plates 42a and 42b.
[94] Ibid. 61–2; see below, p. 197.
[95] *Survey of Lond.* xvii. 94–5.
[96] Ibid. 77, 89–91.
[97] E. Chamberlayne, *Angliae Notitia* (1694–1707); J. Chamberlayne, *Magnae Britanniae Notitia* (1710).

Newcastle-upon-Tyne in 1694, who died in 1711.[98] His house is not known, although Francis, Lord Holles of Ifield (d. 1690), briefly owned and altered Throckmorton's old mansion between 1686 and 1688.[99] Francis, Lord Holles, was a kinsman of John Holles, later duke of Newcastle, himself a great-nephew of the marquess of Dorchester who had died in 1680.[1]

Eighteenth-century Highgate, no longer aristocratic, continued to attract the rich. Its reputation for healthy air and fine prospects was secure. The panorama over London, admired by Defoe,[2] was celebrated in 1743, in verse,[3] and in the 1760s,[4] when it made James Boswell 'all life and joy'.[5] The engraver John Chatelaine, who showed Highgate from the south in 1745 and 1752, was the first of many to depict the village on its wooded heights; by the 1790s views from the top of the hill were equally popular.[6] Advertisements for houses, dating at least from 1728,[7] stressed the convenience, beauty, and gentility of the village.[8] The rebuilding of the alms-houses[9] and enlargements of the chapel, itself a favoured subject for artists,[10] enhanced Highgate's claims to elegance.

Evidence of 18th-century growth survives in many genteel houses.[11] Ireton House and Lyndale House were built as a single residence on the site of an older one next to Cromwell House,[12] facing Hertford House, where one dwelling may have replaced two as early as 1725. The present Ivy and Northgate houses, a substantial semi-detached pair,[13] were refitted. Nos. 17, 19, and 21 High Street (the Gould charity estate) were rebuilt *c.* 1733, probably after Englefield House had filled a gap in the street frontage. Along the south side of the green Throckmorton's old mansion was split up and in 1715 made way for a pair which included Moreton House; Russell House was built at about the same time and Church House later in the century. South Grove House, bought in 1720 by the high church preacher Henry Sacheverell who died there in 1724,[14] was afterwards extended towards the road. Later residences included Cholmeley Lodge, replacing the Mermaid inn on the later north corner of Cholmeley Park and High Street.[15] Humbler buildings also multiplied: there were thirteen on the chapel field in 1717[16] and eight new ones adjoined the White Lion in 1749.[17] In North Road, opposite the school's estate, a strip was acquired for one house in 1713, occupied by two houses in 1752 and by six cottages in 1784; between 1788 and 1790 a local builder, William Anderson, replaced them with a row known as York Buildings in 1815 and numbering twenty cottages from *c.* 1830.[18] Demand for sites diminished the grounds of even the largest houses in High Street; of 18 a. attached to Cromwell House in 1664 only 1 a. was retained, as a garden, from 1742.[19] The one small estate comparable to that of Cholmley's school comprised three cottages with curtilages and meadows left to Christ's Hospital by Jane Savage by will dated 1669. The property lay on the north-east side of High Street, containing 3½ a. with seven tenements in 1840;[20] Christ's Hospital sold nos. 42 and 62 in 1915, nos. 20 and 22 (Broadbent's Yard) in 1922, nos. 6 and 8 in 1928, and the rest of the estate in 1960.[21]

Houses began to line the roads approaching the village and by 1754 stretched a short way along Hornsey and Southwood lanes, and along North Road to a point a little beyond Castle Yard on the east and much farther, almost half-way down the hill, on the west.[22] In Hornsey Lane the houses stood on both the Hornsey and Islington sides of the boundary.[23] At the corner of the lane and Highgate Hill the later Winchester Hall, presumably named after Susannah Winch who held property there before 1691,[24] was called Winches House by 1738, when it was bought by Thomas Rogers.[25] In Southwood Lane John Raymond had a house as early as 1687 and held a forerunner of Southwood in 1707.[26] To the north Field-Marshal George Wade (d. 1748) rebuilt a house which existed by 1736[27] and which he had acquired with 2 a. of Highgate common between Southwood and Jackson's lanes in 1745;[28] afterwards known as Southwood House, it had a three-storeyed centre and was later extended with two two-storeyed wings. In Jackson's Lane itself a rambling house of two storeys and attics, later known as Southwood Lawn, probably dated from the 17th century but was much altered in the 18th.[29]

Travellers increasingly contributed to Highgate's prosperity. The Black Dog, mentioned from 1735,[30] was presumably the inn on Highgate Hill which later made way for St. Joseph's retreat.[31] Opposite stood the Crown, slightly below the existing Old Crown,[32] which marked the southern end of Highgate village in 1774.[33] The Mitre, at the corner of Hampstead Lane facing the Gatehouse, was so named by 1727[34] and licensed by 1717.[35] In North Road, in addition to the Red Lion, a building called

98 G.E.C. *Complete Peerage*, iii. 249.
99 *Survey of Lond.* xvii. 42.
1 *Complete Peerage*, iii. 249; vi. 546–7.
2 *Tour through Eng. and Wales*, ii. 3.
3 *Gent. Mag.* xiii. 491.
4 *London and its Environs Described*, iii (1761), 190.
5 *Boswell's Lond. Jnl. 1762–3*, ed. F. A. Pottle, 43.
6 Potter Colln. 9/31–40. See also below, plate facing p. 144.
7 Sale parts. of Edw. Pauncefort's ho. [Lauderdale Ho.]: Potter Colln. 15/29.
8 Ibid. 15/29, 33; Swiss Cottage libr., Heal Colln., A III, 4, 15.
9 See p. 203.
10 See p. 180.
11 Except where otherwise stated, the para. is based on *Survey of Lond.* xvii.
12 Norman, *Cromwell Ho.* 27.
13 Hist. Mon. Com. *Mdx.* 80.
14 *D.N.B.*
15 *The Times*, 21 May 1931; cuttings and note in Hornsey libr.
16 M.L.R. 1717/2/116; 1717/2/272.
17 Potter Colln. 10/25.
18 *Hornsey Jnl.* 10 Feb. 1933.
19 Norman, *Cromwell Ho.* 26, 29.
20 Marchams, *Ct. Rolls*, 178 n.; *32nd Rep. Com. Char. pt. 6*, H.C. 219, p. 210 (1840), xix (1).
21 Ex inf. the clerk, Christ's Hosp.
22 J. Rocque, *Map of Mdx.* (1754).
23 One was acquired in 1798 by the Idle family: M.R.O., Acc. 953/6.
24 Marchams, *Ct. Rolls*, 249.
25 Guildhall MS. 10465/53.
26 R. B. Pugh, *Site of Southwood Park* (reprinted from *Hornsey Hist. Soc. Bull.* xii), 1.
27 Guildhall MS. 10465/52.
28 Prickett, *Highgate*, 113 and map.
29 Min. of Town and Country Planning, List of Bldgs. (1950).
30 Potter Colln. 15/103.
31 Jealous, *Highgate Village*, 18.
32 Potter Colln. 7/11. Both inns were in Islington par.
33 See p. 128.
34 *T.L.M.A.S.* xii. 318.
35 M.R.O., MR/LV3/3.

the Red Heart stood on the chapel field estate in 1717.[36] The White Hart at the top of West Hill was leased with 5 a. to William Bowstread in 1780; Bowstread had a nursery there in 1804, the inn having closed, and William Cutbush by 1822.[37] Inns in the Hornsey part of Highgate in 1786[38] were the Castle and the Green Dragon, both on the chapel field estate[39] and existing by 1765,[40] the Bull, the Bull and Wrestlers (one of them presumably the Black Bull in North Hill where the artist George Morland stayed in 1802),[41] the Wrestlers, the Assembly House (as the Gatehouse had been temporarily renamed), the Bell, the Coach and Horses, the Coopers' Arms, the Duke's Head, the Mitre, the Rose and Crown, the Red Lion, and the Red Lion and Sun.[42] On the St. Pancras side there were only the Angel, the Flask, and the Fox and Crown,[43] all three of them used on occasion for courts or vestry meetings.[44] Highway robberies, many near the foot of Highgate Hill, led to the establishment of evening patrols from the Rose and Crown to Islington.[45]

The demands of traffic led to widening of the road up Highgate Hill to the Gatehouse in 1767, when the roadside elms were felled and the footways levelled.[46] The narrow archway of the Gatehouse, supporting two storeys[47] and said to be the cause of many accidents, was probably taken down at that time.[48] Aided by the governors of the free school, Highgate had supported its own fire service and anti-robbery fund in the 1730s. By 1720 there was a cage, presumably on the High Street site adjoining the watch-house in 1811.[49] It was a natural step, emphasizing that it had outstripped its neighbours, for the 'populous' hamlet to obtain a Lighting and Watching Act in 1774. The provisions applied to an area from the Crown as far north as the Black Bull, around the Grove and South Grove, and some way down Hornsey, Southwood, and Hampstead lanes, although the last had only to be watched.[50] Highgate thus acquired the amenities of a small town and, with assemblies and a theatre, soon enjoyed a corresponding social life.[51] Patrons for local activities were found in the families of the earl of Mansfield and Lord Southampton,[52] whose estates stretched towards Hampstead. By 1800 Highgate and its westerly neighbour were unrivalled on the north side of London, except perhaps by Stoke Newington, as select residential villages and summer retreats. Busy roads, however, made Highgate more convenient for city men and more of a commercial centre than Hampstead.[53]

Although restricted in its early growth, Highgate by 1800 bore a much more straggling appearance than Hampstead, presumably because it had been easier to encroach on the common or the waste bordering the bishop of London's lands than on estates such as Ken Wood.[54] In 1815 there were detached houses and gardens along most of Hornsey Lane to the new Archway, in much of Southwood Lane, and at the top of Jackson's Lane. Buildings also stretched half-way along the north-east side of North Hill and formed two more groups beyond, probably including the Wellington inn at the junction with Archway Road. On the south-west side they stretched nearly the whole way down the hill but stopped short of its foot. North of the junction, by contrast, Lord Mansfield's Manor Farm stood by itself on the west side of Archway Road. Hampstead Lane, after passing a few houses next to the Gatehouse, led westward from the village between Lord Southampton's grounds and the fields of Hornsey park.[55]

The opening of Archway Road in 1813 was opposed by the innkeepers of Highgate village, whose custom consequently dwindled before the coming of the railways.[56] The new road, with no houses between the Archway and the Wellington in 1815, delayed the north-eastern penetration of Highgate into Hornsey. It was, however, probably responsible for the opening of the Wellington (in 1826 perhaps the only new inn since 1786),[57] for the spread of housing along North Hill,[58] and the opening by 1828 of the Woodman[59] opposite the junction with Southwood Lane. Building continued on the remaining central sites. On the western side of High Street a fire-engine house was to be provided in 1811 and the cage was moved from one side to another of the watch-house, which faced the entrance to Southwood Lane.[60] In the Grove the line of Blake's fashionable row was extended northward over the grounds of Grove House, when Lord Southampton granted building leases for nos. 7 to 12 from 1832.[61] Much of the land in the triangle between the Grove and Collett's causeway (itself called Highgate Grove in 1804)[62] was nursery ground by 1842[63] and later taken for a waterworks.[64]

Near the top of West Hill the first leases for Holly Terrace, on part of the land attached to Hollyside, were granted in 1806. Immediately south stood Holly Lodge, new in 1809[65] when it was leased to the actress Harriot Mellon (d. 1837), afterwards wife of the banker Thomas Coutts (d. 1822) and of William de Vere Beauclerk, duke of St. Albans (d. 1849).[66] Itself a modest villa of two storeys and attics, in the Regency style, Holly Lodge stood in

36 Highgate Sch. rec., box 3, bdle. 1.
37 *Survey of Lond.* xvii. 68; see below, p. 137.
38 M.R.O., MR/LV9/140.
39 Highgate Sch. rec., box 3, bdle. 1.
40 M.R.O., MR/LV8/40.
41 G. C. Williamson, *George Morland* (1907), 89.
42 M.R.O., MR/LV9/140.
43 Ibid. 142.
44 See pp. 163–4.
45 Potter Colln. 15/39–40, 44–5; see p. 165.
46 Lloyd, *Highgate*, 162–3.
47 See frontispiece.
48 Swiss Cottage libr., Heal Colln., A III, 24.
49 See p. 165.
50 15 Geo. III, c. 43.
51 See p. 158.
52 e.g. both families provided governors of the free sch.: *Highgate Sch. Reg.* (5th edn.), pp. lxxxix–xci.
53 F. M. L. Thompson, *Hampstead* (1974), 26.
54 Ibid. 27.
55 M.R.O., MR/DE Hornsey.
56 J. Livingstone, 'Intrinsic Value of Highgate Village' (R.I.B.A. thesis 1975 in Highgate Lit. and Sc. Inst.), 30–1.
57 Only the Bull and Wrestlers and the Bell had gone since 1786, possibly replaced by the Lord Nelson and the Bell and Horns.
58 M.R.O., MR/DE Hornsey.
59 Print by J. Pollard: Potter Colln. 6/89.
60 *Survey of Lond.* xvii. 106.
61 Ibid. 94.
62 Ibid. plate 1.
63 Prickett, *Highgate*, map of 1842.
64 O.S. Map 6″, Mdx. XII. SW. (1873 edn.); see below, p. 168.
65 *Survey of Lond.* xvii. 70.
66 *D.N.B.*

Lauderdale House from the south-west *c.* 1835

Ashurst House from the south in 1715

HIGHGATE

View from the south. Rock House is on the left

View from the north. Church House, of five bays, is in the background

HIGHGATE: POND SQUARE *c.* 1790

well stocked grounds of 21 a. which were to be made available for many local fêtes by Harriot's step-daughter Angela, later Baroness, Burdett-Coutts (d. 1906).[67] The estate, broken up in 1922, stretched down the slope to cover Holly Village and higher up to include the roadside houses from Voel to Holly Terrace.[68]

Whereas Archway Road affected Highgate's economic life, it helped to stimulate a sense of exclusiveness. So too, perhaps, did the closure of the free school's chapel in 1832.[69] Cut off from the rest of Hornsey and no longer able to rely on the funds of the school, residents concentrated on the village's own problems and societies multiplied.[70]

Although Highgate was praised in 1849 for its air, scenery, well lit streets, and water supply mainly from wells,[71] it had pockets of urban squalor. Lack of water was considered a deterrent to builders in 1819[72] and the poor had to rely on the polluted ponds on the green. The two ponds were made into one in 1845, with help from St. Pancras parish and local subscriptions,[73] but drainage remained inadequate.[74] Reports of 1848 revealed overcrowded and insanitary conditions, particularly in Townsend's Yard and York Buildings, which persisted for another 20 years.[75]

Highgate became more sedate with the decline of its coaching trade, the closure of its theatre *c.* 1825, and an attack on Sunday business.[76] In 1840 it was said to present a picture of desolation, whence visitors had to seek refreshment in Hampstead.[77] The zeal which enforced Victorian Sundays also tackled bad drainage and slums, and produced schools, chapels, allotments, and societies for the benefit of the poor. In 1864 a local committee was formed to improve the crown of Highgate Hill and the Highgate Dwellings Improvement Co. was established to repair or build houses for letting to the working class.[78]

The crown of Highgate Hill had first been altered in 1845 when the road from High Street, which had curved between the two ponds,[79] was realigned south of the new pond to form the modern South Grove.[80] At the same time the prebendary of Cantlowes had vested Pond Square in locally chosen trustees.[81] The arrival of piped water from the New River Co. in the 1850s left the pond to be used for rubbish, until in 1863 it was proposed to build over the site. Opposition from the surviving trustees, under Dr. Nathaniel Wetherell,[82] led to the establishment of an improvements committee[83] and its adoption of a plan by Rawlinson Parkinson for filling in the pond and planting it with shrubs.[84] The committee also planted two small plots forming a triangle opposite the church, which were received from the prebendary of Cantlowes in 1865.[85] It was thus responsible for all that remained of Highgate green but, lacking funds, failed to keep it tidy. In 1877 there were abortive plans to rebuild Highgate Literary and Scientific Institution there, as part of a community centre,[86] in 1881 there were complaints about encroachment, and in 1885 St. Pancras vestry took over the square, which it paved with tar.[87]

The Highgate Dwellings Improvement Co. was managed by Alderman (later Sir) Sydney Waterlow of Fairseat, who, with the Congregationalist minister Josiah Viney and Col. J. W. Jeakes of Winchester Hall, was also prominent in saving Pond Square.[88] Viney had already completed the model Verandah Cottages in North Hill and Waterlow had recently erected flats in Finsbury. The aim was not only to build but to renovate and, by competition, force landlords to spend more on their property.[89] An early result was the terrace called Springfield Cottages near the foot of North Hill. At the other side of Highgate, opposite the corner of Archway Road and Jackson's Lane, Coleridge Buildings was opened in 1867 as a four-storeyed block with 96 rooms and survived until 1944. Owners reduced rents at York Buildings and carried out improvements at Townsend's Yard, although *c.* 1868 the one place was still described as a plague-spot and the other as an eyesore.[90]

Meanwhile the restriction of the free school's funds to educational purposes, after making necessary the building of St. Michael's church, had enabled the school itself to expand. Two classrooms had been added to the old school-house in 1820 and a library and fourth classroom were built in 1845. The playground, entered from the present North Road, stretched southward to the ruined chapel and eastward to a wall along Southwood Lane.[91] On the opposite side of the lane the 18th-century Cholmeley House was bought in 1845[92] as the headmaster's residence. The main site began to assume its modern appearance with the opening of the Big School block in 1866. Two boarding houses were in use by the 1850s and two more in the 1860s.[93]

In the mid 1860s Highgate, away from its hilltop centre, still straggled along the old roads.[94] Park- and farm-land stretched behind the houses. The Wellington and some brick-fields were all that bordered the Highgate side of Archway Road except at the foot of Southwood Lane, where there were a few cottages. The genteel villas of the Grove extended a little way across Hampstead

[67] *Camden History Rev.* i. 15–16.
[68] Sales parts. *penes* Messrs. Prickett & Ellis. Holly Village is reserved for treatment under St. Pancras.
[69] See p. 178.
[70] See pp. 158–60.
[71] S. Lewis, *Topog. Dict. of Eng.* ii (1849), 509.
[72] Hunter, *Environs*, ii. 85; see below, p. 168.
[73] Lloyd, *Highgate*, 412–13.
[74] Drainage from the hos. in Pond Sq. is shown on a plan of *c.* 1845: Potter Colln. 10/28.
[75] See p. 169.
[76] See p. 161.
[77] Potter Colln. 15/110–13.
[78] *Camden History Rev.* iii. 8.
[79] See plate facing p. 129.
[80] Potter Colln. 10/31 (plan).
[81] Ibid. 10/30.
[82] See p. 138.
[83] *Camden History Rev.* iii. 6–8.
[84] Potter Colln. 10/29.
[85] Potter Colln. 10/32–4.
[86] Ibid. 10/37; *Camden History Rev.* iii. 8–9; see below, p. 158.
[87] Potter Colln. 10/22.
[88] Except where otherwise stated, the para. is based on *Camden History Rev.* iii. 6–8.
[89] *St. Mic.'s Par. Mag.* Apr. 1867.
[90] Cuttings in Prickett and Cassini, *Highgate*, ii (grangerized copy in Highgate Lit. and Sc. Inst.).
[91] *Highgate Sch. Reg.* (6th edn., 1965), 17, 20.
[92] Highgate Sch. rec., box 4, bdle. 2.
[93] *Highgate Sch. Reg.* (6th edn.), 20, 22, 24.
[94] Except where otherwise stated, the following three paras. are based on O.S. Map 6″, Mdx. XII. SW. (1873 edn.), for which the survey was carried out in 1863–9.

Highgate in 1873

Lane, to form North Grove, and St. Michael's Vicarage had been built to the west. Opposite the Vicarage was Caen Terrace and farther west stood Dufferin Lodge, home of the song-writer Helen Selena, Lady Dufferin, afterwards countess of Gifford, who died there in 1867.[95] Beechwood and Fitzroy House, well back from Hampstead Lane, were in St. Pancras parish, as were some large houses in Lord Southampton's Fitzroy Park.[96]

Other large houses in the 1860s included Farquhar and Linden houses in Hornsey Lane, the three-storeyed Winchester Hall[97] at the corner of Highgate Hill, Southwood Lodge, Southwood Cottage, the Limes, Southwood, Southwood House, all east of Southwood Lane, and Southwood Lawn and Oak Lodge in Jackson's Lane. The Limes had been built by 1815[98] and for most of the early 19th century belonged to the owners of Southwood. Southwood itself, altered by 1842 and further extended by the 1860s, stood in grounds which stretched south-east of the Limes; they were improved for Mark Beauchamp Peacock (d. 1862) and commanded a noted view,[99] depicted by the antiquary F. W. Fairholt.[1]

In North Hill the largest house, and the farthest back from the road, was Park House, which had been converted into a refuge for prostitutes in 1848 and leased as the London Diocesan Penitentiary (later the House of Mercy) in 1855. It had beds for 60 girls in 1877, was taken over by the Clewer Sisters in 1900, and closed in 1940,[2] although the building survived until the flats of Hillcrest were laid out.[3] An adjoining chapel, designed by Arthur Blomfield, was opened in 1877[4] and dismantled in 1946.[5] On the fashionable Hampstead side of the village Dufferin Lodge was demolished in 1869 to make way for Caen Wood Towers, a gabled and battlemented mansion designed by E. Salomons & J. P. Jones, which also replaced the neighbouring Fitzroy House and stood in St. Pancras.[6] Public buildings included a police station in High Street, succeeded by one in the northern arm of South Grove,[7] and offices for the local board in Southwood Lane.[8]

Model dwellings were needed not only for existing slum-dwellers but for railway construction workers and railwaymen. To serve the poorer district that was growing up around the foot of North Hill and the newcomers who were attracted by the railway, All Saints' church was opened in 1864 in a new road (later Church Road) linking North Hill with Archway Road.[9]

Elsewhere building on land away from the old roads, although encouraged by the opening of Highgate station in 1867, had to await the sale of large houses or of the Ecclesiastical Commissioners' lands. The death of Col. J. W. Jeakes in 1874 was followed by his son's sale of Winchester Hall to the Imperial Property Investment Co. in 1881. The house was pulled down in 1881–2, its fittings, including 1½ mile of iron park fencing, were sold, Hornsey Lane was widened, and Cromwell Avenue driven north-eastward through the estate to Archway Road. Houses of two classes, faced with Suffolk brick, were being built and offered in 1882,[10] when their construction presumably led to the opening of the cable tramway up Highgate Hill and furthered the foundation of St. Augustine's church, on the far side of Archway Road. A smaller but more central scheme was started in 1883, when Bisham House was demolished and 30 terraced houses and two larger ones were planned for Bisham Gardens, with eight shops fronting High Street. Property values were expected to rise because of the tramway[11] but neighbouring land was saved from building by the creation of Waterlow Park.[12] In Hornsey Lane Linden and Farquhar houses did not long survive the sale of Winchester Hall, whose land had surrounded them on three sides. Waterlow Park itself was cited as an attraction when houses were offered on the Linden House estate in 1894.[13]

A small working-class area grew up around the Wellington at the foot of North Hill,[14] opposite land acquired by the local board as a depot in 1869,[15] and the G.N.R.'s sidings east of Archway Road. In 1877 a board school was opened next to Springfield Cottages[16] and by 1894 larger houses, most of them terraced or semi-detached, had spread around All Saints' church to fill Bishop's and Bloomfield roads, although none stood in Talbot Road and only a few along the north side of Park House Road (later the Park), facing the grounds of the penitentiary. A building lease for detached or semi-detached houses in part of Talbot Road had been granted by the Ecclesiastical Commissioners in 1892 and other leases, for Talbot and Church roads, were granted in 1896. Terraces were also permitted in Archway Road, near the corner of Talbot Road, in 1892.[17] By 1894 they lined the west side of Archway Road from the foot of North Hill to Southwood Lane and there were more houses from the foot of Jackson's Lane to the Archway cutting. There remained a gap between the foot of Southwood Lane and Jackson's Lane, since the housing that had grown up near the station and church had not yet met the more southerly block formed by the Cromwell Avenue estate. Jackson's Lane itself contained only Southwood House and cottages at the corner of Southwood Lane, on its northern side, and Southwood Lawn and Oak

95 *Complete Peerage*, iv. 493–4; *D.N.B.*

96 The hos. in Fitzroy Pk. are not treated as part of Highgate village.

97 Potter Colln. 7/35–8.

98 M.R.O., MR/DE Hornsey.

99 Pugh, *Southwood Pk.* 2.

1 *D.N.B.*; lithograph in Highgate Lit. and Sc. Inst.

2 Potter Colln. 14/21; *St. Mic.'s Par. Mag.* Jan., Aug., 1864; *Hornsey Jnl.* 19 July 1940.

3 O.S. Maps 6″, 51/28 NE. (1951 edn.), TQ 28 NE. (1958 edn.).

4 *St. Mic.'s Par. Mag.* Aug. 1877.

5 K. U. Platt, *Hist. of All Saints* (1964 centenary booklet), 58.

6 Potter Colln. 12/106. In 1977 it was part of the Middlesex hosp.

7 See p. 170.

8 See p. 167.

9 Platt, *Hist. All Saints*, 9–11, 13, 25–6; see below, p. 182.

10 Potter Colln. 7/35, 39–40, 15/32.

11 Ibid. 7/58.

12 See p. 136.

13 *Highgate Catholic*, July 1894.

14 Except where otherwise stated, the following two paras. are based on O.S. Maps 6″, Mdx. XII. SW. (1873 and 1894–6 edns.).

15 Guildhall MS. 12377.

16 See p. 193.

17 Guildhall MS. 12379.

Lodge on the south side, although detached villas on the Southwood Lawn estate had been projected as early as 1876.[18] Southwood Court had been built by 1882 on land leased from the Peacocks by John Grove Johnson (d. 1908); it was a red-brick house in the Tudor style, of two storeys, basement and attic, with gables, twisted chimneys, and black-and-white infilling. The neighbouring Southwood was much altered and given a third storey at about the same time.[19] Southwood Lawn Road led only a short way from Southwood Lane, past the northern side of Southwood Court, and Cholmeley Park, from High Street, similarly ended near two isolated houses, Lilford House and Copley Dene. There was thus an open tract, with nursery gardens behind High Street, bounded by building along Cromwell Avenue, High Street, Southwood Lane, and Archway Road. A footpath across the fields, from Southwood Lane to Tile Kiln Lane, was neglected by 1891[20] and soon afterwards disappeared.

While Highgate spread eastward to Archway Road, more widely spaced houses were built north-west of the village on the Ecclesiastical Commissioners' land. In the 1860s the bishop's former park still consisted of farm-land along Hampstead Lane west of the Vicarage, except for some allotments[21] and a cricket ground (later the Senior field) leased to Highgate School in 1858. The allotments were bought in 1869 and afterwards converted into the Junior field.[22] On the edge of the Senior field a pavilion was built in 1870, a block of fives courts *c.* 1880, and a swimming bath (from 1896 also a gymnasium) in 1885.[23] A building lease for large houses in Broadlands Road was granted in 1878 to John Groom, architect, who was also to construct two northerly offshoots, later Grange and Denewood roads.[24] In 1879 Highgate School was authorized to buy the freeholds of several new houses in Bishopswood Road, which curved round the Senior field, together with the playing fields, and to build School House for the headmaster and 40 boarders.[25] Both sides of Broadlands Road were built up in the 1880s; the Grange had been built and Grange Road so named by 1882 and the house called Denewood by 1888.[26] North-west of Bishopswood Road the country remained open as far as the Finchley boundary.

Although much extended on the north side by late Victorian housing for the middle classes, Highgate remained distinct from the rest of Hornsey. Physical barriers were perpetuated when an open tract to the north-west was preserved as Highgate golf course and when Highgate and Queen's woods passed into public ownership.[27] The old village was further protected by its elevation. When Shepherd's Hill was at last built up, as an expensive suburb, its residents were regarded as living on the wrong side of Archway Road and in the 1890s they preferred to shop in Highbury rather than to ascend the lanes to Highgate.[28] On the London side building spread to Dartmouth Park and the Archway district of Upper Holloway; it crept up the slopes, where a smallpox and vaccination hospital was built in 1850, followed by St. Joseph's retreat in 1858 and an infirmary for St. Pancras (later part of the Highgate wing of the Whittington hospital), in 1870,[29] but only on the east side did it join Highgate along Hornsey Lane. The village itself was shielded by the reservation of land for Highgate cemetery, opened in 1839,[30] by the formation of Waterlow Park to the east, and to the west by the grounds of Holly Lodge and its neighbours, whose owners contributed to the purchase of Parliament Hill Fields, acquired by the Metropolitan Board of Works as an extension to Hampstead Heath in 1889.[31] Events thus did not vindicate William Howitt, tenant of the Hermitage (replaced by Hermitage Villas) and afterwards of the neighbouring West Hill Lodge: in 1866 when writing *The Northern Heights of London*, Howitt had left for Surrey, dreading the rapid advance of suburban London, that 'monster of burnt clay'.[32]

Most of the remaining space north and east of Highgate had been taken for housing by 1914.[33] Talbot Road was built up and so was the west side of Archway Road between Southwood and Jackson's lanes. Hillside Mansions, an early four-storeyed block of flats[34] near the foot of Jackson's Lane, and the similar Southwood Mansions, at the foot of Southwood Lane, had been built in 1897.[35] Hillside Gardens skirted the grounds of Southwood House. The grounds of Southwood Court still bordered the western end of Southwood Lawn Road but the road itself had been carried eastward to meet Highgate Avenue, which cut across the site of Oak Lodge and where new houses had been advertised in 1897.[36] Houses lined the south side of Jackson's Lane, Southwood Avenue, Highgate Avenue, the east end of Southwood Lawn Road, and Causton Road, as well as the northern end of Cholmeley Park, which had been extended beyond Copley Dene. The Santa Claus home for sick children moved from a private house in South Grove (later Highgate West Hill) to Cholmeley Park in 1900; it stood next to Lilford House, a school from 1886, and was to survive until after 1948, when the L.C.C. acquired it for tuberculous patients.[37] Two nursery-gardens remained behind High Street and the slopes from the back of Southwood Lane towards Causton Road and Cholmeley Park remained open.

Building north-west of Highgate was slower. Stormont Road led north from Hampstead Lane

[18] *Building News*, xxx. 116.
[19] Pugh, *Southwood Pk.* 5.
[20] Potter Colln. 6/87.
[21] See p. 159.
[22] *Highgate Sch. Reg.* (5th edn.), p. xxxix.
[23] Ibid. xli, xliii, xlvi.
[24] Guildhall MS. 12378.
[25] Highgate Sch. rec., box 1, bdle. 7.
[26] Guildhall MSS. 12378–9.
[27] See p. 154.
[28] 'Nineteenth-cent. Highgate: interview with Miss Edith Walker, 1975' (TS. in Highgate Lit. and Sc. Inst.).
[29] Thorne, *Environs*, 354–5. The institutions are reserved for treatment under St. Pancras and Islington.
[30] Lloyd, *Highgate*, 494. The cemetery is reserved for treatment under St. Pancras.
[31] Thompson, *Hampstead*, 333.
[32] A. Lee, *Laurels and Rosemary. The Life of Wm. and Mary Howitt* (1955), 218–19, 243.
[33] Except where otherwise stated, the para. is based on O.S. Maps 6″, Mdx. XII. SW. (1894–6 edn.) and 1/2,500, Mdx. XII. 9 (1914 edn.).
[34] Highgate Lit. and Sc. Inst. photo colln., Ea 58.
[35] Ex inf. Sir Jas. Brown.
[36] Potter Colln 6/90.
[37] *The Times*, 19 June 1900, 14 Dec. 1907; ex inf. Sir Jas. Brown.

in 1915, when woodland still stretched from Finchley along the north side of the lane, opposite Kenwood. Large houses were being built on both sides of View Road in 1898 but by 1915 had spread no farther north-west than Stormont Road.[38] Gaskell Road and its offshoots, in contrast, formed a rectangle of cramped terraces around Highgate board school, off North Hill. The depot was immediately to the north and beyond stood Manor Farm, backing upon fields.[39]

The biggest changes near the centre of the village in the late 19th century were effected by Highgate School. In Southwood Lane the former British school was bought in 1877[40] and used for science lessons, a sanatorium was built at no. 87 in 1884,[41] a new sorting office was leased to the G.P.O. by the governors in 1888,[42] and the headmaster's house was turned into a junior school, known as Cholmeley House, in 1889 and extended in 1894. A new block facing North Road and containing the hall was opened in 1899 and a separate block was added to Cholmeley House in 1904.[43] The governors also rebuilt old houses in North Road: the Castle lost its licence and became a working men's club,[44] cottages between Castle Yard and the Red Lion were demolished in 1888, building leases were offered in 1898,[45] and the Red Lion itself was demolished *c.* 1904.[46] Castle Yard, formerly the yard of the inn, was opened as a road in 1892[47] and Green Dragon Alley, linking North Road with Southwood Lane, was closed in 1898 after the school had agreed to surrender land for widening Castle Yard and Southwood Lane.[48]

Isolated changes took place elsewhere in the village. In High Street the forge at Dodd's Corner, named after the blacksmith's family, was replaced in 1896 by a printing works, which survived until a turning ground for trolley-buses was made *c.* 1947.[49] The Angel inn was rebuilt *c.* 1880[50] and the Gatehouse *c.* 1900.[51] Red-brick flats, similar to those at the foot of Southwood Lane and named Chesterfield Mansions and Burlington Mansions, were built in South Grove between 1898 and 1903.[52] On West Hill Walter Scrimgeour rebuilt the early-18th-century Parkfield and after 1892 demolished the Fox and Crown, where the royal arms had been displayed since the landlord had rescued Queen Victoria and her mother after their carriage had run away in 1837; the site of the inn was taken for stables.[53] On the slopes south of the village two paths between Swain's Lane and Dartmouth Park Hill were stopped up before Lady Burdett-Coutts secured the closure of Bromwich Walk, in return for improvements to Swain's Lane, in 1905.[54] The east wing of Fairseat was demolished for widening the top of Highgate Hill in 1909,[55] and Parkfield, renamed Witanhurst, was enlarged on a grand scale as late as 1913.[56]

The period between the World Wars saw the last fields and woodland along the north side of Hampstead Lane give way to Courtenay, Compton, and Sheldon avenues, all of them laid out by 1920. A few large houses thus linked Highgate with the eastern part of Hampstead. Highgate School opened new science buildings in Southwood Lane in 1928.[57] Ingleholme, in Bishopswood Road on the corner of Hampstead Lane, was later acquired for junior boys and the neighbouring Dormy House was replaced by Cholmeley House; the junior school moved there in 1938, whereupon its old building in Southwood Lane was renamed Dyne House.[58] Farther north, beyond the golf course, Manor farm still belonged to United Dairies in 1932. Aylmer Road had been constructed across the farm from the foot of North Hill to East Finchley by 1935, when the three-storeyed Manor Court, containing 36 flats, stood on its north side next to a shopping parade. On its south side Aylmer Court had been built by 1936 and Whittington Court by 1937. Near the village much of the remaining space east of High Street was also built up by 1938, to complete Cholmeley Crescent.[59] It was overlooked by a three-storeyed house and studio, designed by Tayler and Green, which was completed behind High Street in 1940.[60]

From 1921 the gardens of Southwood Court were improved by Mrs. Elias, whose husband Julius Salter Elias, newspaper proprietor and later Viscount Southwood (d. 1946), demolished the neighbouring Southwood *c.* 1932.[61] More typical of the period than such private embellishments was the replacement of large houses by smaller ones or, more frequently, by blocks of flats. Furnival House had been built in Cholmeley Park as early as 1916;[62] designed by J. H. Pott, it was used by female staff of the Prudential Assurance Co. until *c.* 1928 and thereafter as a home for nurses from the Whittington hospital.[63] The Holly Lodge estate was sold in 1922[64] after the death of Lady Burdett-Coutts's husband, W. L. A. Bartlett-Burdett-Coutts,[65] the house itself making way for part of Holly Lodge Gardens, where detached pseudo-Tudor houses in 'London's loveliest garden colony' were advertised by the Central London Building Co. in 1926.[66] Grove Bank was pulled down *c.* 1933.[67] The

38 O.S. Map 1/2,500, Mdx. XI. 12 (1915 edn.); Guildhall MS. 12378.
39 O.S. Map 1/2,500, Mdx. XII. 9 (1914 edn.). Illus. of Manor Fm., 1888, in Potter Colln. 14/44.
40 Highgate Sch. rec., box 4, bdle. 4.
41 *Highgate Sch. Reg.* (5th edn.), pp. xli, xliii.
42 Highgate Sch. rec., box 3, bdle. 9.
43 *Highgate Sch. Reg.* (5th edn.), pp. xlvi, lxiii.
44 Ex inf. Sir Jas. Brown and see p. 159.
45 Potter Colln. 14/20.
46 *The Times*, 10 Sept. 1904.
47 Ex inf. Sir Jas. Brown.
48 Highgate Sch. rec., box 3, bdle. 11.
49 *Survey of Lond.* xvii. 105; Highgate Lit. and Sc. Inst. photo colln., Ba 29.
50 Highgate Lit. and Sc. Inst. photo colln., Ba 20, 22 (*c.* 1874 and *c.* 1885).
51 Ibid. Cd 6–9.
52 *P.O. Dir. N. Suburbs* (1898); *Kelly's Dir. Hornsey* (1901–2).
53 *Survey of Lond.* xvii. 74–5 and plate 49. The coat of arms has been preserved in the Highgate Lit. and Sc. Inst.: Kitchener, *Old Highgate*, 15.
54 Jealous, *Highgate Village*, 14–15.
55 Potter Colln. 7/64.
56 See p. 138.
57 *Highgate Sch. Reg.* (5th edn.), p. li.
58 Ibid. lxiii.
59 *Kelly's Dir. Hornsey* (1930–7); O.S. Maps 6", Mdx. XI. SE., XII. SW. (1920 and 1938 edns.).
60 *Architectural Rev.* lxxxviii. 71–80.
61 Pugh, *Southwood Pk.* xii. 6–9.
62 Datestone.
63 Ex inf. the asst. chief surveyor, Prudential Assurance Co.
64 Sales parts. *penes* Messrs. Prickett & Ellis.
65 *Who Was Who*, 1916–28.
66 A. Latimer, *Story of Highgate* (1926), 23 and advert.
67 *Survey of Lond.* xvii. 74.

demolition of South Grove House in 1934 and the erection of 50 flats, in a block of three storeys in front and four behind, which began in 1935, threatened the skyline of the northern heights and the centre of the village.[68] Protests from Mr. J. B. Priestley and other eminent residents[69] brought assurances that the natural contours would be respected[70] and perhaps prevented further inroads on what Lady Ottoline Morrell called the simplicity and harmony of the Grove.[71]

People also protested at the building of flats at the top of Highgate Hill, where Cholmeley Lodge was auctioned in 1931[72] and replaced by the block of that name,[73] and in North Road, where the expensive Highpoint One and Two were built between 1936 and 1938.[74] Less obtrusive flats included Rowlands Close, North Hill, replacing the sixteen dwellings known as Ward's Cottages which were condemned in 1932, and twenty-four flats at Grimshaw Close, replacing twenty-one cottages in North Road which were condemned in 1933.[75] Both closes existed by 1935, as did the eight flats forming Cholmeley Court[76] in Southwood Lane.[77] A 150-ft. wooden television mast, later replaced in metal, was built by the B.B.C. at the top of Swain's Lane in 1939.[78] Even with its new flats Highgate, with 17·2 persons per acre, had a lower population density than any ward in Hornsey except Muswell Hill in 1921 and the lowest of all, 18·7, by 1931.[79]

After the Second World War the process of infilling and rebuilding continued but on a limited scale and generally in an unobtrusive form.[80] The longest stretch of new building was Sheldon Avenue's north-easterly extension beyond Denewood Road. A few houses stood on both sides in 1958 and its length had been built up by 1968, although allotments survived to the east in 1976. Similarly, on the slopes below the south-east end of Southwood Lane, the yellow-brick terraced houses of Kingsley Place had been built by 1968, while a small nursery ground was left to the south. The population density remained the lowest for any ward in Hornsey or Haringey: Highgate had 40·32 persons per hectare in 1971 (16·3 per acre), when the average for Hornsey was 79·21.[81]

The bomb-damaged Coleridge Buildings were replaced by Goldsmith Court and a small public garden in 1950.[82] Goldsmith Court, containing sixteen flats, was built by Hornsey Housing Trust with help from the National Corporation for the Care of the Old and the Goldsmiths' Company of London.[83] The court-house and police station, at the corner of Archway and Bishop's roads, had also been bombed but were rebuilt in 1955 and 1960.[84] Council building was planned at Hillcrest in 1947 and finished by 1949.[85] Its architect, T. P. Bennett, also designed two-storeyed terraces in North Road before 1957;[86] they replaced the former Castle inn, in 1919 used as tea-rooms, and neighbouring properties.[87] Near by in Southwood Lane the old municipal offices had gone by 1958 and a terraced row (nos. 99–109) existed in 1968, while Southwood House, empty in 1950[88] but still standing in its own grounds in 1958, made way for terraces of 30 houses in Southwood and Jackson's lanes.[89] Southwood Lawn, which had survived the sale of its gardens, was demolished in 1964.[90] The most striking change was at Southwood Court, which was sold on Lady Southwood's death in 1949 to Mrs. Bohener, who in turn sold it to Ross Hammond Investments (later renamed) in 1962. The house was demolished in 1965 and in its grounds was built Southwood Park, a large block of flats. Some of the land which Lord Southwood had leased from the Limes was laid out for the flats' residents, but the southern part was bought in 1970 by M. P. Kent (Homes) and built up as Somerset Gardens, where the first house was occupied in 1975.[91]

Apart from a new house on the site of the Lawns (no. 16), South Grove, there was little building after 1945 in the centre of Highgate village. Plans to divert heavy lorries there in 1962 were abandoned after the 'Save Highgate' campaign and in 1967–8 both Camden and Haringey councils declared the village a conservation area under the Civic Amenities Act.[92] In Southwood Lane Highgate School replaced the old National school building with two-storeyed flats in 1963[93] and rebuilt Dyne House, with five storeys, between nos. 12 and 16 in 1967.[94] The former Vicarage in Hampstead Lane survived in 1958 but had been replaced by Highgate Close by 1968. Private dwellings farther afield included the three-storeyed flats called Heron's Lea, at the north-eastern end of Sheldon Avenue, by 1960[95] and houses in View Close, under construction in 1962,[96] and Broadlands Close by 1968; exceptionally, two seven-storeyed towers containing 45 flats and called High Sheldon had been erected almost opposite Heron's Lea by 1964.[97] Building land was more readily found in Shepherd's Hill,[98] although some property along the intervening Archway Road was dilapidated in 1977, when long-delayed plans to widen the road were causing dissension.[99]

68 *Hornsey Jnl.* 21 June 1935.
69 *The Times*, 16, 18, 23, 31 Aug., 5 Sept. 1934.
70 Ibid. 8 Sept. 1934.
71 Ibid. 17 Aug. 1934.
72 Ibid. 21 May 1931; photo and plan in Hornsey libr.
73 See p. 136.
74 See p. 139.
75 *Annual Rep. of M.O.H.* (1938).
76 *Kelly's Dir. Hornsey* (1930, 1935).
77 *Builder*, cxlv. 576.
78 Highgate Lit. and Sc. Inst. photo. colln., Bb 6, 7.
79 *Census*, 1921–31.
80 Except where otherwise stated, the following three paras. are based on O.S. Maps 6″, Mdx. 51/28 NE. (1951 edn.) and TQ 28 NE. (1958, 1968, and 1976 edns.).
81 *Census*, 1951–71.
82 M. C. Borer, *Hampstead and Highgate* (1976), 238.
83 Hornsey Housing Trust Ltd. *Chairman's Reps.* (1949); ex inf. the sec. and housing manager.
84 See p. 171.
85 *Builder*, clxxiii. 206–9; clxxvii. 42–5.
86 *Ideal Home*, lxxvi. 112.
87 Jealous, *Highgate Village*, 55.
88 Min. of Town and Country Planning, List of Bldgs. (1950).
89 *Hornsey Jnl.* 26 Aug. 1960.
90 Highgate Lit. and Sc. Inst. photo colln., Ed 4.
91 Pugh, *Southwood Pk.* 9–10.
92 *Buzz* (Highgate Soc. mag.), May 1976; see below, p. 160.
93 Highgate Lit. and Sc. Inst. photo colln., Ea 8, 20.
94 L. Clark, *Prospect of Highgate and Hampstead* (1967), 107.
95 *Hornsey Jnl.* 9 Sept. 1960.
96 Ibid. 12 Oct. 1962.
97 *Hampstead and Highgate Express*, 4 Oct. 1964.
98 See p. 120.
99 See p. 103.

In the Hornsey part of Highgate 83 adult males took the protestation oath in 1642.[1] The village's 161 houses in 1664[2] may have supported more than 800 inhabitants.[3] In 1841 St. Michael's chapelry had 4,302 inhabitants, 3,018 of them in the Hornsey part, compared with only 2,919 in the rest of Hornsey. The population of the Hornsey side of St. Michael's had risen very little, to 3,180, by 1861 and that of the whole village was said to be 5,339 in 1876. St. Michael's contained in all only 4,069 inhabitants in 1891 but north Highgate was then included in the new parish of All Saints, with 4,741. Later growth was slow: Highgate ward had 12,385 inhabitants in 1921 and 13,479 in 1931, when it covered 719 a., and 14,994 in 1951 and 15,580 in 1961, when the area was slightly larger. In 1971 it contained 736 a. (298 hectares) and 12,014 persons.[4]

Most of Highgate's well known residents lived in houses which have been described above, or were connected with churches, chapels, or schools.[5] Natives included the miscellaneous writer and oculist John Taylor (b. 1757), the educational reformer Charles Richson (b. 1806), and the ophthalmic surgeon George Critchett (b. 1817). Charles (afterwards Sir Charles) Scudamore (d. 1849), the physician, spent ten years as an apothecary at Highgate and later, *c.* 1814, practised there.[6] The painters Richard Corbould (d. 1831) and Dean Wolstenholme the younger (d. 1883) both died at Highgate. The aeronaut Charles Green (d. 1870) lived at Naomi Cottage, North Hill, in 1845[7] and the poet Coventry Patmore (d. 1896) at a house called Bowden Lodge, whence he moved in 1866.[8] Later the scientific writer Charles Tomlinson (d. 1897) lived at no. 7 North Road, the theosopher Christopher Walton (d. 1877) at no. 9 Southwood Terrace, and Talbot Baines Reed (d. 1893), writer of boys' books, in Cholmeley Park. In 1884 Robert Hammond publicized the lighting at his house Hilldrop[9] (probably no. 4 North Grove),[10] which was later claimed as the first in Europe to have been lighted throughout by electricity.[11] The cartoonist William Heath Robinson, who was born in Hornsey Rise, Islington, died in 1944 at no. 25 Southwood Avenue.[12] Highgate is described in the autobiography of Sir John Betjeman, whose childhood home was no. 31 West Hill,[13] beyond the village as treated here.

Buildings of Highgate. In 1977 Highgate still evoked strong local pride. Few changes of scene in greater London were so complete as that which accompanied an ascent from Archway station (Islington), with its new buildings and road works, to Highgate High Street. The street itself was better preserved as a whole than its counterpart in Hampstead,[14] having original brick upper storeys, with a few doorways, railings, and even canopied shop-fronts;[15] heavy traffic was the chief contribution of the 20th century. The transition was complete at the top of the hill, where the trees and dignified houses of the Grove, South Grove, and Pond Square formed a peaceful centre on the triangle that had once been Highgate green.

Cromwell House (no. 104 Highgate Hill)[16] is the first building on the Bank, a raised walk along the north-east side of the hill, towards the summit and ending at Cholmeley Park, near the foot of High Street. The house got its name in 1833, apparently on no better grounds than that the builder, Sir Richard Sprignell, was a neighbour of the Iretons. Sir Richard's son Sir Robert sold the house and its 19-a. estate separately in 1664. Alvares Da Costa (d. 1716), a Portuguese Jewish merchant, acquired the house in 1675 and regained the land in 1705, but his son Anthony (d. 1747) sold 18 a. in 1742. A succession of owners followed Anthony's son Abraham, who sold the house in 1749: the last resident owner was Richard Cumberlege Ware from 1821 to 1823 and the last private occupant probably a Mr. Rougemont in 1833. After 1833 Cromwell House served as a school.[17] Great Ormond Street hospital for sick children used it as a convalescent home from 1869[18] and sold the remainder of its lease to the Mothercraft Training Society, which bought the freehold in 1924 and built the four-storeyed Princess Elizabeth hostel, by Richardson & Gill, in the grounds in 1930.[19] The society sold Cromwell House in 1953 to the Church of England Zenana Missionary Society,[20] which in turn sold it in 1970 to the Roman Catholic Montfort Missionaries.[21]

Cromwell House is built of deep red brick and consists of basement, two storeys, and an attic. The symmetry of the main, roadside frontage is affected by a south-eastern extension over a carriage arch, carried out by the Da Costas; presumably they also inserted the main doorway, with its Doric columns and entablature, and added the north wing on the garden side. The lower part of the forecourt wall and the gate piers are also 18th-century, as are the sash windows, while the brick parapet and the roof with its dormers and cupola are of the 1860s, perhaps reconstructions. Despite such changes and patching with lighter materials the original seven-bay front is noted for its proportions, having a slightly projecting centre and bold cornices to define the main floors, with their broad windows, and for the details of its brickwork. The interior contains an elaborate oak staircase of the earlier 17th century, some contemporary

[1] H.L., Mdx. Protestation Rets.
[2] See p. 125.
[3] M.R.O., MR/TH/1–2.
[4] *Census*, 1841–1971. Highgate was included with Hornsey and St. Pancras in the census returns until 1841.
[5] Except where otherwise stated, the following para. is based on *D.N.B.* and Kitchener, *Old Highgate*.
[6] A. M. W. Thomson, *Life of Dr. Wm. Mackenzie* (1973), 21.
[7] *P.O. Dir. Six Home Cnties.* (1845).
[8] B. Champneys, *Memoirs of Coventry Patmore* (1900), i. 223.
[9] R. Hammond, *Electric Light in our Homes* (1884), 87.
[10] *Kelly's Dir. Essex, Herts. and Mdx.* (1890).
[11] Potter Colln. 10/9.
[12] W. Heath Robinson, *My Line of Life* (1938), 3; *D.N.B.* (1941–50).
[13] J. Betjeman, *Summoned by Bells* (1960), 5, 25.
[14] Borer, *Hampstead and Highgate*, 236.
[15] See plate facing p. 144.
[16] Except where otherwise stated, the following two paras. are based on Norman, *Cromwell Ho.* Shorter accounts are in Hist. Mon. Com. *Mdx.* 79–80 and Pevsner, *London, Except Lond. and Westr.* (1952 edn.), 376.
[17] See p. 198.
[18] *St. Mic.'s Par. Mag.* Oct. 1872.
[19] *Builder*, cxxxviii. 474–8.
[20] Newspaper cuttings in Hornsey libr.
[21] Ex inf. the rector.

panelling, and several carved doorcases. Earlier panelling on the ground floor possibly includes survivors of George Crowther's house,[22] rebuilt by Richard Sprignell. The main, south, room on the ground floor (in 1977 a chapel) has a 17th-century plaster ceiling and the main front rooms on the first floor have rich plaster ceilings, reconstructed after the fire of 1865.

Immediately north-west of Cromwell House are Ireton House and Lyndale House (nos. 106 and 108 Highgate Hill) where a cottage of George Crowther was acquired by the Sprignells in 1640 and sold as a house in 1663.[23] They formed a single residence in the late 17th century, the date of a plaster ceiling and a door in Lyndale House, but were largely rebuilt *c.* 1730.[24] Each half has doorways with Tuscan pilasters like that of the adjoining no. 110, also of *c.* 1730 but with its third storey and attic rebuilt. The Cottage, a two-storeyed extension to no. 110, with its ground floor built out in the 19th century, completes the group of old houses on the Bank. The main buildings of Channing school stretch to the entrance to Cholmeley Park, which is flanked by a small lodge and a curving six-storeyed block of 48 flats, built in 1934 to a design by Guy Morgan and called Cholmeley Lodge.[25] Higher up another pair, Ivy House and Northgate House, is late-17th-century, with 18th-century alterations.[26] Charles Knight (d. 1873), author and publisher,[27] came to live at Highgate in 1835[28] and was at Ivy House in 1845.[29]

Almost opposite Cromwell House stands Lauderdale House, of late-16th-century origins but much altered by Charles II's minister John Maitland, earl (afterwards duke) of Lauderdale, and later occupiers.[30] The property, divided by the sons of Sir William Bond (d. 1617), was bought in 1641 by Mary, countess of Home (d. 1645), whose daughter Anne (d. 1671) married Lauderdale. John Ireton had possession from 1649 until the Restoration. Lauderdale apparently left in 1669 and in 1674 Anne's daughter Mary, Lady Yester, surrendered the house, which eventually was bought by Sir William Pritchard, a former lord mayor of London. It remained with Pritchard's heirs the Uthwatts and, from 1757, the Knapps, until sold by Matthew and Arthur John Knapp in 1865 to Sir Sydney Waterlow, who gave it to the L.C.C. in 1889. Famous visitors, in addition to Arabella Stuart,[31] included Charles II, who gave Lauderdale's daughter in marriage to John Hay, Lord Yester (later marquess of Tweeddale), at Highgate in 1666,[32] Samuel Pepys, who found the earl and his Scottish supper guests 'pretty odd company',[33] and Grand Duke Cosimo III of Tuscany in 1669.[34] A story that Nell Gwynne there forced the king to acknowledge their son Charles (later earl of Burford and duke of St. Albans) is probably apocryphal, although it is possible that she followed Lauderdale in residence. The last owner-occupier was Sir William Pritchard; later tenants included Edward Pauncefort (d. 1726), rebuilder of the alms-houses, three successive keepers of private schools,[35] Richard Bethell, the Lord Chancellor (created Lord Westbury),[36] and finally the antiquary James Yates, who died there in 1871. The house became a convalescent home for St. Bartholomew's hospital in 1872[37] and was used by the L.C.C. for shelter, refreshments, and accommodating the council's staff in 1936. It has been owned since 1971 by Camden L.B.[38] and is leased to the Lauderdale House association, formed in 1976.[39]

Lauderdale House is two-storeyed and has walls covered by cream-washed pebbledash.[40] The L.C.C., whose parks committee had urged demolition,[41] removed many Victorian additions and completed the building's restoration by 1893.[42] More repairs were undertaken in 1961 and again after a fire destroyed the roof and much of the upper floor in 1963. Entrance is from a north-eastern range, facing the road and at right angles to a longer range, which looks south-east over the garden and whose projecting upper storey may have been an Elizabethan gallery. A later range faces south-west and there are traces of one to the north-west. The original entrance may therefore have been elsewhere and the plan that of a half-H or quadrangle. A late-16th-century timber-framed house on brick foundations forms the core of the existing building. There is an early brick basement beneath the entrance hall and there is vaulting beneath the courtyard. Some panelling of the 17th century survives in the house. The ground floor's long garden apartment was created in the 1790s; at an earlier time the upper storey was extended over a loggia on the south-west, the windows were replaced by sashes, the walls rendered, and the roof pedimented. The staircase balusters on the landing and the upper flight of steps were destroyed in 1963, together with an octagonal lantern surrounded by rich plasterwork. The gallery, however, has been given a late-17th-century plaster ceiling, removed from no. 72 Leadenhall Street (London) in 1968.

The garden of Lauderdale House, since 1891 part of Waterlow Park, contains early walling, ornaments (some of them resited), and gates.[43] A wall-plaque by the road north of the house commemorates the site of the cottage where Andrew Marvell was said to have lived. Between the cottage and Fairseat stood a house occupied by the architect Sir James Pennithorne (d. 1871) and pulled down by 1889.[44]

[22] See p. 124.
[23] Norman, *Cromwell Ho.* 27.
[24] Hist. Mon. Com. *Mdx.* 80.
[25] *Architectural Rev.* lxxvii. 250–3.
[26] Pevsner, *London, Except Lond. and Westr.* 376; Min. of Town and Country Planning, List of Bldgs. (1950).
[27] *D.N.B.*
[28] C. Knight, *Passages of a Working Life*, iii (1873), 24.
[29] *P.O. Dir. Six Home Cnties.* (1845).
[30] Except where otherwise stated, the following three paras. are based on *Survey of Lond.* xvii. 7–15 and illus.
[31] See p. 124.
[32] *Complete Peerage*, xii(2), 78.
[33] *Diary of Sam. Pepys*, ed. R. Latham and W. Matthews, v. 224.
[34] *Camden History Rev.* iv. 11–12.
[35] See p. 197.
[36] *D.N.B.*
[37] Swiss Cottage libr., Heal Colln., A III, 87.
[38] *Camden History Rev.* iv. 12.
[39] *Highgate Soc. News*, Nov. 1976, Jan. 1977.
[40] See plate facing p. 128. Except where otherwise stated, the para. is based on information supplied by G.L.C., Historic Bldgs. Div. and Mr. David Sturdy.
[41] Swiss Cottage libr., Heal Colln., A III, 6.
[42] Plaque on bldg.
[43] The 18th-cent. garden is reconstructed on a plan *penes* G.L.C., Historic Bldgs. Div.
[44] *Survey of Lond.* xvii. 16.

Highgate High Street contains many 18th-century brick houses, most of three storeys. Nos. 2 and 10 are early-18th-century, although the second has late-18th-century alterations.[45] Nos. 18 to 40, with shop-fronts on the ground floor, present an unusual line of late-18th- or early-19th-century roofs and upper windows.[46] The hooded doorway of no. 42 is surmounted by a cartouche bearing the arms of Sir William Ashurst, presumably a relic of Ashurst House; no. 42 itself is 18th- or early-19th-century, as are the much altered nos. 46 and 48. The weatherboarded no. 60 is early-18th-century and nos. 62, 64,[47] and 66 are late-18th-century; no. 64 houses the long established Highgate pharmacy,[48] inserted between the doorcase and carriage arch of the former White Lion. Nos. 68 to 82 form a row of low, plain, 18th-century houses, mostly refaced and converted into shops but with roofs and window lines adding to the uniform character of the street. They are continued around the corner of Southwood Lane by the 19th-century fronts of nos. 84 and 86 and the modern nos. 88, 90, and 90A. Other survivals are Townsend's Yard, between nos. 42 and 44 but without its former weatherboarded cottages,[49] and the canopied shop-fronts of nos. 62 and 82. On the south side of High Street the site of nos. 17, 19, and 21 was occupied by 1636 and later formed Lady Gould's charity estate. The existing houses were built in 1733 as a terrace, with an extension to no. 17 apparently planned as a shop.[50] The lower and broader Englefield House (no. 23) was probably built by 1710[51] and appears to fill a gap only because the adjoining houses have been rebuilt.[52] Elsewhere the south side of the street has been more thoroughly rebuilt than the north. The Angel and its neighbours are 19th-century, as are most of the buildings with shop-fronts facing High Street and taller backs overlooking Pond Square.

In South Grove the buildings which form Angel Row have been much altered.[53] At the end the relatively low Russell House (no. 9 South Grove) is early-18th-century and of three bays, with a street front rendered *c.* 1800. An 18th-century staircase survives in no. 8 and panelling in Russell House. The adjoining Church House (no. 10) is of five bays and has a staircase which is probably of George I's reign. Sir John Hawkins (d. 1789), Samuel Johnson's biographer,[54] owned the house in the right of his wife Sidney, but apparently never lived there. Church House is said to have been the model for Mrs. Steerforth's residence in *David Copperfield*.[55]

Beyond Highgate Literary and Scientific Institution and the Congregational chapel is Moreton House (no. 14), the survivor of a pair built in 1715. Like Church House it has a front of five bays and an almost identical doorcase. Occupiers have included the Prussian ambassador Count Maltzan in 1781 and from 1809 Dr. James Gillman, with whom Samuel Taylor Coleridge came to live in 1816. Coleridge attracted many literary figures to Highgate: John Keats, on a walk from Hampstead, met him in 1819 and both Southey and Wordsworth visited Moreton House in 1820.[56]

The largest residence in South Grove is Old Hall (no. 17), the main part of which was rebuilt by Sir William Ashurst on the site of the western half of Arundel House. On the east is a one-storeyed wing on part of the site of the Lawns (no. 16), whose basement may contain brickwork from Arundel House, and on the west are modern additions. The central block is five-bayed, with a rain-water head dated 1691, and has been re-fronted, extended by a slightly recessed block on the east side, and given an early-19th-century porch. The interior, much altered, contains some 18th-century woodwork and two panelled rooms, one dated 1595, brought from an inn at Great Yarmouth by William Kemp, Lord Rochdale (d. 1945). Old Hall is shielded from the road by a tall garden wall, with rendered piers and a fine 18th-century wrought-iron gate. Robert Whipple (d. 1953), maker and collector of scientific instruments, lived at no. 13 Holly Lodge Gardens and later at no. 6 Old Hall.[57]

Beyond the approach to St. Michael's church is a milestone, behind which the line of houses is continued by Voel (no. 18), built in the 17th century but refronted on both the road and garden sides in the 18th. The house is three-storeyed and presents an austere front of only three bays. The neighbouring South Grove House stood closer to the road than Voel and, having many windows, contrasted with it. The flats called South Grove House, by Guy Morgan, present an elevation of seven bays to the road but are of greater length.[58]

At the top of Highgate West Hill no. 79 (formerly nos. 45 and 46)[59] occupies a site mentioned in 1493, where the White Hart stood by 1664, and is a conversion from three cottages. The White Hart itself, where 17th-century timbering has been found, was the easternmost of the cottages.[60] The nursery-gardening firm of William Cutbush had a shop at no. 80 (formerly no. 47) until 1918. No. 82 (Hollyside, formerly no. 49) and no. 81 were originally one house, on the site of property sold by William Cholmley to Sir James Harrington in 1656. Hollyside, facing west and on a half-H plan, contains chimney-stacks of that date, although the internal features are mostly 18th-century. From 1712 its estate was extended to include a house and 13 a. which later became the site of Holly Terrace and the northern part of the Holly Lodge estate.

45 Hist. Mon. Com. *Mdx.* 80.
46 Except where otherwise stated, the rest of the para. is based on Min. of Town and Country Planning, List of Bldgs. (1950).
47 See plate facing p. 144.
48 Potter Colln. 8/127.
49 Highgate Lit. and Sc. Inst. photo colln., Ba 15.
50 *Survey of Lond.* xvii. 19–20 and illus.
51 Pevsner, *London, Except Lond. and Westr.* 376.
52 *Survey of Lond.* xvii. 22–6 and illus.
53 Except where otherwise stated, the following four paras. are based on *Survey of Lond.* xvii. 27–71 and illus.
54 *D.N.B.*
55 A. L. Hayward, *Dickens Encyclopaedia* (1924), 81. Similar claims have been made for Old Hall (A. Moreland, *Dickens Landmarks in Lond.* (1931), 74) and for no. 82 Highgate West Hill (ex inf. Sir Jas. Brown).
56 E. K. Chambers, *Samuel Taylor Coleridge* (1938), 294, 299–300. For the Gillmans, see A. W. Gillman, *Gillmans of Highgate* (1895).
57 *D.N.B.* 1951–60; *P.O. Dir. Lond.* (1947, 1952).
58 *Builder*, cxlvii. 331.
59 The numbering of the hos. was changed after their description in the *Survey*, prob. in 1945: ex inf. Sir Jas. Brown.
60 Ex inf. Sir Jas. Brown.

It passed to the family of John Cooke, for whom Holly Terrace was built by George Smart *c.* 1806. On the opposite side of the road a plaque in the wall of an outbuilding of Witanhurst commemorates the Fox and Crown.[61]

The south-west wing of Witanhurst survives from Parkfield, but the rest was built by George Hubbard[62] for Sir Arthur Crosfield, Bt.[63] The mansion overlooks 13 a. of well timbered grounds, which offered a chance of a last significant addition to Hampstead Heath. Proposals to build over the grounds started a *cause célèbre* in 1967,[64] resolved temporarily in 1977 when the house was sold again and refurbished for private occupation.[65]

The oldest part of Witanhurst,[66] dating from *c.* 1700, is of red and brown brick and consists of semi-basement, two storeys, and attics. Hubbard's grandiose building, in a similar style, is two- and three-storeyed, with attics. It has a service wing projecting from the north-east and is therefore L-shaped, the forecourt being entered from the Grove through a gatehouse and the main front, with an Ionic colonnade, facing west. Nothing of the 18th century survives internally in the old part, where much of the ground floor served as a billiard room after decoration had been carried out for Sir Arthur Crosfield by Percy McQuoid and White, Allom & Co. The mansion contains more than 50 rooms, including a baroque staircase hall and a large north-western music room, with richly carved details.

Perhaps the most elegant row in Highgate is the Grove, where nos. 1–6 were built by William Blake but mortgaged to Sir Francis Pemberton.[67] Ownership passed in 1714 from Pemberton's widow to John Schoppens (d. 1728), brother-in-law of John Edwards, and in 1782 from Edwards's granddaughter Mary Preston to Lord Southampton. The houses were sold, mostly to their lessees, in 1863, on the death of the Revd. Thomas William Coke Fitzroy.[68] At the end of 1823 the Gillmans moved from Moreton House to no. 3 the Grove. Coleridge had a study-bedroom in the attic overlooking Kenwood, where he was visited by James Fenimore Cooper and Walter Savage Landor and where he died in 1834.[69] The author Mr. J. B. Priestley bought no. 3 in 1931, renovated it, and sold it at the end of the Second World War.[70] No. 2 was bought by the musician Mr. Yehudi Menuhin in 1959.[71] The judge Sir Edward Fry (d. 1918) moved to no. 6 in 1863, while still a barrister,[72] and his son Roger, the art critic and artist, was born there in 1866.[73]

The three pairs forming nos. 1–6, the Grove, are early semi-detached houses.[74] Each consisted of a basement, ground and first floors, and attics lighted by dormers, with a string course to mark the first floor and a moulded cornice just above the first floor windows; two parallel roofs ran across each pair from north to south, terminating in twin gables between groups of chimney stacks. All have been much altered internally and externally: nos. 1 and 2 were converted into a single residence in 1930–1 by Seely and Paget,[75] who also worked on no. 3, and no. 5 was entirely rebuilt by C. H. James, who removed a second storey and square bay window to restore something of its first appearance. The best preserved is no. 4, with almost the original plan on the ground floor, late 17th- and early-18th-century panelling, and a staircase with twisted balusters.[76] Four examples of wall-paper of *c.* 1700, found in the upper rooms of no. 5 during its rebuilding, are preserved in the Victoria and Albert Museum.

The remaining houses in the Grove, nos. 7 to 12, were built on plots leased by Lord Southampton from 1832.[77] John Drinkwater (d. 1934), the playwright, lived at no. 9.[78] Fine iron railings stand in front of nos. 7 and 8. The Flask, almost opposite no. 5 but facing south-west, has a modern plaque dated 1665. The existing three-storeyed inn is 18th-century, with a former outbuilding which has been refronted to form a two-storeyed extension by South Grove.[79] Behind the Flask 19th-century housing, on the old bowling green, faces both South Grove and the road to the Gatehouse (formerly the northern arm of South Grove but renamed to form a continuation of Highgate West Hill). At the corner of Pond Square the 18th-century Rock House has a pedimented Doric doorcase and two canted bay-windows which project boldly from the first floor. Nos. 1–5 Pond Square are smaller 18th-century houses, nos. 1 and 2 having been partly reconstructed.[80]

Immediately west of the Gatehouse the former no. 52 South Grove has a cistern dated 1789 and a small easterly extension of before 1800. There is an imposing south elevation, with a well-moulded cornice and central pediment. The house was bought by its lessee William Wetherell, an apothecary, in 1788, was later the home of the geologist Dr. Nathaniel Thomas Wetherell (d. 1875),[81] and was still owned by his family in 1936. Its westerly neighbours, formerly nos. 53 and 54 South Grove, form a pair, with a rain-water head dated 1729 and each with three storeys and an attic.[82] They were connected internally to accommodate Grove House school.[83] Most of the humbler houses on the other side of the road have been rebuilt, but the former nos. 46 and 47 are 18th-century.[84]

Although Highgate's oldest houses are mostly south-west of High Street and the Gatehouse, a

[61] *Survey of Lond.* xvii. 72, 75.
[62] Ex inf. G.L.C., Historic Bldgs. Div.
[63] *Who Was Who, 1929–40*, 311.
[64] *The Times*, 27 Sept. 1971; *Buzz* (Highgate Soc. magazine), Sept. 1970, Summer 1971, May 1976.
[65] Ex inf. G.L.C., Historic Bldgs. Div.
[66] The para. is based on report, plans, and photographs *penes* G.L.C., Historic Bldgs. Div.
[67] See p. 126.
[68] *Survey of Lond.* xvii. 90–1.
[69] Chambers, *Coleridge*, 306, 325, 329. An oil painting of Coleridge, apparently done at the Gillmans', is in Highgate Lit. and Sc. Inst.
[70] Ex inf. Mr. J. B. Priestley.
[71] Ex inf. Sir Jas. Brown.
[72] *Survey of Lond.* xvii. 92.
[73] *D.N.B.* 1931–40.
[74] Except where otherwise stated, the para. is based on *Survey of Lond.* xvii. 77–87.
[75] *Country Life*, 30 May 1931, 674–9.
[76] Pevsner, *London, Except Lond. and Westr.* 377.
[77] *Survey of Lond.* xvii. 94.
[78] *St. Pancras Jnl.* iii(x), Mar. 1950, 188.
[79] *Survey of Lond.* xvii. 111.
[80] Ibid. 109–10 and illus.
[81] *D.N.B.*
[82] *Survey of Lond.* xvii. 95–102 and illus.
[83] Ibid. 97; see below, p. 197.
[84] *Survey of Lond.* xvii. 107.

few survive, with some noteworthy modern buildings, in Southwood Lane and in North Road, leading into North Hill. At the top of High Street the tip of the triangular site between Southwood Lane and North Road is occupied by the old graveyard and the Victorian chapel and buildings of Highgate School. Castle Yard, linking the two roads farther north, contains the village's last row of 19th-century working-class cottages.

The south end of Southwood Lane is urban in character. Buildings of Highgate School rise on the west side. On the east are a row of late-18th- and early-19th-century brick houses,[85] Dyne House, which includes a hall and music and art schools,[86] and Highgate Tabernacle. Adjoining the tabernacle no. 22 (formerly Avalon), bears a plaque to the explorer and writer Mary Kingsley (d. 1900), whose father George (d. 1892), the traveller and author, moved there in 1863.[87] Beyond is a range of two- and three-storeyed late-18th-or early-19th-century houses (nos. 24 to 50, even, and 54); the road fronts are rendered and most have been altered, but the backs form an almost symmetrical brown-brick terrace. Southwood Lodge, three-storeyed and early-19th-century, survives with its road frontage altered in Kingsley Place, from which the backs of nos. 24 to 50 can be seen. Opposite no. 22 are the alms-houses, with an inscription recording their rebuilding in 1722 by Edward Pauncefort.

The northern stretch of Southwood Lane, shaded and steep, includes Southwood hospital (the Limes with later additions) and Southwood Park, comprising a four-storeyed row along Southwood Lawn Road and two conjoined tower-blocks, each of seven tiers of flats. The flats, designed by Douglas Stephen and Partners,[88] are of red brick and concrete in a style which has been thought reminiscent of Le Corbusier's and praised for its 'high intellectual modernism'.[89] The whitewashed Bank Point Cottage, with two storeys at the corner of Southwood Lane and three facing Jackson's Lane, is perhaps late-18th-century with successive alterations. Farther down, fronting both lanes, is a private housing estate built in 1960–2; it is of purple brick and concrete, with a stepped roof-line dictated by the steep site.[90] Hillside, a rambling two-storeyed house in Jackson's Lane, is 18th-century but much altered, with a double-bowed garden front and an early-19th-century wing. No. 123 Southwood Lane, with a weatherboarded extension, is a conversion of Well Cottages, an 18th-century pair.[91]

North Road is wider than Southwood Lane, lined with plane trees and made seemingly yet more spacious by front gardens and the playground of Salvin's National school. The south end, opposite the rebuilt Gatehouse inn and Hampstead Lane, is dominated by the red-brick buildings of Highgate School. The chapel (the Crawley memorial chapel) was consecrated in 1867. Built over the vault of its predecessor, it is by F. P. Cockerell in a French middle Gothic style, with an apsidal chancel, a north cloister, and a slender flèche;[92] the interior is richly decorated with coloured bricks and tiles. Cockerell's Big School (1866) is hemmed in by later buildings, designed by C. P. Leach and opened in 1899. Big School, in a scholastic Tudor style, housed the library until 1928. Soon afterwards it was redecorated by A. E. Mumby, architect of the Science Buildings in Southwood Lane, and in 1937 a new library was opened on the top of the science block. Big School is approached by a double stairway of stone (the Shakespeare Steps, named after Sir Geoffrey Shakespeare, Bt.) dated 1949. The main buildings are visible from North Road behind a wrought-iron gateway commemorating the two World Wars; it has replaced a gateway by Leach, which had been surmounted by stone griffins from an earlier structure.[93]

An irregular group of 18th- and 19th-century houses on the east side of North Road includes no. 92, three-storeyed, where a plaque commemorates Charles Dickens's stay in 1832. A more distinguished row is formed on the west side by nos. 13 to 21 (odd), all of them 18th-century except possibly Byron House (no. 13), which has an early-19th-century stuccoed façade and additions on the south side.[94] Byron Cottage (no. 15) has a plaque to the poet A. E. Housman (d. 1936), who lived there from 1887 until 1905, during which time he wrote *A Shropshire Lad*.[95] The Sycamores (no. 21) is of five bays, extended to the north, with an imposing doorway of Doric pilasters and a curved pediment. A few houses, mostly two-bayed, survive from a former row between the Sycamores and no. 37. Nos. 37 & 39 and 41 & 43 are early-19th-century pairs of unusual appearance, with pilaster strips rising to a cement entablature. Nos. 47, 49, and Gloucester House (no. 51) are of similar date. Beyond, where the road bends to descend North Hill, tower the celebrated white blocks of Highpoint One and Two, designed by Lubetkin and Tecton. The first, praised by Le Corbusier as the vertical garden city, is on a double cruciform plan, cement-rendered but with some brick on the ground floor, and contains eight flats, with curving balconies, in each of its 7 storeys. Number Two, to the south, has a porch with caryatids and is ornamented with black brick and cream tile infilling.[96] Among the first tenants, in 1939, was the artist Sir William Rothenstein.[97] Highpoint has been favourably compared for originality with the neo-Georgian Hillcrest, almost opposite, designed by T. P. Bennett & Son.[98] Hillcrest provides 116 flats in seven blocks[99] and is itself notable for its free grouping amid trees on the 5½ a. formerly belonging to Park House.[1]

North Hill contains many early-19th-century houses, either much altered or in short, plain

85 Except where otherwise stated, the following two paras. are based on Min. of Town and Country Planning, List of Bldgs. (1950).

86 Ex inf. the headmaster.

87 *D.N.B.* and Suppl.

88 Pugh, *Southwood Pk.* 9.

89 *Architectural Rev.* cxlii. 363.

90 I. Nairn, *Modern Bldgs. in Lond.* (1964), 42.

91 For the wells, see p. 168.

92 *T.L.M.A.S.* xviii(2), no. 135.

93 *Highgate Sch. Reg.* (5th edn.), pp. xxxvii–xxxviii, xlvi, li; ex inf. the headmaster.

94 Except where otherwise stated, the rest of the para. and the following para. are based on Min. of Town and Country Planning, List of Bldgs. (1950).

95 *D.N.B.* 1931–40.

96 Nairn, *Modern Bldgs. in Lond.* 42; Pevsner, *London, Except Lond. and Westr.* 378–9; F. R. S. Yorke and F. Gibberd, *Modern Flat* (1937), 133–9.

97 *Kelly's Dir. Hornsey* (1939).

98 Pevsner, op. cit. 379.

99 *Builder*, clxxvii. 42.

1 *Architectural Rev.* cvi. 319, 321.

terraces. St. George's House (no. 6) is of *c.* 1800 and has three storeys and a basement, with a lower extension to the south; the front has been rendered and is rusticated on the ground floor, where a semicircular porch with Tuscan columns supports a wrought-iron balcony across the wall at the first floor. Both Albion Cottage (no. 8), with a bow to the north and a later porch, and no. 60 are yellow-brick and early-19th-century. Nos. 62 and 64, a brown-brick pair, are of that date or earlier. On the west side of the road nos. 3, 5, and 7 form an irregular block of 18th-century red- and brown-brick cottages, much altered, no. 3 probably having been two dwellings. The stuccoed Bull inn (no. 13) is 18th-century but greatly changed. Nos. 47 and 49, of red brick and perhaps originally one house of five bays, may be early-18th-century, with later twin doorcases. Prospect Place (nos. 109-19) is a yellow-brick three-storeyed terrace, dated 1811, and Prospect Terrace (nos. 133–9) is grey-brick, of three storeys, and 19th-century.[2] On the same side of the hill are the three-storeyed block built as Verandah Cottages and, near the foot, the yellow-brick terrace of Springfield Cottages (nos. 145–91), dated 1877; both represent mid-Victorian efforts to improve working-class housing.

Highgate junior school's Cholmeley House, in Bishopswood Road, has a datestone of 1937 and is a pale brick neo-Georgian building, designed by Oswald Milne.[3] Mansfield Heights, on a landscaped slope between the Great North Road and Aylmer Road, is an estate of two- and three-storeyed terraces, overlooked by a six-storeyed tower. It is mainly of purple brick, built to the designs of the Metropolitan Police architect's department in 1954,[4] and contrasts with the neo-Georgian flats of Manor Court to the east.

MANORS. The manor of *HARRINGAY* or *HORNSEY* was said in 1294 to have been held by the bishops of London from time immemorial as a member of the manor of Stepney.[5] It was presumably included in Stepney in Domesday Book but by 1241–2 was accounted for separately by a reeve.[6] Before the alienation of the Muswell estate in 1152–3[7] the bishops may have held the whole of Clerkenwell detached and Hornsey except the manor of Brownswood. Except during the Interregnum, when Sir John Wollaston bought the manor and demesne,[8] the manor was held by the bishops until 1868. It then passed to the Ecclesiastical Commissioners, who bought out the lessees' rights in exchange for 137 a.[9]

There is no evidence of a manor-house but there was a lodge in the park, which may have been at Lodge Hill on the boundary with Finchley, where a moat or ditch was visible in 1797.[10] It was mentioned in 1441 and 1464[11] and overgrown with trees by 1576,[12] but remains survived in 1593.[13] Seven episcopal visits to Hornsey are recorded between 1306 and 1335:[14] bishops may have used the house which was acquired in 1293 from Thomas of Banbury and Joan his wife by Richard de Gravesend, bishop 1280–1307, and which descended to his brother Stephen, bishop 1318–38.[15] There was no episcopal residence at Hornsey in 1539[16] or 1579, when John Aylmer, bishop 1577–94, had the lease of a copyhold house in Hornsey manor, which he had repaired and sometimes visited.[17]

The agistment of the park, farmed separately from the demesne *c.* 1390,[18] and the Highgate tolls, administered independently in 1409,[19] were leased together by 1438;[20] from at least 1509 the great park had a different lessee from the little park and the tolls.[21] Most of the demesne was let as a block from the mid 15th century: the exceptions were High Reding[22] and from 1634 the cottage known as the Lord's House in the Bushes.[23]

The demesne farm called Rowledge consisted of the four closes of Lolridge, Withiots, Southfield, and Berryfield in 1464,[24] and of nine closes of 175 a. by 1539;[25] it had grown to 250 a. in 1647, when it included 40 a. of woodland, to 271 a. in 1795, and to 294 a. in 1833.[26] By then Rowledge farm was a block stretching between Hornsey Lane, Crouch End Hill, and Park Road. It was leased to a syndicate in 1407,[27] to John Mollesle in 1438,[28] to Elizabeth Mollesle, widow, to Thomas Marshall by 1464,[29] to Thomas Alderton from 1509 to 1518,[30] to Nicholas Puncheon in 1527,[31] and to Thomas Staunton, perhaps as under-tenant, in 1542–3.[32] Thomas Sherley of Redmarley D'Abitot (Worcs.), a servant of Thomas Cromwell, held Rowledge on preferential terms by 1539,[33] when he and Richard Lechmere (d. 1569) of Hanley Castle (Worcs.) were granted a 50-year lease.[34] From 1547 they also leased the great park. Lechmere's widow Margery sued Sherley for Rowledge[35] but in 1585 Sherley devised the issues of the unexpired term to the wives of Robert Cockshott and John Wylfe.[36] It was presumably the reversion that was leased to John Scott and others in 1569 and to

[2] Pevsner, op. cit. 379.
[3] *Highgate Sch. Reg.* (5th edn.), p. lxiii.
[4] Nairn, op. cit. 43.
[5] *Plac. de Quo Warr.* (Rec. Com.), 475.
[6] E 372/87 rot. 3.
[7] Madge, *Early Rec. of Harringay*, 61–3.
[8] Marchams, *Ct. Rolls*, pp. xix–xxi.
[9] Guildhall MSS. 12386, 12399.
[10] Lysons, *Environs*, iii. 47.
[11] *Eng. Chron. 1377–1461*, ed. J. S. Davies (Camd. Soc. [1st ser.], lxiv), 57; S.C. 6/1140/24 m. 4d.
[12] St. Paul's MS. C (I Nowell), f. 151.
[13] Norden, *Spec. Brit.* 36.
[14] Lloyd, *Highgate*, 76.
[15] Madge, *Med. Rec. of Harringay*, 78–9, 96.
[16] S.P. 1/153 no. 242.
[17] S.P. 12/137 f. 139. The bishop's ho. damaged by fire was not at Hornsey but Fulham, *pace* J. Strype, *Life of Aylmer* (1821 edn.), 48; S.P. 12/137 f. 13.
[18] S.C. 6/1140/18.
[19] Guildhall MS. 10306, m. 3.
[20] S.C. 6/1139/15 m. 1.
[21] S.C. 6/1140/24 m. 2d.
[22] See below.
[23] Guildhall MS. 12370.
[24] S.C. 6/1140/24 m. 4d.
[25] St. Paul's MS. C (Sampson), f. 100v.; but see also C 1/1055/36.
[26] Guildhall MS. 10464A, p. 29.
[27] Ibid. 10306, m. 3.
[28] S.C. 6/1139/15 m. 1.
[29] S.C. 6/1140/24 m. 4d.
[30] S.C. 6/Hen. VIII/2109 m. 2d.; Guildhall MS. 10123/2.
[31] Guildhall MS. 10123/3.
[32] C 1/1055/36.
[33] S.P. 1/153/242.
[34] St. Paul's MS. C (Sampson), ff. 100v.–101.
[35] C 3/109/70.
[36] Prob. 11/68 (P.C.C. 15 Brudenell).

Scott alone in 1580,[37] but it was the actual farm that in 1581 was leased to John Scott of Bromley,[38] who held it initially for years but later for lives. By will dated 1612 he devised it to his second son Stephen, later Sir Stephen, Scott (d. 1658),[39] on the death of whose son John in 1670 Rowledge was leased to Sir Paul Paynter (d. 1688), lord of Muswell, who also held 38 a. of copyhold of Hornsey manor.[40] Paynter's widow Rachel (d. 1694) devised the lease to her husband's great-nephew Paul Paynter, a minor,[41] and her copyhold estate was sold to meet legacies.[42] The lease was held in trust by Rachel's executors, of whom Thomas Dickens became lessee by 1704. In 1724 it was renewed by Francis Dickens, lawyer, whose widow Rachel was lessee from 1747 and had devised it by 1761 to a cousin Anthony Dickens (d. 1795). On the death of Anthony's widow Sally (*née* Scrase) the estate passed in 1801 to their son Charles Scrase Dickens of Brighton (Suss.). By will proved 1833 he devised it to his son and namesake, who in 1856 surrendered the lease of 173 a. to the bishop of London for the freehold of 121 a.[43] In 1861 he enfranchised 71 a. copyhold of the manor of Hornsey.[44]

John Westneys (d. 1784) was under-lessee of the largest part and was succeeded by Philip Booth (d. 1818) and then by John Gillyatt Booth,[45] who in 1833 leased 154 a. By then the old farm-house at Crouch End Hill had been converted into servants' quarters and the adjoining Crouch Hall had been built, with an ornamental water of 6 a. and a park of 52 a.[46] Booth had commissioned a pavilion in 1832 and a façade for the older house in 1835 from J. B. Papworth.[47] In 1847 Booth assigned his under-lease to James Vaudry of Liverpool, who sold it to William Bird, ironmaster, who leased a further 14 a. from C. S. Dickens in 1849. In 1856 Bird surrendered his under-lease but resided at Crouch Hall until 1882, when he sold it.[48] In 1888 the Imperial Property Investment Co. demolished Crouch Hall, a two-storeyed rectangular house with a portico, heavy entablature, and projecting bays.[49] Ground-rents on 142 properties belonging to C. R. Scrase Dickens were sold in 1948.[50]

The agistment of Hornsey park was farmed *c.* 1390[51] and in 1439 was held by Thomas Robert.[52] By 1464 it had been divided between the parts east and west[53] of Southwood Lane, creating the great and little parks. The woods themselves remained in hand until 1645[54] and leases after 1439 referred specifically to pannage, herbage, and agistment.[55] They related increasingly to closes in the park, which contained 235 a. by 1647 and 323 a. by 1787. The great park was leased to Nicholas Johnson in 1461,[56] to his successor Thomas Urgle in 1464,[57] and until at least 1518 to the widow of Sir Thomas Frowyk (d. 1506).[58] In 1527–8 the great park was farmed by a consortium[59] and from 1540 by Thomas Sherley and Richard Lechmere.[60] In 1585 Sherley devised it equally to the children of Anne Cockshott and Elizabeth Wylfe.[61] In the 1570s the under-tenant was John Gilpin of Highgate,[62] who was still lessee in 1590 but whose widow Thomasina and her second husband William Querry held it between 1596 and 1606.[63] From 1638 it was leased to John Oldbury (d. 1680) of Lambeth (Surr.) and to his nephew John Oldbury, merchant of London, who left two daughters.[64] They had assigned it by 1707 to Edward Jennings of the Inner Temple, who assigned it in 1720 to Samuel Strode of London,[65] from whom it passed to his widow Anne and their grandson William Strode (d. 1809) of Northaw (Herts.) by 1775. In 1788, without licence, William Strode sold his rights in lots and apportioned the rent among the purchasers, mainly his under-tenants. The chief purchasers were John Bacon (116 a.), Robert Jordan (56 a.), and Thomas Isherwood (55 a.), but 29 a. were sold to Mrs. Mary Cox, 12½ a. to James Groves, 5½ a. to William Worley, 5 a. to James Baggaley, 8 a. to the earl of Mansfield, and 35 a. to John Thomas.[66] Rather than await the expiry of the remaining two lives the bishop granted individual leases to the occupiers in 1815.[67]

Thomas Isherwood's 55-a. estate was bounded on the north by the demesne woods and on the south by Hampstead Lane. In 1796 he devised it to John Ramsbottom, on whose death it was conveyed to Henry Willmer, who assigned the lease to Peter Truefitt in 1826. Truefitt surrendered it in 1847 to the use of Sarah, Elizabeth Anne, and Maria Jones, three sisters who in 1847 assigned 9 a. to George Abraham Crawshay of Fitzroy Farm, St. Pancras. Maria Jones had died by 1856, when the lease was renewed, but following Elizabeth Anne's death her executors were licensed in 1857 to sell the estate in lots. By that date the bishop had sold the reversion to Charles Bloom and J. B. Dyne.[68]

The tolls belonging to the bishop in Hornsey in 1318[69] were probably at Highgate, where they were afterwards associated with the gatehouse, later the

[37] St. Paul's MSS. C (I Nowell), f. 284; (II Nowell), ff. 207v.–208.
[38] Except where otherwise stated, the rest of the para. and the following para. are based on Guildhall MSS. 12372, 12386.
[39] C 10/56/214.
[40] C 7/535/26; C 7/263/63.
[41] Prob. 11/384 (P.C.C. 99 Lloyd); Prob. 11/433 (P.C.C. 131 Bond).
[42] C 7/263/63; Marchams, *Ct. Rolls*, 246.
[43] See p. 115.
[44] Guildhall MS. 10465/176, pp. 282–7.
[45] *T.L.M.A.S.* xiii. 49.
[46] Guildhall MS. 10418.
[47] Architect's drawings in R.I.B.A., Papworth Colln.
[48] C. R. Watson, *A Hundred Years of Crouch End, 1862–1962*, 13.
[49] Potter Colln. 20/55.
[50] *The Times*, 26 July 1948; sales parts. in B.L., Maps Dept., ref. 33G. 40.
[51] S.C. 6/1140/18.
[52] S.C. 6/1139/15 m. 1.
[53] S.C. 6/1140/24 m. 5.
[54] See p. 153.
[55] S.C. 6/1139/15 m. 1; Guildhall MSS. 10234/1, pp. 510–11; 12400.
[56] Marchams, *Ct. Rolls*, pp. xx–xxi; Guildhall MS. 10418; St. Paul's MSS., box B 74.
[57] S.C. 6/1140/24 m. 5.
[58] Guildhall MS. 10123/2.
[59] Guildhall MS. 10123/3.
[60] St. Paul's MS. C (Sampson), ff. 109v.–110.
[61] C 3/109/70; Prob. 11/68 (P.C.C. 15 Brudenell).
[62] St. Paul's MS. C (I Nowell), ff. 453–4.
[63] Req. 2/41/82; Req. 2/144/77; Guildhall MSS. 10123/15–17; 10312/92, m. 7.
[64] Guildhall MS. 10234/1, pp. 510–11; S. J. Madge, 'Rec. relating to hist. of Hornsey' (original lease, 1687) in Hornsey libr.; C 8/611/6.
[65] M.L.R. 1720/3/141–2.
[66] Guildhall MS. 12418.
[67] Ibid. 10410, 12405.
[68] Ibid. 12373, 12405.
[69] Madge, *Med. Rec. of Harringay*, 65.

Gatehouse tavern.[70] From 1464 until 1807 they were leased with the herbage of Hornsey little park.[71] By 1744 the lease consisted of the Gatehouse, a brewhouse, the tolls, and 69 a.[72] The tolls were already farmed *c.* 1390 by William Payable.[73] In 1409 they were let to Henry Smith,[74] in 1438 to John Dette,[75] in 1464 to John Wiking of Highgate,[76] in 1509 to Stephen Everton,[77] between 1517 and 1527 to Alice Shay, widow,[78] and until *c.* 1536 to Robert Hawkes and Alice his wife. It was later alleged that they were then leased to John Tyson and Alice his wife.[79] By *c.* 1555 Alice Tyson had married John Vaughan, lessee in her right until at least 1578.[80] The lease was held in 1590 by Thomas Parsons and William Mountjoy, under a lease of the reversion in 1559,[81] and from 1601 to 1606 by Thomas Mountjoy.[82] In the late 1570s Henry Linford the elder was apparently subtenant;[83] his son Henry the younger devised the under-lease in 1600 to his son George Linford, who was in possession in 1602.[84] In 1602 the little park and tolls were leased to John Bowyer of London, from 1607 to John Langley of Lambeth (Surr.), in 1611 to Abraham Haynes of London, in 1627 to James Livingstone, groom of the bedchamber, and from 1631 to Abraham Haynes,[85] who in 1639 assigned them to his daughter Elizabeth and her husband Henry Brown of Westminster (d. by 1673). The lease was held by Brown's widow in 1686 and following her death by Abraham Brown and his sister Frances Markham until at least 1709. It was renewed by Abraham Brown and Sarah Brown, spinster, in 1717, by Sarah and her husband Percival Chandler in 1722 and 1730, and by her alone in 1737. She was dead by 1744 when the lessee was Sarah Brown of Barnet, spinster, later wife of Thomas Gregg of the King's Remembrancer's office. Sarah Gregg or her trustees held it until at least 1793 and Thomas Day from 1800. In 1807 he renewed the lease of the Gatehouse and tolls alone, which were leased by Benjamin Richards from 1811 to 1835[86] and then by Samuel Attkins, whose widow Etty held them from 1846 until 1868.[87] Richard Folkes was lessee in 1870 and F. H. Salmon in 1890, when Salmon and the City of London Brewery bought the freehold of the tavern from the Ecclesiastical Commissioners, to whom they remitted the tolls.

In 1807[88] the five closes of 54 a. formerly in the little park were leased to John Addison of Homerton in Hackney, who devised them in 1817 to his widow Elizabeth Catherine Addison (d. 1854). They were then held in trust for her daughters by her executor Thomas Merriman Coombes, whose own executors assigned 39½ a. to the Edgware, Highgate & London Railway Co. in 1864 and the remainder to the G.N.R. in 1868.

High or Rote Reding, in 1536 six closes of 52 a. east of the Great North Road bounded by Finchley wood, Fortis Green, and Hornsey little park,[89] stretched across the boundary into Finchley and were first mentioned in 1395.[90] Like other readings, the closes probably originated as clearings in the demesne woods. Although lessees covenanted to preserve young trees, it was found in 1720 that woodland had been converted to pasture.[91] Such encroachment probably accounts for the growth from 52 a. in 1536 to 76 a. in 1647 and 85 a. in 1792.[92] High Reding was still administered directly by the bishop in 1439, when Rote Reding was first mentioned,[93] but was let as three crofts to John Copwood in 1509.[94] He still occupied it in 1527[95] but in 1536 it was leased to Walter Knight, yeoman of London, at double the rent and therefore may have increased in area. Knight still occurred as lessee in the 1570s[96] in spite of a lease to John Goodwin, merchant-tailor of London, in 1558.[97] Leases were made to Nicholas Kemp of London in 1603,[98] Sir George Paul in 1611,[99] Richard Welby, leatherseller of London, in 1617,[1] Edmund Stile of Beckenham (Kent) in 1619,[2] Francis Paul of Bridgnorth (Salop.) in 1626,[3] and John Juxon of London, lessee of the Bibwell estate in Finchley,[4] in 1634.[5] The lease then descended with Bibwell until 1792, when Susannah, Viscountess Fane, devised it to Thomas Reade.[6] It passed to Robert Johnson of Bloomsbury, to whom the freehold was sold in 1800.[7]

The manor of *TOPSFIELD*, *TOPSFIELD HALL*, or *BROADGATES* apparently originated in an estate at Crouch End subinfeudated by the bishop, as it was held of Hornsey manor for relief, rent, fealty, and suit of court in 1610.[8] It may have been the 1½ hide and 1 virgate acquired from the bishop before 1086 by William the chamberlain[9] and held by Walter the chamberlain in 1201.[10] It may also have been the estate held by Manfred of Harringay in 1318.[11] A London merchant

[70] Guildhall MS. 12371 (lease, 1639); see below.
[71] S.C. 6/1140/24 m. 5.
[72] Guildhall MS. 10243, p. 121.
[73] S.C. 6/1139/15 m. 1; see below.
[74] S.C. 6/1140/18.
[75] S.C. 6/1140/19 m. 3.
[76] S.C. 6/1139/15 m. 1.
[77] S.C. 6/Hen. VIII/2109 m. 2d.
[78] Guildhall MSS. 10123/2–3.
[79] Req. 2/174/24.
[80] S.C. 6/P. & M./193 m. 14; Guildhall MS. 10123/8.
[81] Guildhall MSS. 10123/15–16.
[82] Ibid. 17–18.
[83] Ibid. 10312/92, m. 7.
[84] Prob. 11/97 (P.C.C. 5 Woodhall); Req. 2/174/24.
[85] St. Paul's MSS. C (III Nowell), f. 254; (Overall), ff. 120v., 184 and v.; (Wynnyff), ff. 298–9; (Donne), ff. 90 and v., 172.
[86] Lysons, *Environs* (Suppl.), 200.
[87] The rest of the para. is based on Guildhall MSS. 12371, 10234/1–2, 10242–4.
[88] The para. is based on ibid. 10418, 12375.
[89] St. Paul's MS. C (Sampson), f. 373.
[90] S.C. 2/188/66 m. 15.
[91] Guildhall MS. 10237, p. 65; for the covenants see, e.g., ibid. 10234/2, pp. 33–4.
[92] Guildhall MSS. 10464A; 10234/7, pp. 331 sqq.
[93] S.C. 2/188/72 m. 5d.
[94] S.C. 6/Hen. VIII/2109 m. 2d.
[95] Guildhall MS. 10123/3, f. 26.
[96] Ibid. 4, f. 59; 6, ff. 17–18.
[97] St. Paul's MS. C (Sampson), f. 373.
[98] Ibid. C (Overall), ff. 104–5.
[99] Ibid. (Overall), ff. 231 and v.
[1] Ibid. (Carey), ff. 277v. sqq.
[2] Ibid. f. 425v.
[3] Ibid. (Donne), ff. 102v.–103.
[4] See p. 62.
[5] St. Paul's MS. C (Wynnyff), ff. 301v.–303.
[6] Guildhall MS. 10234/7, p. 331.
[7] M.L.R. 1800/3/628.
[8] Marchams, *Ct. Rolls*, 25; for the following two paras., see *T.L.M.A.S.* xiii. 393–405.
[9] *V.C.H. Mdx.* i. 120.
[10] *Cur. Reg. R.* ii. 77, where it is described as two carucates.
[11] Madge, *Med. Rec. of Harringay*, 67 n.

Richard of Topsfield, who allegedly paid rent for the manor in 1342,[12] may have given it its name, but the first undoubted lord was Stephen Maynard of Islington in 1374. Maynard received 41 a. and rent in Hornsey[13] in 1356 and acquired Payntersfield, which descended with Topsfield until 1773.[14] By 1379 he had been succeeded by William Maynard. In 1398 Topsfield was conveyed by trustees to the use of John Ougham of London,[15] who in 1408 devised it to his wife Margaret for life. It later passed to his brother Eli[16] and to Eli's son John Ougham of Wokingham (Berks.), who in 1431 enfeoffed it to the use of his mother Margaret.[17] In 1457 she conveyed it to her executors, who, in accordance with her will, sold it in 1462 to John Guybon, gentleman of London, and others.[18] Following successive enfeoffments, Topsfield was held in 1467 by Guybon, in 1469 by James Bradman, gentleman of London,[19] and in 1504 by the latter's son John Bradman, salter of London, who conveyed it to William Heron of Alford (Lincs.), John Heron the elder, and John Heron the younger.[20] It was acquired from the Herons by Richard Spencer (d. 1509), who held copyhold land at Crouch End and Highgate and left Topsfield to a younger son Gregory.[21] During the life estate of Gregory's widow Margery, his brother Nicholas sold the reversion to their sister Agnes, widow of Robert Tickill of Kentish Town.[22] At an unknown date it passed to the Ive family, relatives of Agnes's husband. William Ive (d. 1608) of London devised it to Richard Sanderson, fishmonger of London, and his wife for life, but William's son Nicholas was lord in 1619. On the death of Richard Ive the manor passed to his sisters Mary, wife of John George, and Martha, wife of Robert Cutler, who sold it in 1657 to Nicholas Colquitt (d. 1660). Colquitt left it to his mother Margaret Fairclough (d. 1669), who settled it in 1663 on her granddaughter Hester Tyther (d. 1665), later wife of Sir Edward Graves, Bt. Since their daughter Margaret married Edward Maddison without parental consent, the manor passed to Hester's brother Anthony Tyther, to her sister Anne, wife of John Anger, in 1699, and only in 1714 to Margaret Maddison as heir general. In 1718 Margaret sold it to Charles Eyre (d. 1748), haberdasher of London,[23] whose executors sold it in 1749 to John Areskine (d. 1758), merchant of Holborn. It passed from Areskine's widow Rose (d. 1763) to her daughters Elizabeth and Eleanor Baston, respectively wives of Frederick Balthasar Heinzelmann and John Worgan. They sold it in 1773 to Samuel Ellis (d. 1791), tenant of the Three Tuns,[24] whose executors sold it in 1792 to Thomas Smith of Gray's Inn, who was succeeded by his son George (d. 1835). George's nephew and namesake sold it in 1855 to Henry Weston Elder, bristle-merchant (d. 1882), and the trustees of Elder's widow Sarah sold the manor to builders in 1894.

The demesne contained four houses and 305 a. in 1529[25] and only four tenements and 50 a. in 1659.[26] It comprised two inns and 43–50 a. between 1718 and 1773[27] and *c.* 1780 was not the largest freehold estate in the manor.[28] Property including the Bear inn was alienated in 1773[29] but the Elder family acquired other land at Crouch End.[30] No manor-house was mentioned in 1509, when Richard Spencer devised his great tenement of Broadgates with the manor.[31] Between 1718 and 1773 the only houses on the demesne were the Bear and Three Tuns,[32] the second of which was sometimes the meeting-place of the court.[33] The house in the angle of Tottenham and Middle lanes called Topsfield Hall was built after 1781 by Samuel Ellis[34] and sold to John William Paul in 1791. He devised it to his nephew John William Vogel, whose widow Anne sold it in 1812 to Sir Felix Booth, Bt., and John Gillyatt Booth (d. 1849),[35] the distiller, who sub-let it. In 1853 his executors sold it and 6 a. to H. W. Elder, who resided there. A large rectangular stuccoed building of three storeys, it was demolished in 1895.

The estate called *FARNFIELDS* or *FERNFIELDS*, reputed a manor in 1549,[36] had probably been subinfeudated by the bishop: in 1324 it included a carucate held by rent and suit of court at Stepney.[37] It lay between the manor of Topsfield, Brownswood, and Tottenham Lane.[38] Since it was held with the advowson of St. Clement Danes from 1273, like the advowson it may formerly have been held by the Knights Templar.[39] It was held by the priory of St. Sepulchre, Warwick, in 1273, when it was awarded to Hugh the English, a brother of the Holy Sepulchre of Jerusalem, although the priory regained the estate in 1277.[40] In 1324 Farnfields and the advowson of St. Clement Danes were exchanged by the priory with the bishop of Exeter.[41] In 1340 it was conveyed as five houses, 70 a. of land, 2 a. of meadow, and 2 a. of wood to William of Notton and Isabel his wife, who remitted their rights to the bishop.[42] In 1419 the bishop died seised of 15 a. of wood and 140 a. of pasture[43] and in 1511 a long lease was made of 80 a. of land and 30 a. of wood.[44] In 1548 the bishop granted it to Thomas Fisher and in 1549 the king provided that it should be held in free socage.[45] Farnfields was

12 Madge, *Med. Rec. of Harringay*, 45.
13 C.P. 25(1)/151/66 no. 345.
14 C 146/2616; see below.
15 C 146/6447; St. Paul's MSS., box A 62.
16 Guildhall MS. 9171/2, ff. 129v., 130.
17 C 146/6532; C 146/6570.
18 C 146/6466; C 146/6537; C 147/141.
19 S.C. 2/191/65B; C 146/324; C 146/1063; C 146/1403; C 146/6124; C 146/6548; C 146/6571; C 146/6941; C 146/7070; C 263/2/1/8.
20 C 146/7070; C 263/2/1/8; see also C 146/6941.
21 C 1/910/66.
22 Ibid.; C.P. 25(2)/27/181 no. 10.
23 M.L.R. 1718/3/54–6.
24 Ibid. 1773/7/48–51.
25 C.P. 25(2)/27/181 no. 10.
26 C.P. 25(2)/575/1659 Hil.
27 M.L.R. 1718/3/54; 1743/3/65; 1749/2/142; 1773/7/48.
28 M.R.O., Acc. 1289/2.
29 M.L.R. 1773/7/225.
30 See p. 15.
31 Prob. 11/16 (P.C.C. 13 Bennett).
32 M.L.R. 1718/3/54; 1773/7/48.
33 M.R.O., Acc. 1289/1/1.
34 Ibid. 2.
35 Guildhall MS. 1972.
36 *Cal. Pat.* 1549–51, 19; see also C 146/6367 (1489).
37 C 143/67/4/3–4.
38 M.R.O., Acc. 1025; Acc. 237/2; B.L. Maps 3465 (36); Madge, *Med. Rec. of Harringay*, plate VII.
39 Madge, *Med. Rec. of Harringay*, 52–60.
40 E 315/42/257 f. 75, transl. in Madge, *Med. Rec. of Harringay*, 57–60.
41 *Cal. Pat.* 1321–4, 390; C 143/167/4/3–4; C.P. 25(1)/286/33 no. 257; *V.C.H. Warws.* iii. 171.
42 C.P. 25(1)/150/58 no. 126.
43 E 153/1013/1.
44 C 1/1468/30.
45 *Cal. Pat.* 1549–51, 19.

held in 1552 by Sir William Cavendish, who exchanged it with the Crown,[46] and was granted in 1604 to John Erskine, earl of Mar (d. 1634).[47] By 1665 it had been acquired by Sir Thomas Proby, Bt. (d. 1689).[48] In 1713 Sir Thomas's ultimate heir William Proby leased it for 99 years at peppercorn rent to his brother Dr. Charles Proby (d. 1728),[49] and in 1726 John Proby, William's heir, released his right to James Colebrook of London,[50] whose estate comprised 121 a.[51] and who in 1727 apparently acted as trustee of Mary Eyre of London and her husband.[52] In 1729, in a transaction involving William and John Proby, Colebrook was conveyed rights under the will of Sir Thomas Proby[53] and in 1750 the trustees of Mary Eyre conveyed Farnfields to William Harvey of London.[54] In 1757 he mortgaged or conveyed it to Sir Robert Ladbrook (d. 1773), alderman of London,[55] and in 1763 they released it to Sarah Nicoll of Hillingdon, widow,[56] whose devisee John Osborne settled it in 1773 on trustees.[57] At least 85 a. were held by Edward Gray of Harringay House in 1801 and presumably until his death, but they were not then bought by Edward Henry Chapman with Harringay House.[58] At least 60 a. belonged by 1835 to the Revd. John Jankyn (d. 1863), who sold 11 a. to Chapman in 1850[59] and whose son George Faulkner Jankyn leased 7 a. for building in 1880 and sold a further 42 a. in 1884.[60] As the manor was often called Harringay in the 18th century, it probably gave its name to Harringay House and the later district and wards.

The reputed manor of *MUSWELL* originated between 1152 and 1159 in the grant of land at Muswell by Richard de Belmeis, bishop of London (d. 1161), to the Augustinian priory of St. Mary, Clerkenwell.[61] The land probably corresponded to the later 61½ a. of Clerkenwell detached,[62] but the priory may have acquired additional lands in Hornsey:[63] in 1539 part of the estate adjoined Rowledge farm.[64] In 1540 the prioress demised to John Avery, yeoman of the bottles, the farmhouse, chapel, gatehouse, a house, a storehouse, and all lands not already leased;[65] the estate was granted in 1543 to William Burnell, to be held in fee for rent following Avery's death.[66] In 1544 Burnell conveyed his estate to the Augmentations official William Cowper and Cecily his wife,[67] who in 1545 alienated it to Thomas Golding of London.[68] In 1549 Golding sold it to John Goodwin (d. 1574), merchant-tailor of London.[69] In 1554 the reserved rent and other property were bought by Thomas Rowe, probably Sir Thomas Rowe (d. 1570), lord mayor in 1568–9, and George Cotton of London,[70] evidently on behalf of Goodwin, who held them at his death. He devised part of his property including his capital messuage to his wife Anne and part to his son William. Anne, with Thomas Wighel, conveyed her share in 1577 to William (later Sir William) Rowe (d. 1593), later lord mayor, who by 1592 also acquired William Goodwin's share.[71] The Rowes's tenure was not affected by a royal grant of the whole manor to Sir Patrick Murray on the forfeiture of William Goodwin. Sir William Rowe also acquired Stonyfield, part of the demesne which was held at farm in 1540 by John Twyford and bought in 1553 by Thomas Cecil and John Bell to hold in free socage.[72] By 1578 he also had a copyhold estate there.[73] The demesne descended to Sir William's son Nicholas Rowe (d. 1616), who devised it to his wife Elizabeth for life. In 1633 she joined her son Sir Nicholas Rowe and his wife in selling Muswell farm alias Muswell chapel, 4 houses, and 10 closes to George (later Sir George) Benyon of London,[74] whose lands were later sequestrated and in 1650 sold to Colonel Robert Thorpe.[75] In 1655 Thorpe conveyed the whole estate to trustees for his stepdaughters, Philadelphia and Anne Hill,[76] who sold it that year to John Stone, girdler of London.[77] The estate, comprising 2 houses and 56 a., was recovered by Benyon in 1664 after a suit in Chancery[78] and conveyed, under the description of 3 tenements, 4 orchards, and 64 a. in Hornsey and Clerkenwell, to Sir Paul Paynter (d. 1688) in 1665.[79] In 1682 Paynter conveyed nearly half the estate to William Dyke of Ratcliff in Stepney, sea-captain,[80] leaving the rest to his widow Rachel (d. *c.* 1694).[81] The other part passed on William Dyke's death in 1685 to his mother Mary Dyke,[82] occupier in 1692.[83] Only the occupiers were recorded until in 1826 the larger portion was bought by Thomas Bird and on his death *c.* 1834 passed to Thomas Rhodes, together with the smaller portion and the neighbour-

46 E 318/26/1473; Lysons, *Environs*, iii. 50.
47 C 66/1611 m. 25.
48 C.P. 25(2)/760/16 Chas. II Trin.; cf. *V.C.H. Hunts.* iii. 160.
49 M.L.R. 1726/3/15; see also M.L.R. 1720/4/88–9.
50 M.L.R. 1726/5/147–9.
51 Lloyd, *Highgate*, 81.
52 M.L.R. 1727/4/264–5, 268–9.
53 M.L.R. 1734/3/66–7. There is no registration of the will in P.C.C.
54 M.L.R. 1750/3/368–9.
55 M.L.R. 1760/3/91–2.
56 M.L.R. 1763/3/553–4.
57 M.L.R. 1773/2/338–9.
58 M.L.R. 1804/2/18; for Harringay Ho. see p. 149.
59 M.L.R. 1850/9/629.
60 B.L. Maps 3465 (36); M.R.O., Acc. 1025; Acc. 237/2; Madge, *Med. Rec. of Harringay*, plate VII.
61 Madge, *Early Rec. of Harringay*, 60–4. Except where otherwise stated, the following two paras. are based on J. F. Connolly and J. H. Bloom, *An Island of Clerkenwell* (1933), 45–6; *T.L.M.A.S.* xii. 633–50; xiii. 610–15.
62 O.S. Map 6″, Mdx. XII. NW. (1873 edn.).
63 See e.g. C.P. 25(2)/27/185 no. 11; C.P. 25(2)/27/186 no. 12. Between 1533 and 1536 the priory held 1½ a. in Hornsey: S.C. 6/Hen. VIII/2120; S.C. 6/Hen. VIII/2119 m. 3.
64 St. Paul's MS. C (Sampson), ff. 100v.–101.
65 *L. & P. Hen. VIII*, xv, p. 541; S.C. 6/Hen. VIII/2396 m. 100.
66 *Cal. Pat.* 1553–4, 124–5; *L. & P. Hen. VIII*, xviii (1), p. 539.
67 C.P. 25(2)/27/185/11.
68 C.P. 25(2)/27/186/12.
69 *Cal. Pat.* 1549–51, 59; C 54/463 mm. 13–14.
70 *Cal. Pat.* 1553–4, 124–5.
71 Lysons, *Environs*, iii. 51; C 142/291/108; see also C.P. 25(2)/261/33 Eliz. East.
72 *Cal. Pat.* 1553, 131.
73 Guildhall MS. 10312/94, m. 9d.
74 C.P. 43/205 m. 5.
75 *Cal. Cttee. for Compounding*, iv. 2422; C 54/3808 no. 16.
76 C 54/3863 no. 32.
77 C 54/3863 no. 26.
78 C 54/4169 no. 29.
79 C.P. 25(2)/689/17 Chas. II Trin.; B.L. Add. Ch. 71493.
80 C.P. 25(2)/692/34 Chas. II East.
81 Finsbury libr., Clerkenwell rate bk. 1691–2.
82 Prob. 11/379 (P.C.C. 42 Cann).
83 Finsbury libr., Clerkenwell rate bk. 1691–2.

Highgate Hill from the north in 1822. Cromwell House, with a cupola, is on the left

High Street from the north-west

HIGHGATE

Finchley: Lodge Cottage, Nether Street

Highgate: no. 57 Cholmeley Park

Highgate: no. 16 Broadlands Road

Hornsey: house in Crescent Road, Crouch End

SUBURBAN HOUSES

ing Tottenham Wood farm, which had been held with it. Following Rhodes's death in 1856 the whole farm[84] was intended to form Alexandra Park but most of the Clerkenwell part was ultimately built on.

Muswell chapel was apparently demolished soon after the Dissolution and its paving of glazed tiles left exposed.[85] It is not clear whether it occupied the site of the mansion built by Sir William Rowe by 1593,[86] where the cellar enclosed the Mus well;[87] that house was inhabited by Sir Nicholas Rowe in 1631[88] and excluded from the sale of 1633. In 1664 Sir Thomas Rowe's house contained eighteen hearths.[89] He demolished it in 1677 and sold the materials[90] but evidently retained the site,[91] as buildings said to have been the grange of the Rowes were apparently blown down in 1707. Thomas Bird erected Wellfield House on the southern boundary in Wellfield,[92] where a later owner Cornelius Nicholson, miscellaneous writer,[93] excavated foundations reputedly of the chapel.[94]

The manor of *BROWNSWOOD* was the endowment of the prebend of Brownswood in St. Paul's, which probably existed before its holders were first recorded in the early 12th century.[95] The manor probably originated in a division of property between the bishop of London and the chapter of St. Paul's, which may be reflected in entries in Domesday Book under Stepney.[96] The name refers to the demesne wood called Brownswood in 1569[97] and may derive from one Brand, a king's clerk, who was prebendary *c.* 1200.[98] In 1577 the manor covered all of Hornsey south of Topsfield and Farnfields, including the detached portions in Stoke Newington.[99]

The manor was held by prebendaries of Brownswood until 1840, when it passed to the Ecclesiastical Commissioners;[1] during the Interregnum, it was bought by the London draper Richard Utber.[2] It was valued at 5 marks in 1254[3] and 20 marks in 1535.[4] In 1532 all the lands except possibly the woods were leased to Peter Turner, grocer of London, and in 1548 they were leased in reversion.[5] Turner's term had expired in 1569 when Robert Harrington, prebendary 1561–1610, leased manor and woods for 99 years to his brother John Harrington of Witham (Lincs.).[6] John Harrington apparently assigned the lease between 1594 and his death in 1599,[7] presumably to the Draper family who were said to have been lessees for 70 years in 1681. The lease was presumably held by Thomas Draper (d. 1631), whose widow had it in 1649,[8] and was devised by his brother Roger in 1659 to their nephew Thomas Draper (d. 1703), later Sir Thomas Draper, Bt. Dr. Joseph Crowther, prebendary 1642–89, tried to resume the courts and royalties, since from total revenues of £355 in 1681 there was a reserved rent of only £19. During Chancery suits between Draper and Crowther or his representatives from 1664 to 1692 Crowther was imprisoned in the Fleet, where he died.

Draper retained the lease at the old rent[9] and in 1717 his widow Mary devised it for life to her daughter Elizabeth, wife of Sir Henry Ashurst, Bt. (d. 1732), with remainder to the issue of her other daughter Mary Baber.[10] Following Elizabeth's death in 1738 it descended to John Draper Baber, who assigned it in 1750 to John Jennings, a Quaker from Crouch End.[11] On his death in 1758 it was held by his executor Richard Saunders, who was dead by 1766, when it was held in trust for Saunders's sons Thomas and Richard.[12] Richard had died by 1775 and the lease was sold by Thomas[13] in 1789 to John Willan of South Weald (Essex).[14] He left it to his nephew William Willan (d. 1849) of Preston Candover (Hants), with remainder to the latter's son John James Willan.[15] In 1821 an Act authorized the prebendary to lease the demesne to the Willans for 99 years, in order that they could grant building leases, rendering him 44 per cent of the gross revenues.[16] In 1826 a second Act[17] confirmed a building lease of 295 a., made ineffective by the builder's bankruptcy.[18] In 1855 the Ecclesiastical Commissioners[19] conveyed the freehold of the 189 a. north of Seven Sisters Road and the manorial rights to William Willan's executors, in exchange for 156 a. to the south.[20] Under the Finsbury Park Act, 1857,[21] the Metropolitan Board of Works acquired most of the Willans' share and some copyhold land, laid out 115 a. as Finsbury Park,[22] and built up Endymion Road on the remainder.[23] The park passed in 1889 to the L.C.C. and in 1965 to the G.L.C., which administered it in 1976.

84 Ibid. rate bks. 1691–1870; Connolly and Bloom, *Island of Clerkenwell*, 26 sqq.; B.L. Add. MS. 31323, BBB (Map, 1860).
85 W. Camden, *Britannia* (1806 edn.), 108.
86 Norden, *Spec. Brit.* 36.
87 J. Weever, *Ancient Funerall Monuments* (1631), 499; W. J. Roe, *Ancient Tottenham* (1956), 113.
88 Weever, *Monuments*, 499.
89 M.R.O., MR/TH/1.
90 J. Aubrey, *Miscellanies* (1696 edn.), 56.
91 Finsbury libr., Clerkenwell rate bk. 1691–2.
92 Connolly and Bloom, *Island of Clerkenwell*, 29.
93 Cornelia Nicholson, *A Well-Spent Life* (1890).
94 C. Nicholson, *Scraps of Hist. of a Northern Suburb of Lond.* (1879), 12.
95 Le Neve, *Fasti, 1066–1300, St. Paul's*, 29–31.
96 Madge, *Early Rec. of Harringay*, 49.
97 Guildhall MS. 11816B (copy of lease).
98 Le Neve, *Fasti, 1066–1300, St. Paul's*, 29 n. Roger Brun, said to have given the prebend its name, is not known to have held it: Madge, op. cit. 51; Le Neve, *Fasti, 1066–1300, St. Paul's*, 29–31.
99 S.P. 12/113/17.
1 *Lond. Gaz.* 20 Aug. 1852, pp. 2252–3.
2 C 54/3540 no. 16.
3 *Val. Norw.* ed. Lunt, 496.
4 *Valor Eccl.* (Rec. Com.), i. 364.
5 St. Paul's MS. C (Sampson), ff. 198–199v.
6 Ibid. ff. 320–321v.
7 Prob. 11/93 (P.C.C. 32–3 Kidd): Guildhall MS. 9537/9, f. 62. For what follows see *T.L.M.A.S.* xxviii. 333–45.
8 Lysons, *Environs*, iii. 48, quoting lost survey.
9 *T.L.M.A.S.* xxviii. 339.
10 Prob. 11/561 (P.C.C. 228 Whitfield).
11 M.L.R. 1721/1/269; 1722/4/341; 1724/6/423; 1726/2/355; 1733/2/210; 1742/3/241; 1750/1/522.
12 Guildhall MSS., Church Com. 1960.
13 Ibid. 1961.
14 Lysons, *Environs*, iii. 49; M.L.R. 1789/3/301.
15 Brownswood Estate Act, 1 & 2 Geo. IV, c. 44 (Local and Personal).
16 Ibid.
17 Brownswood Estate Act, 7 Geo. IV, c. 36 (Local and Personal).
18 Guildhall MSS., Church Com. 184830.
19 *Lond. Gaz.* 20 Aug. 1852, pp. 2252–3.
20 Guildhall MSS., Church Com. 19254.
21 20 & 21 Vic. c. 150 (Local and Personal).
22 J. J. Sexby, *Municipal Pks. of Lond.* (1898), 311.
23 See p. 115.

The manor-house of Brownswood was called Copthall and stood north-west of the later Seven Sisters Road on part of the park.[24] First mentioned in 1649, it contained a hall, parlour, kitchen, cellar, and two chambers, besides outbuildings;[25] in 1664, when it was unoccupied, there were only four hearths.[26] It may have survived in 1792 as the humble building of two floors with a single storeyed extension, which was soon afterwards rebuilt and came to be well known as Hornsey Wood House.[27] A little brick house, already existing in 1649, was resumed by Dr. Crowther in 1665, presumably for his own use.

OTHER ESTATES. Among the estates of Simon Francis (d. 1357), merchant of London, was land at Hornsey, of which 60 a. were held in dower by his widow Maud (d. 1384). In 1368 her daughter Alice and her husband Sir Thomas Travers conveyed the reversion to feoffees to the use of the heirs of John de Middleton.[28] The feoffees settled it on Sir Thomas in 1373[29] and by 1376 he had conveyed it to Nicholas Brembre (d. 1388), later mayor of London,[30] on whose forfeiture in 1388 it passed to the Crown.[31] In 1394 the estate, 60 a. of land and 4 a. of wood, was granted to Thomas Goodlake and Joan his wife.[32]

William Horne (d. 1496), alderman of London, built up an estate most of which was at Crouch End. In 1482 he acquired Godfreys tenement and 20½ a. copyhold of Hornsey from William Halmer, pouch-maker of London;[33] in 1484 other copyhold from the guardian of Thomas, son of John Bury, a London tailor;[34] in 1486 more copyhold of Topsfield from Richard Spencer and Isabel his wife;[35] in 1487 a freehold estate from Cecily, wife of Thomas Walker;[36] also in 1487 from the parents of Henry Marshall, butcher of London (d. 1480), property which may have been the Triangle estate;[37] and at an unknown date Crouch End croft, late of Henry Quarles.[38] Horne's lands constituted a substantial block, which was sold by his executors in 1497 to John Meautis, the king's secretary.[39] From at least 1497 Meautis accumulated other lands, all of which he quitclaimed *c.* 1503 to John Heron and his father William.[40]

Most of the freehold land in Hornsey lay east of Tottenham Lane and Crouch End near the manors of Brownswood, Topsfield, Farnfields, and Ducketts in Tottenham and sometimes disputed between them. In 1287 William le Brun of Ebury in Westminster, heir of Master William le Brun, acquired 40 a. in Hornsey which the elder William had settled on his sister Isabel and her husband Everard the goldsmith and which they had apparently given to the priory of St. Sepulchre, Warwick, before dying childless.[41] In 1294 the priory unsuccessfully sued the younger William for the lands,[42] which he had conveyed in 1293 to Lawrence Duckett and later formed part of Ducketts manor.[43]

The Brokhersts of Islington held land in Hornsey by 1382, when Richard Brokherst occurred.[44] Land in Downhills granted to Henry Brokherst in 1420 was sold to Thomas Edrich in 1422[45] but in 1437 William Brokherst was granted lands including Lightlond's croft by John Kingsdon, goldsmith of London.[46] Part of William Brokherst's estate, a house and 88 a. in Islington and Hornsey, was alienated in 1464 by his daughter Joan and her husband William Underhill,[47] but the residue descended to their daughter Cecily (d. 1497), wife of Thomas Walker, grocer of London. Cecily sold property to Alderman Horne in 1487[48] and was succeeded by her son Richard, a ward of his brother-in-law Richard Rowlow, a London grocer.[49] In 1503 Richard Walker declared void all conveyances of land in Hornsey and near-by parishes made by himself as a minor to Sir Thomas Frowyk,[50] but feoffees held 80 a. in a wood called Ushers to Sir Thomas's use until his death in 1506.[51] Sir Thomas's estates descended to his daughter Frideswide (d. 1528), first wife of Sir Thomas Cheyney, K.G., who later held them for life. The reversion was divided between Cheyney's daughters Frances Crisp, Catherine Kempe, and Anne Parrott. Eighty acres of woodland were allotted to Catherine, who had borne three daughters, Margaret, Anne, and Alice, and predeceased her father. Margaret, wife of William Cromer, had also died leaving a daughter Anne before Sir Thomas Cheyney's death in 1558,[52] when the wood was divided between the three heirs. One share was apparently among the third of a house and 84 a. in Hornsey, Hendon, and Finchley which Richard Boyce and Margaret his wife conveyed in 1568 to Thomas Sherley and Anne his wife, with warranty against the heirs of Sir Thomas Frowyk.[53] In 1570 the third share of Boyce and by 1576 that of Christopher and Merlian Rythe in two houses and 80 a. in Hornsey, Finchley, and Hendon (including Ushers) had been acquired by John Draper (d. 1576), brewer of London,[54]

24 Rocque, *Map of Mdx.* (1754); see also P. Gosnell, 'Hornsey Wood and Finsbury Pk.' (TS. in Shoreditch libr.), the source for what follows.
25 Guildhall MS. 11816B.
26 M.R.O., MR/TH/1.
27 *Low Life* (1764), 4–6; Guildhall MSS., Church Com. 184832, f. lv; see below, p. 157.
28 M.L.R. 1800/3/628; C.P. 25(1)/151/71 no. 460.
29 *Cal. Close*, 1369–74, 536.
30 Ibid. 1374–7, 357; C.P. 25(1)/152/74 no. 536.
31 *Cal. Inq. Misc.* v, no. 192.
32 *Cal. Pat.* 1391–6, 403.
33 C 146/6555.
34 C 146/10003; see also C 146/9781.
35 C 146/7107.
36 C 146/10842; C 146/7117; C 146/6982; C 146/7130; C 146/7092; C.P. 25(1)/152/100 no. 6.
37 C 146/10840–1; C 146/6982; see also Guildhall MS. 9171/7, f. 94 and v.
38 C 146/7017.
39 C 146/707; C 146/872; C 146/6992; C 146/7017; see also C 146/7089.
40 C 146/7008; C 146/7069; C 146/7073; see also Prob. 11/21 (P.C.C. 1 Bodfelde).
41 C.P. 40/68 rot. 63d.
42 J.I. 1/543 rot. 3.
43 *V.C.H. Mdx.* v. 329.
44 C 146/6443.
45 C 146/4144; C 146/10175; C 146/4423; C 146/1207; C 146/4094; C 146/4531.
46 C 146/2589; C 146/3528–30; C 146/3585; but see *T.L.M.A.S.* xiii. 396.
47 C.P. 25(1)/152/96 no. 12.
48 See above; C 146/7117.
49 C 1/273/27.
50 *Cal. Close*, 1500–9, 113.
51 *Cal. Inq. p.m. Hen. VII*, iii, p. 113; Prob. 11/15 (P.C.C. 15 Adeane).
52 C 142/119 no. 114; Prob. 11/42B (P.C.C. 1 Cheyney).
53 C.P. 25(2)/171/10 Eliz. Trin.
54 Prob. 11/58 (P.C.C. 8 Carew); *Inq. p.m. Lond.* ed. S. J. Madge (1901), ii. 204; C.P. 25(2)/171/12 Eliz. Mich.

lessee of the woods and chief copyholder of Brownswood.[55] The freehold in Hornsey was devised to his son Jasper,[56] who in 1601 conveyed 39 a. to Richard Welby, leatherseller of London.[57] He had also acquired at least 6 a. copyhold from Nicholas (d. 1616) and William, coheirs of Sir William Rowe, 33 a. from Thomas Rotch, and 41 a. from Thomas Sands.

In 1624 Welby sold a mansion, nine cottages, and 127 a. freehold and copyhold in Hornsey and Clerkenwell detached to Cecily (d. 1634), widow of Giles Duncombe, leatherseller of London,[58] who in 1629 surrendered them to her daughter Sarah, wife of Sir Henry Rowe (d. 1662), lord mayor of London, with remainder to their second son Thomas (later Sir Thomas) Rowe (d. 1696).[59] Thomas, then the eldest surviving son, was admitted in 1658[60] and left the estate, which had greatly increased in value, to his son Thomas (d. *c.* 1705).[61] It then passed to the younger Thomas's uncle Anthony Rowe (d. *c.* 1707) and the latter's daughters Mary, wife of Sir Edmund Denton, Bt., and Charlotte Rowe.[62] In 1705 the estate was grossly encumbered[63] and by 1711 it was to be sold under the will of Henry Guy, who had acquired the rights of the coheirs.[64] In 1726 Guy's surviving executors surrendered the estate to William Pulteney (d. 1764), later earl of Bath, with remainder to his brother Harry.[65] In 1767 Harry, by then a general, devised it to his cousin Frances Pulteney (d. 1782), wife of William Johnstone, later Sir William Pulteney, Bt., from whom it descended to her daughter Henrietta Laura Pulteney (later countess of Bath).[66] On the death of the childless countess of Bath in 1808[67] the estate devolved on William Harry Vane (d. 1842), earl of Darlington and later duke of Cleveland,[68] who sold it in seven lots in 1810.[69]

At his death in 1576 John Draper's copyhold estate at Brownswood consisted of 73 a. between Stroud Green Road and Brownswood and 32 a. between the latter and Green Lanes. It was held by his heirs, presumably his sons, in 1577,[70] by his widow in 1594,[71] and by his eldest son Thomas (d. 1612), descending to the latter's sons Thomas (d. 1631), Robert (d. 1642), and Roger. In 1636 it was held jointly by Lady (Sarah) Kemp, widow of the younger Thomas, Robert, and Roger and in 1656 by Roger alone.[72] It was apparently among the lands that he devised to his brother Robert's son Thomas (d. 1703), later a baronet,[73] who apparently alienated it. Sir William Paul of Bray (Berks.), Bt. (d. 1686), held 110 a. The estate was held by his widow, who married Sir Formedon Penystone, Bt., *c.* 1709,[74] and passed under Sir William's will to the Paul family. It was presumably among the property inherited from William Paul before 1727 by his daughter Catherine, wife of Sir William Stapleton, Bt. (d. 1740), which apparently descended to her son Sir Thomas Stapleton, Bt. (d. 1781).[75] By 1796, however, the western portion of 81 a. was held by a Mr. Lucas, who was succeeded in 1808 by John Lucas, the owner in 1822.[76] It belonged to William Lucas in 1823[77] and was enfranchised for James Lucas in 1856.[78] It was owned by Joseph Lucas[79] between 1861 and 1876 and was built over by 1880.

A house mentioned in 1577[80] was extended or rebuilt in 1609,[81] apparently by Sir Thomas Stapleton whose initials appear on datestones and panelling. Known as Stapleton Hall, it stands near the north-west end of Stapleton Hall Road and presumably was occupied by Stapleton as a tenant. In 1765 it was licensed as the Stapleton Hall tavern.[82] William Lucas is said to have divided the house into two[83] and in his time it was surrounded by farm-buildings.[84] Between 1856 and 1884 it was occupied by Charles Turner (d. 1892), member of a prominent farming family and later of Womersley House.[85] It was the Stroud Green Conservative club by 1888[86] and in 1962 was bought by the club,[87] which occupied it in 1978. Some early-17th-century panelling has been reset in a short back wing and parts of the building may be of that date. The main range is probably 18th-century but was refronted in the early or mid 19th century. More recent alterations have included the demolition of an annexe towards the street and the addition of a modern clubroom at the rear.

In 1461 one Adam Turvey had settled copyhold of Hornsey on his wife Alice and son Robert[88] and in 1465 Adam's widow and son settled two cottages and 8 a. on Robert's wife Margaret, with remainder to his daughters Marion and Isabel. Robert also surrendered land to Giles Eustace in 1465 and 1474[89] and in 1474 with his mother to John (later Sir John) Elrington, treasurer of the king's household.[90] Robert Turvey had died by 1475, whereupon Isabel, who married Richard

55 S.P. 12/113/37.
56 Prob. 11/58 (P.C.C. 8 Carew); *Inq. p.m. Lond.* ii. 204.
57 C.P. 25(2)/173/43 Eliz. Trin.
58 Marchams, *Ct. Rolls*, 62; C.P. 25(2)/324/22 Jas. I Mich.
59 Marchams, *Ct. Rolls*, 75.
60 Ibid. 132.
61 Prob. 11/430 (P.C.C. 37 Bond).
62 Connolly and Bloom, *Island of Clerkenwell*, 24–5; Guildhall MS. 10465/26.
63 C 8/598/109; *Cal. Treas. Bks.* 1711, 153; see C 7/283/30; C 8/294/12; C 9/598/109.
64 Guildhall MS. 10465/26.
65 Ibid. 41.
66 Ibid. 80, pp. 109–12.
67 Ibid. 124, pp. 266–82.
68 Ibid. 125, pp. 1–8.
69 Ibid. 125, pp. 8–24.
70 S.P. 12/113/17.
71 Guildhall MS. 9537/9, f. 63v.
72 C 5/23/76.
73 Prob. 11/293 (P.C.C. 356 Pell).
74 St. Paul's MS. F.B. 3, ff. 18v.–20.
75 G.E.C. *Baronetage*, iv. 111; *Hist. Parl., Commons, 1715–54*, ii. 442.
76 Guildhall MSS., Church Com. 184832, ff. 4v.–5; 184829; 184833, p. 17.
77 J. Nelson, *Hist. Islington* (1823), 167.
78 M.A.F. 9/164.
79 Met. Bd. of Wks. *Mins. of Proc.* (1861), 895.
80 St. Paul's MS. C (II Nowell), f. 10v.; M.R.O., Acc. 237/2.
81 The para. is based on Potter Colln. 20/2, pp. 4–5 (cutting); *Islington Daily Gaz.* 5 July 1909; *Hornsey Jnl.* 17 May 1935; Lloyd, *Highgate*, 297; Madge, *Early Rec. of Harringay*, 52–5.
82 M.R.O., MR/LV8/40.
83 S. Lewis, *Hist. and Topog. of Par. of St. Mary Islington* (1842), 281.
84 Sketches of 1824–36 in Hornsey libr.
85 *N. Mdx. Chron.* 25 June 1892; *P.O. Dir. N. Suburbs* (1884).
86 *P.O. Dir. N. Suburbs* (1888 and later edns.).
87 *Hornsey Jnl.* 20 July, 23 Nov. 1962.
88 C 146/6450.
89 C 146/6526; C 146/6627.
90 C 146/6627.

Spencer, may have been admitted to her share but Marion, a minor, was placed in the custody of her mother, who married Thomas Corbrond. Marion died by 1479, when Isabel and her husband were admitted to the other purparty of her father's lands, which were released by the Corbronds.[91] Richard Spencer (d. 1509) was active in the local land market before acquiring the manor of Topsfield.[92] Apart from Topsfield he left property at Hornsey, Highgate, Crouch End, and Muswell Hill to be divided among his sons Gregory, Hugh, and Nicholas, with remainder in default of issue to Nicholas as eldest son. The testator's residence by the gate to the church, his houses in Hornsey, and all his copyhold land at Crouch End were left for life to his widow Isabel. Some was bought by William Cholmley of Lincoln's Inn, probably before 1513: at William's death in 1546 it was divided between his stepdaughters.[93] In 1513 Gregory and Nicholas Spencer sold the reversion on their mother's death and all their customary land in Middlesex to Sir Richard Cholmley; Nicholas had not surrendered it in 1519 and it was not paid for at Sir Richard's death in 1521.[94] He devised it to his illegitimate son Roger, later Sir Roger, Cholmley (d. 1565) whose title was disputed by the testator's brother Roger. Arbiters awarded only a third of the land to the son,[95] who later seems to have held the whole estate. Some was sold[96] and the rest was divided between his daughters, the wives of Christopher Kenn and John Russell, who surrendered some to Sir Roger's servant Jasper Cholmley (d. 1588), whose sons held it in 1608.[97] Kempe's house at Highgate left in 1509 to Nicholas Spencer may be the house and 4 a. held there by his son *c.* 1535.[98] Between 1578 and 1587 Richard's sons John Spencer of the Middle Temple and Roger Spencer alienated five houses, including one at Crouch End then called the Green Lettuce but later Old Crouch Hall;[99] in 1577 John Spencer also held 20 a. copyhold of Brownswood.[1]

Land in the manor of Ducketts in Tottenham and Hornsey, formerly of St. Bartholomew's hospital, was acquired in 1554 by William Parker, draper of London,[2] who conveyed it in 1556 to Ranulph Cholmley, recorder of London.[3] The land was probably Sistersfield, left to the hospital in 1563,[4] when Ranulph's copyhold estate passed to his brother Sir Hugh Cholmley (d. 1596), the military commander,[5] who lived in Hornsey in 1574,[6] perhaps at Brick Place or Tower Place, which he surrendered in 1578 to Thomas Aglionby of Hornsey together with ten houses and 58 a.[7] Aglionby devised them in 1583 for life to his wife Cecily (later Cecily Payne).[8] In 1603 she settled 14 a. on their son Ambrose, who held 26 a. by 1605,[9] mortgaged the estate in 1622, and sold the house and 32 a. in 1631 to Richard Chambers the younger, alderman of London, and Catherine his wife.[10] Chambers also inherited lands acquired by his parents Richard (d. 1632–3) the elder and Susannah (d. 1641), and in 1645 settled Brick Place, nine cottages, and 36 a. on himself and his prospective second wife Judith.[11] At his death in 1658 he left five sons to share his encumbered estate: eight houses and 15 a. were conveyed in 1662 to Christopher Joyner (d. 1690), merchant of London.[12] On the death of Judith in 1668 the four surviving brothers surrendered Brick Place and 21 a. to Sir John Musters (d. 1690), from whom they descended to his four grandsons.[13] Brick Place itself was damaged in a storm and demolished in 1703,[14] although the moat remained. In 1704 the surviving coheirs surrendered the property to Thomas Joyner, merchant of London,[15] Christopher's son and ultimately his sole heir,[16] who also bought land from Thomas Priestly in 1711–12[17] and left the united estate to his sons Christopher and Thomas, who sold some of it.[18] In 1721 Christopher was admitted to his late brother's share[19] and by will dated 1727 he left eleven houses and *c.* 40 a. to his aunt Elizabeth Joyner,[20] who devised them in 1738 to John Bicknell of the Inner Temple.[21] In 1740 Bicknell left the estate equally to his brothers Charles (d. by 1762) and Robert and his sisters Elizabeth Hay and Jane and Dorothea Bicknell.[22] Robert acquired the whole estate,[23] which in 1763 he surrendered to George Wright,[24] in whose family it had descended to George Jasper Wright by 1836. In 1839 it was said to belong to George Edward Smythe, a lunatic, and *c.* 1847 was acquired by the G.N.R.[25]

In 1592 John Cage acquired from William Bromfield a freehold house and 37 a.,[26] which he conveyed in 1599 to Nicholas Cage,[27] who also held 68 a. copyhold of Hornsey at his death in 1607.[28] He devised all his estates in Hornsey and Tottenham for life to his widow Anne,[29] who married Robert Barker.[30] In 1626 the freehold was conveyed to Richard Sprignell, later a baronet,[31] to whom the copyhold was also surrendered in 1627.[32] In 1625 Richard had inherited *c.* 50 a. of

91 C 146/6468.
92 C 146/6468; C 146/7107; see p. 143. Except where otherwise stated, the para. is based on *T.L.M.A.S.* xiii. 321, 400, 427; Prob. 11/16 (P.C.C. 13 Bennett).
93 Prob. 11/31 (P.C.C. 7 Allen); C 1/1152/42.
94 C 54/387 m. 27; C 54/395 m. 15.
95 Prob. 11/20 (P.C.C. 22 Maynwaring); *D.N.B.*; C 54/395 m. 15.
96 C 1/1157/40–1.
97 Marchams, *Ct. Rolls*, 20; Lloyd, *Highgate*, 139–40.
98 C 1/718/5.
99 Guildhall MS. 10312/94, mm. 6, 44.
1 S.P. 12/113/37.
2 *V.C.H. Mdx.* v. 329.
3 C.P. 25(2)/74/630 no. 20; *Cal. Pat.* 1555–7, 413.
4 Prob. 11/51 (P.C.C. 23 Chayre). Sistersfield belonged to Ric. Draper in 1613 and by 1617 to Fran. Benning, occupier of Ducketts: Marchams, *Ct. Rolls*, 38, 45, 74.
5 *D.N.B.*; Guildhall MS. 10312/94, mm. 6–7.
6 *Mdx. Cnty. Rec.* i. 86.
7 Guildhall MS. 10312/94, mm. 6–7.
8 Ibid. 95; Prob. 11/66 (P.C.C. 25 Butts).
9 Marchams, *Ct. Rolls*, 7, 15.
10 Ibid. 59 n., 80–1; C 8/54/53.
11 Marchams, *Ct. Rolls*, 36, 48, 101–2.
12 Ibid. 136–7, 139.
13 Ibid. 158, 211.
14 Lysons, *Environs*, iii. 52.
15 Guildhall MS. 10465/20; see also ibid. 22.
16 Marchams, *Ct. Rolls*, 187, 215, 229.
17 Guildhall MS. 10465/26–27.
18 Ibid. 34.
19 Ibid. 36; see also ibid. 35.
20 Ibid. 47.
21 Ibid. 54.
22 Ibid. 56.
23 Ibid. 77, pp. 82–4; 78, pp. 114–16.
24 Ibid. 79, pp. 1–3.
25 M.R.O., D.R.O. 20/H/1, pp. 48, 61.
26 C.P. 25(2)/173/35–6 Eliz. Mich.
27 C.P. 25(2)/173/41–2 Eliz. Mich.
28 Marchams, *Ct. Rolls*, 19, 69.
29 Prob. 11/110 (P.C.C. 68 Huddlestone).
30 Marchams, *Ct. Rolls*, 68.
31 C.P. 25(2)/457/3 Chas. I Mich.
32 Marchams, *Ct. Rolls*, 69.

copyhold accumulated by his father Robert between 1605 and 1615,[33] in 1629 he bought 13 a. of freehold from Thomas Wilson,[34] and in 1631 12 a. (probably Sistersfield) from William Benning of Ducketts in Tottenham.[35] Although he sold 35 a. of freehold to Michael Johns in 1654[36] he still possessed the freehold closes of Downhills, Sistersfield, Highlands, and Farmersfield, amounting to 49 a.[37] In 1651 he settled Cromwell House and 23 a. jointly on his son Robert and Anne Livesey his wife,[38] with whom nine other children disputed the remaining four houses and 160 a. on Sir Richard's death in 1659.[39] In 1663 the copyhold and the freehold estates were sold to Philip Jemmett (d. 1678), alderman of London,[40] who devised the copyhold to his daughter Anne and her husband Sir Jonathan Raymond (d. 1711), also an alderman. Their second son John Raymond succeeded to only eight cottages and 10 a., which descended to his grandson and namesake in 1796.[41] The main estate passed to the elder son Sir Jemmett Raymond, who sold the freehold in 1712 and the copyhold in 1718 to David Mitchell of Westminster.[42] In 1719 Mitchell alienated it to Thomas Bishop of West Drayton,[43] who in 1724 conveyed it to William King of Clapham (Surr.).[44] In 1729 King conveyed the freehold to his nephew William Cole of Magdalen Laver (Essex)[45] and left the copyhold to William and his heirs male, with remainder to his other nephew Henry Cole. By 1731 King and William Cole had died and the copyhold had passed to Henry Cole.[46] It was inherited in 1765 by his cousin Thomas Wilcox of Westminster, bookseller,[47] whose widow surrendered it in 1800 to William Wilcox,[48] who in 1808 sold it to Edward Gray of Harringay House.[49] The freehold estate passed to John Cozens, nephew and devisee of William Cole, and in 1772 to his eldest son John Cozens of Magdalen Laver.[50]

Sir John Skeffington (d. 1525), alderman of London, left most of his freehold and copyhold estate in Hornsey to his wife Elizabeth, who later married Sir John Dauncy.[51] In 1552, after the death of Skeffington's son William, William's eldest son John Skeffington was heir to the freehold;[52] the copyhold was divided between John and his brothers George (d. 1581), merchant of the staple, Thomas (d. 1592), Richard (d. 1597), who all died childless, and James.[53] In 1607 James Skeffington (d. 1607–8) surrendered a house and 24 a. to John's son William Skeffington of Fisherwick (Leics.).[54] William apparently acquired the whole estate, which included Sir John Skeffington's house, five cottages, and 91 a. of copyhold land situated mainly between Park Road, Middle Lane, and Hornsey High Street or by Hornsey Lane. In 1619 he sold it to William Priestly (d. 1620),[55] who already occupied land in the parish.[56] Priestly's son William (d. 1664) left a house, ten cottages, and 100 a. to his son Thomas,[57] who settled them on himself and his wife Hester in 1694.[58] On her death in 1720 they descended to their son William Priestly (d. 1744) of Bloomsbury, the lessee since 1694.[59] He sold a house and 22 a. in 1736[60] and his widow held the remainder in 1749.[61]

In 1789 Edward Gray, linen-draper of London, acquired several fields in the east part of the parish, where in 1792 he was erecting Harringay House,[62] reputedly on the site of a Tudor mansion[63] in a loop of the New River. He was rated for 55 a. in 1796.[64] By 1801 he also possessed at least 85 a. of the manor of Farnfields or Harringay[65] and in 1809 he acquired from Mary Wilcox and William Stebbing 93 a. lying together in the north-west part of the parish.[66] He was assessed on 192 a. in 1829[67] and at his death in 1838 ordered that the estate should be sold.[68] Cockfields, 27 a. north of Turnpike Lane, was sold to William Bradshaw[69] but in 1840 the house itself and 52 a. of freehold and 43 a. of copyhold in Hornsey and Tottenham were sold to Edward Henry Chapman,[70] who had held 37 a. as copyhold of Brownswood since at least 1822. Following his death in 1869 the estate was sold,[71] most if not all of it to W. C. Alexander, who lived there in 1876[72] and sold it to the British Land Co. in 1880–1, when it consisted of 91 a. bounded by Green Lanes, Turnpike Lane, the G.N.R., and the T. & H.J.R.[73] The land was rapidly built upon and Harringay House itself was demolished in 1885.[74] Standing in extensive gardens and a park laid out between 1800 and 1809,[75] it was probably the largest house in Hornsey.

ECONOMIC HISTORY. Agrarian history. In

33 Ibid. 13, 42–4.
34 C.P. 25(2)/457/5 Chas. I Trin.
35 C.P. 25(2)/457/7 Chas. I Trin.
36 C.P. 25(2)/575/1654 Mich.
37 C 6/143/164; see also C.P. 25(2)/689/15 Chas. II Mich.
38 Marchams, *Ct. Rolls*, 112.
39 C 6/143/164.
40 C.P. 25(2)/689/15 Chas. II Mich.; Marchams, *Ct. Rolls*, 142–3.
41 Guildhall MSS. 10465/34; 46; 111, pp. 226–34.
42 M.L.R. 1712/4/126; Guildhall MS. 10465/35.
43 Guildhall MS. 10465/35; M.L.R. 1719/4/344–5.
44 M.L.R. 1724/6/433–4; Guildhall MS. 10465/46.
45 M.L.R. 1729/1/318–19.
46 Guildhall MS. 10465/46.
47 Ibid. 80, pp. 263–5.
48 Ibid. 115, pp. 145–8.
49 Ibid. 124, pp. 158–61.
50 M.L.R. 1772/5/389–90; 1782/1/51; see below.
51 C 1/977/12; Prob. 11/21 (P.C.C. 40 Bodfelde); *L. & P. Hen. VIII*, iv (1), p. 952.
52 E 40/15023.
53 Prob. 11/63 (P.C.C. 28 Darcy); Prob. 11/80 (P.C.C. 75 Harrington); Prob. 11/91 (P.C.C. 3 Lewyn); but see also Guildhall MS. 10312/94, m. 43d.
54 Marchams, *Ct. Rolls*, 7; Prob. 11/113 (P.C.C. 13 Dorset).
55 Marchams, *Ct. Rolls*, 52–3.
56 Ibid. 29, 34, 37, 44, 50, 51.
57 Ibid. 56 n., 152 n.
58 Ibid. 152, 229–31.
59 Ibid. 229.
60 M.R.O., Acc. 616/1.
61 C 78/1867 no. 2.
62 *Ambulator* (1793); it was complete by 1796: ibid. (1796).
63 Sherington, *Story of Hornsey*, 43.
64 Bruce Castle Mus., D/PH/2B/6.
65 M.L.R. 1804/2/18.
66 Guildhall MS. 10465/154, p. 142.
67 M.R.O., D.R.O. 20/E2/3.
68 Madge, *Origins of Name of Hornsey*, 20.
69 Guildhall MS. 10465/124, pp. 153–7; see also ibid. 169, pp. 517–21.
70 Hornsey libr., Madge MSS., quoting abs. of title (1882).
71 Hornsey libr., Madge MSS.
72 Thorne, *Environs*, 364.
73 Madge, *Origins of Name of Hornsey*, 20; see also B.L. Maps 3465 (36), nos. 1–11; Madge, *Med. Rec. of Harringay*, plate VII.
74 *Hornsey Hist. Soc. Bull.* v (1974).
75 Madge, *Origins of Name of Hornsey*, 19; Keane, *Beauties of Mdx.* 48–51.

1241–2, 1273–4, and 1298 the demesne of Hornsey manor was leased[76] but it was exploited directly in 1304 and 1318, when it was managed directly with that of Finchley. In 1318 there was a separate grange of Hornsey, probably the later Rowledge farm. The *famuli* consisted of a herdsman, a ploughman, and a ploughleader, and there were six oxen; there were eight oxen in 1304 and thirteen in 1339, when there was only one complete plough. In 1318 five other ploughs were provided by villeins rendering labour services.[77] Apparently the demesne was still in hand in 1375[78] but *c.* 1390 Rowledge farm was leased as a whole and the herbage of the parks and High Reding were leased separately.[79] Farnfields was already leased in 1369[80] but the demesne of Muswell was in hand between 1488 and 1535.[81] The first known lease of Brownswood demesne dates from 1547.[82]

There were 63 freehold and copyhold tenants of Hornsey manor in 1406.[83] The majority were probably copyholders: freehold land was almost confined to the eastern fringe of the parish. The tenements recorded between 1318 and 1406 varied from 1 to 28 a. in size.[84] Bondmen and bondlands were recorded in 1375[85] and in 1318 a sower, 2 scatterers, 5 ploughmen, and 5 ploughleaders rendered boon-works.[86] The tenants owed rents of assize, Romescot, smokepennies, palfrey money,[87] heriots,[88] and, by 1384, 4*s.* as their share of the 64*s.* common fine due to the bishop from the manor of Stepney.[89] There were nine copyhold tenants of Brownswood in 1577, when they owed rents of assize and hen-silver of 3*s.* 4*d.* on each house.[90] On Hornsey manor in 1406 and on Brownswood manor *c.* 1580 holdings were subject to partible inheritance,[91] as on the manor of Stepney itself. On Hornsey manor subdivision of holdings was frequently averted by surrenders in tail and to the use of tenants' wills or reversed by the purchase of all purparties by a single individual.[92]

In the 15th century some copyhold and freehold land in a small area east of Crouch End consisted of strips in larger fields; one such strip contained five ridges in 1478.[93] There is no evidence of open fields elsewhere in the parish: estates already in closes at the earliest dates for which concrete evidence survives were Muswell demesne in 1488,[94] Brownswood demesne in 1547,[95] the copyhold of Brownswood manor in 1577,[96] and the copyhold of Hornsey manor in the early 17th century.[97] By 1318 the field called Little Redings (in Finchley) existed in the woods, and assarting continued after the leasing of the demesne:[98] those fields were probably fenced off from the woodland by 1303.[99] A field on Hornsey demesne was fenced during 1318.[1]

In 1318 wheat was delivered to the bishop's reeve from the grange at Hornsey. On Hornsey demesne 58 a. were sown with wheat in 1304 and 54½ a. were under rye, when little of either was in store. In 1304 the granary contained 109 bu. of maslin, 104 bu. of oats, 24 bu. of dredge, and 8 bu. of rye, in 1318 there were 115 bu. of wheat and 11 bu. of oats, and in 1339 there remained 47 bu. of rye, 64 bu. of peas, 72 bu. of beans, and 570 bu. of oats, probably as winter feed for livestock. In 1304 there had been hay worth 24*s.* Of the 1318 harvest, 61 bu. of wheat and oats were threshed and winnowed on the manor, 34 qr. of wheat were delivered to Stepney for milling, and the remainder was consumed locally. Wheat and oats were supplied to the *famuli.* Villeins of Hornsey had five ploughs in 1318[2] and were growing wheat and oats in 1375.[3] A rector bequeathed 4 qr. of wheat in 1428,[4] arable was under cultivation at Muswell in 1488,[5] and in 1557 a resident possessed a fully equipped plough and harrows.[6]

Part of Hornsey demesne in 1318,[7] all of Farnfields demesne in 1419,[8] and most of Muswell demesne between 1488 and 1535 were pasture.[9] Open-field arable in Topsfield manor was converted to pasture by 1478[10] and conversion was complete on High Reding by 1536[11] and Rowledge farm by 1543.[12] In 1547 the demesne of Brownswood manor was under grass.[13]

A herdsman was employed on Hornsey manor in 1318.[14] There were 6 carthorses and 4 stots in 1304 and 2 carthorses and 4 stots in 1339. There were 2 bulls, 47 cows, and 5 bullocks in 1304 and 2 bulls and 25 cows in 1339. By then goats and pigs had been replaced by 138 ewes and 189 lambs.[15] No stock was leased with the demesne in 1396 or

[76] E 372/87 rot. 3; E 372/117 rot. 7d.; E 352/36 rot. 5.
[77] Madge, *Med. Rec. of Harringay*, 62–71 (*sede vacante* accts. 25 Aug.–13 Nov. 1318, misdated 1283–4 by Madge); ibid. 99–102 (executors' accts. 1304); E 154/1/47 m. 3 (inventory, 8 Dec. 1339).
[78] St. Paul's MSS., box A 62/2.
[79] See pp. 140–1.
[80] *Cal. Inq. p.m.* xii, p. 341.
[81] Connolly and Bloom, *Island of Clerkenwell*, 46–9; S.C. 6/1140/18; S.C. 6/Hen. VIII/396 m. 13; S.C. 6/Hen. VIII/2116 m. 2; S.C. 6/Hen. VIII/2117 m. 2; S.C. 6/Hen. VIII/2118 m. 4; S.C. 6/Hen. VIII/2120.
[82] St. Paul's MS. C (Sampson), f. 279v.
[83] St. Paul's MSS., box A 62/2.
[84] Ibid. box A 62; box A 62/2; box B 79/53.
[85] Ibid. box A 62/2.
[86] Madge, *Med. Rec. of Harringay*, 68.
[87] S.C. 6/1139/15 m. 1; Guildhall MS. 11927.
[88] St. Paul's MSS., box A 62. Heriots had disappeared by 1667: Marchams, *Ct. Rolls*, 154.
[89] P. Taylor, 'Estate of bp. of Lond. from 7th to early 16th cent.' (Lond. Univ. Ph.D. thesis, 1976), p. 18.
[90] S.P. 12/113/17.
[91] St. Paul's MSS., box A 62/2; Sta. Cha. 8/182/21; see also *T.L.M.A.S.* xii. 317–18.
[92] St. Paul's MSS., box A 62; C 146/6124; C 146/6627; C 146/10324.
[93] C 146/6414.
[94] S.C. 6/1140/18.
[95] St. Paul's MS. C (Sampson), f. 279v.
[96] S.P. 12/113/17.
[97] Marchams, *Ct. Rolls, passim.*
[98] Madge, *Med. Rec. of Harringay*, 70; see above.
[99] E 372/149 rot. 39d.
[1] Madge, *Med. Rec. of Harringay*, 69.
[2] Ibid. 69–71; 99–101; E 154/1/47 m. 3. For the dates of the sources see note 77 above.
[3] St. Paul's MSS., box A 62/2.
[4] Guildhall MS. 9171/3, f. 190.
[5] S.C. 6/1140/18.
[6] Guildhall MS. 9171/14, ff. 31v.–32.
[7] Madge, *Med. Rec. of Harringay*, 71.
[8] E 153/1013/1.
[9] Connolly and Bloom, *Island of Clerkenwell*, 46–9; S.C. 6/1140/18; S.C. 6/Hen. VIII/396 m. 13; S.C. 6/Hen. VIII/2116 m. 2; S.C. 6/Hen. VIII/2117 m. 2; S.C. 6/Hen. VIII/2118 m. 4; S.C. 6/Hen. VIII/2120.
[10] C 146/6414.
[11] St. Paul's MS. C (Sampson), f. 373.
[12] C 1/1055/36.
[13] St. Paul's MS. C (Sampson), f. 279v.
[14] Madge, *Med. Rec. of Harringay*, 71.
[15] Ibid. 101–2; E 154/1/47 m. 3.

1404.[16] Two tenants possessed oxen in 1375[17] and teams of oxen were in use in 1524 and 1557;[18] a team of carthorses occurred in 1461[19] and other horses in 1396 and 1557.[20] Four tenants owned cows in 1318[21] and individual residents bequeathed from 1 to 6 cows between 1402 and 1533.[22] A tenant had a sheep-pen in 1375[23] and in 1428 a resident bequeathed 5 stone of wool.[24] Between 1488 and 1535 St. Mary's priory, Clerkenwell, pastured cattle on its Muswell demesne.[25] Pigs grazed in the park in 1318 and 1375 and were said to number 1,000 in 1359.[26]

From *c.* 1550 to 1850 there was continual expansion of the cultivated area at the expense of woodland and waste. Probably little more than a quarter of Hornsey demesne was farmed in 1540, little less than a half in 1647, and over two-thirds in 1820.[27] Similarly the area of the manor of Brownswood excluding waste amounted to 536 a. in 1577,[28] when waste was not surveyed, but in 1796 there were 597 a., including only 1 rod of waste. The demesne grew from 313 a. in 1577 to 320 a. in 1649 and 329 a. in 1796, and the copyhold from 223 a. in 1577 to 268 a. in 1796. Moreover, much of Brownswood and various copyhold groves were cleared during the same period. Finally, in 1816, the commons were added to the cultivable area.

About 1600 the copyholders of Brownswood manor tried unsuccessfully to fix entry fines.[29] Arbitrary fines persisted on Topsfield manor[30] but were fixed on Hornsey manor in 1667.[31]

There are few references to arable after 1550 but there was a mill-house at Muswell Hill in 1574[32] and a short-lived windmill was erected shortly before 1601 on the north side of chapel field, Highgate.[33] Little of the parish was said to be under the plough in 1795[34] and in 1796 only 36 a. or 6 per cent of Brownswood manor was arable. The area had doubled by 1822[35] but in 1869 only 95 a. or 4 per cent of farmed land in the parish was arable, mainly under wheat but including fodder and root-crops.[36]

From the late 16th century rents for grassland rose rapidly, apparently stimulated by demand from London. After 1569 rents on the manor of Brownswood rose 13 times by 1649, 20 times by 1681, and 75 times by 1821.[37] High prices encouraged investment, especially manuring: in 1664 a lessee sought allowance for improvements[38] and in 1822 a tenant's rent was reduced because he had manured his land highly.[39] Manuring was expected on the Hornsey demesne in 1837, when the low yield of 130 a. of good grassland was attributed to inadequate investment.[40]

There were sheep on Rowledge farm in 1543[41] and in 1599 a small copyholder left 100 sheep.[42] Three thefts in 1613–15 were of sheep[43] and large flocks overcharged the waste in 1629 and 1632.[44] In the 1840s J. G. Booth concentrated on sheep farming on his Crouch Hall estate, which included Shepherd's Hill, on which stood the Shepherd's Cot.[45] Milch cattle occurred in 1531 and 1599, when a tenant possessed six,[46] and unspecified cattle in 1610, 1694, and 1774.[47] In 1610 a London innkeeper pastured 120 horses on 21 a. at Brownswood of which he had bought the herbage.[48]

Hay was grown for sale *c.* 1500[49] and by the early 17th century haymaking was sufficiently widespread to occupy a migrant worker throughout the summer.[50] Sixty loads of hay were sold for consumption in the City of London *c.* 1500[51] and 80 loads were sold at Smithfield in 1651.[52] About 1728 a farmer lost hay worth £770[53] and at Muswell Hill in 1774 a farm of 130 a. had 200 loads for sale.[54]

The common land of Hornsey manor, mainly at Muswell Hill, Fortis Green (so called in 1558),[55] and Highgate (Southwood), totalled 600 a. in 1647.[56] Tenants also had rights of pasture in the demesne woods[57] but they failed to establish rights on the neighbouring Finchley common in 1812.[58] There was waste on the manor of Topsfield[59] and at Brownswood there may have been 60 a. of waste in 1577, probably at Stroud Green.[60] Pounds existed at Highgate and Stroud Green in 1576–7[61] and Hornsey manor had poundkeepers by 1617.[62] From 1637 the homage elected overseers of the

16 St. Paul's MSS., boxes B 94, A 67/58.
17 Ibid. A 62/2.
18 Guildhall MSS. 9171/10, f. 49v.; 9171/14, ff. 31v.–32.
19 Ibid. 9171/5, f. 309.
20 Ibid. 9171/1, f. 386; 9171/14, ff. 31v.–32.
21 St. Paul's MSS., box B 79/53.
22 Guildhall MSS. 9171/2, f. 17; 9171/4, f. 26; 9171/5, ff. 91, 309; 9171/8, f. 35v.; 9171/9, f. 62v.; 9171/10, ff. 49v., 210v.
23 St. Paul's MSS., box A 62/2.
24 Guildhall MS. 9171/3, f. 204Av.
25 Connolly and Bloom, *Island of Clerkenwell*, 46–9; S.C. 6/1140/18; S.C. 6/Hen. VIII/396 m. 13; S.C. 6/Hen. VIII/2116 m. 2; S.C. 6/Hen. VIII/2117 m. 2; S.C. 6/Hen. VIII/2118 m. 4; S.C. 6/Hen. VIII/2120.
26 St. Paul's MSS., box A 62/2; K.B. 9/66/70.
27 See p. 154.
28 S.P. 12/113/17; St. Paul's MS. C (II Nowell), ff. 9v.–11. The copies are not identical. For what follows see ibid.; Guildhall MSS. 9537/9, ff. 62–63v. (1594); 11816B (1649); Church Com. 184832, ff. 1v.–7 (1796, 1821); St. Paul's MS. F.B. 3, ff. 11–21v. (1709).
29 S.P. 44/55 pp. 155–6.
30 M.R.O., Acc. 1289/1/1.
31 *T.L.M.A.S.* xii. 318.
32 Prob. 11/57 (P.C.C. 2 Pyckering).
33 It had disappeared by 1641: Marchams, *Ct. Rolls*, 53; Highgate Sch. rec., box 3, bdle. 1; box 1, bdle. 2.
34 Lysons, *Environs*, iii. 46.
35 Guildhall MSS., Church Com. 184832, ff. 1v.–7.
36 M.A.F. 68/193.
37 *T.L.M.A.S.* xxviii. 334; Guildhall MSS., Church Com. 184832, f. 72.
38 C 10/488/73.
39 Guildhall MSS., Church Com. 184832, f. 2.
40 Guildhall MS. 12418.
41 C 1/1055/36.
42 Prob. 11/96 (P.C.C. 65 Wallopp, will of George Ray).
43 *Cal. Mdx. Sess. Rec.* ii. 297, 282; i. 147.
44 Marchams, *Ct. Rolls*, 74, 80.
45 *Hornsey Jnl.* 10 Mar. 1911.
46 Req. 2/14/161; Prob. 11/96 (P.C.C. 65 Wallopp, will of George Ray).
47 Sta. Cha. 8/182/21; C 8/354/237; Potter Colln. 20/94 (advert.).
48 Sta. Cha. 8/182/21.
49 C 1/161/42.
50 Sta. Cha. 8/202/14.
51 C 1/161/42.
52 C 7/143/116.
53 M.R.O., Cal. Mdx. Sess. Bks. 1727–9, 109.
54 Potter Colln. 20/94.
55 St. Paul's MS. C (Sampson), f. 375.
56 Marchams, *Ct. Rolls*, p. xx.
57 See p. 153.
58 M.R.O., D.R.O. 20/J/5.
59 M.R.O., Acc. 1289/1/1, pp. 135–8.
60 St. Paul's MS. C (II Nowell), f. 11.
61 Ibid. ff. 151, 11.
62 Marchams, *Ct. Rolls*, 45. The para. is based on ibid. *passim.*

commons, who took fees from the owners of beasts and controlled demands on the waste. In 1585 no drover was to pasture his beasts there[63] and in 1638, 1640, 1659, 1699, 1717, and 1719[64] inhabitants of other manors and parishes were presented for pasturing their livestock, the people of Friern Barnet being particularly troublesome. In 1650, 1658, and 1717[65] tenants were presented for pasturing other people's beasts. In 1584,[66] 1623, 1629, and 1632 individual tenants were found to have overcharged the commons, but the main users, as in 1791, were probably the poor.[67] The homage was concerned to protect its own animals and made frequent orders against infected stock, including geese (1650), asses (1699, 1719), and goats (1719):[68] unringed pigs were a perennial problem. The value of the commons for grazing was endangered by the poor, who took the dung for sale in 1637–8, and by those who used it as a dumping ground or took gravel, loam, fern, furze, or turf. Tenants were permitted to take fern and furze only in the winter but presentments reveal frequent infringements. There were many disused pits by 1815, when the commons were declared to be incapable of improvement without inclosure.[69]

The most serious threat arose from encroachments, frequent from at least 1579.[70] In the 17th century the poor built many cottages on the waste, until in 1676 the homage forbade further grants for that purpose. In 1686 the court found that Thomas Rowe had deceived it into granting 30 a. From 1791 it allowed grants of the waste at 22-years' purchase and sold turf and loam, the proceeds going to the wastelands fund;[71] a similar policy had been tried in 1671. By 1816 only 232 a. remained and Brownswood had no waste. Although there were many trespassers from other parishes, only the poor of Tottenham were allotted land under the inclosure award published in that year, when allotments were made to four tenants of Topsfield and eighteen of Brownswood.[72] The bishop received 30 a., the prebendary of Brownswood 24 a., the rector 46½ a., and the copyholders the rest.[73] Some common at Hornsey, still used for grazing, was not inclosed, in order to preserve the beauty of the village.[74] Waste at Topsfield in 1820 may have survived for the same reason.[75] To make such allotments productive was expensive: one of 23 a. on Hornsey common, consisting mainly of disused gravel pits, had been levelled and fenced by 1821.[76] Many others were very small. Several allotments on Muswell Hill common, copyhold of Brownswood, had not been thought worth improving in 1831.[77] The commons were used for dumping rubbish in 1863[78] and most of them later were built upon.

Grain production had ceased by 1877.[79] Farmland, which totalled 2,179 a. in 1869, was reduced to 1,432 a. in 1877, 542 a. in 1897, 169 a. in 1917, 15½ a. in 1937, and 9 a. between 1957 and 1962. Grazing land totalled only 187 a., 17 per cent of the grassland, in 1869, but increased to 738 a. (55 per cent) in 1877 and to 79 per cent in 1887; by 1907 it represented little more than a third of the grassland. Meanwhile the number of cattle rose from 241 in 1869 to 388 in 1877 and 360 in 1887 before declining to 160 in 1897, 63 in 1907, and 5 in 1917. They were mainly dairy cows, for whose products a shop was opened in Stanhope Road, Crouch End, in 1885.[80] The number of sheep fell from 324 in 1869 to 56 in 1877, and 24 in 1907. There were 179 pigs in 1867, 167 in 1887, and 105 in 1907; none remained in 1917. Some 70 pigs were kept in a small field behind Archway Road in 1893, when the farmer was ordered to remove them, and a similar number behind Townsend's Yard, Highgate, in the 1890s.[81] Horses, mainly draught animals, still numbered 116 in 1869 but with the end of grain production their number fell to 38 in 1877 and 9 in 1977; 59 recorded in 1917 included 47 vanners.

In 1869 1,997 a. or 83 per cent of the grassland was for mowing, but the total and proportion fell sharply by 1877 owing to the advance of buildings and grazing. Nevertheless the 1,105 a. under hay in 1877 vastly exceeded local demand. There were haystacks at Clissold Park and Brownswood Park in 1873[82] and at North Hill, Highgate, in 1869[83] but in 1887 the fields adjoining Hampstead Lane were said to be the hayfields nearest London.[84]

There was an orchard at Crouch End in 1465[85] and a hop yard at Muswell Hill in 1574.[86] Seven acres of hops existed in 1869 but had disappeared by 1877, when there were 9 a. of orchard and ¾ a. of nursery garden. The nursery had probably included part of one that was being established on the corner of Mountgrove Road and Green Lanes in 1821 by James Smith,[87] who had failed by 1838.[88] The nursery disappeared between 1872, when the frontages were taken for building, and 1894.[89] At Highgate a nursery which had existed in 1804 became that of William Cutbush; in 1881 the firm had 4 a. at Highgate, where it remained until 1918, 20 a. at Barnet, and 7 a. at Finchley.[90] A nursery in Wightman Road, Harringay, included a vinery,

63 Guildhall MS. 10312/96, m. 2d.
64 Ibid. 10465/32, 34.
65 Ibid. 10465/32.
66 Ibid. 10312/95.
67 M.R.O., D.R.O. 20/H/79.
68 Guildhall MS. 10465/32, 34.
69 M.R.O., MR/DE Hornsey.
70 Guildhall MS. 10312/94, m. 44.
71 M.R.O., D.R.O. 20/H/69–70, 83; see Guildhall MS. 10465/108 sqq.; *Hornsey Jnl.* suppl. 12 Dec. 1903; see below, p. 165.
72 M.R.O., MR/DE Hornsey. The inclosure Act had been passed in 1813: 53 Geo. III, c. 7 (Local and Personal, not printed).
73 Lloyd, *Highgate*, 173.
74 M.R.O., D.R.O. 20/J/4.
75 M.R.O., Acc. 1289/1/1, pp. 135–8.
76 Guildhall MSS., Church Com. 184832, f. 2.
77 Ibid. f. 82.
78 Bruce Castle Mus., D/PH/4A/4, p. 1.
79 M.A.F. 68/535. For what follows see M.A.F. 68/193 (1869); M.A.F. 68/1105 (1887); M.A.F. 68/1675 (1897); M.A.F. 68/2245 (1907); M.A.F. 68/2815 (1917); M.A.F. 68/3358 (1927); M.A.F. 68/3837 (1937); M.A.F. 68/4576 (1957); M.A.F. 68/4777 (1962).
80 Guildhall MS. 12382.
81 Hornsey loc. bd. *Ann. Rep. of M.O.H.* (1893); *Min. Bk. 1892–4*, p. 445; W. E. Atkins, 'Memories of Highgate', i (TS. *penes* Sir James Brown).
82 Shoreditch libr., HOR/2, pp. 241, 250.
83 *The Times*, 16 Aug. 1869.
84 Foley, *Lanes and Meadow Paths*, 21–2.
85 C 146/6495.
86 Prob. 11/57 (P.C.C. 2 Pyckering, will of John Goodwin).
87 Guildhall MSS., Church Com. 184832, f. 3.
88 Ibid. f. 89.
89 Guildhall MSS., Church Com. 156978; O.S. Map 6", Mdx. XII. SE. (1873 edn.).
90 *Survey of Lond.* xvii. 67–8; *Seven Sisters & Finsbury Pk. Jnl.* 13 Jan. 1881.

cucumber- and peach-houses, and glass forcing-pits in 1885; it too had gone by 1894.[91] In 1880 there were at least two other nurseries at Hornsey and four at Highgate[92] and in 1887 there were 17½ a. of nurseries and orchards. The area shrank from 5 a. of small fruit in 1897 to 1 a. in 1907,[93] but there were still 4 holdings in 1947, 2 with small areas of glass-houses and 3 with small frames.[94] In 1887 the local board opened its own nurseries at Irish Corner with 4 glass-houses to supply the isolation hospital and public gardens.[95] The nurseries had been considerably enlarged by 1963[96] and survived in 1976.

WOODS.[97] The bishop of London's woods once covered most of the west and central areas of Hornsey and the eastern part of Finchley, probably merging into Finchley common, itself a demesne wood, and even the commons of Hornsey manor. If the bishop's lodge of 1464 was at Lodgehill on the boundary with Finchley[98] it was in the middle of his woods. Besides Rowledge grove of 40 a. he had 650 a. of demesne woods in 1647. There were also closes of 380 a. in the great and little parks and High Reding,[99] apparently assarted from the surrounding woodland. Repairs were made to closes in the parks *c.* 1390[1] and the names Oxleas and High Reding, mentioned *c.* 1540,[2] indicate clearings. Before the formation of such closes the demesne woods of Hornsey manor covered not less than 1,070 a., of which *c.* 380 a. were in Finchley. They had dwindled to 700 a. in 1647,[3] 450 a. by 1746,[4] 394 a. by 1820,[5] and 278 a. in 1885. In 1841 131 a. of the remaining woodland was in Finchley.[6] In 1976 only Queen's wood of 51 a., Highgate wood of 69 a., and Coldfall wood of 32 a. survived.

First mentioned in 1241,[7] Hornsey park was already fenced by 1303.[8] In 1241–3 and 1263 grants of deer and timber were made by the Crown *sede vacante*.[9] In 1406 the chapter took 32 spars for the belfry of St. Paul's cathedral and 1,000 faggots as firewood.[10] Of 15 trespassers in the park in 1318, 13 had felled oaks and one had taken 600 faggots.[11] Commissions were issued in 1318–19 and 1354 against those who had taken deer, fish, or timber during vacancies.[12] Trespasses were also recorded in 1375,[13] 1577,[14] 1618–19, and 1631,[15] and destruction was beyond the control of the officers by 1646.[16] The lord employed a parker or woodward by 1318[17] and protected the deer.[18] In 1318, when the reeve was allowed a tenth of receipts from the pannage and herbage towards his wages, ten colts were pastured in the park.[19] It was customary by 1375 for copyholders to attend 'at the cross' on 11 November to pay the lord for pannage.[20] In 1374 the parker was to keep the wood and collect the issues of agistment and pannage, for which in addition to his fee he might take underwood, branches, and windfalls, and stint 4 cattle, 4 colts, and 5 pigs in the park.[21] By *c.* 1390 the pannage, agistment, and herbage were farmed[22] but the woods were kept in hand. The bishop's palace was supplied with 4,000 faggots in 1464–5[23] but by 1579, to preserve the woods, the bishop used coal not only at Fulham but at Hornsey.[24] The lease of the great park in 1540 reserved brushwood and dead wood to the bishop.[25]

Henry of Sandwich, bishop 1263–73, sold timber to the Franciscans and Dominicans of London.[26] In 1423–4 oaks and underwood were sold[27] and in 1464–5 timber, underwood, and logs were sold locally.[28] For systematic exploitation the woods were organized in falls by 1577,[29] which numbered *c.* 28 in 1647.[30] In 1570 the woods seem to have been well maintained,[31] but Richard Putto of Highgate, the under-tenant, had been licensed to clear part of Finchley fall.[32] In 1576 John Gilpin was licensed to clear a large triangle at the Highgate end of the great park,[33] and in 1577 *c.* 60 a. had been felled, mainly by Gilpin and his lessees.[34] In 1579 Bishop Aylmer admitted selling 800 trees and 24 a. woodland in Hornsey alone but asserted that the trees had been pollarded or were in decay. He was accused of selling £1,000-worth of timber and he admitted receipts of £600, which was nearly equal to the value set on all the remaining timber in 1647.[35] Aylmer, ordered by the council to desist from waste, appointed his son Samuel as woodward.[36] Richard Fletcher, bishop 1594–6, left £60-worth of wood felled at Highgate.[37]

In 1645 the bishop leased all the woods, consisting of 650 a., to John Smith of Hornsey, whom he appointed woodward.[38] The office descended with the lease until *c.* 1743.[39] In 1662 the woods were

[91] M.R.O., Acc. 804.
[92] *P.O. Dir. N. Suburbs* (1880).
[93] M.A.F. 68/1105; M.A.F. 68/1675; M.A.F. 68/2245.
[94] L. G. Bennett, *Horticultural Ind. of Mdx.* (1952), 38.
[95] Hornsey loc. bd. *Rep. on Property of Bd.* (1894).
[96] *Hornsey Jnl.* 13 Sept. 1963.
[97] The para. is based on the section below.
[98] S.C. 6/1140/24; Madge, *Early Rec. of Harringay*, 46–7.
[99] Guildhall MS. 10464A, pp. 25–6, 29.
[1] S.C. 6/1140/18.
[2] St. Paul's MS. C (Sampson), f. 109v.
[3] Guildhall MS. 10464A, pp. 26, 29.
[4] Ibid. 10243.
[5] Ibid. 10418.
[6] See p. 147.
[7] *Cal. Close*, 1237–42, 373.
[8] E 372/149 rot. 39d.
[9] *Cal. Close*, 1237–42, 373, 380, 385, 397, 414; 1242–7, 75, 117; *Cal. Lib.* 1240–5, 153; 1263, 118.
[10] St. Paul's MSS., box A 62.
[11] Ibid. box B 79/53.
[12] *Cal. Pat.* 1317–21, 292, 307; 1354–8, 127.
[13] St. Paul's MSS., box A 62/2.
[14] Guildhall MS. 10312/94, m. 33.
[15] Marchams, *Ct. Rolls*, 47, 49, 77.
[16] Guildhall MS. 12395.
[17] Madge, *Med. Rec. of Harringay*, 70.
[18] *Cal. Pat.* 1370–4, 462–3.
[19] Madge, *Med. Rec. of Harringay*, 68.
[20] St. Paul's MSS., box A 62/2.
[21] *Cal. Pat.* 1370–4, 462–3.
[22] S.C. 6/1140/18.
[23] S.C. 6/1140/24 m. 4d.
[24] Strype, *Life of Aylmer*, 48.
[25] St. Paul's MS. C (Sampson), f. 110.
[26] *Cal. Close*, 1272–9, 32; see also ibid. 36.
[27] St. Paul's MSS., box B 90.
[28] S.C. 6/1140/24 m. 4d.
[29] S.P. 12/137 *passim*.
[30] Guildhall MS. 10464A, pp. 25–6.
[31] S.P. 12/137 f. 82.
[32] St. Paul's MS. C (I Nowell), ff. 240–1.
[33] Ibid. (II Nowell), f. 151.
[34] Guildhall MS. 10312/92, m. 7. For what follows see Strype, *Aylmer*, 46–8; S.P. 12/137 ff. 13–16, 139–40.
[35] Guildhall MS. 10464A, p. 26.
[36] Req. 2/64/60.
[37] Lambeth Pal. MS. 661, f. 283.
[38] Guildhall MSS. 12395; 10464A, p. 26.
[39] Ibid. 10234/2, pp. 542–4.

leased to Rees Gwyn of Highgate,[40] from whom they passed in 1692 to John Russell and after 1702 to Thomas Russell, whose heirs conveyed them in 1708 to Edward Jennings. By 1715 the lease was held by Silvanus Horton and Richard Hodgson, apparently in trust for John Sherwood until 1737, when Sherwood became lessee. Following his death it was renewed to William Abbot, coal-merchant of Highgate, in right of his wife Jane, Sherwood's executrix. After Jane's death it passed to her husband and then to their four daughters. The lease was renewed in 1754 to their guardians. In 1769[41] it was held by James Way as agent for William Murray (d. 1793), Lord Mansfield (later earl of Mansfield).[42] The lease was renewed for his heirs until in 1885 the earl's trustees acquired the freehold of 16 a. and sold their rights in 683 a. to the Ecclesiastical Commissioners.[43]

As early as 1647 the lessee felled 18 a. in breach of the lease.[44] The lessees alleged that in 1727, while making charcoal, they had accidentally burnt 20–30 a. of underwood, which they asked permission to plough up.[45] It was found that in 1726 they had grubbed up much woodland and that a clause requiring the planting of 300 trees had been omitted from the lease;[46] 205 a. had been grubbed up by 1746,[47] 273 a. by 1759,[48] and 328 a. by 1819. In 1817 the fences, ditches, gates and hedges of Coldfall (formerly Great Coldfall) wood were in disrepair. Copyholders had long depastured their animals there and in 1815 they failed in their claim that it was part of the commons only because it featured in leases. There was no replanting of trees and in 1819 the bishop was urged to resume possession and either to manage the woodland efficiently or convert it to agriculture.[49] There were only 168 trees in all the woods in 1823, among them 154 oaks: 83 were too small to fell.[50] Nevertheless 278 a. remained in 1885, when the largest woods were Coldfall (111 a.), Gravel Pit, and Churchyard Bottom.[51] The trees had apparently recovered by the period 1886–97, when, apart from oaks, there was a dense foliage of larches, willows, and hornbeams. The woods were frequented by sportsmen, birdcatchers, and walkers[52] until the Ecclesiastical Commissioners closed them.[53] From 1884 H. R. Williams campaigned locally and in the national press to preserve the woods as open spaces, which would be more rural than Finsbury Park. In 1885 the Ecclesiastical Commissioners gave Gravel Pit wood to the Corporation of London, which renamed it Highgate wood and maintained it in 1976. Churchyard Bottom wood was bought by Hornsey U.D. with help from other local authorities and opened in 1898 as Queen's wood,[54] a condition of purchase being that Wood Lane should be extended through the south part as Queen's Wood Road. In 1920 Coldfall wood, bounded on the south by Fortis Green and on the west by Finchley, stretched northward and eastward almost to Coppetts Wood hospital and Coppets Road and Tetherdown respectively.[55] Most of it was cleared in the 1920s for council housing.[56] In 1976 there remained 32 a. north of Creighton Avenue.[57]

Rowledge grove, mentioned in 1528,[58] in 1647 comprised 40 a. that had long been leased with Rowledge farm[59] but were not recorded later.

The bishop retained hunting rights until 1662, when they were leased with fishponds in Hornsey and Finchley for 21 years to Sir Thomas Rowe. The rent included three brace of partridges and two brace of pheasants annually.[60] The lease was renewed for Thomas Rowe the younger in 1676 and 1682 and in 1700 for Charles Bonython, serjeant-at-law, and Richard his son. It was renewed in 1732 for Francis Dickins, whose widow Rachel devised it to Anthony Dickins (d. 1795), and in 1814 for Henry Berry, who appointed a game-keeper in 1822.

Brownswood, the manor's largest demesne wood, was known as Hornsey wood by 1745[61] and covered 122 a. both in 1548[62] and 1577.[63] The wood was leased out from 1569[64] and had diminished to 119 a. by 1594, to 92 a. by 1649,[65] and to 52 a. by 1709.[66] To make room for pleasure grounds it was reduced to 27 a. by 1796.[67] The flora attracted botanists from the 16th century[68] and the wood, although divided, still seemed wild in 1866.[69] As part of the grounds of Hornsey Wood House it was incorporated in Finsbury Park, where the forest trees had been felled by 1869.[70]

In 1294 the prior of St. Sepulchre, Warwick, accused Roger of Arderne of taking wood from his manor of Farnfields, where Roger was found to have taken only what he had been sold.[71] The woods of Farnfields contained 16 a. in 1419[72] and 30 a. *c.* 1557[73] and survived in 1577, when there were also demesne woods of Topsfield.[74]

Excluding the demesnes the largest wooded

[40] Guildhall MS. 10234/1, pp. 249–50. Except where otherwise stated, the para. is based on ibid. 10234/1–5, *passim*; 10242, pp. 122–3; 10243, p. 119; 10244, f. 44v.; 12395.
[41] But see ibid. 10234/5, pp. 279 sqq.; Lysons, *Environs*, iii. 47.
[42] Guildhall MS. 10243.
[43] Ibid. 12399.
[44] Ibid. 10464A, p. 26.
[45] Ibid. 10242, p. 498.
[46] Ibid. 10242, pp. 529–30.
[47] Ibid. 10243, p. 119.
[48] Ibid. p. 120.
[49] Ibid. 10418.
[50] Ibid. 12799.
[51] Ibid. 12399.
[52] Foley, *Lanes and Meadow Paths*, 24–7; *The Times*, 22 Oct. 1891; 8 Mar. 1897.
[53] *Hornsey & Finsbury Pk. Jnl.* 18 Nov. 1899; *N. Mdx. Chron.* 20 Nov. 1886.
[54] *Opening of Queen's wood* (programme) in Hornsey libr.; *The Times*, 25 July 1898, 5 Feb. 1883; for the next para. see index to *The Times*, 1883–98; cuttings in Hornsey libr.; Lloyd, *Highgate*, 495–506.
[55] O.S. Map 6", Mdx. XII. NE. (1920 edn.).
[56] See p. 117.
[57] Ex inf. chief supt. of parks, Haringey L.B.
[58] C 1/674/24.
[59] Guildhall MS. 10464A, p. 29.
[60] The para. is based on Guildhall MSS. 12393–4; 10234/1, pp. 255–7; 10234/2, pp. 97–9, 114 sqq.; 10234/5, pp. 41–2.
[61] Rocque, *Map of Mdx.* (1745).
[62] St. Paul's MS. C (Sampson), ff. 198v.–199v.
[63] S.P. 12/113/17.
[64] Guildhall MS. 11816B, p. 86; S.P. 12/113/17.
[65] Guildhall MSS. 11816B, p. 86; 9537/9, f. 62v.
[66] St. Paul's MSS., F.B. 3, f. 15.
[67] Guildhall MSS., Church Com. 184832, f. 2; W. and A. E. Wroth, *London Pleasure Gdns. of 18th cent.* (1896), 170.
[68] P. Gosnell, 'Hornsey Wood and Finsbury Park', 1–2, in Hackney libr.
[69] *Hornsey Hornet*, 15 Dec. 1866.
[70] Gosnell, 'Hornsey Wd. and Finsbury Pk.'.
[71] J.I. 1/543 rot. 26.
[72] E 153/1013/1.
[73] C 1/1468/30.
[74] S.P. 12/113/17.

areas were the various commons, which in 1647 on Hornsey manor carried trees worth £295 belonging to the bishop.[75] The largest of the many freehold and copyhold groves was apparently Ushers, which contained 30 a. in 1576.[76] Such groves were gradually cleared, such as the 7 a. of wood that George Crowther converted to pasture between 1586 and 1604.[77] In 1667 the homage of Hornsey declared that a tenant should have all trees that were so close to his lands that a cart with a woolpack could not pass between them and the perimeter.[78]

Trade and industry. Tilers were digging at Highgate by 1485.[79] Bricks, used in the tower of Hornsey church *c.* 1500[80] and in a forerunner of Lauderdale House, probably accounted for the name of Brick or Tower Place in 1578.[81] Cholmley's school and its chapel were to be repaired by John Weatherley, lessee of the chapel field, in 1601[82] and thereafter many houses in Highgate, including Cromwell House, were of brick. A cottage of brick existed at Brownswood by 1647[83] and another at Hornsey by 1648.[84] Weatherley, who was already making bricks at Highgate in 1595,[85] had a works on the waste ground near Southwood Lane in 1604, where he dug holes which were a danger to travellers, and in 1608 he took soil from the great park, of which he was under-tenant.[86] Weatherley's son also took materials from the commons, as was permitted until 1619 when the homage forbade soil to be removed from Crouch End Hill. Repeated efforts were made to punish offenders, many of them from St. Pancras. By 1667 tenants were allowed to dig earth or sand to repair their tenements, and both in 1686 and 1793 licences to dig were granted.[87] Tilekilnfield and its kilns were mentioned in 1654 and other kilns in 1614 at Southwood Lane and in 1793.[88] Sawpits occurred in 1609, 1648, and 1797, and there were 3 sawyers in Hornsey Side in 1831.[89] Brick-makers occurred in 1648, 1684, and 1691, and in 1829 there were two brick-works at Highgate, one of 25 a. and one in Southwood Lane.[90] In 1831 there were 6 brick-makers, 22 bricklayers, 11 glaziers and plumbers, and a plasterer in Highgate Side and 7 bricklayers, 4 brick-makers, 12 house-painters, and 31 carpenters in Hornsey Side.[91] In 1901, near the peak of building in Hornsey, 1,915 people were employed in building, including 467 carpenters and joiners, 320 bricklayers and their labourers, 145 plasterers, and 323 painters, glaziers, and decorators. As many as 1,877 were still employed in the trade in 1931 and 2,455 in 1951.[92] No works produced bricks or tiles in 1976 but there were several large firms of builders' merchants, notably off Summersby Road, Highgate.

Gravel for the roads was available in most parts of the parish from Hornsey Wood House[93] to Irish Corner. The name Gravelpit wood occurred in 1863, when there was a Gravel Walk at Crouch End, and the glebe included a Gravelpit field in 1804.[94] The supply had diminished by 1650, when the Hornsey surveyors took 600 loads from Clerkenwell detached,[95] in 1684 the homage needed to extract it gratis from the bishop's woods, and by 1817 the surrounding commons were virtually exhausted of gravel.[96] In 1815, to make up new roads, 1,078 loads were extracted from the demesne wood of Coldfall,[97] which had long provided good gravel for the turnpike road.[98] From 1819 the price was raised and in 1824 the pit there was the only one open in the parish.[99]

Stock-raising gave rise to related trades. There were several butchers in the early 17th century[1] and tanners in 1607 (2), 1616 (3),[2] and 1697. In 1611 a watercourse was polluted by a tanner who used lime-pits and ponds on the common.[3] A blacksmith's forge occurred in 1577[4] and wheelwrights in 1633 and 1701. In 1831 5 blacksmiths, 4 wheelwrights, a harness-maker, 2 saddlers, a horse-dealer, and a carrier resided at Hornsey Side and 3 blacksmiths, 12 coachmen, 3 wheelwrights, and a horse-dealer at Highgate Side.[5] The forges at Crouch End and Highgate survived until *c.* 1844[6] and 1896 respectively.[7]

At Highgate a new brewhouse was leased from Joseph Townsend in 1749.[8] 'Highgate brewhouse', so called in 1783,[9] may have been John Addison's brewery, recorded between 1800 and 1808.[10] Fortis Green brewery was a large building between the entrances of the modern Fortis Green Avenue and Lynmouth Road in 1869.[11] It was occupied by Charles Green, brewer and grocer, from at least 1845 to 1855,[12] by Mrs Susan Green & Son from 1859 to 1884,[13] and by Norman & Co. from 1888 until 1901, when it may already have belonged to Ind Coope & Co., whose district office was next door.[14] Brewing had probably ceased by 1902, when Ind Coope occupied the whole site,[15] which *c.* 1910 became H. W. Wilson's Fortis Green brewery stores.[16]

Hornsey brewery at no. 27 Clarendon Road was run in 1884 by S. F. Rhodes.[17] In 1886 it was

[75] Marchams, *Ct. Rolls*, p. xx.
[76] See p. 146.
[77] Marchams, *Ct. Rolls*, 10.
[78] *T.L.M.A.S.* xii. 321.
[79] See p. 123.
[80] See p. 174.
[81] Guildhall MS. 10312/94, mm. 6–7.
[82] See p. 124.
[83] Guildhall MS. 11816B.
[84] Marchams, *Ct. Rolls*, 109. The following paras. are based on ibid. *passim*.
[85] Req. 2/144/77.
[86] Prob. 11/160 (P.C.C. 132 St. John).
[87] Guildhall MS. 10465/108, p. 114.
[88] Ibid. 103, pp. 239–45.
[89] M.R.O., D.R.O. 20/E5/4A.
[90] M.R.O., D.R.O. 20/E2/3.
[91] M.R.O., D.R.O. 20/E5/4A; E5/5.
[92] *Census*, 1901, 1931, 1951.
[93] Guildhall MSS., Church Com. 184832, f. 2.
[94] O.S. Map 6", Mdx. XII. NW. (1873 edn.); M.L.R. 1804/3/436.
[95] *Cal. Cttee. for Compounding*, i. 233.
[96] Guildhall MS. 10418, but see M.R.O., MR/DE Hornsey.
[97] Guildhall MS. 12799.
[98] Guildhall MS. 10418.
[99] Guildhall MS. 12799; Bruce Castle Mus., D/PH/2B/12.
[1] *Cal. Mdx. Sess. Bks.* ii. 149; *Cal. Mdx. Sess. Rec.* i. 147; iii. 299.
[2] *Cal. Mdx. Sess. Rec.* iii. 267.
[3] *Cal. Mdx. Sess. Bks.* vii. 91.
[4] Guildhall MS. 10312/94, m. 6d.
[5] M.R.O., D.R.O. 20/E5/4/5; E5/4A.
[6] Hornsey libr., sales partics.
[7] See p. 133.
[8] M.R.O., Acc. 600.
[9] M.R.O., MJ/SPC/W263.
[10] *P.O. Annual Dir.* (1800); *Holden's Triennial Dir.* (1808).
[11] O.S. Map 6", Mdx. XII. NW. (1873 edn.).
[12] *P.O. Dir. Six Home Cnties.* (1845, 1851, 1855).
[13] Ibid. (1959); *P.O. Dir. N. Suburbs* (1884).
[14] *P.O. Dir. N. Suburbs* (1888); *Kelly's Dir. Wood Green* (1900–1).
[15] *Kelly's Dir. Wood Green* (1901–2).
[16] Ibid. (1909–11).
[17] *P.O. N. Suburbs* (1884)

occupied by Alexander & Co.[18] and between 1888 and 1920 by R. Caffyn & Son (later F. P. B. Caffyn & Co.), perhaps as lessees. The brewery may have belonged to the Rhodes family throughout: an adjoining house was occupied by Samuel Rhodes in 1880 and S. F. Rhodes from 1917 to 1939,[19] and from 1923 the brewery itself was managed by V. F. Rhodes.[20] Caffyn's were brewing ale and 'Invalid Stout' in 1895.[21] Brewing may have continued until 1957 and bottling until 1959[22] but from 1960 Rhodes & Co. dealt only in wines and spirits made elsewhere.[23]

Soda water was made at Highgate in the 1820s by Thomas Dunn of the pharmacy and in 1845 by his successor.[24] Early-19th-century bottles and the remains of a brick-lined container and pipes were found beneath a shed behind no. 64 High Street in 1977.[25]

Hornsey was said to have no trade in 1904[26] and no industry in 1933,[27] with some exaggeration, and had no large factories either in 1921 or 1954.[28] More people were employed in handicraft than in agriculture by 1821,[29] and crafts accounted for most of the 297 workshops registered under the Factory Act of 1901 in 1905, when there were 68 dress-makers, 23 milliners, 29 launderers, 42 bake-houses, and 6 bicycle-makers.[30] In 1901 Hornsey residents included 925 textile workers, 293 of them women, and 2,046 others engaged in making clothes, of whom 1,190 were women; they included 277 tailors and 829 milliners, and presumably were all employed locally.[31] By 1906 61 workshops had been added and 51 closed[32] and by 1911 the total number had risen to 377, before falling steadily to 275 in 1918,[33] while the trades scarcely altered. By 1954, however, 75 of the 246 workshops were engaged in light engineering, including 39 in the motor trade. Among the four factories employing over 100 people were the gas-works and the Myddelton and Alexandra Park Laundry (M.A.P.). The others processed films (probably Kay Films) and made hollow metalware. As only eight other firms employed more than 50 and another sixteen more than 25,[34] industry remained relatively unimportant. By 1963 there were only 233 factories, of which 41 lacked mechanical power.[35]

Hill & Son and Norman & Beard, church organ-builders, is an amalgamation of two firms: William Hill & Son, formed in the 1840s and tracing its origins to John Schneytler *c.* 1748, and the East Anglian firm of Norman & Beard, incorporated in the 1890s. After the merger in 1916 the company used a factory in Islington until 1943 and Manor works at Eagle Cottage, Hornsey High Street, from 1947. It later employed *c.* 120 indoor craftsmen, themselves training apprentices, and a similar number throughout the country. Among the organs built between 1950 and 1974 were those for seven English and eight Canadian cathedrals. The firm moved to a former branch at Thaxted (Essex) in 1974, leaving the Hornsey premises empty.[36]

Brian Taylor's, garment-makers, occupied Woodside works in Summersby Road until 1951, when half the factory was taken over by Gauges and Instruments, a family business founded in 1941 at Palmers Green. Gauges and Instruments needed more accommodation by 1963, when there were 75 staff, and later expanded into the rest of the factory, formerly occupied by Austin & Hayes. In 1976 *c.* 40 employees were engaged in precision engineering, making components for the aircraft, motor, and electronic industries, and the firm's own power press equipment.[37]

Johnson Roberts, founded *c.* 1900 and re-formed in 1940 in Stoke Newington, moved to Pembroke Road, Hornsey, in 1951 and to a new factory in the near-by Myddelton Road in 1965 following its purchase by Dental Manufacturing (later Hawtin Industries and in 1976 Hawtin Ltd.). Since 1951 it has specialized in the repair of internal combustion engines, mainly road vehicles but also including stationary engines. In 1976 there were 27 employees.[38]

Robert Deard's, haulage and refuse contractors, was founded *c.* 1875 at Finchley and moved to north Hornsey detached *c.* 1954. The offices and parking area for lorries occupied a large site on the corner of Colney Hatch Lane and the North Circular Road in 1976.[39]

Henley's Medical Supplies was founded by D. F. Henley in 1948. In 1949 it moved from Alexandra Road, Hornsey, to the Alexandra works in Clarendon Road, where it was initially housed over the stable of the former Hornsey brewery. Adjoining premises had been acquired by 1976, when a two-storeyed block, to contain storage space, a print room, and offices, was being erected. The company manufactures a range of surgical disposable sundries, in which it claimed to be Great Britain's leading specialist, and waterproof bedding and protective clothing. It also distributed in Britain many surgical and X-ray supplies manufactured abroad. In 1976 there were 150 employees at the Alexandra works and 130 others in the Hornsey area, Harlow (Essex), and Westbury (Wilts.), most of them employed in warehouses.[40]

Mr. A. C. B. (Colin) Chapman adapted vehicles as Lotus sports cars at Muswell Hill and at Vallance Road, Wood Green, before moving into a former stable at no. 7 Tottenham Lane in 1951, when he established the Lotus Engineering Co. which was incorporated in 1953. The staff had grown to 30

[18] *Hutchings & Crowsley's Dir. Hornsey* (1886).
[19] *P.O. Dir. N. Suburbs* (1880, 1888); *Kelly's Dir. Hornsey* (1917–18 and later edns.).
[20] *Kelly's Dir. Hornsey* (1923 and later edns.).
[21] Ibid. (1895–6).
[22] *P.O. Dir. Lond.* (1957–9); but see *Kemp's Dir. Hornsey* (1955–60).
[23] *P.O. Dir. Lond.* (1960 and later edns.).
[24] *Pigot's Com. Dir.* (1826–7); *P.O. Dir. Six Home Cnties.* (1845)
[25] Ex inf. Dr. Joan Schwitzer.
[26] *Hornsey Jnl.* 30 Apr. 1904.
[27] D. H. Smith, *Industries of Gtr. Lond.* (1933), 73.
[28] Hornsey Boro. *Ann. Reps. of M.O.H.* (1921, 1954).
[29] *Census*, 1821.
[30] Hornsey Boro. *Ann. Rep. of M.O.H.* (1906–7).
[31] *Census*, 1901.
[32] Hornsey Boro. *Ann. Rep. of M.O.H.* (1906–7).
[33] *Census* (1911 and later censuses).
[34] Hornsey Boro. *Ann. Rep. of M.O.H.* (1954).
[35] Ibid. (1963).
[36] Ex inf. Mr. Herbert Norman.
[37] Ex inf. Mr. A. S. Villeneuve, Gauges & Instruments Ltd.; Hornsey Boro. *Official Guide* [1963].
[38] Ex inf. Mr. G. R. Matthews.
[39] Ex inf. Mr. E. A. S. Dennis.
[40] Ex inf. Mr. D. F. Henley.

by 1959 and the premises were extended with new offices and workshops in 1953 and again in 1957. Lotus cars, which won several motor-racing trophies, were designed and entirely built in Hornsey until 1957, when the body-building was done at Edmonton, but in 1959 the company moved to Cheshunt (Herts.).[41]

There were 121 tradesmen in Hornsey Side in 1831, of whom 55 were in the building trades, 25 dealt in food and drink, 18 made footwear, 8 sold clothing, and 11 were associated with horses and transport.[42] None plied luxury trades of the kinds found at Highgate, where there had been a tailor's shop in 1605,[43] a wig-maker's in 1749,[44] and an apothecary's (the Highgate pharmacy) before 1800.[45] Highgate Side provided employment for 6 barbers, a bookseller, a cabinet-maker, 3 chemists, 2 clock-makers, 2 opticians, a confectioner, 2 printers, a chimney-sweep, 2 tinmen, an upholsterer, 3 white-smiths, and 3 pipe-makers among its 205 tradesmen in 1831. Most nevertheless fell into the same categories as in Hornsey Side, for there were 32 dealing in food and drink, including 16 publicans, 21 coachmen, 66 in the building trades, 21 cobblers, and 20 dealing in clothing, among whom 8 were drapers or haberdashers.[46] A ban on Sunday trading in Highgate, apparently effective *c.* 1840, was made the object of a further campaign under the Revd. T. H. Causton, Harry Chester, and other leading residents, in 1842–3.[47]

In 1867 it was claimed that Hornsey's shopkeepers did not satisfy local demand[48] and *c.* 1880 it was worthwhile for London costermongers to hawk fish and other commodities in the new suburbs of Finsbury Park and Crouch Hill.[49] As building spread, several new shopping areas appeared and in 1891 it was claimed that no useful trade was lacking at Muswell Hill.[50] That was before the construction of Crouch End Broadway and Muswell Hill Broadway with their high-quality shops. Muswell Hill was particularly well equipped with drapers *c.* 1926.[51] By 1914 there were 1,174 shops of 41 distinct types, grocers numbering 103 and being followed by confectioners, boot-makers, drapers, and butchers.[52] The number of shops grew to 1,325 by 1934[53] and 1,356 by 1949.[54] Apart from Woolworth's at Crouch End and Sainsbury's at Muswell Hill relatively few chain stores or large supermarkets had been opened by 1976 and except at Crouch End and Muswell Hill most of the shops were small and specialized.

SOCIAL AND CULTURAL ACTIVITIES. In 1552 there were five licensed victuallers at Highgate, only three at Hornsey, and one at Muswell Hill.[55] Evidence for Highgate's growth as a separate place of resort lies in a rhyme about morris dancing on the green in 1601,[56] in an indictment for evil rule on the Sabbath in 1616,[57] and in the inclusion of the Mermaid among the taverns of London by the 'water poet' John Taylor in 1636.[58] Festivities, perhaps indicating a fair, took place in 1676[59] and in the Grove in 1744.[60] The Cave at Highgate, 'a nursery of profaneness', was suppressed after its owners had been indicted in 1714.[61]

There was a bowling alley near Hornsey church in 1622. A bowling green was being laid out at Muswell Hill in 1668[62] and existed in 1717, when a nearby skittle alley on the waste was ordered to be levelled.[63] At Highgate there was a bowling green south of the Red Lion by 1757[64] and the opening of another was announced by the landlord of the Castle in 1769, when it was to be used by a local society. Highgate gentlemen were also seeking members for a cricket club at about that time.[65] Foot races were held from Barnet to the Gatehouse in 1697 and down Highgate Hill, with one contestant on stilts, in 1740. Three days of horse-racing, on a new course at Highgate, were advertised in 1735.[66] Brief revivals of archery led to meetings near Highgate Hill in the 1730s[67] and to the formation in 1790 of the society of Woodmen of Hornsey, which competed at Blackheath in 1793.[68] In 1817 game around Hornsey offered a 'tolerable' day's shooting early in the season and harriers were kept by a gentleman of Muswell Hill.[69]

In 1761 the Rowes' old 'manor-house' of Muswell Hill had been converted some time ago into a place of entertainment.[70] Away from Highgate, however, the most popular Sunday resort by 1758 was Hornsey Wood House,[71] probably the Little Hornsey where citizens' ladies drank tea in 1755. It remained a genteel tea-house on the edge of Hornsey wood until 1796, when the building was extended as Hornsey Wood tavern,[72] some of the trees were felled, the gardens were enlarged, and a lake was formed.

41 I. V. H. Smith, *Lotus—The First Ten Years* (1958), *passim*; ex inf. the publ. relations man., Lotus Cars Ltd.
42 M.R.O., D.R.O. 20/E5/4A.
43 Hist. MSS. Com. 9, *Hatfield House*, xvii, p. 506.
44 Potter Colln. 10/25.
45 Ibid. 8/127.
46 M.R.O., D.R.O. 20/E5/4/5.
47 Potter Colln. 10/25.
48 *Hornsey Hornet*, 15 Jan. 1867.
49 *Finsbury Pk. Weathercock*, 13 July 1877; *Hornsey & Finsbury Pk. Jnl.* 28 July 1881.
50 *Muswell Hill Advertiser*, June 1891.
51 St. J. Adcock, *Wonderful London* [*c.* 1926].
52 Hornsey Boro. *Ann. Rep. of M.O.H.* (1914).
53 Ibid. (1934).
54 *Hornsey Jnl. Annual* (1949).
55 *Mdx. Cnty. Rec.* i. 11.
56 In *Jack Drum's Entertainment*: R. Simpson, *School of Shakespeare*, ii. 137.
57 *Mdx. Sess. Rec.* iv. 81. Also at Hornsey: ibid. 92.
58 *Mdx and Herts. N. & Q.* iv. 78.
59 M. S. Briggs, *Mdx. Old and New*, 111.
60 *Home Cnties. Mag.* v. 198.
61 J. P. Malcolm, *Anecdotes of Manners and Customs of Lond.* (1810), i. 100.
62 Marchams, *Ct. Rolls*, 57, 157.
63 Guildhall MS. 10465/32.
64 Plan on lease of 19 Sept. 1757 in Highgate Sch. rec., box 3, bdle. 1.
65 Potter Colln. 14/61.
66 Ibid. 15/103. Presumably the race-course was not that at Green Street, at the foot of Highgate West Hill, mentioned in Lloyd, *Highgate*, 409–11.
67 Swiss Cottage libr., Heal Colln., A III 3.
68 *Muswell Hill Rec. and Friern Barnet Jnl.* 29 May 1956.
69 Hassell, *Rides and Walks*, i. 37.
70 *Lond. and its Environs Described* (1761), v. 19.
71 Except where otherwise stated, the rest of the para. is based on Wroth, *Lond. Pleasure Gdns. of 18th Cent.* 169–71, which includes a list of views of the tavern. A further list is in P. Gosnell, 'Hornsey Wood and Finsbury Pk.' (TS. in libr.) and many illus. are in Potter Colln. 20/24, 20/26–31.
72 Guildhall MS. Church Com. 184832, f. 2; early-19th-cent. illus. show that the old ho. was not demol., *pace* W. S. Scott, *Bygone Pleasures of Lond.*

Thereafter it attracted a wide clientele: families, dinner parties, anglers, who found the lake better stocked than the New River,[73] and aristocratic pigeon-shooters, who held a match there in 1863.[74] The buildings were demolished in 1866 and their grounds absorbed in Finsbury park.[75]

Hornsey wood was a favourite haunt of the poet George Crabbe (1754–1832)[76] and could be reached by walkers from Islington who came first to a sluice-house over the New River, east of what was later the end of Blackstock Road.[77] The sluice-house, depicted from the late 18th century[78] and partly surviving in 1874, was often confused with a resort popular among working-class Londoners[79] and known as Highbury Sluice tea-house, formerly Eel-Pie house, in 1804. The old eel-pie house was called Highbury Sluice-House tavern by 1847, when its pleasure grounds stretched along the west bank of the river to the sluice-house.[80] A large two-storeyed building with dormers,[81] the tavern survived into the 1870s. The New Sluice-House inn had been built in Blackstock Road by 1890.[82]

Meanwhile, apparently at least from the early 17th century, the inns of Highgate were noted for a burlesque oath which was required of strangers and known as 'Swearing on the horns'. The custom may have originated among graziers, who halted on their way to Smithfield, or simply as the invention of an inn-keeper.[83] It was known to the poet Richard Brathwaite in 1638,[84] derided in 1681,[85] deplored as a popular distraction in 1754,[86] described in a pantomime song in 1782,[87] mentioned by Byron,[88] and depicted by several artists,[89] including George Cruikshank.[90] An early-19th-century licensee recalled as many as 120 applicants in one day, when gentry and London tradesmen had come to be sworn freemen of Highgate and guards officers had celebrated at the Gatehouse.[91] In 1795 every inn kept a pair of horns on which the oath was administered, although swearing had already become less common[92] and by 1830 was of antiquarian interest.[93] The ceremony was confined to one inn by 1857[94] and soon afterwards died out, until revived outside the Gatehouse in 1898[95] and again in 1906.[96] It was later practised by the Highgate Thirty club[97] and, from 1959, at the Wrestlers and other inns.[98]

At Highgate, which had a theatre in the early 19th century,[99] exclusive groups were formed by the better-off. Assemblies, presumably at the Gatehouse, were instituted or renewed in 1779, with as many as nine meetings in a season attended by subscribers' families and up to 24 non-members. The cost of tickets was raised from 1800 and assemblies came to be held monthly during the winter. Meetings were less frequent from 1819 and may have ceased after 1822.[1] Highgate book society, limited to eighteen members who each paid one guinea a year and an entrance fee, was formed in 1822. It met at subscribers' houses, included Dr. Gillman[2] who reputedly borrowed books which were annotated by Coleridge,[3] and later was served as treasurer by J. B. Dyne, headmaster of Highgate School. Dinners were held ten times a year in 1901. The society was wound up in 1922, when its remaining funds were given to Highgate School to found a prize.[4]

Highgate Literary and Scientific Institution was established in 1839, with 76 subscribers and Harry Chester as its president.[5] During its first year, at no. 1 Southwood Terrace, 400 books were acquired and lectures inaugurated. The institution began as another genteel society, observing social distinctions among its members, but it admitted working men at reduced rates from 1848. Supported by well-to-do residents and many distinguished officers and speakers, the institution soon became the axis of the social and cultural life of Highgate, as was still claimed in 1956. Through its publications it helped to preserve the village,[6] whose situation on a hill-top, at a distance from municipal libraries and meeting-places, itself enabled the institution to survive. Presidents included Charles Tomlinson and Robert Whipple, the second of whom was a generous benefactor. Premises in South Grove, originally outbuildings of Church House and then a Jewish school,[7] were leased in 1840 and bought in 1932. The former schoolroom served as a library, with a new lecture theatre behind, until in 1880 the library moved to the rear and a bigger lecture hall was built by roofing

73 W. Hone, *Every-Day Bk.* (1830), i. 761–2.
74 *The Times*, 1 July 1863.
75 See p. 111.
76 *Life of Geo. Crabbe by his son* (1932 edn.), 51.
77 Except where otherwise stated, the rest of the para. is based on Potter Colln. 20/6–12.
78 A lithograph in Potter Colln. 20/8 is ascribed to 1808 but is earlier, as it shows Hornsey Wood Ho. in the background without its extensions.
79 T. Cromwell, *Walks through Islington* (1835), 137.
80 Potter Colln. 20/13 (plan).
81 See also Hornsey libr., N. Mdx. Photo. Soc. nos. 542, 546, 549–51.
82 *Kelly's Dir. Essex, Herts. and Mdx.* (1890).
83 *N. & Q.* 15th ser. clxxx. 376–7; W. K. Jealous, *Highgate Village*, 78–9.
84 'Barnabee's Journal, by Corymbaeus' [Ric. Brathwaite], 2nd part, pub. in W. Carew Hazlitt, *Barnabae Itinerarium* (1876 edn.).
85 Swiss Cottage libr., Heal Colln., A III.
86 G. Rudé, *Hanoverian Lond.* 95.
87 *Songs, Airs etc. in the Entertainment of Harlequin Teague* (1782). An earlier date is mistakenly given in Hone, *Every-Day Bk.* ii. 378.
88 *Childe Harold's Pilgrimage*, canto 1, stanza lxx.
89 e.g. prints of 1784 and 1796 in Potter Colln. 9/5–7. See also cuttings in Swiss Cottage libr., Heal Colln., A III 22–30.
90 Hone, *Every-Day Bk.* ii. 78–9.
91 Ibid. 86.
92 Lysons, *Environs*, iii. 78.
93 Hone, *Every-Day Bk.* ii. 81.
94 R. Bell, *Ancient Poems, Ballads and Songs of the Peasantry of Eng.* 189.
95 Jealous, *Highgate Village*, 83, 85.
96 Photo. in Potter Colln. 9/2.
97 *N. & Q.* 15th ser. clxxx. 376.
98 *Hornsey Jnl.* 13 Oct. 1961. A plaque at the Wrestlers stated that the ceremony was held twice yearly in 1976.
99 See p. 161.
1 Highgate assembly bk. 1812–22 in Highgate Lit. and Sc. Inst. The bk. begins with an account of the assembly as conducted since 1779.
2 Highgate bk. soc. min. bk. 1822 in Highgate Lit. and Sc. Inst.
3 *N. & Q.* 6th ser. i. 277.
4 Highgate bk. soc. min. bk. 1887 in Highgate Lit. and Sc. Inst.; ex inf. Sir Jas. Brown.
5 Except where otherwise stated, the para. is based on *Highgate Literary and Scientific Institution, 1839–1956* (pamphlet reprinting articles in *Hornsey Jnl.*) and on min. bks. in the inst.
6 Prickett's *Hist. Highgate* gained second place in a competition organized by the inst. and won by W. S. Gibson, whose *Prize Essay* was pub. in 1842. Lloyd's *Hist. Highgate* was written by the sec. to mark the jubilee of the inst.
7 See p. 197.

the courtyard; the enlargement, with an entrance lobby, was apparently the work of Rawlinson Parkinson.[8] The institution housed *c.* 40,000 books and had a resident librarian in 1976.[9]

Highgate supported a two-company loyal association from 1798 until 1802. The Loyal Highgate Volunteers, of four companies, were formed in 1803 and probably disbanded in 1813.[10] In 1804 several officers were fined and others dismissed for non-attendance.[11] The 14th Middlesex (Highgate) Volunteer Rifle Corps[12] first met in 1859 and was soon followed by the 13th (Hornsey) corps. In 1880 the two corps amalgamated in the 3rd Middlesex Rifle Volunteers, later the 1st Volunteer Battalion of the Duke of Cambridge's Own (Middlesex Regiment) and, on the formation of the Territorial Army in 1908, the 7th Battalion.[13] At Highgate the volunteers moved in 1878 from the old infants' school in Castle Yard[14] to the new Northfield hall,[15] whither a commemorative stone was taken after the demolition of the older building in 1955.[16] At Hornsey they used a small drill-hall at Crouch End[17] and from 1888 the National hall in High Street[18] until the Elms was bought as headquarters for the 3rd Middlesex Rifle Volunteers in 1896; after the county council had paid the remaining debt in 1900 the old house was replaced by a drill-hall.[19]

The Good Intention benefit society met at the Mitre inn, Highgate, from 1794 and later at the Gatehouse, and another friendly society met at the Three Compasses, Hornsey, from 1795 until 1797. The Well Wishers' friendly society met at the Angel, Highgate, from 1806 until 1814, the True Britons' friendly society at the King's Head, Crouch End, from 1811 until 1820, and the United Friends' society at the Compasses, Hornsey, from 1813. Later associations included the True Britons' benefit society (later amalgamated with Finchley Provident society) from 1837, a court of the Ancient Order of Foresters from 1842, and Crouch End philanthropic institution from 1869, all at Crouch End inns, and the Loyal Rose and Crown Lodge of Old Friends and the Friendly Whittingtonians' benefit society, at Highgate from 1851 and in 1853 respectively.[20] The Highgate, Hornsey and Stoke Newington benefit building society was formed in 1860, with offices at no. 4 Highgate High Street. It moved to Bisham Gardens in 1895, to no. 16 Weston Park in 1903, to no. 4 Crouch End Broadway in 1934, and finally to High Road, Whetstone, in 1965. The society, renamed the Highgate building society in 1933, became part of the Abbey National building society in 1974.[21]

Other organizations for the poor, as for the gentry, at first were particularly numerous in Highgate. A savings bank at the infants' school was established in 1840[22] and a penny bank, under the same management, at Highgate Literary and Scientific Institution in 1861.[23] The Philanthropic Society for Highgate and Hornsey was formed in 1833 and survived in 1842,[24] although many such groups proved short-lived.[25] A working men's association, with its own library, was founded in 1861 in the old British school in Southwood Lane by Congregationalists.[26] St. Michael's working men's institute, meeting first at the National school, was founded in 1862. It used a club-house in Southwood Lane from 1864[27] before joining the Congregational association as Highgate Working Men's club in 1871[28] and moving to part of the old Castle inn in 1872.[29] By 1882 the club no longer existed, although winter meetings were held in North Hill and a Highgate Youths' Institute had been established in 1881 by the vicar of All Saints.[30] At Crouch End subscriptions were raised for a working men's club and coffee tavern, which was opened in Park Road, as the China Cup, in 1880.[31]

Highgate cottage gardens were established in 1847[32] by Harry Chester and others, who leased two blocks of land totalling *c.* 5½ a. and abutting Hampstead Lane west of the Vicarage. In 1865, after Cholmley's school and W. Piper had bought the freehold and required part of the land for building, the allotments near the road were exchanged for ground to the north-west.[33] The area was divided into 84 plots in 1888,[34] ten years before the school assumed possession.[35] Tenants could exhibit at Highgate horticultural society, established in 1859[36] and catering for all classes, whose summer show in 1863 was 'the great annual fête of Highgate'.[37] The society, which used large private gardens and was widely known through the patronage of Miss Burdett-Coutts,[38] still existed in 1976.

An Athenaeum, for assemblies and all the activities carried on at Highgate Literary and Scientific Institution, was proposed in 1859[39] but ambitious plans were only partly realized with the opening of Northfield hall, North Hill, in 1878.[40] The premises, leased by a company which had been promoted

[8] Plans dated 1879 and of internal alterations in 1851 in Highgate Lit. and Sc. Inst.
[9] Ex inf. the chairman.
[10] Jealous, *Highgate Village*, 55.
[11] Swiss Cottage libr., Heal Colln., A III 55.
[12] Uniforms illus. in coloured lithograph, ascribed to 1870, in Potter Colln. 15/121.
[13] Lloyd, *Highgate*, 470–1; Jealous, *Highgate Village*, 55–6.
[14] E. T. Evans, *Rec. of 3rd Mdx. Rifle Volunteers*, 119, 131, which dates the move 1879.
[15] See below.
[16] *Hornsey Jnl.* 1 Jan. 1956; inscriptions on hall.
[17] Prospectus of Hornsey Nat. Hall Co. in Hornsey libr., Heal Colln.
[18] *Kelly's Dir. Essex, Herts. and Mdx.* (1890).
[19] *Hornsey Jnl.* 26 May 1961.
[20] F.S. 2/7.
[21] Ex inf. the branch manager, Abbey Nat. bldg. soc., Whetstone.
[22] Potter Colln. 15/115 (rules and bk.). It was est. in 1840 according to Prickett, *Highgate*, 98.
[23] *Highgate Cong. Chap. Yr. Bk.* (1861), 58, (1862), 66 (copy in Highgate Lit. and Sc. Inst.).
[24] Prickett, *Highgate*, 99.
[25] Lloyd, *Highgate*, 476.
[26] *Highgate Cong. Chap. Yr. Bk.* (1861), 44. Rules in Potter Colln. 10/126.
[27] *St. Mic.'s Par. Mag.* Jan. 1863, May 1864 et seq.
[28] *Highgate Cong. Chap. Yr. Bk.* (1871), 9.
[29] *St. Mic.'s Par. Mag.* Feb. 1872; *The Times*, 23 Jan. 1872.
[30] *St. Mic.'s Par. Mag.* Jan. 1882; Lloyd, *Highgate*, 476 478.
[31] Leaflet and ticket in Hornsey libr., Heal Colln.
[32] Swiss Cottage libr., Heal Colln., A III 5.
[33] *St. Mic.'s Par. Mag.* Apr. 1863, June 1865; deeds in Highgate Sch. rec., box 4, bdle. 6.
[34] Lloyd, *Highgate*, 484–5.
[35] New lease, 1899, in Highgate Sch. rec.
[36] Lloyd, *Highgate*, 482. Min. bks. from 1903 are at Highgate Lit. and Sc. Inst.
[37] *St. Mic.'s Par. Mag.* July 1863.
[38] *The Times*, 17 July 1873; min. bk. 1903 in Highgate Lit. and Sc. Inst.
[39] Plan and elevation of a spacious building, with a Greek Doric portico, in Highgate Lit. and Sc. Inst.
[40] *St. Mic.'s Par. Mag.* July, Dec. 1878.

largely by members of the institution, included a dwelling-house and two committee rooms. They provided a headquarters for the volunteers and a public meeting-place and in 1879 provoked suggestions that they might replace the institution itself.[41] At Hornsey, hitherto served only by the drill-hall at Crouch End, a company opened the National hall in High Street in 1888. The building, on three floors and including a hall for 500, was to accommodate a new Conservative association and the volunteers, as well as public meetings.[42] Hornsey constitutional club, founded in 1889,[43] also met there.[44]

A debating society used Highgate Literary and Scientific Institution from 1863 until 1873.[45] Highgate also had a choral society by 1868 and a new one from 1873.[46] Many musical, dramatic, literary, debating, and temperance groups were encouraged by the churches: Crouch End choral society, founded *c.* 1874, met in the early 1880s at Christ Church schoolroom[47] and Hornsey young men's society, founded *c.* 1875, had a committee chaired by the minister of Park chapel.[48] New areas produced their own societies: a Conservative club at Hornsey was formed after the success of one at Stroud Green, started in 1886,[49] and by 1888 a Stroud Green institute met in an iron room in Granville Road.[50] From 1886 Finsbury Park had a working lads' institute, which acquired premises in Poole's Park (Islington).[51]

By 1903 Muswell Hill had five literary societies, a social club, and orchestral and musical societies, most of them connected with the churches and all of recent date.[52] The parish's most imposing centre of entertainment was the Athenaeum, a florid, balustraded building[53] erected in 1900 by Edmondson[54] in St. James's Parade, Fortis Green Road. The Muswell Hill Club, a conservatoire of music, and the Muswell Hill Parliament all met there from 1909 until after the First World War and a girls' school was there from 1910. The Athenaeum, with halls seating 466 and 200, was also used as a cinema from 1922.[55]

The Highgate Preservation Society was founded in 1934 and joined with members of the successful 'Save Highgate' campaign in 1966 to form the Highgate Society, which met in a room leased from the Highgate Literary and Scientific Institution.[56] The new group, although largely concerned with traffic through the village, had the broad aim of improving the quality of local life.[57] Plans to widen Archway Road gave rise to the Archway Road Campaign in 1968, the Shepherd's Hill Association in 1969, and the North Highgate Group in 1970.[58] The Hornsey Historical Society, whose interest in Highgate was shared by the Camden History Society, was founded in 1971.[59]

Cricketers from Highgate played at Westminster in 1790[60] and travelled to Woodford (Essex) in 1795.[61] A match between teams from Hornsey and Highgate took place in 1843.[62] A Hornsey club of the 1840s, which used a field opposite the Priory, was succeeded by the Harringay club, playing at the north-east end of Shepherd's Hill, and *c.* 1856 by another Hornsey club, which played near Wood Green and later opposite the Priory until 1861. The existing Hornsey cricket club prospered because of the shortage of land nearer London. It was so named from 1870, after the Phoenix club from Tufnell Park had taken over a small local club, the Hanover, and merged with another former Tufnell Park club, the Carlton, in 1875. The old Harringay club's ground was leased from the Ecclesiastical Commissioners in 1874 and vacated for an adjoining field, later part of Crouch End playing fields, in 1883.[63] Matches between Cholmley's school and Highgate village took place regularly in the 1860s.[64] By 1888 there were cricket clubs named Harringay, Hornsey Rise, Hornsey Vale, Hornsey Priory, and the Highgate Bohemians.[65]

Highgate lawn tennis club was established in 1881[66] and had six courts west of North Hill by 1888, when there were also football, skating, and gymnastic clubs.[67] The Highgate club, formed in 1883 for indoor and outdoor amusements, played football and cricket at Manor Farm and encouraged bicycling.[68] There were tennis clubs for Hornsey Rise in 1884[69] and Ferme Park in 1888.[70] Crouch End Vampires football club was established in 1885 and used a ground in Coppetts Road, in 1976.[71] Hornsey ladies' football club won national attention in the 1890s.[72] Highgate golf club, founded in 1904, moved to links west of Bishop's wood in 1905, when its former course between Highgate wood and Fortis Green was required for building by the Ecclesiastical Commissioners.[73] After a fire in 1926 the club-house was rebuilt on its old foundations.[74] The course and club-house, approached from Denewood Road, covered *c.* 84 a. in 1976.[75] The course of Muswell Hill golf club, serving the north-eastern part of the parish, lay in Wood Green.[76]

Highgate ponds, in St. Pancras parish, were used for swimming and skating and, from *c.* 1852, by

41 *St. Mic.'s Par. Mag.* Mar. 1879.
42 *The Times*, 25 June, 19 Nov. 1888; prospectus in Hornsey libr., Heal Colln.
43 4th ann. rep. 1892–3 in Hornsey libr., Heal Colln.
44 *Kelly's Dir. Hornsey* (1898–9).
45 *St. Mic.'s Par. Mag.* Dec. 1863, Dec. 1873.
46 Ibid. Feb. 1868, Mar. 1873.
47 Programmes for 10th season (1883–4) etc. in Hornsey libr., Heal Colln.
48 Programme for 7th session (1881–2) in Hornsey libr., Heal Colln.
49 Beaconsfield hall draft prospectus in Hornsey libr., Heal Colln.
50 *Crouch End and Hornsey Weekly News and Highgate Advertiser*, 12 May 1888.
51 *The Times*, 30 Apr. 1900.
52 *Hornsey and Finsbury Pk. Jnl.* 14 Mar. 1903.
53 Illus. in *Muswell Hill Rec.* 1 Oct. 1907.
54 *Hornsey and Finsbury Pk. Jnl.* 10 Feb. 1900.
55 *Kelly's Dir. Hornsey* (1909–10 and later edns.).
56 *Buzz* (Highgate Soc. magazine), May 1976.
57 Ex inf. the chairman.
58 Collins and Pharaoh, *Transport Org.* 367–72.
59 Ex inf. Dr. Joan Schwitzer.
60 Potter Colln. 15/103.
61 Swiss Cottage libr., Heal Colln., A III 3.
62 Potter Colln. 21/109.
63 *Hist. Hornsey Cricket Club* (pamphlet, 1908).
64 *St. Mic.'s Par. Mag.* July 1864 and later edns.
65 *Crouch End and Hornsey Weekly News and Highgate Advertiser*, 5, 12, 26 May 1888.
66 *St. Mic.'s Par. Mag.* Dec. 1881.
67 Lloyds, *Highgate*, 475, 478.
68 Potter Colln. 15/107.
69 Concert programme in Hornsey libr., Heal Colln.
70 *Crouch End and Hornsey Weekly News and Highgate Advertiser*, 16 June 1888.
71 Notice at grounds.
72 Interview with capt. in *Daily Graphic*, 2 Mar. 1895.
73 *Hampstead and Highgate Express*, 25 Feb. 1905; ex. inf. the sec.
74 *Builder*, cxxxiii. 612.
75 Ex inf. the sec.
76 *V.C.H. Mdx.* v. 341.

Highgate model yacht club, which held races there until 1914.[77] A municipal swimming pool was opened in 1929 in Park Road, next to Crouch End playing fields. Public baths and wash-houses were built in 1932.[78] A new indoor pool had been built in Park Road by 1975.

A theatre was advertised by the Highgate press of an actor named H. Jackman in 1812 and 1816. The building contained boxes, a pit, and a gallery,[79] was apparently known as Larne's theatre,[80] and was recalled as having been a converted barn or wheelwright's workshop on the free school's land in Southwood Lane.[81] It may have closed by 1825, when actors were said to have been patronized by Mrs. Coutts (formerly Harriot Mellon) and to have played at the White Lion.[82]

A hall at no. 31 Topsfield Parade, Crouch End, was adapted to seat 1,200 and opened in 1897 as the Queen's opera house.[83] The theatre, which had no gallery, belonged to Messrs. Morell and Mouillot until *c.* 1903. It then became a music hall, with an upstairs room occupied by a social club before and after a fire necessitated reconstruction in 1905. Soon renamed the Hippodrome, it included a cinematograph room from 1910[84] and was described as a cinema in 1926,[85] although live performances were still staged. The building closed as a result of bomb damage in 1942, housed a school of dancing in 1948, and was used for storage before its demolition by Grattan Ltd. in the early 1950s.[86] Finsbury Park had an open-air theatre in the park itself, where a variety of light entertainments was provided by the L.C.C. between 1945 and 1953.[87] A company which had been formed in 1945 opened the private Mountview theatre at no. 104 Crouch Hill in 1947. The freehold was bought by the principal, Peter Coxhead, in 1949, when a theatre school was founded, and vested in the Mountview arts centre in 1966. The North London film theatre and the Phoenix theatre club rented parts of the centre in 1976, when the Mountview theatre school had 125 full-time students and 225 part-time students and younger members.[88]

The Picture House in Broadway Parade, Crouch End, was open by 1911.[89] It closed *c.* 1915 but was succeeded in 1922 by the Perfect picture house, which was apparently on the same site and which in 1930–1 was renamed the Plaza.[90] Hornsey National hall served as a cinema[91] in 1920–1 and the Hippodrome, after its conversion, continued as one until the Second World War.[92] A cinema at Finsbury Park in 1918, owned by North Metropolitan Theatres,[93] was probably the Rink, at the corner of Stroud Green and Seven Sisters roads,[94] where the first talking film was shown in England to representatives of the film industry.[95] The cinema was renamed the Gaumont in 1950[96] and, as the Top Rank club, was used for bingo in 1977. At Muswell Hill the Summerland cinema in the Broadway was open from 1921 to 1938,[97] the Odeon in Fortis Green Road by 1937,[98] and the Ritz (later the ABC) by 1940.[99] Both the Odeon and the ABC remained open in 1976.

A large hostel for the Y.M.C.A. was opened in 1929 at the corner of Tottenham Lane and Elmfield Avenue, aided by a bequest from Mrs. Palmer Thomas,[1] and was extended in 1958.[2] Harringay boys' club, established in 1958, moved from North Harringay school into a new building in Tottenham Lane in 1961.[3] A social centre for Muswell Hill Methodist church was provided by Guy Chester on land at Pages Lane, which he had bought in 1924. Later he contributed towards a hostel and headquarters of the Methodist Youth Department, which was built to the design of Charles Pike, opened in 1960, and named Chester House.[4]

A free library was opened in 1860 by Highgate Congregational chapel and moved in 1861 to the new premises of the working men's association in Southwood Lane.[5] The vicar of Highgate had a parochial library at the infants' school by 1863 and used[6] a legacy to establish a library for St. Michael's working men's institute, also in Southwood Lane, in 1864.[7] Christ Church, Crouch End, opened a library *c.* 1877[8] and by 1895 there were libraries managed by Park chapel, St. James's, Muswell Hill, and St. Paul's, Harringay. Highgate Literary and Scientific Institution retained its cheap subscriptions and in 1895 there were circulating libraries, mostly connected with Mudie's, at Hornsey, Crouch End, Harringay, Stroud Green, and Muswell Hill.[9] In South Hornsey, after unsuccessfully seeking a poll on the Public Libraries Act, subscribers opened a reading room and lending library for householders within ½ mile of Finsbury Park station in 1894. The library was at no. 1 Blackstock Road and so was transferred, after the adoption of the Act, to Stoke Newington borough, which moved it to Milton Road.[10]

77 Potter Colln. 13/50–1; ex inf. Sir Jas. Brown.
78 *Hornsey Boro. 1903–53*, 16, 25.
79 *N. & Q.* 6th ser. iii. 307; play bill and copies in Potter Colln. 14/61, 64.
80 Lloyd, *Highgate*, 190.
81 Potter Colln. 14/61, 64–5.
82 Ibid. 14/59. *Complete Peerage*, xi. 292–3.
83 Illus. in the *Sketch*, 18 Aug. 1897.
84 P. G. Andrae, *Those were the Days* (pamphlet hist. in the possession of Mr. W. G. Campbell).
85 Hornsey Boro. *Official Guide* [1926].
86 Andrae, op. cit.
87 W. E. Jackson, *Achievement: Short Hist. of L.C.C.* 120–1; *The Times*, 22 June 1945. The Finsbury Pk. Empire theatre was in Islington.
88 Ex inf. the principal.
89 *Kelly's Dir. Hornsey* (1911–12). There were also 'electric' theatres across the boundary in Highgate Hill and Green Lanes: ibid.
90 Ibid. (1916–17, 1922, 1931).
91 Ibid. (1920, 1921).
92 *The Times*, 13 Apr. 1950.
93 Ibid. 19 July 1918.
94 *Kelly's Dir. Hornsey* (1920 and later edns.). The nearby Astoria, Finsbury Pk., was in Islington.
95 Ex inf. Sir Jas. Brown.
96 *Hornsey Jnl.* 4 Aug., 11 Aug. 1950; Mdx. Loc. Hist. Council, *Bull.* xviii. 14.
97 *Kelly's Dir. Wood Gn. and Muswell Hill* (1921); *Kelly's Dir. Hornsey* (1938).
98 *Kelly's Dir. Hornsey* (1937).
99 *Hornsey Jnl.* 5 Jan. 1940.
1 *The Times*, 13 May 1929.
2 Inscription on bldg.
3 *Hornsey Jnl.* 28 Dec. 1962.
4 Ibid. 26 Mar. 1959, 22 Apr. 1960, 20 May 1960.
5 *Highgate Cong. Chap. Yr. Bk.* (1860), 45; (1861), 44.
6 *St. Mic.'s Par. Mag.* June 1864, Jan. 1863; Prickett and Cassini, *Highgate*. After the closure of the working men's club (see above, p. 159) the libr. was reserved for church workers: *St. Mic.'s Par. Mag.* Jan 1882.
7 *St. Mic.'s Par. Mag.* June 1864.
8 5th–8th ann. reps. in Hornsey libr., Heal Colln.
9 Cutting from *N. Mdx. Chron.* in Stoke Newington libr.
10 Finsbury Pk. Free Libr. min. bk. and newspaper cuttings in Stoke Newington libr. For Hornsey's municipal libraries, see below, p. 171.

Highgate museum of sanitary appliances, displaying old and modern drainage, was opened in 1892 by Hornsey local board, after public inspection of its work during a cholera scare.[11] The building stood in the council's coal depot at the foot of North Hill.[12] It was open once a week in 1908[13] and closed in 1928.[14]

The weekly *Hampstead and Highgate Express*,[15] established at Hampstead in 1860, circulated in Hornsey and survived in 1976, as did the *Hampstead and Highgate Record and Chronicle*, founded in 1889 as the *Hampstead Record* and renamed in 1918. The *Hornsey Hornet*, first published monthly from Tottenham Lane in 1866, enjoyed initial success but soon moved to London and, as the *Hornet*,[16] ceased to be a local newspaper.[17] The *Seven Sisters' and Finsbury Park Journal*, founded in 1879 with offices in Crouch Hill, became the *Hornsey and Finsbury Park Journal* in 1881 and, through several changes of name, was generally known as the *Hornsey Journal*, with offices in Tottenham Lane and Fleet Street in 1975. The *Muswell Hill Record* appeared from 1908 to 1919, continued as the *Muswell Hill Record, Alexandra Park and Friern Barnet Journal* until 1954, then as the *Record* until 1957, and finally was amalgamated in the short-lived *London Chronicle*. The parish was also covered by the *North Middlesex Chronicle*, published at Islington from 1868 until 1940.

The *Finsbury Park, Crouch Hill and Hornsey House and Property Register and Local Advertiser* appeared in 1880 and was soon renamed the *North London Advertiser*, which survived until 1884. Other short-lived newspapers included the *Weathercock of Finsbury Park*, covering much of south-eastern Hornsey as well as Islington, in 1876–7; the *Hornsey and Middlesex Messenger* in 1888, continued as the *Middlesex Messenger* in 1889; the *Crouch End and Hornsey Weekly News and Highgate Advertiser*, in 1888; the *Hornsey Hawk Eye* in 1897; the *Crouch End and District Review* in 1898; the *North London Mercury and Crouch End Observer* from 1899 to 1905; and the *Crouch End and District Advertiser* in 1922. The *Finchley Free Press*, founded in 1893, was also issued in 1896 as the *Highgate and Muswell Hill Post*. In 1908 the Hornsey and Tottenham Press, with offices in Seven Sisters Road and in Grand Parade, Muswell Hill, owned the *Highgate Times*, the *Muswell Hill Times*, and the *Hornsey and Harringay Mercury*.

LOCAL GOVERNMENT. MANORIAL GOVERNMENT. In 1294 the bishop of London claimed to have possessed in Hornsey as member of his manor of Stepney view of frankpledge, infangthief and outfangthief, the chattels of fugitives and outlaws and waste of their lands, pillory, cucking stool, gallows, amercements in local courts, and assizes of bread and ale from time immemorial. Except for gallows his right was admitted by a jury.[18] In 1318–19 there was a separate court for Hornsey,[19] which may have met at Stepney where the lord of Farnfields owed suit of court in 1324.[20] By 1575 it was held at Highgate in October.[21] In 1375 there was a court every three weeks[22] and from the 17th to the 19th centuries there was normally a view of frankpledge and general court baron in April and sometimes a special court baron.[23]

Between 1374 and 1885 there were also courts for the manor of Topsfield.[24] Its court rolls were lost in 1703, when minutes and drafts from 1683 were copied into a book in which subsequent courts were recorded. The court baron was held from time to time, but not annually, within the manor from 1750 to 1820, usually at the King's Head and sometimes at the Three Tuns. Only after the longest gap of 20 years did it become active in local government between 1820 and 1833, when the homage presented encroachments and waste.

No courts were recorded for Muswell or Farnfields. The court for Brownswood, which was a court leet and court baron from 1649 to 1795,[25] existed from at least 1569. The last known enfranchisement occurred in 1870.[26] Under a demesne lease of 1569 it was to be held quinquennially,[27] but it met every three years by *c.* 1709[28] and annually in 1795.[29] In 1649 it was held at the manor-house[30] and in 1795 at Hornsey Wood House.[31] In 1682 the lessee had custody of some court rolls over 60 years old[32] but none is known to survive.

The court of Topsfield was concerned only with the conveyance of copyhold land,[33] which was also the main business of the courts of Brownswood and Hornsey. In 1577 an ordinance of the Hornsey court regulated lawsuits concerning copyholds.[34] Local government was the preserve of the two principal manors and probably the court of Brownswood exercised similar jurisdiction to that of Hornsey. In 1318–19, 1375, and 1577 offenders against the lord's woods were presented at the Hornsey court[35] but later infringements were ignored. The homage still protected communal rights in 1797, when it ordered the reopening of two blocked footpaths;[36] dunghills on the highways were denounced as late as 1728[37] and clearance of a ditch was decreed in 1717.[38] By-

[11] *The Times*, 26 Sept. 1892; cat. and plan in Hornsey libr.
[12] O.S. Map 1/2,500, Lond. III. 41 (1894 edn.).
[13] *Kelly's Dir. Essex, Herts. and Mdx.* (1908).
[14] *Hornsey Jnl.* 9 Apr. 1928.
[15] The following two paras. are based on B.L. Newspaper Cat.; *Kelly's* and *P.O. Dirs.*; and *Willing's Press Guide* (1896 and later edns.).
[16] Sherington, *Story of Hornsey*, 120–1.
[17] Copies from 1871 in B.L.
[18] Madge, *Med. Rec. of Harringay*, 80–1.
[19] St. Paul's MS., box B 79/53. Ct. rolls survive for 1318–19, 1376, 1406, 1442–3, 1534–5, 1577–8, 1584–5, and with gaps from 1603 to 1819: ibid. A 62, B 68, B 70, B 79/53; Guildhall MSS. 10312/92–6, 10312/98–117, 10312/122; 10832/1–138; S.C. 2/191/4–12. Those for 1603–1701 are calendared in Marchams, *Hornsey Ct. Rolls*. There are ct. bks. 1684–1951, Guildhall MSS. 10465/1–228, and draft ct. bks. 1681–1847, ibid. 10466/1–17.
[20] *T.L.M.A.S.* xiii. 394.
[21] Guildhall MS. 10312/92, m. 7.
[22] St. Paul's MS., box A 62.
[23] Marchams, *Ct. Rolls, passim*; Guildhall MSS. 10465/17–175.
[24] *T.L.M.A.S.* xiii. 393–4. There is a ct. roll for 1467, S.C. 2/191/65B, and a ct. bk. for 1683–1885, M.R.O., Acc. 1289/1/1. For the next three sentences see ibid.
[25] Guildhall MS. 11816B, p. 87; Lysons, *Environs*, iii. 48.
[26] Guildhall MS. 11816B, p. 87; M.A.F. 9/164.
[27] Guildhall MS. 11816B, p. 87.
[28] St. Paul's MS., F.B. 3, f. 14.
[29] Lysons, *Environs*, iii. 48.
[30] Guildhall MS. 11816B, p. 89.
[31] Madge, *Early Rec. of Harringay*, 51.
[32] *Cal. S.P. Dom.* 1682, 83.
[33] M.R.O., Acc. 1289/1/1; S.C. 2/191/65B.
[34] Guildhall MS. 10312/93, m. 3d.
[35] St. Paul's MSS., boxes A 62, B 79/53; Guildhall MS. 10312/92, m. 6d.
[36] Guildhall MS. 10465/112, pp. 195–6.
[37] Ibid. 10465/43.
[38] Ibid. 10465/32.

laws, each with a fixed penalty, were frequently promulgated and offenders indicted.[39] From 1637 there were irregular appointments of overseers of the commons; they were supported by a tariff of fines,[40] as were the pound-keepers mentioned in 1617, when it was an ancient custom to impound strays.[41] The Highgate pound mentioned in 1629 needed repair by the lord in 1676.[42] Another common pound existed at Stroud Green in Brownswood in 1577.[43] The Hornsey homage also frequently presented those who took gravel, loam, fern, turf, or furze outside the manor;[44] in 1671 furze was to be taken only for repairs to the highways.[45] Usually the court ordered the frequent encroachments on the waste to be laid open and unlicensed buildings to be demolished. From 1786 encroachments were permitted on condition that the full purchase price should be paid into the wastelands fund.[46] Such activity suggests that the court's authority was effective with tenants of the manor. The numerous presentments may indicate inability to exact fines from non-residents, who were the worst offenders, rather than a level of fines too low to deter profitable activities.

There were two pledges for Hornsey in 1406[47] and an ale-taster occurred in 1442–3.[48] In 1577 there were two constables, two chief pledges, later called headboroughs, and two ale-tasters, one of each being elected for Hornsey Side, the other for Highgate Side.[49] Those officers were appointed annually, unlike the driver of the commons who occurred irregularly from 1694.[50] By 1701 there was one driver for Highgate Side[51] and from 1711 there were two for the whole manor.[52] There was usually only one after *c.* 1770,[53] who was paid by the parish in 1803 and appointed by it from 1855 until 1868, when the local board dispensed with him.[54] From 1637 to 1712 overseers of the commons were elected intermittently:[55] in 1700 there was one for Hornsey Side and another for Highgate Side.[56] No ale-tasters were appointed after 1750.[57] Constables and headboroughs were elected by the court until 1840, when they were superseded by the metropolitan police.[58]

The St. Pancras part of Highgate was administered by courts of the prebend of Cantlowes, recorded from 1479 and at which three headboroughs, two rent collectors, two affeerers, an ale-taster, and a constable were normally sworn.[59] It was rare for officers to be assigned specifically to an area, as they were on Hornsey manor from 1577. Some division nonetheless existed within Cantlowes: several officers were Highgate residents and there were elections of constables for Highgate in 1531 and 1533 and of a headborough in 1624.[60] Eighteenth- and 19th-century courts were often held at the Angel, High Street, as well as in Kentish Town;[61] in 1768 the court met at the Flask.[62]

Hornsey manor court ordered the expulsion of some sub-tenants in 1578[63] and was active in enforcing the poor law in the 17th century. A by-law of 1612 forbade any inhabitant to accept a tenant or inmate unless he gave surety to discharge the parish of relief. Between 1604 and 1674 the homage presented at least 34 offences: in 1674 six families were involved and in 1676 a tenant was indicted for dividing his tenement.[64]

It was probably to avoid paying expenses that Hornsey vestry did not permanently take over the appointment of officers, although it supervised them. Probably in 1644, when there was no court leet, and on occasions such as 1755 when those nominated refused to serve, the vestry appointed constables.[65] In 1742 it tried to compel those elected as constables to serve and in 1794 it decided to hold a special vestry whenever manorial officials failed to act.[66] In 1746 the vestry asked the justices to fine the constables and headboroughs for not attending the vestry but by the 1780s they were rarely present.[67] The justices ordered the provision of a watch-house in 1682,[68] and in 1687–8, when there were no stocks, whipping post, or cage, the homage petitioned the lord to provide timber for them. The vestry, however, was responsible for the cage in 1773 and the stocks in 1792.[69]

PARISH GOVERNMENT TO 1837. Hornsey vestry was mentioned in 1688.[70] Minute books from 1739[71] record meetings in the vestry room at the church and occasionally at public houses or Highgate chapel. From 1740, when there were 3 vestries a year, their frequency increased. There were often as many as 7, in 1786 there were 12, but 3 or 4 were more common from 1835. Attendance increased from an average of 10 in 1740–5 to *c.* 20 in 1820. There were exceptional years, such as 1855, when two vestries attracted 56 and 47 parishioners. The rector normally chaired meetings from 1830 but had rarely attended before 1820, although his curate sometimes had done so. Churchwardens were present most frequently, followed after 1820 by the overseers. Non-officeholders were usually in a majority and in 1866

39 Marchams, *Ct. Rolls, passim*, esp. 153–5.
40 Ibid. 89.
41 Ibid. 45.
42 Ibid. 73, 174.
43 S.P. 12/113/17.
44 Marchams, *Ct. Rolls, passim*; Guildhall MSS. 10465/31; 112, p. 194.
45 Marchams, *Ct. Rolls*, 253.
46 M.R.O., D.R.O. 20/G/69–70, C1/1; Guildhall MSS. 10465/108, pp. 113–14; see below, p. 165.
47 St. Paul's MS., box A 62.
48 S.C. 2/191/62.
49 Guildhall MS. 10312/92, m. 7.
50 Marchams, *Ct. Rolls*, 225.
51 Ibid. 250.
52 Guildhall MS. 10465/26.
53 Ibid. 94.
54 M.R.O., D.R.O. 20/C1/4; Bruce Castle Mus., D/PH/2A/1; O/H/1/1.
55 Marchams, *Ct. Rolls*, 89, 93, 126, 246, 250; Guildhall MS. 10465/27.
56 Marchams, *Ct. Rolls*, 246.
57 Guildhall MS. 10465/66.
58 Ibid. 155, p. 216; *Lond. Gaz.* 13 Oct. 1840, p. 2250.
59 Ct. rolls survive for 1479–1534, 1593–4, and 1609–85 and ct. bks. for 1686–1950: Guildhall MSS. 14220/1–54. A TS. transl. of the rolls to 1632, by W. McB. Marcham, is in G.L.R.O., rm/50.15.
60 Marcham, 'Cantlowes Ct. Rolls', pp. 100, 103, [pt. 2] 30.
61 e.g. Guildhall MSS. 14220/41, 46, 48 *passim*.
62 Ibid. 41, p. 80
63 Guildhall MS. 10312/94.
64 Marchams, *Ct. Rolls*, 30 and *passim*.
65 *T.L.M.A.S.* xvi. 42.
66 M.R.O., D.R.O. 20/C1/1, f. 11; C1/4, f. 216v.
67 Ibid. C1/1, esp. f. 31.
68 M.R.O., Cal. Mdx. Sess. Bks. 1679–82, 129.
69 Marchams, *Ct. Rolls*, 205, 207; see below, p. 165.
70 M.R.O., D.R.O. 20/C4/1.
71 Except where otherwise stated, the para. is based on ibid. C1/1–4, and Bruce Castle Mus., D/PH/2A/1–3.

it was alleged that a minority of the well-to-do dominated the morning vestries that most inhabitants could not attend:[72] after several motions, evening meetings were at last introduced in 1889.[73] Elections were often disputed, as during the years 1748 to 1751, particularly when they were remunerative: in 1833 a beadle was elected with 125 votes of 256 cast.

Minute books of St. Pancras vestry survive from 1718.[74] Meetings were announced at Highgate chapel,[75] like those of Hornsey vestry, and occasionally took place near by at the Flask or the Fox and Crown,[76] although more frequently in Kentish Town. St. Pancras vestry gradually encroached on the duties of the steward of Cantlowes manor, who in 1775 was asked not to dispute the nominations of constables.[77] Officers were appointed for the southern and northern divisions of St. Pancras, the second in 1718 being termed the Highgate division.[78]

Churchwardens for Hornsey occurred from 1421[79] and one was intermittently described as upper or senior churchwarden from 1674[80] until at least 1855, when it was decided that the one for Hornsey Side should be senior. Separate churchwardens for Highgate and Hornsey Sides were established by 1782. Early churchwardens performed some of the functions of overseers,[81] who first occurred in 1612.[82] Four overseers were elected in 1742 and eight in 1861 but from 1740 there was normally one each for Hornsey Side and Highgate Side. The function of deputy overseer was added in 1788 to that of vestry clerk, mentioned from 1739, whose duties in 1774 embraced attendance, the preparation of accounts, and legal business. In 1853 it was recommended that all his duties should be included in his salary, as he supplemented his income by performing the legal business through his own firm, Thomas Tatham & Sons. Instead, however, his salary, which had grown from £20 in 1791 to £100 in 1832, was reduced. In 1861 the octogenarian Thomas Tatham, only the second vestry clerk since 1788, was succeeded by his son, who died in 1889. Only from 1889 did the vestry clerk have an office in the parish.[83] The clerk of Highgate chapel was paid from 1792 for posting vestry notices and the Hornsey parish clerk was salaried from 1739.

The Hornsey homage elected two surveyors of the highways for Hornsey and Highgate Sides in 1606 but not afterwards.[84] Presumably the surveyor for Hornsey Side mentioned in 1668 was elected by the vestry,[85] like his successors after 1739. Four surveyors were nominated to the justices in 1740, three in 1745, and thereafter generally two. In 1797, at the request of the justices, ten were named, five for each division. There had been a single salaried surveyor between 1772 and 1777, an assistant surveyor in 1821, and two assistant surveyors, one for each division, from 1825.

An apothecary for the poor occurred from 1750, a master of the workhouse after 1743, and a beadle from 1774. In addition to his salary, the beadle received a new hat and coat every three years from 1788 and an allowance for brooms as church cleaner in 1792. Initially responsible only for supervising the poor in the workhouse, he was required from 1789 to keep order at church and in the village on Sundays and from 1790 to attend vestries and assist the officers. Separate beadles were appointed for the two divisions in 1812. In 1825 the Highgate beadle was to go to church every Sunday, escort the poor from Highgate division, attend all meetings, and execute orders. An engine-keeper was appointed for each division from 1813, a collector of rates from 1817, and a public health inspector from 1853.

The cost of salaries increased from £42 in 1776 to *c.* £200 in 1836–7. Accounting was often slow: in 1821 the vestry ordered that officers should produce their accounts within the statutory time limit and should justify each item with a voucher; in 1853, when it was impossible to audit any accounts, all parish officers were directed to reveal their annual balance.

In 1674–5 the churchwardens were passing the poor and prevented the settlement of a pregnant woman.[86] Small sums were paid to relieve the sick and poor in 1664–5[87] and in 1669–70 there were apparently five regular pensioners.[88] Besides casual relief, £37 of the total expenses of one churchwarden in 1680–1 consisted of pensions.[89] Poor-rates levied up to three times a year amounted to between 2*d.* and 12*d.* in the £ in the years 1740 to 1749. By 1785–7 they had risen to between 2*s.* 2*d.* and 2*s.* 6*d.* and by 1800–2 to between 2*s.* 9*d.* and 5*s.*, but they had fallen slightly by 1820–1. Over the period receipts and expenses grew enormously. In 1749 a rate of 8*d.* yielded the overseer of Hornsey Side *c.* £110; between 1773 and 1823 the income of his successors rose from £216 to £1,501 and that for Highgate division from £170 to £1,248.[90] In 1834–5 expenditure by the whole parish was £1,576.[91]

It was only in 1730 that the parish leased a house in Hornsey Lane as a temporary workhouse.[92] A permanent site of 1 a. of copyhold land in Hornsey High Street, with out-buildings, was acquired in 1735[93] and by 1743 a workhouse stood there.[94] The out-buildings were ruinous in 1778 and eight rooms were added by 1779, when improvements were made to the old building. In 1779, however, four more rooms had to be added and in 1781 a further extension was needed. A committee was appointed to consider improvements in 1812. The population of the workhouse increased from 60 in 1823 to 83 in

72 Cutting from *Hornsey Hornet* in Hornsey libr.
73 *Hornsey & Finsbury Pk. Jnl.* 3 Aug. 1889.
74 Min. bks. are in the care of the mace-bearer, Camden town hall.
75 St. Pancras vestry min. bk. 1718–80, f. 206.
76 Ibid. ff. 4, 16.
77 Ibid. f. 440.
78 Ibid. f. 1.
79 Guildhall MS. 9171/3, f. 80v. Except where otherwise stated, the following four paras. are based on M.R.O., D.R.O. 20/C1/1–4 and Bruce Castle Mus., D/PH/2A/1–3.
80 M.R.O., D.R.O. 20/E1/1.
81 e.g. ibid.
82 Ibid. E1/1, 7; Marchams, *Ct. Rolls*, 30.
83 *Hornsey & Finsbury Pk. Jnl.* 3 Aug. 1889.
84 Marchams, *Ct. Rolls*, 15.
85 M.R.O., D.R.O. 20/F1/1; see also ibid. C4/1.
86 M.R.O., D.R.O. 20/E1/5.
87 Ibid. E1/1.
88 Ibid. E1/3.
89 Ibid. E1/7.
90 Ibid. E1/8, 23; C1/3.
91 *Second Ann. Rep. of Poor Law Com.* H.C. 595–II, p. 212 (1836), xxix(2).
92 M.R.O., D.R.O. 20/E4/1.
93 Ibid. E4/2.
94 Except where otherwise stated, the following two paras. are based on M.R.O., D.R.O. 20/C1/1–4; Bruce Castle Mus., D/PH/2A/1–3.

1827, when there were 104 others receiving outdoor relief and an extension to house 50–60 was necessary. After rejecting a proposal for a workhouse on a different site, the vestry added a wing for *c.* 80 poor in 1827–8.

The workhouse was directly administered through a master and mistress and from 1812 it was supervised by a committee of the vestry, which met monthly from 1813. The assent of the churchwardens or overseers had been necessary hitherto for the admission or discharge of inmates. In 1753 the vestry wanted to keep the paupers as well as possible and in 1783 they were provided with beer. In 1744 a fence was built to prevent them from wandering, in 1754 none was to live out, and in 1748 they were to be badged and in 1782 clothed in uniform. In 1781 the clerk was to seek suitable employment and receive the income from the work of the able-bodied who refused to be discharged. Several who did not work were referred to the justices in 1782 and in 1804 an agreement was reached to farm the idle and disorderly to the master of the City workhouse in Islington. The mistress was allowed 10 per cent of the issues of the poor's work in 1785 and the master as much as 50 per cent in 1803.

By will proved 1608 James Skeffington devised to the parish a cottage inhabited by two widows[95] but in 1623 the homage presented that John Richardson had no licence to devise his cottage on the waste to the poor.[96] There was a parish house in 1668–9, when the occupant was evicted by a churchwarden.[97] Ten parish houses were occupied by the poor in 1697[98] and five from 1725 to 1773,[99] when two stood on the ½-a. site of the former manorial bowling green in Hornsey High Street and the others in Southwood Lane.[1] Repairs were made by the vestry in 1758, 1766, and 1810. Two of the cottages in Southwood Lane were demolished in 1815 and replaced by one in 1818. Seven new cottages were built in 1818 there and near by in Muswell Hill Road,[2] three being for the poor of Highgate and four for those of Hornsey. Two more were erected in 1828. Unlike the older cottages, rent-free in 1795,[3] the new ones were let cheaply. Four cottages at Muswell Hill built by 1817 and devised to the parish by James Wright were refused by the vestry, as they were subject to fines at the will of the lord of Topsfield. The Southwood Lane cottages were paid for out of the wastelands fund, established in 1786 from fines for licences to inclose the waste.[4] The fines were fixed in 1810 at £80 per acre by the vestry and the fund was used for the poor under a trust deed of *c.* 1790. In 1806 a lawyer advised that the proceeds could not serve to reduce the poor-rate. One suggested use had been to provide cottages: in 1803 the vestry asked the bishop of London for a site and in 1806 trustees were admitted to 1 a. in Southwood Lane.[5] The fund had grown to £730 by 1817, mainly in stock, of which £600 was spent on building the cottages; afterwards their rents swelled the fund. As both cottages and fund remained the responsibility of the parish after the formation of Edmonton union, their later history belongs with that of parish charities.

Rates in 1750 occasioned an appeal to quarter sessions. Assessment by 5 per cent of the purchase price, although customary, was considered unfair to owner occupiers. After an appeal to the justices in 1793 the rate was quashed and the vestry appointed an impartial committee, which carried out a general survey but overruled the objectors, for whom in 1796[6] another rate was quashed. A further appeal occurred in 1803 and there were more disagreements about assessment in 1817. The vestry of Hornsey also opposed the Bill to turnpike Green Lanes in 1789[7] and Bills to extend the metropolitan sewer system in 1814 and 1822.[8]

Hornsey parish's cage stood on the west side of Highgate High Street. In 1770 St. Pancras vestry agreed to contribute towards its repair and in 1775 both cage and stocks were to be moved nearer the watch-house,[9] presumably to the site later occupied by no. 59, from which the cage was moved in 1811 to the site of no. 61.[10] Offenders were also kept in the Gatehouse.[11] Highgate residents subscribed to a fund for the conviction of robbers from 1737, when they bought stock which had doubled in value, to £80, by 1761. Rewards were advertised and payments made for feeding and escorting prisoners before trial.[12] Later the Highgate and Whetstone turnpike trust maintained horse patrols:[13] on winter evenings they operated between Highgate and Islington, whence another patrol led travellers to and from London, and Kentish Town.[14]

In 1803 Hornsey decided to erect its own stocks by the church and a cage in the workhouse garden.[15] In 1825 the cage was repaired[16] but in 1833, after prisoners had escaped, it was found unsuitable for even temporary confinement. To make better use of its restricted site, shared with the watch-house, the vestry agreed to its rebuilding.[17]

From 1774 local trustees were reponsible for lighting and watching Highgate except Caen Wood Lane, which had only to be watched. The trustees, who had to own or occupy property in the village worth at least £20 a year, initially numbered 48, besides the minister of Highgate chapel. Five or more were to appoint officers and fix an annual rate not exceeding 2*s.* in the £, from which persons paying rent of less than £6 a year were to be exempt.[18]

LOCAL GOVERNMENT AFTER 1837. On Hornsey's

95 Prob. 11/113 (P.C.C. 13 Dorset).
96 Marchams, *Ct. Rolls*, 58.
97 M.R.O., D.R.O. 20/E1/2.
98 Highgate Sch. rec., box 1, bdle. 2.
99 Ibid.; M.R.O., D.R.O. 20/H/1, p. 165; B.L. Add. MS. 5836, f. 91.
1 See below, p. 202.
2 Ibid.
3 Lysons, *Environs*, iii. 59.
4 M.R.O., D.R.O. 20/C1/1; Guildhall MS. 10465/108, pp. 113–14.
5 Guildhall MS. 10465/121, p. 144.
6 Bruce Castle Mus., D/PH/2B/6.
7 Rep. to vestry (1851) in Hornsey libr.
8 J. T. Smith, *The Parish* (1851), 533.
9 St. Pancras vestry min. bk. 1718–80, ff. 405, 445.
10 *Survey of Lond.* xvii. 106.
11 Swiss Cottage libr., Heal Colln., A III 24 (cutting attributed to 1763).
12 Highgate Sch. rec., box 1, bdle. 11.
13 Swiss Cottage libr., Heal Colln., A III 71 (cutting attrib. to 1782).
14 Potter Colln. 15/39.
15 M.R.O., D.R.O. 20/C1/3–4.
16 Ibid. C1/4; B1/2.
17 Ibid. C1/4.
18 15 Geo. III, c. 43.

inclusion in Edmonton poor law union from 1837 the parish workhouse was demolished and its site was sold.[19] Hornsey tried unsuccessfully to join the separate union formed by Hampstead in 1898 and still had 66 paupers at Edmonton workhouse in 1903.[20]

A highway board[21] was established by the vestry under the Highways Act, 1835.[22] Initially of 20 surveyors, it was reorganized in 1855 with 12 members representing equally the Hornsey, Highgate, and Stoke Newington divisions. It met 33 times in 1854–5 and had offices at no. 17 Highgate High Street and in 1862 at Highgate post office. The board appointed a salaried clerk, a rate collector, and an assistant surveyor and public health inspector. In 1855 it claimed to be more efficient than its predecessor, making a 6*d*. rate suffice for all purposes, and promised continued improvements as well as essential maintenance.

Rates still caused controversy. When in 1856 the highway board tried to finance internal drainage by assessing the beneficiaries, it was obstructed by technical objections, forcing it to levy a highway-rate and exact payment by litigation, which served as the test case for the Nuisance Removal Act (1855).[23] A rate proposed in 1856 to balance the churchwardens' accounts was defeated in vestry but was subsequently approved in a poll.[24] When the highway board petitioned against the Parochial Assessments Bill, it feared that those with local responsibility would be excluded from assessment and that the right to appeal against the rate would be curtailed.[25]

Hornsey's vigorous defence of communal rights from 1848 was inspired by Joshua Toulmin Smith of Wood Lane, Highgate (d. 1869), constitutional lawyer and opponent of centralization, as member of committees and chairman of the highway board and local board.[26] In 1858 the highway board prevented the inclusion of the Stoke Newington division in the metropolis for the purposes of paving, cleaning, and lighting.[27] It decided in 1857 not to adopt the Vestry Clerk's Act in order to keep him answerable to the parish.[28] The vestry was unable to prevent the filling-in of the New River and tried in vain to stop the construction of the G.N.R. through the parish. A Bill introduced in 1852 by the G.N.R.[29] would have enabled it to close footpaths but Hornsey succeeded in having the clause struck out and safeguards inserted. Footpaths were also preserved by indicting the G.N.R. and the Archway Road Co. The vestry carefully reviewed plans of the T. & H.J.R. in 1857 and the highway board appointed a railway committee to investigate proposed lines in 1860.[30] In 1860 Hornsey again petitioned against a Bill to extend the metropolitan sewer system, whereupon a clause saving its rights was substituted.[31] Apart from objecting to the Parochial Assessments Bill, in 1861 the highway board opposed the Highway Bill, which threatened the inhabitants' powers to manage affairs that required local knowledge.[32] By such resistance Hornsey gave a lead to neighbouring parishes.

The growth in population of the parts of Hornsey imbedded in Stoke Newington led in 1855 to their receiving equal representation in the vestry with Highgate Side and Hornsey Side. From 1871 a third overseer for South Hornsey was appointed. Ratepayers' meetings adopted the lighting provisions of the Lighting and Watching Act, 1834, for one estate in 1847[33] and another in 1854;[34] the estates were amalgamated in 1858 in the Hornsey (Stoke Newington) district, which covered all the parish south of Hornsey Wood House.[35] Its lighting inspectors considered adopting the Local Government Act, 1858, from 1861, with or without the rest of Hornsey,[36] and in 1865 South Hornsey local board of health was established for the area south of Seven Sisters Road.[37] Disputes with neighbouring authorities resulted in attempts to annexe the area to the metropolis[38] but were resolved by a public inquiry in 1873 and the Metropolitan Board of Works Act, 1874.[39] South Hornsey became a U.D. in 1894, a separate civil parish in 1895,[40] and, under the London Government Act, 1899, a ward in the Metropolitan Borough of Stoke Newington, whereupon it was transferred to the county of London.[41] Under the London Government Act, 1963, it was incorporated in Hackney L.B. in 1965,[42] when Brownswood Park became Brownswood ward and Clissold Park was part of Defoe ward.

Hornsey escaped inclusion in the metropolitan sewer system on several occasions. In 1848 the ratepayers of Highgate elected a sanitary committee[43] and in 1851 the vestry appointed a standing drainage committee, which was superseded in 1854 by the highway board. In 1867 the parish had a bad system of drainage, apparently because the powers of committee and board were insufficient,[44] the vestry in 1864 having refused to adopt the Local Government Act, 1858. When South Hornsey local board was established, a similar application by the district of St. Michael, Highgate, failed because sewage could not be disposed of within the district.[45] Early

19 S. I. Richardson, *Edmonton Poor Law Union* (Edmonton Hund. Hist. Soc.), 11, 24–5.
20 Hornsey Boro. *Ann. Rep. of M.O.H.* (1903).
21 Except where otherwise stated, the para. is based on Bruce Castle Mus., D/PH/2A/1.
22 5 & 6 Wm. IV, c. 50.
23 Bruce Castle Mus., D/PH/4A/1, pp. 347 sqq.; J. T. Smith, *Local Self-Govt. Unmystified* (1857), 14–15; idem., *Practical Procs. for Removal of Nuisances* (1861), 138–44.
24 J. T. Smith, *True points at issue in the 'Church Rate' question*, Manchester Church Defence Assoc. (1860).
25 Bruce Castle Mus., D/PH/4A/3, p. 186.
26 J. T. Smith, *Law of Eng. relating to Pub. Health* (1848), iii; *D.N.B.*; see also W. H. Greenleaf, 'Toulmin Smith and Brit. Political Tradition', *Public Administration* (1975), esp. 33–4.
27 Bruce Castle Mus., D/PH/4A/3, p. 223.
28 Smith, *The Parish*, 209–10.
29 For the next two sentences see ibid. 537–41.
30 Bruce Castle Mus., D/PH/4A/3, pp. 174–5, 178.
31 Ibid. p. 141.
32 Ibid. p. 186.
33 Bruce Castle Mus., D/PH/2B/1, 27.
34 Shoreditch libr., HOR/L/1; Bruce Castle Mus., D/PH/2B/2, 27.
35 Shoreditch libr., HOR/L/2.
36 Ibid.
37 *Lond. Gaz.* 30 June 1865, p. 3306.
38 Bruce Castle Mus., D/PH/4A/3, p. 223; Shoreditch libr., HOR/L/2 [1861, 1863, 1864].
39 37 & 38 Vic. c. 97; Shoreditch libr., HOR/2, pp. 148–50, 152, 192–3, 256–7, 332–3.
40 'Rep. on prop. division into 2 pars.' (1895) in M.R.O., *Reps. of Local Inqs.* (1895–1907).
41 Bruce Castle Mus., D/PH/4A/4, pp. 215–16.
42 Lond. Govt. Act, 1963, c. 33.
43 Reps. in Hornsey libr.
44 *Hornsey Hornet*, 15 Jan. 1867.
45 Bruce Castle Mus., D/PH/4A/4, pp. 215–16; Prickett and Cassini, ii (cuttings and papers).

in 1866 a similar proposal was rejected by Hornsey ratepayers.[46] Under the Sanitary Act, 1866, Edmonton union appointed a committee to remove nuisances and the vestry appointed a drainage committee.[47] There were thus three committees with overlapping functions, inadequate powers, and authority to levy rates, and in 1867 the parish adopted the Local Government Act. At that juncture the *Hornet* considered Hornsey the 'worst governed parish about London'.[48]

Hornsey local board consisted of fifteen members, who met fortnightly and had committees for nuisance removal, sewers and water, for roads and works, and for finance. It retained the highway board's officers and appointed a treasurer, a clerk, an assistant surveyor and inspector, and a rate collector.[49] During the 1880s F. D. Askey, founder of Hornsey radical association and town clerk 1890–1924, repeatedly attacked the board for extravagance but by 1903 it was considered efficient.[50] Hornsey became a U.D. under the Local Government Act, 1894, and was divided into the 8 wards of Highgate, Muswell Hill, Crouch End, Hornsey (divided in 1903),[51] North and South Harringay, Stroud Green, and Finsbury Park, each with 3 members.[52] The wards varied from 109 a. to 709 a. and in population from 4,859 to 19,044 in 1901,[53] when Clerkenwell detached was added to Hornsey and Middlesex.[54] After a campaign started in 1897 Hornsey was incorporated as the second municipal borough in Middlesex in 1903[55] but it failed to become a county borough in 1904 and 1915.[56] The new borough had a mayor, 3 aldermen, and 27 councillors elected from 9 wards[57] and in 1907 there were 30 councillors and 10 aldermen.[58] From 1936 there were 8 wards: Highgate, Muswell Hill, Central Hornsey and Stroud Green each returned 6 councillors, and Crouch End, North and South Harringay, and Finsbury Park returned 3.[59] In 1956 councillors were elected for 3 years and aldermen for 6, the full council met 8 times a year, and there were 8 main committees.[60] At the first borough elections there was a contest in 7 wards and a 63 per cent poll. The first council included Liberals and nonconformists but dominance was rapidly achieved by the new Municipal Reformers (later Conservatives). There were 43 Conservative and 5 Labour councillors in 1950.[61] In 1965 Hornsey joined Tottenham and Wood Green in Haringey L.B.

Hornsey local board used the old highway board offices,[62] until in 1869 it moved into the purpose-built no. 99 Southwood Lane[63] on land leased from the London Diocesan Penitentiary. The offices were greatly enlarged in 1885 and 1916[64] but were considered ill situated by 1894 and unsuitable in 1934–5.[65] A more central town hall, which would

BOROUGH OF HORNSEY. *Per chevron argent and gules, in chief two oak trees eradicated proper and in base two swords in saltire proper, the latter pommelled and hilted or* [Granted 1904]

also house the school board, was accordingly built at Crouch End.[66] Designed by R. H. Uren, it won the bronze medal of the R.I.B.A. in 1936 for the best street frontage built in London during the previous three years. It is of pinkish grey bricks with dressings of Portland stone, forming two freely grouped blocks linked by a slim 80-ft. tower and including an assembly hall for 1,000 people.[67] In 1976 it housed Haringey's departments of town planning and electoral registration, the offices of the borough architect, surveyor, engineer, town safety, area housing and youth employment officers, the registrar of births and deaths, and the school welfare clinic.

LONDON BOROUGH OF HARINGEY. *Sable, eight rays issuing from the fess point throughout or* [Granted 1965]

Under the Parliamentary Reform Act, 1885, the Hornsey Division of Middlesex was established.[68] In 1918, under the Representation of the People's Act,[69] Hornsey became a parliamentary borough.[70] Both constituencies have returned only Unionist and Conservative M.P.s,[71] although in 1945 Hornsey was one of three constituencies where a Communist,

[46] *Hornsey Hornet*, 15 Jan. 1867.
[47] Ibid.; Bruce Castle Mus., D/PH/2A/2.
[48] Bruce Castle Mus., O/H/1/1, p. 77; *Hornsey Hornet*, 1 Sept. 1867.
[49] Bruce Castle Mus., O/H/1/1, pp. 1–5.
[50] Cuttings in Hornsey libr.; *Lond. Argus*, 10 Oct. 1903.
[51] Hornsey Boro. *Ann. Rep. of M.O.H.* (1903).
[52] Bruce Castle Mus., Hornsey U.D. min. bk. 1892–4, pp. 699, 711, 775; see also 'Rep. on application for division of dist. into wards' (1894) in M.R.O., *Reps. of Local Inqs.* (1889–97).
[53] Hornsey Boro. *Ann. Rep. of M.O.H.* (1901).
[54] *Stat. Rules & Orders 1903*, no. 137.
[55] *Hornsey Boro. 1903–53*, 5–7.
[56] *Hornsey Jnl.* 30 Apr. 1904; 'Bill to constitute the Boro. of Hornsey a Cnty. Boro.' in Hornsey libr.
[57] *The Times*, 2 Nov. 1907; see also Hornsey Boro. *Official Guide* [1926].
[58] *The Times*, 2 Nov. 1907.
[59] Order in Council in Hornsey libr.
[60] Hornsey Boro. *Official Guide* [1956].
[61] Cutting (1928) in Hornsey libr.; *The Times*, 3 Nov. 1936, 12 May 1950.
[62] Bruce Castle Mus., O/H/1/1, p. 1.
[63] Potter Colln. 14/77.
[64] Hornsey loc. bd. *Rep. on Property of Bd.* (1894); *Hornsey Jnl.* 18 Nov. 1925.
[65] *The Times*, 16 Aug. 1933; 'Rep. on division betw. Hornsey and Sth. Hornsey dists.' (1894) in M.R.O., *Reps. of Local Inqs.* (1889–97).
[66] *The Times*, 26 Oct. 1934; 5 Nov. 1935. The old bldgs. were sold; ibid. 18 Dec. 1934.
[67] Ibid. 12 May 1936; Pevsner, *Mdx.* 114; *Builder*, cxlv. 573, 610.
[68] 48 & 49 Vic. c. 15.
[69] 8 & 9 Geo. V, c. 50.
[70] *Whitaker's Almanack* (1918 and 1919).
[71] Ibid. (1885 and later edns.).

despite Labour opposition, won more than 20 per cent of the votes.[72]

PUBLIC SERVICES. A well at Muswell existed in 1159[73] and plentiful springs near by in 1544,[74] but until the late 19th century much of the parish depended on wells bored through the thick London Clay: in 1871 a well at Hornsey Wood House was 200 ft. deep and another was over 160 ft. deep.[75] At Crouch End water was drawn from a small common pond, which became polluted *c.* 1820 and was filled up in 1828.[76] A well and pump had been built without licence in 1820.[77] In 1828 a public meeting decided on the immediate provision of a public well and pump. The vestry's contribution was withdrawn on opposition from Highgate Side but the well was built in 1830 from private subscriptions.[78] Several houses at Muswell Hill had wells dating from *c.* 1780[79] but as they contained inferior water and belonged mainly to the wealthy, most people relied on springs in Tottenham and on the well at Muswell, whose closure in 1861 led to legal proceedings, whereby the inhabitants' customary right was vindicated. The Muswell Estate Act, 1866, guaranteed access to St. Dunstan's well in Tottenham, which was reconstructed and supplied with a pump.[80] Hornsey itself may have been supplied by the New River but in 1850 a well and pump near Church Path were maintained by neighbouring property-owners.[81] In 1868 small houses in St. James's Lane depended on a private well at the Priory.[82]

Highgate, in spite of chalybeate springs in Southwood Lane,[83] had poor natural supplies of water.[84] The rich could use their own wells or lay pipes, as Dr. Elisha Coysh had done from Swain's Lane in 1659;[85] water was also carted uphill from deep wells on either side of Southwood Lane, whose lower stretch was known as Wells Hill, until *c.* 1870.[86] In 1800 Robert Kilby Cox possessed the right to convey spring water on the highway from Barnet to a reservoir at Highgate.[87] Ponds were the sole source for the poor in 1819, when they were polluted, and in 1857, of 159 dwellings surveyed, only fourteen had water piped by the New River Co.; 75 depended on a parish pump and nine private pumps, of which that for York Buildings was polluted and another was often dry.[88] In 1851 the water from eight Highgate wells contained nitric acid which corroded lead tanks; in at least one case the acid represented contamination from the old chapel cemetery.[89] In 1857 four other dwellings depended on a pond teeming with frogs and many households bought water by the pail.[90] Model cottages under construction at North Hill in 1863 were to rely on a parish well.[91]

The New River Co., from 1904 the Metropolitan Water Board, supplied water to the workhouse in 1814,[92] to St. Mary's church in 1841–2,[93] and to houses in Highgate in 1857.[94] In 1858 the company and vestry agreed on a supply to 119 dwellings at Highgate at the owners' cost; all were connected in 1859.[95] In 1875 New River water had replaced the pumps in Highgate and the Crouch End pump was no longer needed.[96] The whole parish had some supply by 1894[97] but only during the years 1902–4 was a regular supply extended everywhere.[98] Between 1852 and 1855 the New River Co. built a pumping station east of Green Lanes, in Stoke Newington, which received water from filter beds on the west side in Brownswood Park. Two covered reservoirs were constructed in 1908 at Woodside Avenue, Fortis Green, and in 1953 a new contact tank was added;[99] in 1976 the station pumped 30 million gallons daily from the Thames to the Lea valley reservoirs or for local consumption. The New River and a well in the Campsbourne supplied filter beds north of Hornsey High Street by 1863, when a pumping station existed. In 1932 seven engines pumped 15 million gallons daily to the Hornsey Lane and Crouch Hill reservoirs for local consumption.[1] Covered reservoirs were built at Mount View Road, Crouch Hill, by 1885[2] and at Finsbury Park *c.* 1867.[3] Water was supplied by the Thames Water Authority in 1976.

At Highgate in 1840 Dr. Robert Moger reported numerous deaths from infectious diseases in an overcrowded lodging-house, inhabited largely by Irish beggars.[4] In 1848 ratepayers appointed a sanitary committee,[5] whose four sub-committees found houses served by drains intended merely for the roads and that there were many open drains, including one from the wells to the foot of Southwood Lane; in York Buildings four privies were shared by 40 families.[6] In 1863, after an epidemic

[72] D. E. Butler, *Electoral System in Britain since 1918* (1963), 156.
[73] Madge, *Early Rec. of Harringay*, 61–3.
[74] 35 Hen. VIII, c. 10.
[75] H. Walker, *Saturday Afternoon Rambles round Lond.* (1871), 11, 41.
[76] *T.L.M.A.S.* xiii. 414–16; M.R.O., Acc. 1289/1/1, pp. 160, 210.
[77] *T.L.M.A.S.* xiii. 415; M.R.O., Acc. 1289/1/1, p. 160.
[78] *T.L.M.A.S.* xiii. 415; M.R.O., D.R.O. 20/C1/4; H1/1, pp. 58–9 (printed rep.).
[79] *The Times*, 24 Feb. 1936.
[80] Howitt, *Northern Heights*, 424.
[81] M.L.R. 1850/1/273.
[82] Bruce Castle Mus., O/H/1/1.
[83] S. Sunderland, *Old London's Spas, Baths and Wells* (1915), 53.
[84] Hunter, *Environs*, ii. 85–6.
[85] *Survey of Lond.* xvii. 39.
[86] Potter Colln. 14/83. An iron cover near Well Cottages and four granite pillars near the boundary wall of Southwood Ho. formerly marked the sites: ex inf. Sir Jas. Brown and see Highgate Lit. and Sc. Inst. photo colln. Ea 42.
[87] Guildhall MS. 10465/115, p. 138.
[88] Bruce Castle Mus., D/PH/4A/2, pp. 233–7; Lloyd, *Highgate*, 412–13.
[89] *The Times*, 8 Jan. 1851.
[90] Bruce Castle Mus., D/PH/4A/2, pp. 233–7.
[91] Ibid. 4A/4, pp. 10, 33.
[92] M.R.O., D.R.O. 20/C1/4.
[93] Ibid. B1/1, p. 40.
[94] See above.
[95] Bruce Castle Mus., D/PH/2A/1; 4A/2, p. 339.
[96] *N. Mdx. Chron.* 9 Jan. 1875; see also Potter Colln. 20/18.
[97] Hornsey loc. bd. *Ann. Reps. of M.O.H.* (1894, 1897–8).
[98] Bruce Castle Mus., O/H/3/2; *Hornsey Jnl.* 30 Apr. 1904.
[99] *London's Water Supply 1903–53*, 88, 221.
[1] O.S. Map 6″, XII. Mdx. NW. (1894–6 and later edns.); *Hornsey Jnl.* 2 Sept. 1932.
[2] *Hutchings & Crowsley's Dir. Hornsey* (1885).
[3] Met. Bd. of Wks. *Mins. of Proc.* (1867), ii. 1142, 1321.
[4] *The Times*, 23–25 July, 29 July, 5 Aug. 1840. Except where otherwise stated, the para. is based on Bruce Castle Mus., D/PH/4A/1–4; 2A/1–2.
[5] Reps. in Hornsey libr.
[6] Highgate sanitary cttee., reps. of sub-cttees. 1848 in Highgate Lit. and Sc. Inst.

of scarlet fever, Moger drew attention to the poor sanitation, which was complicated by the division of Highgate between three parishes. The drain towards Holloway was often blocked, others had no suitable outlets, and there were badly sited slaughter houses, offal pits, and pigsties. An inquiry placed the main responsibility on St. Pancras and Islington parishes but also blamed Hornsey and suggested that wider powers were required. Hornsey highway board decided that the drainage of Highgate was easily remedied but in 1868 Townsend's Yard and York Buildings, housing 135 people, were still served by only six open privies not connected to water.[7]

In 1853 the vestry considered that the Stoke Newington division had the worst sanitation in the parish in spite of its temporary inclusion in the metropolitan system under the Metropolitan Sewers Act, 1848. Hornsey had avoided absorption and in 1860 had amended the Metropolitan Local Management Act Amendment Bill, which provided for a sewer to Hornsey. Vigilance was needed to avoid interference: a drainage committee was appointed in 1850 and a highway board in 1854. The main problem, arising from new houses in Hornsey High Street and at Muswell Hill, was serious in 1851 but was not thought expensive to solve. The necessary works, considered to be nearly finished in 1856, were ready only in 1860. Committee and board opposed in principle 'imposing works' to relieve individuals at public expense[8] and emphasized private responsibilities. They purified public ditches and encouraged the maintenance of private cess-pits, prosecuting offenders, but even in 1866 open sewers were common.[9]

Sewage was discharged into the Moselle before it flowed into Tottenham. After the local board had vacillated over a scheme to co-operate with Tottenham,[10] its drains were connected to the northern high-level sewer of the metropolis under the Hornsey Local Board Act, 1871.[11] The internal and out-fall system were designed by Baldwin Latham.[12] A pumping station was built in 1884 to raise the sewage from the Wright's Park estate[13] and in 1888 the smallest farm in the country was built to handle the drainage of 300 a. at Muswell Hill.[14] Clerkenwell detached had paid metropolitan sewer-rates from their inception[15] but its sewage was a nuisance to its neighbours by 1882 and the Clerkenwell vestry could not afford a separate system. By 1893 houses were connected to public drains which discharged via a roadside ditch into the sewers of Friern Barnet and Wood Green. Hornsey had received the sewage in 1887 and Friern Barnet accepted it under a 30-year agreement until 1899, when the district was included in Hornsey. In 1902 Coppetts Wood sewage farm was enlarged to meet the extra demand.[16]

In 1904 Hornsey was claimed to have as perfect a drainage system as any part of the country.[17] South Hornsey had used the metropolitan system from its construction but paid no sewer-rates after 1855.[18] The local board built no sewers itself, requiring builders in Brownswood Park to connect their drains to the Hackney board of works' sewer in Green Lanes, but it was acquitted of gross neglect in 1873.[19] Threats by Hackney to have South Hornsey annexed to the metropolis under the Metropolis Local Management Act, 1855, resulted in the Metropolitan Board of Works Act, 1874, by which South Hornsey was connected to the high- and middle-level sewers and was subjected for the first time to sewer-rates.[20] The Coppetts Wood sewage farm was closed *c.* 1970[21] and in 1976 a depot of British Road Services stood on the site.

An Act of 1774 authorized trustees to light the streets of the hamlet of Highgate, whether in St. Pancras, Islington, or Hornsey, and to levy rates.[22] By 1868 the trustees had an income of *c.* £400[23] and from at least 1825[24] they bought gas from the Imperial Gas Light and Coke Co., which also supplied the lighting districts in the Stoke Newington division (later South Hornsey) from 1854.[25] The 1774 Act was repealed in 1868 and the fittings of the trust were vested in Hornsey local board.[26] The rest of the parish was unlit in 1866[27] but in 1868 Hornsey adopted the lighting provisions of the Lighting and Watching Act, 1834; 120 lamps were bought in 1868 and the streets were lit from 1869,[28] although the provision was remembered as sparse in 1904.[29] Gas was supplied by the Hornsey Gas Co., which was incorporated in 1857 to supply Hornsey (except South Hornsey) and Clerkenwell detached. It started trading in 1861 and served Muswell Hill, Fortis Green, and Crouch End in 1862, and North Hill, Highgate.[30] In 1865 the G.N.R. bought back the site of the gas-works, which in 1866 was replaced by a new works in Clarendon Road, Hornsey.[31] The company was authorized to enlarge its capital in 1866, 1884, and 1902, gradually extending the works into Wood Green, and in 1929 completed a new gasholder.[32] In 1937 it was controlled by SEGAS and after nationalization in 1949 by the North Thames Gas Board. From 1957 the works has been a gasholder station.[33] The Imperial Gas Light and

[7] Bruce Castle Mus., O/H/1/1.
[8] See also Smith, *Law of Eng. relating to Pub. Health*, iii.
[9] Sherington, *Story of Hornsey*, 102, citing *Hornsey Hornet*, Aug. 1866.
[10] Bruce Castle Mus., O/H/1/1, pp. 28–31, 33–4.
[11] 34 & 35 Vic. c. 129 (Local Act); *The Times*, 2 Sept. 1871.
[12] *The Times*, 8 Sept. 1871.
[13] Hornsey loc. bd. *Rep. on Property of Bd.* (1894), 24.
[14] Ibid. 8–9; 50 Vic. c. 15 (Local Act).
[15] The next three sentences are based on *N. Mdx. Chron.* 27 Sept. 1884, 28 Oct. 1882, 28 Apr. 1883; *N. Lond. Herald & Crouch End Observer*, 21 Oct. 1899.
[16] Hornsey U.D. *Ann. Rep. of M.O.H.* (1902).
[17] Sherington, *Story of Hornsey*, 103.
[18] Except where otherwise stated, the next three sentences are based on Shoreditch libr., HOR/1, 2; for agreement (1858) with Hackney bd. of wks. see 'Rep. of Hornsey Highway Bd. 1859' in Hornsey libr.
[19] 37 & 38 Vic. c. 97 (Local Act).
[20] 18 & 19 Vic. c. 120.
[21] O.S. Maps 6″, TQ 29 SE. (1962 and 1973 edns.).
[22] 15 Geo. III, c. 43.
[23] Bruce Castle Mus., O/H/1/1, p. 100.
[24] S. Everard, *Gas Light and Coke Co.* (1949), 160.
[25] Shoreditch libr., HOR/L/1.
[26] 31 & 32 Vic. c. 153 (Local Act).
[27] *Hornsey Hornet*, 15 Nov. 1866.
[28] Bruce Castle Mus., O/H/1/1, pp. 89, 103, 116; M.R.O., Acc. 880/47, pp. 224, 228–9, 238–9.
[29] Sherington, *Story of Hornsey*, 101.
[30] M.R.O., Acc. 880/46, pp. 77, 84; 47, p. 61.
[31] Ibid. 46, pp. 138 sqq.; 47, p. 61.
[32] 29 & 30 Vic. c. 33 (Local Act); 47 & 48 Vic. c. 51 (Local Act); 2 Edw. VII, c. 188 (Local Act); programme (1928) in Hornsey libr.
[33] E. G. Stewart, *Historical Index of Gasworks 1806–1957* (1957), 52–3.

Coke Co. was taken over in 1876 by the Gas Light and Coke Co., which was nationalized in 1949.[34]

In 1883 the Metropolitan (Brush) Electric Light and Power Co. was authorized to supply electricity in Hornsey, starting in Highgate.[35] In 1900 Hornsey U.D. opposed the North Metropolitan Electricity Supply Co. and decided to supply electricity itself.[36] Under powers of 1898 the borough assumed responsibility in 1903 and built a generating station in Tottenham Lane.[37] By 1904 lighting was mainly by electricity.[38] The plant was extended between 1923 and 1927 and sub-stations were opened at Muswell Hill *c.* 1920 and Highgate in 1924.[39] After 1936, when a change from direct to alternating current began, six new sub-stations were built.[40] The borough co-operated with the Central Electricity Generating Board from *c.* 1931[41] and its service was nationalized in 1947.[42] The former generating station was damaged in 1944 and later demolished but the battery room was converted into the C.E.G.B. Radiochemical Laboratory in 1964[43] and there was also a transformer station on the site by 1976, when responsibility for supply rested with the Eastern Electricity Board. South Hornsey was supplied from 1908 by the Stoke Newington municipal generating station and after nationalization by the London Electricity Board.[44]

Subscriptions for a fire-engine were collected at Highgate in 1731, after Dr. Lewis Atterbury had left money towards its purchase and the governors of the free school had agreed to keep it in the chapel yard. An engine-house was built, two engines were bought, and in 1739 there were efforts to establish a fund for expenses.[45] A fire-engine for Hornsey parish was mentioned in 1775–6.[46] In 1811 the vestry bought two engines,[47] for Hornsey and Highgate Sides, and in 1813 appointed two engine keepers. The Highgate engine-house thereafter stood immediately north of the watchhouse, on copyhold land of Cantlowes.[48] Both engines functioned efficiently in 1839[49] but in spite of more expenditure in 1842[50] the Highgate one was in disrepair in 1851 and in 1860 it was alleged that neither could put out fires; the Hornsey engine was then found to be satisfactory and the Highgate machine to be unsuitably housed. In 1869 a new manual engine of the type used in the metropolitan areas was acquired for the Highgate volunteer fire brigade, which had been formed in 1868 with a hired machine; the local board was also given two escapes.[51] As engines from neighbouring parishes could no longer attend, the Stoke Newington divisional lighting inspectors acquired a new engine and employed a keeper in 1861; there was a volunteer fire brigade by 1864.[52] Hornsey Side had a volunteer fire brigade by 1874[53] and a new central fire station on land south of Hornsey High Street from 1885. A room in North Road, Highgate, was hired in 1882 and a portable fire station was opened in 1887. By 1894 there was a street fire station in Stapleton Hall Road, Stroud Green, and there were 26 alarm posts throughout the district.[54] A brick station was built at Muswell Hill in 1899 and in 1904 there were also iron rooms at Highgate and Stroud Green.[55] The latter was manned only at night and later moved to Alroy Road, Harringay, before being closed on the adoption of self-propelled vehicles and motor pumps.[56] The North Road fire station was rebuilt in 1906.[57] In 1926 there was a central station, with new branches at Muswell Hill and Highgate,[58] and in 1956 there was only a single branch at Fortis Green.[59] In 1963 a new central station was opened on the corner of Priory Road and Park Avenue South, the site of St. George's church, which was to replace stations in Tottenham Lane and Fortis Green.[60] In 1953 the county council became the fire authority.[61]

In 1774 the hamlet of Highgate acquired its own watchmen, but in 1840 both Hornsey and Highgate were included in the Metropolitan Police District.[62] The old lock-up at Priory Road, Hornsey, was retained as a police station until 1868, when it was returned to the parish, which used it as a mortuary.[63] It was not replaced until the opening of a new station at Tottenham Lane in 1884.[64] There was a police station in High Street, Highgate, in 1845,[65] at no. 51 South Grove (later no. 49 Highgate West Hill) from 1850 until *c.* 1900,[66] and in Archway Road by 1902.[67] By 1886 Hornsey was in Y division, which included Wood Green and Islington in 1903. An additional station was erected at Fortis Green in 1904–5 and in 1915 the Tottenham Lane station was rebuilt.[68] The Archway Road station was bombed in the Second World War and rebuilt in 1960.[69] A station was opened at Blackstone Road, Brownswood Park, in 1958–60.[70]

Petty sessions were held at Highgate police station

[34] Everard, *Gas Light and Coke Co.* 247, 382.
[35] 46 & 47 Vic. c. 217 (Local Act).
[36] *N. Lond. Mercury*, 17, 24 Mar., 20 Oct. 1900.
[37] *Hornsey Boro. 1903–53*, 15; Hornsey Boro. *Partics. of Property of Corp.* (1904), 29.
[38] Sherington, *Story of Hornsey*, 101.
[39] *Electrical Times*, 21 July 1927.
[40] *Hornsey Boro. 1903–53*, 115; Hornsey Boro. *Rep. of Boro. Electrical Officer* (1938), 9.
[41] Hornsey Boro. *Rep. of Boro. Electrical Officer* (1938), 5.
[42] *Hornsey Boro. 1903–53*, 15.
[43] *Regional Power*, Oct. 1964.
[44] Stoke Newington M.B. *Official Guide* [1950, 1958].
[45] Highgate Sch. rec., box 1, bdle. 11.
[46] M.R.O., D.R.O. 20/C1/3. The para. is based on ibid. C1/4; Bruce Castle Mus., D/PH/2A/1–2.
[47] M.R.O., D.R.O. 20/H/1, p. 107; K1/4.
[48] T. Chapman, *Acct. of Hornsey Chars.* (1853), 6; Guildhall MS. 14220/46, pp. 40–1.
[49] M.R.O., D.R.O. 20/H/1, p. 108.
[50] Ibid. B1/7/26.
[51] Bruce Castle Mus., O/H/1/1, pp. 166, 174; *Hornsey Jnl.* 31 Dec. 1937.
[52] Shoreditch libr., HOR/L/2.
[53] *P.O. Dir. Mdx.* (1874).
[54] Hornsey loc. bd. *Rep. on Property of Bd.* (1894), 21–3; *St. Mic.'s Par. Mag.* June 1882; see also 'Rep. on division betw. Hornsey and S. Hornsey dists.' (1894) in M.R.O., *Reps. of Local Inqs.* (1889–97).
[55] See plate facing p. 177.
[56] Hornsey Boro. *Partics. of Property of Corp.* (1904); *Hornsey Jnl.* 9 Nov. 1928.
[57] Inscription on bldg.
[58] Hornsey Boro. *Official Guide* [1926].
[59] Ibid. [1956].
[60] Ibid. [1963].
[61] *Hornsey Boro. 1903–53*, 14.
[62] *Lond. Gaz.* 13 Oct. 1840, p. 2250.
[63] Bruce Castle Mus., D/PH/4A/1; O/H/1/1, p. 45; illus. in Hornsey libr.; *N. Mdx. Chron.* 22 Mar. 1879. For its eventual fate see ibid. 25 Apr. 1885.
[64] Bruce Castle Mus., O/H/1/1, p. 338; *P.O. Dir. N. Suburbs* (1884).
[65] *P.O. Dir. Six Home Cnties.* (1845).
[66] Lloyd, *Highgate*, 465; *P.O. Dir. Mdx.* (1870); *Kelly's N. Suburban Dir.* (1900). The bldg. was at the eastern end of a range and known as no. 1 Grove Place.
[67] *Kelly's N. Suburban Dir.* (1902).
[68] *Hornsey Boro. 1903–53*, 14–15.
[69] *Hornsey Jnl.* 20 May 1960.
[70] Stoke Newington M.B. *Official Guide* [1958, 1960].

from 1870[71] and later at the Gatehouse and, *c.* 1888, Northfield hall. In 1898 a police and petty sessional court-house, in the style of the Middlesex Guildhall at Westminster, was built in Archway Road on part of the site which was soon afterwards used for the new police station.[72] After damage during the Second World War courts were held at Hornsey town hall until the completion of the modern building, designed by the county architect's department, in 1955.[73] A coroner's court was opened at High Street, Hornsey, in 1886[74] and rebuilt in 1972.[75]

The Libraries Act was adopted by Hornsey in 1896 and a library was opened in 1899 in Tottenham Lane[76] on a site shared with the fire station. The existing libraries at Shepherd's Hill and Quernmore Road, Stroud Green, were opened in 1902 and by 1903.[77] A site in Duke's Avenue was given in 1899 by Edmondson & Son for a library but in 1910 reverted to the donor; a branch was finally opened in Muswell Hill in 1931.[78] Although enlarged in 1935, the central library was too small in 1949, when the site at Haringey Park was acquired for Hornsey central library, which opened in 1965.[79] Highgate branch library, built by St. Pancras M.B. in 1906,[80] stood south of the village, in Chester Road. In 1948 a temporary library at Queen's Drive, Brownswood Park, was opened by Stoke Newington M.B.; it was rebuilt in 1960–1.[81]

A dispensary for the poor was established at Highgate in 1787 by 61 subscribers of Highgate, Hornsey, Muswell Hill, Crouch End, and Holloway. It was managed by elected officers and employed a surgeon and an apothecary. Subscribers could nominate patients, whose number increased from 159 in 1787–8 to 406 in 1817. Treatment ceased to be free in 1840, when a self-supporting principle was adopted. It was at Rock House in 1873 and survived in 1887.[82] The vestry, which contributed towards the dispensary in 1818,[83] employed a medical officer for the poor from 1750.[84] Edmonton union employed two until 1849, whereupon the doctor's residence at Highgate was held to be inconvenient for Hornsey Side.[85]

Coppetts Wood hospital originated in 1888 as an isolation hospital for Hornsey on former waste land at Irish Corner. When new it was regarded as a model institution. Additions in 1893–4,[86] 1906, and 1926–7 increased its capacity to 130.[87] From 1922 responsibility was shared with Finchley and Wood Green, whence patients had been admitted since 1899 and *c.* 1906. After nationalization in 1948 it was included in the Northern hospital group until 1963 and then in the Archway group. One ward was reconstructed in 1957–8 and the other four were reconstructed in 1963, when one was adapted for general medicine. The others were taken over by the infectious diseases department of the Royal Free hospital on its move from Hampstead and in 1968 Coppetts Wood became an integral part of the Royal Free hospital. In 1976 there were 109 beds, 87 for infectious diseases.[88]

Hornsey Central hospital in Park Road was opened in 1910 as Hornsey Cottage hospital. On 1½ a. given by the Ecclesiastical Commissioners,[89] it was extended in 1920 and 1938 and had 61 beds in 1956;[90] in 1962 a physiotherapy wing was opened.[91] In 1948 it was included in the Archway and from 1963 in the North London group. In 1976 38 beds were occupied by geriatric patients of the former Highbury Home and 22 more had been given as a unit to the local general practitioners.[92]

St. Luke's Woodside hospital was founded by St. Luke's charity, which ran asylums in London until 1916–17. In 1928–30, with proceeds from the sale of its Old Street premises, the charity adapted three villas in Woodside Avenue, Fortis Green, as a 50-bed hospital for nervous disorders. The hospital was enlarged to hold 100 beds to qualify as a teaching hospital in 1948, when it became part of the Middlesex hospital's department of psychological medicine.[93] The Noel Harris wing for acutely disturbed psychiatric patients was added in 1964 and Simmons House for adolescent drug dependency patients in 1968.[94] In 1975 there were 80 beds.[95]

A home for the aged was opened in conjunction with Hornsey Housing Trust at no. 47 Cecile Park in 1939 by a committee chaired by Margaret Hill, wife of the Nobel prize-winner Professor A. V. Hill.[96] It was moved to no. 21 View Road (later Delia Grotten Home, accommodating 24) in 1940, when homes for bomb refugees were opened at nos. 9–11 Hampstead Lane (Gate Home), Southwood Home for the more infirm, and no. 14 Bishopswood Road (later Woodlands, accommodating 34). After the incorporation of the committee as Hill Homes Ltd. with charitable status in 1944, it established the Trees, extended in 1949, at no. 2 Broadlands Road, and in 1945 took over Woodlands and Gate and Delia Grotten homes. Gate Home had been closed by 1948 but Nuffield Lodge, no. 22 Shepherd's Hill, and Stanhope residential club, no. 22 Stanhope Road, had been opened and there were altogether

71 *P.O. Dir. Mdx.* (1870).
72 *Hornsey Boro. 1903–53*, 14; Potter Colln. 6/90.
73 Hornsey Boro. *Official Guide* [1956]; *Builder*, clxxxix. 343.
74 *The Times*, 2 Dec. 1886.
75 Haringey L.B. *Environmental Health Service Rep.* (1974).
76 Hornsey Boro. *26th Ann. Rep. of Pub. Libr. Cttee.* (1924–5).
77 Datestone on bldg.; *Hornsey Boro. 1903–53*, 27.
78 Ibid. 28; *26th Ann. Rep. Pub. Libr. Cttee.*; *Muswell Hill Record*, 11 Feb. 1910.
79 *Hornsey Boro. 1903–53*, 28; datestone on bldg.
80 *The Times*, 20 Oct. 1906.
81 Stoke Newington M.B. *Official Guide* [1960].
82 Min. and subscr. bks. in Highgate Lit. and Sc. Inst.; J. C. Marriott, 'An A.B.C. of Highgate' (1904), 142–3 (MS. in Bruce Castle Mus.); Hutchings & Crowsley, *Hampstead and Highgate Dir.* (1873).
83 M.R.O., D.R.O. 20/C1/4.
84 Ibid. C1/1, f. 48.
85 Bruce Castle Mus., D/PH/2A/1.
86 Hornsey loc. bd. *Rep. on Property of Bd.* (1894); *Ann. Rep. of M.O.H.* (1894).
87 *Hornsey Jnl.* 9 Nov. 1928; programme in Hornsey libr.
88 Ex inf. Dr. R. T. D. Emond.
89 *The Times*, 27 Sept. 1907; bazaar programme and leaflet in Hornsey libr.
90 Hornsey Boro. *Official Guide* [1956].
91 *Hornsey Jnl.* 25 May 1962.
92 Ex inf. the hosp. sec.
93 C. N. French, *Story of St. Luke's Hosp.* (1951), esp. 149–59, 173.
94 *Hornsey Jnl.* 16 Sept. 1964; ex inf. the hosp. sec.
95 *Hospitals Yr. Bk.* (1975).
96 The para. is based on *Chairman's Acct. of Hill Homes* (1948); M. Hill, *Experiment in Care of Mentally Ageing* (*c.* 1955); Hill Homes, *31st Ann. Rep.* (1975); *Geriatrics*, Sept. 1960, offprint and information from the sec., Hill Homes Ltd.

131 inmates in five homes. Designed for those in fairly good health, the charity co-operated closely with hospitals. In 1950 the King Edward's Hospital Fund established Whittington Home as a halfway stage between home and hospital and leased it to Hill Homes until 1967, when it was taken over by the National Health Service. Gwendolen Sim, no. 22 Broadlands Road, was opened in 1954 as a home for the mentally ageing and worked closely with Friern hospital. The only purpose-built home is Goldsmiths of 1964 in Denewood Road, where 15 of the 30 beds were assigned to the local geriatrician in 1976. There were seven homes with 230 inmates in 1960 and 216 in 1976, when Homfray House at no. 4 Broadlands Road had replaced Stanhope residential club. To permit the conversion of Nuffield Lodge into self-contained flats, Hill Homes was registered in 1975 as a housing association.

CHURCHES. The living of Hornsey was assessed in 1291[97] and had a priest in 1302, when it was a rectory.[98] Except during the Interregnum, when Sir John Wollaston was patron,[99] it has been in the gift of the bishop of London from at least 1321.[1] There were chapels at Muswell from *c* 1190 and Highgate from *c.* 1387. The Muswell estate of the nuns of St. Mary, Clerkenwell, already subject to special arrangements, was annexed to Clerkenwell parish *c.* 1540. Part of Hornsey parish was assigned to St. Michael's, Highgate, in 1834.[2] South Hornsey detached was included in the consolidated chapelry of St. Matthias, Stoke Newington, in 1849.[3] Districts were formed from Hornsey parish for Muswell Hill in 1843, Crouch End in 1862, Brownswood Park in 1875, Ferme Park in 1877, Stroud Green in 1880, and Cranley Gardens in 1910, and from Hornsey and Tottenham in 1892 and 1898 for North and South Harringay respectively. Another four chapelries were formed between 1834 and 1940. In 1976 the old parish was divided between 16 districts and contained 14 churches. Whereas a total of 4,611 attended 4 churches in Hornsey and Highgate on census Sunday 1851,[4] there were 13,808 at 13 churches and 4 missions in 1903, of which 11,848 were in Hornsey and 1,960 in Highgate.[5] In 1976 the demolition of several churches was threatened.

The living was worth 8 marks in 1291 and 1340,[6] £22 in 1535,[7] and £30 in 1547.[8] The income was £92 in 1649[9] but £20 extra was assigned to the incumbent by the committee for plundered ministers in 1656.[10] It was worth *c.* £140 in 1749 and £426 in 1851.[11] Tithes amounted to only 22*s.* in 1535.[12] The relatively low income was due to a modus of 4*d.* an acre, which yielded £17 in 1726.[13] In 1749 it was believed that an earlier rector had been prevented from challenging it only by death.[14] The composition was said to be customary in 1765, when it was confirmed after the rector had tried to levy tithes in kind.[15] In 1815 tithes from common lands were extinguished[16] and in 1845 and 1850 the rector dissuaded the Tithe Commissioners from making an award, which would have been expensive but not remunerative.[17] The modus, assessed on 2,100 a., yielded only £35 in 1851[18] and had fallen to £10 by 1889, when it was dwindling annually because it was applied only to land not built on.[19] In 1610 there were 37 a. of glebe and in 1663 40 a.[20] The glebe lay south of Hornsey High Street and east of the modern Church and Tottenham lanes.[21] By 1749 *c.* 40 a. were leased and there were 5 a., probably the Rectory garden, in hand.[22] In 1804 a strip along Tottenham Lane was sold in redemption of land tax;[23] under the inclosure award 46½ a. were allotted in two fields on Muswell Hill common[24] and in 1851 the total glebe was 89½ a.[25] Some was leased for building in 1881, more was added in 1883, and 75 a. remained in 1889.[26] Offerings of £140 amounted to a third of the stipend in 1851, when they were falling,[27] and *c.* £100 in 1889.[28]

A rector's house existed in 1320[29] and a house and outbuildings in 1610,[30] shortly before they were encompassed by the New River. The rectory house, almost ruined in 1660, was repaired before 1673 at the incumbent's expense. It contained six hearths in 1664.[31] In 1750, when the previous rector had been non-resident, £400 was needed, but not spent, to make it habitable.[32] In 1830–4, after having been held by another absentee,[33] the Rectory was again in disrepair.[34] In 1826 it was a two-storeyed timber-framed building of lath and plaster.[35] A new Rectory existed by 1851[36] and was extended *c.* 1890.[37] A large gabled building of brick with stone dressings,[38] in 1½ a. of garden in 1889,[39] it made way in 1962 for St. David's school.[40] A red-brick house was erected

97 *Tax. Eccl.* (Rec. Com.), 17.
98 Madge, *Med. Rec. of Harringay*, 76–7, 91; see also *Reg. Winchelsey* (Cant. & York Soc.), ii. 963.
99 *Home Cnties. Mag.* i. 57.
1 Hennessy, *Novum Rep.* 223–4.
2 See p. 178.
3 *Lond. Gaz.* 5 Jan. 1849, pp. 33–4; 9 Jan. 1849, p. 71.
4 H.O. 129/9/6/1/3; H.O. 129/137/1/1/1–3.
5 Mudie-Smith, *Rel. Life*, 161, 175, 407.
6 *Tax. Eccl.* (Rec. Com.), 17; *Inq. Non.* (Rec. Com.), 195.
7 *Valor Eccl.* (Rec. Com.), i. 433.
8 Hennessy, *Novum Rep.* 223.
9 *Home Cnties. Mag.* i. 57.
10 *Cal. S.P. Dom.* 1655–6, 320.
11 M.R.O., D.R.O. 20/H/1, p. 6.
12 *Valor Eccl.* (Rec. Com.), i. 433.
13 M.R.O., Cal. Mdx. Sess. Bks. 1722–7, 303–4.
14 B.L. Add. MS. 5836, ff. 73, 75.
15 Ibid. f. 70 (newspaper cuttings); E 13/1027 mm. 2–3; M.R.O., D.R.O. 20/C1/2 (1766).
16 M.R.O., MR/DE Hornsey.
17 Bruce Castle Mus., D/PH/4A.
18 M.R.O., D.R.O. 20/H/1, p. 6.
19 M.R.O., D.R.O. 20/B4/4.
20 Newcourt, *Rep.* 652.
21 Marchams, *Ct. Rolls*, p. xxiv.
22 B.L. Add. MS. 5836, f. 73.
23 M.L.R. 1804/3/436.
24 M.R.O., MR/DE Hornsey.
25 M.R.O., D.R.O. 20/H/1, p. 6.
26 Ibid. A7/1; B4/4.
27 M.R.O., D.R.O. 20/H/1, p. 6; H.O. 129/137/1/1/3.
28 M.R.O., D.R.O. 20/B4/4.
29 Madge, *Med. Rec. of Harringay*, 127–9; Guildhall MS. 9171/5, f. 349.
30 Newcourt, *Rep.* 652.
31 M.R.O., MR/TH/1; J. Walker, *Sufferings of the Clergy* (1714), ii. 295; Guildhall MS. 9537/20, p. 1.
32 B.L. Add. MS. 5836, ff. 71–2.
33 See below, p. 173.
34 M.R.O., D.R.O. 20/A6/2/1–2.
35 Sketch (1826) *penes* the rector.
36 H. O. 129/137/1/1/3.
37 Potter Colln. 21/70.
38 Photos. *penes* the rector.
39 M.R.O., D.R.O. 20/B4/4.
40 *Hornsey Jnl.* 16 Feb. 1962.

on part of the site *c.* 1964[41] and provision was made in 1969 for a future Rectory on the churchyard.[42]

Failure to pay papal tenths resulted in excommunication of the rector in 1302[43] and an interdict on the church in 1303.[44] The fraternity of Holy Trinity mentioned in 1401[45] presumably worshipped in the Trinity chapel. Apart from that of the Holy Trinity, there were lights to the Holy Cross in 1411,[46] the rood in 1478,[47] and All Hallows in 1480.[48] A rent-charge of 3*s.* 4*d.* from Pitmansacre was left by John Hill in 1500 to endow an obit for himself and his family[49] but in 1547 it had been spent for five years on the poor and the highways.[50] In 1533 another testator sought inclusion on the bederoll and left two cows to the fabric.[51] The origin is not known of the 7-a. copyhold close called Churchfield from which 13*s.* 4*d.* rent was being spent partly on church repairs in 1547.[52] Farmed respectively by William and Robert Shepherd,[53] Pitmansacre and Churchfield passed to the Crown on the dissolution of the chantries.[54] The parish lost its rent-charge from Pitmansacre permanently[55] but Churchfield later became a charity estate.[56]

In 1592 Dr. Thomas Skeffington left a £1 rent-charge from copyhold land in Highgate to provide sermons at the parish church at Christmas and Whitsun each year.[57] Robert Willanton, rector 1556–60, was deprived[58] and Thomas Lant (d. 1688), rector from 1637 and said to have been of blameless character, was ejected *c.* 1645. In 1649 the cure was served by a minister chosen by the parishioners but Lant was restored in 1660.[59] Between 1719 and 1810 there was a monthly communion and children were catechized in Lent.[60] In 1791, after the curate was so drunk that the congregation asked him not to preach, the vestry complained that it had long desired a curate of whom it could approve; it also tried to influence the rector's choice.[61] In 1850 it memorialized Queen Victoria against the re-establishment of the Roman Catholic hierarchy in England.[62]

The hymn tune 'Hornsey' was composed by S. S. Wesley, a friend of Canon Richard Harvey, rector 1829–81,[63] who founded six daughter churches and was described as equally unsympathetic towards ritualism and the extreme Low Church.[64] His successor Prebendary J. Jeakes and his curates were considered ultra-Protestant in 1888[65] and St. Clair Donaldson, rector 1901–4, tried to broaden the services and abolished evening communion.[66] The choice of his successor, Francis Norman Thicknesse, rector 1904–11, was criticized as that of a moderate High Churchman, since Hornsey had an evangelical tradition.[67] The changes which he introduced, including a reredos, a cross on the altar, and a monthly choral communion, were resisted by some choristers and were denounced as idolatrous in a lengthy controversy in the local press.[68] In 1851 736 people attended morning service and 425 in the evening[69] and on one Sunday in 1903 the total congregation at all services was 1,555.[70]

Among the numerous rectors who held other preferments were Walter of London, rector in 1302–3,[71] Robert Harrington, rector 1560–1610, and Richard Harvey, who were prebendaries of Brownswood. Among absentees were Charles Sheppard, rector 1780–1829, who lived at Northampton[72] and William Cole (d. 1782), rector 1749–50, the antiquary.[73] Lewis Atterbury, rector 1719–31 and for 37 years lecturer at Highgate chapel, published sermons and theological tracts.[74] Thomas Westfield, rector 1615–37 and a noted preacher, became bishop of Bristol,[75] St. Clair Donaldson was in turn archbishop of Brisbane and bishop of Salisbury,[76] and H. C. Montgomery-Campbell, rector 1926–33, became bishop of London.[77] There was a curate in 1547,[78] 1749, and 1851.[79] James Moorhouse, curate between 1859 and 1861, was later bishop of Manchester.[80] In 1933 it was considered that rectors of Hornsey were destined for preferment.[81]

The existing church of *ST. MARY*, a converted hall, is at least the fourth building of that name to serve the parish; only the tower survives from previous churches. The 'ragged surface' of the first known church, the result of the rubble, bricks, and irregular stones in its construction,[82] may explain a belief that old materials had been re-used.[83] No part appears to have been older than the 13th century. By 1401 the Trinity chapel had been added to the south side of the undivided nave and chancel.[84] Money was left for it to be roofed in 1428,[85] work was in progress in 1452,[86] and in 1460 the Trinity

41 Ex inf. the rector.
42 1969 c. i.
43 W.A.M. 5810, 5817.
44 Ibid. 5820.
45 Guildhall MS. 9171/2, f. 17.
46 Ibid. f. 201v.
47 Guildhall MS. 9171/6, f. 220.
48 Ibid. f. 305.
49 Guildhall MS. 9171/8, f. 228v.
50 E 36/258 f. 149v.
51 Guildhall MS. 9171/10, f. 210v.
52 Hennessy, *Novum Rep.* 223; E 36/258 f. 149v.
53 E 36/258 f. 149v.
54 *Cal. Pat.* 1549–51, 96–7.
55 Marchams, *Ct. Rolls*, 20 sqq.
56 See p. 200.
57 Prob. 11/80 (P.C.C. 75 Harrington).
58 Hennessy, *Novum Rep.* 223.
59 *Walker Revised*, 260; *Home Cnties. Mag.* i. 57–8.
60 Guildhall MSS. 9550; 9557, f. 23.
61 M.R.O., D.R.O. 20/C1/1, ff. 162 sqq.
62 Bruce Castle Mus., D/PH/2A.
63 *Hornsey Jnl.* 1 Sept. 1933.
64 *Holloway Press*, 4 Oct. 1873; *Gloucester Chron.* 29 June 1889.
65 *N. Mdx. Chron.* 11 Aug. 1888.
66 *Hornsey Jnl.* 17 Nov. 1939.
67 *The Record*, 19 Aug. 1904; *English Churchman*, 2 Feb. 1905.
68 *Hornsey Jnl.* 13, 27 Jan. 1905; *N. Mdx. Chron.* 21, 28 Jan. 1905; bk. of cuttings (1904–5) *penes* the rector.
69 H.O. 129/137/1/1/3.
70 Mudie-Smith, *Rel. Life*, 407.
71 Madge, *Med. Rec. of Harringay*, 76–7; *Reg. Winchelsey* (Cant. & York Soc.), ii. 962. Except where otherwise stated, the para. is based on Hennessy, *Novum Rep. passim.*
72 *Story of Hornsey Par. Ch.* (1949), 13.
73 B.L. Add. MS. 5836, f. 73.
74 Lysons, *Environs*, iii. 57.
75 *Cal. Close*, 1389–92, 163, 309; 1392–6, 110; 1396–9, 287.
76 *Hornsey Jnl.* 1 Sept. 1933.
77 *Crockford* (1965–6).
78 Hennessy, *Novum Rep.* 223.
79 M.R.O., D.R.O. 20/H/1, p. 6.
80 *Crockford* (1896).
81 *Hornsey Jnl.* 1 Sept. 1933.
82 *Gent. Mag.* cii (2), 12–14. Except where otherwise stated, the para. is based on B.L. Add. MS. 5836, ff. 70v.–82 (1749); *Gent. Mag.* lxxx (2), 17; cii (2), 12–14.
83 Norden, *Spec. Brit.* 21.
84 Guildhall MS. 9171/2, f. 17.
85 *Fifty Earliest Eng. Wills*, ed. F. J. Furnivall (Early Eng. Text. Soc. lxxiii), 80.
86 Guildhall MS. 9171/5, ff. 91, 309.

aisle was mentioned,[87] then or later of six bays. The most westerly bay, which served as the vestry from 1749 to 1832, was narrower and opened into the contemporary base of the tower to the north. The tower, towards which a bequest had been made in 1429,[88] contained a bell in 1460[89] but was unfinished in 1481–2.[90] Money was left towards the steeple in 1499 and the first three stages were apparently completed *c.* 1501, as they bore the arms of Bishops Savage (1496–1501) and Warham (1501–3), who also glazed the east window. Further legacies were made in 1517–18[91] towards the tower and in 1533 for finishing the church,[92] but the additional stages apparently contemplated[93] were never built. Of brick faced with stone, the steeple was too big for the church in 1749. Money was left in 1462 for the rood-loft,[94] complete by 1478,[95] and there was a rood-stair to the south. Round-headed windows were substituted for the Gothic ones in nave and aisles between 1810 and 1832, and by 1749 dormer windows had been inserted in the nave roof to light the galleries.[96] In 1631 Samuel Armitage, girdler of London, erected a west gallery and in 1714, when the church was 'beautified', a small south gallery was added. In 1793 there was seating for only 200 and demand for pews greatly exceeded the number unappropriated.[97] In 1800 it was decided to erect a bigger south gallery and to install the organ given by John William Paul (d. 1795) at the west end of the north gallery.[98] The south gallery, which accommodated singers and servants in 1810, was slightly enlarged in 1815 and eventually covered the whole aisle[99] but in 1831, with only 220 sittings, the church was too small and in disrepair.[1] Except for the tower, of which the top stage was rebuilt to a different plan,[2] the whole fabric was demolished.

In 1832–3 a new church by George Smith was built adjoining the tower. Commended by contemporaries,[3] it was of white Suffolk brick with stone dressings in a Gothic style and consisted of a six-bay clerestoreyed nave and chancel with clerestorey and north and south aisles.[4] It stood on a platform containing 38 private vaults, of which 12 were sold towards the building costs.[5] The bishop, the rector, and three others each subscribed £1,000 towards the total cost of £8,400.[6] There was seating nominally for 960 in box-pews or in galleries on three sides, where most of the 480 free places were, but only 600 places were considered tolerable in 1887, when the working classes were practically excluded. The building, considered unfit to be the mother church of such an important parish,[7] was replaced in 1888 but survived unused until 1927, when all of it except the tower was demolished and the vaults were filled in.[8] The site was made into a Garden of Remembrance in 1950[9] and the bells were later removed from the tower, which had become dangerous.[10] In 1966 money for the tower's maintenance was contributed by the council[11] but both tower and graveyard remained ecclesiastical property.

To avoid disturbing graves a site was taken from the glebe on the corner of Hornsey High Street and Church Lane, where the new church could not be oriented.[12] Designed in the Perpendicular style by James Brooks, it was of elaborately worked stone and consisted of nave with clerestorey and aisles of six bays, transepts, two-bay chancel and side chapels, and two-storeyed east porch. The body of the church was consecrated in 1889 and the west front and first stage of an intended lofty tower were added by Sir Charles Nicholson *c.* 1900. The tower was never completed, from shortage of money[13] and later because of the instability of the subsoil.[14] The church contained 1,200 seats, half of them free, and was potentially the finest 19th-century church in Middlesex. As early as 1904 cracks appeared in the masonry and in the 1960s scaffolding was required internally.[15] The church was demolished under the St. Mary, Hornsey, Act, 1969,[16] and the site was used for a school. From 1969 services have been held in the church hall, formerly the National hall, acquired in 1916.[17] Planning permission was repeatedly refused for a church adjoining the old tower.[18]

A secular Dutch table of *c.* 1700 was used in turn as an altar and credence table.[19] An organ by Henry Willis was restored in 1928 and 1946. A 15th-century brass inscription commemorates Richard Ruggevale and there is a complete brass for the infant John Skeffington (d. *c.* 1520) and part of one for Thomas Priestley (d. 1613) and his brother and namesake.[20] Monuments include an incised stone

[87] Guildhall MS. 9171/7, f. 111v.
[88] Ibid. 9171/3, f. 223v.
[89] Ibid. 9171/5, f. 309.
[90] Guildhall MSS. 9171/6, f. 311; 9171/7, f. 111v.
[91] Prob. 11/12 (P.C.C. 7 Moone, will of Henry Chicheley).
[92] Guildhall MSS. 9171/9, ff. 62v., 88; 9171/10, f. 210v.
[93] *Gent. Mag.* lxxx (2), 17.
[94] Guildhall MS. 9171/5, f. 317v.
[95] Ibid. 9171/6, f. 220.
[96] See plate facing p. 193.
[97] Bk. of cuttings (1904–5) *penes* the rector.
[98] M.R.O., D.R.O. 20/C1/1, ff. 155v.–265, *passim*; D.R.O. 20/B2/1A; see also printed rep. of 'Groves and Wright v. Rector . . . and Inhabitants of Hornsey' in Bk. of cuttings (1905–6) *penes* the rector.
[99] M.R.O., D.R.O. 20/C1/4; illus. in B.L., Potter Colln. 21/22.
[1] M.R.O., D.R.O. 20/C1/4; B2/3.
[2] Compare *Gent. Mag.* lxxx (2), 17 (print) and prints in Hornsey libr. with bldg.; see also M.R.O., D.R.O. 20/B2/27; H.O. 129/137/1/1/3.
[3] *The Times*, 26 July 1833, 20 July 1835.
[4] H.O. 129/137/1/1/3; W. E. Trotter, *Sel. Topog. of 30 Miles around Lond.* (1839), 88. See below, plate facing p. 192.
[5] M.R.O., D.R.O. 20/B2/3; C1/4.
[6] Ibid. C1/4.
[7] Photo. and subscription leaflet in Hornsey libr.; *N. Mdx. Chron.* 31 July 1869.
[8] M.R.O., D.R.O. 20/B2/13; *The Sphere*, 14 May 1927 (illus.).
[9] 1969, c. i.
[10] Architect's rep. (1959) in Hornsey libr.; *Hornsey Jnl.* 25 Aug. 1961, 30 Mar. 1962.
[11] Ex inf. the rector.
[12] The para. is based on subscription leaflet (1887) and postcards in Hornsey libr.; Pevsner, *Mdx.* 113; Hennessy, *Novum Rep.* 223; Robbins, *Mdx.* 298; T. F. Bumpus, *London Chs.: Ancient and Modern* (1907), 227; elevations in Hornsey libr., Heal Colln.; *Builder*, liv. 340 and illus. See also plate facing p. 192.
[13] St. Mary, Hornsey, *Bazaar Souvenir* (1908) in Hornsey libr.
[14] *Muswell Hill Rec.* 4 Nov. 1948.
[15] Photos. *penes* the rector.
[16] 1969, c. i; *Hornsey Jnl.* 3 Dec. 1904; ex inf. the rector.
[17] See above, p. 160; Char. Com. files.
[18] Ex inf. the rector; 1969, c. i.
[19] Except where otherwise stated, the para. is based on *Story of Hornsey Par. Ch.* (1949); Hist. Mon. Com. *Mdx.* 78; C. J. Sidey, *Short Hist. Hornsey Old Ch.* (1911); Pevsner, *Mdx.* 113.
[20] In 1977 the brasses were at the Rectory: *T.L.M.A.S.* xxviii. 309–14. Other fittings were at St. Peter's, N. Harringay: see below.

slab of *c.* 1613 for George Rey of Highgate and his two wives, an obelisk of 1601 for Richard Candish, a wall monument with kneeling figure, broken pediment, and cartouche for Francis Musters (d. 1680), and memorials to Samuel Rogers (d. 1855) by William Behnes and to Mrs. Gazeley, 1795, by Henry Rouw.[21] Richard Ruggevale left 33*s.* 4*d.* for a chalice in 1462[22] and in 1547 there were a silver-gilt chalice, copper-gilt pipe and paten, and other vessels of laten.[23] The present silver plate includes two flagons of 1641 given by Lady Musters and William Thatcher's gift in 1713[24] of cup and stand-paten of 1694 and plate of 1700. In 1557 the church had a sanctus and three large bells[25] and from 1749 six bells, rehung in 1775. In 1937 they were treble, (ii), (iii), (iv), (v), T. Janaway, 1775; tenor, J. Warner, recast in 1880. The churchyard, the burial place of Trotwood in *David Copperfield*,[26] was several times enlarged and was closed for burials in 1892. Many graves were full of water then and in 1750,[27] when all the poor of the parish were buried there. In 1808 the rector was selling plots for private vaults.[28] Among those interred there was Samuel Rogers (d. 1855), poet.[29] There are registers of births from 1653 and of marriages and burials from 1654.[30]

By 1159 there was a chapel at Muswell,[31] later dedicated to *ST. MARY*. The chaplain or priest was appointed by the priory of St. Mary, Clerkenwell and first mentioned in 1476, when the priory's tenants had rendered their tithes and offerings at the chapel or St. James's church at Clerkenwell and worshipped at the chapel from time immemorial, with the consent of the rector of Hornsey.[32] By 1526–7 the rector was paid 6*s.* 8*d.* as annual composition for his tithes.[33] The priory's bailiff accounted for the oblations, which had totalled £6 9*s.* 10*d.* in the previous year.[34] They included the offerings of pilgrims, whom miracles had attracted to Muswell by the late 15th century, particularly at the Assumption (15 August) and Nativity (8 September) of the Blessed Virgin Mary and on Good Friday.[35] Norden recorded an image of the Virgin there and the association of Muswell spring with miraculous cures from the time of a king of Scots,[36] possibly Malcolm IV (1153–65), lord of Tottenham.[37] Papal indulgences, allegedly lost or damaged, were confirmed in 1476[38] and in 1477 an indulgence was granted to all pilgrims who visited the chapel or priory church and contributed towards the rebuilding of the latter.[39] The priory paid a hermit for selling wax at Muswell[40] and in 1531 pilgrimage there was denounced for 'bawdry'.[41] In 1540 the priest occupied a chamber in the gatehouse.[42] The chapel was included in grants of the dissolved priory's estate,[43] and by 1598 the district was regarded as a detached part of Clerkenwell parish.[44]

The church of *ST. JAMES*, Muswell Hill, stands on the corner of St. James's Lane and Muswell Hill Road on land given by Henry Warner.[45] A chapel committee was formed in 1839[46] and in 1842 an unoriented church was built. Of white brick and in an Early English style, it was designed by Samuel Angell and had a nave seating 432, a shallow chancel, and diminutive tower and spire.[47] The consolidated chapelry assigned in 1843 included Clerkenwell detached;[48] the chapel stood by itself at an equal distance from several growing settlements. In 1874 the nave was extended and a north aisle added, at a cost larger than that of the original building, to increase the number of sittings to 550. Since the church was too small and in a dangerous condition in 1898, J. S. Alder designed a new church of Ancaster stone, with Bath stone dressings in a Perpendicular style.[49] Chancel, vestries, chapels, and two bays of the nave were consecrated in 1901, the rest of the nave, west end, and base of the west tower in 1902, and the tower and spire in 1910.[50] It was gutted during the Second World War but by 1952 had been restored by Caroë and partners with seating for 800;[51] in the interim services were held in a temporary structure in the nave. In 1978 the church consisted of a chancel with side chapels, an aisled and clerestoreyed nave, and a tower and spire 179 ft. high. In 1851 259 people were at morning service and 198 at evening service[52] and on one Sunday in 1903 677 attended in the morning and 419 in the evening.[53] The living was always in the gift of the bishop of London. Thomas Jackson, the first vicar, later became bishop himself. Prebendary E. A. Dunn, vicar 1931–58, was a noted preacher and Edmund Courtenay Pearce, assistant curate 1899–1900, was later master of Corpus Christi College, Cambridge, and bishop of Derby.[54] There were new organs in 1842, 1853, 1889, and 1913 and the choir, from 1892 under distinguished choirmasters, enjoyed a national reputation between the World Wars.

The church of *ST. MATTHEW* was founded as a chapel of ease of St. James's, with the aid of the Missionary Society, to serve the Coldfall estate. The site, on the corner of Coppetts Road and Creighton

21 R. Gunnis, *Dict. of Brit. Sculptors*, 48, 33.
22 Guildhall MS. 9171/5, f. 334.
23 E 315/498 f. 35v.
24 M.R.O., D.R.O. 20/H/1.
25 *T.L.M.A.S.* xvii. 41; xix. 58.
26 Draper, *Literary Assocs. of Hornsey*, 3.
27 *The Times*, 1 Feb. 1892; B.L. Add. MS. 5836, f. 71.
28 M.R.O., D.R.O. 20/C1/4.
29 *D.N.B.*
30 *T.L.M.A.S.* xviii (2), no. 123.
31 Madge, *Early Rec. of Harringay*, 73. The charter confirms one granted by 1159: ibid. 61–2.
32 *Cal. Pap. Reg.* xiii (1), 224–5.
33 Connolly and Bloom, *Island of Clerkenwell*, 13; S.C. 12/19/4.
34 Connolly and Bloom, op. cit. 47, 49.
35 *Cal. Pap. Reg.* xiii (1), 224–5.
36 Norden, *Spec. Brit.* 36–7; the pilgrimage is also mentioned in J. Heywood, 'Play of the Four PP', *Chief Pre-Shakespearean Dramas* (1924), 368.
37 *T.L.M.A.S.* xii. 635.
38 *Cal. Pap. Reg.* xiii (1), 224–5.
39 Ibid. 244–5.
40 S.C. 6/Hen. VIII/2117 m. 3d.
41 J. Foxe, *Acts and Monuments* (1576), 1016.
42 S.C. 6/Hen. VIII/ 2396 m. 100.
43 See p. 144.
44 J. Stow, *Survey of Lond.* (1598), 360; *T.L.M.A.S.* xii. 649.
45 Except where otherwise stated, the following two paras. are based on *Church on the Hill* (1951) (commem. booklet); *T.L.M.A.S.* xviii (2), nos. 130, 132.
46 J. C. Marriott, 'Muswell Hill' (1903), 311 (MS. in Bruce Castle Mus.), citing 'Epitome of the Hist. of the Ch.'.
47 *Illus. News of the World*, 3 July 1858.
48 *Lond. Gaz.* 6 Oct. 1843, pp. 3253–4; see also M.R.O., D.R.O. 20/H/1, p. 74 (plan).
49 *Hornsey Jnl.* 16 June 1900; *N. Mdx. Chron.* 18 June 1898.
50 *Muswell Hill Record*, 11 Feb., 18 Feb. 1910.
51 Ex inf. the vicar.
52 H.O. 129/137/1/1/2.
53 Mudie-Smith, *Rel. Life*, 407.
54 *Hornsey Jnl.* 30 Oct. 1964.

Avenue, had been given by the Ecclesiastical Commissioners in 1908.[55] A wooden mission hall of 1925[56] was replaced in 1940 by a brick church to a plain design by Caroë and Passmore. It consists of a chancel, north vestry, south chapel and tower, and aisled nave and west porch. St. Matthew's had its own minister from 1932 and became a vicarage in 1940, with the Church Pastoral Aid Society as patron.[57] The parish was described as difficult in 1963, when the electoral roll had fallen from the peak of 200 members.[58]

CHRIST CHURCH, Crouch End, stands on the corner of Crouch End Hill and Crescent Road on a site given by Charles Scrase Dickens.[59] Services in the rented Broadway hall during the rebuilding of the parish church continued after 1833. The hall seated only 170 but on Census Sunday 1851 evening service was attended by 193.[60] A new church was consecrated in 1862, when a district was assigned.[61] A. W. Blomfield initially built a nave, north aisle, and chancel to seat 450, adding a south aisle with a further 243 seats in 1867. A tower and spire were built in 1873, substantial repairs were undertaken in 1881, and, with the impending closure of St. Andrew's in 1906–7, the south aisle was widened for 120 extra seats and a vestry and three porches were added.[62] War damage was repaired between 1949 and 1952 by P. Willoughby, who presumably whitewashed the coloured brick arcades.[63] In 1976 Christ Church consisted of a chancel, with north tower and spire above a vestry, another north vestry, south organ-chamber, and an aisled and clerestoreyed nave with north and west porches. Of Kentish Rag outside and brick within, it is in a restrained Decorated style. On one Sunday in 1903 attendances were 509 in the morning and 345 in the evening.[64] There was an organist in 1863 and new organs were provided in 1871 and 1898; organ and choir were prominent in services in 1892 and the church had a fine musical tradition in the years 1914 to 1917 and 1962 to 1964.[65] In 1914 the Revd. C. J. Sharp prevented his own succession by a dogmatic Anglo-Catholic or Evangelical,[66] but Canon Bryan Green, vicar 1934–8, established a militant evangelical tradition.[67] W. R. Matthews, vicar 1916–18, was later dean of St. Paul's, and W. F. P. Chadwick, vicar 1938–47, became suffragan bishop of Barking.[68] The patron is the bishop of London.

The church of *ST. ANDREW*, Shepherd's Hill, stood on a site near Montenotte Road given by the Ecclesiastical Commissioners.[69] An iron and wooden building by A. E. Billing with seating for 400 and a south-east tower and belfry, it opened in 1890. It was attended on one Sunday in 1903 by 295 people in the morning and 193 in the evening.[70] The population did not grow as expected and there was competition with St. Augustine's, Highgate. St. Andrew's therefore remained a chapel of ease to Christ Church and was closed in 1907, whereupon the building became the first Anglican church of St. Andrew, Felixstowe (Suff.).

The church of *ST. JOHN THE EVANGELIST*, Brownswood Park, stands on the corner of Queen's Drive and Gloucester Road. The district chapelry created in 1875,[71] after changes in 1880 and 1915, has lain almost entirely in the peninsular part of Hornsey south of Seven Sisters Road. Work on the building, to a grandiose design by F. Wallen in a Venetian Gothic style, began in 1869 but was delayed by the builder's bankruptcy. Two-thirds of the church was consecrated in 1874 and the west end in 1878, when Wallen's services were dispensed with,[72] and the adjoining Vicarage was erected in 1876. The church has an apsidal chancel with side chapels, transepts, a central tower, of which the upper stages were not built, an aisled and clerestoreyed nave with north and south porches, and an apsidal western baptistery. Extensive repair was needed in 1920 and under-pinning from 1928, and severe war damage was not remedied until 1951. Although founded at popular request in a growing area, St. John's suffered from dwindling congregations by 1885. In 1903 only 199 attended a service in the morning and 172 another in the evening,[73] in a church that sat 900, and expenses could hardly be met in 1895 and 1913. George Birkett Latreille, first vicar, held the benefice for 47 years. His successor A. C. Turberville was noted for his advanced churchmanship. In 1928 the patronage was transferred from the bishop to the Corporation of London.

The church of *HOLY INNOCENTS*, on the corner of Tottenham Lane and Rokesley Avenue, was built in 1876–7 to a design by A. W. Blomfield.[74] Of yellow brick with red-brick and stone dressings in a Gothic style, it has a chancel, north chancel, and south tower surmounting an organ-chamber, and an aisled and clerestoreyed nave with south porch, at the west end of which two vestries and a hall are screened off. It contained 860 seats,[75] all free, and on one Sunday in 1903 was attended by morning and evening congregations of 440 and 721.[76] In 1973–4 the western bay was refashioned as a hall, reducing the seating for services to *c.* 300.[77] In 1877 a district was assigned from the parish of Hornsey[78] and the patronage of the living was vested in the bishop.[79]

The church of *HOLY TRINITY*, Stroud Green,[80] on the corner of Granville and Stapleton

[55] *Muswell Hill Record*, 31 Jan. 1908.
[56] S. J. Kitchener, 'MS. Notes' in Hornsey libr.
[57] *Crockford* (1935 and later edns.).
[58] *Hornsey Jnl.* 8 Feb. 1963.
[59] Except where otherwise stated, the para. is based on C. R. Watson, *A Hundred Yrs. of Christ Ch., Crouch End*, (jubilee booklet); *T.L.M.A.S.* xviii(2), no. 125
[60] H.O. 129/137/1/1/1.
[61] *The Times*, 30 June 1862; see also *Lond. Gaz.* 4 Nov. 1862, pp. 5228–9.
[62] *The Times*, 13 July 1906.
[63] Pevsner, *Mdx.* 114.
[64] Mudie-Smith, *Rel. Life*, 407.
[65] M.R.O., D.R.O. 23/I/C1/1; *Hornsey Jnl.* 6 July 1962, 19 June 1964; W. R. Matthews, *Memories and Meanings* (1969), 93.
[66] Matthews, op. cit. 83–4.
[67] *Hornsey Jnl.* 6 July 1962; Watson, *Christ Church*, 42; *Crockford* (1973–4).
[68] *Hornsey Jnl.* 21 Feb. 1962.
[69] *Crouch End & Hornsey Weekly News*, 16 June 1888.
[70] Mudie-Smith, *Rel. Life*, 407.
[71] *Lond. Gaz.* 19 Mar. 1875, p. 1710. For what follows see W. G. Lewis, *St. John Brownswood Pk. 1874–1974* (jubilee booklet). See also illus. facing p. 193.
[72] *Finsbury Pk. Weathercock*, 29 June 1877, 13 July 1877.
[73] Mudie-Smith, *Rel. Life*, 407.
[74] *T.L.M.A.S.* xviii(2), no. 126; Pevsner, *Mdx.* 114; M.R.O., D.R.O. 20/A10/1.
[75] Doc. *penes* Revd. B. K. Lunn.
[76] Mudie-Smith, *Rel. Life*, 407.
[77] Ex inf. the vicar.
[78] *Lond. Gaz.* 27 Nov. 1877, pp. 6670–1.
[79] M.R.O., D.R.O. 20/A10/1.
[80] Except where otherwise stated, the para. is based on *T.L.M.A.S.* xviii(2), no. 127.

Finchley: St. Marylebone Burial Ground in 1855

Highgate: St. Michael's Church from the south-east in 1832

Fire station at Stroud Green *c.* 1900

Railway sidings south of Hornsey station, from the south-west

HORNSEY

Hall roads, replaced a crowded temporary hall[81] in stages between 1880 and 1885. Designed by E. B. Ferrey in a 13th-century style, it was of brick with stone dressings and had a nave, south aisles, transepts, vestry, south porch, and west spirelet.[82] Although built at only moderate cost, the interior was dignified and spacious.[83] There were 1,200 seats in 1903,[83] when a morning service was attended by 1,051 and an evening service by 1,210.[85] Following war damage the church was declared unsafe *c.* 1951 and pulled down in 1960. The site was re-used for a hall, Vicarage, and public garden. The adjoining red-brick hall in Granville Road was adapted as the church, with a western portico and spirelet.[86] The congregation was evangelical in 1885, when 2,266 signatories opposed the presentation of the ritualist, Dr. Robert Linklater, vicar 1885–1911. By 1888, however, Holy Trinity was the only Hornsey church with Anglo-Catholic services,[87] which were retained in 1976. In 1881 a district was assigned from the chapelries of Holy Innocents and St. John and from Hornsey parish.[88] The patron is the bishop of London.

The church of *ST. PAUL*, South Harringay, and its Vicarage and hall occupy the site between Wightman, Cavendish, and Burgoyne roads. An iron church stood in 1883 in Burgoyne Road[89] and by 1886 was served by the London Diocesan Home Mission.[90] The nave of the permanent church was consecrated in 1891 and the chancel and chapel were finished in 1903. Designed by G. M. Silley and built of Peterborough red brick with Bracknell stone dressings, it has a chancel, south-east chapel and bellcot, north vestries, and an aisled and clerestoreyed nave of six bays with north-west and south-west porches. When built the church seated 700[91] and congregations on one Sunday in 1903 totalled 671 in the morning and 834 in the evening;[92] in 1976 there were no pews in the north aisle. In 1892 a consolidated chapelry was formed from Hornsey and part of Tottenham,[93] with the bishop as patron of the living.

The church of *ST. PETER*, North Harringay, stands with its Vicarage between Wightman, Frobisher, and Lausanne roads. It originated in 1884 as a chapel of ease to the parish church.[94] The iron chapel was replaced by the present Gothic structure designed by James Brooks and Godsell, of which the western part was consecrated in 1897 and the chancel, organ-chamber, side chapel, and vestries were finished in 1905.[95] The church was of red brick with stone dressings and consisted of a chancel, a north chapel, an aisled and clerestoreyed nave, and south-west and north-west turrets. Extensive war damage had not been repaired in 1958. On one Sunday in 1903 congregations were 559 in the morning and 707 in the evening,[96] and the additions of 1905 increased the seating to almost 1,000,[97] but in 1976 only the south aisle was used for worship and the rest of the building contained fittings from the demolished parish church. In 1898 a consolidated chapelry was formed from Hornsey and part of Tottenham,[98] with the bishop as patron of the living. In 1977 St. Peter's parish was combined with that of Christ Church, West Green, Tottenham.[99]

The church of *ST. LUKE*, Mayfield Road, originated in the work of the London Diocesan Home Mission in 1898.[1] An iron church was built in 1898–9 and replaced by the permanent church designed by J. E. K. and J. P. Cutts. Six bays of the nave and aisles seating 500 were completed in 1903, and the chancel, organ-chamber, chapel, and clergy's vestry were consecrated in 1908. The church is of red brick with stone dressings and consists of a chancel, south chapel and north organ-chamber, an aisled and clerestoreyed nave of five bays, western baptistery, and north-west vestry and south-west entrance; the sacristy and another vestry are beneath the organ-chamber and north aisle. A central turret has been removed. The Vicarage of 1910 stands immediately to the north. As completed the church seated 750, a number since reduced: on one Sunday in 1903 359 people attended in the morning and 326 in the evening.[2] A densely populated district of only 123 a. was taken from those of Christ Church, Holy Trinity, and Holy Innocents in 1903. Pew rents were falling by 1902 and closure was first threatened in 1929.[3] Presentations were suspended in 1968, since which date there has been a priest-in-charge.[4] Incumbents changed from an evangelical to a High Church tradition and in 1976 professed Second Vatican Council Catholicism. The patron is the bishop of London.

The existing church of *ST. GEORGE*, Cranley Gardens, on the corner with Park Road, occupies a site given by the Ecclesiastical Commissioners *c.* 1900.[5] Dr. St. Clair Donaldson, however, acquired land on the corner of Priory Road and Park Avenue South, where J. S. Alder designed a church with a chancel, transepts, and aisled nave.[6] The nave and aisles of 1907 seated 400 and were of red brick with yellow Taynton stone dressings, in a late Decorated style with Perpendicular details.[7] In 1910 a district was assigned with the bishop as patron of the living.[8]

[81] *The Times*, 26 Apr. 1880.
[82] Illus. in *Holy Trinity, Stroud Green, Fête Programme* (1908) in Hornsey libr.
[83] *The Times*, 1 Jan. 1881; Pevsner, *Mdx.* 114.
[84] Doc. *penes* Revd. B. K. Lunn.
[85] Mudie-Smith, *Rel. Life*, 407.
[86] *Hornsey Jnl.* 10 Mar. 1961.
[87] *Hornsey & Finsbury Pk. Jnl.* 18 July 1885; *N. Mdx. Chron.* 11 Aug. 1888. See also *Hornsey Jnl.* 20 Jan. 1926.
[88] *Lond. Gaz.* 24 June 1881, p. 3182.
[89] Except where otherwise stated, the para. is based on *Ch. of St. Paul, Harringay* (1951) (diamond jubilee booklet); *T.L.M.A.S.* xviii (2), no. 133.
[90] *Kelly's Dir. Hornsey* (1886).
[91] Ex inf. the vicar.
[92] Mudie-Smith, *Rel. Life*, 407.
[93] *Lond. Gaz.* 1 July 1892, pp. 3796–7.
[94] *Kelly's Dir. Hornsey* (1886); *Hornsey Jnl.* 4 July 1958. The para. is otherwise based on ibid.; *T.L.M.A.S.* xviii (2), no. 134.
[95] *Hornsey Jnl.* 7 July 1905; *The Guardian*, 6 July 1905; see also *Builder*, lxxi. 40.
[96] Mudie-Smith, *Rel. Life*, 407.
[97] *The Guardian*, 6 July 1905.
[98] *Lond. Gaz.* 25 Oct. 1898, pp. 6222–3.
[99] Ex inf. the vicar of Chr. Ch. with St. Peter (1977).
[1] The para. is based on docs. *penes* Revd. B. K. Lunn, priest-in-charge. See also illus. facing p. 193.
[2] Mudie-Smith, *Rel. Life*, 407.
[3] St. Luke's Hornsey, *7th Crouch End Guide Jubilee 1925–75* (1975).
[4] Ex inf. the Revd. B. K. Lunn.
[5] Except where otherwise stated, the para. is based on *T.L.M.A.S.* xviii (2), no. 129; *Hornsey Jnl.* 8 Nov. 1935, 9 Oct. 1959; bk. of cuttings *penes* Revd. P. E. Brassell.
[6] Illus. in St. Mary, Hornsey, *Bazaar Souvenir* (1908) in Hornsey libr.
[7] *Kelly's Dir. Hornsey* (1927).
[8] *Lond. Gaz.* 9 Aug. 1910, pp. 5788–9.

The site proved ill chosen but in 1928 a chancel, chapel, and organ-chamber by W. C. Waymouth were added. In 1940 the church was bombed, from 1945 only the chancel and chapel were used for worship,[9] and in 1956 the building was demolished and the site sold.[10] The modern church by Randall Morris was consecrated in 1959.[11] It is not oriented. Of red brick on a reinforced concrete frame with transverse elliptical arches, it has a sanctuary, aisled nave with east vestries, south-east chapel and bell turret, and south porch. The 16th-century font from St. Mary's was moved from the old to the new St. George's church.[12] The church was served from 1907 until 1949 by Dr. C. E. Simpson (d. 1961) as curate, priest-in-charge, and vicar.[13]

Highgate did not form an ecclesiastical district until the 19th century, when a consolidated chapelry was created after the building of St. Michael's church on the St. Pancras side of the boundary.[14] Previously there had been only the chapel of Cholmley's school, on the Hornsey side, which itself had replaced a chapel of the hermitage. Both chapels had come to serve local inhabitants remote from their own parish churches.

The hermit's chapel at Highgate existed perhaps in the 1350s and 1360s[15] and certainly in 1387,[16] its keeper being responsible by 1464 for repairing roads. Miracles at Highgate attracted great devotion and resort in 1464, when the pope granted an indulgence to those who would support the chapel, which was dedicated to St. Michael.[17] Local inhabitants, in both Hornsey and St. Pancras, used it for worship in 1503. In that year the vicar of St. Pancras led a procession to Highgate, presumably to assert his own rights.[18] The hermits were appointed by the bishop,[19] who in 1540 made a lease of the former hermitage along with the great park.[20] He gave the chapel and 2 a. to Cholmley's school in 1565[21] but in 1577 the Crown granted the chapel, as a concealed chantry,[22] to John Farnham.[23] Farnham soon sold his title to Roger Puleston, the school's receiver general, who in turn conveyed it to the governors.[24]

The school's statutes of 1571 required the master to read prayers every Sunday except the first in the month, when worshippers should attend their own parish churches.[25] The governors raised subscriptions for a new chapel, towards which Hornsey parish made a small contribution, and completed it in 1578.[26] From 1593 Highgate chapel was often called a chapel of ease.[27] The master continued to act as reader and there was also a lecturer from 1637, when William Platt left him £10 a year by a codicil, or earlier.[28] The lecturer or preacher was sometimes called the chaplain[29] and was appointed, presumably from the first and certainly from 1731, by the governors.[30] By the 1630s the chapel was used as a parish church, where baptisms, marriages, and burials were performed.[31] In 1639 it served the inhabitants on Highgate Hill who otherwise would have to go to Hornsey or St. Pancras, in 1719 people seldom travelled to their own churches, and in 1781 a former resident who had moved to Muswell Hill was asked to give up his pew.[32] The status of the chapel was questionable, and was complicated by disputes between reader and lecturer,[33] by claims of the rector of Hornsey[34] and vicar of St. Pancras,[35] and by doubts whether school funds should be spent on the periodic enlargements of the chapel[36] or the master's time on pastoral work as reader.[37] The question who should receive the fees was resolved by a governors' order of 1720, dividing them proportionately.[38] The division of pastoral responsibility between reader and lecturer was much at issue in the 1720s when the lecturer, Dr. Lewis Atterbury (d. 1731) was rector of Hornsey.[39] Thereafter the lecturers tended to hold benefices at a distance and, being often styled simply 'morning preacher' from 1750,[40] to yield some of their preaching duties to the reader.[41] The division between the reader and the two parochial incumbents, however, remained in contention.[42]

When in 1821 the governors promoted a private Bill for a larger chapel, the resulting controversy ended in a judgement that the chapel had not been intended for general use. It was accordingly replaced in 1832 by a new church, which also served the school until 1867[43] and in 1834 was assigned a consolidated chapelry from Hornsey and St. Pancras parishes.[44] The last master to serve as reader, appointed in 1816, served the church until 1838.[45] Thereafter the living was a perpetual curacy, styled a vicarage from 1868, in the bishop's patronage.[46]

The hermits presumably depended on small

[9] *Hornsey Jnl.* 21 Sept. 1945, 11 Nov. 1949.
[10] Cutting in Hornsey libr.
[11] Datestone on bldg.; see also *Hornsey Jnl.* 29 May 1959, 18 Sept. 1959, 9 Oct. 1959.
[12] M.R.O., D.R.O. 20/B4/6; Sidey, *Short Hist. Hornsey Old Ch.* 7.
[13] *Hornsey Jnl.* 21 Sept. 1945.
[14] See below.
[15] See p. 103.
[16] The year 1386 is given in Newcourt, *Repertorium*, i. 654; see Guildhall MS. 9531/3, f. 51v.
[17] *Cal. Papal Reg.*, xii. 411. The dedic. was recorded in 1462: Guildhall MS. 9171/5, f. 317v.
[18] The hermit sued the vicar in Star Chamber: *Home Cnties. Mag.* xii. 49–53.
[19] Newcourt, *Repertorium*, i. 654.
[20] St. Paul's MS. C (Sampson), f. 109v.
[21] *Highgate Sch. Reg.* (5th edn.), pp. x–xi.
[22] E 178/2913/1.
[23] Highgate Sch. rec., box 1, bdle. 1.
[24] *Highgate Sch. Reg.* p. xvi.
[25] Highgate Sch. rec., governors' min. bk. 1576–1810, f. 41v.
[26] Ibid. f. 3 and v.
[27] Norden, *Spec. Brit.* 22.
[28] Platt had also left 20*s.* for a sermon in 1632: Prob. 11/175 (P.C.C. 158 Goare) and Lysons, *Environs*, iii. 70. The reader alone apparently served the inhabitants in 1615: governors' min. bk. 1576–1810, f. 53.
[29] Guildhall MS. 9537/20, f. 1.
[30] Governors' min. bk. 1576–1810, f. 99.
[31] See p. 181.
[32] Governors' min. bk. 1576–1810, ff. 60, 84v., 281v.
[33] Highgate Sch. rec., box 1, bdle. 3.
[34] Governors' min. bk. 1576–1810, f. 61.
[35] Ibid. ff. 97–8.
[36] Memo. by Wm. Felton at back of Highgate chap. reg. 1633–1753 in St. Mic.'s ch.
[37] *Highgate Sch. Reg.* p. xxvii.
[38] Highgate Sch. rec., box 1, bdle. 5.
[39] Ibid. box 1, bdle. 3; governors' min. bk. 1576–1810, f. 97.
[40] B.L. Add. MS. 5836, f. 96.
[41] Governors' min. bk. 1576–1810, ff. 278v., 285v.; Lysons, *Environs*, iii. 70.
[42] Highgate Sch. rec., box 1, bdle. 5. Lloyd, *Highgate*, 155, wrongly says that the vic. of St. Pancras delayed the opening of St. Mic.'s ch. until 1834.
[43] *Highgate Sch. Reg.* pp. xxix–xxx.
[44] *Return of Pars. Divided . . . 1818–65*, H.C. 557, p. 9 (1861), xlviii; *Lond. Gaz.* 3 Oct. 1834, p. 1767.
[45] *Highgate Sch. Reg.* pp. xxx, xcv.
[46] *Crockford* (1868, 1870).

bequests, recorded from 1461,[47] and on alms. Under the statutes of 1571 the master received £10 a year for all his duties. By 1586 the governors paid slightly more[48] and bonuses thereafter were occasionally granted. A master was appointed in 1746 at a salary of £20, soon increased by one half and in 1757 to £100 on account of higher rents obtained for the chapel estate. A further rise was refused in 1771, when the profits from still higher rents were devoted to building repairs.[49] As reader he was entitled to £10 a year by the gift of Edward Pauncefort[50] and also profited from pew rents and chapel fees. In 1728 the master complained that his fees were being taken by Lewis Atterbury and suggested that gifts by Platt, John Smith (d. 1655), and Sir John Wollaston (d. 1658) had been misappropriated.[51] The lecturer enjoyed annual payments of £10 from Platt and Wollaston and £1 from both Platt and Smith for a sermon,[52] in addition to whatever the governors might offer. A statement in 1750 that the chapel was endowed with *c.* £80 a year[53] presumably referred to the salaries of both reader and lecturer.[54] Atterbury received £60 a year by 1723 and his successors the same until in 1789 Dr. John Strachey, having given great satisfaction for 16 years, was granted an additional £30.[55] When a consolidated chapelry was formed the lecturer's endowment was transferred to it.[56] In 1859 the income of St. Michael's was £550 a year and in 1892 it was £600.[57]

There was no glebe,[58] although a parsonage house was built in 1856 on land given by the bishop of London[59] on the north side of Hampstead Lane,[60] where a datestone survived in 1977. The house, with 4 a. of garden, was sold in 1936 and later replaced by Highgate Close. No. 68 Southwood Lane was the Vicarage from 1936 until its sale in 1972. The vicar then moved to no. 10 the Grove, which had been left to the parish by Miss A. Barber.[61]

Thomas Carter, master and reader from 1639, was accused of opposing the protestation oath in 1641[62] and of drunkenness in 1644. He was then ejected by the parliamentarian governors,[63] who included Wollaston, Sir Richard Sprignell, and later Henry Ireton.[64] In 1661 Carter complained that he had been imprisoned for having read the prayers laid down in the school's statutes and was reinstated.[65] Although the governors asserted in 1729 that the master ought to serve no cure but Highgate chapel,[66] William Felton, master 1746–81, was also rector of Wenden Lofts and Elmdon (Essex). In 1750 Felton, 'Methodistically inclined', was not allowed to preach by the lecturer[67] but there is no sign that any master was thought inadequate as a pastor.

Daniel Latham, who had been rector of Orsett and vicar of Grays Thurrock (Essex), apparently held no other position when lecturer at Highgate, where he made his will.[68] Most of his successors, however, were pluralists who obtained the lectureship early in their careers. Lewis Atterbury preached at Highgate before his appointment on Latham's death in 1695[69] and Edward Yardley (d. 1769), who married a beneficiary under Atterbury's will,[70] preached there before succeeding Atterbury in 1731.[71] Yardley was soon rector of St. Florence (Pemb.) and from 1739 archdeacon of Cardigan.[72] John Strachey, appointed in 1773,[73] was already rector of Erpingham (Norf.); he had become a royal chaplain, archdeacon of Suffolk, and prebendary of Llandaff[74] before surrendering the lectureship in 1793. James Saunders, who followed,[75] was the son of Thomas Saunders, a governor of the free school.[76] The last lecturer was Charles Mayo, formerly Rawlinsonian professor of Anglo-Saxon, who was appointed in 1803 and lived mainly at Cheshunt (Herts.).[77] Two later incumbents of St. Michael's, C. B. Dalton, 1854–78, and H. Edwards, 1946–73, were prebendaries of St. Paul's.[78] From the late 19th century there has normally been an assistant curate.[79]

A salaried clerk was paid by the governors for 1640–1[80] and was probably the man who received two years' wages for 'his pains about the chapel' in 1636.[81] John Hartwell was churchwarden in 1670, when another man was clerk of the chapel, but by 1672 had apparently secured the clerkship for himself.[82] In 1692 the governors appointed his son and namesake[83] and in 1731 a William Hartwell was succeeded by his son, William, who was still clerk in 1759.[84] A man was paid yearly for minding the clock in 1648[85] and also for ringing the bell on winter evenings in 1669, although the clerk was responsible for the clock in 1709.[86] There was a salaried organist before 1747, when a new one was appointed at the same rate.[87]

The statutes of 1571, reaffirmed in 1729, enjoined the master to say morning and evening prayers on every Sunday and holy day, except the first Sunday in the month, morning prayers with the litany on Wednesday and Friday, and evening

47 Guildhall MSS. 9171/5, f. 322v.; 7, f. 134v.; 8, f. 91v.
48 Governors' min. bk. 1576–1810, ff. 42, 134.
49 Memo. at back of Highgate chap. reg. 1633–1753.
50 Governors' min. bk., f. 113v.
51 Highgate Sch. rec., box 1, bdle. 3.
52 Lysons, *Environs*, iii. 70.
53 B.L. Add. MS. 5836, f. 96.
54 Governors' min. bk., f. 99.
55 Ibid. ff. 99, 237, 283.
56 *Highgate Sch. Reg.* p. xxx.
57 *Clergy List* (1859, 1892).
58 *Return of Glebe Lands,* H.C. 307, p. 86 (1887), lxiv.
59 Lloyd, *Highgate*, 156.
60 O.S. Map 6", Mdx. XII. SW. (1865 edn.).
61 Ex inf. the Revd. H. Edwards.
62 *Walker Revised*, 259.
63 Governors' min. bk., f. 62v.
64 *Highgate Sch. Reg.* pp. xxii–xxiii.
65 Governors' min. bk., f. 67.
66 Ibid. f. 97v.
67 B.L. Add. MS. 5836, f. 96. Felton was a graduate of Queen's Coll. Oxf. (Governors' min. bk., f. 109v.), not of St. John's Coll., Camb., as in *Alumni Cantab. to 1751*, ii. 129.
68 *Calamy Revised*, 315.
69 *D.N.B.*
70 B.L. Add. MS. 5836, f. 96.
71 Governors' min. bk., f. 99; E. Yardley, *The Rational Communicant . . . in four sermons preached at the Chapel in Highgate, 1728*.
72 *Alumni Cantab. to 1751*, iv. 487.
73 Governors' min. bk., ff. 276v., 278v.
74 *Alumni Cantab. 1752–1900*, vi. 62.
75 Governors' min. bk., f. 284.
76 *Highgate Sch. Reg.* p. lxxxix; *Alumni Oxon. 1715–1886*, 1256.
77 *D.N.B.*
78 Le Neve, *Fasti, 1541–1847, St. Paul's*, 47; *Crockford* (1973–4).
79 *Crockford* (1892 and later edns.).
80 Governors' min. bk., f. 145.
81 Ibid. f. 140v.
82 Ibid. ff. 167, 171.
83 Ibid. f. 180.
84 Ibid. ff. 98, 128.
85 Ibid. f. 147v.
86 Ibid. ff. 69v., 187.
87 Ibid. f. 111v.

prayers on Saturdays and the eve of holy days.[88] The altar was deemed to have been suitably railed off in 1637[89] but ritualism was discouraged by William Platt, who stipulated that the gospel should be 'powerfully and purely preached'.[90] A book of homilies and other works were required in 1685.[91] In addition to the two Sunday services there was a monthly communion in the mid 18th[92] and early 19th centuries.[93] An anti-ritualist tradition at St. Michael's in the mid 19th century was perhaps inspired by the Evangelical T. H. Causton, perpetual curate 1838–54.[94] Causton was followed by C. B. Dalton, son-in-law of Charles Blomfield, bishop of London.[95] Dalton, who confessed that he could not love dissenters, caused offence by placing a small cross on the altar.[96] On his death the living was offered to Daniel Trinder, vicar 1878–88, as a moderate High Churchman free from ritualism.[97] Dalton established a fund in 1857 for a scripture reader, who also taught evening classes at the National school, and in 1860 a parochial nurse was appointed.[98] A railway labourers' mission, with a chaplain appointed by the London Diocesan Home Mission from 1863, was also supported by Dalton and included Highgate's high street among its weekly meeting-places.[99] The parish magazine, founded in 1863, had a circulation of more than 8,000 by 1871.[1] Attendances at St. Michael's were said to average 1,300 in the morning, 500 in the afternoon, and 1,000 in the evening in 1851,[2] when the church was still used by Cholmley's school, and were 527 in the morning and 279 in the evening on one Sunday in 1903.[3]

The hermitage was thought by Norden to have stood on the site of Cholmley's school.[4] Probably it did so, having been next to the bishop's park in 1387[5] and close to the parish boundary in 1503, when the hermit barred the way to the procession from St. Pancras.[6] The chapel seems to have been substantial, perhaps as a result of the gifts solicited in 1464,[7] since the hermit sought refuge in its steeple in 1503.[8] A garden and orchard formed part of the premises in 1531[9] but the building itself was ruinous by 1577.[10] There was no known connexion with the Hermitage in West Hill, where William and Mary Howitt lived.[11]

Work on the chapel for the free school started in 1576 and ended in 1578.[12] The building was of brick,[13] with its north wall abutting the schoolhouse.[14] It was enlarged with help from local subscribers in 1616, consecrated in 1617, perhaps for the first time, and again enlarged in 1628.[15] Soon afterwards it had a battlemented west tower and a gabled south wall,[16] which presumably survived until further additions were made in 1719–20, largely at the expense of Edward Pauncefort. An easterly extension measuring 40 ft., apparently the breadth of the old chapel, by 24 ft. was consecrated in 1720,[17] forming a 'sort of chancel' with a higher ceiling and the altar in a semi-domed recess. Probably the south wall was refaced at that time and its square-framed windows were replaced by tall round-headed windows beneath oval lights. Such was the appearance of the chapel in 1750, when it was as large as Hornsey church and also had a vestry north of the chancel and porches flanking the tower. There were north and south aisles, a gallery along the north wall, and another gallery, with an organ, at the west end; the altar stood on a marble step beneath an 'arched cupolo' with gilded lettering.[18] A new organ was installed in 1753.[19] The roof of the older, main, part of the chapel was lower than that of the east end until 1772, when the whole structure was reroofed out of the accumulated funds of the school estate.[20] Thereafter hipped roofs ran the length of the building, rising behind a plain parapet which had replaced the gables along the south wall; the battlements on the tower were also replaced by a parapet, with globes at the corners.

In the 18th and early 19th centuries Highgate chapel was often portrayed, perhaps because it stood opposite the Gatehouse and had links with eminent residents.[21] William Cole remarked on its fine monuments in 1750, when he singled out those to William Platt (d. 1637) and his wife, Sir Francis Pemberton (d. 1697), and Lewis Atterbury (d. 1731),[22] although in 1816 the building itself was considered humble and to have a 'trifling' tower.[23] On the chapel's closure in 1832 five 18th-century monuments were transferred to the new church, as were the plate and registers.[24] The Platts' monument, restored at the expense of St. John's College, Cambridge, was installed in the old church of St. Pancras,[25] while Pemberton's memorial was moved to Trumpington (Cambs.)[26] and Atterbury's to Hornsey parish church.[27] The old chapel was then

88 Governors' min. bk., ff. 41v., 97v.
89 *Cal. S.P. Dom.* 1636–7, 545.
90 Prob. 11/175 (P.C.C. 158 Goare).
91 Guildhall MS. 9537/20, f. 90.
92 Guildhall MS. 9550.
93 Highgate Sch. rec., box 1, bdle. 5.
94 *Camden Hist. Rev.* ii. 12.
95 K. U. Platt, *Hist. of All Saints* (centenary booklet, 1964).
96 *The Times*, 15 Sept. 1934.
97 Ibid. 3 Sept. 1878.
98 *St. Mic.'s Par. Mag.* Jan., Sept. 1869.
99 Ibid. Oct., Dec. 1863; July 1864.
1 Ibid. Jan. 1871.
2 H.O. 129/9/6/1/3.
3 Mudie-Smith, *Rel. Life*, 175.
4 Norden, *Spec. Brit.* 22.
5 Newcourt, *Repertorium*, i. 654.
6 He was ordered to clear the way betw. the green and the chapel: Marcham, *Cantlowes Ct. Rolls* (TS. in G.L.R.O.), 50.
7 See p. 178. 12*d.* was left to the fabric in 1462: Guildhall MS. 9171/5, f. 317v.
8 *Home Cnties. Mag.* xii. 49–51.
9 Newcourt, *Repertorium*, i. 654.
10 Highgate Sch. rec., box 1, bdle. 1.
11 *pace* W. Howitt, *Northern Heights*, 418.
12 Governors' min. bk., f. 3.
13 Norden, *Spec. Brit.* 22.
14 Cf. later prints in Potter Colln. 8/13, 8/19.
15 Governors' min. bk., f. 4 and v. The second enlargement is wrongly dated 1623 in *V.C.H. Mdx.* i. 303.
16 Sketch attrib. to Hollar in Potter Colln. 8/14.
17 Governors' min. bk., ff. 85–87v., 92; plan in ibid. f. 88.
18 B.L. Add. MS. 5836, f. 96. Sketches, 1750, by Wm. Cole in ibid. f. 95v. and by Chatelaine in Potter Colln. 8/13. A later lithograph, showing the interior, is in Potter Colln. 8/15.
19 Governors' min. bk., ff. 119, 122.
20 Memo. at back of Highgate chap. reg. 1633–1753.
21 Prints in Potter Colln. 8/17, 20–3, in Swiss Cottage libr., Heal Colln., A III 16a–19, and in Hornsey libr. See above, frontispiece.
22 B.L. Add. MS. 5836, ff. 96, 97, 99.
23 Brewer, *Beauties of Eng. and Wales*, x (5), 220.
24 See below.
25 B. Clarke, *Par. Churches of Lond.* 137.
26 Hist. Mon. Com. *Cambs.* ii. 298, which merely says that the memorial was reputed to have come from Highgate parish [sic] church. Illus. in ibid. i, plate 16.
27 Pevsner, *Mdx.* 113.

dismantled, part of it becoming overgrown with ivy and part serving as a fives court until the site was cleared for rebuilding in 1865.[28] The burial ground, closed in 1857,[29] contained 17th-century slabs[30] in 1976 but the remains of Coleridge, in a vault beneath the new school chapel, were removed to St. Michael's church in 1961.[31]

The existing church of *ST. MICHAEL* is set back from South Grove on the crest of Highgate Hill, facing south-east and, with its spire, dominating the skyline. The building is of pale stock brick with stone dressings and consists of an aisled and clerestoreyed nave with three galleries, western tower with octagonal spire, and chancel with vestries beneath.[32] A plan of 1822 to rebuild the old chapel a little farther north was abandoned when the school's governors had to end their responsibility and in 1830 Charles Barry proposed a church on the site of Sir William Ashurst's decayed mansion.[33] There the new church, built to the design of Lewis Vulliamy, was consecrated in 1832.[34] Half of the total cost was met by the Church Building Commissioners and one-fifth by the governors of the school.[35] Vulliamy's mixed Gothic style has generally won praise for its elegance,[36] although in the late 19th century many considered it impure.[37] The nave, with its octagonal piers, is light and spacious. Buttresses and crocketed pinnacles adorn both the spire and the body of the building, increasing its resemblance to Vulliamy's demolished Christ Church, Woburn Square.[38]

The original seating capacity was for 1,520,[39] including places for the poor and for Cholmley's school. There was an eastern vestry until 1880–1, when the chancel was built by C. H. M. Mileham under a faculty of 1878 and seating for the choir was introduced.[40] The nave and aisles were reseated at that time. A new reredos had been installed in 1873 and enrichment and further alterations at the east end were begun in 1903 under Temple Moore and included the provision of a side chapel at the end of the south aisle. The spire was struck for the third time by lightning in 1903, when the church had temporarily to be closed,[41] and was again damaged, with much of the fabric, by a flying bomb in Waterlow Park in 1944. Restoration was carried out in stages between 1946 and 1954.

An organ was installed in the west gallery in 1842, lowered in 1859,[42] and replaced by one behind the choir in 1885. The original east window[43] was replaced in 1889 by one by C. E. Kempe, who later designed glass for the side chapel. Temple Moore's embellishments included the addition of saints' figures and colouring the reredos in 1903 and the erection of a screen on the south side of the chancel in 1905. Kempe's east window was largely destroyed in 1944 but some pieces were placed behind the organ in the east wall of the chancel aisle and a new east window, one of the last works of Evie Hone, was dedicated in 1954.[44] The first memorial designed for the church was that to Coleridge (d. 1834). The most imposing of the monuments from the old chapel is one for John Schoppens (d. 1720) and his wife. The others commemorate Rebecca Pauncefort (d. 1719), Sir Edward Gould (d. 1728), Samuel Forster (d. 1752) and his wife, and John Edwards (d. 1769).[45] The church has one bell, cast in 1847 by G. Mears and given, with the clock, by George Crawshay of Ivy House.[46]

By 1676 Highgate chapel possessed a cup and cover, bought by the governors in 1636, a paten, perhaps acquired at the same time, and two flagons given by Mrs. Jane Savage. The plate was all of silver and was the responsibility of the lecturer, who in 1695 deposited it at Sir William Ashurst's house. William Thatcher later presented a silver paten, Edward Pauncefort paid for all the plate to be gilded, and a silver-gilt spoon of 1773 was inscribed to the chapel with the date 1774. Much if not all of the old plate passed to the churchwardens of St. Michael's, who in 1900 held a paten datemarked 1636, a flagon of 1668, Thatcher's plate of 1710, and the spoon of 1773.[47] In 1908 the vestry declined to return them to the school, on legal advice,[48] and thereafter retained them,[49] with other pieces presented in the 19th century.[50] The registers, which are complete, contain baptisms from 1634, marriages from 1635, and burials from 1633.[51]

The needs of new residents after the opening of Highgate station led to evening services at Francis House, North Hill, in a room rented from a carrier named Cokeham, in 1863.[52] The Ecclesiastical Commissioners and Lord Mansfield gave a site where the church of *ALL SAINTS*, with a curate-in-charge, was consecrated in 1864. It remained within St. Michael's parish until 1874, when the building's enlargement secured the creation of a consolidated chapelry out of St. Michael's, St. Mary's, Hornsey,

28 *Highgate Sch. Reg.* p. xxxv. Fragments of the south wall, *c.* 1840, are depicted in Potter Colln. 8/23.
29 *Lond. Gaz.* 26 June 1857, p. 2199.
30 Hist. Mon. Com. *Mdx.* 79. A plan of the old burial ground, with a list of the graves in 1899, is at St. Mic.'s ch.
31 N. Fruman, *Coleridge, the Damaged Angel*, 433.
32 Pevsner, *London, Except Lond. and Westm.* 362.
33 Plans by Sam. Ware and Chas. Barry among Highgate Sch. rec., box 1, bdle. 5.
34 Clarke, *Par. Churches*, 140. A drawing of the ch. from the NW. by Vulliamy, 1831, is in Potter Colln. 10/160 and various views are in ibid. 10/155, 161–8.
35 Prickett, *Highgate*, 81.
36 E. Smith, O. Cook, and G. Hutton, *Engl. Par. Churches*, 217.
37 e.g. Thorne, *Environs*, i. 348; T. F. Bumpus, *Lond. Churches*, 134.
38 Pevsner, *London, Except Lond. and Westm.* 362. See above, plate facing p. 176.
39 Except where otherwise stated, the following two paras. are based on Clarke, *Par. Churches*, 140; Sir Jas. Brown, *St. Mic.'s Highgate* (pamphlet, 1977); and information from Sir Jas. Brown.
40 A litho. of the interior before alteration is in Potter Colln. 10/149.
41 Potter Colln. 10/168.
42 *St. Mic.'s Par. Mag.* Oct. 1873.
43 Prickett, *Highgate*, 81.
44 Nairn, *Mod. Bldgs. in Lond.* 41. A colln. of cuttings on the window, with photographs, is at the church.
45 L.C.C. *Survey of Lond.* xvii. 55–60.
46 *T.L.M.A.S.* xix. 58.
47 Highgate Sch. rec., box 1, bdle. 5 (memo. on plate, 1900). See also descriptions in ibid. bdle. 2 (tables of gifts, 1697 and 1771) and governors' min. bk., ff. 80v., 81v.
48 Potter Colln. 10/159; some of the pieces are inaccurately described in the newspaper cuttings.
49 Pevsner, *London, Except Lond. and Westm.* 362.
50 E. Freshfield, *Communion Plate of . . . County of Lond.* 25.
51 In 1976 the registers were kept at the church.
52 Except where otherwise stated, the following two paras. are based on K. U. Platt, *Hist. of All Saints* (centenary booklet, 1964).

and St. James's, Muswell Hill.[53] The living then became a vicarage, in the patronage of the bishop.[54] Heavy expenses were incurred by the need to provide access from both North Hill and Archway Road along All Saints' (later Church) Road, where tolls were levied by lessees of the Archway Road Co. until 1876.[55] Consequently the church was built with only *c.* 300 sittings, although William Gladstone paid for a plan that allowed for future additions.[56] The church, of stone, was designed in a 14th-century style by A. W. Blomfield, the Revd. C. B. Dalton's brother-in-law, as a small cruciform building with an eastern bell-turret.[57] A north porch was added in 1864 and an organ-chamber in 1865, while the north transept served as a clergy vestry. In 1874 Blomfield added the south aisle and increased the seating to *c.* 550.[58] There were attendances of 345 in the morning and 219 in the evening on one Sunday in 1903.[59] John Stockdale added a north aisle and south-east vestries in 1912 and the chancel was restored in 1938, but damage was caused during the Second World War and by a fire in 1945. The church, whose north aisle had been blocked off, was restored by W. C. Waymouth[60] and rededicated in 1953. In 1977 the north aisle, separated from the body of the church by folding doors, served as a parish hall.

A Sunday school and institute opened in 1866 in Cokeham's rooms, an iron schoolroom was dedicated in 1873 on land bought by Dalton at the corner of All Saints' Road and North Hill, and in 1876 no. 1 North Hill Terrace (later no. 109 North Hill) was rented as a mission house. In 1880 the mission used a new building adjoining the iron room and designed by C. H. M. Mileham, who was a churchwarden. A brick schoolroom was built in 1882, when the iron one moved to become the first church of St. Augustine.[61] A convalescent home occupied the upper floor of the mission house from 1880 and was extended over the schoolrooms in 1884. It was further extended in 1911, accommodated 20 in 1921,[62] and closed in 1924. The vicarage, immediately east of the church, was dedicated in 1875 and replaced by a smaller house in 1963, when most of the old garden was sold to Middlesex C.C.

In 1881 the vicar of All Saints bought a part of the former Winchester Hall estate in Archway Road, with help from the Bishop of London's Fund. All Saints' iron schoolroom was moved there in 1882 and consecrated as the temporary church of *ST. AUGUSTINE*,[63] a few weeks after services had started at no. 4 Northwood Road.[64] The iron church was enlarged in 1884. The chancel and one bay of the nave of an adjoining permanent church were consecrated in 1888 and the nave, with a temporary façade towards Archway Road, was opened in 1896. A consolidated chapelry was formed in 1898 out of All Saints' and St Michael's parishes, with the curate of All Saints as vicar and the bishop as patron.[65] There were attendances of 174 in the morning and 242 in the evening on census Sunday 1886[66] and of 283 in the morning and 307 in the evening in 1903.[67] The church, of red and yellow brick with stone dressings, was designed in a 14th-century style by J. D. Sedding. It was to seat more than 700 and to have an aisled nave, a north chapel, and a clergy vestry south of the sanctuary, with rooms underneath. The chapel was completed by Henry Wilson in the 1890s and the west end, with a bell-tower higher than originally planned and a two-storeyed north-west porch, was dedicated in 1914. J. H. Gibbons, who designed the west end, restored the fabric after a fire in 1924. The west front is adorned with a life-size stone Calvary, which, with the church's ceremonial, led to a Protestant demonstration in 1914. Most of the fittings were replaced after the fire by the Revd. J. H. Hodgson, 'an absolute Catholic', and in 1976 included the Stations of the Cross and many carved figures.

The foundation stone of St. Augustine's Vicarage, Langdon Park Road, was laid in 1901. Both the Vicarage and the red-brick parish hall, opened between it and the church in 1905, were designed by J. S. Alder, who was a churchwarden.

ROMAN CATHOLICISM. A seminary priest, Leonard Hyde, was arrested at Highgate in 1585.[68] Recusant gentry included Francis Yates of Highgate in 1587, and, from Hornsey, George Mackworth in 1589,[69] Mary Jerningham in 1593–4,[70] and Catherine, wife of Anthony Kitchen, in 1594.[71] The foremost was Sir John Arundell (d. 1591), of Lanherne (Cornw.), confined for three years to Alderman Rowe's house at Muswell Hill but in 1590 allowed to choose another place near to London.[72] Sir John was host to young Mr. Stourton and young Mr. Arundell, both listed as papists, in 1588[73] and his daughter Elizabeth married John Charnock,[74] a local gentleman fined for recusancy in 1593–4.[75] Another prominent recusant was Jane, Lady Lovell, of Highgate.[76] In 1608 the rector presented Walter and Nicholas Henningham for non-attendance at Highgate chapel.[77] Arundel House was also suspect as a centre of Roman Catholic intrigues: inquiries were made in 1615 about food which had been procured by the earl of Arundel's servants for Henry, prince of Wales (d. 1612), on the May Day before his death.[78]

After Lord Arundel's public profession of Pro-

53 *Lond. Gaz.* 20 Oct. 1874, p. 4775.
54 *St. Mic.'s Par. Mag.* Dec. 1874.
55 Ibid. Oct. 1879.
56 Potter Colln. 14/41.
57 Illus. in Platt, *All Saints.*
58 *St. Mic.'s Par. Mag.* Dec. 1874.
59 Mudie-Smith, *Rel. Life*, 407.
60 *T.L.M.A.S.* xviii (2), no. 124.
61 See below.
62 S.P.C.K. *Official Yr. Bk. of Ch. of Eng.* (1921), p. 234.
63 Except where otherwise stated, the following two paras. are based on A. Sanders, *St. Augustine of Canterbury* (jubilee booklet, 1975).
64 Platt, *All Saints*, 35.
65 *Lond. Gaz.* 8 Mar. 1898, p. 1427.
66 *British Weekly*, 19 Nov. 1886.
67 Mudie-Smith, *Rel. Life*, 407.
68 *Cath. Rec. Soc.* v. 105.
69 *Mdx. Cnty. Rec.* i. 171, 187.
70 *Cath. Rec. Soc.* lvii. 93.
71 *Mdx. Cnty. Rec.* i. 219.
72 *Acts of P.C.* 1588–9, 410; 1590, 393.
73 *Cath. Rec. Soc.* xxii. 123.
74 Ibid. xviii, pp. xxi, 146.
75 *Mdx. Cnty. Rec.* i. 221, 224.
76 Hist. MSS. Com. 9, *Hatfield House*, xvii. 613–14. Lady Lovell may have been Jane, dau. of John Roper, Ld. Teynham, and w. of Sir Rob. Lovell.
77 M.R.O., Cal. Mdx. Sess. Rec. 1608–9, 159.
78 *Cal. S.P. Dom.* 1611–18, 324, 334.

testantism in 1615[79] there was little evidence of recusancy, even in Highgate. The gardener of one Heveningham was said to be in touch with visiting papists in 1679[80] but the parish contained no reputed Roman Catholics in 1706.[81] A 'few' were recorded later in the century and sixteen in 1767.[82] Martin Hounshill, chaplain to the duke of Norfolk, was buried at Hornsey in 1783[83] and two French emigré priests lived at Highgate in 1797.[84]

For most of the 19th century Roman Catholics worshipped outside Hornsey. From 1858 a wide area was served by St. Joseph's retreat, on Highgate Hill. In 1869 its chapel was often crowded, especially with Irish from Upper Holloway,[85] many of whose children attended St. Joseph's or, later, St. Aloysius's schools.[86] The Passionists of St. Joseph's opened St. Mary's chapel and school in Tottenham Lane in 1871 but apparently did not maintain them for long.[87]

Many new residents of Stroud Green had no desire to retain links with the mission at Eden Grove, in less prosperous Holloway.[88] In 1892 they formed a committee, which in 1893, as Stroud Green Catholic association, began to raise funds for a church. Coombe House, at the corner of Womersley and Dashwood roads, was bought in 1894, when mass was celebrated there. It was designated St. Augustine's, since canons regular of St. Augustine were intended to serve the mission, but was soon committed to canons regular of the Lateran, who changed the name to St. Peter-in-Chains. A red-brick church, in a Gothic style, was founded in 1898 and completed in 1902.[89] There were attendances of 473 in the morning and 125 in the evening on one Sunday in 1903.[90] The church was still served by canons regular of the Lateran in 1976.

Muswell Hill was included in the new East Finchley parish from 1898.[91] Sisters of St. Martin of Tours arrived in 1904, a separate parish was formed in 1917, and the temporary church of Our Lady of Muswell opened in 1920. The church, accommodating 300 and designed for future conversion into a hall, was so called because it stood in Colney Hatch Lane, near the medieval estate of the nuns of Clerkenwell. A permanent church was first used for worship in 1938 and consecrated in 1959. It was built of brick in the Byzantine style, to the designs of T. H. B. Scott,[92] and seated 600.

Harringay was served from West Green in Tottenham,[93] originally called the parish of West Green and Harringay, until the purchase of the Methodists' church in Mattison Road.[94] Mass was celebrated in the adjoining hall in 1963, when a priest-in-charge of Harringay district was appointed, and the parish of St. Augustine of Canterbury was created in 1964. The former Methodist church was used for worship from 1964.

Pastoral work among West Indians in Haringey and neighbouring boroughs was undertaken by the Revd. John Robson from 1972. No. 416 Seven Sisters Road was later acquired as the Caribbean pastoral centre and adapted for worship and social activities.[95]

PROTESTANT NONCONFORMITY. Highgate, the home of Parliamentarians[96] and just beyond the limits imposed by the Five Mile Act, was a natural resort for dissenters. John Storer, formerly lecturer at Stowmarket (Suff.), was licensed as a Presbyterian at his house in Highgate in 1672, when Hezekiah King, ejected from Fowlmere (Cambs.), was similarly licensed in Hornsey.[97] The Quaker William Mead entertained George Fox at Highgate in 1677 and 1678[98] and Daniel Latham, ejected from Orsett (Essex), made his will there in 1691.[99] A meeting-house in Southwood Lane was said to have been founded in 1662,[1] although the first recorded minister was Josiah Sprigge (d. 1684).[2] His successor William Rathband had property in Highgate from 1662,[3] was registered as a preacher in 1689, when he had no particular charge, and was buried there in 1695.[4]

The 18th-century congregation in Southwood Lane[5] claimed descent from that of 1662, although the next known minister, Thomas Sleigh, was recorded only *c.* 1729.[6] Among its regular members was John Wilkes's father Israel (d. 1761), a rich Clerkenwell distiller.[7] Ministers included David Williams, founder of the Royal Literary Fund, Rochemont Barbauld, husband of the writer Anna Letitia Barbauld, the biographer John Towers, and the philologist Alexander Crombie. Many were unorthodox and none stayed for long: the deistic Williams withdrew in 1773, Towers left on the opening of a rival chapel in 1778, and dissension grew when a successor introduced his own liturgy.[8] The old and new meeting-houses, on opposite sides of the lane, were described as Presbyterian and Methodist respectively.[9] The first closed on Crombie's departure in 1798, to be reopened briefly by Unitarians in 1806 and sold to the Baptists by 1814. Its later history was that of a Baptist tabernacle, while the rival meeting-house, where Methodists probably did not worship for long, was replaced by a forerunner of Highgate Congregational church.

At Crouch End, a village previously 'without the

79 *D.N.B.*
80 *Cal. S.P. Dom.* 1679–80, 44–5.
81 Guildhall MS. 9800/2.
82 Ibid. 9557.
83 Lysons, *Environs*, iii. 55.
84 Mdx. Local Hist. Council, *Bull.* xiii. 2.
85 Howitt, *Northern Heights*, 405. The chap. was in Islington.
86 See p. 199.
87 Potter Colln. 20/50; see above, p. 193.
88 Except where otherwise stated, the para. is based on min. bks. of the Stroud Green Catholic Assoc. i (1892), ii (1893–5), and TS. notes *penes* the par. priest.
89 S. J. Kitchener, 'Hist. Hornsey, Chapter 4' (MS. *penes* Hornsey libr.).
90 Mudie-Smith, *Rel. Life*, 408.
91 Except where otherwise stated, the para. is based on J. A. Goodall, *Our Lady of Muswell* (pamphlet, 1959) and information from the par. priest.
92 *Muswell Hill and Friern Barnet Jnl.* 20 Jan. 1939.
93 *V.C.H. Mdx.* v. 355.
94 The rest of the para. is based on *St. Augustine of Canterbury* (souvenir brochure, 1965).
95 Ex inf. the director.
96 See p. 125.
97 *Calamy Revised*, 308, 465.
98 *Short Jnl. and Itinerary Jnls. of Geo. Fox*, ed. N. Penney, 232, 270.
99 *Calamy Revised*, 315.
1 Prickett, *Highgate*, 167.
2 *Trans. Cong. Hist. Soc.* v. 8; *D.N.B.*
3 Marchams, *Hornsey Ct. Rolls*, 135 sqq.
4 *Calamy Revised*, 404; A. Gordon, *Freedom after Ejection*, 3, 72, 338.
5 Except where otherwise stated, the para. is based on *Trans. Cong. Hist. Soc.* v. 8–9, 13, and *D.N.B.*
6 Dr. Williams's Libr., Evans MS. 34.4.
7 *Gent. Mag.* lxviii (1), 126.
8 Ibid.; *D.N.B.*
9 Guildhall MSS. 9557, f. 23; 9558, f. 452.

gospel', a small building was opened for worship in 1806.[10] It might have been the place attended by a few Methodists in 1810[11] or that registered by Baptists in 1819,[12] and was later known as Broadway chapel.[13] John Wesley had preached at Highgate in the 1780s[14] and Independents had registered rooms at Hornsey in 1794, 'Highgate House', jointly with Baptists, in 1797, and a greenhouse at Hornsey in 1806.[15] At Muswell Hill, where the Baptist Dr. Samuel Stennett (d. 1795) had lived,[16] part of a house was registered by dissenters in 1822.[17] Stennett's house was bought in 1826 by the philanthropist William Brodie Gurney (d. 1855), who attended Highgate Baptist chapel but held Sunday evening services in his own drawing-room until 1830. Worshippers at Muswell Hill, led by Gurney's missionary friend Eustace Carey (d. 1855), were said to number 150–200 in the summer months.[18]

Baptists,[19] at Crouch End and in Southwood Lane from the early 19th century, Methodists, earlier but more briefly in Southwood Lane and at Crouch End in 1810, and Congregationalists, arising from groups of Independents, were the longest established denominations. All three opened chapels as housing spread and in 1873 the Methodists created a Highgate circuit out of part of the area served from Islington.[20] The Hornsey and Highgate Free Church Council was formed in 1896; it was renamed after the withdrawal of Highgate's churches in 1901 and a separate council for Muswell Hill was established in 1903.[21]

The attraction of churches just outside the parish, such as the Methodist churches in Archway Road and Holly Park, obscures the strength of nonconformity in Hornsey and the relative popularity of the sects. In 1903 slightly more than half of the 29,329 worshippers were Protestant nonconformists, the Anglicans accounting for 13,015 and the Roman Catholics for 598. Baptists had as many as 5,056, followed by Congregationalists with 3,983 and Wesleyan Methodists with 3,566. Presbyterians numbered 1,652, Brethren 674, and Primitive Methodists 428.[22] Later arrivals included the Moravians, the Salvation Army, Christian Spiritualists, and Mennonites. A few churches were closed or rebuilt after the Second World War and others were closed on the union of Congregationalists with Presbyterians as the United Reformed Church.

BAPTISTS.[23] Crouch End chapel, afterwards Broadway hall, was opened by Baptists in 1806 and soon used for two Sunday services, a weekday lecture, and a Sunday school.[24] Dissenters at Crouch End had a small place of worship in 1810[25] and 1816[26] but it is not known if they used the later Broadway hall or the meeting-place registered by Baptists in 1819[27] and made the centre of an open communion in 1822.[28] The later Broadway hall was used in turn by Congregationalists, by Anglicans during the rebuilding of St. Mary's, and again by Baptists from 1879 until the opening of Ferme Park chapel in 1889. The hall had once been a farm building of Crouch Hall and had only 170 sittings in 1851 when under lease to the rector,[29] who added Gothic windows and a short tower with a cupola.[30] Broadway hall afterwards served the Universalist Church and the British Legion, until a fire in 1923 led to its demolition in 1925. Its site was covered by the forecourt of Hornsey town hall.

Campsbourne Road church first met in an iron chapel, leased in 1873 and registered in 1876.[31] After dissension[32] a group left to found Westbury Avenue church, Wood Green,[33] and in 1892 Campsbourne's remaining members joined Ferme Park church, which rebuilt the chapel in Campsbourne Road as a mission, started several institutions, and by 1903 had raised the attendance to 158 in the morning and 195 in the evening.[34] In 1907 a brick hall, seating 600, and two smaller halls were opened in the Campsbourne, next to three houses (nos. 3 to 5) which had been given to the mission. The hall in Campsbourne Road was thereafter used for adult education and, later, as an institute and a scouts' headquarters. In 1954, with help from Ferme Park, Campsbourne chapel again became independent. It retained the hall and two converted houses in the Campsbourne in 1976.

Ferme Park Baptist church was formed largely through the efforts of John Batey, minister at Broadway hall. Land had been bought at the corner of Weston Park and Ferme Park Road in 1888 and a chapel, with schoolrooms and seating 630, was opened in 1889. A building on the plan of a Greek cross, seating 1,250 and with marble baptistery and vestries, was opened in 1900, when the older one was converted into halls and a flat. Ferme Park, which administered many societies, had Hornsey's largest Baptist attendances in 1903, with 1,052 on one morning and 1,036 in the evening.[35] Members, who belonged to the London Baptist Association in 1928,[36] numbered 1,205 in 1914 and 1,029 in 1939. From 1973 they worshipped in Park chapel, belonging to the United Reformed Church, while awaiting the rebuilding of their own church, which was demolished in 1974.[37]

Archway Road Baptist church, on the later corner

10 *Evangelical Mag.* xiv. 476.
11 Guildhall MS. 9558, f. 455.
12 G.R.O. Worship Returns, iii, no. 1137.
13 S. W. Kitchener, 'Hist. Hornsey. Chapter 4' (MS. notes in Hornsey libr.); *Hornsey Jnl.* 8 Nov. 1935.
14 See p. 197.
15 G.R.O. Worship Returns, iii, nos. 351, 359, 423, 643.
16 *Baptist Mag.* xlvii. 598; *D.N.B.*
17 G.R.O. Worship Returns, iii, no. 1293.
18 *Baptist Mag.* xlvii. 598; *D.N.B.*
19 For the hist. of individual chs. see below.
20 *Hall's Circuits and Ministers* (1897), 129, 181.
21 *Ferme Park Retrospect* (75th anniv. booklet, 1964), 22.
22 Mudie-Smith, *Rel. Life*, 408.
23 Except where otherwise stated, the following three paras. are based on *Ferme Park Retrospect*, 5 sqq.
24 The chapel was opened by Bapt. preachers, incl. Jos. Ivimey (see below, n. 55): *Evangelical Mag.* xiv. 476. A statement that it had also been used by Quakers cannot be verified.
25 Guildhall MS. 9558, f. 455.
26 Brewer, *Beauties of Eng. and Wales*, x (5), 213.
27 G.R.O., Worship Returns, iii, no. 1137.
28 *T.L.M.A.S.* xiii. 417.
29 H.O. 129/137/1/1/1.
30 Illus. (1898) in *T.L.M.A.S.* xiii. 413. A watercolour and photograph, ascribed respectively to 1880 and 1883, are in Potter Colln. 20/49, 57.
31 G.R.O. Worship Reg. no. 23000. In 1928 its date of origin was given as 1875: W. T. Whitley, *Baptists of Lond.* 213–14.
32 J. E. Ellis, *John Wm. Kirton*, 173.
33 *V.C.H. Mdx.* v. 360.
34 Mudie-Smith, *Rel. Life*, 407.
35 Ibid. 407.
36 Whitley, *Baptists of Lond.* 283.
37 Ex inf. the minister, Park chap.

of Wembury Road, was promoted by the London Baptist Association.[38] Building began in 1885[39] and continued in 1888[40] but the congregation temporarily disbanded before the opening of a new chapel, on the same site, in 1894.[41] Attendances numbered 323 in the morning and 398 in the evening on one Sunday in 1903[42] and there was seating for 700 in 1928.[43] The chapel had closed by 1941[44] and later was replaced by Highgate district synagogue.[45]

Emmanuel church, Duckett Road, probably originated as Hornsey Park Baptist chapel, registered at no. 114 Turnpike Lane in 1892 but vacated by 1896.[46] In 1903 there were 166 worshippers on one Sunday morning and 178 in the evening at Duckett Road.[47] Emmanuel church had closed by 1928.[48]

Muswell Hill Baptist church was also promoted by the London Baptist Association.[49] A chapel in Duke's Avenue, with a hall beneath, was founded in 1901[50] and registered in 1902.[51] It was attended by 314 on one Sunday morning and 372 in the evening in 1903[52] and had seating for *c.* 800,[53] later reduced to 750. The building is of red brick with stone dressings, in a Decorated style; its tower is surmounted by an octagonal lantern, with a spirelet. A hall for young people was opened at the rear of the church in 1957.[54]

STRICT BAPTISTS. Highgate Baptist chapel or tabernacle originated in a mission sent by the church of Eagle Street, Holborn, in 1809.[55] The old meeting-house in Southwood Lane stood empty in 1811[56] but had been acquired for worship, with help from Eagle Street, by 1814.[57] It may have been the Ebenezer chapel registered by Christopher Miller, a Highgate butcher, in 1829[58] but was later rebuilt[59] and was registered by Particular Baptists in 1861.[60] In 1851 there were 190 sittings, 50 of them free, and a congregation on census Sunday of 95 in the morning, 55 in the afternoon, and 118 in the evening.[61] By 1903 attendances were 66 in the morning and 122 in the evening, the smallest at any of Hornsey's six Baptist churches.[62] After numbers had fallen further,[63] the chapel was registered as Highgate tabernacle[64] by members of the London Baptist Association.[65] Although refurbished in 1960–1,[66] the building was disused in 1971[67] and served as a photographic studio in 1977, when it retained its galleries[68] and presented a stuccoed and pedimented front, with round-headed windows, to Southwood Lane. It was bought by Highgate School in 1977.[69]

Stroud Green chapel, Stapleton Hall Road, was established in 1878[70] and registered as Crouch Hill chapel by Particular Baptists in 1884.[71] A red-brick building in the Gothic style, with adjoining halls, was founded in 1889.[72] There were 280 worshippers in the morning and 396 in the evening on one Sunday in 1903.[73] There were 475 seats in 1928, by which date the church had joined the London Baptist Association,[74] and 460 in 1975.[75]

CONGREGATIONALISTS. Highgate Congregational chapel was founded in Southwood Lane, where in 1827 a site was sub-leased by the Revd. John Thomas to trustees who were to erect a chapel for the Village Itinerancy or Evangelical Association for the Propagation of the Gospel. The chapel was built in 1834, when the neighbouring building of 1778 was demolished, and in 1844 was called Highgate Congregational church.[76] In 1851 there were 400 sittings, 300 of them free, and the average attendance was 320 in the morning, including 70 Sunday-school children, and 200 in the evening.[77] It housed a British school from 1860 until 1874.[78] A building in South Grove, with a schoolroom underneath, was opened in 1859[79] to replace the chapel of 1834 and was later enlarged.[80] It seated 720 by 1894[81] and was attended by 312 in the morning and 203 in the evening on one Sunday in 1903.[82] Under Josiah Viney, minister in 1859, the chapel was active in local life.[83] The building was retained for regular worship, with seating reduced to 600,[84] until the formation of Highgate United Reformed church in 1967. The stone Gothic chapel in South Grove in 1976 temporarily housed Highgate district synagogue.[85] Highgate chapel established a mission at no. 33 North Hill in 1872;[86] it

38 Whitley, *Baptists of Lond.* 242.
39 Datestone.
40 Lloyd, *Highgate*, 466.
41 Whitley, *Baptists of Lond.* 283, 242.
42 Mudie-Smith, *Rel. Life*, 407.
43 Whitley, *Baptists of Lond.* 283.
44 G.R.O. Worship Reg. no. 34980.
45 Kitchener, 'Hist. Hornsey'.
46 G.R.O. Worship Reg. no. 33168.
47 Mudie-Smith, *Rel. Life*, 407.
48 Whitley, *Baptists of Lond.* 236.
49 Ibid. 250.
50 Ex inf. the church sec. Mrs. Jas. Edmondson laid one of the foundation stones.
51 G.R.O. Worship Reg. no. 39022.
52 Mudie-Smith, *Rel. Life*, 407.
53 Whitley, *Baptists of Lond.* 283.
54 Ex inf. the church sec.
55 J. Ivimey, *Hist. of Eng. Baptists*, iv. 409–10. The author was pastor of Eagle Street ch.: *D.N.B.*
56 Lysons, *Environs* (Suppl.), 200.
57 Ivimey, *Eng. Baptists*, iv. 409–10.
58 G.R.O. Worship Returns, iii, no. 1628.
59 Although it was said to have been rebuilt in 1836, when the freehold was bought (Lloyd, *Highgate*, 189 and Potter Colln. 14/70), the 17th-cent. building survived in 1851: H.O. 129/137/1/1/5. It was 'enlarged' in 1867: *Mdx. Dir.* (1870).
60 G.R.O. Worship Reg. no. 12413.
61 H.O. 129/137/1/1/5.
62 Mudie-Smith, *Rel. Life*, 407.
63 *Hornsey Jnl.* 3 Feb. 1961.
64 G.R.O. Worship Reg. no. 48311.
65 Whitley, *Baptists of Lond.* 283.
66 *Hornsey Jnl.* 3 Feb. 1961.
67 G.R.O. Worship Reg. no. 48311.
68 *Highgate Soc. News*, Jan. 1977.
69 Ex inf. the headmaster.
70 Whitley, *Baptists of Lond.* 222.
71 G.R.O. Worship Reg. no. 23811.
72 Date on building.
73 Mudie-Smith, *Rel. Life*, 407.
74 Whitley, *Baptists of Lond.* 283.
75 *Baptist Union Dir.* (1975–6).
76 Deeds in Highgate Sch. rec., box 4, bdle. 4; Lloyd, *Highgate*, 187.
77 H.O. 129/137/1/1/4.
78 See p. 193.
79 *Kelly's Dir. Essex, Herts. and Mdx.* (1908); *Highgate Cong. Chap. Yr. Bk.* (1859) (copy in Highgate Lit. and Sc. Inst.).
80 Thorne, *Environs*, 349.
81 *Cong. Yr. Bk.* (1894).
82 Mudie-Smith, *Rel. Life*, 176.
83 *Highgate Cong. Chap. Yr. Bk.* (1859 et seq.) (copies in Highgate Lit. and Sc. Inst.).
84 *Cong. Yr. Bk.* (1951).
85 Ex inf. the sec., Highgate Utd. Ref. ch.
86 *Cong. Yr. Bk.* (1894, 1951).

was described as undenominational in 1936[87] but again as Congregationalist in 1951, when it seated 180.[88] The hall was later acquired by Jehovah's Witnesses.[89]

Park chapel,[90] at the foot of Crouch Hill, was opened in 1855 and registered by Independents in 1856.[91] Alterations raised its seating to 1,017 in 1877[92] and 1,430 by 1894.[93] After further extensions it had 816 worshippers in the morning and 671 in the evening on one Sunday in 1903, the largest Congregationalist attendances in Hornsey.[94] The chapel and its halls formed a popular social centre, accommodating Hornsey British school until 1877 and later being described as a 'great church'.[95] From 1973 Baptists from Ferme Park shared Park chapel, by then a United Reformed church and still seating *c.* 1,400. The original Gothic building, with a corner turret and small spire,[96] had faced east along Haringey Park. In 1976 it formed part of an impressive stone range and was the northern end of a larger north–south chapel; at the southern end stood a church parlour, built in 1886, and on the north the Corbin hall, dated 1892. The Grove mission was apparently established in 1881 and served from Park chapel in 1951,[97] although a Grove united mission was also listed as undenominational.[98]

Mount View Congregational church was founded to serve Stroud Green, where land on the corner of Mount View and Granville roads was acquired with help from Park, Highgate, and Tollington Park chapels. A hall was opened in 1887 and used for worship until the completion of a building in the Decorated style, of red brick faced with terracotta, which in 1893 was to seat 1,000.[99] The pastorate was said to be prosperous[1] and on one Sunday in 1903 there were attendances of 330 in the morning and 231 in the evening.[2] The church was closed and demolished in 1935.[3]

Muswell Hill Congregational church presumably originated in Union church, Tetherdown, registered in 1891.[4] Union church stood opposite Page's Lane[5] and may have been only a hall, as a church at the corner of Queen's Avenue was begun in 1898 and the first registration of 1891 was cancelled in 1912. The new church, on land given by James Edmondson,[6] was registered in 1901[7] and was a Gothic building of brown roughcast with stone dressings. There were 850 sittings[8] and attendances on one Sunday in 1903 of 603 in the morning and 568 in the evening.[9] The building accommodated members of the former Presbyterian church from 1973 and seated 257 in 1976.[10]

METHODISTS. Middle Lane Wesleyan Methodist church[11] was founded in 1873, with help from the new Highgate circuit. The iron Trinity church in Hornsey High Street[12] was used until the opening of a brick building at the corner of Middle Lane and Lightfoot Road in 1886. It seated 1,000 and on one Sunday in 1903 there were attendances of 322 in the morning and 427 in the evening.[13] The church, in an early Gothic style, was demolished in 1975 and replaced by one of red brick and concrete, seating 200.[14]

Finsbury Park or Wilberforce Road Wesleyan Methodist church opened in 1871 in an iron building on land bought by Sir Francis Lycett at the corner of Wilberforce and Seven Sisters roads. A permanent church was used from 1875, being assigned to the new Finsbury Park circuit, and near-by stables, acquired for a Sunday school, were replaced by a hall in 1901. An offshoot was founded in 1878 in Gillespie Road, Islington.[15] The main church, later in Stoke Newington, had attendances of 630 in the morning and 495 in the evening on one Sunday in 1903.[16] The building, seating 1,000 in 1894,[17] was of brick with stone dressings, in the Gothic style, and had a north-west tower and spirelet. Between 1959[18] and 1976 it was replaced by a yellow-brick block, with the church behind, near the corner site.

A Wesleyan mission room at no. 66 Gordon Road, Hornsey Vale, was registered from 1884 until 1896.[19] Possibly the same room was used by the Church of England in 1908.[20]

Willoughby Road Wesleyan Methodist church[21] opened as a Sunday school chapel in 1885, on land acquired in 1882 near the corner of Hampden Road. Classrooms were built in 1889 and a church, perhaps replacing an iron one, was opened on the corner site to the east in 1893. A lecture hall and more classrooms were added to the north in 1903, when on one Sunday there were attendances of 822 in the morning and 1,124 in the evening.[22] The congregation, which belonged to the Finsbury Park circuit, was joined by many from Mattison Road in 1963.[23] After a fire in 1973 Willoughby Road church was replaced by a yellow-brick structure which, with the adjoining schoolroom in Hampden Road, seated 300. The

87 *Kelly's Dir. Hornsey* (1936).
88 *Cong. Yr. Bk.* (1951).
89 See below.
90 Except where otherwise stated, the para. is based on Kitchener, 'Hist. Hornsey', and information from the church sec.
91 G.R.O. Worship Reg. no. 7672.
92 *N. Mdx. Chron.* 3 Feb. 1877.
93 *Cong. Yr. Bk.* (1894).
94 Mudie-Smith, *Rel. Life*, 407.
95 W. R. Matthews, *Memories and Meanings*, 86.
96 Lithograph by T. Packer, 1859, in Potter Colln. 20/63.
97 *Cong. Yr. Bk.* (1951).
98 *Kelly's Dir. Hornsey* (1936); see below, p. 188.
99 *Independent and Nonconformist*, 2 Nov. 1893; G.R.O. Worship Reg. no. 30078.
1 A. Porritt, *A Home of Fellowship*, 46–7.
2 Mudie-Smith, *Rel. Life*, 407.
3 Kitchener, 'Hist. Hornsey'.
4 G.R.O. Worship Reg. no. 33028.
5 O.S. Map 6", Mdx. XII. NW. (1894–6 edn.).
6 Newspaper cuttings, 27 Oct. 1898, in Hornsey libr.
7 G.R.O. Worship Reg. no. 38288.
8 Cutting, 27 Oct. 1898, in Hornsey libr.
9 Mudie-Smith, *Rel. Life*, 407.
10 Ex inf. the sec., Muswell Hill Utd. Ref. ch.
11 Except where otherwise stated, the para. is based on *Middle Lane Meth. Ch. 1873–1973* (booklet), where the iron ch. and its successor are illus.
12 See p. 188.
13 Mudie-Smith, *Rel. Life*, 407.
14 Ex inf. the minister.
15 L. F. Church, *Finsbury Pk. Wesl. Ch. Jubilee Souvenir* (1925).
16 Mudie-Smith, *Rel. Life*, 161.
17 O.S. Map 1/2,500, Lond. III. 75 (1894 edn.).
18 *Finsbury Pk. Wesl. Ch.*; Stoke Newington, *Official Guide* [1947, 1959].
19 G.R.O. Worship Reg. no. 28049.
20 *Kelly's Dir. Essex, Herts. and Mdx.* (1908).
21 Except where otherwise stated, the para. is based on *Willoughby Rd. Meth. Ch.* (booklet, 1974) and information from Mrs. Dorothy Simpson.
22 Mudie-Smith, *Rel. Life*, 407.
23 *Hornsey Jnl.* 27 Sept. 1963; see below.

brick hall opened in 1903[24] was bought with the empty corner site by Haringey L.B. and survived in 1976.

Mattison Road, later Harringay, church opened as an iron tabernacle in 1891 and was replaced by a permanent church and halls in 1901.[25] A schoolroom was registered in 1900.[26] Originally sponsored by the Caledonian Road circuit of the Primitive Methodists, it joined the Finsbury Park circuit after the Methodists' union in 1931. There were attendances of 188 in the morning and 240 in the evening on one Sunday in 1903,[27] when membership was rising and Mattison Road was described as the chief Primitive Methodist church in London. A minister was shared with Grange Park from 1931 to 1942 and thereafter with Finsbury Park. The church, seating 400,[28] was of brick with stone dressings, in a Decorated style. It closed in 1963 and became a Roman Catholic church.[29]

A Wesleyan church in Inderwick Road belonged to the Finsbury Park circuit by 1898[30] and had attendances of 70 in the morning and 147 in the evening on one Sunday in 1903.[31] It belonged to the Highgate circuit in 1906[32] and apparently closed soon afterwards.

Muswell Hill Wesleyan Methodist church occupied a wooden building at the foot of the Avenue, Wood Green, in 1898 and moved to the corner of Colney Hatch Lane and Alexandra Park Road in 1899. The nave and transepts were built in that year and other parts in 1904.[33] The church belonged to the Highgate circuit[34] and had attendances of 349 in the morning and 305 in the evening on one Sunday in 1903.[35] The building is of red brick with stone dressings, in a Gothic style, and has a corner turret terminating in an octagonal lantern.

Highgate or Jackson's Lane Wesleyan Methodist church was opened in 1905, twelve years after a site had been obtained at the corner of Archway Road. The building included a Sunday school and was of red brick with stone dressings, designed in an early Gothic style by W. H. Boney of Highgate; the church seated 650 and the schoolroom 400.[36] Although well known in the 1960s for its counselling centre,[37] the church had closed by 1976.

PRESBYTERIANS. Highgate Presbyterian church, at the corner of Hornsey Lane and Cromwell Avenue, was built by the church extension committee of the London presbytery and opened in 1887.[38] There were attendances of 473 in the morning and 362 in the evening on one Sunday in 1903.[39] The building, of stone in a Decorated style, was known as Highgate United Reformed church from 1967 and seated 400 in 1976.[40]

Muswell Hill Presbyterian church, at the corner of Prince's Avenue and the Broadway, was registered in 1899[41] and completed in 1903,[42] when on one Sunday there were attendances of 489 in the morning and 328 in the evening.[43] The church was built of flint and terracotta, to the designs of G. Baines,[44] with late Gothic and *art nouveau* features, including a corner tower surmounted by a copper spirelet. Its materials and style later won widespread attention[45] and led to a campaign for its preservation after the Presbyterians joined the Congregationalists in 1973. The building, seating *c.* 600, was unused in 1976.[46]

BRETHREN. Cholmeley hall, in Archway Road opposite Cholmeley Park, was registered in 1890 by undesignated Christians.[47] Brethren worshipped there in 1903, when on one Sunday there were 195 in the morning and 200 in the evening.[48] Their fellowship, believed to have come from Clapton hall, Hackney, was renamed Cholmeley Evangelical church in 1966. The yellow-brick building, seating *c.* 250, included a hall and youth centre in 1976.[49]

By 1886 Plymouth Brethren, perhaps unconnected with Cholmeley hall, had a mission room in Archway Road.[50] In 1903 Brethren also met at no. 88 North Hill and no. 45 Woodstock Road, with morning attendances of 85 and 43 and evening attendances of 68 and 32 respectively; smaller groups worshipped in the drill hall, Southwood Lane, and no. 33 Stroud Green Road.[51] Plymouth Brethren registered the assembly rooms in Middle Lane, Crouch End, from 1916 until 1922 and a mission hall at no. 59 Park Road from 1921 until 1934.[52] They also met at Coleridge hall, Coleridge Road, in 1936, when no. 45 Woodstock Road was used by an unspecified denomination.[53] Alexandra hall, built on the parish boundary in Alexandra Road by 1901,[54] was a meeting-place of Brethren in 1968.[55]

In 1923 Brethren from Cholmeley hall had an iron room in St. James's Lane, Muswell Hill, which was registered from 1929 until 1935. After its demolition they used temporary meeting-places before buying a site in Wilton Road, Friern Barnet, where Wilton chapel was opened in 1952.[56]

THE SALVATION ARMY. Assembly rooms in Middle Lane were registered by Salvationists in 1907. The registration was cancelled in 1912,[57] presumably on the foundation of a citadel in Tottenham Lane,

[24] Datestone 1902.
[25] Except where otherwise stated, the para. is based on *St. Augustine of Canterbury* (souvenir brochure, 1965).
[26] G.R.O. Worship Reg. no. 37585.
[27] Mudie-Smith, *Rel. Life*, 408.
[28] *Hornsey Jnl.* 2 Aug. 1963.
[29] See p. 183.
[30] *Kelly's Dir. Hornsey and Wood Green* (1898–9).
[31] Mudie-Smith, *Rel. Life*, 407.
[32] *Kelly's Dir. Hornsey and Crouch End* (1905–6).
[33] *Beauty in the Sanctuary* (pamphlet on new windows, 1937); *Hornsey Jnl.* 17 Apr. 1959.
[34] *Kelly's Dir. Essex, Herts. and Mdx.* (1908).
[35] Mudie-Smith, *Rel. Life*, 407.
[36] *The Times*, 15 Sept. 1905.
[37] *Hornsey Jnl.* 28 Oct. 1960.
[38] Ibid. 5 Oct. 1962.
[39] Mudie-Smith, *Rel. Life*, 408.
[40] Ex inf. the sec.
[41] G.R.O. Worship Reg. no. 36982.
[42] Pevsner, *Mdx.* 114; there is a datestone of 1902.
[43] Mudie-Smith, *Rel. Life*, 408.
[44] *Hornsey Hist. Soc. Quarterly Bull.* June 1975, 9.
[45] J. Barnard, *Decorative Tradition*, 73 and plate 62.
[46] Ex inf. the sec., Muswell Hill Utd. Ref. ch.; *Hampstead and Highgate Express & News*, 30 Apr. 1976.
[47] G.R.O. Worship Reg. no. 32444.
[48] Mudie-Smith, *Rel. Life*, 408.
[49] Ex inf. the sec.; *P.O. Dir. Lond.* (1975).
[50] *Kelly's Dir. Hornsey* (1886); *Kelly's Dir. Mdx.* (1890).
[51] Mudie-Smith, *Rel. Life*, 408.
[52] G.R.O. Worship Reg. nos. 46775, 48171. A hall in Park Rd. was reg. by 'unsectarian Christians' in 1929: see below, n. 92.
[53] *Kelly's Dir. Hornsey* (1936).
[54] Ibid. (1901–2).
[55] *Free Ch. Dir.* (1968–9).
[56] G.R.O. Worship Reg. no. 51998; ex inf. Mr. J. E. Small.
[57] G.R.O. Worship Reg. no. 42712.

opposite Elmfield Avenue,[58] which was registered in 1913.[59] The building, of red brick with stone dressings, was damaged in the Second World War but it reopened in 1944[60] and remained in use in 1976.

MORAVIANS.[61] Hornsey Moravian church, in Priory Road, was founded in 1907[62] and consecrated in 1908.[63] Its congregation separated from the Moravian church in Fetter Lane, London, in 1910.[64] The church, of red brick with stone dressings in a 14th-century style, has a corner turret and spire. In 1976, when the first major alterations were planned, there was seating for *c.* 270. An adjacent hall was rebuilt in the 1930s.

SPIRITUALISTS. Felix hall, Crouch End, was used briefly by Spiritualists from 1925 and a shop in Church Lane, Hornsey, from 1936.[65] Christian Spiritualists registered nos. 56 and 58 Wightman Road for a few months in 1933.[66]

Muswell Hill Spiritualists met at a house in Tetherdown in 1936 and at the Athenaeum from 1939[67] until its demolition. From 1965 they hired a hall of Crescent Lodge hotel, Crouch End, until in 1968 they moved to no. 36 Waldegrave Road. In 1976 the house, also used as a dancing school, seated *c.* 40.[68]

SOCIETY OF FRIENDS. Meetings were held at the Athenaeum, Muswell Hill, in 1924[69] and a meeting-house in Church Crescent was built in 1926[70] and survived in 1976. At Highgate Quakers were established in 1953[71] and rented part of Davies's school of English, at no. 17 North Grove, in 1975.[72]

MENNONITES. During the Second World War relief work was undertaken by Mennonites in Shepherd's Hill, where, at no. 14, the London Mennonite Centre was founded in 1954. It served as an information centre and students' hostel, and had a chapel with an average Sunday attendance of 20 in 1976.[73]

OTHER DENOMINATIONS AND UNSPECIFIED MISSIONS. Highgate Wood Cottage, Jackson's Lane, was registered by Christians in 1851[74] and Christ Church, in Coach and Horses Lane, by Episcopalian dissenters from 1853 until 1896.[75] The Free English Church built the iron Trinity church in Hornsey High Street *c.* 1872 but sold it to the Methodists in 1873.[76] The drill hall in Southwood Lane, later used by Brethren, was registered by home missionaries in 1882.[77]

The Grove united mission registered a room at no. 14 the Grove, Crouch End, in 1878.[78] Perhaps it occupied premises near the corner of the Grove and Lynton Road, recorded in 1886[79] and attended by 51 in the morning and 58 in the evening on one Sunday in 1903,[80] although the original registration was cancelled in 1896 and a hall in the Grove was again registered, by undesignated Christians, in 1912.[81] The Grove united mission survived in 1936[82] and presumably was not connected with the Congregationalists' mission, which still existed in 1951.[83]

Shortly before the foundation of Highgate Unitarian church in Despard Road, Islington,[84] in 1885 Unitarians, including girls from Channing House school, worshipped in the drill hall at Crouch End.[85]

Hornsey tabernacle, Wightman Road, was registered for undenominational worship in 1893.[86] In 1903 it was used by 'disciples of Christ', with an average attendance on one Sunday of 58 in the morning and 118 in the evening,[87] and in 1912 it was registered as Hornsey Church of Christ.[88] Members joined Harringay Congregational church to form Harringay United church, Tottenham, in 1969,[89] whereupon the Wightman Road site was sold to the United Apostolic Faith Church.[90]

Broadway hall served the Universalist Church by 1903 and in 1910.[91] Unspecified Christians registered Park Road hall in 1929,[92] a room at no. 44 Coleridge Road from 1942 until 1949,[93] and no. 88 North Hill from 1944 until 1949.[94]

Christian Scientists were at no. 137 Stroud Green Road from *c.* 1912 until 1923 and thereafter at nos. 60 or 58 Crouch Hill until the Second World War.[95] They also had a reading room at no. 13 Topsfield Parade, Crouch End, in 1936.[96]

The Chapel of the Divine Love, a room at no. 83 Claremont Road, Highgate, was registered by the Evangelical Catholic Communion from 1938 until 1964.[97]

Jehovah's Witnesses acquired no. 33 North Hill as a Kingdom hall by 1964 and retained it in 1976.[98]

The United Apostolic Faith Church bought and renovated the former Hornsey tabernacle in 1970.

58 Datestone 1912.
59 G.R.O. Worship Reg. no. 45612.
60 *Hornsey Jnl.* 4 Feb. 1944.
61 Except where otherwise stated, the para. is based on information from the min.
62 Datestone on ch.
63 *Hornsey Jnl.* 3 Oct. 1958.
64 Ibid. 1 Nov. 1929.
65 Kitchener, 'Hist. Hornsey'.
66 G.R.O. Worship Reg. no. 54231. The near-by sanctuary at no. 65 Duckett Rd. was in Tottenham: *V.C.H. Mdx.* v. 363.
67 Kitchener, 'Hist. Hornsey'.
68 Ex inf. the church sec.
69 *Kelly's Dir. Hornsey* (1924).
70 Kitchener, 'Hist. Hornsey'.
71 Ex inf. Friends' Ho. libr.
72 *P.O. Dir. Lond.* (1975).
73 Ex inf. the warden.
74 G.R.O. Worship Returns, iii, no. 2392.
75 G.R.O. Worship Reg. no. 721.
76 *Middle La. Meth. Ch.* 4; see above, p. 186.
77 G.R.O. Worship Reg. no. 26292.
78 Ibid. 24012.
79 *Hutchings & Crowsley's Dir. Hornsey* (1886).
80 Mudie-Smith, *Rel. Life*, 408.
81 G.R.O. Worship Reg. nos. 24012, 54144.
82 *Kelly's Dir. Hornsey* (1936).
83 See p. 186.
84 *P.O. Dir. Lond.* (1934).
85 Dalton, *Channing Ho. Sch.* 10; undated newspaper cutting in Hornsey libr., Heal Colln.
86 G.R.O. Worship Reg. no. 33639.
87 Mudie-Smith, *Rel. Life*, 408.
88 G.R.O. Worship Reg. no. 45072.
89 *V.C.H. Mdx.* v. 362.
90 Ex inf. the gen. overseer, Utd. Apostolic Faith Ch.
91 *Kelly's Dir. Hornsey* (1903–4, 1910–11).
92 G.R.O. Worship Reg. no. 52069.
93 Ibid. 60021.
94 Ibid. 60892. In 1903 the premises had been used for undenominational services, as well as by Brethren.
95 *Kelly's Dir. Hornsey* (1912–13 and later edns.).
96 Ibid. (1936).
97 G.R.O. Worship Reg. no. 58302.
98 Ex inf. the branch manager, Watch Tower Bible and Tract Soc. of Pennsylvania; *P.O. Dir. Lond.* (1975).

A hall, offices, and premises for the Evangel Press were added in 1971 and flats in 1972. The church was called the Gospel Centre in 1977, when it seated *c.* 200 and was the headquarters of the group, which belonged to the Pentecostal movement.[99]

JUDAISM. Defoe found Highgate a favourite retreat of wealthy Jews, who lived there 'in good figure', served by their own butchers and other tradesmen. He also heard that there was a private synagogue,[1] which presumably was part of a house. Jewish residents, such as the Da Costas,[2] probably led Hyman Hurwitz to open his school by 1802.[3] A synagogue adjoined Hurwitz's buildings[4] but did not survive the school's closure.[5]

Public worship was confined to neighbouring parishes until a temporary building was opened by Hornsey and Wood Green affiliated synagogue in 1920. A new building on the same site in Wightman Road, seating *c.* 200, was founded in 1958 and opened in 1959.[6] In 1976 the congregation remained a local synagogue, affiliated to the United Synagogue in Upper Woburn Place, St. Pancras.[7]

Highgate district synagogue, so called from 1947,[8] originated in a community which bought no. 88 Archway Road in 1929. A synagogue for *c.* 400 was opened in 1937[9] but superseded by no. 200, on the corner of Wembury Road, in 1950. The building, a converted Baptist chapel partly refaced with yellow bricks, was damaged by fire in 1975.[10] Services thereafter were held in a room attached to St. Augustine's church and in the former Congregational church in South Grove, while new premises were sought.

Muswell Hill Jews at first worshipped in hired halls and a house in Methuen Park.[11] In 1946 they registered a hall on the ground floor of the Athenaeum[12] and in 1962 they bought a site at no. 31 Tetherdown, for a synagogue to hold 500. The congregation formed a district synagogue of the United Synagogue by 1962[13] and a constituent synagogue from 1976.[14]

EDUCATION. From 1791 occasional payments were made for teaching children in the workhouse to read and write.[15] Until the early 19th century, however, the poor received regular education only at Highgate, where Sir Roger Cholmley's free school, founded in 1565, catered for 40 local boys.[16] A late-17th-century school, to be supported by ladies' subscriptions, proved short-lived but a girls' charity school survived from *c.* 1719.[17] The master of the free school taught private pupils in 1819.[18] In that year his school was enlarged, with aid from the National Society,[19] and there were also boys' and girls' National schools at Hornsey, presumably of recent foundation. The parish, with a population of *c.* 4,000, had 170 places at four schools to support a claim that the poor possessed the means of education. There were also two day-academies and about a dozen boarding schools,[20] most of them at Highgate.[21]

From 1829 Cholmley's school was allowed to charge for extra subjects, so beginning its transformation, as Highgate School, into the modern public school. St. Michael's National school was built near by in compensation, and it soon absorbed the girls' charity school.[22] In 1835 the new school took 98 pupils and three nonconformist Sunday schools an additional 85, while 365 attended 20 private establishments.[23] A National school opened at Muswell Hill in 1850 and British schools at Highgate by 1854 and Hornsey in 1865. Evening classes were started at the National schools in Highgate[24] and Muswell Hill[25] in 1856 and at a room in North Hill by Highgate Congregational church in 1868.[26] From 1861 Roman Catholic children from Highgate could attend St. Joseph's schools, on the Islington side of the boundary,[27] but Cholmley's foundation grew too expensive for the lower middle class, for whom a 'semi-classical or commercial day-school' was needed.[28] A small offshoot of St. Joseph's was established at Crouch End in 1871 and another National school, Holy Innocents', arose from a rebuilding of 1872. In South Hornsey detached, a day-school opened in 1868 at a Sunday school built by Milton Road Congregational church. Children from there also went to National schools attached to the churches of St. Matthias and St. Faith, in Stoke Newington.[29]

A school board for the whole parish was formed amid general agreement in 1874, after a rising population in South Hornsey combined with decisions to close the British schools to threaten a deficiency of some 1,600 places. The board, initially of nine members headed by the rector, met at Southwood Lane.[30] Its most urgent problem was in South Hornsey detached, where Milton Congregational school was about to close: the London board refused to help pay for new accommodation,

[99] Ex inf. the gen. overseer.
[1] D. Defoe, *Tour through Eng. and Wales* (Everyman edn. 1928), ii. 3.
[2] *Trans. Jewish Hist. Soc.* xxi. 80; see above, p. 135.
[3] See p. 197.
[4] Brewer, *Beauties of Eng. and Wales*, x(5), 216.
[5] Howitt, *Northern Heights*, 398.
[6] *Hornsey Jnl.* 20 June 1958; 15 May 1959.
[7] Ex inf. the hon. sec.
[8] Except where otherwise stated, the para. is based on information from the rabbi.
[9] *The Times*, 23 Aug. 1937.
[10] Ibid. 31 Oct. 1975.
[11] Ex inf. the sec.
[12] G.R.O. Worship Reg. no. 61365.
[13] *Hornsey Jnl.* 28 Sept. 1962.
[14] Ex inf. the sec.
[15] M.R.O., D.R.O. 20/C1/1, ff. 157, 176, 240.
[16] For the hist. of Highgate Sch. see *V.C.H. Mdx.* i. 302–4.
[17] For individual schs. see below. Schools in S. Hornsey are reserved for treatment under Stoke Newington.
[18] *Educ. of Poor Digest*, 538.
[19] *Camden Hist. Rev.* ii. 9.
[20] *Educ. of Poor Digest*, 538.
[21] For private schs. see below.
[22] *Camden Hist. Rev.* ii. 9, 11.
[23] *Educ. Enquiry Abs.* 565.
[24] St. Mic.'s sch., mins. of managers, Mar. 1856.
[25] I. T. Plant, *Story of St. James's Sch.* (centenary booklet), 6.
[26] *Highgate Cong. Chap. Yr. Bk.* (1868), 28.
[27] *Buzz*, May 1969; *Rep. of Educ. Cttee. of Council, 1865–6* [3666], p. 555, H.C. (1866), xxvii.
[28] *Schs. Enquiry Com. 1867–8* [3966–X], p. 35, H.C. (1867–8), xxviii (9).
[29] Hornsey sch. bd. mins. i. 31–2, in Bruce Castle Mus.
[30] Lloyd, *Highgate*, 459–60; *N. Mdx. Chron.* 19, 26 Dec. 1874. Except where otherwise stated, the rest of the para. is based on Hornsey sch. bd. mins. i–ii, *passim*.

the Education Department opposed the choice of any site which might affect Stoke Newington's schools, and land had to be compulsorily purchased. T. Chatfeild Clarke was appointed architect in 1876 and building started at Crouch End and Highgate, as well as in South Hornsey. After charges of profiteering, several members pledged to economy were elected to the board in 1877. They took control by forcing resignations and were themselves accused of proposing a general reduction in salaries and the employment of unqualified teachers, and of suppressing the fact that 478 South Hornsey children attended elementary schools outside the parish.[31] In 1880 a more liberal board was returned, of eleven members and with H. R. Williams as chairman.

In 1881 there were 4,602 children aged three to fourteen, almost half of them in South Hornsey, and 3,917 places, of which 2,000 were at the board's, 1,447 at the National, and 470 at private schools. The figures excluded the rapidly growing districts of Finsbury Park and Stroud Green, partially served by sixteen private establishments,[32] where middle-class families around Oakfield Road opposed any public elementary school.[33] Similar hostility was shown on the Harringay Park estate, where purchasers were not told by the British Land Co. that the board as early as 1883 had bought a site between Falkland and Frobisher roads. Attacked by builders and householders in both areas and by the vicars of St. Paul's and Holy Trinity, the board wavered throughout the 1880s. Meanwhile the problem of 'border children' grew worse: Tottenham had over 100 Hornsey pupils in 1889[34] and the London board, which refused admission to 200 in 1892, prompted the Education Department to remonstrate with Hornsey.[35]

Deficiencies near the eastern boundary were largely met during the 1890s with the building of Harringay, Stroud Green, and Campsbourne schools. By 1900 there were vacancies at Highgate and Muswell Hill, although places were still short at Harringay. Stroud Green school had been sited well south of Oakfield Road, to serve Brownswood Park in the peninsular part of South Hornsey. The board therefore opposed the transfer of that part, with the detached portions farther east, to London in 1899. At the same time Hornsey received the outlying portion of Clerkenwell at Muswell Hill.[36]

Secondary education for the poor was provided in 1890 only at denominational halls in Stroud Green.[37] In 1882, however, H. R. Williams had suggested that the district might support a higher grade school,[38] as residents soon confirmed,[39] and in 1888 his retirement had been commemorated by a scholarship tenable at a secondary school.[40] There was also a proposal to devote Roger Draper's charity to technical education.[41] Hornsey National schools were 'upper-grade' in 1899, when Col. J. W. Bird conveyed £1,500 in trust to support scholarships there.[42] The board itself in its final months began to build a higher elementary school and a special instruction school next to its new South Harringay school.[43] Truants were sent to the Bath industrial school until in 1884 the board joined Tottenham and Edmonton in establishing the North London Truants' industrial school at Walthamstow,[44] where 169 Hornsey boys had gone by 1900. Land for a polytechnic was offered by the board to Middlesex county council.[45] From 1904 the Hornsey educational foundation offered 12–16 exhibitions for boys and girls at technical schools. The exhibitions, in wide demand,[46] were normally tenable outside Hornsey but in 1926, in spite of objections that they should be restricted to trade schools, they were extended to special courses at Hornsey council schools.[47] It was decided to abandon them in 1933 and plans to assist technical or commercial schools with a substantial scientific curriculum and to pay pupils' incidental expenses[48] were embodied in a Scheme of 1937.[49]

Hornsey became a Part III authority, responsible for elementary education, under the Act of 1902. The board's successor, the education committee, met from 1903 until 1920 at no. 206 Stapleton Hall Road.[50] The committee took pride in relatively small classes, taught only by qualified teachers with good salaries.[51] It vainly sought responsibility for secondary education in 1904[52] and conducted its own census into the needs of children beyond the age of 15 in 1905–6.[53] Finding that provision was dependent on private schools, Hornsey co-operated closely with Middlesex in taking over and enlarging the poorer ones.[54] Funds from the Pauncefort charity were available from 1903 to support three, later five, girls at secondary schools[55] and a further income was derived from the Hornsey educational foundation.[56] Advanced courses were introduced at elementary schools, Stroud Green and South Harringay, in 1920[57] and extended in 1923.[58] By the late 1920s between 25 and 30 per cent of Hornsey's children received secondary education. The proportion exceeded that aimed at for Middlesex as a whole,[59] partly because many children were educated privately. Over 7,000 pupils attended public elementary schools *c.* 1932, when there were *c.* 2,000 at six secondary schools and a similar number at private schools. Most elementary schools had been organized into senior and junior sections and nine offered

31 *N. Mdx. Chron.* 12 Apr. 1880.
32 Ibod. 18 Mar. 1882.
33 Ibid. 13 Oct. 1888.
34 *Hornsey Hist. Soc. Quarterly Bull.*, ii (7), 4–5; ii (8), 3–6.
35 Hornsey libr., Heal Colln., election address.
36 Hornsey sch. bd. *Rep. by Chairman* (1898–1900), 7–8, 11 (copy in Hornsey libr.).
37 See p. 195.
38 *N. Mdx. Chron.* 2 Dec. 1882.
39 Hornsey sch. bd. mins. iii. 318–19.
40 TS. notes in Hornsey libr.
41 *N. Mdx. Chron.* 28 Apr. 1888.
42 Char. Com. files.
43 *Hornsey Boro. 1903–53*, 26.
44 Hornsey sch. bd. mins. iii. 318, 347–52, 361 and *passim.*
45 *Rep. by Chairman* (1898–1900), 17.
46 Hornsey Par. Chars. *Chairman's Reps.* (1904–5, 1912–21).
47 *Hornsey Jnl.* 28 Jan. 1927.
48 Ibid. 10 Feb. 1933.
49 See p. 202.
50 Hornsey educ. cttee. min. bk. i et seq., in Bruce Castle Mus.
51 H. B. Brackenbury, *Boro. of Hornsey. Review of Wk. of Educ. Cttee. 1903–12*, in Hornsey libr.
52 Petition for cnty. boro. status in Hornsey libr.
53 Hornsey educ. cttee. min. bk. iv. 101–25.
54 *Hornsey Boro. 1903–53*, 26.
55 Hornsey educ. cttee. min. bk. i. 115, ii. 51.
56 Hornsey par. chars., *Chairman's Rep.* 1913.
57 Hornsey educ. cttee. *Memo. by Chairman* (1924), 8.
58 Hornsey educ. cttee. min. bk. xxi. 83–4, 155.
59 *Hornsey Jnl.* 6 Nov. 1964.

commercial and practical courses to senior pupils.[60] The county council supported Hornsey School of Art from 1904[61] and four evening institutes in the 1930s.[62]

Under the Act of 1944, Hornsey became an 'excepted district'.[63] After further building and amalgamation the education committee in 1963 was responsilbe for 23 primary schools, of which 6 were for juniors and infants combined, 6 secondary modern schools, and 3 grammar schools. Five of the primary schools and one secondary school were Voluntary Aided, and one primary and one grammar school were Voluntary Controlled.[64] The 10,500 children in state schools included *c.* 1,500 immigrants, of whom over a third were Cypriot and a quarter West Indian; nearly a quarter of the infants were immigrants, mostly at Crouch End, Harringay, and Stroud Green.[65] The Hornsey parochial charities (educational and vocational foundation) was established in 1955, out of the educational foundation and the apprenticing charities. By 1960 it had an income of over £4,000, devoted to exhibitions for higher education and assisting institutions not provided by the local authority.[66] Applications increased from 1964, until by 1975 grants to individuals exceeded £1,000 and those to institutions were £4,300, divided mainly between Harringay boys' club, the Y.M.C.A., and Church of England schools.[68]

From 1965 Hornsey was joined with Tottenham and Wood Green in Haringey L.B., which reorganized secondary education on comprehensive lines in 1967.[69] In 1975 the former borough contained 11 schools for infants, 11 for juniors, and 5 for infants and juniors together, and 5 secondary schools.[70]

Elementary schools founded before 1874.[71] The Ladies' school or hospital at Highgate was described in 1680 by its founder, William Blake, as a 'charity school',[72] apparently the earliest use of that term.[73] Blake was a London vintner, who bought the old banqueting house annexed to Arundel House.[74] He published an architect's engraving[75] and later drew a detailed bird's-eye view[76] of his proposed school, on the site of Old Hall and no. 16 South Grove; his own house stood farther west, opposite Dorchester House, which he acquired as accommodation for girls. In the event he built only a house[77] on the green, behind the Flask, began to fill it with 40 fatherless boys from Highgate, Hornsey, and Hampstead, and in 1679 asked some noble ladies and rich merchants' wives to contribute to the first year's costs. Pupils were clothed as at London's Bluecoat school; apart from reading and writing, the boys would learn painting, gardening, accounts, and navigation, and the girls domestic crafts. A public appeal was launched in 1680,[78] shortly before the purchase of Dorchester House with help from Sir Francis Pemberton and William Ashurst. Six London vestries promised to send children and in 1683 the school was described as famous,[79] but it lacked local support and foundered through family hostility and the indifference of fashionable subscribers.[80] In 1682 Blake was imprisoned for debt in Newgate, whence he issued a vain appeal[81] in 1685. His own house had been sold to Ashurst and Dorchester House had passed to Pemberton, together with nos. 1–6 the Grove, which had been built to secure an income for the school and remained its only memorial.[82]

Highgate girls' charity school was founded by the governors of the free school, who had chosen 24 girls and appointed a mistress by 1719.[83] Among the governors was Edward Pauncefort, who soon built a classroom and a house for the mistress in the middle of his row of alms-houses in Southwood Lane and who, by will dated 1723, ordered the purchase of land worth £60, to provide £30 a year for the alms-people, £10 for the reader at Highgate chapel, and the residue for the school. No land was bought and the school received only £5 p.a. from stock paid for by Pauncefort's heir under a decree of 1751, when the other beneficiaries enjoyed their full payments. The school saved enough from contributions to buy £1,000 stock but sold it in 1812 to meet the debts of Pauncefort's charity, which thereafter paid a dividend from the general fund. In 1819 the school's income was £112, of which £77 came from an annual sermon. Twenty-six girls were taught reading, writing, arithmetic, and plain work but only 20 were also clothed.[84] There were still 26 pupils in 1843,[85] shortly before the institution was absorbed in St. Michael's schools. The school-house survived, with the alms-houses, in 1976.

60 Boro. of Hornsey, *Rep. of Special Cttee. on Pub. Educ.* 39–41.
61 *Hornsey Jnl.* 4 Dec. 1936.
62 *Rep. of Special Cttee. on Pub. Educ.* 42.
63 *Hornsey Boro. 1903–53*, 27.
64 Mdx. C.C. educ. cttee. *List . . . 1963*.
65 *Hornsey Jnl.* 8 Mar. 1963, 3 Jan. 1964.
66 Hornsey par. chars., Scheme of Min. of Educ. 1955, in Hornsey libr.
67 Ex inf. Revd. P. E. Brassel.
68 Char. Com. files.
69 *V.C.H. Mdx.* v. 365.
70 Ex. inf. Haringey L.B., chief educ. offr.
71 In the following accounts of individual schs., attendance figures for 1898 are from *Schs. in Receipt of Parl. Grants, 1898–9* [C. 9454], p. 169, H.C. (1899), lxxiv; figs. for 1906 are from *Public Elem. Schs. 1906* [Cd. 3510], p. 452, H.C. (1907), lxiii; and those for 1919, 1932, and 1936 from *Bd. of Educ., List 21, 1919, 1932, 1936* (H.M.S.O.). Except where otherwise stated, figs. for 1975 have been supplied by the headmaster or headmistress.
72 [W. Blake], *The Ladies Charity School-house Roll*, 40. The work, a description of the sch. with an appeal for continued support, prefaces a sermon called *Silver Drops or Serious Things* by Blake, 'house-keeper' to the sch. A copy, apparently owned by Blake, is at Highgate Lit. and Sc. Inst.
73 J. Jennings, *Pol. Theory of Elem. Educ.* 3. Except where otherwise stated, the rest of the para. is based on Sir Jas. Brown, 'The Ladyes Hospital' (TS. copy of lecture in Highgate Lit. and Sc. Inst.), which amplifies and in some respects corrects L.C.C. *Survey of Lond.* xvii. 52–4, 89–90.
74 See p. 126.
75 *Survey of Lond.* xvii, plate 40.
76 Ibid., plate 39.
77 The sch. is illus. in Blake's appeal (see above, n. 72) and in *Gent. Mag.* lxx (2), facing p. 721.
78 See above, n. 72. The letters sent in 1679 were printed as part of the appeal.
79 *Diary of Ralph Thoresby*, ed. J. Hunter, i. 161.
80 M. G. Jones, *Char. Sch. Movement*, 53.
81 *Charity Martyrd*: copy in Highgate Lit. and Sc. Inst. Blake died in 1690 or 1691.
82 See p. 126.
83 Highgate Sch. rec., governors' min. bk. 1576–1810, f. 84r. The bk. also records later appts. of the mistress.
84 *2nd Rep. Com. for Educ. of Poor*, H.C. 547, pp. 105–6 (1819), x-B.
85 *Digest of Schs. and Chars. for Educ.* H.C. 435, p. 177 (1843), xviii. Collections were recorded in the churchwardens' accts. until 1842: M.R.O., D.R.O. 20/B1/1.

St. Mary's or Hornsey National schools, for 60 boys and 55 girls in 1835,[86] may have originated in a girls' establishment founded in 1800.[87] By 1819 there was a school for boys, supported by subscriptions totalling £70 a year, and another for girls, supported by £90 and by £45 from their needlework.[88] The boys' school stood on the north side of Priory Road and was ½ mile from the girls',[89] built by 1815[90] and rebuilt in 1832[91] in Tottenham Lane on former glebe land. An infants' school was opened near the girls' in 1848,[92] raising the total accommodation to 210, and a government grant was made to all three schools from 1849.[93] In 1850, after enlargement, the boys' school was reported to be much improved and the girls' to be excellent.[94] Combined attendance was 224 in 1865 and 266 in 1872,[95] before the opening of new buildings for the boys in 1873[96] and infants in 1884,[97] both in High Street, and extensions to the girls' school. There were places for 300 boys, 235 girls, and 250 infants by 1890[98] and vacancies, notably among the infants, in 1906 and 1919. All three departments were classed as upper-grade schools by 1899[99] but the description was abandoned in 1904 and they were regarded as one school from 1905.[1] Both boys and girls used a building which opened with 428 places in High Street in 1929, whereupon accommodation for 240 infants was provided in Tottenham Lane.[2] The rebuilding was paid for largely by the grocer David Greig, a former pupil, who in 1932 endowed a trust fund.[3] Seniors and juniors were separated in High Street in 1953 and the juniors took over the whole site in 1964, on the dispersal of the senior girls and removal of the boys to St. David's school in Rectory Gardens. St. David's joined St. Katharine's in 1976 and St. Mary's junior school took over Rectory Gardens, leaving the High Street buildings to be demolished. Meanwhile St. Mary's infants' school moved to Church Lane in 1971, the Tottenham Lane buildings also being demolished. Both schools were Voluntary Aided in 1976, when there were 220 juniors and 209 full-time infants on the rolls.[4]

St. Michael's National school, Highgate,[5] started with classes in a room rented from Cholmley's school. A school-house, similarly leased, was built in 1833 next to the alms-houses in Southwood Lane, with classrooms for *c.* 100 boys and 100 girls.[6] In 1839 an infants' school, holding *c.* 125, was erected at the corner of Castle Yard. Voluntary contributions and school pence provided a total income of £207 in 1848.[7] On the school's move in 1852 its old premises were leased out by Cholmley's school and by 1885 those in Southwood Lane were houses known as nos. 1–3 School Place.[8]

St. Michael's school was transformed through local enthusiasm for the 'industrial' system, stimulated in 1850 by Harry Chester of South Grove, assistant secretary to the Privy Council committee on education, and the Revd. T. H. Causton. Subscribers included the bishop of London, Miss Burdett-Coutts, and Lord Mansfield, and Chester secured an unprecedentedly large government grant.[9] Premises in North Road, designed by Anthony Salvin with accommodation for 150 boys, 120 girls, and 150 infants,[10] were opened in 1852; three teachers' houses and twelve dormitories were included and 4 a. were reserved for a farm.[11] It was hoped that the curriculum, to include husbandry for boys and domestic training for girls, would encourage the poor to keep their children at school. St. Michael's National and Industrial schools were managed by a distinguished committee and continued in the 1850s to be a showplace. Almost immediately, however, there were arguments over teaching dissenters' children the catechism,[12] which led to the establishment of a rival British school. From the 1860s the farming side was reduced: idealism waned, practical experience was lacking, parents demanded a more conventional education, and the government eventually ceased to subsidize 'industrial work'. Later there were many vacancies, since accommodation was for 505 in 1880–1,[13] 602 in 1898, and 656 in 1906, when the attendances were 341, 401, and 396. The school, however, took some children from the St. Pancras side of Highgate until 1906.[14] It was reorganized into senior and junior mixed departments in 1922, with total accommodation for 430 and an attendance of 304, and then into junior mixed and infants' departments, with 364 places and 172 pupils in 1938.[15] St. Michael's was later given Voluntary Aided status and enlarged to hold 437 pupils on the roll in 1975,[16] when part of it still occupied Salvin's grey-brick, stone-dressed buildings.

St. James's National school, Muswell Hill,[17] was built and opened in 1850. It stood in Fortis Green near the corner with Tetherdown,[18] on land given

86 *Educ. Enquiry Abs.* 565.
87 Drawing of later sch. and note by John Buckler: B.L. Add. MS. 36369, f. 195.
88 *Educ. of Poor Digest*, 538.
89 Ed. 7/87; Nat. Soc. files.
90 M.R.O., MR/DE Hornsey.
91 B.L. Add. MS. 36369, f. 195. It is not clear if the 'old sch.-ho. at Crouch End', ibid. f. 194, was a predecessor of the boys' or girls' schs.
92 Ed. 7/87; Nat. Soc. files. Prints of the boys' and girls' (*recte* infts'.) schs., from *Illus. Lond. News*, are in Hornsey libr.
93 *Mins. of Educ. Cttee. of Council, 1848–9* [1215], pp. li, ccxvi, H.C. (1850), xliii.
94 Ibid. *1850–1* [1357], p. 49, H.C. (1851), xliv.
95 *Rep. of Educ. Cttee. of Council, 1865–6* [3666], p. 555, H.C. (1866), xxvii; ibid. *1872–3* [C. 812], p. 457, H.C. (1873), xxiv.
96 Ex inf. the headmaster, St. Mary's jnr. sch. The bldg., dtd. 1872, survived in 1976.
97 Ed. 7/87. The former inf. sch. became Holy Innocents'; see below.
98 *Kelly's Dir. Essex, Herts. and Mdx.* (1890).
99 *Schs. in Receipt of Parl. Grants, 1898*, 169.
1 Hornsey educ. cttee. min. bk. iii. 23, 134.
2 *Bd. of Educ., List 21, 1932* (H.M.S.O.).
3 *Hornsey Jnl.* 25 Oct. 1929; *The Times*, 12 Dec. 1932.
4 Ex inf. the headmaster and the headmistress.
5 Except where otherwise stated, the following two paras. are based on *Camden Hist. Rev.* ii. 11–12.
6 *Educ. Enquiry Abs.* 565.
7 Ed. 7/87.
8 Leases in Highgate Sch. rec., box 3, bdle. 3.
9 Nat. Soc. files (list of subs.).
10 Ibid. (report). Reps. and circulars of Highgate schs. bldg. cttee. in Highgate Lit. and Sc. Inst.
11 *St. Mic.'s Par. Mag.* Apr. 1903.
12 Nat. Soc. files; Potter Colln. 14/45–7; circular letter by vicar, 1853, in Hornsey libr.
13 *Rep. of Educ. Cttee. of Council, 1880–1* [C. 2948–I], p. 634, H.C. (1881), xxxii.
14 Hornsey educ. cttee. min. bk. ii. 135; iv. 77.
15 *Bd. of Educ., List 21, 1922, 1938* (H.M.S.O.).
16 Ex inf. the headmaster.
17 Except where otherwise stated, the para. is based on I. T. Plant, *Story of St. James's Sch.*
18 Guildhall MS. 1281.

The second church *c.* 1835

Interior of the third church in 1968

ST. MARY'S CHURCH, HORNSEY

The first church of St. Mary in 1798

St. John's church, Brownswood Park

Interior of St. Luke's church, Mayfield Road

HORNSEY

by the bishop of London. The building was designed by Salvin and intended for infants who would later go to Hornsey National schools. By 1858, however, when the income came mainly from voluntary contributions and weekly pence, 58 infants and older girls were taught by an uncertificated mistress.[19] Older boys followed and by 1870 St. James's took 100 of Muswell Hill's 164 children aged 5 to 13, while Hornsey took 21. Enlargements raised the accommodation to 124 by 1878[20] and 292 by 1898, although attendances reached only 88 and 144. There was temporary overcrowding in 1912 and reduced accommodation, for 269, by 1919. St. James's was reorganized as a primary school, for pupils aged 5 to 11, after extensions in 1931. It moved to Woodside Avenue in 1968 and was Voluntary Aided, with 220 children on the roll, in 1975. The old buildings appeared unaltered from the front in 1950, except for bomb damage to a spire, and were demolished in 1969.[21]

Highgate British school was founded in 1852,[22] as a result of nonconformist disillusion with St. Michael's, and by 1854 received a government grant for a certificated master.[23] In 1859, when the treasurer was James Yates, the school occupied cramped premises in Southwood Lane, with 85 boys and 87 girls on the roll. It took over the old Congregational chapel in 1860[24] and had a headmaster, an assistant, and two mistresses in 1870.[25] Average attendance was 140 in 1873,[26] shortly before its replacement by Highgate board school.[27]

Hornsey British school was built in 1864 and opened in 1865, largely through the efforts of Russell Maynard, a member of Park chapel and active in the British and Foreign Schools Society. The schoolrooms, for boys, girls, and infants, adjoined the chapel on the site of the later Corbin hall. The school was supported by voluntary contributions and pence in 1870[28] but received a parliamentary grant from 1871. Between 1871 and 1873 the average attendance rose from 94 to 177.[29] Hornsey school board took over the premises in 1875 and later moved the pupils to Park Road.[30]

Crouch End Roman Catholic, or St. Mary's, school opened in 1871 next to the new chapel and priest's house in Tottenham Lane. It was an old building, leased from the Passionists of St. Joseph's Retreat and consisting of a schoolroom for boys and girls and another for infants. The income came from voluntary contributions and pence and the management was like that of St. Joseph's schools.[31] The school received no parliamentary grant and apparently was short-lived.

Holy Innocents' National school was the name later given to the old St. Mary's infants' school, which was rebuilt in 1872 before the opening of Holy Innocents' church.[32] It was for infants only and received a parliamentary grant by 1888, when there were 127 places.[33] The school was rarely full, with 114 places in 1893,[34] but in 1907 its proposed closure was resisted by the managers, who stressed its benefits to the poor of Hornsey Vale. From 1919 there were 101 places and in 1922 control passed to the education committee. The premises, by that time overcrowded, were thereafter leased from the trustees, the vicar of Holy Innocents' and the archdeacon of Middlesex,[35] until their replacement by Rokesly school in 1934.[36] The core of the old brick building, on the corner of Rokesly Avenue and Tottenham Lane, was used as a public convenience and shelter in 1976.

Elementary schools founded 1874–1903. Crouch End board school[37] moved from the former British school to Park Road in 1877. The accommodation, originally for 602,[38] rose to 984 by 1884[39] and 1,442 in 1888,[40] but had fallen to 1,259 by 1898, after transfers to the new Stroud Green and Campsbourne schools. After renovation and the removal of older girls to Campsbourne, Crouch End school reopened in 1935 with places for 400 mixed juniors and 360 senior boys.[41] Under the Act of 1944 the boys formed a separate secondary modern school, later absorbed by Priory Vale.[42] Crouch End junior school closed in 1975, when it had 110 pupils on the roll.

Highgate board school, which leased the former British school in 1875, moved to a new building in North Hill in 1877.[43] The old premises were thereupon sold by Highgate Congregational chapel to Cholmley's school,[44] to become laboratories.[45] Extensions, the largest being in 1893–4,[46] raised the accommodation from 213 in 1880[47] to 877, in mixed and infants' departments, by 1898. In 1919 there were only senior and junior mixed departments, which were progressively reduced to accommodate 592 by 1936, when further reorganization produced 464 places for juniors and 192 for infants. North Hill junior and infants' schools remained at North Hill in 1975, with 220 and 130 children on their respective rolls.

[19] Ed. 7/87.
[20] *Rep. of Educ. Cttee. of Council, 1878–9* [C. 2342–I], p. 958, H.C. (1878–9), xxiii.
[21] Ex inf. the headmaster.
[22] *Roger Draper's Char.* (1863) in Hornsey libr.
[23] *Mins. of Educ. Cttee. of Council, 1854–5* [1926], p. 200, H.C. (1854–5), xlii.
[24] *Highgate Cong. Chap. Yr. Bk.* (1859), 15; (1860), 40. Lease to Yates and other trustees, 1860, in Highgate Sch. rec., box 4, bdle. 4.
[25] *Hampstead and Highgate Express Dir.* (1870).
[26] *Rep. of Educ. Cttee. of Council, 1873–4* [C. 1019–I], p. 374, H.C. (1874), xviii.
[27] The premises are described in a letter from the surveyor of Highgate Sch., 1876, *penes* Messrs. Bower, Cotton & Bower.
[28] Ed. 7/87; T. E. Turkington, 'Brief Hist. of Crouch End Sch.' (duplicated centenary booklet).
[29] *Rep. of Educ. Cttee. of Council, 1871–2* [C. 601], p. 303, H.C. (1872), xxii; ibid. *1872–3*, p. 457.
[30] Turkington, op. cit.
[31] Ed. 7/87.
[32] *Kelly's Dir. Essex, Herts. and Mdx.* (1890); O.S. Map 6", Mdx. XII. NW. (1873–6 edn.). Postcard and photo. in Hornsey libr.
[33] *Rep. of Educ. Cttee. of Council, 1888–9* [C. 5804–I], p. 601, H.C. (1889), xxix.
[34] Ibid. *1893–4* [C. 7437–I], p. 911, H.C. (1894), xxix.
[35] Hornsey educ. cttee. min. bk. v. 110, 122; xxi. 45, 86–7.
[36] *Bd. of Educ., List 21, 1936* (H.M.S.O.).
[37] Except where otherwise stated, the para. is based on Turkington, 'Crouch End Sch.'.
[38] *Rep. of Educ. Cttee. of Council, 1880–1*, 635.
[39] Ibid. *1884–5* [C. 4483–I], p. 592, H.C. (1884–5), xxiii.
[40] Ibid. *1888–9*, 601.
[41] *Bd. of Educ., List 21, 1936* (H.M.S.O.); *Hornsey Jnl.* 18 Nov. 1935.
[42] See p. 195.
[43] Ex inf. the headmaster, Highgate jnr. sch.
[44] Deeds in Highgate Sch. rec., box 4, bdle. 4.
[45] C. A. Evors, *Hist. Highgate Sch.* (1938 edn.), 13.
[46] Ex inf. Mrs. R. E. Jobson.
[47] *Rep. of Educ. Cttee. of Council, 1880–1*, 635.

Harringay board school, between Falkland and Frobisher roads, opened in 1893. It accommodated 1,475 boys, girls, and infants in 1898, when they occupied separate floors and when there was also a temporary mixed department for 480, making it the largest of Hornsey's schools.[48] The school, called North Harringay from 1903,[49] accommodated only 1,160 by 1932 and was reorganized into junior mixed and infants' schools in 1934; senior girls were transferred, while senior boys continued to use the top floor as a secondary modern school, later absorbed into Priory Vale.[50] In 1976 the upper floors of the board school building were occupied by North Harringay junior school, with 411 on the roll, and the ground floor and extensions by the infants', with 258 enrolled.

Stroud Green board school opened in temporary buildings in Stroud Green Road in 1894. From 1896 it used a new building in Woodstock Road,[51] with accommodation for 1,351 boys, girls, and infants on separate floors.[52] There were 1,052 places by 1932, when the school was reorganized into a senior mixed or secondary modern school with 346 places, a junior mixed with 408, and an infants' with 344. The seniors were later absorbed into Bishopswood, leaving the board's building to Stroud Green junior and infants' schools,[53] with 320 and 180 children on their rolls in 1975.

Campsbourne board school, Boyton Road, opened in 1897. It consisted of a building for 450 boys and 450 girls and of another for infants.[54] The school was full in 1906 but by 1919 the number of places had been reduced to 1,373 and by 1932 to 1,176. After reorganization in 1935[55] there was a senior girls' school for 320, later renamed Clemence Cave school, a junior mixed school for 420, and an infants' for 400.[56] In 1975 the junior school had 322 pupils enrolled and the infants' 208.

Elementary schools founded 1903–1945. South Harringay council school, planned by the board, opened in 1904.[57] It consisted of a building with 600 places for junior mixed pupils and another for 300 infants, on a site between Mattison and Pemberton roads which also housed new higher elementary and special instruction schools.[58] After 1919 the accommodation was for only 400 juniors and 240 infants, until reorganization in 1934 created a junior mixed and infants' school for 340,[59] while senior girls used the old higher elementary school block facing Pemberton Road. When the senior girls moved into Hornsey grammar school in 1952, their block was occupied by some of the juniors, who shared their own building with the infants. In 1974 the infants took over the Pemberton Road block, leaving the juniors the whole of the old junior school and part of the original infants' school.[60] There were 339 children on the roll of the junior school in 1976 and 263 on that of the infants' in 1975.

Muswell Hill council school was built and opened in Alexandra Place in 1913, when a few children were transferred there from St. James's school.[61] It accommodated 88 in the juniors' department and 132 in the infants' in 1927, shortly before its reorganization into a junior mixed and infants' school for 200, and was described as temporary until after the Second World War.[62] Junior and infants' schools, with 411 and 184 pupils enrolled, occupied the old site in 1976.

St. Gilda's Roman Catholic school, Dickenson Road, opened in 1915. It remained a private school for mixed children of all ages, under the Sisters of Christian Instruction, until 1971. Rebuilding was taking place in 1975, when there were 260 juniors on the roll.[63]

Coldfall council school opened in 1928 to serve the new Coldfall housing estate north-west of Muswell Hill.[64] The two-storeyed building, for 440 senior pupils and 400 juniors and infants,[65] was to take a few children from Friern Barnet.[66] There were 520 seniors by 1936 but in 1954 the upper storey was left to juniors alone on the opening of William Grimshaw school.[67] In 1975 Coldfall junior school, with 185 children enrolled, occupied the upper storey and the infants' school, with 192 including a nursery, remained on the lower floor.

Rokesly council school, on the south corner of Rokesly Avenue and Hermiston Avenue, opened for 480 infants in 1934.[68] An adjoining junior school for 480, on a restricted site and with a circular assembly hall,[69] opened in 1953.[70] In 1975 there were 397 juniors and 280 infants on the rolls.

Primary schools founded after 1945.[71] Tetherdown junior mixed and infants' school opened in 1947, in buildings formerly used by Tollington preparatory school. In 1958 it moved to the old Tollington girls' school in Grand Avenue, where in 1975 there were 270 children on the roll.

St. Aidan's junior mixed and infants' school, Albany Road, was formed in 1948 when senior girls moved from St. Aidan's, formerly Stroud Green and Hornsey, high school. A new building was opened in 1972 but the old yellow-brick hall was retained in 1975, when St. Aidan's was Voluntary Aided and had 215 children on the roll.

St. Peter-in-Chains Roman Catholic school for infants was open by 1959[72] in Elm Grove, close to St. Gilda's junior school. Originally independent, it was Voluntary Aided in 1969[73] and had 206 infants on the roll in 1975.

Our Lady of Muswell Roman Catholic school

48 Ed. 7/87; Hornsey sch. bd. *Rep. by Chairman* (1898–1900), 18, 34.
49 Hornsey educ. cttee. min. bk. ii. 40.
50 Ex inf. the headmaster, N. Harringay jnr. sch.
51 Ed. 7/87.
52 Newspaper cutting in Hornsey libr., Heal Colln.
53 *Bd. of Educ., List 21, 1936* (H.M.S.O.); ex inf. the headmistress, Stroud Green jnr. sch.
54 Ed. 7/87; *Builders' Jnl.* 24 Nov. 1897.
55 Ex. inf. the headmaster, Campsbourne jnr. sch.
56 *Bd. of Educ., List 21, 1936* (H.M.S.O.).
57 Ed. 7/87.
58 Programme of opening and plan in Hornsey libr.; *Hornsey Jnl.* 30 Apr. 1904.
59 *Bd. of Educ., List 21, 1932, 1936* (H.M.S.O.).
60 Ex inf. the headmaster, S. Harringay jnr. sch.
61 Ed. 7/87.
62 *Bd. of Educ., List 21,1927, 1932, 1938* (H.M.S.O.).
63 Ex inf. the headmistress; *Westm. Yr. Bk.* (1969).
64 *Hornsey Boro. 1903–53*, 26.
65 *Bd. of Educ., List 21, 1932* (H.M.S.O.).
66 *Hornsey Jnl.* 14 Dec. 1928.
67 Ex inf. the headmistress, Coldfall inf. sch.
68 *Bd. of Educ., List 21, 1936* (H.M.S.O.).
69 Official opening programme in Hornsey libr.
70 Ex inf. the headmaster, Rokesly jnr. sch.
71 Except where otherwise stated, the following six paras. are based on information from the head teachers.
72 *Westm. Yr. Bk.* (1959).
73 Ibid. (1964, 1969).

opened in 1959 in the former buildings of St. Martin's convent school, Page's Lane. It was a Voluntary Aided junior mixed and infants' school, with 350 children on the roll in 1975.

Coleridge school opened in new buildings in Crescent Road in 1971. Juniors and infants formed separate schools from 1972 and had 240 and 190 full-time pupils on their rolls in 1975.

Secondary and senior schools founded before 1967. A grammar school for 'sons of parents of limited means' occupied an iron room adjoining Holy Trinity church, Stroud Green, in 1890. It had a junior department in 1909, when prospectuses were available at the Vicarage. A Baptist grammar school used the Victoria hall, Stapleton Hall Road, also in 1890.[74]

The Stationers' Company's school opened in 1861 at Bolt Court, Fleet Street (London).[75] In 1895 it moved to 2 a. in Mayfield Road, as a grammar school for boys aged 8 to 16,[76] and in 1906 it accommodated 400.[77] From 1909 it was managed by a committee appointed by the company and the county and borough councils,[78] which approved the opening of a preparatory department in 1913[79] and built extensions in 1912 and 1939. Its status changed from Voluntary Aided to Voluntary Controlled in 1966, a year before its reorganization as a comprehensive school.[80]

St. Aidan's school, as Stroud Green and Hornsey high school for girls, was opened by the Church Schools' Co. in 1887. It occupied a cramped site, on the corner of Stapleton Hall and Albany roads, and had no playground in 1906, when there were 150 places and 111 pupils. The school, subsidized by the company to supplement the fees,[81] was taken over by local governors in 1919 and grant aided by Middlesex from 1928.[82] It became an elementary school in 1948 on the removal of older girls to Hornsey high school.[83]

Hornsey high school for girls originated in the private Stroud Green high school, founded *c.* 1887 by Mrs. Mills-Carver and comprising a new building at the corner of Addington and Oakfield roads, with its grounds backing those of a teachers' and boarders' house at the corner of Stapleton Hall and Oakfield roads. In 1906 there were 150 places and 130 pupils of all ages, including six boarders whose payments were needed for solvency. Competition with the Church Schools' Co.'s establishment was mutually damaging but plans for amalgamation failed. In 1908 Stroud Green high school was taken over by the county[84] as a girls' counterpart to the Stationers' school and in 1915 it moved to new buildings in Weston Park.[85] Hornsey high school was reorganized as part of the comprehensive Hornsey school for girls and in 1972 its former premises passed to the Stationers' school.[86]

Tollington grammar school opened in 1902 as a branch of Tollington Park college, Islington. A building was erected in Tetherdown, in the grounds of an older house inhabited by the joint proprietor, W. Campbell Brown.[87] There were 225 fee-paying boys aged 7 to 16 in 1903[88] and, after extensions, 293 by 1906.[89] The school was taken over by Middlesex, as a Muswell Hill counterpart to the Stationers' school, in 1919 and a preparatory department was then opened.[90] Tollington girls' school, in Grand Avenue by 1911,[91] was also acquired[92] and continued as a separate grammar school until joined with the boys' in a four-storeyed block on part of the Tetherdown playing fields in 1958.[93] The girls' former premises were taken over by Tetherdown primary school and later the new grammar school block became part of Creighton comprehensive school.

Hornsey county school opened in 1904, as Hornsey higher elementary school, on land which had been acquired by the board east of South Harringay school. It accommodated 340 mixed pupils in 1906, when average attendance was 127, and changed its name on passing to the county council in 1908.[94] The school was converted from a grammar to a girls' secondary modern in 1951[95] and was absorbed into the comprehensive Hornsey school for girls in 1967.

William Grimshaw school opened as a mixed secondary modern school in Creighton Avenue in 1955.[96] From 1961 it offered extended courses, attended by older pupils from other secondary modern schools.[97] It was amalgamated into Creighton comprehensive school in 1967.

Clemence Cave secondary modern school for girls was so named in 1955.[98] It stood in Boyton Road and previously had been Campsbourne girls' secondary modern school. From 1967 it formed part of Hornsey school for girls.

Bishopswood school opened on part of Crouch End playing fields in Montenotte Road in 1961. It accommodated 680 mixed pupils and replaced Stroud Green secondary modern school.[99] Bishopswood was absorbed into Highgate Wood comprehensive school in 1967.

Priory Vale school was formed in 1962 out of North Harringay and Crouch End boys' secondary modern schools. It was divided into eastern and western halves, since pupils continued to use the old board schools' premises in Falkland and Park roads[1]

[74] *Kelly's Dir. Essex, Herts. and Mdx.* (1890); *Hornsey and Crouch End Dir.* (1909–10).
[75] C. Glagden, *Stationers' Co.* 256–7. Land was acquired in 1858, a year often given as that of the sch.'s foundation.
[76] *Kelly's Dir. Essex, Herts. and Mdx.* (1908); *Stationers' Co.'s Sch. Prospectus* [1969].
[77] Hornsey educ. cttee. min. bk. iv. 116.
[78] Ex inf. the headmaster.
[79] Hornsey educ. cttee. min. bk. xi. 157.
[80] Ex inf. the headmaster. Except where otherwise stated, information on reorganizations in 1967 has been supplied by the comprehensive schs.
[81] Hornsey educ. cttee. min. bk. iv. 119–20.
[82] *Hornsey Jnl.* 18 June 1937.
[83] Ex inf. the headmaster, St. Aidan's jnr. and inf. sch.
[84] Hornsey educ. cttee. min. bk. iv. 120–3; vii. 18.
[85] *Hornsey Boro. 1903–53*, 26.
[86] Ex inf. the headmaster, Stationers' sch.
[87] Hornsey educ. cttee. min. bk. iv. 118.
[88] *V.C.H. Mdx.* i. 274.
[89] Hornsey educ. cttee. min. bk. iv. 118.
[90] Ibid. iv. 119; xvii. 19.
[91] *Wood Green and Muswell Hill Dir.* (1911–12).
[92] *Hornsey Boro. 1903–53*, 26.
[93] *Hornsey Jnl.* 25 July 1958; programme of opening in Hornsey libr.
[94] E. M. Burke, *Hornsey Cnty. Sch. 1904–29*, 1, 6, 13; programme of opening in Hornsey libr.
[95] Ex inf. the headmistress, Hornsey sch. for girls.
[96] Invitation card in Hornsey libr.
[97] *Hornsey Jnl.* 7 Apr. 1961.
[98] Ibid. 22 July 1955.
[99] Ibid. 19 Aug. 1960, 7 Apr., 10 Nov. 1961.
[1] Ibid. 6 July, 7 Dec. 1962.

until Priory Vale was absorbed into Highgate Wood and other schools in 1967.

St. David's Church of England school opened in 1964 in new buildings on the site of Hornsey Rectory.[2] Plans for it to replace St. Mary's mixed secondary modern school were altered for it to take boys only in order that the new London Borough of Haringey, which would also contain St. Katharine's in Tottenham, should have two single-sex Anglican schools. It was therefore renamed, partly in honour of David Greig whose fund had made possible the rebuilding of a denominational school.[3] St. David's, designed for some 300 pupils, became a comprehensive school in 1967.[4]

Comprehensive schools founded after 1967.[5] After the Stationers' Company's school had been reorganized in 1967, the company continued to appoint a third of the governors. Juniors used an annexe in Falkland Road[6] until the former Hornsey high school buildings were added to the Stationers' site in 1972. There were 1,325 boys enrolled in 1975.

Hornsey school for girls was formed in 1967 out of Hornsey high, Hornsey county, and Clemence Cave schools. It used Hornsey high and Clemence Cave schools' premises, with huts and the halls of Ferme Park Baptist church, before moving to a new building in Inderwick Road in 1971. There were 1,400 girls on the roll in 1975.

Highgate Wood school in 1967 replaced Bishopswood and Priory Vale lower schools, whose premises it thereafter used. There were 1,132 boys and girls on the roll in 1975.

Creighton school in 1967 replaced William Grimshaw and Tollington schools, whose buildings thereafter constituted the north and south wings. There were 1,498 mixed pupils on the roll in 1975.

St. David's Church of England school, with 330 boys in 1975, continued in Rectory Gardens until 1976. It was then absorbed into the new mixed school of St. David and St. Katharine, whereupon the buildings were taken over by St. Mary's junior school.

The school of St. David and St. Katharine opened in new buildings in St. Mary's Road in 1976, when it replaced St. David's school and St. Katharine's, Tottenham. It started with 750 boys and girls, whose numbers were to rise to 1,320 by 1980.

Special school.[7] Greenfields school, for maladjusted children, occupied new buildings in Coppetts Road from 1975. The school had opened in White Hart Lane as the New Day school in 1972[8] and afterwards had used the former Page Green board school in Broad Lane, Tottenham.[9] There were 40 boys and girls, aged 7 to 16, on the roll in 1976.

Hornsey College of Art originated, as Hornsey School of Art, in private classes under Frank Swinstead. A school and residence opened in Waverley Road in 1882,[10] with government help,[11] but remained self-supporting until 1904; thereafter the county council gradually assumed control, taking over the residential part as a school in 1907 and buying the freehold in 1925. The building, which faced a side road and in appearance had to conform with neighbouring housing,[12] was reconstructed and joined to a new extension in 1931.[13] Numbers rose from *c.* 60 full-time and 200 part-time students in 1926, when Swinstead retired, to 365 full-time, 100 part-time day, and nearly 1,000 part-time evening students by 1947.[14] As the only art school in east Middlesex and a training college for teachers, the school was overcrowded by 1953.[15] After expansion at Crouch Hill had been banned, the fine art department moved to Alexandra Palace in 1964[16] and the teachers' training department later acquired an annexe in Tottenham.[17] The school was widely known for its 'Hornsey' designs. Unrest among its students in the late 1960s was publicized in *The Hornsey Affair*. In 1973 the college was combined with Hendon and Enfield technical colleges to form the Middlesex Polytechnic.[18]

Private schools. Crouch End or Hornsey[19] academy presumably opened when John Yeo of Hornsey, who kept several boarders, was licensed to teach in 1686.[20] In 1741 Jane Lovell, schoolmistress, left John Lee, apparently her assistant, the lease of property where the school was held. The wood engraver John Bewick (d. 1795)[21] taught there and the philologist John Grant[22] was tenant in 1810. W. C. Smith, Grant's successor and perhaps his associate by 1819, took foreign boys[23] and in 1844 offered an education to 40–50 young gentlemen, under a principal, four tutors, and a music teacher.[24] There were 42 pupils, aged 7 to 15, in 1851.[25] Crouch End school was said to be nearly 200 years old in 1872[26] and still advertised in 1879,[27] but the site was sold to the Imperial Property Investment Co. in 1882. The last principal, T. Knight, moved with some pupils to Fairfield, Tottenham Lane, which was sold with the Topsfield estate in 1894, and then to the Chestnuts in Middle Lane, later replaced by Chestnut Court.[28] The original school building, with its playground on the corner of Park Road and Crouch End Broadway,[29] was described as in the Elizabethan style in 1844; the three-storeyed, weatherboarded house then stood east of a later, two-storeyed school block, with

2 Ex inf. the headmaster.
3 *Hornsey Jnl.* 27 July 1962, 24 Jan., 18 Sept. 1964.
4 *St. Mary's Par. Mag.* July 1964.
5 Except where otherwise stated, the following six paras. are based on information from the headmaster or headmistress.
6 *Prospectus* [1969].
7 The para. is based on information from the headmaster.
8 *V.C.H. Mdx.* v. 374.
9 Ibid. 370.
10 *Hornsey Jnl.* 4 Dec. 1936.
11 *The Times,* 9 Nov. 1883.
12 *Hornsey Jnl.* 4 Dec. 1936.
13 Ibid. 27 Nov. 1931.
14 Ibid. 7 Mar. 1947.
15 Mdx. C.C. *Scheme of Further Educ.* (1953).
16 *Hornsey Jnl.* 5 Aug. 1960, 6 Nov. 1964.
17 *V.C.H. Mdx.* v. 372.
18 Ibid. 257.
19 *V.C.H. Mdx.* i. 243.
20 Except where otherwise stated, the rest of the para. is based on *T.L.M.A.S.* xiii. 420–7.
21 *D.N.B.*
22 E. L. Greenberg, 'Contribution to Educ. by Private Academies' (Lond. Univ. M.A. thesis, 1953), 26.
23 Illus. advert. in Guildhall libr., PR V HOR.
24 *Illus. Lond. News,* 13 July 1844.
25 H.O. 107/1702/1/3/22–25.
26 F. S. de Carteret-Bisson, *Our Schs. and Colls.* 270.
27 Idem., *Our Endowed and Priv. Schs.* 710.
28 *Hornsey Jnl.* 17 July 1953.
29 Sale parts. and plan, 1882, in Potter Colln. 20/52.

Dutch gables. The buildings had changed little by 1882, shortly before their demolition.[30] An establishment under J. Lynn was called Old Crouch Hall school for a short time after 1882.[31]

George Spragg kept a school at Hornsey in 1686[32] but the earliest master of whom anything more is known was the calligrapher and mathematician Humphry Johnson (fl. 1713), who moved from London to teach boarders in Hornsey, where he died.[33] Many fee-paying pupils were attracted by the large houses and healthy situation of Highgate. The nonconformist Elizabeth Tutchin, widow of the pamphleteer John Tutchin, moved there from Newington Green and opened a girls' school after 1710.[34] Philippa Jeynson kept a girls' boarding school, which moved from near Hornsey Lane to Pemberton Row (later the Grove) *c.* 1740,[35] a schoolmaster named John Rosier occupied Englefield House in 1783,[36] and in the 1780s Messrs. Dower and Rogers offered boys a polite education at a long established academy.[37] In 1787 and 1788 John Wesley visited Miss Teulon's school on the hill, presumably Lauderdale House where he had first preached in 1782.[38] Another nonconformist, the Revd. Edward Porter, kept a school at no. 9 South Grove (Russell House) in 1799[39] and 1801.[40]

A Jewish academy[41] had been established at Highgate by 1802 under Hyman Hurwitz, who leased no. 10 South Grove (Church House) from the antiquary John Sidney Hawkins. It had *c.* 100 boys in 1820 and there was thought to be nothing like it in England except at Brighton.[42] From 1810 to 1812 Hurwitz also leased the adjoining no. 9, perhaps for a short-lived girls' school kept by his sister.[43] In 1821 Hurwitz, later the first professor of Hebrew at London University, renewed his lease of no. 10 and of property to the west, abutting on Swain's Lane. He apparently did so for the benefit of his successor Leopold Neumegen, whose Jewish academy survived until 1832[44] and perhaps until the lease expired in 1837. The premises on the west were converted into Highgate Literary and Scientific Institution in 1840[45] and Church House, where Neumegen still lived in 1842,[46] was leased to Kilham Roberts in 1843.[47] Roberts kept a school there in 1845.[48]

By 1820 Highgate had several eminent schools.[49] Daniel Dowling, a writer on mathematics, had sought pupils in 1810[50] and probably occupied Sir William Ashurst's old house from 1812.[51] In 1818 Dowling kept the Mansion House academy there and offered a broad liberal education, with social accomplishments and a choice of vocational and scientific courses. His boarding school moved to Hammersmith between 1826 and 1829.[52] On the north side of the green the later no. 53 South Grove had apparently been extended as a school by 1804 and from 1809 was occupied by Louis Beauvais,[53] who trained boys for the professions[54] until between 1813 and 1817.[55] Lauderdale House was a school, under Mrs. Sheldon in 1804[56] and William Gittens in 1812[57] and 1828.[58] South Grove seminary, later the Lawns, opened *c.* 1812[59] and occupied a wing of Old Hall and a gabled building to the east.[60] It was run as a girls' finishing school by the Misses Grignon and Hull in 1832[61] and 1845.[62]

Dr. Benjamin Duncan took over an academy *c.* 1814[63] on the Bank, Highgate Hill,[64] where his advanced views were shared by his chief language teacher Joachim De Prati, a follower of Saint-Simon and former colleague of Pestalozzi. Duncan offered a broad, practical education, with no corporal punishment, and did not observe vacations and so made no extra charge for boys from the colonies.[65] On his move to Hammersmith in 1829 he was succeeded by George and Frances Kieckhofer, who by 1851 had made way for the Revd. Alfred Barrett.[66] Described as preparatory in 1845,[67] the school had 26 boys aged 7–12 in 1851[68] and probably survived, as Highgate commercial academy and under other names, until the 1870s.

Grove House school opened in 1825 at no. 53 South Grove. It became well known as 'Fenner's' after its first principal, Zachariah Fenner, whose sister conducted a girls' school[69] and who retired in 1872.[70] The premises were bought from Nathaniel Wetherell in 1842[71] and housed *c.* 40 boys, mostly

30 Illus. in adverts. (see above, nn. 23, 24) and *T.L.M.A.S.* xiii, facing p. 420. Photos. of 1882–3 are in Potter Colln. 20/56–7 and Hornsey libr., Heal Colln.
31 Potter Colln. 20/53, 56; prospectus in Hornsey libr., Heal Colln.
32 Guildhall MS. 9537/20, f. 91.
33 *D.N.B.*; A. Heal, *English Writing-Masters . . . 1570–1800*, 66.
34 *D.N.B.* s.v. John Tutchin.
35 Potter Colln. 15/31 (cuttings ascribed to 1733 and 1740).
36 *Survey of Lond.* xvii. 25.
37 Potter Colln. 15/31 (cuttings ascribed to 1782, 1786).
38 Journal in *Works of John Wesley*, iv. 241, 342, 406, 442.
39 *V.C.H. Mdx.* i. 249. Edward Porter preached at the new chapel, Southwood Lane, in 1792: Potter Colln. 14/69.
40 *Survey of Lond.* xvii. 30.
41 Except where otherwise stated, the para. is based on *Trans. Jewish Hist. Soc.* xxi. 232–8 and *Survey of Lond.* xvii. 37.
42 *Ambulator* (1820), 168.
43 Howitt, *Northern Heights*, 398.
44 *Pigot's Com. Dir.* (1832–4), with ref. to Louis [sic] Neumegen.
45 See p. 158.
46 Prickett, *Highgate*, 117.
47 *Survey of Lond.* xvii. 38.
48 *P.O. Dir. Six Home Cnties.* (1845).
49 *Ambulator* (1820), 168.
50 Greenberg, 'Private Academies', 206.
51 *Survey of Lond.* xvii. 62.
52 Greenberg, 'Private Academies', 44, 59, 122–4.
53 *Survey of Lond.* xvii. 97, 102.
54 Greenberg, 'Private Academies', 203.
55 *Survey of Lond.* xvii. 102.
56 Ibid., plate 1.
57 Ibid. 15.
58 *Boarding Schs. Dir.* (1828).
59 *Camden Hist. Rev.* ii. 10.
60 *Survey of Lond.* xvii. 46 and plate 36b.
61 *Pigot's Com. Dir.* (1832–4).
62 *P.O. Dir. Six Home Cnties.* (1845).
63 Except where otherwise stated, the para. is based on *Camden Hist. Rev.* ii. 10–11.
64 Prickett and others wrongly state that the sch. was on the site of Arundel Ho. It is illus. on the Bank in Potter Colln. 7/16.
65 Adverts. in the *European Mag.* May 1820, commented on in the *Cholmeleian*, June 1903, and in Swiss Cottage libr., Heal Colln., A III, 6.
66 H.O. 107/1702/1/5/13–14.
67 *P.O. Dir. Six Home Cnties.* (1845).
68 H.O. 107/1702/1/5/13–14.
69 *Camden Hist. Rev.* ii. 9.
70 Jealous, *Highgate*, 36.
71 *Survey of Lond.* xvii. 102.

boarders, in 1872[72] and 60 in 1879.[73] The school closed in 1930 on the retirement of A. E. C. Dickinson, the third headmaster.[74]

Cromwell House[75] was a boys' boarding school in 1840 when under lease to William Addison, who had taught in Highgate at least since 1826.[76] In 1843 he was succeeded by the Revd. Gerard van de Linde, an anglicized Dutchman who helped to organize the first national educational exhibition in 1854 and whose school was known as the 'Collège français'. Van de Linde prepared boys for the professions and had 31 pupils, aged 11 and over, in 1851.[77] His widow sold the school in 1858 to the Revd. Henry Stretton, who, after a fire in 1865,[78] moved to St. Albans in 1866.

In the early 19th century the popularity of Highgate probably restricted private education elsewhere. At Muswell Hill part of the Rowes' old property was sold in 1810 as Bath House academy, lately occupied by a schoolmaster named Hunt.[79] At Crouch End, in addition to the boys' academy, the Misses Lobb kept boarders and a day-school in 1826[89] and Elizabeth Lobb still had 32 girls, aged from 9 to 16, in 1851.[81] Highgate had 12 private schools in 1826 and 19, excluding fee-paying pupils of the master of Cholmley's school, by 1832,[82] whereas the rest of the parish had merely the 2 Crouch End establishments. There were 2 new seminaries at Crouch End by 1845, when Highgate's 14 schools included only 5 that had existed in 1830.[83]

The spread of housing produced a more even distribution of schools. Among the longest lived was Oakfield, a preparatory school opened at Crouch End in 1859 and with 40 boarders and 40 day-boys in 1879.[84] By 1890 it had moved from Hornsey Lane to Haslemere Road,[85] where there were 108 boys in 1911 and it closed in 1933.[86] Alexandra Park college, a boarding and day-school which stressed science and modern languages, opened in Middle Lane in 1868[87] and survived in 1890.[88] Early schools in Stroud Green included Hornsey Rise college, Victoria Road, in 1872, Rothbury House college, for day-boys, in 1879,[89] and Victoria college, Florence Road, in the 1880s.[90] At Highgate boarders and day-boys attended Sutherland House, on the Bank, in the 1870s.[91] All Saints' Middle Class school, for girls and small boys, was opened in North Hill by the vicar in 1876[92] and survived in 1890.[93] St. Mary's ladies' day-school was opened in 1886 by the Sisters of the Union of the Sacred Hearts at Lilford House, Cholmeley Park. In 1921 it moved to Hornsey Lane, where it became a junior school in 1944 and, as Birklands, continued until 1961.[94] The house in Cholmeley Park, no. 53, served as a nursing home until at least 1939.[95]

Channing House,[96] the most successful of Highgate's 19th-century private foundations, opened in Sutherland House in 1885 under the Revd. Robert Spears,[97] later the first minister of Highgate Unitarian church. The school was endowed by the Misses Matilda and Emily Sharpe, primarily for the daughters of Unitarian ministers, and named after William Ellery Channing. Private benefactions assisted six pupils. Numbers rose to *c.* 90 after a year and reached *c.* 125 by 1925, by which date barely half of the girls were boarders. Ivy House, higher up the hill, was leased for dormitories and offices in 1885. The school also leased the semi-detached West View, immediately below Sutherland House, in 1885 and extended the frontage of both in 1887. West View was bought in 1901, followed by Slingley, the southerly half of the pair, in 1921 and by the neighbouring Hampden House in 1925 and Arundel House, forming another pair, in 1930. Fairseat, leased with 2 a., was used from 1926. A hall was opened in 1927[98] and the school known simply as Channing from 1931. The main frontage was further extended in 1954, when Haigh House replaced Hampden and Arundel houses, which had been demolished in 1945, and the bombed Betchworth House. A junior school opened in 1943 at no. 12 Southwood Lane, which was sold in 1955, and later occupied Fairseat. There were 250 girls in 1950, few of them Unitarians, and 390, aged 5 to 18, in 1975.[99]

The new suburb of Stroud Green had at least 21 private schools in 1890,[1] including the forerunners of St. Aidan's and Hornsey high schools and the two denominational grammar schools for boys.[2] The Anglo-French high school, established *c.* 1884, had 100 pupils of all ages in Ferme Park Road in 1889[3] and opened a girls' branch in Ridge Road in 1890. Stapleton Hall school for girls, at no. 54 and later also at no. 34 Stapleton Hall Road, lasted from 1898 or earlier until 1935.[4] There were a further six schools in Harringay and many more in Finsbury Park, although some lay outside Hornsey's boundary. At the northern end of Crouch Hill by 1898 there were schools at nos. 102 and 104, called Durham House and Cecile House, no. 110, preparatory and kindergarten departments of Cecile House, and no. 112, Darra House.[5]

72 Bisson, *Schs. and Colls.* 269.
73 Bisson, *Endowed and Priv. Schs.* 709.
74 Jealous, *Highgate*, 36; *Hampstead and Highgate Express*, 20 Dec. 1974.
75 Except where otherwise stated, the para. is based on Norman, *Cromwell Ho.* 30–4, and *Camden Hist. Rev.* ii. 10.
76 *Pigot's Com. Dir.* (1826, 1832–4).
77 H.O. 107/1702/1/5/8–10.
78 See p. 135.
79 Guildhall MS. 10465/12, pp. 210–12.
80 *Pigot's Com. Dir.* (1826).
81 H.O. 1702/1/3/25–7.
82 *Pigot's Com. Dir.* (1826–7, 1832–4).
83 *P.O. Dir. Six Home Cnties.* (1845).
84 Bisson, *Endowed and Priv. Schs.* 710. Prospectuses, 1884 and 1891, in Hornsey libr., Heal Colln.
85 *Kelly's Dir. Essex, Herts. and Mdx.* (1890).
86 *Hornsey Jnl.* 28 July 1933.
87 Prospectuses in Hornsey libr., Heal Colln.
88 *Kelly's Dir. Essex, Herts. and Mdx.* (1890).
89 Bisson, *Schs. and Colls.* 270; *Endowed and Priv. Schs.* 708–9.
90 E. Monk, *Memories of Hornsey* (Hornsey Hist. Soc 1976), 15, 38.
91 Bisson, *Schs. and Colls.* 270; *Endowed and Priv. Schs.* 709.
92 *St. Mic.'s Par. Mag.* Aug. 1876.
93 *Kelly's Dir. Essex, Herts. and Mdx.* (1890).
94 Ibid.; *Hornsey Jnl.* 10 Feb. 1961.
95 *Kelly's Dir. Hornsey* (1922, 1939).
96 Except where otherwise stated, the para. is based on T. E. Dalton, *Channing Ho. Sch. 1885–1960*.
97 *D.N.B.*
98 *Builder*, cxxxv. 972.
99 Truman and Knightley, *Schools* (1975).
1 Except where otherwise stated, the following two paras. are based on *Kelly's Dir. Essex, Herts. and Mdx.* (1890, 1908).
2 See p. 195.
3 *Hornsey and Mdx. Messenger*, 11 Jan. 1889.
4 *Kelly's Dir. Hornsey* (1898–9, 1935).
5 Ibid. (1898–9).

The number of schools in the south-east part of the parish halved between 1890 and 1908, following the spread of public education, but a new demand arose farther north. In 1890 Fortis Green had two private schools and Muswell Hill had none; in 1908 there were still the two at Fortis Green and at least seventeen at Muswell Hill, including an offshoot of Tollington Park college and a school which had been opened in Tetherdown in 1904 by the Sisters of St. Martin of Tours.[6] Frederick Newcombe, who conducted a collegiate school in Muswell Hill Road, apparently had moved from Stroud Green.[7]

Two preparatory schools opened in 1897: Byron House, in North Grove, Highgate,[8] and Norfolk House, at no. 10 Muswell Avenue.[9] The first, co-educational and attended by John Betjeman,[10] closed in 1962.[11] The second was claimed as Muswell Hill's only purpose-built school in 1910, when it had boys' and girls' departments and agreed to accommodate Tollington's preparatory pupils.[12] It contained 150 boys in 1975.[13] Crouch End college, later high school, for girls was founded in 1900 in Weston Park.[14] After periods in Fairfield Road and Middle Lane[15] it moved in 1936 to no. 125 Hornsey Lane,[16] where it accommodated girls of all ages and a kindergarten,[17] and to no. 51 Shepherd's Hill for its final year in 1973.[18] Southwood Hall was a girls' school from *c.* 1905 to 1930.[19] King's House school for girls, founded in 1898,[20] was in Muswell Hill Road by 1912 and survived in 1939; its premises, nos. 152 and 154, were used as a home for the blind in 1955 but stood empty in 1977.[21]

Among more recent schools was Highfield, opened at no. 1 Bloomfield Road in 1947 and with 176 boys and girls, aged 3 to 11, in 1976.[22] In 1949 no. 109 Hornsey Lane was bought for St. Aloysius's junior school,[23] which opened in 1950 and had no official connexion with St. Aloysius's college,[24] founded by the Brothers of Mercy in 1879 on the Islington side of Hornsey Lane.[25] While the college passed to the De La Salle Brothers the junior school remained under the Brothers of Mercy[26] and in 1961 it acquired no. 111, formerly the convent of the Union of the Sacred Hearts. In 1975 there were 120 children on the roll.[27] Whittingham school, originally a nursery at no. 271 Colney Hatch Lane, opened in 1952 at no. 208 Muswell Hill Road and gradually acquired nos. 206, 204, and 202. Later it took pupils to the age of 8 and, for a short time, girls to the age of 15. In 1977 there were *c.* 275 mixed pupils, aged $2\frac{1}{2}$ to 12, on the roll.[28] Northern Heights, at the corner of North Road and Hampstead Lane, was a school of dancing in 1930; after the Second World War it was also a preparatory school[29] until the building's demolition in 1962. Shepherd's Hill school, also preparatory, closed in 1973; its former premises, no. 51, were briefly used by Crouch End college and from 1974 by St. Giles's college.[30] The former Byron House was renamed Charlotte House in 1963 by Davies's school of English.[31] There was a preparatory academy for R.A.D.A., with mixed pupils age 15–17, at no. 55 Shepherd's Hill from 1945 until 1957.[32]

CHARITIES FOR THE POOR. The charities of Hornsey and Highgate divide between those once administered by the parish and those that were not.[33] Although some of the former were intended for Hornsey Side alone, they have all been used for the whole parish. Those subject to the governors of Cholmley's school (except John Smith's) or other Highgate trustees have been applied solely by Highgate even when intended for the whole parish. In 1976 most of the parochial charities were divided between the Hornsey Parochial Charities and the Hornsey Parochial Charities (educational and vocational foundation), which had the same trustees. The Highgate charities consisted of the Wollaston and Pauncefort alms-houses and Lady Gould's charity, managed by Cholmley's school, and distributive charities, several of them administered by the vicar of St. Michael's.

PARISH CHARITIES. The charities administered by the parish[34] were consolidated from the late 18th century under the heads of apprenticing, alms-houses, and the distribution of fuel, bread, blankets, and money, regardless of the founders' intentions. In 1853 all surpluses were kept by the treasurer of the charities, Thory Chapman, in his private bank account,[35] and after that date accounting was extremely lax[36] and large balances were allowed to accumulate. In 1886, when there was no treasurer and balances were held by various parish officers,[37] the vestry appointed a committee to manage the

6 J. A. Goodall, *Our Lady of Muswell* (pamphlet, 1959).
7 Prospectus for University sch., 1884, in Hornsey libr., Heal Colln.
8 *Hornsey Jnl. Annual* (1950).
9 Hornsey Boro. *Official Guide* [1956].
10 J. Betjeman, *Summoned by Bells*, 25.
11 *Hornsey Jnl.* 19 Jan., 3 Aug. 1962.
12 *Muswell Hill Record*, 18 Mar. 1910.
13 Truman and Knightley, *Schools* (1975).
14 Hornsey Boro. *Official Guide* [1956].
15 Ex inf. Dr. Joan Schwitzer.
16 *The Times*, 22 Oct. 1936; *P.O. Dir. Lond.* (1942).
17 Hornsey Boro. *Official Guide* [1956].
18 Ex inf. Dr. Joan Schwitzer.
19 *Kelly's Dir. Hornsey*. (1905–6, 1930); magazine, 1907, in Potter Colln. 14/89.
20 *Paton's Schs.* (1933).
21 *Kelly's Dir. Hornsey* (1912–13, 1939); *Kemp's Dir. Hornsey* (1955).
22 Truman and Knightley, *Schools* (1975); ex inf. Mrs. R. Jobson.
23 *The Aloysian*, Dec. 1949.
24 Ex inf. the headmaster.
25 *V.C.H. Mdx.* i. 262.
26 *Westm. Yr. Bk.* (1966).
27 Ex inf. the headmaster.
28 Ex inf. the headmaster.
29 *Kelly's Dir. Hornsey* (1930); *Kemp's Dir. Hornsey* (1955).
30 Ex inf. Dr. Joan Schwitzer.
31 *Hornsey Jnl.* 15 Nov. 1963.
32 *Kemp's Dir. Hornsey* (1955); ex inf. Dr. Joan Schwitzer.
33 Except where otherwise stated, the section below is based on Char. Com. files; *18th Rep. Com. Char.* H.C. 62, pp. 383–404 (1828), xx; *Gen. Digest of Endowed Chars.* H.C. 433 (11), pp. 4–5 (1867–8), lii (1); *Endowed Chars. Mdx.* H.C. 306, pp. 8–9 (1899), lxx; Thory Chapman, *Acct. of Chars. of Par. of Hornsey* (1853); H. Warner, *Acct. of Chars. of Par. of Hornsey* (1869); E. C. Price, 'Acct. of Chars. of Ancient Par. of Hornsey' (TS. of 1922 in Hornsey libr.).
34 Recorded in tables of benefactors, e.g. Highgate Sch. rec. box 1, bdle. 2 (1697, 1771); B.L. Add. MS. 5836, ff. 89–91 (1725); Lysons, *Environs*, iii. 58–9, 75–6.
35 *N. Mdx. Chron.* 27 Nov. 1886.
36 Bruce Castle Mus., D/PH/2A/1.
37 *N. Mdx. Chron.* 27 Nov. 1886.

charities. South Hornsey's relatively small share of the distributive charities and the mismanagement of Draper's charity were especially criticized. A Scheme of 1890 established the Hornsey Parochial Charities, combining twenty foundations. The poor's share of Churchfield and the Fuel fund, which could not be included in 1890, were added in 1954 and 1960 respectively. Tame's charity was added in 1967 and Bird's in 1972.

Churchfield. Rent from a close called Churchfield was used by the parish on the poor and highways in the 5 years before 1547, when it passed to the Crown.[38] Leased to Robert Shepherd, the land was sold in 1549 to Robert Wood to hold of the manor of Stanton Lacy in free socage.[39] Shepherd later claimed to have bought it from Wood but it was adjudged to be copyhold of Hornsey manor, rented to him by parochial trustees.[40] When new trustees were admitted in 1627, the income was declared to be for the maintenance of the church and the relief of the poor at the churchwardens' discretion. From 1687[41] a succession of trustees was maintained. Churchfield was let at £33 in 1827. In 1847 3 a. were sold to the G.N.R. for £1,000, which was invested in stock, and the remaining 4 a. were leased at £14 and from 1853 at £24. In 1878 the G.N.R. bought the remaining land for £3,750, which was also invested.[42] The total income was £145 in 1886,[43] when, as in 1827, it was included in the churchwardens' accounts for repairs to the church.[44] In 1894 the Charity Commissioners ordered that half the income be paid to the Hornsey Parochial Charities for pensions but only in 1953 did a Scheme divide it equally between the Churchfield ecclesiastical charity and the Churchfield charity for the poor. The former was still spent on the church in 1976.[45]

Bread fund. Susannah Chambers (d. 1641) of London, widow, left a rent-charge of £4 2*s.*, of which £2 12*s.* was to be distributed each Sunday in shilling instalments in bread or money to the poor of Hornsey.[46] Payment had ceased by 1827, when it was resumed. In 1897 the rent was redeemed for £125, which yielded a slightly increased income when invested.

In accordance with the will dated 1732 of Catherine Joyner of the parish of St. George the Martyr, spinster, her sister Elizabeth Joyner by will dated 1738 left a rent-charge of £4 for the poor of Hornsey Side to be distributed monthly in bread. Payment of the rent was disputed in 1864 but had resumed by 1869.

Holland and Evans's charity apparently originated in a gift of £6 a year by William Evans, probably made in 1758. Richard Holland, by testamentary paper proved in 1760, asked Evans, his residuary legatee, to secure a like sum for ever to the parish, both sums to be distributed monthly in bread among the poor of Hornsey Side not receiving relief.

Samuel Ellis (d. 1791), of Topsfield Hall, bequeathed £300 to buy stock, the dividends to be distributed weekly in bread among the poor of Hornsey. In 1827 the income was £9 18*s.* 6*d.*

By will dated 1797 Isaac Crunden gave the poor of Hornsey £150 stock for distribution in bread each Sunday. His devise of land for the same purpose was invalid, but the stock yielded £4 10*s.* in 1827.

In 1816 Richard Patmore of Hornsey gave £200 stock, the interest to be distributed in bread among those not receiving relief.[47] In 1827 the dividends amounted to £6 10*s.*

The vestry was administering all the bread charities together in 1793, contrary to the donors' intentions. The consolidated fund was divided equally between Highgate Side and Hornsey Side and was given away weekly and on two feast-days. The senior churchwarden was made responsible for the fund and the beadle for distribution.[48] In 1827 3*d.* and 6*d.* loaves were distributed to about 40 of the most needy following Sunday afternoon service at Hornsey church and probably also at Highgate chapel. In 1856 distributions were made at St. Michael's church in St. Pancras to recipients from Highgate Side[49] and in 1869 distribution occurred after morning service in the churches of the several ecclesiastical districts. By vestry order of 1824 bread worth only £11 1*s.* was dispensed in Hornsey Side and the same amount in Highgate Side,[50] although the total income of the fund was £36 18*s.* 6*d.* in 1827 and £45 between 1853 and 1886. By 1837 the savings had been invested in stock and consolidated with the bread fund itself, which received dividends from £1,081 stock[51] and was further consolidated in 1853.[52] In 1886 ten paupers of Highgate Side and twenty of Hornsey Side received a 6*d.* loaf weekly, and the recipients were appointed for life. The arrangement, which made it difficult to meet the suggestion that more should be distributed in South Hornsey, was censured by the Charity Commission. Distribution of bread ceased in 1890 on the formation of the Hornsey Parochial Charities.

Apprenticing charities. In 1659 Roger Draper of Stroud Green left £120 to apprentice six poor boys of Hornsey to freemen of London in trades other than those of silkweaver, tailor, and vintner; premiums of £15 for the master and £5 for clothing and equipping the boy were to be paid, not more than two each year,[53] and it is clear that the principal was to be spent. Following a Chancery decree of 1661 Draper's heir and executor Sir Thomas Draper, Bt., in 1668 surrendered to parochial trustees, in return for a full discharge and £20,[54] 2 a. of copyhold of the manor of Canonbury in Islington. The land was let at £7 in 1670[55] and at £10 by 1765. None of the issues was spent on premiums between 1740 and 1755.[56] In 1765 the land was let on a building lease at £10 rent for the first 8 years and £20 thereafter. Trustees admitted as copyholders in 1787 did not

[38] E 36/258 f. 149v.; see above, p. 173.
[39] *Cal. Pat.* 1549–51, 96–7.
[40] Req. 2/274/24; see also Guildhall MS. 10312/95.
[41] Marchams, *Ct. Rolls*, 61, 68, 205.
[42] Cutting in Hornsey libr.
[43] *Standard*, 12 Nov. 1886.
[44] Ibid.; *N. Mdx. Chron.* 13 Nov. 1886.
[45] Ex inf. the Revd. P. E. Brassell.
[46] Prob. 11/186 (P.C.C. 93 Evelyn).
[47] M.R.O., D.R.O. 20/H/1, p. 79.
[48] Ibid. C1/1, ff. 195v., 201v.
[49] Bruce Castle Mus., D/PH/2A/1.
[50] M.R.O., D.R.O. 20/H1/1, pp. 50, 54.
[51] Ibid. p. 50.
[52] Bruce Castle Mus., D/PH/2A/1.
[53] Prob. 11/293 (P.C.C. 356 Pell).
[54] B.L. Add. MS. 5836, f. 89.
[55] M.R.O., D.R.O. 20/H/1, p. 27.
[56] Ibid. C1/1, ff. 2–68, *passim.*

devote the rent to the charity, and the costs of a suit in Chancery consumed arrears up to 1798. In 1841 the admission of new trustees to ten houses in Hornsey Row (later Upper Street) and eight in Canonbury Lane cost more than the annual income. The exclusion of certain trades was not observed before or after 1824 in apprenticing boys at premiums fixed by custom at £5. The balance grew[57] and premiums were £15 or more from 1858.[58] New leases of the Islington property in 1863[59] increased net income to £660 a year in 1869. A Scheme of 1866 authorized premiums of £30 for boys and £20 for girls for apprenticing them in trades, including that of pupil teacher but not excluding those of silkweaver, tailor, or vintner. Alternatively industrial exhibitions of £10 or £5 a term for five years might be granted to learn trades in which apprenticeship was not customary. In 1867 two special vestries approved 32 apprenticeships, including one as pupil teacher and 21 for additional fees, and two exhibitions.[60]

The Islington properties were enfranchised in 1883,[61] when the trustees' report incorporated surveyors' advice[62] which the vestry accepted under the mistaken impression that it represented the trustees' intentions. The trustees let the Upper Street frontage for eighty years at less than the current rent or highest bid, permitted unsuitable shops to be built, and allowed the erection of a factory which depressed the value of housing. Their mismanagement, condemned in local newspapers,[63] necessitated the buying back of a lease and litigation which absorbed three-quarters of the income in 1889.[64] A new lease was made in 1948 of property in Canonbury Lane, and all the property was sold between 1955[65] and 1970, the proceeds being invested in stock.

In 1662 Anne, widow of John Smith of Highgate, conveyed to six trustees property worth £80 a year in Canterbury and Westbere Marsh (Kent) for charities there and in Hornsey. From the issues £20 a year was to be paid to Hornsey to apprentice four poor children annually. Originally the whole issues of the estate were for charity but growing revenues were not matched by disbursements. Hornsey's share of the charity increased to £49 in 1866, when the estate was worth £364,[66] and further increased to £60 *c.* 1880.[67] Although more used than the other apprenticing charities, there was a balance of £11 in 1827 and £45 by 1853.[68] By a Scheme of 1867 Anne Smith's charity was administered like Roger Draper's charity. The Canterbury property was sold in 1919 and the proceeds were invested.

Daniel Midwinter (d. 1756) of Hornsey bequeathed £1,000 to the Stationer's Company of London on condition that £14 a year was paid to apprentice and clothe a boy and girl of Hornsey. The bequest took effect on the death of his widow in 1770. In 1822 the Stationers' Company owed 12 years' arrears, which was reduced to 5 by 1838[69] and 2 in 1853.[70] In 1866 the Company paid over the capital and arrears of fees, which were invested to yield £14 18*s.* 6*d.* in 1869. In 1867 a Scheme provided that Midwinter's charity should be administered like Draper's charity.

In 1783 and 1789 the vestry restricted the apprenticing charities to children of parishioners, past and present,[71] and in 1789 and 1823 ordered that nobody should take his own child as apprentice,[72] although the order was reversed in 1824.[73] In 1856 not all the children apprenticed were poor.[74] From the late 18th century the charities were administered jointly and the expenses of drawing up indentures and of visiting apprentices, at a rate fixed in 1783,[75] were met from Draper's and Anne Smith's charities.[76] The £7 premium from the Stationers' Co. was reserved by 1827 for more respectable masters or for cases of extreme poverty, when the sum was used as an extra allowance on clothes. In 1813 the vestry authorized payment of an extra £5 at the end of the first year of apprenticeship,[77] in order to attract better masters. By 1827 the extra came from Draper's and Anne Smith's charities, even when the initial premium was from Midwinter's charity. Until *c.* 1860 most premiums were paid from Anne Smith's charity and as early as the 1740s, when up to four premiums were granted annually,[78] supply exceeded demand. Twenty-three boys from Hornsey Side and 37 from Highgate Side were apprenticed between 1835 and 1853, when there was a combined surplus from Draper's and Anne Smith's charities of £176.[79] That was before the great increase of income in 1863 and foreshadowed the accumulation of surpluses for which successive Schemes failed to find a use over the next 120 years.

From 1853 onwards there was criticism of apprenticing as a way of using charitable funds[80] and from 1880 the trustees suggested devoting the whole proceeds to education.[81] The Scheme of 1890, by which the charities became a separately administered part of Hornsey Parochial Charities, nonetheless retained premiums for apprenticeship while widening the scope for expenditure on technical and industrial education. No more than half the income was to be used for apprenticing and by an Order of 1904 the old apprenticing charities were divided equally between an apprenticing fund and the Hornsey educational foundation; any surplus from the former was paid to the latter. From 1904 to 1905 and 1912 to 1921 about twelve apprenticeship

57 Ibid. H/1, pp. 35–6, 38.
58 Bruce Castle Mus., D/PH/2A/1.
59 Hornsey par. *Roger Draper's Char.* (1863) (copy in Hornsey libr.).
60 Bruce Castle Mus., D/PH/2A/2, pp. 175, 184–6, 191–3, 236, 243.
61 *N. Mdx. Chron.* 21 July 1883.
62 *Rep. of trustees of Hornsey Row estate* (1883) (copy in Hornsey libr.).
63 *N. Mdx. Chron.* 25 Aug. 1883, 26 Mar. 1887, 7 Apr. 1888; *Standard*, 4 Apr. 1888.
64 *N. Mdx. Chron.* 7 Aug. 1888, 27 Oct. 1894.
65 Hornsey Par. Chars. *Ann. Rep. and Abs. of Accts.* (1960).
66 Bruce Castle Mus., D/PH/2A/2.
67 Cutting in Hornsey libr.
68 Bruce Castle Mus., D/PH/2A/1.
69 M.R.O., D.R.O. 20/H/1, pp. 39–41.
70 Bruce Castle Mus., D/PH/2A/1.
71 M.R.O., D.R.O. 20/H/1, p. 18; C1/1, ff. 96v., 143v.
72 Ibid. C1/1, f. 143v.
73 Ibid.
74 Hornsey par. *Acct. of Apprenticeship Chars.*
75 M.R.O., D.R.O. 20/C1/1, f. 99.
76 Hornsey par. *Acct. of Apprenticeship Chars.*
77 M.R.O., D.R.O. 20/C1/4.
78 Ibid. C1/1, ff. 2–68, *passim.*
79 Bruce Castle Mus., D/PH/2A/1.
80 Ibid.; 2A/2, p. 92.
81 Cuttings in Hornsey libr.; see also *N. Mdx. Chron.* 10 June 1876, 28 Apr. 1888.

premiums were granted each year for such trades as dress-making or motor repairs and in 1921 ten girls were apprenticed to a telegraphist. As many successful candidates did not take up their apprenticeships, there were 53 premiums unused in 1914.[82] By 1933 premiums absorbed only a quarter of the apprenticing fund, the balance being paid to the educational foundation,[83] but by a Scheme of 1937 they were retained and the maximum premium was raised to £50. In 1955 they were abolished, when a Scheme merged the two funds as the Hornsey Parochial Charities (educational and vocational foundation).[84]

Fuel fund or the Poor Allotments charity. Under the Hornsey Inclosure Act (1813) the poor were allotted 17 a., consisting of 12½ a. at Irish Corner, 1 a. at Wood Lane, Highgate, and two copyhold allotments of 3½ a. at Fortis Green.[85] The Wood Lane allotments were divided by 1834 into eight plots,[86] which were let for cultivation at nominal rents to paupers not in receipt of relief.[87] The other land was let to the best bidder. The charity received only £20 10*s*. rent in 1853. A small part of the Irish Corner allotment was sold in 1869 and the remainder was compulsorily purchased for £3,000 by Hornsey local board in 1887.[88] The proceeds were invested in stock. After enfranchisement in 1868 the Fortis Green allotments were to let on 99-year building leases in 1869 and the Wood Lane allotment was similarly let in 1867. By 1886 there was an income of £143. All the lands had been sold by 1940 except nos. 43 and 45 Wood Lane,[89] which were sold in 1960,[90] and the proceeds were invested. The Fuel fund was omitted from the Scheme of 1890 because it was regulated by Act of Parliament but under an Act of 1940 management passed to the Hornsey Parochial Charities, which could appropriate up to £100 extra towards distribution of fuel[91] and with which in 1960 the Fuel fund was amalgamated.

Under the inclosure award the income was to be distributed among the poor in coals.[92] The first gifts, worth £14, were made in 1818 and 50 sacks were divided equally between Hornsey and Highgate sides *c*. 1840.[93] In 1886 1,351 sacks were delivered: 347 in South Hornsey, 290 in Highgate, 65 in Muswell Hill, 75 in Crouch End, and 344 and 230 respectively in the districts of St. Mary and Holy Innocents, Hornsey.[94] There were complaints that coal was not always given and that it was sometimes sub-standard. South Hornsey, the poorest area, demanded a larger share and a committee was established to supervise distribution there.[95] Distribution had much improved by 1900[96] and continued until 1960.

Alms-house charities. Land called the Bowling Alley estate was given for the benefit of the poor before 1697, when it yielded £5 2*s*. in rent. Near by, fronting Hornsey High Street, were two cottages which in 1828 belonged to the same charity and were let rent-free to two widows. In Southwood Lane, near Wollaston's alms-houses, there were three cottages belonging to the parish in 1697. They had been rebuilt or converted into four by 1771;[97] two were pulled down in 1815 and one was rebuilt in 1818.[98] Eight cottages called the Wastelands Cottages were built on waste land given in 1806 by the bishop of London to provide sites for housing the poor.[99] The parish therefore owned twelve cottages for the poor in 1828. Six were for Highgate and six for Hornsey Side. The Wastelands Cottages were let at low rents, the vestry in 1854 ordering the eviction of a tenant because he was not in employment, and the other four were rent-free.[1] The cottages in Southwood Lane were double cottages, each housing two widows, in 1853.[2] The vestry neglected the maintenance of its cottages, which in 1886 were considered unsuitable for alms-houses[3] and in 1894 were beyond economical repair.[4] In that year the Hornsey Parochial Charities agreed to sell the cottages in Southwood Lane to Cholmley's school, which bought them in 1898, and to pension off the inmates. Against strong local opposition,[5] the trustees arranged for building leases for the sites of the others, which were accordingly pulled down. The freehold of the High Street property was sold by 1940 and that of all but three of the 27 houses on or adjoining the site of the Wastelands Cottages, in Muswell Hill Road, between 1969 and 1975.

Other charities. William Priestly (d. 1620), merchant-tailor of London, devised £250 to the Merchant Taylors' Company to pay four nobles (£1 6*s*. 8*d*.) a year quarterly to eight poor men, four of them from Hornsey.[6] The charity was unaltered in 1827 and in the two decades from 1835 the recipients were old men.[7]

William Platt of Highgate green, by codicil proved 1637, devised land to St. John's College, Cambridge, subject to annual payments which included £20 to the overseers of St. Pancras and Hornsey for the poor. The poor of St. Pancras were to receive £14, of which £10 was for those living at or near Highgate and £4 for those at Kentish Town or between there and Highgate. The poor of Hornsey were to have £6 subject to the satisfactory location of the testator's monument in Highgate chapel.[8] There were no trustees in 1827, when the income was distributed in money and bread. In 1867–8 the whole £6 was distributed as fuel, in accordance with the supposed wishes of the donor. Hornsey's share of the charity was included in the Hornsey Parochial

82 Hornsey Par. Chars. *Chairman's Reps*. (1904–5, 1912–21).
83 *Hornsey Jnl*. 10 Feb. 1933.
84 See pp. 190–1.
85 M.R.O., MR/DE Hornsey.
86 M.R.O., D.R.O. 20/E5/5; E5/13 (plan).
87 Ibid. E5/5.
88 *N. Mdx. Chron*. 3 Nov. 1886; 50 Vic. c. 15 (Local Act).
89 3 & 4 Geo. VI, c. 17 (Local Act).
90 Hornsey Par. Chars. *Rep. and Abs. of Accts*. (1960).
91 3 & 4 Geo. VI, c. 17 (Local Act).
92 M.R.O., MR/DE Hornsey.
93 M.R.O., D.R.O. 20/H/1.
94 *N. Mdx. Chron*. 12 June 1886.
95 Ibid. 15 May 1886, 7 Apr. 1888; cutting in Hornsey libr.
96 Cutting in Hornsey libr.
97 Highgate Sch. rec., box 1, bdle. 2.
98 See p. 165.
99 Cutting in Hornsey libr.
1 Bruce Castle Mus., D/PH/2A/1.
2 Cutting in Hornsey libr.
3 *Standard*, 12 Nov. 1886; *N. Mdx. Chron*. 13 Nov. 1886.
4 *N. Mdx. Chron*. 27 Oct. 1894.
5 *N. Mdx. Chron*. 27 Oct. 1894; *The Times*, 11 June 1895.
6 Prob. 11/135 (P.C.C. 39 Soame).
7 M.R.O., D.R.O. 20/H/1, pp. 1–4.
8 Prob. 11/175 (P.C.C. 159 Goare).

Charities in 1890; the rent-charge was reduced in 1970 and the proceeds were invested in stock.

Charles Brown (d. 1826), surgeon of Hornsey, left £100 stock, the income to provide blankets for eight paupers at Christmas. The stock yielded £2 14*s*. in 1836, when blankets were given to eight paupers with large families.[9]

George Buckton of Hornsey, by will proved 1847, gave £200 stock, the residue, after the maintenance of his family vault and monuments, to provide blankets and clothing for the poor of Hornsey not receiving relief. In 1867–8 the income was £6.

Brown's and Buckton's charities were spent on blankets and clothing among the most deserving poor of Hornsey Side in 1886.[10]

Sophia Mitchell, by will proved 1868, left £100, the income to maintain her tomb and any surplus to be distributed among the poor of Hornsey. In 1886, when £20 had been spent on her tomb, no income had been received by the churchwardens since 1879.

The Wastelands fund originated *c.* 1790 with fines paid for the use of the poor for inclosing commons. The balance left after the building of the Wastelands Cottages[11] was invested, and rent from the poor's cottages was also paid into the fund. In 1864 £150 was appropriated for public health from the fund.[12] Rent and dividends were still accruing in 1886, when nobody could remember any charitable application of the money.[13]

Also paid into the fund was the rent of £13 13*s*. received for Fermee's Tuke, that part of a piece of ground, given to the parish in 1811 as a site for a fire-engine house, which was surplus and was let on a building lease in 1850. The house, later no. 65 High Street, was sold in 1954.

Hornsey Parochial Charities. Hornsey Parochial Charities were established in 1890 by a Scheme uniting all the parish charities except Churchfield and the Fuel fund, which were added later. The Highgate charity of Maria Tame was added in 1967. The apprenticing charities were always managed independently by the same trustees. The income of all the charities was £64 in 1890 but building leases of the sites of the parish cottages raised it to £520 by 1905.[14] In 1962 the total income was £2,025. Between 1969 and 1975 all but three of the houses were sold. The proceeds were invested and in 1975 yielded an income of £8,241, of which £2,544 was unspent.

Distribution in kind ceased under the 1890 Scheme, which provided for at least four pensions of 6*s*. or 8*s*. a week, grants to dispensaries, hospitals, convalescent homes, and provident clubs, and to individuals preparing for a trade or in temporary distress. The parish cottages had been demolished by 1898 and the rents for their sites devoted to additional pensions, which were the main source of expenditure until the 1960s. The total spent on pensions fluctuated from £300 to £425 between 1904 and 1921, when the number of pensioners ranged from 24 to 47.[15] As beneficiaries were not to be in receipt of poor-relief, the number and the level of pensions was restricted:[16] in 1949, when the trustees had difficulty in applying the income, there was a large surplus. The basic level of pension was raised from 6*s*. a week in 1960 to £4 a month by 1975. Between 1960 and 1975 there were from 18 to 25 pensioners and the total expenditure on pensions ranged from £375 to £582. Small grants were made to nursing associations and hospitals between 1904 and 1921.[17] Payments to institutions for old people totalled £100 in 1960 and rose to £990 in 1969 and £1,350 in 1975. Occasional grants to individuals were insignificant until 1969 but amounted to £714 in 1975. Following the union with the Poor Allotments charity in 1960, the Hornsey Parochial Charities distributed money for fuel, which by 1975 was the largest item of expenditure. Each beneficiary received 15*s*. in 1960 and £3 in 1975, between which two dates the number of beneficiaries almost doubled to 932.

Col. John William Bird, by deed of 1899, provided that if St. Mary's upper grade school should cease to exist the income from his scholarship fund of £1,500 should be distributed among the poor of Hornsey.[18] The school closed in 1964 and a Scheme of 1972 vested Col. Bird's charity in the Hornsey Parochial Charities.

HIGHGATE CHARITIES. *Alms-house charities.* Sir John Wollaston (d. 1658) built six alms-houses at the south end of Southwood Lane for six paupers living at Hornsey or Highgate in Hornsey. By his will he devised the alms-houses to the governors of Cholmley's school, who were to nominate the inmates, and also left a rent-charge of £16, to provide £1 for repairs and a pension of £2 10*s*. for each inmate.[19] His heirs suspended payments after three years, until Chancery ordered them to be resumed.[20] In 1886 the rent-charge was redeemed for £683, which was invested in stock.

The Wollaston alms-houses had decayed by 1722 when Edward Pauncefort rebuilt them[21] as part of a range of twelve single-storeyed alms-houses, in the centre of which stood the schoolmistress's house and the schoolroom of the girls' charity school.[22] Wollaston's six alms-houses and Pauncefort's six were regarded as separate. By will dated 1723 Pauncefort directed his executors to buy land yielding £60 a year and to convey it to trustees for charitable purposes: £30 of the income was to be paid as £5 pensions to the six poor widows of his own foundation, £10 to the reader of Highgate chapel, and the residue to the girls' charity school. Until the land had been settled £60 income was to be paid from his personal estate. In 1728 Chancery appointed the six governors of Cholmley's school as trustees. Robert Pauncefort, the founder's executor, paid £60 each year until 1749, when Chancery directed him to hand over £1,500, which the

[9] M.R.O., D.R.O. 20/B1/1, p. 1; H/1, pp. 149–50.
[10] *N. Mdx. Chron.* 13 Nov. 1886.
[11] See pp. 165, 202.
[12] Bruce Castle Mus., D/PH/2A/1.
[13] *N. Mdx. Chron.* 13 Nov. 1886.
[14] Hornsey Par. Chars. *Chairman's Rep.* (1904–5).
[15] Hornsey Par. Chars. *Chairman's Reps.* (1904–5, 1912–21).
[16] *Hornsey Jnl.* 28 Jan. 1927, 10 Feb. 1933.
[17] Hornsey Par. Chars. *Chairman's Reps.* (1904–5, 1912–21).
[18] See p. 190.
[19] Prob. 11/276 (P.C.C. 248 Wootton).
[20] Marchams, *Ct. Rolls*, 150–1.
[21] Lysons, *Environs*, iii. 75–6; stone on bldg.
[22] See above, p. 191.

trustees invested in stock yielding only £45. Payments to the girls' charity school were accordingly reduced but those to the curate and alms-houses remained undiminished.

Hannah Boise, by will dated 1746, bequeathed to the governors of Cholmley's school £150 stock, the dividends to be distributed among the six women in Wollaston's alms-houses. The income fluctuated and in 1811 the stock was sold, although payment of the pensions continued. In 1827 they totalled £6.

Samuel Forster, by will dated 1752, left £300 to the governors of Cholmley's school to augment the incomes of the inmates of Wollaston's and Pauncefort's alms-houses. The principal was invested in stock, which yielded a gradually higher dividend, and in 1827 consisted of £510 stock yielding £12 a year.

Robert Bootle, by will dated 1757, left £300 to the governors of Cholmley's school for Wollaston's and Pauncefort's alms-houses. It was used in 1758 to buy £320 stock, which yielded £9 12*s.* in 1824.

John Edwards, by will dated 1768, gave £300 to the governors of Cholmley's school to augment the pensions of the inmates of Wollaston's alms-houses or otherwise benefit that charity. The sum was invested in 1770 in stock which was sold in 1773 to pay for repairs to Highgate chapel. Only in 1822 was it replaced with £398 stock, which yielded £10 7*s.* 2*d.* in 1827. Edwards also left £50 for distribution at his death, including £12 for the almswomen,[23] which may have been the £50 invested in 1771 and of unknown origin in 1827.

Thomas Bromwich, by will dated 1787, was said to have left £100 stock to the almswomen[24] but it is not clear whether it was ever received.

Tobias Kleinert, by will dated 1784, devised the reversion of property[25] at Highgate to the governors of Cholmley's school. The devise was declared void but the governors received income from the property from Kleinert's successor, who tried to realize the donor's wishes but was later found to have only a life interest. The income, estimated at £100 a year in 1797,[26] totalled £922 up to 1816.[27] After spending £1,011 in a lawsuit over the property, the governors were required to refund £459 received wrongly. Half the property escheated to the Crown, which gave the governors £323 from the proceeds of sale. In 1824 the income from stock bought therewith contributed £7 5*s.* 7*d.* to the almspeople's pensions.

Thomas Cooke, by will dated 1810, bequeathed to the governors of Cholmley's school £2,100 stock, to increase the pensions of Wollaston's and Pauncefort's almspeople. In 1827 it yielded £63.

In 1814 William Bloxam, a governor of Cholmley's school, bought £100 stock for the poor of Highgate, of which the dividends were distributed among the inmates of the alms-houses by his daughters for many years. In 1872 his son C. J. Bloxam, then treasurer of the school, transferred the capital to the governors but asked that during their lifetime his sisters might continue the distribution.

In 1881 William's daughter Emily Bloxam gave £100 stock to augment the pensions of the almswomen but continued to distribute the sums herself.

James Robert Bullen, by will dated 1899, bequeathed money to augment the pensions which was invested in £907 stock.

In 1907 the £186 stock of John Schoppens's charity was transferred to the alms-houses. In 1728 Schoppens had bequeathed £150 to his brother-in-law John Edwards (d. 1769) to buy land for the maintenance of his monument in Highgate chapel and, after Edwards's death, for the poor. Edwards bought no land but bequeathed £150 in Schoppens's name to the governors of Cholmley's school, who bought stock and spent the income in 1773 on repairing the chapel.

Miss Anne de Vismes Bloxam (d. 1935) of Westgate-on-Sea (Kent) gave the residue of her estate to the alms-houses in reversion.

Regulations for the Wollaston alms-houses were drawn up by the governors of Cholmley's school *c.* 1669. No married couple was to be admitted, no inmate might marry, and all must attend services in Highgate chapel.[28] The inmates seem always to have been women, whose selection took a prominent place in governors' meetings from 1701.[29] By 1827 they were normally tradesmen's widows, aged 50 or above. Wollaston had intended that the alms-houses should also serve Hornsey but in 1869 his charity was exclusively for residents of Highgate. Until at least 1770 the almswomen received the pensions given to the distinct Wollaston and Pauncefort foundations but all were paid £7 a year, mainly from bequests, in 1797.[30] In 1827 *c.* £277 was due to each foundation and there was a slight surplus above the pensions. The charities were administered jointly with Cholmley's school, Highgate chapel, and the girls' charity school: all stock was held in common and all income was paid into a common fund. The greatest loser was the girls' charity school[31] and the main beneficiary was the chapel. On balance the alms-houses benefited from the system of accounting. In 1827 the Charity Commissioners made detailed proposals to restore each charity and recommended that in future each should be accounted for separately. There was an accumulated surplus by 1950, when it was spent on repairs, but there were deficits in 1956 and in 1957, when the income was *c.* £350. Repairs and modernization were carried out in 1961–2 with the aid of £1,751 from Lady Gould's charity. As the almswomen received old-age pensions and other benefits, the trustees reduced the pensions, ceased contributing towards fuel, and put the savings towards the electricity bill. The cost of maintenance reached £470 in 1972, by which date the income had increased to £1,173.

Other charities. By deed dated 1636, Thomas Coventry, later Lord Coventry (d. 1661), granted rent-charges to the Merchant Taylors' Company of London subject to the annual payment of £10 for distribution in fuel and clothing equally among the poor of Highgate in both Hornsey and St. Pancras. It seems that, because one of the rent-charges was not paid, no income was received in the mid 17th

[23] Lysons, *Environs*, iii. 76.
[24] Ibid.
[25] Ibid.
[26] Ibid.
[27] Brewer, *Beauties of Eng. & Wales*, x (5), 221.
[28] Highgate Sch. rec., governors' min. bk. 1576–1810, f. 71.
[29] e.g. ibid. ff. 186v.–7.
[30] Lysons, *Environs*, iii. 76.
[31] See p. 191.

century,[32] and before 1691 a churchwarden had failed to account for £71 of the charity's money. In 1824 the charity was distributed among 24 women from each parish, who enjoyed it for so long as they remained in Highgate. The payment was later replaced by £286 stock. A Scheme of 1961, when the income was £10 a year, provided for distribution in kind or money.

John Smith of Highgate, whose wife Anne gave him £100 for an annual sermon and payments to the 20 poorest men and women of Highgate in Hornsey, in addition gave £4 a year for the 20 poorest people of Hornsey. By codicil to his will proved 1655 he left a rent-charge on the later Barton Court estate near Canterbury (Kent) to the governors of Cholmley's school, to spend £1 on a lecture on 10 December, £6 on 20 poor of Highgate in Hornsey, and £4 on 20 poor of Hornsey.[33] The rent-charge was sold in 1902 and the proceeds were invested in stock yielding £11 5*s.* in 1972; £1 was paid to the vicar of St. Michael's, Highgate, and £6 5*s.* was divided among 25 poor of Highgate and £4 among 20 poor of Hornsey.

Elizabeth, wife of Edward (later Sir Edward) Gould, by will dated 1691 left the reversion of three houses, afterwards nos. 17, 19, and 21 High Street, for the rent to be distributed among those poor of Highgate in Hornsey and St. Pancras who were not in receipt of relief. Following Sir Edward's death in 1728 the trust took effect. The three houses were let at £76 in 1824. The income was distributed, generally among people who had been reduced from better circumstances, in sums of £5 or less. The properties yielded £70 rent in 1867–8. No. 19 was sold in 1956 for £2,405 and the proceeds invested in stock. In 1964 there was a total income of £550, £165 being spent on repairs and administrative expenses and £399 distributed.

In 1715 John Beaker gave a rent-charge of 12*s.* for distribution in bread among the poor of Highgate. The property was identifiable in 1725 but nothing thereafter is known of the charity.[34]

Dame Sarah Pritchard (d. 1718) devised £800 stock, the income of £32 to be distributed among seven parishes in Middlesex and elsewhere. It included £2 10*s.* to be divided equally among ten poor maids or widows of Highgate. By 1824 £2 17*s.* 8*d.* was paid to the minister of Highgate, who added to it and distributed £3 among the twelve inmates of the Wollaston and Pauncefort alms-houses. By a Scheme of 1871, the income was apportioned to give Highgate £3. In 1972 the income of £2·88 was expended by the vicar of St. Michael's.

In 1856 Elizabeth Annè Jones bequeathed £150 to the vicar of St. Michael's for charitable purposes. The Revd. C. B. Dalton invested the capital and used the income to pay for a girl's attendance at Highgate industrial school. The income amounted to *c.* £5 in 1867–8 and £4·80 in 1972, when it was expended at the vicar's discretion.

Maria Tame (d. 1857) gave a sum to Highgate dispensary, after the closure of which the charity was transferred in 1915 to a nursing association and in 1967 to the Hornsey Parochial Charities for aiding the sick of Highgate in Hornsey.

William Hale of Kentish Town in St. Pancras and a native of Highgate, by will proved 1870, gave £100 stock to maintain his family vault, any residue to be distributed among the poor of Highgate at Christmas. The Charity Commissioners ordered in 1871 that the whole income be divided among the poor. The income was £2·66 in 1972, when it was dispensed by the vicar.

In 1972 the incomes of the Coventry charity and the Highgate part of John Smith's charity were doubled by the vicar of St. Michael's and given away each December in sums of 25p. The income of Jones's, Hales's, and Pritchard's charities, totalling £10·34, was dispensed in sherry, tobacco, and discretionary payments.

32 *Cal. Cttee. for Compounding*, iii. 2191–2.

33 Prob. 11/256 (P.C.C. 211 Berkeley).

34 B.L. Add. MS. 5836, f. 91.

INDEX

NOTE: An italic page-number denotes an illustration on that page or facing it.

Among the abbreviations used in the index, sometimes with the addition of an *s* to indicate plurality, the following may need elucidation: agric., agriculture; Alb., Albert; Alex., Alexander; Alf., Alfred; alms-ho., alms-house; And., Andrew; Ant., Anthony; Art., Arthur; Assoc., Association; Bart., Bartholomew; bd., board; Benj., Benjamin; bldg., building; bldr., builder; boro., borough; bp., bishop; Bros., Brothers; bt., baronet; Capt., Captain; Cath., Catherine; Cathm., Catholicism; ch., church; chars., charities; Chas., Charles; Chris., Christopher; co., company; Col., Colonel; Coll., College; Colln., Collection; ct., court; cttee., committee; ctss., countess; Dan., Daniel; dau., daughter; dist., district; dom., domestic; Edm., Edmund; Edw., Edward; Eliz., Elizabeth; Ern., Ernest; fam., family; Fran., Francis; Fred., Frederick; gdn., garden; Gen., General; Geo., George; Geof., Geoffrey; Gilb., Gilbert; govt., government; Hen., Henry; Herb., Herbert; ho., house; hosp., hospital; Humph., Humphrey; ind., industry; Jas., James; Jos., Joseph; jr., junior; Kath., Katharine; Lawr., Lawrence; ld., lord; libr., library; Lond., London; m., married; man., manor; Marg., Margaret; Mat., Matthew; mchss., marchioness; Mic., Michael; mkt., market; Nat., Nathaniel; Nic., Nicholas; nonconf., nonconformity; par., parish; Pat., Patrick; Pet., Peter; Phil., Philip; pk., park; pop., population; pub., public; *q.v.*, *quod vide*; Reg., Reginald; Revd., Reverend; Ric., Richard; rly., railway; Rob., Robert; Rog., Roger; Rom., Roman; s., son; Sam., Samuel; sch., school; Sim., Simon; soc., social *or* society; Sq., Square; sr., senior; sta., station; Steph., Stephen; svce., service; Thos., Thomas; Vct., Viscount; Vctss., Viscountess; w., wife; Wal., Walter; wkho., workhouse; wks., works; Wm., William.

CORRIGENDA TO VOLUMES III AND V

Earlier lists of corrigenda will be found in Volumes I, III, IV and V

Vol. III, page 15*a*, line 12, *for* '1884' *read* '1887'
104*b*, line 13 from end, *for* 'John' *read* 'Richard'
113*a*, line 28, *for* 'John' *read* 'Richard'
145*a*, line 8 from end, *for* 'probably in 1872' *read* 'in 1873'
145, note 26, *delete whole footnote and substitute* 'Ex inf. Mr. H. V. Borley.'
190*a*, lines 3–4, *for* 'between 1878 and 1881' *read* 'in 1884'
190, note 57, *delete whole footnote and substitute* 'Ex inf. Mr. H. V. Borley.'
208*b*, lines 2–3, *for* 'Marylebone to High Wycombe' *read* 'Paddington to Park Royal'
208, note 43, *delete whole footnote and substitute* 'Ex inf. Mr. H. V. Borley.'
290*c*, s.v. Fox, *delete* 'John, bp. of Winchester, iii. 104, 113' *and after* '325' *add* '; iii. 104, 113.'

Vol. V, page ix, last line, *for* 'III and IV' *read* 'I, II, and IV'
5*a*, line 12 from end, *for* 'west' *read* 'east'
5*b*, line 28, *for* 'Wembley' *read* 'West Hampstead'
6*a*, line 17, *delete* 'later'
9*b*, line 30, *for* 'Olympia' *read* 'Olympus'
12*b*, lines 8–9, *delete from* 'near' *to* 'London.'
15*a*, lines 8–9 from end, *for* 'the Underground group at once' *read* 'John Laing & Sons'
15*b*, line 16, *delete* 'As at Golders Green,'
15*b*, line 17, *for* 'in the station forecourt' *read* 'at the station'
15, note 74, *delete whole footnote and substitute* 'Jackson, *Semi-det. Lond.* 142.'
35*b*, line 14 from end, *for* 'Hood' *read* 'Flood'
37*a*, line 26, *for* 'Sherman' *read* 'Shearman'
37*b*, line 3, *for* 'architect' *read* 'architects'
37*b*, line 5, *for* 'was' *read* 'were C. Nicholas and'
54*b*, line 20 from end, *for* 'Co.' *read* 'Country'
62*a*, line 19 from end, *for* 'Co.' *read* 'Country'
93*a*, line 35, *for* '1847' *read* '1843'
93, note 87, *delete whole footnote and substitute* 'W. Keane, *Beauties of Mdx.* 194.'
94*a*, lines 30–1, *for* 'London Passenger Transport Board' *read* 'Metropolitan Railway'
95, note 26, *for* '95' *read* '98'
109, note 1, *for* 'Gaz.' *read* '*Observer*'
111*a*, line 3 from end, *delete* 'opposed by Edgware vestry[27]'
111*b*, line 4, *for* 'that date' *read* '1912/13'
113*b*, line 18, *for* 'Court' *read* 'House'
114*b*, line 8 from end, *for* 'message' *read* 'messuage'
120, note 34 *to read* 35
120, note 35 *to read* 34
124, note 45, *for* '*Harmoniuous*' *read* '*Harmonious*'
133, note 62, *for* 'Gillan' *read* 'Gillam'
136, note 96, *for* 'Helen' *read* 'Henrietta'
136, note 7, *delete from* 'The London' *to* 'Cockfosters'
137*a*, line 7, *delete* 'Steam and'
143, note 14, *for* '1912' *read* '1907'
161*b*, line 32, *for* 'by' *read* 'in the style of'
186*a*, line 11, *for* 'western bellcot' *read* 'bellcot over the chancel arch'
186*a*, line 29, *for* 'red' *read* 'stock'
212, note 42, *for* 'N. P.' *read* 'H. P.'
212*b*, line 13, *for* '1852' *read* '1850'
212*b*, line 19, *for* 'at' *read* 'via'
214*a*, line 5 from end, *for* 'Corinthian' *read* 'Tuscan'
219, note 8, *for* 'below' *read* 'above'
255*a*, lines 1–2, *for* 'Aiar' *read* 'War' *and for* 'Wded' *read* 'Aided'
257, note 67, *for* 'Radcliff' *read* 'Radcliffe'
291*b*, line 6, *for* '1971' *read* '1917'
312, note 92, *delete* '*Kelly's Dir. Mdx.* (1926);'
319*b*, line 7, *for* 'ten' *read* 'nine'
345*a*, lines 23–4 from end, *for* 'Taylor and A. R. Jennett' *read* 'Tayler and A. R. Jemmett'
348*a*, line 3, *for* 'Curtiss' *read* 'Curtis'
381*c*, s.v. architects, *for* 'Jennett' *read* 'Jemmett' *and insert* 'Nicholas, C.'
382*a*, s.v. architects, *for* 'Sherman' *read* 'Shearman' *and insert* 'Tayler'
401*c*, s.v. Jennett, *for* 'Jennett' *read* 'Jemmett'
403*a*, s.v. Laing, *insert* '15'
404*c*, s.v. London Passenger Transport Board, *delete* '94'
406*a*, s.v. Metropolitan Railway, *insert* '94'
406*a*, s.v. Metropolitan Railway Co. Estates, *for* 'Co.' *read* 'Country'
408*a*, s.v. Nicholas, *insert* 'C., architect, 37;'

CORRIGENDA TO VOLUMES III AND V

Vol. V, page 409*a*, s.v. Page, *for* 'Sam. Hood' *read* 'Sam. Flood'
413*b*, s.v. Sherman, *for* 'Sherman' *read* 'Shearman'
415*c*, s.v. Stanmore, Little, *delete* 'Stone Grove Court, 113'
416*a*, s.v. Stanmore, Little, Stone Grove Ho., *for* '112' *read* '112–13'
416*c*, *insert* 'Tayler, A. S., architect, 345'
416*c*, s.v. Taylor, *delete* 'A. S., architect, 345'